DRAMA
for Students

DRAMA
for Students

**Presenting Analysis, Context and Criticism on
Commonly Studied Dramas**

Volume 5

David Galens, Editor

The Gale Group

DETROIT • SAN FRANCISCO • LONDON • BOSTON • WOODBRIDGE, CT

National Advisory Board

Drama for Students

Staff

Editorial: David M. Galens, *Editor*. Christopher Busiel, Clare Cross, John Fiero, David M. Galens, Lane A. Glenn, Carole Hamilton, Elizabeth Judd, Sheri Metzger, Annette Petrusso, Arnold Schmidt, *Entry Writers*. Tim Akers, Brigham Narins, Kathy Wilson, *Contributing Editors*. James Draper, *Managing Editor*. Kathy Wilson, *''For Students'' Line Coordinator*. Jeffery Chapman, *Programmer/Analyst*.

Research: Victoria B. Cariappa, *Research Team Manager*. Andy Malonis, Barb McNeil, *Research Specialists*. Tamara C. Nott, Tracie A. Richardson, Corrine A. Stocker, Cheryl L. Warnock, Robert Whaley, *Research Associates*. Patricia T. Ballard, Phyllis P. Blackman, *Research Assistants*.

Permissions: Maria Franklin, *Interim Permissions Manager*. Kimberly F. Smilay, *Permissions Specialist*. Kelly A. Quin, *Permissions Associate*. Sandra K. Gore, *Permissions Assistant*.

Graphic Services: Randy Bassett, *Image Database Supervisor*. Robert Duncan and Michael Logusz, *Imaging Specialists*. Pamela A. Reed, *Imaging Coordinator*. Gary Leach, *Macintosh Artist*.

Product Design: Cynthia Baldwin, *Product Design Manager*. Cover Design: Michelle DiMercurio, *Art Director*. Page Design: Pamela A. E. Galbreath, *Senior Art Director*.

Table of Contents

The Study of Drama

We study drama in order to learn what meaning others have made of life, to comprehend what it takes to produce a work of art, and to glean some understanding of ourselves. Drama produces in a separate, aesthetic world, a moment of being for the audience to experience, while maintaining the detachment of a reflective observer.

Drama is a representational art, a visible and audible narrative presenting virtual, fictional characters within a virtual, fictional universe. Dramatic realizations may pretend to approximate reality or else stubbornly defy, distort, and deform reality into an artistic statement. From this separate universe that is obviously not "real life" we expect a valid reflection upon reality, yet drama never is mistaken for reality—the methods of theater are integral to its form and meaning. Theater is art, and art's appeal lies in its ability both to approximate life and to depart from it. By presenting its distorted version of life to our consciousness, art gives us a new perspective and appreciation of reality. Although, to some extent, all aesthetic experiences perform this service, theater does it most effectively by creating a separate, cohesive universe that freely acknowledges its status as an art form.

And what is the purpose of the aesthetic universe of drama? The potential answers to such a question are nearly as many and varied as there are plays written, performed, and enjoyed. Dramatic texts can be problems posed, answers asserted, or moments portrayed. Dramas (tragedies as well as comedies) may serve strictly "to ease the anguish of a torturing hour" (as stated in William Shakespeare's *A Midsummer Night's Dream*)—to divert and entertain—or aspire to move the viewer to action with social issues. Whether to entertain or to instruct, affirm or influence, pacify or shock, dramatic art wraps us in the spell of its imaginary world for the length of the work and then dispenses us back to the real world, entertained, purged, as Aristotle said, of pity and fear, and edified—or at least weary enough to sleep peacefully.

It is commonly thought that theater, being an art of performance, must be experienced—that is, seen—in order to be appreciated fully. However, to view a production of a dramatic text is to be limited to a single interpretation of that text—all other interpretations are for the moment closed off, inaccessible. In the process of producing a play, the director, stage designer, and performers interpret and transform the script into a work of art that always departs in some measure from the author's original conception. Novelist and critic Umberto Eco, in his *The Role of the Reader: Explorations in the Semiotics of Texts,* explained, "In short, we can say that every performance offers us a complete and satisfying version of the work, but at the same time makes it incomplete for us, because it cannot simultaneously give all the other artistic solutions which the work may admit."

Thus Laurence Olivier's coldly formal and neurotic film presentation of Shakespeare's *Hamlet* (in which he played the title character as well as directed) shows marked differences from subsequent adaptations. While Olivier's Hamlet is clearly entangled in a Freudian relationship with his mother, Gertrude, he would be incapable of shushing her with the impassioned kiss that Mel Gibson's mercurial Hamlet (in director Franco Zeffirelli's 1990 film) does. Although each of the performances rings true to Shakespeare's text, each is also a mutually exclusive work of art. Also important to consider are the time periods in which each of these films were produced: Olivier made his film in 1948, a time in which overt references to sexuality (especially incest) were frowned upon. Gibson and Zeffirelli made their film in a culture more relaxed and comfortable with these issues. Just as actors and directors can influence the presentation of drama, so too can the time period of the production affect what the audience will see.

A play script is an open text from which an infinity of specific realizations may be derived. Dramatic scripts that are more open to interpretive creativity (such as those of Ntozake Shange and Tomson Highway) actually require the creative improvisation of the production troupe in order to complete the text. Even the most prescriptive scripts (those of Neil Simon, Lillian Hellman, and Robert Bolt, for example), can never fully control the actualization of live performance, and circumstantial events, including the attitude and receptivity of the audience, make every performance a unique event. Thus, while it is important to view a production of a dramatic piece, if one wants to understand a drama fully it is equally important to read the original dramatic text.

The reader of a dramatic text or script is not limited by either the specific interpretation of a given production or by the unstoppable action of a moving spectacle. The reader of a dramatic text may discover the nuances of the play's language, structure, and events at their own pace. Yet studied alone, the author's blueprint for artistic production does not tell the whole story of a play's life and significance. One also needs to assess the play's critical reviews to discover how it resonated to cultural themes at the time of its debut and how the shifting tides of cultural interest have revised its interpretation and impact on audiences. And to do this, one needs to know a little about the culture of the times which produced the play as well as the author who penned it.

Drama for Students supplies this material in a useful compendium for the student of dramatic theater. Covering a range of dramatic works that span from the fifth century B.C. to the 1990s, this book focuses on significant theatrical works whose themes and form transcend the uncertainty of dramatic fads. These are plays that have proven to be both memorable and teachable. *Drama for Students* seeks to enhance appreciation of these dramatic texts by providing scholarly materials written with the secondary and college/university student in mind. It provides for each play a concise summary of the plot and characters as well as a detailed explanation of its themes and techniques. In addition, background material on the historical context of the play, its critical reception, and the author's life help the student to understand the work's position in the chronicle of dramatic history. For each play entry a new work of scholarly criticism is also included, as well as segments of other significant critical works for handy reference. A thorough bibliography provides a starting point for further research.

These inaugural two volumes offer comprehensive educational resources for students of drama. *Drama for Students* is a vital book for dramatic interpretation and a valuable addition to any reference library.

Source: Eco, Umberto, *The Role of the Reader: Explorations in the Semiotics of Texts,* Indiana University Press, 1979.

Carole L. Hamilton
Author and Instructor of English
Cary Academy
Cary, North Carolina

Introduction

Purpose of Drama for Students

The purpose of *Drama for Students* (*DfS*) is to provide readers with a guide to understanding, enjoying, and studying dramas by giving them easy access to information about the work. Part of Gale's "For Students" literature line, *DfS* is specifically designed to meet the curricular needs of high school and undergraduate college students and their teachers, as well as the interests of general readers and researchers considering specific plays. While each volume contains entries on "classic" dramas frequently studied in classrooms, there are also entries containing hard-to-find information on contemporary plays, including works by multicultural, international, and women playwrights.

The information covered in each entry includes an introduction to the play and the work's author; a plot summary, to help readers unravel and understand the events in a drama; descriptions of important characters, including explanation of a given character's role in the drama as well as discussion about that character's relationship to other characters in the play; analysis of important themes in the drama; and an explanation of important literary techniques and movements as they are demonstrated in the play.

In addition to this material, which helps the readers analyze the play itself, students are also provided with important information on the literary and historical background informing each work.

This includes a historical context essay, a box comparing the time or place the drama was written to modern Western culture, a critical overview essay, and excerpts from critical essays on the play. A unique feature of *DfS* is a specially commissioned overview essay on each drama by an academic expert, targeted toward the student reader.

To further aid the student in studying and enjoying each play, information on media adaptations is provided, as well as reading suggestions for works of fiction and nonfiction on similar themes and topics. Classroom aids include ideas for research papers and lists of critical sources that provide additional material on each drama.

Selection Criteria

The titles for each volume of *DfS* were selected by surveying numerous sources on teaching literature and analyzing course curricula for various school districts. Some of the sources surveyed included: literature anthologies; *Reading Lists for College-Bound Students: The Books Most Recommended by America's Top Colleges;* textbooks on teaching dramas; a College Board survey of plays commonly studied in high schools; a National Council of Teachers of English (NCTE) survey of plays commonly studied in high schools; St. James Press's *International Dictionary of Theatre;* and Arthur Applebee's 1993 study *Literature in the Secondary School: Studies of Curriculum and Instruction in the United States.*

Input was also solicited from our expert advisory board (both experienced educators specializing in English), as well as educators from various areas. From these discussions, it was determined that each volume should have a mix of "classic" dramas (those works commonly taught in literature classes) and contemporary dramas for which information is often hard to find. Because of the interest in expanding the canon of literature, an emphasis was also placed on including works by international, multicultural, and women playwrights. Our advisory board members—current high school teachers—helped pare down the list for each volume. If a work was not selected for the present volume, it was often noted as a possibility for a future volume. As always, the editor welcomes suggestions for titles to be included in future volumes.

How Each Entry Is Organized

Each entry, or chapter, in *DfS* focuses on one play. Each entry heading lists the full name of the play, the author's name, and the date of the play's first production or publication. The following elements are contained in each entry:

- **Introduction:** a brief overview of the drama which provides information about its first appearance, its literary standing, any controversies surrounding the work, and major conflicts or themes within the work.

- **Author Biography:** this section includes basic facts about the author's life, and focuses on events and times in the author's life that inspired the drama in question.

- **Plot Summary:** a description of the major events in the play, with interpretation of how these events help articulate the play's themes. Subheads demarcate the plays' various acts or scenes.

- **Characters:** an alphabetical listing of major characters in the play. Each character name is followed by a brief to an extensive description of the character's role in the plays, as well as discussion of the character's actions, relationships, and possible motivation.

  Characters are listed alphabetically by last name. If a character is unnamed—for instance, the Stage Manager in *Our Town*—the character is listed as "The Stage Manager" and alphabetized as "Stage Manager." If a character's first name is the only one given, the name will appear alphabetically by the name.

Variant names are also included for each character. Thus, the nickname "Babe" would head the listing for a character in *Crimes of the Heart,* but below that listing would be her less-mentioned married name "Rebecca Botrelle."

- **Themes:** a thorough overview of how the major topics, themes, and issues are addressed within the play. Each theme discussed appears in a separate subhead, and is easily accessed through the boldface entries in the Subject/Theme Index.

- **Style:** this section addresses important style elements of the drama, such as setting, point of view, and narration; important literary devices used, such as imagery, foreshadowing, symbolism; and, if applicable, genres to which the work might have belonged, such as Gothicism or Romanticism. Literary terms are explained within the entry, but can also be found in the Glossary.

- **Historical and Cultural Context:** This section outlines the social, political, and cultural climate *in which the author lived and the play was created.* This section may include descriptions of related historical events, pertinent aspects of daily life in the culture, and the artistic and literary sensibilities of the time in which the work was written. If the play is a historical work, information regarding the time in which the play is set is also included. Each section is broken down with helpful subheads.

- **Critical Overview:** this section provides background on the critical reputation of the play, including bannings or any other public controversies surrounding the work. For older plays, this section includes a history of how the drama was first received and how perceptions of it may have changed over the years; for more recent plays, direct quotes from early reviews may also be included.

- **For Further Study:** an alphabetical list of other critical sources which may prove useful for the student. Includes full bibliographical information and a brief annotation.

- **Sources:** an alphabetical list of critical material quoted in the entry, with full bibliographical information.

- **Criticism:** an essay commissioned by *DfS* which specifically deals with the play and is written specifically for the student audience, as well as excerpts from previously published criticism on the work.

In addition, each entry contains the following highlighted sections, set separate from the main text:

- **Media Adaptations:** a list of important film and television adaptations of the play, including source information. The list may also include such variations on the work as audio recordings, musical adaptations, and other stage interpretations.

- **Compare and Contrast Box:** an "at-a-glance" comparison of the cultural and historical differences between the author's time and culture and late twentieth-century Western culture. This box includes pertinent parallels between the major scientific, political, and cultural movements of the time or place the drama was written, the time or place the play was set (if a historical work), and modern Western culture. Works written after the mid-1970s may not have this box.

- **What Do I Read Next?:** a list of works that might complement the featured play or serve as a contrast to it. This includes works by the same author and others, works of fiction and nonfiction, and works from various genres, cultures, and eras.

- **Study Questions:** a list of potential study questions or research topics dealing with the play. This section includes questions related to other disciplines the student may be studying, such as American history, world history, science, math, government, business, geography, economics, psychology, etc.

Other Features

DfS includes "The Study of Drama," a foreword by Carole Hamilton, an educator and author who specializes in dramatic works. This essay examines the basis for drama in societies and what drives people to study such work. Hamilton also discusses how *Drama for Students* can help teachers show students how to enrich their own reading/viewing experiences.

A Cumulative Author/Title Index lists the authors and titles covered in each volume of the *DfS* series.

A Cumulative Nationality/Ethnicity Index breaks down the authors and titles covered in each volume of the *DfS* series by nationality and ethnicity.

A Subject/Theme Index, specific to each volume, provides easy reference for users who may be studying a particular subject or theme rather than a single work. Significant subjects from events to

broad themes are included, and the entries pointing to the specific theme discussions in each entry are indicated in **boldface.**

Each entry has several illustrations, including photos of the author, stills from stage productions, and stills from film adaptations.

Citing Drama for Students

When writing papers, students who quote directly from any volume of *Drama for Students* may use the following general forms. These examples are based on MLA style; teachers may request that students adhere to a different style, so the following examples may be adapted as needed.

When citing text from *DfS* that is not attributed to a particular author (i.e., the Themes, Style, Historical Context sections, etc.), the following format should be used in the bibliography section:

> "Our Town," *Drama for Students.* Ed. David Galens and Lynn Spampinato. Vol. 1. Detroit: Gale, 1997. 8–9.

When quoting the specially commissioned essay from *DfS* (usually the first piece under the "Criticism" subhead), the following format should be used:

> Fiero, John. Essay on "Twilight: Los Angeles, 1992." *Drama for Students.* Ed. David Galens and Lynn Spampinato. Vol. 1. Detroit: Gale, 1997. 8–9.

When quoting a journal or newspaper essay that is reprinted in a volume of *DfS,* the following form may be used:

> Rich, Frank. "Theatre: A Mamet Play, 'Glengarry Glen Ross'." *New York Theatre Critics' Review* Vol. 45, No. 4 (March 5, 1984), 5–7; excerpted and reprinted in *Drama for Students,* Vol. 1, ed. David Galens and Lynn Spampinato (Detroit: Gale, 1997), pp. 61–64.

When quoting material reprinted from a book that appears in a volume of *DfS,* the following form may be used:

> Kerr, Walter. "The Miracle Worker," in *The Theatre in Spite of Itself* (Simon & Schuster, 1963, 255–57; excerpted and reprinted in *Drama for Students,* Vol. 1, ed. Dave Galens and Lynn Spampinato (Detroit: Gale, 1997, pp. 59–61.

We Welcome Your Suggestions

The editor of *Drama for Students* welcomes your comments and ideas. Readers who wish to suggest dramas to appear in future volumes, or who have other suggestions, are cordially invited to contact the editor. You may contact the editor via E-mail at: **david.galens@gale.com.** Or write to the editor at:

David Galens, *Drama for Students*
The Gale Group
27500 Drake Rd.
Farmington Hills, MI 48331-3535

Literary Chronology

525 B.C.: Aeschylus is born in Eleusis, Greece.

456 B.C.: *Prometheus Bound* by Aeschylus is first performed at the Great Dionysia.

456 B.C.: Aeschylus dies in the Greek colony of Gela, Sicily; according to legend, he is killed when an eagle, trying to crack an animal's shell, drops a tortoise on the playwright's head.

1564: Christopher Marlowe is born in Canterbury, England.

1593: *Edward II* by Christopher Marlowe debuts; it is published the following year. Marlowe is also stabbed to death this year, while awaiting trial for atheism and blasphemy.

1860: Anton Chekhov is born on January 29 in the port village of Taganrog in the Ukraine.

1888: Eugene O'Neill is born on October 16 in New York City.

1897: *Uncle Vanya* by Anton Chekhov is written, a revision of the playwright's earlier, failed play *The Wood Demon.* The play makes is stage debut at the Moscow Art Theatre on October 26, 1899.

1898: Bertolt Brecht is born Eugen Bertolt Friedrich Brecht on February 10 in Augsburg, Bavaria, Germany.

1904: Anton Chekhov dies of tuberculosis on July 2 in Badenweiler, a German health resort; he is buried in Moscow, Russia.

1905: Jean-Paul Sartre is born on June 21 in Paris, France.

1913: William Motter Inge is born May 3 in Independence, Kansas.

1917: Carson McCullers is born Lula Carson Smith on February 19, in Columbus, Georgia.

1930: Peter Shaffer is born May 15 in Liverpool, England.

1930: Harold Pinter is born on October 10, in Hackney, a section of London, England.

1937: Tom Stoppard is born Tomas Straussler in Zlin, Czechoslovakia, on July 3.

1939: *Mother Courage and Her Children* by Bertolt Brecht debuts in Zurich, Switzerland. As an exile from the Nazi government, Brecht would not be able to stage the work in his native Germany until after World War II.

1940: Luis Valdez is born June 26 in Delano, California.

1944: *No Exit* by Jean-Paul Sartre debuts in Paris, France.

1946: *The Iceman Cometh* by Eugene O'Neill debuts in New York City, it is the playwright's first work on Broadway in twelve years.

1950: Following the 1946 publication of her novel of the same name, Carson McCullers's play *The Member of the Wedding* debuts on Broadway at the Empire Theatre.

1950: Wendy Wasserstein is born in Brooklyn, New York, on October 18.

1953: *Picnic* by William Inge debuts on Broadway in February to uniformly positive reviews.

1953: Eugene O'Neill dies of pneumonia on November 27.

1956: Tony Kushner is born in Manhattan, New York.

1956: Bertolt Brecht dies on August 14 in East Berlin, East Germany, from a coronary thrombosis.

1958: *The Birthday Party,* Harold Pinter's first commercially produced full-length play, debuts in Cambridge, England, at the Arts Theatre, on April 28.

1967: Following a series of health problems, Carson McCullers suffers a fatal stroke on September 29 in Nyack, New York.

1973: William Inge dies of asphyxiation from carbon monoxide fumes in Los Angeles, California, on June 10; the death is ruled a suicide.

1973: *Equus* by Peter Shaffer debuts in London, England, at the Old Vic Theatre on July 26.

1978: *Zoot Suit* by Luis Valdez debuts in Los Angeles, California, to wide popular acclaim; the play moves to Broadway later in the year, to harsher critical judgement.

1980: Jean-Paul Sartre dies in Paris, France, on April 15 of uremia.

1988: *The Heidi Chronicles* by Wendy Wasserstein is first produced Off-Broadway at the Playwrights Horizons theatre on December 11, where it runs for three sold-out months; the play moves to the Plymouth Theater on Broadway on March 9, 1989.

1991: The first segment of Tony Kushner's *Angels in America, Millennium Approaches,* debuts at the Mark Taper Forum in Los Angeles, California; the second segment, *Perestroika,* bows the following year.

1993: *Arcadia* by Tom Stoppard debuts at the Lyttelton stage of the Royal National Theatre in London, England, on April 13; the play debuts on Broadway two years later, March 31, 1995, at the Lincoln Center Theater.

Acknowledgments

The editors wish to thank the copyright holders of the excerpted criticism included in this volume and the permissions managers of many book and magazine publishing companies for assisting us in securing reproduction rights. We are also grateful to the staffs of the Detroit Public Library, the Library of Congress, the University of Detroit Mercy Library, Wayne State University Purdy/Kresge Library Complex, and the University of Michigan Libraries for making their resources available to us. Following is a list of the copyright holders who have granted us permission to reproduce material in this volume of *DFS*. Every effort has been made to trace copyright, but if omissions have been made, please let us know.

COPYRIGHTED EXCERPTS IN *DFS*, VOLUME 5, WERE REPRODUCED FROM THE FOLLOWING PERIODICALS:

Classical Quarterly, v. 46, June, 1996 for "Chains of Imagery in Prometheus Bound," by J. M. Mossman. Reproduced by permission of Oxford University Press and the author.—*Commonweal*, v. LVII, March 20, 1953; v. CXVI, May 5, 1989. Copyright 1953, 1989 Commonweal Publishing Co., Inc. Both reproduced by permission of Commonweal Foundation.—*Modern Drama*, v. XV, September, 1972; v. XXII, March, 1979. © 1972, 1979 University of Toronto, Graduate Centre for Study of Drama. Both reproduced by permission.—*New York*, Magazine, v. 22, March 27, 1989; v. 22, April 10, 1989; v. 24, September 2, 1991; v. 27, May 2, 1994. Copyright © 1989, 1991, 1994 K-III Magazine Corporation. All rights reserved. All reproduced with the permission of *New York* Magazine.—*The Nation*, New York, v. 176, March 7, 1953; v. 228, April 7, 1979; v. 246, May 21, 1988; v. 248, June 12, 1989; v. 256, February 22, 1993; v. 260, May 1, 1995. Copyright 1953, 1979, 1988, 1989, 1993, 1995 *The Nation* magazine/The Nation Company, Inc. All reproduced by permission.—*The New Republic*, v. CXIV, April 29, 1946; v. 115, October 21, 1946; v. 148, April 13, 1963; v. 193, October 28, 1985. Copyright 1946, 1963, 1985. All reproduced by permission of *The New Republic*.—*The New Yorker*, v. LV, April 2, 1979; v. 64, December 26, 1988. © 1979, 1988 by Mimi Kramer. All rights reserved. Both reproduced by permission.—*The Saturday Review*, v. 4, January 25, 1975. © 1975 General Media Communications, Inc. Reproduced by permission of Saturday Review Publications, Ltd.—*Theatre History Studies*, v. XV, June, 1995. Reproduced by permission.

COPYRIGHTED EXCERPTS IN *DFS*, VOLUME 5, WERE REPRODUCED FROM THE FOLLOWING BOOKS:

Lahr, John. From *Light Fantastic: Adventures in the Theatre*. Dial Press, 1996. Copyright © 1996 by John Lahr. Bloomsbury Publishing Plc, 1996. Reproduced by permission of Dial Press/Dell Publishing a division of Random House, Inc. In the

British Commonwealth by Bloomsbury Publishing plc.

PHOTOGRAPHS AND ILLUSTRATIONS APPEARING IN *DFS,* VOLUME 5, WERE RECEIVED FROM THE FOLLOWING SOURCES:

Aeschylus, photograph. The Library of Congress.—Brecht, Bertolt, photograph. Archive Photos, Inc. Reproduced by permission.—Chekhov, Anton, photograph. The Library of Congress.—From a movie still of *Zoot Suit* by Luis Valdez, Directed by Luis Valdez, with Rose Portillo as Della, Daniel Valdez as Henry Reyna, John Anderson as the Judge and Edward James Olmos as El Pachuco, 1981, Universal, Della, Henry and friends flash-back to re-create a dance before the Judge and the mythical El Pachuco, photograph. Universal. Courtesy of The Kobal Collection. Reproduced by permission.—From a movie still of *Zoot Suit* by Luis Valdez, Directed by Luis Valdez, with Edward James Olmos as El Pachuco, Rose Portillo as Della and Daniel Valdez as Henry Reyna, 1981, Universal, El Pachuco is sitting in the car where Della sits holding the badly beaten Henry after the brawl at Sleepy Lagoon, photograph. Universal. Courtesy of The Kobal Collection. Reproduced by permission.—From a theatre production of *Angels in America* by Tony Kushner at New York's Walter Kerr Theatre on Broadway, with Ellen McLaughlin as the Angel and Stephen Spinella as Prior Walter, May 17, 1993, photograph. AP/Wide World Photos. Reproduced by permission.—From a theatre production of *Arcadia* by Tom Stoppard, Directed by Eric Forsythe at University Theatres Mainstage production, The University of Iowa, November, 1997, photograph. University of Iowa. Reproduced by permission.—From a theatre production of Bertolt Brecht's *Mother Courage and Her Children* with Diana Rigg at the National Theatre, London, November, 1995, photograph by Robbie Jack. CORBIS/Robbie Jack. Reproduced by permission.—From a theatre production of Bertolt Brecht's *Mother Courage and Her Children* with Diana Rigg, Bohdan Poraj and Brett Fancy at the National Theatre, London, November, 1995, photograph by Robbie Jack. CORBIS/Robbie Jack. Reproduced by permission.—From a theatre production of Christopher Marlowe's *Edward II* with Ian McKellan as Edward II and James Laurenson as Gaveston at the Picadilly Theatre, London, January 26, 1970, a homosexual love scene between Edward II and Laurenson, photograph. CORBIS/Hulton-Deutsch Collection. Reproduced by permission.—From a theatre production of Harold Pinter's *The Birthday Party* with John Alderton as Stanley and Paula Wilcox as Lulu at the Shaw Theatre, London, 1975, Lulu is applying makeup while Stanley in his PJ's looks on, photograph. CORBIS/Hulton-Deutsch Collection. Reproduced by permission.—From a theatre production of *No Exit* by Jean-Paul Sartre, Directed by Jeff Bell, at Performance Network, with (l-r) Wendy Wright as Inez, Troy F. Sill as Joseph Garcin and Nancy Wright as Estelle, December, 1997, photograph by Wayne M. Fager. © Wayne M. Fager. Reproduced by permission.—From a theatre production of *Picnic* by William Inge, Directed by Joshua Logan at the Music Box Theatre, with Janice Rule, Peggy Conklin, Kim Stanley and Ralph Meeker, May 5, 1953, photograph by Zinn Arthur. AP/Wide World Photos. Reproduced by permission.—From a theatre production of *The Iceman Cometh* by Eugene O'Neill in New York, with (l-r) James Barton as Hickey the Traveling Salesman, Dudley Digges as the Saloon Keeper, Jeanne Cagney and Ruth Gilbert in a cheap gin-mill on New York's West Side, October 4, 1946, photograph. AP/Wide World Photos. Reproduced by permission.—From a theatre production of *The Member of the Wedding* by Carson McCullers, with (l-r) Julie Harris, Ethel Waters and Branden de Wilde, photograph. AP/Wide World Photos. Reproduced by permission.—From a theatre production of Wendy Wasserstein's *The Heidi Chronicles,* Directed by Norman W. Johnson, Jr., at Ithaca College Theatre, December 4-6, 1997, photograph by Rachel Hogancamp. ITHACA COLLEGE THEATRE. Reproduced by permission.—From a theatre production of Wendy Wasserstein's *The Heidi Chronicles,* Directed by Norman W. Johnson, Jr., at Ithaca College Theatre, December 4-6, 1997, photograph by Rachel Hogancamp. ITHACA COLLEGE THEATRE. Reproduced by permission.—Inge, William R., photograph. The Library of Congress.—Kushner, Tony, photograph. AP/Wide World Photos. Reproduced by permission.—Man in wire horse mask, holding woman, from the play *Equus,* by Peter Shaffer, 1974, photograph by Zoe Dominic. Reproduced by permission of the photographer.—Marlowe, Christopher, engraving. Corbis-Bettmann. Reproduced by permission.—McCullers, Carson, photograph. AP/Wide World Photos. Reproduced by permission.—O'Neill, Eugene G., photograph. The Library of Congress.—Pinter, Harold, photograph. AP/Wide World Photos. Reproduced by permission.—Prometheus Brings Fire from The Heavens to Humanity, photograph. Corbis-Bettmann. Reproduced by permission.—Sartre, Jean-Paul, photograph. AP/Wide World Photos. Reproduced by permission.—Shaffer, Peter, photograph by Jerry Bauer. © Jerry Bauer. Reproduced by permission.—Stoppard, Tom, photograph. AP/Wide World Photos. Reproduced by permission.—Valez, Luis, photograph. Arte Público Press—University of Houston. Reproduced by permission.—Wasserstein, Wendy, photograph. AP/Wide World Photos. Reproduced by permission.

Contributors

Christopher Busiel: Doctoral candidate, University of Texas, Austin. Entry on *Equus*.

Clare Cross: Doctoral candidate, University of Michigan, Ann Arbor. Entry on *The Iceman Cometh*.

John Fiero: Professor Emeritus of Drama and Playwriting, University of Southwestern Louisiana. Entry on *The Birthday Party*.

Lane A. Glenn: Author, educator, director, and actor, Lansing, Michigan. Entries on *Arcadia* and *Angels in America*.

Carole Hamilton: Freelance writer and instructor at Cary Academy, Cary, North Carolina. Entries on *Edward II* and *Zoot Suit*.

Elizabeth Judd: Freelance writer, Washington, D.C. Entry on *Uncle Vanya*.

Sheri Metzger: Freelance writer and Ph.D., Albuquerque, NM. Entry on *Picnic*.

Annette Petrusso: Freelance author and screenwriter, Austin, TX. Entries on *The Heidi Chronicles*, *Member of the Wedding*, *Mother Courage and Her Children*, and *No Exit*.

Arnold Schmidt: Ph.D. affiliated with the English department at California State University, Stanislau. Entry on *Prometheus Bound*.

Angels in America

TONY KUSHNER

1991

Angels in America is the first major work of playwright Tony Kushner, and its astounding success has turned the man and his writing into cultural icons of the late-twentieth century. Referred to by scholar John M. Clum in *Acting Gay: Male Homosexuality in Modern Drama* as "a turning point in the history of gay drama, the history of American drama, and of American literary culture," *Angels* has received numerous awards and critical accolades, including the Pulitzer Prize for drama and the Antoinette Perry (Tony) Award for best play. It has been produced in dozens of countries around the world and translated into several languages, including Chinese.

Interestingly, *Angels in America* began as a work made for hire. After writing only a handful of plays, and experiencing only one major production, Kushner was approached by Oskar Eustis, a resident director at the Mark Taper Forum in Los Angeles, who had been impressed by the playwright's first drama, *A Bright Room Called Day.* In 1987, Eustis asked Kushner to write a play about the impact of AIDS on the gay community in San Francisco for the Eureka Theater. The two applied for grants, conducted workshops, and developed the work, which became *Angels in America,* at the Mark Taper Forum. The play then went on to the Eureka and later to the National Theatre of Great Britain, where it began to attract its global following.

Angels in America is an "epic" drama, which means its plot unfolds over great distances of time

and place, involves many characters, and more than one story line. Two complete plays form the entire plot: the first part, *Millennium Approaches* and its second installment, *Perestroika.* Together, they present more than thirty characters in eight acts, fifty-nine scenes, and an epilogue.

Kushner subtitled his play "A Gay Fantasia on National Themes." Like a "fantasia," which is a medley of familiar tunes with variations and interludes, the play's scenes often seem musical, like operatic arias, playful duets, or powerful trios. Characters move in and out of conversations with each other, sometimes even overlapping other vignettes, which occur onstage at the same time, and the settings change rapidly from offices to bedrooms, from hospital wards to the imaginary South Pole.

For all its intricacies, however, the plot of the play is quite simple. It is the story of two couples whose relationships are disintegrating, set in America in the 1980s against a backdrop of greed, conservatism, sexual politics, and the discovery of an awful new disease: AIDS. It is this backdrop that provides *Angels in America* its magnitude and sets it apart from other love stories. In this play, the plot is largely driven by its themes, which are viewed from different characters' perspectives, as through a kaleidoscope, as the story unfolds.

AUTHOR BIOGRAPHY

Tony Kushner was born in Manhattan, New York, in 1956. While he was still an infant, his musician parents moved the family to Louisiana, where they played with the New Orleans Philharmonic. He developed an appreciation for opera and literature from his father and learned a passion for theatre from his mother, who acted in local plays. Kushner's views on religion, politics, and sex, hallmarks of his later work as a playwright, began to take shape during his early childhood. He attended Hebrew school, where he developed an attraction toward his teacher but would struggle to hide his homosexual feelings for several years. He felt further isolated as a Jew in the American South, where he regularly encountered anti-Semitism. When he left Lake Charles to attend Columbia University in New York he was, by his own estimation, liberal, ardently Zionist, and extremely closeted.

While at Columbia, he discovered new intellectual influences that changed his perspectives and would later shape his writing. He delved into the Middle Ages, found his own fantastical, spiritual side, and thought for a time he would become a medieval studies professor. It wasn't until after he received his B.A. that Kushner "came out" and began to live as an openly gay student and artist. He went on to study directing at New York University's Tisch School of the Arts. Kushner read Bertolt Brecht and Karl Marx and realized the awesome potential of a politically charged theatre. He credits Brecht, particularly the German's play *Mother Courage and Her Children,* with guiding him toward a career as a playwright.

A Bright Room Called Day (1985) was Kushner's first foray into professional theatre. The play, which initially received only a brief run at London's Bush Theatre, concerns a group of friends in pre-World War II and their responses to Hitler and Nazism. Critics were not kind to the work, especially in the United States where it was called "fatuous" and "an early front-runner for the most infuriating play of 1991." Kushner himself called the production a "catastrophe." The writer's next efforts were adaptations: *The Illusion* (1988), taken from Pierre Corneille's play *L'illusion comique;* and *Widows,* adapted from a book by fellow playwright Ariel Dorfman (*Death and the Maiden*) and produced in Los Angeles in 1991.

Kushner's next work would catapult him to the forefront of the American theatre and earn him praise on stages around the world. More than one critic labeled the AIDS drama *Angels in America* a spectacular, monumental achievement, and marveled at Kushner's ability to capture the mood of an era. As a result of his success the playwright emerged as a widely respected spokesperson for many marginalized groups, including not only gays and lesbians but blacks, Jews, agnostics, socialists, and artists, all of whom he depicted in a struggle for dignity, respect, and survival in his play.

Since *Angels in America* took the theatre world by storm in 1992, Kushner has continued writing and adapting plays, including *Slavs!* and his version of the popular Yiddish drama *The Dybbuk.* He has also become a prolific and highly respected essayist and lecturer, articulating his views on politics, race, class, and the arts in books and magazines and at conferences and college campuses around the country.

PLOT SUMMARY

Millennium Approaches: Act I, scene 1

It is late-October, 1985, and Rabbi Isidor Chemelwitz stands alone next to a small coffin, conducting the funeral service for Sarah Ironson. In his eulogy for the deceased, he describes her as a caring, devoted wife and mother who traveled from Eastern Europe to America to make a home for herself and the Jewish people in "the melting pot where nothing melted." Rabbi Chemelwitz says Sarah was "the last of the Mohicans," and warns that soon, "all the old will be dead."

Millennium Approaches: Act I, scene 2

The same day as the funeral, Roy Cohn is visited in his office by Joseph Porter Pitt. Roy is a vulgar man, who screams and swears as he juggles three different conversations on his office phone. Joe is a Mormon, sensitive to Roy's foul language but eager to advance his career. He is an attorney who has been working as a law clerk in the Court of Appeals, and Roy is ready to give him his big break: He wants the younger man to go to Washington and work for the Justice Department, where he can be Roy's eyes and ears. Joe is stunned, appreciative, and agrees to discuss the opportunity with his wife.

Millennium Approaches: Act I, scene 3

Joe's wife, Harper, spends her days alone, often in a haze from sedatives she takes, and longing for a closer relationship with her husband, who is drifting further and further away from her. This scene begins with Harper sitting at home, listening to the radio, and talking to herself. She fantasizes about the ozone layer, and what it must look like from space, where "guardian angels, hands linked, make a sort of spherical net, a blue-green nesting orb, a shell of safety for life itself." Alternately paranoid and visionary, Harper is like the canary in a coal mine. She is more sensitive to danger than ordinary people, yet unable to save herself from the trouble ahead.

She is caught in the midst of her reverie by Mr. Lies, an imaginary travel agent who offers to take her on a vacation away from her worries—perhaps to Antarctica or the ozone layer. Harper complains to Mr. Lies that she is worried about the coming third millennium, when all sorts of strange things could happen.

Tony Kushner

This time, her fantasy is interrupted by the abrupt appearance of Joe. Once again late coming home, Joe claims to have been "out walking" and pitches his news to Harper: Would she like to move to Washington?

Millennium Approaches: Act I, scene 4

Back at the funeral, Louis and Prior are sitting outside the funeral home, waiting for the service to continue at the cemetery. Louis is Sarah Ironson's grandson, though he hadn't visited her much since she moved into the Bronx Home of Aged Hebrews ten years earlier. The two men have been in a committed relationship for four years and banter with each other about their cat, who has run away, and Louis's closeted homosexuality at family gatherings, where he insists on calling himself "Lou" (to avoid the sibilant S, Prior jokes).

As the couple reflects on life and loss, Prior reveals something startling: He has developed a purple lesion on his arm. It is Kaposi's sarcoma, "the wine dark kiss of the angel of death," and an early visual sign of the Acquired Immune Deficiency Syndrome (AIDS). He has been hiding the mark for awhile, afraid that Louis might leave him when he found out. Louis reacts angrily.

Millennium Approaches: Act I, scene 5

This scene is split between Joe and Harper at home and Louis at the cemetery with the Rabbi and his grandmother's coffin. It is at this point that the relationships of the central couples—Joe and Harper, Louis and Prior—begin to disintegrate.

Joe pursues the subject of his new career opportunity with Harper, trying to convince her that Washington, D.C., would be a fine place to live. Harper is afraid of more change, however, and insists on staying put. Joe observes that her medication may be the cause of her anxiety.

Meanwhile, in the cemetery, Louis quizzes the Rabbi on the church's view of someone who abandons a loved one in great need. He is planning to leave Prior because he cannot face life with Prior's disease. The Rabbi, however, is more concerned with getting himself home, across town, than with counseling the confused Louis.

At the Pitt house, Joe speaks idealistically about the new America, led by the Republican conservatism of Ronald Reagan, a chord struck again later in the play by Roy and his assistant, Martin. Harper has no room for political idealism in her life. She is suspicious of Joe's "walks" and tries to rekindle desire between them by offering him sexual favors and asking for a baby. Joe turns away, obviously uncomfortable with her suggestions, and Harper drifts back into her troubled delirium, mumbling, "The world's coming to an end."

Millennium Approaches: Act I, scene 6

Joe finds Louis crying in the men's room of the offices of the Brooklyn Federal Court of Appeals, where they both work. Louis is mourning the sickness of his companion and upset about his decision to leave the AIDS-stricken Prior. Joe tries to comfort him and is "outed" by Louis, who recognizes immediately that the self-proclaimed Reaganite attorney is gay. On his way out the door, Louis playfully kisses Joe on the cheek.

Millennium Approaches: Act I, scene 7

Sometime after Joe and Louis meet in the men's room, Harper and Prior find each other in a mutual dream scene. In his dream, Prior is seated at a table, applying drag makeup and musing about the distance between the life he longs to lead and the one his sickness has handed him, when Harper appears in a valium-induced hallucination. They confront each other with "revelations." She sees

the disease in him but insists there is a part deep inside that is still clean and healthy. He drops the news that her husband, Joe, is a homosexual, something she has been suspecting for a while.

After Harper leaves the dream, a feather floats to the ground and a voice from above calls to Prior, telling him to "prepare the way" for the "infinite descent."

Millennium Approaches: Act I, scene 8

In another split scene, the two couples are back with their respective partners—Harper and Joe at home, Louis and Prior in bed. Harper summons the courage to confront her husband with the truth they have both been denying. She begs him to confess to her that he is a homosexual, that their marriage has been a facade and a sin against their Mormon religion. Still, given the opportunity to reveal his secret, Joe resists and will say only that he is "a very good man who has worked very hard to become good."

In the other part of the scene, Prior's illness is getting worse, his symptoms more severe, yet Louis cannot even bear to hear him talk about it, let along comfort his lover. Looking for an opportunity of his own, Louis asks Prior if he would hate him for walking out. "Yes," Prior responds.

Millennium Approaches: Act I, scene 9

In a doctor's office, Henry, Cohn's physician, breaks the news to his patient that Roy has AIDS. The lawyer, however, refuses the diagnosis. He does so not because he is afraid of death or disease but because of the social stigma attached: "Roy Cohn is not a homosexual," he tells Henry, "Roy Cohn is a heterosexual man who fucks around with guys."

Millennium Approaches: Act II, scene 1

A month has gone by, and Prior is deteriorating rapidly. In the middle of the night, late in December, Louis finds him on the floor, incontinent and in terrible pain. Louis wants to call for an ambulance, but Prior is afraid if he goes to the hospital he won't return. He faints in Louis's arms.

Millennium Approaches: Act II, scene 2

The same night, a similar crisis occurs at the Pitt home. Harper's mental anguish is beginning to match Prior's physical suffering. She tells Joe that she feels herself "going off again," slipping away into her pills and troubled dreams. She even suggests it is time for him to leave her, to go off to Washington alone, but he refuses.

Millennium Approaches: Act II, scene 3

It is one in the morning the next day and Louis is sitting near Prior's bed in a hospital, discussing his condition with Emily, a nurse. He tells her about the significance of Prior's name. It is an old, respected name in the Walters family, which dates back to the Norman Conquest (the overthrow of the government of England in 1066 by the forces of Normandy).

Louis's musings on Prior's family history agitates his despair. While Prior's ancestors have been clinging to each other for generations, through wars, death, and the long march of history, Louis can't stand the suffering he sees now. On his way out the door, for a walk in the park, he asks the nurse to tell Prior goodbye for him.

Millennium Approaches: Act II, scene 4

An hour later, Louis is in Central Park, having sex in the bushes with a stranger. When their condom breaks, the harried Louis tells the man, "Keep going. Infect me. I don't care." But the man is frightened away by Louis's strange behavior.

Meanwhile, in a scene that overlaps Louis's park misadventure, Joe is at a bar with Roy, seeking some solace of his own. He is torn between the sense of duty he feels as a Mormon and as a husband to Harper and the sense of dedication he has, to his work and to Roy. The elder attorney goads him, telling him that, "Everyone who makes it in this world makes it because somebody older and more powerful takes an interest." Roy would like to be that somebody for Joe, helping him establish himself in the big time politics of Washington, D.C. To further leverage his position, and take advantage of Joe's sensitivity, Roy admits that he his dying, though he tells Joe it is cancer that is killing him.

Millennium Approaches: Act II, scene 5

A few days later, Prior is still in his hospital bed, sick but improving. He is visited by Belize, the duty nurse, who is a black former drag queen and, coincidentally, former lover of Prior's. Belize tries to comfort him with an assortment of herbal "voodoo" remedies and a listening ear. Prior is distressed about Louis's absence and confused about a voice he keeps hearing—a voice that is a little frightening but strangely comforting and arousing. After Belize leaves, the Voice is heard. It tells Prior to prepare for a marvelous work that must be done, then disappears.

Millennium Approaches: Act II, scene 6

It is January, 1986, a few weeks later, and Joe and Roy are meeting Martin, a Reagan Administration Justice Department lawyer in a Manhattan restaurant. The purpose of the rendezvous is to give Joe the hard sell. Because he borrowed half a million dollars from a client (and failed to repay it), Roy is being threatened with disbarment by the New York State Bar Association, and he desperately wants Joe to take a job with the Justice Department, where he can help Roy's case. Joe is disturbed by the ethics of the situation and still concerned about Harper, but he agrees to think about it some more.

Millennium Approaches: Act II, scene 7

Joe and Louis run into each other during lunch on the steps of the Hall of Justice building in Brooklyn. Both men are feeling extreme anxiety, which shows itself in different ways. Louis jokes about Republican politics and his spontaneous behavior. Joe admits to feeling overwhelmed and wishing sometimes that everything he was obligated to, including justice and love, would just go away. For a moment they connect and Louis offers to keep Joe company, but Joe retreats and they go their separate ways.

Millennium Approaches: Act II, scene 8

That night, drunk and desperate, Joe stands at a payphone in Central Park and calls his Mormon mother in Salt Lake City to confess that he is a homosexual. Confused and angry, his mother tells him he's being ridiculous, drinking is a sin and he should go home to his wife. She hangs up on him.

Millennium Approaches: Act II, scene 9

The next morning, Joe nearly confesses the truth to Harper. He admits he has never been attracted to her and that he is the source of many of her problems and hallucinations. She gets more and more agitated by his confession and finally calls for Mr. Lies to take her away. He shows up, dressed in Antarctic explorer's gear, and they promptly disappear. At the same time, Louis breaks the news to Prior that he will not be coming back; as much as he loves Prior, he can't cope with his disease.

Millennium Approaches: Act II, scene 10

Nearly a continent away, in Salt Lake City, Utah, Joe's mother, Hannah, stands in front of her house with Sister Ella Chapter. Hannah has decided to sell the house and move away and has enlisted her friend Sister Ella to help with the sale. They discuss the Mormon life in Salt Lake, and Sister Ella warns Hannah that the world outside is a dangerous place.

Millennium Approaches: Act III, scene 1

Alone in his apartment, Prior wakes from a nightmare to find an apparition dressed in the clothes of a thirteenth-century British squire seated next to his bed. The ghost introduces himself as another Prior Walter (Prior 1)—the fifth in the Walter family line. He is soon joined by another Prior Walter (Prior 2), a ghost from seventeenth-century London. Both men died young from plagues—as it seems Prior will as well—and they have been sent to prepare the way for "the messenger." They call Prior a prophet and seer, chant mysteriously, and disappear, echoing the same words as the Voice from earlier scenes: "Prepare, prepare, The Infinite Descent, A breath, a feather, Glory to. . . ."

Millennium Approaches: Act III, scene 2

In a split scene, Louis and Belize sit in a coffee shop, passionately discussing race, sexual identity, and politics, while, at the hospital, Emily delivers a medicated IV drip to Prior. In the middle of a frenzied tirade, Louis tells Belize that one of America's problems is its lack of spirituality. "There are no angels in America," he rants, "no spiritual past, no racial past, there's only the political." Louis's contradictory opinions, particularly his views on the importance of race, anger Belize, who is running out of patience with Louis's hysterics. Although Louis calms down, expresses his love for Prior, and asks about his condition, he is still afraid to be near him. Belize leaves Louis behind, frustrated and confused.

Meanwhile, Prior describes the current state of his illness to Emily. Many of his physical symptoms have receded, but he fears he is losing his mind. In the middle of their conversation, he imagines she is speaking Hebrew to him. Then, while she is writing her report, he sees a giant book with a flaming Aleph (the first letter of the Hebrew alphabet) rise up through the floor, slam shut, and disappear. Emily notices nothing, and Prior runs away.

Millennium Approaches: Act III, scene 3

Fleeing a reality she cannot confront, and caught up in her own hallucination, Harper appears in Antarctica with Mr. Lies. A light snow is falling, and she is imagining how she can build a city of her own in the ice, befriend an Eskimo, and give birth to a baby girl with thick white fur and a marsupial pouch. Mr. Lies observes that what she is experiencing is "a retreat, a vacuum, its virtue is that it lacks everything; deep-freeze for the feelings."

Millennium Approaches: Act III, scene 4

Hannah Porter Pitt, Joe's mother, arrives in New York after selling her home in Salt Lake City. She waited several hours at the airport for her son to meet her, then took a bus in search of Brooklyn, and ended up being deposited at the final stop on the driver's route: the Bronx. She meets a homeless woman, mumbling to herself and warming her hands by a trash fire in an oil drum. The Woman gives her directions to the Mormon Visitor's Center and sends her on her way with the suggestion that, "In the new century I think we will all be insane."

Millennium Approaches: Act III, scene 5

While Hannah is in search of Joe, he is across town at Roy's house, breaking some bad news to the ailing attorney: Joe will not be going to Washington on Roy's behalf. He explains to Roy that his wife is missing, his mother is on her way, and he finds himself unable to break the law, even for the mentor he claims to love as a father. Angry and toying with Joe, Roy smiles at first, accepting his decision, then shouts insults at him and pushes him across the room. After Joe leaves, Roy collapses on the floor. His own illness is beginning to overtake him. In his delirium he sees the ghost of Ethel Rosenberg—the woman he sent to the electric chair years before as a traitor to her country. She warns Roy that she will be seeing him soon, in death, then calmly picks up the phone and dials an ambulance for him.

Millennium Approaches: Act III, scene 6

Prior is in his bedroom with the ghosts of his ancestors—Prior 1 and Prior 2. They are trying to help him prepare for the mysterious arrival he has been warned about. To help him relax, they conjure a spectral image of Louis for him to dance with. As

Prior and the imaginary Louis dance, the two ghosts disappear. Then, suddenly, Louis vanishes and the sound of wings fills the room.

Millennium Approaches: Act III, scene 7

Louis and Joe meet in the park. Each man is desperate for some kind of meaningful contact but filled with doubt and self-hatred for their recent actions. Finally, they kiss, then walk away together, as the scene's focus changes to Prior's apartment. The sound of the wings is getting louder and louder, until finally a deafening din fills the room, the lights flicker, change colors, then plunge into darkness. There is a tremendous crash, followed by a brilliant white light, and the Angel of America appears, floating over Prior's bed. "Greetings, Prophet," she addresses him, "The Great Work begins: The Messenger has arrived."

Perestroika: Act I, scene 1

The second part of *Angels in America* begins in Moscow at the Soviet Kremlin, where Aleksii Antedilluvianovich Prelapsarianov, the world's oldest living Bolshevik, is delivering a passionate speech about the need for a practical political theory to guide his country. Near the end of his oration, a great crashing sound is heard, and the scene changes to reveal the tableau at the end of *Millennium Approaches:* Prior cowering in his bed with the Angel of America hovering in the air above him. Once again she tells him, "The Messenger has arrived" Prior replies, "Go away."

Perestroika: Act I, scene 2

Louis and Joe appear at Louis's apartment. There is an initial awkward moment, as Joe nearly loses his resolve and leaves; but Louis manages to seduce him with kindness and tenderness. As the two men begin kissing and caressing each other, the scene changes to Harper's imaginary Antarctica.

Perestroika: Act I, scene 3

Mr. Lies is sitting by himself, playing the oboe, when Harper appears with a small pine tree. The sounds in the background keep changing from the sea and the wind to the din of city traffic, as Harper begins to fade in and out of her fantasy. In her dream, Joe appears, wrapped only in Louis's bed sheet. She accuses him of falling out of love with her and begs him to come back. He refuses and

vanishes, leaving her alone in the park with the flashing lights of a police car.

Perestroika: Act I, scene 4

Hannah has managed to find Joe and Harper's apartment in Brooklyn. As she walks in the door, the phone rings. The call is from the police, who have found Harper in Prospect Park with the pine tree she apparently chewed down. Hannah asks the caller not to send Harper to the hospital and agrees to come and collect her "peculiar" daughter-in-law.

Perestroika: Act I, scene 5

Back in his apartment, Prior has turned a corner in his battle with disease. His encounter with the Angel, which he now thinks was a dream, caused him to have an orgasm in his sleep, and for the first time in months he is feeling exhilarated. He calls Belize at the hospital to tell him the good news. Shortly afterward, Belize calls him back with some news of his own: Roy Cohn has just checked in with AIDS.

Perestroika: Act I, scene 6

Lying in his hospital bed, sick and scared, Roy is as irascible as ever. When Belize comes in to administer an IV drip, Roy hurls a string of foul-mouthed, bigoted epithets at him that causes Belize to bristle and threaten the dying man. As offensive as Roy is, and as much as Belize hates him for what he represents, the nurse can't help but feel sorry for the patient. He warns Roy not to accept the radiation his doctor will surely prescribe and suggests he use whatever contacts he has to secure a trustworthy supply of azidothymidine (AZT), the only drug being prescribed that seems to have some effect on the AIDS virus. After Belize leaves, Roy phones Martin and blackmails him into finding the AZT he needs.

Perestroika: Act I, scene 7

A split scene between Louis's bedroom in Alphabetland and the Pitt apartment in Brooklyn shows three weeks in the lives of Joe and Louis, Harper and Hannah. After finally breaking through to one another, Louis and Joe are spending as much time as they can in bed, in each other's arms. They have sex, argue politics and religion, and try to forget the relationships they have left behind. At the same time, Hannah is working on Harper, trying to retrieve her from her madness by getting her to go to work at the Mormon Visitor's Center. Though he claims to be happy and sleep peacefully through the night, Joe is haunted by visions of Harper, who appears to taunt him for being in love with Louis.

Perestroika: Act II, scene 1

Prior accompanies Belize to the funeral of a mutual friend, who happened to be a well-known New York City drag queen. Prior's appearance and demeanor have changed. He is dressed all in black, wearing a long coat with a fringed scarf wrapped around his head, and he has become very introspective. He explains to Belize that the Angel he thought he dreamt was actually real and that he has become a prophet of some kind.

Perestroika: Act II, scene 2

To illustrate Prior's story, the scene changes to his bedroom three weeks earlier and the arrival of the Angel. While Belize stands nearby and watches, Prior replays his encounter with the celestial being. She has come to instruct Prior in the ways of prophecy, to reveal to him the hidden location of the implements of divination (under the tile near his kitchen sink). She explains to him that God created the world for His pleasure, then split it into two parts—men and women—in order to release the potential for *change*. As people evolved and sought more and more change, God grew fascinated with his creation's curiosity and eventually left Heaven to pursue the experience for himself. Prior has been charged with spreading the word to humanity: They must stop moving, stop changing, in order to restore God to Heaven and put the universe right again.

The flashback disappears, and Prior rejoins Belize in front of the funeral home. Belize thinks Prior's vision is simply a reaction to his illness and the loss of Louis, but Prior is nearly convinced. ''Maybe I am a prophet,'' he tells his friend, ''Maybe the world has driven God from Heaven, incurred the angels' wrath.'' And it has been left to Prior to run away or help find God again.

Perestroika: Act III, scene 1

It is February, 1986, a week later. Roy is in his hospital room trying to manage his disbarment hearing by telephone, with the ghost of Ethel Rosenberg standing a deathwatch over him. Belize appears with Roy's prescribed medication and learns the conniving lawyer has secured his own private stash of AZT—more than he could use in fifty years. Roy refuses to share any of the coveted drugs. He and Belize exchange racial insults, and Belize

simply takes a few bottles, leaving Roy alone with Ethel and convulsed with pain.

Perestroika: Act III, scene 2

The same day, across town, Prior pays a visit to the Mormon Visitor's Center, where Hannah and Harper have become volunteer caretakers. He tells Harper he is an ''Angelologist'' conducting research on Angels and his fieldwork has led him to the Mormons. The principal attraction at the Center is the Diorama Room, where mannequins arranged in a wagon-train tableau on a little stage depict a Mormon family's trek from Missouri to Salt Lake. Together, they listen to the recorded reenactment.

Fantasy and reality blur as the mechanical figures relate the history of the Mormons' westward journey. The real Louis walks into the scene and argues with the Mormon father, who looks like Joe. It is a hallucination shared by both Prior and Harper, and it ends when both figures walk off the stage together. Harper pulls the curtain closed as Hannah returns to check on her guest. Not understanding Harper's dementia or Prior's visions of angels, she tells them the diorama is closing for repairs and it is time to leave. Left alone, Harper talks to the Mormon Mother in the diorama, who comes to life and escorts her away.

Perestroika: Act III, scene 3

That afternoon, Joe and Louis are sitting in the dunes at Jones Beach, a once-popular spot for homosexual encounters. They are watching the waves roll over the sand. Joe swears his love for Louis and offers to give up anything for him, including his religion. Louis, however, longs to see Prior again and is beginning to realize his love for his sick companion is greater than his fear of Prior's disease.

Perestroika: Act III, scene 4

Joe and Louis remain on stage as the scene splits to include the New York Hospital. It is late at night, and Belize enters Roy's hospital room to administer his medication. The morphine in Roy's IV drip is causing him to hallucinate, and he mistakes the nurse for the incarnation of Death, coming to take him away.

Perestroika: Act III, scene 5

The scene splits again, as Harper and the Mormon Mother from the Visitor's Center diorama appear at the Brooklyn Heights Promenade. Harper is seeking advice from the Mother. She wants to know how people *change*. While the women discuss the pain and suffering change causes, the scene splits a final time to reveal Prior at home, removing his prophet attire and taking his medication. The four separate scenes now include all the major characters in the play. Louis leaves Joe sitting on the beach, walks to a phone booth, and calls Prior.

Perestroika: Act IV, scene 1

It is the next day, and a split scene shows two attempted reconciliations. At the hospital, Joe is visiting Roy, whose condition is deteriorating rapidly. At first the forgiveness Joe seeks seems at hand: The dying Roy offers his blessing of life to his protege. Then Joe, trying to win more approval, tells Roy about his new relationship with Louis. Roy is enraged and leaps from his bed to attack Joe. Belize rushes in to restore order, forcing Roy back into bed and sending Joe away.

At the same time, Louis and Prior meet on a park bench. Prior, who is ready to make Louis's reunion as difficult as possible, is further hurt and angered to discover that Louis does not want to return to him; he merely wants some understanding between them. Prior surprises Louis by telling him he knows about his new lover and even knows he is a Mormon. Louis's defense is that he needed companionship. Disgusted, Prior walks away, leaving Louis alone on the bench.

Perestroika: Act IV, scene 2

In an attempt to face his frustration, Prior drags Belize to the Hall of Justice in Brooklyn to find Joe and confront the man who has replaced him in Louis's life. The duo stumbles into Joe's office, then promptly lose their resolve. Prior sees a handsome, healthy man he can't compete against; Belize recognizes Joe as the law clerk from Roy's hospital room. They scramble away before Joe can catch them.

Perestroika: Act IV, scene 3

The next day, Louis and Belize meet at the Bethesda Fountain in Central Park, one of Prior's favorite spots. Louis wants Belize to help him communicate with Prior, but the nurse is too frustrated with Louis's antics. He tells Louis about their visit to Joe and shocks him with the news that Joe is connected with the villainous Roy Cohn.

Perestroika: Act IV, scene 4

At the same time, in the Mormon Visitor's Center, Joe and his mother, Hannah, appear together for the first time. Like Louis, Joe is hesitantly searching for his mate, seeking some kind of absolution for his terrible behavior but not knowing exactly what he wants. Hannah is stern with him but still wants to help somehow. Between them, they realize that Harper has run away, and Joe leaves to find her.

Prior appears at the Center, passing Joe on his way out. He has come to warn Joe about Louis, that he is weak and unfaithful, but turns to Hannah instead. As he tries to deliver his message, his illness overtakes him and he collapses. Hannah helps him up and they head off to the hospital.

Perestroika: Act IV, scene 5

Late that afternoon Joe finds Harper, barefoot and without a coat, standing in the freezing rain at the Promenade in Brooklyn Heights. She is staring at the Manhattan skyline and trying desperately to come to terms with her scattered life. Joe collects his wounded wife, and they head toward home.

Perestroika: Act IV, scene 6

At the hospital, Emily examines Prior and scolds him for ruining his condition, just when he was getting better. Prior tries to explain his encounters with the Angel to Hannah, who tells him he had a vision like the one the Mormon prophet Joseph Smith had. The two are trying to come to terms with each other, when a roll of thunder warns Prior that the Angel is returning for him. Hannah promises to stay by his side and watch over him.

Perestroika: Act IV, scene 7

Joe and Harper are lying in bed. Apparently, they have just had sex, and Harper tries again to get Joe to admit his homosexual urges to her. They are right back where they were before, which is too much for Joe to handle. He rises, dresses, and again leaves her behind.

Perestroika: Act IV, scene 8

Later that night, Joe visits Louis at his apartment. On Belize's advice, Louis has been researching Roy Cohn and the legal decisions Joe has ghost written for the judge he serves. Many of the decisions have been extremely conservative and, in Louis's estimation, unethical. They argue about the cases, Joe's scruples, and his relationship with Roy Cohn. Their debate turns into a brawl, and, in his rage, Joe beats Louis severely. He tries to apologize, but Louis sends him away.

Perestroika: Act IV, scene 9

Back in Roy's hospital room, the ghost of Ethel Rosenberg has arrived with some terrible news for the near-dead man: he has been disbarred. For all his struggles, he will not be a lawyer when he dies. As his final act of petty revenge, Roy tricks Ethel into singing him a lullaby. When she is finished, he brags that he finally made Ethel Rosenberg sing (to ''sing'' is slang for a confession; this is a reference to the confession the historical Roy Cohn never won from Rosenberg during her trial). Cohn dies.

Perestroika: Act V, scene 1

The Angel returns. It is much later the same night in Prior's hospital room, and Hannah has fallen asleep in a chair near Prior's bed. An eerie light appears, then blackness and thunder, and the Angel materializes. Although terrified, Hannah manages to offer Prior advice: wrestle with the Angel and demand to be released from his role as Prophet. Prior grapples with the Angel, and the two wrestle around the room amidst screeching voices, blasts of music, and strange flashes of light. Finally the Angel relents. A ladder appears, leading up to Heaven, and the Angel invites Prior to climb it and return the Book of Prophecy he has been given.

Perestroika: Act V, scene 2

Prior appears in Heaven, dressed in robes like Charlton Heston in *The Ten Commandments*. Heaven looks like San Francisco after the earthquake of 1906. He meets Harper, who is not dead but merely visiting after her sexual encounter with Joe. Harper disappears and the scenery changes to the Hall of the Upper Orders. The Angel appears to escort Prior to a meeting with the rest of the angelic Continental Principalities.

Perestroika: Act V, scene 3

Down on earth, Belize has called Louis to Roy's deathbed. He wants him to say the Kaddish, the Jewish prayer for the dead, over Roy's body, then take the dead man's stash of AZT. Louis refuses at first, objecting to prayer for such an evil man and protesting that he doesn't remember any Jewish rituals. Guided by the ghost of Ethel Rosenberg, however, Louis manages to recite the entire ceremony.

Perestroika: Act V, scene 4

Joe returns to his apartment in Brooklyn, looking for Harper. Instead he finds the ghost of Roy, who witnessed the fight he had with Louis. Roy commends Joe on his viciousness, kisses him, then vanishes, just as Harper walks through the door.

Perestroika: Act V, scene 5

The scene changes quickly back to Heaven, where the Continental Principalities are gathered in their Council Room. They are huddled around a damaged 1940s model radio, listening to news from earth that tells them what the future holds for God's creation below. A crackling report tells them about a disaster at the Chernobyl Nuclear Power Plant that will occur in two months. The Angel of Antarctica remarks that he/she will be happy to watch the humans suffer, since they are responsible for the misery in Heaven since God left. The group begins arguing about technology, like their radio and nuclear power, and the course of human events, when suddenly the Angel of America appears with Prior.

Prior informs the Angels that he wants to return the book he has been given, abandon his role as prophet, and go back to living his life as before, miserable as he might be. The Angels try to convince him that everyone on earth would be happier if he would help convince them to stop moving and changing, but Prior is determined not to cooperate. Regardless of the suffering it entails, ''I want more life,'' he tells the assembly. He adds that, if God returns, they should sue Him for abandoning everyone. Prior exits.

Perestroika: Act V, scene 6

Out on the streets of Heaven, Prior encounters Sarah Ironson, Louis's dead grandmother, and Isidor Chemelwitz, the Rabbi who performed her funeral service at the beginning of *Millennium Approaches*. They are seated on wooden crates playing cards. The Rabbi helps Prior conjure the ladder back to earth, and Sarah encourages him to struggle with the Almighty, because after all, ''It's the Jewish way.''

Perestroika: Act V, scene 7

In a quick scene, Prior passes Roy on his journey back to earth. Roy is standing waist-deep in a smoldering pit, seemingly talking to God about the abandonment suit the Angels are bringing against him. As the slickest lawyer in Heaven or Hell, Roy agrees to represent God, even though, he tells his holy client, ''You're guilty as hell.''

Perestroika: Act V, scene 8

Back in his bed in the hospital, Prior wakes from his adventure in Heaven like Dorothy in the

The Wizard of Oz. He tries to tell Belize, Emily, and Hannah about the Angels and how he only wanted to go home again, but they are interrupted by the arrival of Louis. Emily leaves to finish her rounds of the hospital wards, Hannah goes to put her life back in order, and on his way out, Belize offers Prior Cohn's AZT horde. Louis tells Prior he wants to come back.

Perestroika: Act V, scene 9

The two troubled couples go their separate ways. Harper confronts Joe in their apartment and demands his credit card so she can go off and start a life of her own. As consolation, she offers Joe her valium and suggests he goes exploring. At the same time, in the hospital room, Prior tells Louis he still loves him, but he can't come back.

Perestroika: Act V, scene 10

The scene splits to include Harper on board a jet plane, headed for San Francisco. She describes a dream she had in which the souls of the dying on earth floated up in the sky, where they took the place of the angels and repaired holes in the ozone.

Perestroika: Epilogue

Prior, Louis, Belize, and Hannah are gathered at the Bethesda Fountain in Central Park, Prior's favorite spot, four years later. The world has changed somewhat—the Berlin Wall has fallen and through the Russian leader Gorbachev's policy of ''Perestroika'' the Cold War seems to be over. Prior is living with his disease and plans to live longer still. Together, the group relates the story of the angel Bethesda, who appeared in the Temple square in Jerusalem long ago. Where the angel landed, a fountain appeared that could heal anyone who walked through its waters. Hopefully, they say, the fountain will appear again when the Millennium comes and everyone will be healed and purified. Prior blesses the audience, wishes them ''More Life,'' and tells them: ''The Great Work Begins.''

CHARACTERS

Angel of America

The Angel is one of seven celestial beings who form the Continental Principalities, one representative in Heaven for each continent on Earth. She is the Continental Principality of America, a beautiful being with magnificent gray wings. In *Millennium*

MEDIA ADAPTATIONS

- While several attempts at adapting *Angels in America* to film have occurred since the play's initial acclaim, the project remains in development, with various directors, including Robert Altman, attached at one time or another.

Approaches her appearance is preceded by strange lights, music, voices, and ghostly messengers. She crashes through Prior's ceiling at the end of *Millennium Approaches* to tell him he has been chosen as the Prophet who will help the world stop changing and return God to Heaven. In *Perestroika* she loses a wrestling match to Prior and is forced to take him up to Heaven, where he confronts the Continental Principalities and demands to be released from prophecy.

Norman Arriaga

See Belize

Belize

Belize, whose real name is Norman Arriaga, is a former drag queen and a former lover of Prior's. He is a nurse at New York Hospital who cares for Roy Cohn when he is admitted with AIDS. Throughout the play he acts as friend and counsel to Prior and adversary to Louis. When Louis abandons Prior it is Belize who visits the sick man, comforts him, and ever secures drugs for him (Cohn's stash of AZT). Each time they meet, he and Louis argue over politics, race, religion, and the meaning of love. Belize is smart, witty, and capable of being dismissive and offensive, but his actions speak louder than his words. In one way or another, he helps everyone he meets, like an angel on earth.

Sister Ella Chapter

Sister Ella Chapter appears only once, briefly, in *Millennium Approaches*. She is a friend of Hannah Pitt's in Salt Lake City, as well as a real estate saleswoman who helps Hannah sell her house for her move out East. Sister Ella, like the angels, believes people should stay put, and in her mind Salt Lake City, the home of the Mormons, is the best place to put down roots.

Rabbi Isidor Chemelwitz

The Rabbi appears twice, once at the beginning of *Millennium Approaches,* when he conducts the funeral service for Sarah Ironson, and once in *Perestroika,* where he plays cards with the dead woman in Heaven and helps Prior find his way back to Earth after his confrontation with the angels. Rabbi Chemelwitz sets the tone for the entire play in his eulogy when he warns that, "Pretty soon . . . all the old will be dead."

Roy M. Cohn

The character of Roy M. Cohn is based on the real-life lawyer who prosecuted Ethel and Julius Rosenberg for treason in 1951 and died of AIDS in 1986. Like the real Cohn, he is loud, vulgar, mean, and treacherous. He is a closeted homosexual who flatters, bribes, and threatens people to get what he wants, both in and out of the courtroom. In the play he is fighting for his professional status and his life, both of which he loses. In spite of Roy's efforts to plant a friend on the inside, the New York Bar Association revokes his license to practice law because of his unethical behavior. At the same time, he is stricken with AIDS, which he tries to pass off as liver cancer. He dies in a hospital bed with the ghost of Ethel Rosenberg watching over him.

Later, in the afterlife, Roy becomes God's attorney, defending the Almighty against the abandonment lawsuit brought by the Continental Principalities. Although Cohn existed in history, Kushner is careful to note that he has invented his character's words in the play and taken liberties with his actions.

Continental Principalities

The Continental Principalities are a group of seven powerful angels who represent each of the continents of Earth. They appear in the play only once, as a group, assembled in their Council Room in Heaven, where they have convened a "Permanent Emergency Council" and stand perpetual watch over the dismal state of human affairs below. They

bicker and fight and are easily distracted. For all their splendor and power they seem oddly human. When Prior arrives in Heaven, escorted by the Angel of America, they try to convince him to be their Prophet who will instruct the world to cease its constant change, but they are unsuccessful. When Prior leaves, he suggests they should sue God for abandonment, which, with Cohn as their lawyer, they do.

Emily

Emily is a nurse at Saint Vincent's Hospital who cares for Prior each time he is admitted. She is tender and sincere and has seen many cases of AIDS in the last few years. She offers hope that Prior's condition is better than many and tries to help him learn ways of living with his illness.

Martin Heller

Martin is a lawyer in the Justice Department in Washington, D.C., and a friend of Cohn's. He appears briefly in *Millennium Approaches* to help Roy convince Joe to move to Washington and take a job in the Justice Department, where he can watch out for Roy's best interests. Appearing in a Manhattan restaurant, Martin is the voice of extreme right-wing Republicans in the play. He boasts about the Republican revolution in Washington and predicts "the end of Liberalism. The end of New Deal Socialism. The end of ipso facto secular humanism. The dawning of a genuinely American political personality. Modeled on Ronald Wilson Reagan."

Doctor Henry

Henry has been Roy's doctor for nearly thirty years and has treated him for a variety of sexually transmitted diseases. He knows Roy is a homosexual in denial, but he has to break the news to him that he has contracted AIDS and will likely die soon. Under threats from Cohn, Henry attempts to cover up the real nature of the lawyer's disease. The doctor gets Cohn admitted to the hospital as a patient with liver cancer.

Louis Ironson

Louis is a word processor for the Second Circuit Court of Appeals in New York and the lover of first Prior then Joe. He is a semi-closeted homosexual, openly gay around his friends but reserved and "butch," as Prior describes his exaggerated macho behavior, around his family and coworkers. Louis's political ideology, religion, and philosophy of life seem as complicated as his sexual identity. In the course of the play he claims that God and angels don't exist yet later finds himself saying the Jewish prayer for the dead in Hebrew over the body of Cohn. He detests bigots and hypocrisy and admits to voting for Jesse Jackson, then claims race is unimportant in America and finds himself in bed with a right-wing Republican Mormon. Louis desperately searches for the underlying, defining meaning of life and continually finds confusion and disappointment.

At the beginning of the play, he has been in a serious, monogamous relationship with Prior for four years, when Prior reveals a terrible secret: he has contracted AIDS and will soon begin to suffer the disease's worst symptoms. Wracked with guilt but panicked that his comfortable, somewhat predictable world is changing, Louis abandons his lover and runs straight into the arms of Joe, who is facing an identity crisis of his own. Louis spends the rest of the play sparring with Joe about his conservative politics and trying to reconcile his love for Prior with his fear of disease and decay. Near the end, when he has finally summoned the courage to ask Prior to let him return, it is too late. Although they remain in love with each other, Prior can't forgive him for the pain he has caused.

Sarah Ironson

Sarah is Louis's grandmother. Although she doesn't appear until late in *Perestroika,* her presence is known from the beginning of the play, when Rabbi Chemelwitz eulogizes her as "the last of the Mohicans." On Earth, she was a Russian-Jewish immigrant who raised a large family in New York before retiring in her old age to the Bronx Home of Aged Hebrews. In Heaven, she plays cards with Rabbi Chemelwitz and tells Prior, "You should struggle with the Almighty! It's the Jewish way."

Mr. Lies

Mr. Lies is Harper's imaginary friend, who appears each time she retreats into fantasy or hallucination. He takes the form of a travel agent dressed like a jazz musician and alternately leads Harper away from her worries and directs her back to them.

Man in the Park

The Man in the Park is a stranger Louis meets after fleeing Prior's hospital room. He lives with his parents, so he tries to get Louis to invite him home. When Louis refuses, he agrees to sex in the park but runs away when their condom breaks and Louis starts acting strangely.

Mannequins

The Mannequins are the principal attraction in the Diorama Room of the Mormon Visitor's Center in New York City. They represent a Mormon family, arranged in a wagon-train tableau on a little stage, trekking westward from Missouri to Salt Lake. The Father Mannequin looks like Joe, and while Prior and Harper are watching the reenactment he comes to life and talks to Louis, then leaves the stage with him. Afterward, Harper strikes up a conversation with the Mother Mannequin, who also comes to life and escorts Harper to the Brooklyn Heights Promenade.

Hannah Porter Pitt

Hannah is Joe's Mormon mother. After her son calls her late at night from a payphone to confess he is a homosexual, she sells her home in Salt Lake City and flies to New York to help him. Her culture shock is traumatic at first, as she encounters the homeless and the eccentric on the streets of New York City, but she summons her inner strength and quickly adjusts to her surroundings. Abandoned by Joe, she takes a job at the Mormon Visitor's Center and tries to help Harper, her daughter-in-law, cope with the crisis.

When Prior wanders into the Center, she thinks his talk about angels is crazy and dangerous, in spite of what her own religion tells her, but later she becomes his protector. When Prior collapses in her arms, she takes him to the hospital and sits near his bed as the Angel approaches. It is Hannah who remembers Jacob's mythical bout with his angel, and she tells Prior if he wants to be free from the burden of Prophecy, he must wrestle the Angel into submission. At the end of the play she has been absorbed into the New York landscape and sits near the Bethesda Fountain with the others, reading the *New York Times*.

Harper Amaty Pitt

Harper is Joe's wife and a link between the real and imagined worlds of the play. In the playwright's words, she is "an agoraphobic with a mild Valium addiction and a much stronger imagination." Her pills and her imagination are her defense against the real world, which she finds overwhelming. Much of her frustration and anger comes from her relationship with her husband. Harper thinks she loves Joe, but he has grown less and less affectionate toward her and spends more and more time away from home. Although she finds it hard to admit to herself, she suspects Joe's homosexuality and is desperately trying to find a way to live her life contentedly, either with or without him.

When the stress of the world becomes too much for her, Harper calls upon her imaginary friend, Mr. Lies, to take her away to some imaginary realm where she can be free and happy. In her mind, she travels to Antarctica, to Heaven, even into other people's dreams. Her journeys have made her one of the more perceptive and poetic characters in the play. She thinks of the ozone layer as ''a kind of gift, from God, the crowning touch to the creation of the world: guardian angels, hands linked, [making] a spherical net, a blue-green nesting orb, a shell of safety for life itself.''

Joseph Porter Pitt

Joe is the chief clerk for Justice Theodore Wilson of the Federal Court of Appeals, Second Circuit, New York. He is a Mormon, married to Harper, and a completely closeted homosexual. For most of his life he has not admitted his homosexuality to his family, friends, wife, or even himself, but a turning point is near. He has been chosen by the great Roy Cohn to be his right hand man in Washington, and Joe now faces a tremendous crisis of conscience: He must decide whether he can transplant his paranoid, delusional wife, who he is growing less and less fond of, from her relatively familiar surroundings in New York to the politic world of Washington; and he must determine whether his own principles will allow him to work for a man as dangerous and unethical as Roy Cohn.

As if to compound his troubles, Joe meets Louis in his self-imposed exile from Prior and is seduced by him. He is both terrified and invigorated by the experience, still unsure of his life's direction but starting to sense his true identity. He turns down Cohn's offer and stays in New York. He admits to his mother, to Roy, to himself, to everyone but Harper, that he is gay. He spends several weeks completely absorbed in his new boyfriend. Still, like Louis, Joe is continually plagued with guilt and drawn back to the relationship he left behind. Also

like Louis, he returns to his mate too late. By the end of the play Harper has found enough resolve, and stability, to leave Joe behind.

Aleksii Antedilluvianovich Prelapsarianov

Introduced as ''the World's Oldest Living Bolshevik,'' Aleksii Antedilluvianovich Prelapsarianov appears briefly at the beginning of *Perestroika* delivering an impassioned speech in Moscow at the Soviet Kremlin. His topic is the need for a practical political theory to guide his country, and the most important quality he asks for in this new theory is one the Angels abhor: Change.

Prior 1

Prior 1 is the ghost of one of Prior's ancestors from the thirteenth century. In life, he was an English farmer, from near Yorkshire. In death, he appears in *Millennium Approaches* as a messenger on behalf of the Angel, come to prepare Prior for her arrival. He recognizes Prior's illness as a form of the pestilence that ravaged England in his day and caused his own death.

Prior 2

Prior 2 is another of Prior's ancestors—a sophisticated seventeenth century Londoner. He also appears in *Millennium Approaches* to prepare Prior for the Angel's arrival and, like Prior 1, he, too, was killed by a form of the plague that wiped out half the city of London. Just before the Angel's arrival, when Prior is deep in despair, the two apparitions summon a vision of Louis for Prior to dance with, then they disappear.

Ethel Rosenberg

Like Roy Cohn, the character of Ethel Rosenberg is based on an actual historical person. Ethel Rosenberg and her husband Julius were convicted of atomic espionage in 1951 and sentenced to death as traitors to the United States. Roy Cohn was instrumental in their prosecution. In the play, Ethel's desire for revenge compels her to haunt Roy from the time he is admitted to the hospital, dying of AIDS. She appears from time to time to taunt him with death and bring him bad news from the outside, where the New York State Bar Association has decided to disbar the treacherous attorney. Just before his death, Roy tricks her into singing him a lullaby.

Prior Walter

As much as any other character in this large ensemble work, Prior is the protagonist of *Angels in America*. He is also the only principal character whose personality seems to be forged by the events of the plot. Early in the play, Prior reveals his illness: He has AIDS and will soon become very sick and probably die. Soon afterward, he hears the first Voice, announcing the impending arrival of the Angel. From that point forward, everything Prior is, and everything he does, is related to his disease and his role as unwilling Prophet.

Prior also faces what may be the most difficult choices in the play and, in the process, grows stronger. He spends most of *Millennium Approaches* as a victim, being acted *upon*. He is battered first by his disease, the physical effects of which are beyond his control. Then he is abandoned by his lover, Louis, and left in mental anguish. Finally he is spiritually assaulted by the ghosts of his ancestors and the arrival of the Angel, who has come to burden him with a task he doesn't want.

The choices he must make define his new personality in *Perestroika*, when instead of being a victim, he becomes a fighter, someone who *acts*. He learns that, although he cannot cure his disease, through discipline and careful care, he can limit its effects on his body. Next, he comes to terms with Louis, who he still loves deeply. Although Louis returns, seeking reconciliation, Prior has found the strength to live by himself and reject Louis for abandoning him in his time of need. Finally, and perhaps most important to the universal scheme of the play, Prior successfully battles the Angel, gains admittance to Heaven, and refuses to serve as Prophet for the Continental Principalities, who wish to stop the forward progress of the world and find God again. It is this encounter with the celestial figures of the play that stands as a metaphor for all of the characters' conflicts, including Prior. In a moving speech to the Angels he sums up the spirit of his own struggles, and all of humankind, when he says, simply, ''We live past hope.''

Woman in the South Bronx

The Woman in the South Bronx appears once, near the end of *Millennium Approaches*. She is a schizophrenic, homeless woman who meets Hannah, fresh from Salt Lake City, getting off the bus at an abandoned lot in the South Bronx. After some uncontrollable, disturbing outbursts, she gives Hannah directions to the Mormon Visitor's Center and tells her, ''In the new century I think we will all be insane.''

THEMES

Change and Transformation

Change and transformation are at the center of *Angels in America*. In one way or another, each strand in the plot is related to change of some kind, and every major character faces some manner of transformation. Some characters are frightened by change and prefer the comfort and familiarity of the world they know.

Harper for example, begins the play terrified by the changes she sees, or thinks she sees, around her. She fears she is losing her husband, her home, and her sanity, and it is all overwhelming. She finds a metaphor for her fear in the ozone layer, high above the earth, which she likens to protective, guardian angels surrounding the planet. ''But everywhere,'' she says, ''things are collapsing, lies surfacing, systems of defense giving way.'' Through the course of the play, Harper does indeed lose everything she held dear, and in the process finds a new perspective on change and transformation. As she sits in a plane, bound for San Francisco and a new life, she suggests, ''Nothing's lost forever. In this world, there is a kind of painful progress. Longing for what we've left behind and dreaming ahead.''

Other characters are encouraged by change, even thrive in it. Louis's view is somewhat Darwinian. He tells the Rabbi that his sense of the world is that it will change for the better with struggle, which is why he can't accept Prior's sickness into his philosophy of life. Instead, Louis runs away, immersing himself in change to avoid deterioration. He finds Joe, who earnestly echoes the sentiments of his newfound right-wing Republican friends, Roy and Martin. Joe tells Harper that things are starting to change for the good in the world. ''America has rediscovered itself,'' he insists, ''Its sacred position among nations.'' To Joe, the country has been reinvented, for the better, during the Reagan years. Interestingly, though, by the end of the play both Louis and Joe are longing to return to the way things were, but both are denied this homecoming.

TOPICS FOR FURTHER STUDY

- Kushner has cited the German playwright Bertolt Brecht as a major influence on his writing. Read one of Brecht's major plays, perhaps *Mother Courage and Her Children* or *The Caucasian Chalk Circle,* and compare and contrast Brecht's style of epic, political theatre with Kushner's. Consider such things as plot structure, depth of characters, and how each man treats important themes in his work.

- *Angels in America* is subtitled ''A Gay Fantasia on National Themes.'' In music, a ''fantasia'' is a free-form composition in which the composer lets imagination, or ''fantasy,'' prevail over rules of a particular musical form. Fantasias may also be a medley of familiar tunes woven together with variations and interludes. Listen to a fantasia, perhaps Johann Sebastian Bach's ''Fantasia in G'' or Ralph Vaughan Williams's ''Fantasia on a Theme by Thomas Tallis,'' and determine ways in which Kushner's play is constructed like a musical fantasia. Consider the number of scenes and characters in *Angels in America,* as well as the play's themes and the way they are woven into the plot.

- The setting for *Angels in America* is extremely important to the plot and its characters. The 1980s are viewed as a time of economic greed and rising political conservatism. It was also the decade in which AIDS was discovered and homosexuals in America had to fight for rights, recognition, and survival. Pick a year during the eighties and research top news stories in politics, economics, and medicine. Then return to Kushner's play and see how your findings may have influenced the characters and their behavior.

- The first part of *Angels in America* is subtitled *Millennium Approaches*. The word ''millennium'' has a dual meaning. It refers to a time span of one thousand years, and, in some religions, it suggests a hoped-for period of joy, prosperity, and justice that will occur near judgment day. Research the significance of changing millennia in history. How did people act near the changing of the last millennium in the year 1000? What events are planned around the changing of the next millennium in 2000? How is the prospect of a new millennium important in Kushner's play?

Prior and the Angels are caught up in the play's biggest struggle over change. On a personal level, Prior is having change after change thrust upon him. First, his disease attacks, changing his body. Then, Louis abandons him, changing his world. Finally, the Angel calls upon him and asks him to become a Prophet on behalf of the Continental Principalities. Stasis, the opposite of change, is what the Angels seek. Prior thwarts their plan, however, and tells them, ''We can't just stop. We're not rocks—progress, migration, motion is . . . modernity. It's *animate,* it's what living things do.''

Identity

A search for identity is underway, beginning with the opening monologue of *Angels in America,* and each of the characters becomes involved, whether they intend it or not. In his eulogy for Sarah Ironson, Rabbi Chemelwitz describes the deceased as one of a special breed of immigrants who crossed the ocean and established a new homeland in America, carrying along bits of the Old World and passing them along to her children. To the Rabbi, Sarah Ironson is part of America's identity; she was an essential ingredient in ''the melting pot where nothing melted.''

On a more personal quest, Joe seeks a different kind of identity. All his Mormon life he has tried to deny the nature of his sexuality: He is attracted to men. In an attempt to change his true identity, he went so far as to marry Harper. Contrary to his beliefs, he helps write decisions in court cases that deny the rights of homosexuals. Through the short relationship he finds with Louis, he is nearly liberated. He admits his longings to himself, and to Louis, but stops short of coming out to the world. At the end of the play he is still torn between his life as a heterosexual, married, Republican law clerk and the fleeting glimpse of happiness he found in Louis's arms.

In keeping with his character traits, Louis's search for identity is more abstract. Though he thinks he has come to terms with the world, and has developed opinions and answers for any situation, his philosophies are constantly being tested, and he, like Joe, lives a life of contradictions. He criticizes Joe for hiding his sexuality, yet he has a ''butch'' side himself, an overtly masculine, heterosexual facade that he assumes around his family. He is a tortured agnostic who was raised Jewish but can't find a religion that accepts him for what he is. Politically, he is an extreme liberal but is attracted to a confused right-wing Republican. Louis's quest for identity does not end with the play: During the Epilogue, he is still arguing religion and politics with Belize (who, as a black ex-drag queen and confidant to both Prior and Louis has an identity crisis of his own).

American Dream

Kushner suggests that his play is ''A Gay Fantasia on *National* Themes,'' and the concept of America—its social dynamics, political identity, and uncertain future—are prominent themes in the play. Set in the 1980s, a decade of greed and conservatism, *Angels in America* can not avoid exploring the impact of Republican politics on the country. Roy Cohn represents the worst the right wing has to offer: political monopoly, economic disparity, discrimination, and censorship. His henchman, Martin, crows, ''It's a revolution in Washington, Joe. We have a new agenda and finally a real leader'' and brags that soon Republicans will control the courts, lock up the White House, regain the Senate, and run the country the way it ought to be run.

In contrast to these conservative combatants, Louis and Belize despair over America's future, each for different reasons. Louis complains that nothing matters in America except politics and power, the very things Roy and his associates covet. ''There are no gods here,'' he rails, ''no ghosts and spirits in America, there are no angels in America, no spiritual past, no racial past, there's only the political.'' To Belize, however, there is a distinct spirit to America, and he doesn't like it. ''I hate this country,'' he counters, ''It's just big ideas and

stories and people dying and people like you.'' To Belize, there is precious little freedom in the land of the free.

These extreme views of America are left unresolved at the end of the play. The Epilogue, which occurs in 1990, four years after most of the play's action, explains that in the intervening years the Berlin Wall has fallen, the Russian leader Mikhail Gorbachev's vision of ''Perestroika'' or ''radical change'' has helped bring an end to the Cold War, and America has emerged as a leader of nations. Still, the ragged band of survivors gathered around Bethesda Fountain in Central Park are both champions and victims of the American Dream.

Hannah left her comfortable Mormon life in Salt Lake City and, like her ancestors before her, migrated to a new land (New York City) to be reinvented. Her struggle will continue. Louis and Belize remain, at best, marginal members of society, still misunderstood, still mistreated, and still struggling for the rights enjoyed by society's heterosexual majority. And Prior, though he has survived his disease much longer than he expected, knows his story is not the end but only a beginning for homosexuals with AIDS in America. ''We won't die secret deaths anymore,'' he warns, ''The world only spins forward. We will be citizens. The time has come . . . The Great Work Begins.''

STYLE

Epic Theatre

Angels in America is built with an epic plot construction. In early storytelling, *epic* referred to the kind of tale Homer told in the *Odyssey* and *Iliad:* stories that cover long periods of time, perhaps months or even years; involve many locations, ranging from small rooms to forests and battlefields; follow many characters through multiple plotlines; and alternate short and long scenes, with a series of crisis points, rather than a single strong climax near the end. Many of Shakespeare's plays follow in the epic tradition, and other notable modern examples include the plays of Bertolt Brecht (*Mother Courage and Her Children*), and Robert Schenkkan's *Kentucky Cycle,* a six-hour, nine-play saga covering two hundred years of history in the lives three eastern Kentucky families.

Kushner's massive undertaking with *Angels in America* is divided into two complete plays: *Millen-*

In the pivotal scene from Millenium Approaches, *the Angel of America descends upon the room of the soon-to-be prophet Prior Walter*

nium *Approaches* and *Perestroika.* Together, they span more than four years, from October, 1985, to February, 1990. Settings range from living rooms, offices, and hospital wards to New York City streets, Antarctica, and even Heaven.

Scenes in *Angels in America* are both long and short and often overlap each other, occurring on the stage simultaneously. This provides two qualities that are important to epic plots: *juxtaposition* and *contrast.* In *climactic* plots, the story moves forward in a cause-and-effect fashion, with the action in one scene influencing the action in the next. In epic

plots, however, the action may alternate between the plot and subplot, with little connection between the two. The effect of two seemingly unrelated scenes placed next to each other is a *juxtaposition* of action, characters, and ideas, which often produces a *contrast* that makes the play more meaningful.

For example, Act II, scene 9 of *Millennium Approaches,* is a split scene involving Joe and Harper at home, and Prior and Louis in Prior's hospital room. The two scenes, juxtaposed together, each present someone abandoning a loved one. Joe has already drunkenly confessed his homosexuality to his mother on the telephone and now seeks a way to escape his wife, who needs him desperately. Louis, on the other hand, still loves Prior but can't stand living with his sickness. Playing the two scenes simultaneously amplifies the confusion and agony each man feels and makes it difficult to simply dismiss their actions as heartless. Similar juxtapositions occur throughout the play.

Perhaps most importantly, the overall effect of an epic plot is *cumulative* rather than catastrophic. In a climactic work, such as Sophocles's *Oedipus Rex* or the plays of Henrik Ibsen (*A Doll's House*) and Arthur Miller (*Death of a Salesman*), events are compressed and occur quite near the end of the story, making an explosive confrontation inevitable. Epic plots allow events, circumstances, and emotions to pile up, one on top of the other, overwhelming the characters and audience alike. Rarely does a single event—a character's error in judgment or an antagonist's vile deed—decide the outcome. Accordingly, *Angels in America* ends in uncertainty. The ultimate fate of the characters is unknown, but the events and emotions that have accrued impart a sense of enormity and importance to the play's ideas—progress, identity, community, and acceptance.

Political Theatre

Theatre has been a forum for political ideas and agendas for as long as audiences have been attending plays. In America, the Federal Theatre Project of the depression-era 1930s mounted "Living Newspapers," short plays integrating factual data with emotional, often melodramatic vignettes. Topics usually addressed some kind of social cause, such as slum housing for the urban poor or the plight of the American farmer. During the radical 1960s, several black theatre groups, such as Imamu Amiri Baraka's (formerly LeRoi Jones) Spirit House and the Negro Ensemble Company, were organized with the goal of producing plays written by, and for, blacks in America, often with anti-white themes. Whatever the cause, political theatre is often driven by the *themes,* or ideas, in the play, as much as by the plot or characters.

Kushner follows in the tradition of large, important, political dramas, influenced mainly, he claims, by Bertolt Brecht, the German playwright who is credited with the creation of a unique brand of *Epic Theatre.* Brecht's theories for his Epic Theatre contain many of the qualities of epic plot structure but also assume a strong political aspect; he was a staunch communist and held virulent anti-

war beliefs. His plays were *didactic,* which means he wanted to *teach* his audiences something, and his lessons were usually stated strongly and openly. Furthermore, Brecht wanted his spectators to be active participants in the theatre and think critically while watching his plays, rather than become absorbed in emotion as passive witnesses. To manage this, he attempted to "alienate" his audiences by exposing theatrical devices (lighting, scene changes, etc.). He also broke up the action of his plays—with disruptive elements such as ironic songs and placards that explained forthcoming plot points—so spectators were not allowed to become absorbed in the story but were instead constantly forced to reevaluate characters and their actions. Through this process, Brecht felt, audiences would better understand and appreciate a play's political messages.

Like Brecht, Kushner strives for a very *theatrical* presentation that doesn't attempt complete illusion. He recommends a minimal amount of scenery for *Angels in America*—with all the rapid changes of location, realistic scenery would be quite cumbersome to a production. Furthermore, Kushner suggests the scene changes be handled quickly, in full view of the audience (without blackouts) using both stagehands and actors, a very Brechtian technique. As for the moments of magic in the play, such as the appearance of the Angel, the ghosts, Mr. Lies, and other fantastic occurrences, the playwright says in his introduction, "It's OK if the wires show, and maybe it's good that they do, but the magic should at the same time be thoroughly amazing."

Kushner is also extremely political, and he, too, wants his audiences to learn something, though he allows more subtlety of expression than Brecht. In Kushner's play, the strong political ideas are woven into the fabric of the plot and sub-plots, and the audience is left with an *impression* rather than an obvious *message.* Controversial ideas are usually presented from both sides, leaving the audience free to draw their own conclusions. While Brecht strongly advocated communism and often hit audiences on the head with his overt pacifist rhetoric, Kushner lets his characters and their philosophies speak for themselves.

The concept of the American Dream, for example, is viewed from several perspectives, none of which is presented as "right:" Roy and Martin find the American Dream in the struggle for political power; Joe harbors an idealistic, perhaps naive vision of America as a land of freedom, opportunity, and justice for all; embittered Belize and Louis, scorned by mainstream society for their openly gay lifestyles, find America oppressive and hypocritical, yet they continue their struggles for rights and recognition. By presenting political ideas in this kaleidoscopic fashion, Kushner opens a political *dialogue* with his audiences, rather than simply shouting messages at them.

HISTORICAL CONTEXT

History, both the near and distant past, echoes throughout *Angels in America.* Prior's ancestors from the thirteenth and seventeenth centuries return to herald the arrival of the Angel. The complex evolution of philosophies, political systems, and religions (such as the Jewish and Mormon faiths) over the years are discussed and debated in the context of the characters' current struggles. The most important era to the play, however, is the one in which it is set: the 1980s.

Often characterized as a decade of greed, conservative politics, and negligent middle-class social policies, the 1980s are an indelible imprint on the plot and characters of *Angels in America.* From Roy, Martin, and Joe, who directly serve the Republican tide that washed across the country during the ''Me'' decade (so named for the self-centered behavior that was tolerated, even encouraged, by 1980s American culture), to Prior, Louis, and Belize, all somehow victims of straight, white America and the AIDS crisis, Kushner's work is an unmistakable product of its time.

The Political 1980s

Angels in America is steeped in politics, particularly influenced by the platforms of the Republican party. Ronald Reagan, Republican President of the United States from 1980-1988, is mentioned often in Kushner's play. He is the era's most recognizable political icon, and the success or failure of economic and political policies from the 1980s is usually attributed to his administration. Reagan's far-reaching economic policies, termed ''Reaganomics,'' were an attempt to correct many of the economic and social problems Americans had been experiencing since the 1970s, when many felt the country had lost its confidence.

During the 1970s and early-1980s, Americans found renewed interest in ecological awareness and demanded that industry take steps to save the imperiled environment. This led congress to pass strict measures that forced American companies to divert profits to environmental controls and cleanup, reducing their ability to modernize and compete with less regulated foreign companies. At the same time, the cost of gas and oil was skyrocketing, unemployment reached 7.1 percent, and the inflation rate soared to 12.5 percent.

America was not doing any better abroad, where the Cold War seemed to be favoring the communists and the Middle East was rapidly becoming a foreign policy embarrassment. The Soviet Union had invaded Afghanistan and installed a communist leader in 1979 and the communist power was also gaining leverage in Africa and Central America. Terrorists from the Middle East hijacked U.S. aircraft, and fifty-three Marines and civilian personnel in the American embassy in Iran were held hostage for more than a year, from November, 1979, to January, 1981.

Amidst all this chaos, Reagan was swept into office on a platform promising a strong national defense and a tough stance against the communist Soviet Union. He also vowed to reduce the size and cost of government, lower taxes by 30 percent, reduce spending, and curb inflation. With the help of a largely Republican senate, Reagan's foreign policy and ''supply-side economics'' met with a mixture of success and failure. On the positive side, inflation and interest rates fell. Between 1983 and 1989, 18 million new jobs were created, and the average price of stocks nearly tripled in value. A lot of Americans grew very rich, and the country experienced what has been called the longest period of peacetime economic growth in the nation's history.

Growth had its downside, however. The national debt tripled, the nation's trade deficit quadrupled, and much of the credit for economic growth was attributed to the burgeoning defense industry. In his first year in office, Reagan convinced Congress to budget nearly $200 billion in defense spending, creating an economic windfall through the largest peacetime defense buildup in American history.

Still, the buildup had its payoff. Kushner took the title for the second part of his epic, *Perestroika,* from the policies of Soviet leader Mikhail Gorbachev who, faced with America's tremendous military might and economic boom under Reagan, chose to radically change the direction of Russian society. Gorbachev sought to reform the Soviet economy through *perestroika,* a Russian word for ''restructuring,'' and he introduced *glasnost,* or ''openness,'' into political and cultural affairs. Within a

COMPARE
&
CONTRAST

- **1980s:** In 1981, the Center for Disease Control in Atlanta, Georgia, identifies a new syndrome initially called "Gay-Related Immune Deficiency." The disease is named AIDS (Acquired Immune Deficiency Syndrome) in 1982. By the end of 1985, AIDS has spread to at least fifty-one countries. In 1988, the United States becomes the last major Western industrialized nation to launch a coordinated education campaign. By the end of the decade, an estimated 1 million people worldwide have contracted AIDS. In the United States, nearly 150,000 cases have been diagnosed and almost 90,000 people have died.

  Today: Globally, an estimated 33.4 million people are living with AIDS. In the worst-affected countries, such as Zimbabwe and Tanzania, more than 10 percent of the adult population might be infected. In developed countries, however, massive education and disease prevention campaigns, along with new experimental drugs, have slowed or even reversed the spread of AIDS. In 1992, the first successful combination drug therapy for the treatment of AIDS begins in the United States; there is still no cure. Education and disease-prevention counseling occur in public schools, and national advertising campaigns promote safe sex or abstinence. In the United States, the number of new cases diagnosed and deaths from the disease have been dropping rapidly since 1993.

  Over 48,000 people die from AIDS-related illnesses in 1994. By 1997, that number falls to just over 14,000.

- **1980s:** The Executive Office is held by Republicans from 1980-92. Republicans also control the Senate, occupying just over half the seats. The House of Representatives is mostly Democrats, as it has been since the end of World War II.

  Today: Embattled Democratic President Bill Clinton is elected to two terms, beginning in 1992. While the Democrats also wrest the majority of Senate seats away from Republicans for a short time (1987-1994), the GOP rallies and gains control of the entire Congress in 1995.

- **1980s:** The eighties "bull market" begins on August 17, 1982, when the Dow Jones Industrial Average rises 38.81 points to 831.24—the biggest one day gain in the hundred-year history of the Dow. Over the next five years the value of most stocks nearly triples as the market soars.

  Today: After climbing steadily since 1990, the market sets a new record—9337.97 points—on July 17, 1998. At that height, rises and drops of hundreds of points a day are not unusual. Investing in stocks is a white knuckle ride enjoyed by more Americans than ever before.

---

few short years the spread of communism around the world, a threat once characterized by Reagan as the "Evil Empire," had reversed itself. The Berlin Wall, a longtime symbol of the division between the communist east and the capitalist west, was dramatically dismantled in 1989. Two years later, in December, 1991, the Soviet Union's communist dictatorship collapsed; the Cold War was over.

AIDS in America

The other "war" that really matters to *Angels in America* was a domestic one that was being

fought between an outnumbered, marginalized, terrified homosexual community and the rest of America, which was largely heterosexual. The discovery of the Acquired Immune Deficiency Syndrome (AIDS) in 1981 threw both sides into a feverish struggle over rights, recognition, and morality in America.

Americans have always been, at best, ambivalent about homosexuals in their midst. It wasn't until 1973 that the American Psychiatric Association removed homosexuality from its list of mental disorders and the U.S. military continues its "don't ask, don't tell'' policy for gays in the military. For a time, AIDS was used by some as justification for anti-gay sentiments (some made outrageous claims that the disease was a biblical curse sent down by God to eradicate homosexuality). In the early-1980s, the disease became known as the ''gay plague,'' in spite of the fact that other groups of heterosexuals— notably Haitians, drug addicts, and hemophiliacs— also suffered the syndrome's debilitating symptoms. The government—and President Reagan in particular—seemed disinterested in the suffering of gay Americans. Serious research at the National Institutes of Health did not begin until early-1983, eighteen months after AIDS had been declared an epidemic in the U.S. Gay rights activists compared their treatment by the United States government to the suffering of Jews in Nazi Germany during the Holocaust.

While there are a great many important themes in *Angels in America,* it is this crisis, at once historical and timely, that Kushner chooses to return to at the end of the epic. Prior closes the play's Epilogue with a direct address to the audience, during which he tells them, ''This disease will be the end of many of us, but not nearly all, and the dead will be commemorated and will struggle on with the living, and we are not going away.'' In many ways, the struggle that began for homosexuals in America with the AIDS crisis in the 1980s defined the relationship between gay and straight America in subsequent decades.

CRITICAL OVERVIEW

Angels in America followed a rapid, if circuitous, route to success. The first part of Kushner's epic work, *Millennium Approaches,* was originally commissioned and planned for San Francisco's Eureka Theater in 1989. The play actually premiered in a workshop production in Los Angeles at the Mark Taper Forum in 1990, then landed briefly at the Eureka Theater in 1991 before getting its first major production at the Royal National Theatre in London in 1992. Later that year, *Perestroika* was added, and the full production was performed for the first time back in Los Angeles. By the time the play reached Broadway in 1993, it had already garnered numerous awards and accolades, including the Pulitzer Prize for drama and the adoring praise of critics around the world. As expected, it won the Antoinette Perry (Tony) Award for best play in 1993.

Sometimes success draws detractors, and many a critic has made his reputation by savagely criticizing what all his colleagues seem to adore. *Angels in America,* however, seemed to carry a special blessing—in spite of what were seen as a few minor flaws, most reviewers agreed that its greatness couldn't be denied. Shortly after the Broadway opening in 1993, and long after the play had already been praised and canonized by writers everywhere it had appeared, Jeremy Gerard wrote in *Variety,* ''Believe the hype: This smartly ambitious, unabashedly sprawling, glintingly provocative, frequently hilarious and urgently poignant play is as revelatory as the title suggests, both in its kaleidoscopic account of life in the Reagan '80s and its confirmation of a young writer's dazzling, generous vision.''

Reviewers found a lot to like in *Angels.* Hal Gelb, writing for the *Nation,* suggested, ''Tony Kushner has written an enormously entertaining play while at the same time treating important matters seriously.'' Gelb also praised the balance Kushner found in his political stance, noting, ''Unlike many playwrights on the left, Kushner does a good job of allowing the characters on the right their humanity.'' In the *New Republic,* Robert Brustein, a critic and scholar known for his rigorous standards and candor, admitted, ''Kushner is that rare American thing, an artist-intellectual, not only witty himself but the gauge by which we judge the witlessness of others. His very literate play once again makes American drama readable literature.''

For many commentators, Kushner's characters, and the opportunity they provide performers, were the most appealing aspect of the play. In the *New York Post,* veteran critic Clive Barnes observed, ''Kushner peoples his phantasmagoria with great, sharply realistic characters—the savagely comic Roy Cohn, played with expectorating, explosive bile by Ron Liebman, Steven Spinella's whimsically wicked, spindly, long-dying prophet and Jeffrey Wright's raw and motherly nurse, are luminously wonderful.'' Audiences and critics alike are often drawn to villains. A good villain, like Shakespeare's Richard III, is articulate, charismatic, and wickedly appealing. Accordingly, much praise was lavished on Kushner's depiction of Roy Cohn, the historical epitome of right-wing conservatism in the 1950s and hypocrisy in the 1980s. In the *New Yorker,* John Lahr asserted, ''As written, Cohn is one of the great evil characters of modern American drama. In him Kushner personifies the barbarity of individualism during the Reagan years, and also the deep strain of pessimism that goes with the territory.''

Other reviewers appreciated the remarkable humor the play contains, in spite of its deadly serious subject matter. ''The big surprise is how funny it is,'' wrote David Patrick Stearns in *USA Today,* ''Hysteria and humor flip back and forth in Marcia Gay Harden's portrayal of the mousy, Valium-addicted Mormon housewife who hallucinates herself into a vacation to Antarctica.'' Referring to *Perestroika* in *New York* magazine, John Simon said, ''Kushner is a funny fellow, and there is both nicely elaborated humor and rapid-fire wit throughout much of the three-and-a-half hour span.''

Perhaps the most complimented aspect of Kushner's play was his ability to create a monumental work of art that deftly handles so many important ideas. In *New York Newsday,* Linda Winer wrote, ''Kushner uses a huge canvas, but a very delicate brush. This is a play of big ideas—politics, religion, love, responsibility and the struggle between staying put and our need to move, preferably forward.'' It's a lot to take in, Winer suggested, ''And, yet, this heretofore almost unknown playwright is such a delightful, luscious, funny writer that, for all the political rage and the scathing unsanitized horror, the hours zip by with the breezy enjoyment of a great page-turner or a popcorn movie.''

Criticism has been leveled at *Angels in America*—though usually leavened by compliments for the play's literary ambition and stage production. Gelb's review in the *Nation,* for example, which was mainly glowing, still noted that, ''despite Kushner's daring theatricality, endlessly fertile imagination and ambitious sense of form, *Angels in America* has its problems, some of them serious. The 'angels' plot itself, for one, isn't as fully imagined or its tone as clear as the earthbound narratives, and the angels' cause—anti-migration, cessation of relentless human movement—isn't compelling.'' Gelb also found parts of the play redundant, noting, ''A still more obvious flaw is the way Kushner hits the same points over and over. For a good long stretch in the middle section, you feel he's taken the angels' enjoinder to heart: Nothing moveth.''

Kushner's epic American drama also managed to raise moral objections in more conservative publications and on some college campuses. In the *Christian Science Monitor,* critic Ward Morehouse III wrote, ''The play, which won this year's Pulitzer Prize for drama, has a power and boldness seldom seen on Broadway, but its homosexual themes may

eliminate it from some theatergoers' agendas.'' Morehouse also warned his readers about the nudity and sexual situations in *Angels in America,* suggesting that director George C. Wolfe may have gone too far, including some scenes the critic felt were inserted solely for shock value. Objections turned into actions at the Catholic University of America, where campus administrators refused to allow advertisements to be posted for a planned production of the play in 1996. The administrators forced a student group to move to an off-campus location for the performance.

CRITICISM

Lane A. Glenn

Glenn is a Ph.D. specializing in theatre history and literature. In this essay he explores the changing nature of faith and spirituality in the twentieth century and the way these changes are reflected in Angels in America.

The characters in Tony Kushner's magnum opus *Angels in America* are reflections of the modern, millennial age. Like so many of us, they are on a quest for *spirituality,* for some kind of inner fulfillment, and their search seems to have taken on a desperate significance in the closing years of the second millennium.

Philosophically, the twentieth century has been called an ''age of uncertainty,'' of individuals seeking meaning for their lives and order in an increasingly chaotic universe. Traditional beliefs are being altered or ignored, while new faiths and new icons appear daily. Some people continue to enrich their lives with the religious doctrines of their ancestors—Catholicism, Judaism, Islam, or Hinduism—while others explore direct experiences through mysticism or paganism. Some find comfort and meaning in newly created, ''cult'' religions or abandon the search entirely and call themselves atheists or agnostics. In America, ''Materialism,'' the quest for money and goods, has often been called a new religion of the age. This sense of anxiety and uncertainty, so prevalent in *Angels in America,* is rooted in the not-so-distant past—the changes in science, philosophy, and technology wrought by the nineteenth century.

The nineteenth century taught the western world uncertainty, and the lesson—as much as any discov-

WHAT DO I READ NEXT?

- More of Kushner's provocative writing can be found in *Thinking about the Longstanding Problems of Virtue and Happiness: Essays, A Play, Two Poems, and a Prayer* (1995). As the lengthy and descriptive title indicates, the work contains another play, *Slavs!*, as well as some of Kushner's thoughts, in essay form, on relationships, sexuality, identity, and American politics.

- Larry Kramer's 1985 drama *The Normal Heart* examines the AIDS epidemic as the public was just becoming aware of the problem. The play dramatizes the early history of the disease and accuses the government, media, and conservative religious groups of ignoring the public health threat by labeling the epidemic a "gay plague."

- Kushner cites the work of German playwright Bertolt Brecht as a strong influence on his writing style. Some of Brecht's better known epic plays are *Mother Courage and Her Children, The Good Woman of Setzuan, The Caucasian Chalk Circle,* and *The Threepenny Opera.*

- *After Heaven: Spirituality in America since the 1950s* (1998) by Robert Wuthnow suggests Americans in the last few decades have shifted away from a "spirituality of dwelling" and toward a "spirituality of seeking." Part of the seeking process means exploring new beliefs and religions, as well as personal encounters with spiritual figures, such as angels.

- *Citizen Cohn* (1988) by Nicholas Von Hoffman is the biography of Roy Marcus Cohn, ruthless lawyer, communist-basher, closeted homosexual, and loathed icon of the Cold War era. The book (a feature film adaptation starring James Woods as Cohn is available on video) provides a disturbing look at the McCarthy hearings of the 1950s, the Rosenberg trial, Cohn's behind-the-scenes manipulations and secret sexual identity, and his death of AIDS in 1986.

---

ery, war, or disaster since—has shaped the identity of the modern age. Charles Darwin published his famous *Origin of Species* in 1859, presenting the world with revolutionary, and troubling, ideas. In suggesting that all forms of life evolved from a common ancestry, and that the evolution of species continues through the "survival of the fittest," the British naturalist pulled the rug out from under many of the world's most cherished faiths. If true, Darwin's theories reduce human beings to the status of natural objects, no more spiritual or glorious than animals, plants, or any other living organism. *Origin of Species* also suggests that humans are shaped primarily by their *heredity* and *environment*. The spiritual concepts of fate and destiny, central to many religious faiths, play no part in the drama of human existence: People have free will, make their own decisions, and are responsible for their own actions.

By the turn of the century, other great thinkers had also widely influenced the way people view the world and their existence in it. The French philosopher Auguste Comte suggested in his *Course of Positive Philosophy* (translated into English in 1853) that only primitive or partially evolved groups of people base their societies on religions or hopeful political theories, and that the ideal society is one governed by the principles of scientific observation. Renowned psychoanalyst Sigmund Freud reinforced some of Darwin's ideas about the primitive origins of human beings when he suggested that many of our actions are guided by deeply-rooted subconscious thoughts. The nineteenth century scientific and political notions of Darwin, Comte, Freud, and others have had a deep and lasting impact on how we view the world today.

Faith shaken by the rigors of science and the heartlessness of politics in the twentieth century fills *Angels in America.* Kushner's epic drama encompasses a variety of beliefs, including Judaism, Mormonism, and Agnosticism, and incorporates supernatural elements such as visions, ghosts, and angels. The play never claims the superiority of one belief over another but suggests that all faiths may be important to the progress of humankind at what is perhaps a crucial moment in history: the dawn of a new millennium.

In a 1991 interview with *Theatre Week* magazine, Kushner suggested, "There are moments in history when the fabric of everyday life unravels, and there is this unstable dynamism that allows for incredible social change in short periods of time. People and the world they're living in can be utterly transformed, either for the good or the bad, or some mixture of the two. . . . During these periods all sorts of people—even people who are passive under the pressure of everyday life in capitalist society—are touched by the spirit of revolution and behave in extraordinary ways." Kushner's belief in climactic moments in time is echoed by Ethel Rosenberg, a character in *Angels in America,* who warns: "History is about to crack wide open. Millennium approaches."

Although Kushner didn't intend it, Judaism is one of his play's most important religious motifs. The playwright himself is a third generation Jew, though he claims he is deeply ambivalent toward his faith and is actually a "serious agnostic." In a 1995 interview with a Rabbi at the Hebrew Union College-Jewish Institute of Religion in New York, Kushner described his own family, the generations after his grandparents, explaining, "We didn't know Yiddish, we didn't know Hebrew, we didn't know prayers. We went to a very, very Reform—I mean sort of reformed out of existence—Jewish congregation."

Angels in America suggests that Kushner's experience growing up Jewish in the American South is shared by many Americans—the children and grandchildren of immigrants who packed their faiths along with their suitcases for their voyage to America. As younger generations make their own way in this "melting pot where nothing melted," they may turn their backs on the traditions and beliefs of their ancestors, but the human spirit, like nature, abhors a vacuum. The empty space left behind must be filled with something—the soul requires it.

Rabbi Isidor Chemelwitz is the first character who appears in *Angels in America.* He stands alone onstage, conducting the funeral service for Sarah Ironson. In memorializing Sarah, he appeals to the assembled mourners to remember their Jewish heritage:

> She was . . . not a person but a whole kind of person, the ones who crossed the ocean, who brought with us to America the villages of Russia and Lithuania—and how we struggled, and how we fought, for the family, for the Jewish home, so that you would not grow up *here,* in this strange place, in the melting pot where nothing melted. Descendants of this immigrant woman, you do not grow up in America, you and your children and their children with the goyische names. You do not live in America. No such place exists. Your clay is the clay of some Litvak shtetl, your air the air of the steppes—because she carried the old world on her back across the ocean, in a boat, and she put it down on Grand Concourse Avenue, or in Flatbush, and she worked that earth into your bones, and you pass it to your children, this ancient, ancient culture and home.

Yet already Sarah Ironson's own grandson Louis, present at her funeral, has strayed far from his Jewish roots. Kushner has called Louis the closest thing to an autobiographical character he has ever created. Like his creator, Louis is Jewish, gay, and deeply ambivalent toward the faith of his family. He finds no comfort in a religion that rejects him for his sexuality, and he doesn't hesitate to criticize the shortcomings of Judaism. "Jews don't have any clear textual guide to the afterlife; even that it exists," he tells Prior. "I don't think much about it. I see it as a perpetual rainy Thursday afternoon in March. Dead leaves." Instead of the organized, traditional faith of his family, Louis has embarked on a lifelong quest to develop his own philosophy of life, one that doesn't demand purity or pass judgment and encompasses his unique experiences and allows for all the political and social vagaries of the world in which he lives. He doesn't believe in God and insists, "It should be the questions and shape of a life, its total complexity gathered, arranged, and considered, which matters in the end, not some stamp of salvation or damnation which disperses all the complexity in some unsatisfying little decision—the balancing of the scales."

Traveling a spiritual path alone is difficult, however. Louis is criticized throughout the play for his unorthodox views on relationships, politics, and religion. Furthermore, like Kushner, who has never completely shaken his Jewish roots, Louis keeps returning to the faith of his ancestors subconsciously or against his will. In one of the play's more haunting scenes, Louis visits Roy Cohn's hospital room and, possessed by the spirit of Ethel Rosenberg, chants the Kaddish, the Jewish prayer for the dead, over Roy's body.

Cohn, while alive, is the play's other prominent Jewish figure, and he, too, has his own unique way of identifying with his faith. For Roy, everything in life is a tool to use to his best advantage. The telephone and the law are equal extensions of his ambitious personality, and he uses and discards people like newspapers. When it comes to his Jewishness, Roy recognizes faith can get in the way of political aspirations. "I'm about to be tried, Joe, by a jury that is not a jury of my peers," he complains. "The disbarment committee: genteel gentlemen Brahmin lawyers, country-club men. I offend them, to these men . . . I'm what, Martin, some sort of filthy little Jewish troll?" Even on his deathbed, salvation and the afterlife are an afterthought. The ghost of Ethel Rosenberg, a restless spirit who has been haunting Roy like a "dybbuk" (from Jewish folklore; a disembodied spirit that possesses the living) materializes to forge some sort of absolution between them, but the cantankerous lawyer chooses a practical joke as his last act on earth. He tricks Ethel into singing him a lullaby, then promptly dies.

The other important faith presented in *Angels in America* is Mormonism. Appropriately enough for the play, both Judaism and Mormonism have histories of dislocation, of rootlessness seeking a physical and spiritual home. Judaism began with God's command to Abraham to remove himself and his family to a new land, while Mormonism started with a westward movement across America, revealed by an angel to the sect's founding prophet, Joseph Smith. In a 1992 discussion at the Royal National Theatre of Great Britain, Kushner told interviewer Adam Mars Jones, "Mormonism is a theology that I think could only really have come from America. . . . The theology is an American reworking of a western tradition that is uniquely American: the notion of an uninhabited world in which it's possible to reinvent."

Like the founders of their faith, the Mormons in the play are constantly on the move, seeking their destinies. Early on, Joe Pitt tries to convince his wife, Harper, to move to Washington to better his career in politics. Harper, who describes herself as a "Jack Mormon," someone who is flawed in her faith, has already followed Joe from Salt Lake City to New York and is afraid of more geographical dislocation. Instead, she travels the world in her mind, ranging as far as Antarctica in her struggles to escape her troubled life at home. After receiving a phone call in the middle of the night from her son, during which he drunkenly confesses his homosexuality, Hannah Pitt sells her house in Utah, the Mormon homeland, and travels to New York to set him "straight."

Kushner illustrates both the positives and negatives of the faiths represented in the play when he juxtaposes them on top of one another and characters with clashing ideologies meet. For example, when Harper and Prior find each other in a mutual dream, Harper asserts, "In my church we don't believe in homosexuals." Prior, patient and tolerant, even in the face of death, jokingly retorts, "In my church we don't believe in Mormons."

The divisions run deeper, however, among some of the play's more serious-minded characters. When Louis discovers Joe's religion, it signals the beginning of the end of their relationship. "I don't like cults," he tells his Mormon lover. "The Church of Jesus Christ of Latter Day Saints is not a cult," Joe insists. Louis becomes unusually conservative and angrily replies, "Any religion that's not at least two thousand years old is a cult."

In spite of all the contrasting views of faith presented, from agnosticism to mysticism to Mormonism to Judaism, one of the most important conflicts in the play occurs on a higher plane, largely unconcerned with categories of belief. The Continental Principalities are one of the play's principal motivating forces. This group of seven angels, representing each of the continents on earth, is a significant spiritual symbol, though they are not allied with any particular faith. Instead, these angels represent history and the unstoppable evolution and progress of human events. Kushner has alluded to the influence of the political theorist and philosopher Walter Benjamin on his work, and it has been noted that a particular passage, from Benjamin's *Theses on the Philosophy of History,* significantly shaped *Angels in America:*

> A Klee painting named "Angelus Novus" shows an angel looking as though he is about to move away from something he is fixedly contemplating. His eyes are staring, his mouth is open, his wings are spread. The angel of history must appear in this way. He has turned his face toward the past. Where a chain of events appears before us, there *he* sees one single catastrophe, which incessantly piles ruin upon ruin and hurls it in front of his feet. The angel would like to stay, awaken the dead, and join together what has been smashed apart. But a storm blows out from

Paradise, which has captured him in his wings and is so strong that the angel can no longer close them. This storm irresistibly propels him into the future, to which his back is turned, while the pile of debris before him grows skyward. That, which we call progress, is *this* storm.

Like the angel of history in Benjamin's description, the Continental Principalities feel battered by the course of human events, particularly in the twentieth century as the pace of change has accelerated to a manic rate. They believe that God has abandoned heaven in pursuit of the thrill that change and progress has provided his creation, which is why they have called upon Prior to be their Prophet. The job he has been given is to convince humankind to *stop* moving, to cease their progress. As the chosen spokesman for creation, however, Prior has other ideas. "We can't just stop," he tells the Angels. "We're not rocks—progress, migration, motion is . . . modernity. It's *animate,* it's what living things do. We desire. Even if all we desire is stillness, it's still desire *for.* Even if we go faster than we should. We can't *wait.* And wait for what? God. . . . He isn't coming back."

If there is an ultimate message within the exploration of twentieth century spirituality in *Angels in America,* it is the concept of *inclusion.* While different faiths, ideologies, and political stances are debated throughout the play, there are no clear victors. For every champion of a cause, whether it is Republicanism, Zionism, or free will, there is an opponent, equally armed and, at least in his own experience of the world, justified. The former prophet Prior Walter's final words suggest just such a common bond:

Bye now.

You are fabulous creatures, each and every one.

And I bless you: *More Life.*

The Great Work Begins.

Source: Lane A. Glenn, for *Drama for Students,* Gale, 1999.

Hal Gelb

In this review of a production encompassing both parts of Kushner's play, critic Gelb praises the playwright's ability to fuse entertainment with important social issues while maintaining an epic scope.

In *Angels in America* (most recently at the Mark Taper Forum in Los Angeles), a two-part, seven-hour workup of the nation's fin-demillennium health, Tony Kushner has written an enormously entertaining play while at the same time treating important matters seriously. Kushner de-ghettoizes the AIDS play, placing the disease, like the destruction of the ozone layer or Americans' flight from mutual responsibility in the Reagan era, at the heart of a national and planetary collapse. Mixing realism, fevered hallucination and otherworldly theatrical effects, he pulls back from the tight close-up of so much American drama to underscore a connection between public destiny and love and responsibility in personal relationships. *Angels in America* stands as a kind of lighthouse on the coast of a new era, signaling renewed feelings of hope and longing for community.

The characters—who are both types and not types, and that's the point—include the revenant Ethel Rosenberg (Kathleen Chalfant), a saintly gay black nurse (K. Todd Freeman) and a Jewish cappuccino intellectual named Louis (Joe Mantello) who is endlessly opinionated about democracy, revolution and other big topics but falls apart when illness and death strike close to home. Early in *Millennium Approaches,* Prior Walter, his lover—so well-born he can trace his roots to the Bayeux Tapestry—announces he has AIDS, and Louis flees.

Meanwhile, on the other side of the political spectrum, a repressed Reaganite attorney, Joe Pitt, also struggles with responsibility. He wavers between accepting his homosexuality and conforming to his Mormon upbringing by remaining with his wife, Harper (who, suffering Joe's indifference, has turned into a Valium visionary). The play's paradigm of Reaganesque evil is Roy Cohn, who denies he's subject to the same laws of nature and society as everyone else, and who crows, "They say terrible things about me in *The Nation.* Fuck *The Nation.*" Strangely, considering Kushner's condemnation of Reagan-era selfishness, his conservatives are intent only on social order and moral decency. They don't talk about deregulation or keeping more of what they've got.

Cohn, who views responsibility and love as a trap—and is represented here without his real-life loyal-to-the-end lover, Peter Fraser—attempts to install Pitt in the Justice Department so he can influence Cohn's disbarment hearing. During the course of the play, Cohn also discovers he has AIDS. These events, along with the disintegrating relationships, Joe and Louis's affair and an attempt to check the unraveling of God's grand design by an angel who flies in, Mary Martin-style, are the play's core.

> KUSHNER'S DIALOGUE IS REMARKABLE IN THE WAY IT REVEALS THE LOVE THE CHARACTERS ARE REQUESTING, REQUIRING, GIVING AND WITHHOLDING"

Yet, despite Kushner's daring theatricality, endlessly fertile imagination and ambitious sense of form, *Angels in America* has its problems, some of them serious. The "angels" plot itself, for one, isn't as fully imagined or its tone as clear as the earthbound narratives, and the angels' cause—anti-migration, cessation of relentless human movement—isn't compelling. A still more obvious flaw is the way Kushner hits the same points over and over. For a good long stretch in the middle section, you feel he's taken the angels' enjoinder to heart: Nothing moveth. And in *Perestroika* , particularly, Kushner generates enough irrelevant material to keep what he's talking about from standing out clearly. The play also conflates different kinds of self-interest. Louis's abandonment of Prior comes from his gut fear of mortality; he can be faulted for spinelessness and betrayal, but not selfishness in the same sense as Reaganite greed. Yet his action comes in for the play's greatest moral heat.

But as Woody Allen movies used to, *Angels in America* generates so much good will that you don't care about its flaws. When it flies—which is much of the time—it *flies*. That has a lot to do with the play's attempt to heal divisions and its penetrating description of the gulfs between us. Kushner's dialogue is remarkable in the way it reveals the love the characters are requesting, requiring, giving and withholding, and I found myself hurting for them in a way I don't for characters in other plays. He also supplies them with a flood of laugh lines.

The writing is complemented by fine ensemble acting under the direction of Taper resident director Oskar Eustis and Tony Taccone. To mention just a few of the wonderful performances, there's Jeffrey King's beautifully revealing portrait of the tortured self-hatred behind Joe Pitt's square-jawed strength; Kathleen Chalfant's dry-as-dust rendering of Joe's

constantly surprising Mormon mom; Ron Leibman's ferocious Cohn, a dog who's sunk his teeth into life and won't let go; and hovering over it all, Stephen Spinella's Prior Walter, an enormously compelling mixture of feistiness and fragility, bitchiness and childlike wonder. The only weakness is Cynthia Mace, who suffers by comparison with Anne Darragh, who in the original San Francisco production played Harper's mental problems as though they could be overcome.

That production in the spring of 1991, at the Eureka Theater, where Eustis and Taccone commissioned the play, offered a fully mounted *Millennium Approaches* and a staged reading of *Perestroika.* (The Taper's was the first full-scale production of both.) At that time, with Reagan/Bush still apparently invincible, the play's apocalyptic vibrations were more than a little disquieting, particularly in the scene where Cohn and a crony picture a conservative dominion lasting well into the next century. Whether it's the new context or rewrites that reshaped the play's outlook, *Angels in America* now seems more optimistic. In front of John Conklin's Federalist facade with its enormous, jagged fault line, Kushner reasserts the interconnectedness of our multicultural, sexually and politically diverse populace. And in an ending that, unfortunately, probably says more about the sweetness of Kushner's heart than about the future, he points to a metaphorical *perestroika* of our own, a passing away of old enmities (well, sort of) and the disappearance of old divisions, with tolerance not just for gays but for Mormons too. Unlike many playwrights on the left, Kushner does a good job of allowing the characters on the right their humanity—except for Cohn, whom he uses for the most part as a focus of conservative evil. But he needs to address the further prejudice of the left—the one that makes the black nurse saintly and the Jewish intellectual the object of greatest moral heat—if the old divisions are to be dealt with.

Source: Hal Gelb, review of *Angels in America* in the *Nation*, Vol. 256, no. 7, February 22, 1993, pp. 246–47.

John Lahr

Lahr is a noted theatre critic and biographer. In this essay, he reviews a complete production of Angels in America *marking the debut of* Perestroika, *the work's second segment. The critic praises the breadth of the play and lauds both Kushner and the cast of this production. Lahr terms the performance a victory for both the playwright and for the dramat-*

ic genre, proving "the transforming power of the imagination to turn devastation into beauty."

High on a hill in downtown Los Angeles, the thirty-six-year-old playwright Tony Kushner stood watching an usher urge the people outside the Mark Taper Forum to take their seats for the opening of "*Angels in America,*" his two-part "gay fantasia on national themes." it was the première of the play's long-awaited second segment, "*Perestroika,*" which was being performed, together with the first part, "*Millennium Approaches,*" in a seven-hour back-to-back marathon. "I never imagined that this was going to come out of sitting down in 1988 to write what was supposed to be a two-hour play about five gay men, one of whom was Mormon and another was Roy Cohn," Kushner said. "The level of attention that's being paid to the plays is completely terrifying." On the first day the Taper opened its box office for Kushner's twin bill, it took in thirty-two thousand eight hundred and four dollars, far exceeding the previous record in the theatre's distinguished history; and just last week "*Millennium Approaches,*" which ran for a year at the Royal National Theatre in England, won the London *Evening Standard's* award for best play. Driving to the Taper for his opening, Kushner said, he had thought, If I have a fiery car crash, the play will probably be really well received and no one will dare trash it, and it would be this legendary thing. Now Kushner was experiencing the actual rush of first-night terror: he couldn't feel the pavement under his feet. "I feel like I'm walking on some cushion, like dry sponge," he said. "Unsteady. Giddy."

Every playwright has a ritual for opening night. Some playwrights walk. Some drink. Some tough it out and watch from the back of the theatre, silently coaxing the players over every production obstacle. Kushner takes himself away for a Chinese meal; in the case of this doubleheader, he'd need two meals. He had already taped his opening-night ticket into his journal. He'd fitted himself out with a lucky ceramic lion given him by his mother and with a medal of the Virgin Mary from Majagure, in what was formerly Yugoslavia. He had one more thing to do. "Once the curtain goes up, I sing 'Begin the Beguine'—it's the longest pop song without a chorus," he explained, shouldering a blue backpack. "I have to sing it *well* from start to finish. If I can get through the whole thing without fucking up the words, it's going to be O.K." I left him to it.

Inside the seven-hundred-and-forty-two-seat auditorium, the Taper's artistic director, Gordon Da-

vidson, shmoozed with the first-nighters like a rabbi with his congregation. Over the twenty-five years of Davidson's stewardship, the Taper has generated a prodigious amount of theatre work, some of which has invigorated Broadway and Off Broadway. Although the local press likes to bite the hand that feeds it, and periodically snaps at Davidson, no other American regional theatre approaches the Taper's creative record. Recently, Davidson and his theatre seem to have had a second lease on creative life, giving George C. Wolfe's innovative musical "Jelly's Last Jam" its first production and staging Robert Schenkkan's "The Kentucky Cycle," which was the first play to win a Pulitzer Prize without being put on in New York. With "*Angels in America,*" which Davidson workshopped, and into which he has already sunk a million three hundred thousand dollars of the theatre's budget, the Taper is poised for another scoop. Davidson worked the room, handing out butterscotch candies, as is his opening-night custom, and smiling the smile that has launched a few hundred shows but none more brazenly ambitious or better produced than Kushner's. The occasion felt more like a feeding frenzy than like a first night. Robert Altman was there, checking out the play as movie material. A good proportion of the New York theatre's high rollers seemed to be there, too, eager to get a piece of Kushner's action: JoAnne Akalaitis, of the Public Theatre, with whom Davidson will produce the cycle in New York in February; Rocco Landerman, of Jujamcyn; the Broadway producers Margo Lion and Heidi Landesman; and a host of critics, including Frank Rich, of the *Times,* and Jack Kroll, of *Newsweek.* As the houselights dimmed, Davidson found his seat and glanced at the copy of "Moby Dick" that Kushner had given him as an opening-night present. "I felt it was appropriate for the occasion," Kushner's inscription read. "It's my favorite book, by my favorite writer, someone who spent years pursuing, as he put it in a letter to Hawthorne, 'a bigger fish.'"

Just how big a fish Kushner was trying to land was apparent as the lights came up on John Conklin's bold backdrop of the facade of a Federal-style building, leached of color and riven from floor to ceiling by enormous cracks. The monumental design announced the scope and elegant daring of the enterprise. It gave a particular sense of excitement to the evening, and bore out one of Kushner's pet theories. "The natural condition of theatre veers toward calamity and absurdity. That's what makes it so powerful when it's powerful," he said before

" FROM ITS FIRST BEAT, *ANGELS IN AMERICA* EXHIBITED A RAVISHING COMMAND OF ITS CHARACTERS AND OF THE DISCOURSE IT WANTED TO HAVE THROUGH THEM WITH OUR SOCIETY"

he decamped to Chinatown. "The greater the heights to which the artists involved aspire, the greater the threat of complete fiasco. There's a wonderfully vibrant tension between immense success and complete catastrophe that is one of the guarantors of theatrical power." From its first beat, "*Angels in America* " exhibited a ravishing command of its characters and of the discourse it wanted to have through them with our society.

Kushner has not written a gay problem play, or agitprop Sturm und Schlong; nor is he pleading for tolerance. "I think that's a terrible thing to be looking for," he told me. Instead, with immense good humor and accessible characters, he honors the gay community by telling a story that sets its concerns in the larger historical context of American political life. "In America, there's a great attempt to divest private life of political meaning," he said. "We have to recognize that our lives are fraught with politics. The oppression and suppression of homosexuality is part of a larger political agenda. The struggle for a cure for AIDS and for governmental recognition of the seriousness of the epidemic connects directly to universal health care, which is connected to a larger issue, which is a social net." Set in 1985, at the height of the Reagan counter-revolution, "Millennium Approaches" maps the trickle-down effect of self-interest as Kushner's characters ruthlessly pursue their sexual and public destinies. Louis, unable to deal with illness, abandons his lover, Prior, who has AIDS; Joe, an ambitious, bisexual Mormon Republican legal clerk, abandons his dippy, pill-popping Mormon wife, Harper ("You, the one part of the real world I wasn't allergic to," she tells him later); and Roy Cohn, in his greed, is faithless to everybody. "There are no angels in America, no spiritual past, no racial past, there's

only the political," Louis says, in one of the idealistic intellectual arabesques meant to disguise his own moral and emotional quandary, which Joe Mantello's droll characterization both teases and makes touching. Louis invokes Alexis de Tocqueville, and it's Tocqueville who put his finger on that force of American democracy whose momentum creates the spiritual vacuum Kushner's characters act out. "Thus not only does democracy make every man forget his ancestors, but it hides his descendants and separates his contemporaries from him," Tocqueville wrote. "It throws him back forever upon himself alone and threatens in the end to confine him entirely within the solitude of his own heart."

This isolation has its awesome apotheosis in the dead heart of Roy Cohn. "Hold," Cohn barks into the phone—his very first word. Turning to Joe (Jeffrey King), whom he's singled out as a potential "Royboy," he says, "I wish I was an octopus, a fucking octopus. Eight loving arms and all those suckers. Know what I mean?" This is a great part, which calls out of Ron Leibman a great performance. Roaring, cursing, bullying, jabbing at the air with his beaky tanned face and at the phone with his cruel fingers, he incarnates all that is raw, vigorous, and reckless in Cohn's manic pursuit of power. "Love; that's a trap. Responsibility; that's a trap, too," he tells Joe while trying to set him up as his man inside the Justice Department and spell out the deep pessimism behind his rapacity. "Life is full of horror; nobody escapes, nobody; save yourself." With his rasping, nasal voice swooping up and down the vocal register, Leibman makes Cohn's evil incandescent and almost majestic. ("If you want the smoke and puffery, you can listen to Kissinger and Shultz and those guys," he confides to Joe at one point. "But if you want to look at the heart of modern conservatism you look at me.") Cohn is the king of control and the queen of denial. He tells his doctor when he learns he has AIDS, "Homosexuals are men who in fifteen years of trying cannot get a pissant anti-discrimination bill through City Council. Homosexuals are men who know nobody and who nobody knows. Does this sound like me, Henry?"

But Cohn's hectoring gusto doesn't overwhelm the piquancy of the other stories. Kushner's humor gets the audience involved in the characters, and the play works like a kind of soap opera with sensibility, whose triumph is finally one of design rather than depth. Kushner doesn't impose personality on ideas but lets ideas emerge through careful observation of personality. He listens to his characters and, with his percolating imagination, blends the quirky logic of their voices with their hallucinatory visions. Prior (played by Stephen Spinella) dances with Louis in a dream. In her lovelorn grief, Harper (Cynthia Mace) fantasizes herself in the Antarctic, and later Joe comes hilariously alive, stepping out of a pioneer tableau, during Harper's vigil in the Diorama Room of the Mormon Visitors' Center in New York City. Ethel Rosenberg, who owed her execution to Cohn's single-handed, improper intervention with the presiding judge, appears at Cohn's bedside. These hauntings are sometimes dramatized as projections of parts of the self that have been murdered in order to survive. "Are you a ghost?" Prior asks Louis as he sways in the arms of his guilty lover to the tune of "Moon River." "No," Louis says. "Just spectral. Lost to myself." The final, ambiguous image of "*Millennium Approaches,*" which brings the play to a halt, if not to a conclusive end, is the appearance of an angel to Prior while he languishes in his sickbed. "*Very* Steven Spielberg," Prior says as the set parts and the angel (Ellen McLaughlin) swings down on wires, to proclaim him Prophet and tell him tantalizingly that his great work is about to begin. With the help of jets of smoke, Pat Collins' evocative lighting, and the strong directorial hands of Oskar Eustis and Tony Taccone, the audience is brought bravoing to its feet. The production is far superior in every scenic and performing detail to the celebrated English version.

"*Perestroika*" is the messier but more interesting of the two plays, skillfully steering its characters from the sins of separation in the eighties to a new sense of community in the embattled nineties. Though "*Perestroika*" should begin where "*Millennium Approaches*" breaks off, it opens instead with an excellent but extraneous preamble by the oldest living Bolshevik, bemoaning this "sour little age" and demanding a new ideology: "Show me the words that will reorder the world, or else keep silent." Kushner can't keep silent; but, while his play refuses ideology, it dramatizes, as the title suggests, both the exhilaration and the terror of restructuring perception about gay life and about our national mission. The verbose Angel that appears to Prior now turns out in "*Perestroika*" to be the Angel of Death or, in this case, Stasis. She takes up a lot of time broadcasting a deadly simple, reactionary message of cosmic collapse. "You must stop moving," she tells Prior. "Hobble yourselves. Abjure the Horizontal, Seek the Vertical." But,

once the characters get back on the narrative track of the plot, "Perestroika" finds its feet and its wisdom.

The real drama of "*Perestroika*" is the fulminating, sometimes funny battle the characters wage in trying to deal with catastrophic loss. Here, as in "*Millennium Approaches,*" Cohn, the fixer, is shrewdly placed at the center of the argument. Cohn will not accept loss, always stacking life's deck to maintain his fantasy of omnipotence. "I can get anyone to do anything I want," he tells his black male nurse, Belize (played with panache by K. Todd Freeman), before picking up the phone to blackmail an acquaintance for the drug AZT. "I'm no good at tests, Martin," he tells the acquaintance. "I'd rather cheat." And later, with his stash of AZT in a locked box in the foreground, he crows at his nurse like a big winner: "From now on, I supply my own pills. I already told 'em to push their jujubes to the losers down the hall." All change requires loss, and Cohn's power is a mighty defense against change. His emptiness is colossal. Significantly, Cohn dies mouthing the same words that introduced him in "*Millennium Approaches.*" Kushner shows his other characters growing through an acceptance of loss. "Lost is best," Harper says, refusing to take Joe back after his fling with Louis, and going with the flow of her aimlessness. "Get lost. Joe. Go exploring." Prior, too, has finally wrestled control of his life and what remains of his momentum from the Angel of Stasis. "Motion, progress, is life, it's—modernity," he says, unwilling to be stoical. "We're not rocks, we can't just wait. . . . And wait for what? God." His task is to make sense of death and, as he says, "to face loss, with grace."

Part of this grace is humor, the often heroic high-camp frivolity that both acknowledges suffering and refuses to suffer. When Cohn brags to his nurse, "Pain's . . . nothing, pain's life," Belize replies, sharpish, "Sing it, baby." Kushner uses laughter carefully, to deflate the maudlin and to build a complex tapestry of ironic emotion. He engineers a hilarious redemption for the politically correct Louis, who is forced by Belize to say Kaddish over Cohn's dead body in order to steal the remaining AZT to prolong Prior's life. Louis prays with Ethel Rosenberg's ghost over the body, and they end the Hebrew prayer with "You son of a bitch." And at another point in his emotional turmoil Prior turns to Louis and accuses him of having taken a Mormon lover. "Ask me how I knew," Prior says. Louis asks, "How?" Prior rounds on him: "Fuck you. I'm a prophet." Even Cohn gets off a cosmic joke, making a last-minute appearance from Purgatory as God's lawyer. ''You're guilty as hell,'' he growls at the Deity. ''You have nothing to plead, but not to worry, darling, I will make something up.''

''*Perestroika*'' ends by celebrating community, not individualism, auguring with eerie serendipity the spirit of the new Clinton era. Even the monstrous Cohn is acknowledged as a fallen victim by the brotherhood. ''The question I'm trying to ask is how broad is a community's embrace,'' Kushner says. ''How wide does it reach? Communities all over the world now are in tremendous crisis over the issue of how you let go of the past without forgetting the crimes that were committed.'' In the play's epilogue, which jumps to 1990, Kushner confronts the audience with the miraculous. Prior has lived four more years. He sits in Central Park in animated conversation with his friends. Then, turning the conversation up and down at his command (Kushner's homage to the ending of ''The Glass Menagerie''), Prior steps out of the play world to talk directly to us. It's an extraordinarily powerful (if haphazardly staged) moment, in which the community of concern is extended by the author to the human family, not just the gay world. ''Bye now,'' Prior says. ''You are fabulous, each and every one, and I love you all. And I bless you. *More life.* And bless us all.''

Backstage, Kushner stood dazed and rumpled among a crowd of well-wishers. ''I've been working on this play for four and a half years,'' he said. ''Tonight, a whole era in my life comes to an end. It's been an incredibly strange ride.'' His exhaustion and the happy fatigue of the cast members, who lingered in doorways, seemed to bear out part of Kushner's opening-night message, which was pinned to the stage-door bulletin board. ''And how else should an angel land on earth but with the utmost difficulty?'' it read. ''If we are to be visited by angels we will have to call them down with sweat and strain, we will have to drag them out of the skies, and the efforts we expend to draw the heavens to an earthly place may well leave us too exhausted to appreciate the fruits of our labors: an angel, even with torn robes, and ruffled feathers, is in our midst.''

Kushner and the excellent Taper ensemble had made a little piece of American theatre history on that cloudless California night. ''*Angels in America*'' was now officially in the world, covered more or less in glory. It was a victory for Kushner, for

theatre, for the transforming power of the imagination to turn devastation into beauty.

Source: John Lahr, ''Beyond Nelly'' in the *New Yorker,* Vol. LXVIII, no. 40, November 23, 1992 , pp. 126–30.

SOURCES

Barnes, Clive. Review of *Angels in America* in the *New York Post,* November 24, 1993.

Benjamin, Walter. ''Theses on the Philosophy of History'' in *Illuminations,* edited by Hannah Arendt, translation by Harry Zohn, Schocken Books, 1969, pp. 257-58.

Brustein, Robert. Review of *Angels in America* in the *New Republic,* May 24, 1993, pp. 29-31.

Cohen, Norman J. ''Wrestling with Angels'' in *Tony Kushner in Conversation,* edited by Robert Vorlicky, University of Michigan Press, 1998, p. 220.

Gelb, Hal. Review of *Angels in America* in the *Nation,* February 22, 1993, pp. 246-48.

Gerard, Jeremy. Review of *Angels in America* in *Variety,* May 10, 1993, p. 243.

Jones, Adam Mars. ''Tony Kushner at the Royal National Theatre of Great Britain'' in *Tony Kushner in Conversation,* edited by Robert Vorlicky, University of Michigan Press, 1998, pp. 24-25.

Kushner, Tony. *Angels in America, Part One: Millennium Approaches,* Theatre Communications Group, 1992, p.5

Lahr, John. Review of *Angels in America* in the *New Yorker,* May 31, 1993.

Morehouse III, Ward. Review of *Angels in America* in the *Christian Science Monitor,* May 17, 1993, p. 12.

Simon, John. Review of *Angels in America* in *New York,* December 6, 1993, p. 130.

Stearns, David Patrick. Review of *Angels in America* in *USA Today,* May 5, 1993, p. 1D.

Szentgyorgyi, Tom. ''Look Back—and Forward—in Anger'' in *Theatre Week,* January 14-20, 1991, p. 16.

Winer, Linda. Review of *Angels in America* in *New York Newsday,* May 5, 1993.

FURTHER READING

Adelman, Deborah. *The 'Children of Perestroika': Moscow Teenagers Talk about Their Lives and the Future,* ME Sharpe, 1992.
    Interviews with Moscow teenagers that describe their views on the former Soviet Union, socialism and

capitalism, the culture of the West, and how they view the future of their society after the Cold War.

Barlett, Donald L., and James B. Steele. *America: What Went Wrong?,* Andrews & McMeel, 1992.
A critical view of the 1980s that faults corporate greed, government short-sightedness, and the social and economic policies of President Ronald Reagan with undermining the American Dream.

Brask, Per, editor. *Essays on Kushner's Angels,* Blizzard (Winnipeg), 1995.
An early collection of essays about *Angels in America,* published shortly after the play was produced, that attempts to view the work from North American, European, and Australian perspectives to see how Kushner's brand of political drama fared around the Western world.

Christie-Dever, Barbara. *AIDS: Answers to Questions Kids Ask,* Learning Works, 1996.
Informative question-and-answer style approach to AIDS awareness and education for teenagers. Includes biographical sketches of Ryan White, Magic Johnson, and other notable AIDS figures.

Geis, Deborah R., and Steven F. Kruger, editors. *Approaching the Millennium: Essays on* Angels in America, University of Michigan Press, 1997.
An anthology of essays about *Angels in America,* written by theatre and film directors, scenic designers, professors, and critics. Topics range from perspectives on racial and sexual politics in Kushner's work, to explorations of religious imagery and postmodern theoretical analysis.

Mann, Jonathan M. *AIDS in the World,* Harvard University Press, 1992.
An analysis of the spread of AIDS around the world, including the effects of the disease on different popu-

lations and the response to the pandemic in different geographical locations.

Pemberton, William E. *Exit with Honor: The Life and Presidency of Ronald Reagan (The Right Wing in America),* ME Sharpe, 1998.
A biography of Ronald Reagan, the iconic president of the 1980s. Describes the life of President Reagan and explores his presidency in detail, along with critiques of his political successes and failures.

Shilts, Randy. *And the Band Played On: Politics, People, and the AIDS Epidemic,* St. Martin's, 1987.
An in-depth examination of the genesis and spread of the AIDS virus that views the disease from cultural, political, and popular perspectives. Shilts was a homosexual journalist and gay-rights activist who died of AIDS in 1994.

Stine, Gerald J. *Acquired Immune Deficiency Syndrome: Biological, Medical, Social, and Legal Issues,* Prentice Hall, 1998.
Informative look at the history and current state of the AIDS/HIV pandemic, including statistics, social reactions, economic costs, recent medical findings, and references.

Twist, Clint. *1980s (Take Ten Years),* Raintree, 1993.
Examines the most important news events of the 1980s, including AIDS, the Cold War, and the fall of the Berlin Wall.

Vorlicky, Robert, editor. *Tony Kushner in Conversation,* University of Michigan Press, 1998.
A collection of accessible, entertaining, and extremely informative interviews and conversations with Kushner, documented by journalists, teachers, directors, and other playwrights. Also includes an afterword by Kushner, in which he wryly describes "the Intelligent Homosexual."

Arcadia

TOM STOPPARD

1993

When asked once about the origins of *Arcadia,* Tom Stoppard replied that he had been reading *Chaos,* a book about mathematical theory and at the same time wondering about the contrasts between Romanticism and Classicism in style, temperament, and art. Few playwrights find source material in subjects as diverse, and unlikely, as Stoppard and his literary achievements are often considered more amazing for someone who left school at the age of seventeen and never attended a university.

For some, *Arcadia* represents a pinnacle in Stoppard's career. After years of writing clever, witty plays with intellectual appeal, he managed to produce one that tugs at the heart as well as the mind. After its Broadway debut, Vincent Canby wrote in the *New York Times,* ''There's no doubt about it. *Arcadia* is Tom Stoppard's richest, most ravishing comedy to date, a play of wit, intellect, language, brio, and, new for him, emotion.''

Arcadia premiered on the Lyttelton stage of the Royal National Theatre of Great Britain on April 13, 1993. It opened on Broadway two years later, March 31, 1995, at the Lincoln Center Theater. Both productions were greeted with tremendous enthusiasm by critics and the public alike. In London, the play garnered the prestigious Olivier Award for best play (comparable to Broadway's Antionette ''Tony'' Perry Award), while in America *Arcadia* received the New York Drama Critics Circle Award. Even the small handful of reviewers who found

fault in *Arcadia* grudgingly hailed it as Stoppard's greatest play to date.

As the action bounces back and forth in time, Stoppard explores the nature of truth and history, the conflict between Classical and Romantic thought, mathematics and chaos theory, English landscape architecture, and, ultimately, love both familial and familiar. In the words of *Time* reviewer Brad Leithauser: "In *Arcadia* we have been given a major English drama, one of those by which, ultimately, the theater of our time may be evaluated. It is a play that holds up beautifully not only on the stage but on the page."

AUTHOR BIOGRAPHY

Tom Stoppard is regularly cited as one of England's greatest playwrights, alongside such national treasures as George Bernard Shaw, Oscar Wilde, John Osborn, David Hare, and Alan Ayckborn. Yet, even among such lauded company, Stoppard's place is considered unique, for he writes plays, and creates worlds, unlike other dramatists. In a career that has spanned three decades and more than two-dozen plays, Stoppard has consistently made his audiences laugh, cry, and think, all at the same time. In a *New Yorker* review of Stoppard's *Arcadia,* critic John Lahr explained, "The three-ring circus of Stoppard's mind pulls them in at the box office, where news of the intellect, as opposed to the emotions, is a rarity. . . . Stoppard's mental acrobatics flatter an audience's intelligence and camouflage the avowed limits of his plotting and his heart."

Stoppard was born Tomas Straussler in Zlin, Czechoslovakia, on July 3, 1937. When he was only two, his family moved to the island republic of Singapore. In 1942, when the Japanese invaded, he was evacuated to India with his mother and brother. His father, who remained behind, was killed. In 1946 his mother married Kenneth Stoppard, a British army major, and the family moved to England. Stoppard attended English public school from the age of nine to seventeen, then left to become a journalist. (Later reviewers suggest that his lack of a complete formal education may be the greatest asset to his work—it is often held that his lack of knowledge in areas such as history and formal literary structure allow his plays to be freewheeling dramatic escapades.) He wrote for a couple newspapers during the next few years, eventually specializing in theatre and film. His first work as a dramatist was on

Tom Stoppard

radio; he had two fifteen-minute radio plays broadcast on the BBC in 1964, *The Dissolution of Dominic Boot* and *"M" Is for Moon among Other Things.*

After only a couple minor productions of his first stage plays were performed in 1965-66, Stoppard became a sort of overnight sensation in 1967 with *Rosencrantz and Guildenstern Are Dead,* a seriocomic absurdist farce about two minor courtiers in Shakespeare's *Hamlet.* The play was given a major staging by the Royal National Theatre of Great Britain and has been playing on stages around the world ever since. In many ways, *Rosencrantz and Guildenstern* set the standard by which Stoppard's future work would be judged. By most critics' estimation, it contains all of the hallmarks of a "Stoppard play." It is intelligent and fiercely philosophical, yet at the same time witty, sometimes physically farcical, and it often appears to not take itself too seriously.

These same qualities are found in other Stoppard successes, such as *The Real Inspector Hound* (1968), in which two theatre critics are murdered on stage by characters in the play they are watching; *Jumpers* (1972), a farcical parody of modern philosophy; and *Travesties* (1974), a fantasy play that imagines the results if communist forefather Vladimir Lenin, author James Joyce, and Dadaist founder Tristan

Tzara all lived together in Zurich during World War I. In all these plays, Stoppard examines similar themes: the relationship of art to life, the frustrating quest for knowledge and ultimate truth, and the fragile bonds formed between all sorts of human beings. They are the same ideas that are brought to fruition in his 1994 work, *Arcadia*. With the debut of this play, many critics heralded Stoppard as one of the most influential and revered playwrights of the twentieth century.

PLOT SUMMARY

Act I, scene 1

The action begins in April, 1809. The setting is Sidley Park, the Derbyshire, England, estate of the Coverly family. Thirteen-year-old Thomasina Coverly is studying with her tutor, the young Septimus Hodge, in a large room facing a garden. Thomasina is exceptionally intelligent for her age, and her current project is a search for proof of Fermat's last theorem, an algebraic conundrum that has perplexed mathematicians since the seventeenth century. Meanwhile, Septimus is reading "The Couch of Eros," a particularly horrible poem written by one of the manor's current guests, Ezra Chater.

Thomasina has an insatiable curiosity, and her main interest for the day, other than her math lesson, is in a phrase she overheard: "carnal embrace." Septimus comically tries to spare his young pupil the adult explanation and convince her that it simply means "hugging a side of beef," but Thomasina is not fooled. She overheard some of the house staff talking about Mrs. Chater, who was discovered in "carnal embrace" in the gazebo. Septimus relents and explains the alternate meaning of the phrase ("sexual congress"); he does not admit, however, that he was the culprit embracing Mrs. Chater in the garden.

As the two resume their studies, Jellaby, the manor's butler, delivers a note from Mr. Chater, calling upon Septimus to meet him immediately to fight a duel over the honor of his wife. Septimus slips Mr. Chater's invitation into the pages of "The Couch of Eros" and returns a message suggesting he will be available later that day, after his lesson with Thomasina. Undeterred, the enraged Chater bursts in, demanding satisfaction.

Chater is boisterous, passionate, and vain but not very bright. Septimus sends Thomasina from the room, then disarms the cuckholded husband by flattering his poetry and praising his wife. He admits making love to the woman but convinces Chater that she did it out of loyalty, in order to persuade Septimus to write a glowing review of her husband's poetry. Septimus lavishes compliments on Chater's writing and promises to publish a review that will make him one of England's most prized poets—though not if he is forced to kill him in a duel. Chater is fooled—and so excited at his good fortune that he inscribes Septimus's copy of his book with the words, "To my friend Septimus Hodge, who stood up and gave his best on behalf of the Author—Ezra Chater, at Sidley Park, Derbyshire, April 10th, 1809." (*Chater's note between the pages of the book, and his inscription inside the cover, become important clues in the mystery that unfolds later in the play.*)

As the two men settle their compact, other members of the household burst into the room, arguing loudly. Lady Croom and her brother, Captain Brice, are protesting the plans of Richard Noakes, a landscape architect who Lord Croom has hired to refashion the grounds of Sidley Park. Noakes has assembled a series of watercolor paintings that depict the gardens of the country house "before" and "after" his recommended treatment. At the moment the gardens are a vision of classical splendor—trees neatly and symmetrically grouped on the hillside and a lake surrounded by meadows "on which the right amount of sheep are tastefully arranged." Noakes's new design transforms Sidley Park into a Gothic wilderness—the Romantic style of the era—complete with gloomy forests, artificial ruins, rampant briars, and a rustic hermitage. Lady Croom and Captain Brice are mortified but young Thomasina, who heard the commotion and returned to the room, judges Noakes's scheme perfect.

The sound of gunfire is heard outside, where the poet Lord Byron is hunting with Lord Croom and his young son, Augustus Coverly. The group marches out of the room to meet the hunters and continue debating the transformation of the Croom estate, leaving Septimus and Thomasina alone again. Innocently, she draws a picture of a hermit in Noakes's hermitage and hands Septimus a note from Mrs. Chater, which he reads then inserts into the pages of "The Couch of Eros." (*Both the drawing and the note also become essential clues later in the play.*)

Act I, scene 2

The next scene takes place nearly two centuries later, at the present day Sidley Park. The room remains the same but its inhabitants change. Hannah Jarvis, an author in her late thirties, is visiting the estate, which still belongs to the Croom family. She has written one bestselling book already and is conducting research for her next work, which she thinks will focus on the breakdown of the Romantic Imagination in the early-nineteenth century.

Hannah's hosts are the current children of the Croom family, who wander in and out of the room throughout the scene, preparing the house for a big costume garden party. The children are Valentine Coverly, an Oxford postgraduate student conducting mathematical research on the number of grouse reported killed in the family's game books over the years; Chloe Coverly, the Crooms' eighteen-year-old daughter; and Gus Coverly, the fifteen-year-old, apparently mute, youngest son.

The mysteries which are at the root of *Arcadia*'s plot develop with the arrival of Bernard Nightingale, a Sussex professor who has come seeking information about Lord Byron. Bernard has stumbled across Septimus's copy of "The Couch of Eros" and discovered the notes and inscription inside. Because the book was found in Byron's personal library, Bernard has taken a few creative—and erroneous—mental leaps. He has developed the theory that Lord Byron, who was visiting the Croom estate at the same time as Chater in 1809, killed the hapless would-be poet in a duel and fled the country. A mistake of sorts is also at the root of Hannah's work. Finding Thomasina's drawing of the "hermit" in Noakes's landscape sketches, Hannah assumed the figure was a real person, who died on the estate in 1834. She is making the "Sidley hermit" the metaphorical centerpiece for her book about the decline of Romanticism in England.

Hannah and Bernard get off to a rocky start when she discovers that the pompous professor is actually the same man who wrote an insulting review of her first book. Two heads appear better than one, however, as they each have information to offer that helps them piece together the clues of their separate puzzles. They declare a truce and spend the day ransacking the estate's library for proof of their theories. At the same time, Chloe expresses an interest in Bernard and tells Hannah she plans to ask him to the party that evening; and young Gus seems to have developed a similar crush on Hannah. At the end of the scene, the silent boy presents her with an apple, freshly picked from the orchard.

Act I, scene 3

The scene changes to the past. It is 1809 once more, a day after the previous skirmish between Septimus and Chater. Thomasina is once again studying in the great garden room, attempting to translate a poem from Latin into English. Septimus is writing his review of Chater's "Couch of Eros." Again Jellaby delivers a note from Chater, which Septimus chooses to ignore. Thomasina reveals that her mother, Lady Croom, is angry with Lord Croom for allowing Noakes to destroy the garden and has become interested in their houseguest, Lord Byron.

Thomasina continues to insist, over Septimus's objections, that the universe can be reduced to a mathematical formula. In order to prove it, she offers to plot the leaf off an apple (the same piece of fruit, left on the set from the previous scene, that Gus gave to Hannah) and deduce its equation.

Chater storms in with Captain Brice, once again demanding a duel with Septimus. He has heard about Septimus's scathing review of his previous work, "The Maid of Turkey," and is convinced the tutor means to insult him again when he writes about his new book. Before the men can take steps to settle the matter, Lady Croom appears and borrows Septimus's copy of "The Couch of Eros" to give to Lord Byron. Byron wishes to satirize Chater and his awful poetry in the next edition of his *English Bards and Scotch Reviewers*. (*An important plot development: This is how Chater's book ends up in Byron's library for Bernard to find generations later.*) Lady Croom remarks with some concern that Byron intends to leave Sidley Park and go adventuring through Europe, right in the middle of the Napoleonic wars.

Lady Croom rushes off with "The Couch of Eros," leaving the quarrelsome men alone again. This time Septimus agrees to duel. He will meet Chater behind the boathouse at five o'clock the next morning, followed by Chater's subsequent duel with Captain Brice five minutes later (the naval officer has also been dallying with Mrs. Chater). Afterward, Hodge rails angrily: he will leave the country, Byron can remain behind to tutor Thomasina, and everybody will be happy.

Act I, scene 4

Present day Sidley Park: Hannah and Valentine are poring over books in the garden room. Hannah is examining Septimus's math primer, while Valentine leafs through Thomasina's lesson book. They have discovered a note Thomasina wrote in the margin of the primer, similar to Fermat's last theorem, that suggests her intent to explain nature through numbers. The graphs in her lesson book, Valentine explains, are primitive iterated algorithms, created using the same mathematical theory Valentine is applying to his study of the grouse population in the game books. He is surprised by the find, since iterated algorithms weren't widely known until computers made them practical, late in the twentieth century.

Bernard sputters into the room, excited about a recent find. He has discovered a copy of Byron's *English Bards and Scotch Reviewers* with a penciled inscription insulting Chater's poetry. To Bernard, this is proof positive that Byron killed Chater. Hannah adds fuel to the fire by telling him about a discovery of her own. She ran across a letter from Lady Croom to her husband that describes the marriage of Captain Brice to Mrs. Chater, again suggesting that Mr. Chater had been recently killed. More crucial, if misleading, information comes from Valentine, who affirms that Lord Byron was indeed a guest at Sidley Park; the game books he has been studying record that Byron shot a hare there in 1809.

Bernard rushes off in search of the records, while Valentine leads Hannah to a new revelation in her own work. He notes that it would take innumerable pencils, stacks of paper, and years and years of concentrated time for someone to complete the iterated algorithm that was started in Thomasina's lesson book. To do so, Valentine wryly remarks, someone would have to be insane. Hannah's thoughtful look suggests she is putting some new pieces together—linking the Sidley hermit to Thomasina's discovery.

Act II, scene 5

Bernard's theory about Lord Byron has rocketed from speculation to spectacular find in a single afternoon. Armed with the "facts" he has been provided by Hannah, Valentine, and the books in the Coverlys' library, he has already prepared a lecture he plans to read at the Byron Society, prior to publishing his version of history in pursuit of wealth and academic fame. He reads the lecture to the smitten Chloe, who listens adoringly; to Valentine, who listens semi-attentively while feeding his turtle; and to Hannah, who punctuates his address with

continuous objections to his findings. In the end, she warns him, "You'll end up with so much *fame* you won't leave the house without a paper bag over your head."

In the course of arguing about his research, Bernard manages to offend everyone in the house except Hannah, who knows his insults and intellectual bullying are only tools of rhetoric—he uses them to win points, not to seriously hurt people. Bernard packs up his research and heads off to town in a cab, promising to return that evening to accompany Chloe to the costume party. On his way out he drops another piece of Hannah's puzzle in her hands: a small book, written in 1832, that describes the hermit of Sidley Park and his pet tortoise, Plautus. She adds this to a letter she found, announcing the death of the hermit at the age of twenty-seven, and is more convinced than ever that the hermit and Septimus Hodge are one and the same, but she has yet to find the final clue that will prove it.

Act II, scene 6

The briefest scene of the play describes how the events of 1809 came to a climax in the middle of the night at Sidley Park. It is early in the morning, just before dawn, and Septimus returns from the boathouse, where he was supposed to have dueled Chater but instead shot only a rabbit. He is met by Jellaby, who explains that Mrs. Chater was caught leaving Byron's room the night before, and in the tumult that followed, Captain Brice, the Chaters, and Lord Byron all left the estate. Lady Croom interrupts the gossip, sending Jellaby off to work. She is infuriated at Septimus for leaving behind two letters to be read in the event of his death. One was a love letter, addressed to her, the other a note of encouragement from teacher to student, addressed to Thomasina.

It turns out that Septimus's real passion all along has been for Lady Croom—Mrs. Chater was merely a diversion. For her part, the Lady has always been fond of Septimus and merely toyed with Lord Byron. She reveals that her brother, Captain Brice, has enlisted the help of Mr. Chater to serve as an amateur botanist on an expedition to the Indies. His ulterior motive, of course, is to be near Mrs. Chater. Septimus and Lady Croom agree to put the events of the past few days behind them. To please her, Septimus even burns a letter he received from Lord Byron without reading it. Grateful for his discretion, Lady Croom invites Septimus to come to her room later that morning. When she is gone, the young tutor burns the two letters he wrote as well, leaving no clues for future detectives like Bernard and Hannah.

Act II, scene 7

The final scene of the play combines the past and present on stage at the same time. In the present, it is the night of the costume garden party, hosted by the Coverlys. Chloe, Valentine, and Gus are all dressed in Regency clothes, typical of Byron's era. Bernard's "discovery" has landed him in all the newspapers, while Hannah still struggles with her hermit. Valentine has fed Thomasina's equations into a computer, taken them a few million steps further than she was able, and produced beautiful pictures out of simple numbers. While looking over Valentine's shoulder at his computer-generated model, Hannah reveals the most startling surprise of the play: Thomasina died in a fire at Sidley Park the night before her seventeenth birthday.

While Valentine and Hannah continue their work in silence, Thomasina and her little brother, Augustus, run onstage. A few years have elapsed in the nineteenth century setting. It is now 1812, and Thomasina is sixteen and nearing her birthday. Septimus joins the children for the daily lesson, which Augustus chooses to abandon. Left alone, Thomasina insists that Septimus should make good on his promise to teach her how to waltz. The piano has been playing in the next room throughout the scene. At the keys (though unseen) is Count Zelinsky, Lady Croom's new piano tuner and, apparently, her new lover. When she whisks into the room Septimus treats her coldly. She ignores his jealousy and remarks on her new dahlias, which Captain Brice recently brought back from his expedition to the Indies, where Mr. Chater died of a monkey bite and Mrs. Chater subsequently became Mrs. Brice.

Switching to present-day action, Bernard appears for his date with Chloe and is hounded immediately by Hannah, who has found the last, and fatal, piece of his puzzle. In one of Lady Croom's garden books, Hannah ran across an entry describing the dahlias and Chater's unfortunate accident in the Indies. Since he was killed picking flowers by a monkey, he obviously could not have been killed in a duel by Lord Byron. Bernard finally realizes he should not have rushed to judgment and that his newfound fame will soon be over when Hannah reports her find in the press. Life, for the moment, goes on, and Chloe assembles a costume for Bernard to wear to the party.

A few hours pass and it is evening. In the offstage room, the Count is playing piano for Lady Croom. Septimus is studying Thomasina's work when she appears in her nightgown for her waltzing lesson. The work she has drawn in her lesson book, it turns out, is a diagram of heat exchange. It suggests what hadn't been discovered yet by scientists: that heat could not work backwards. The second law of thermodynamics, as described by Thomasina, meant the universe must someday wind down, grow cold, and die. Disturbed by the implications, Septimus takes his young pupil in his arms and begins to dance.

While Septimus and Thomasina waltz, and stop to kiss, the action in the present day continues around them. Bernard suddenly rushes in, adjusting his clothes, followed by Chloe. They explain to Valentine and Hannah that Chloe's mother caught them together in the hermitage. A little embarrassed but not very repentant, Bernard dresses himself and prepares his escape, leaving a crestfallen Chloe behind. On his way out the door Hannah tells him she thinks she knows who the hermit of Sidley Park was but still lacks proof. Still his impetuous self, Bernard advises her: "Publish!"

Septimus and Thomasina stop their dancing. He returns her lesson, lights her candle, and tells her she should go off to bed, being careful of the candle's flame. Too in love to leave, she asks for another dance. As they twirl around again, Gus enters with a folio for Hannah. It contains a drawing of Septimus and Plautus, the final piece of her puzzle, linking the tutor to the hermitage. In a gesture of gratitude, she dances, awkwardly, with Gus. The final haunting image of the play is of the past and present dancing together.

CHARACTERS

Captain Edward Brice

Captain Brice is the bold and blustery brother of Lady Croom. He is not as refined or witty as his sister, but he can be equally as stubborn. When on duty, he serves in the British Royal Navy. While off duty, he has been staying at Sidley Park with his sister and pursuing Mrs. Chater, the wife of Ezra Chater. Because Mr. Chater is even less perceptive than he is, Captain Brice has been able to conduct his love affair with Mrs. Chater right under the poor man's nose. At one point, faced with the possibility that Septimus Hodge might be dallying with Mrs.

Chater as well, Captain Brice offers to stand up for Mr. Chater in a duel for her honor. The twice cuckolded Chater never realizes he is caught between two of his wife's lovers. When the Chaters are finally thrown off the property for their scandalous behavior, Captain Brice offers Mr. Chater a job as a botanist on an expedition he is leading to the Indies. Once there, the hapless Mr. Chater dies from a monkey bite, and Captain Brice finally gets to marry the object of his affection.

Ezra Chater

Ezra Chater is one of the play's greatest fools and one of literature's biggest cuckolds. He is quick-tempered, slow-witted, vain, and married to a woman who cannot stay faithful. He ended up at Sidley Park as the guest of Captain Brice who, in amorous pursuit of the lusty Mrs. Chater, flattered his poetry and paid fifty pounds to have him published. Chater views Brice as his doting patron, and Brice views Chater as a nit-wit.

When Chater hears that Septimus Hodge, the estate's tutor, has been seen in "carnal embrace" with his wife, he quickly challenges Septimus to a duel. He changes his mind, however, when Septimus falsely praises his poetry and offers to write a glowing review in a London periodical. Later he discovers he has been fooled again, and reissues his challenge. He is prepared to meet Septimus behind the Coverly's boathouse at dawn, but is rushed off the property in the middle of the night when his wife is caught with yet another man, the rakish poet, Lord Byron. Sometime later, while accompanying his wife and Captain Brice on a voyage to the Indies, Chater is bitten by a monkey and dies abroad. Hardly pausing a day to mourn, the widowed Mrs. Chater marries Captain Brice.

Augustus Coverly

Augustus Coverly is seen only briefly, near the end of the play. He is Thomasina's younger brother, fifteen years old in 1812, and a student at Eton. The first time he appears he is taunting his sister and is rude to Septimus. He returns briefly, however, penitent and hoping the tutor will have a brotherly talk with him about sex.

Chloe Coverly

Chloe Coverly is the daughter of the modern day Croom family at Sidley Park. She is eighteen, extremely impressionable, and immediately falls for Bernard's flamboyant appearance and insistent intelligence. Though not as academically inclined as her older brother, Valentine, or as intuitively gifted as her younger brother, Gus, she manages to supply one of the play's more interesting ideas. While everyone seems determined to find sense, some kind of ordering theory, in chaos, Chloe suggests that sex is the wrench in the works. "The universe is deterministic all right, just like Newton said, I mean it's trying to be," Chloe claims, "but the only thing going wrong is people fancying people who aren't supposed to be in that part of the plan." The human element, as unpredictable as anything chaos could muster, is what the others weren't considering. In the end, Chloe is caught up in the chaos, when her mother finds her in "carnal embrace" with Bernard at the family garden party.

Gus Coverly

At fifteen, Gus is the youngest of the modern Coverly children, the descendants of Thomasina and Augustus Coverly. He is an autistic and mute, given to shyness with unpredictable spurts of sociability. Valentine, his brother, tells Hannah that Gus spoke until he was five, then he mysteriously went silent. The modern day Lady Croom (unseen in the play) believes he is a genius. After spending months, and hiring experts, to help her find the foundations of an old boathouse on her property, Gus led her right to it. The enigmatic boy seems to function as some kind of symbol in the play, perhaps as a representative of intuition over reason. Near the end, it is Gus who provides Hannah with the final clue she needs to solve the puzzle she has been working on: a sketch of Septimus holding Plautus the tortoise.

Thomasina Coverly

The progress Thomasina Coverly makes in *Arcadia* is from precocious to poignant. She begins the play as the nearly fourteen-year-old daughter of Lord and Lady Croom, owners of Sidley Park. Young as she is though, Thomasina knows—and guesses at—truths far beyond her years. While studying her mathematics, she asks her tutor, Septimus Hodge, with mock innocence, "What is carnal embrace?" She is undeterred when he tells her it is "the practice of throwing one's arms around a side of beef," and proceeds to relay a story she heard about one of the house guests caught in carnal embrace in the gazebo. Sometimes she is childlike and impish, while at other times her deadly seriousness is disarming.

In many ways, Thomasina is the central character of *Arcadia*. She searches for truths, in people, in mathematics, and in poetry, and her ideas send the other characters scurrying for answers—or scratching their heads. Her genius is *intuitive*. She struggles to learn things, such as Latin, by rote, but she can *perceive* things and draw conclusions that others cannot. For example, she realizes while eating her rice pudding that the jam can be stirred outward and *into* the pudding, "making red trails like the picture of a meteor in my astronomical atlas." But, she notes, you cannot stir backward and bring the jam together again. From this experiment, Thomasina concludes that if every atom in the universe could be momentarily stopped in its place and examined, a brilliant mathematician could write a formula for all the future, just by predicting the motion of matter.

Thomasina spends much of the play trying to prove her theory to Septimus, who simply tries to keep up with his young protegé and continually challenge her with new ideas. It is not until three years later, during the final scene of the play, that Septimus finally begins to understand what his student has stumbled upon. In trying to explain chaos and thermodynamics, Thomasina has produced a theory that suggests the universe is spiraling outward, cooling off, and will someday grow cold and die. By this time, teacher and student have begun to develop a physical relationship. In the play's haunting final moments, they dance and kiss, just hours before Thomasina's seventeenth birthday, when she is destined to die in a fire in her bedroom.

Valentine Coverly

The oldest of the modern Coverly children, Valentine is a postgraduate student at Oxford, studying biology, mathematics, and, recently, chaos theory. Although he is capable of some dry humor (he jokes, for example, that Hannah is his fiance, and he takes his pet turtle "Lightning" out for a "run"), Valentine is mainly a serious-minded, analytical individual. He draws his inspiration from the wonders of science, and finds Bernard's pursuit of Lord Byron's history "trivial," because, he says, *personalities* don't matter, it's the *knowledge* they produce that is important.

While Hannah tries to find a reason for the collapse of Romanticism as well as a connection to the Sidley Park hermit, and Bernard flails about, grasping at straws to support his wild theories about Lord Byron's escape from England, Valentine occupies himself with cold, clear, calculated statistics—his family's game books. The books are a centuries-old record of all the animals that have been hunted and killed on the estate, and Valentine is analyzing the data to find a pattern for the life cycles of grouse in the area. A formula describing the cycles, he explains, must exist, and it would create some order out of chaos. Like Hannah, Valentine gets caught up in the research Thomasina was conducting in the house two centuries before, though he initially cannot believe she knew what she was doing, since science had yet to discover the theories she put forth. "There's an order things happen in," he insists, "You can't open a door till there's a house." In the end, though, his scientist's resolve is shaken, and he recognizes Thomasina's ideas for genius—and the consequences her ideas have for the rest of the universe.

Lady Croom

Lady Croom is the archly witty resident aristocrat of Sidley Park in the 1809 scenes. Highborn and highbred, she still manages to misquote the painter Nicolas Poussin, insult all her guests, and stoop as low as any other character in the play to satisfy her desires—mostly with any man willing to dally in her dressing room. Lady Croom's principal objective in the play is to prevent Richard Noakes from ruining the countryside around her home with Lord Croom's vision of a Romantic wilderness. She is happy with the current arrangement, which includes trees neatly grouped on the hillside and a winding creek flowing from an artificial lake in the middle of neatly trimmed meadows with just the right amount of sheep "tastefully arranged." In short, she says, "It is nature as God intended." As her view of nature demonstrates, she is often unaware of contradicting herself, despite her cleverness in conversation and incisive wit.

Lady Croom's other objective seems to be casual affairs. In the course of the play she manages to find her name connected with no fewer than three of her guests—Lord Byron, the poet; Septimus Hodge, her daughter's tutor; and Count Zelinsky, an expatriate Polish aristocrat hired as Sidley Park's piano tuner. Septimus seems to take his relationship with Lady Croom seriously, for he wrote her a love letter, to be opened in the event of his death, before going off to duel with Chater and Captain Brice. Like others before him, however, he is abandoned when the Lady's affection turns toward Count Zelinsky at the end of the play.

Septimus Hodge

After studying mathematics and natural philosophy at Cambridge, where Lord Byron was one of his classmates, Septimus Hodge came to Sidley Park to work as the tutor for the Croom family's daughter, Thomasina Coverly. Septimus is young, intelligent, clever, and apparently attractive. He begins the play aged twenty-two. His brief encounter with Mrs. Chater in the estate's gazebo is choice gossip among the servants, and he is conducting an ongoing affair with Lady Croom, his protegé's mother.

For Septimus, the passions of the flesh compete with the quest for knowledge as his most important defining characteristics in the play. His first responsibility is to Thomasina, who is an exceptionally gifted student, and it often takes all his resources to keep up with her questions and ideas. While studying mathematics and trying to find proof for Fermat's last theorem, for example, Thomasina wonders about the meaning of "carnal embrace." Septimus cleverly dodges the uncomfortable question by providing a technically true, if somewhat misleading, answer. "Carnal embrace is the practice of throwing one's arms around a side of beef," he tells his mischievous charge. Septimus's ability to think quickly on his feet gets him out of a few scrapes in the play. When confronted by Ezra Chater, the husband of the woman he was found embracing in the gazebo, he admits to his indiscretion but turns Chater's vanity against him. In exchange for avoiding a duel over Mrs. Chater, whose reputation, Septimus claims, "could not be adequately defended by a platoon of musketry deployed by rota," the young tutor offers to publish a glowing review of Mr. Chater's book of poetry, "The Couch of Eros," which Septimus actually hates.

Like Valentine in the modern scenes, Septimus is initially skeptical of Thomasina's attempts to create order out of chaos in the universe through a simple mathematical theory. He doesn't doubt her creativity or intelligence, but he is more comfortable when she sticks to traditional lessons from her books. Though he doesn't immediately recognize it in Thomasina, Septimus does believe genius exists. To him, it is a property shared by humanity across the ages, and great ideas are part of the continuum of life. "The missing plays of Sophocles will turn up piece by piece or be written again in another language," he reassures Thomasina. "Ancient cures for diseases will reveal themselves once more. Mathematical discoveries glimpsed and lost to view will have their time again." In the end, he realizes Thomasina is right, and her theory suggests the eventual end of the universe. What he mourns, however, is not the end of life but the loss of

innocence. "When we have found all the mysteries and lost all the meaning, we will be alone, on an empty shore," he laments before joining Thomasina in her first, and last, waltz.

Hannah Jarvis

Hannah Jarvis is a cool, capable, and seemingly impenetrable historian who has been invited to Sidley Park by the current Lady Croom to research landscape changes on the estate over the past two centuries. Her specialty area of study is landscape and literature between 1750 and 1834, and she has already written *Caro,* a best-selling book about Lord Byron. Because she is not an academic, but an actual field researcher and writer, her success has infuriated professors and would-be literary pundits around England. Now she is on to something new. While rooting around the libraries and landscape of the Croom estate she has discovered a new topic, a sort of mystery, to work on. She is trying to find clues about the Sidley hermit, who she calls "my peg for the nervous breakdown of the Romantic Imagination."

Hannah's search intensifies when she is joined by an unlikely ally—Bernard Nightingale, a snooty college don who published a scathing review of her last book and has turned up looking for clues to a Lord Byron scandal. Though they seem to be opposite personalities, and quarrel continuously, Hannah and Bernard manage to help one another find pieces to their respective puzzles. One of the biggest differences between them, however, is a proper respect for the process of research and the reporting of history. While Bernard is prepared to rush off to press with his story without all the necessary information, Hannah bides her time, looking for more and more information that will link a small sketch of a hermit found in one of Lady Croom's garden books to Septimus Hodge, author, tutor and, in Hannah's mind, a symbol of the descent of Romanticism into the age of scientific reason.

Jellaby

Jellaby is the butler at Sidley Park in the 1809 scenes. He says little, and his principal part in the play is delivering various notes between Ezra Chater, Septimus, and Mrs. Chater. At one point, Septimus bribes Jellaby into telling him about the events of the previous night, when Mrs. Chater was caught leaving Lord Byron's room and everyone was ushered off the property.

Bernard Nightingale

In his *New Yorker* review, critic John Lahr called Bernard Nightingale "a whirlwind of spurious intellectual connections" and "a literary climber of the first order." Other reviewers have called him greedy, self-centered, and a loose cannon. He is all these and more. Bernard is a professor at Sussex University, though his real passion lies in publishing, not in the classroom. When asked if teaching shouldn't be the first priority for a professor he snidely retorts, "Good God, no, let the brats sort it out for themselves."

In a way, Bernard is a satirical portrait of the worst kind of scholar academia has to offer. He is an irresponsible intellectual snob who is willing to string together scattered clues on the tiniest shreds of evidence in order to produce grand theories that will make him famous and his colleagues jealous. What's worse, he dresses the part. Bernard appears at Sidley Park wearing the typical garb of a Sussex don—suit, tie, and large leather satchel—along with some flamboyant touches of his own, like a peacock-colored display handkerchief bursting out of his jacket pocket.

He has come to assemble evidence for his most recent ambitious theory: a connection between the famous Romantic poet Lord Byron and one of the guests at Sidley Park in 1809. He manages to enlist the help of Hannah Jarvis, a writer who is also studying the history of the estate, and the manor's current occupants, descendants of Thomasina Coverly. One of these, eighteen-year-old Chloe Coverly, he finds time to seduce along the way. Together, they find a series of clues that may or may not support Bernard's idea that Byron shot and killed a shoddy poet in a duel at Sidley Park in 1809, then fled the country for two years. Heedless of Hannah's warning that he doesn't have enough proof yet to take his findings public, Bernard presents a lecture for the Byron Society and even appears on a morning talk show. Immediately afterward, Hannah finds another clue that proves him wrong, and his dreams of lifelong academic fame disappear—for the moment.

Richard Noakes

The part Richard Noakes plays in the plot of *Arcadia* is quite small, only a few lines, yet his presence embodies the Romantic sentiment of his age. He is a landscape architect, hired by Lord Croom to transform the grounds at Sidley Park from their current state, an orderly pastoral paradise in the style of Capability Brown, into a chaotic, Gothic wilderness in the picturesque fashion of Salvator Rosa, a popular Romantic painter. While the unseen Lord Croom seemingly supports Noakes and his designs for unkempt, "natural" surroundings, the rest of the household is barely civil toward him. Lady Croom continually hounds him, complaining of the noise his new steam engine makes and insulting his design ideas, and Septimus refers to him as the Devil, sniping, "In the scheme of the garden he is as the serpent."

THEMES

Enlightenment vs. Romanticism

By setting much of *Arcadia* in 1809, Stoppard pits two opposing historical epochs against each other: Enlightenment and Romanticism. The eighteenth century age of Enlightenment stressed orderly, rational thought, and conformity to accepted rules and forms, and looked to the Classical Greeks and Romans as models of simplicity, proportion, and restrained emotion in culture, art, and literature. Romanticism of the early nineteenth century was a deliberate revolt against Enlightenment ideals. Romantic philosophers and artists experimented with literary forms and stressed individuality, freedom, and the wildness of nature in their work.

The characters in *Arcadia*, in both the past and present scenes, represent both kinds of thought. Lady Croom wants to preserve her classically-inspired gardens where, "The slopes are green and gentle. The trees are companionably grouped at intervals that show them to advantage. The rill is a serpentine ribbon unwound from the lake peaceably contained by meadows on which the right amount of sheep are tastefully arranged." Her adversary in taste is the landscape architect Richard Noakes (hired by the unseen Lord Croom), who is prepared to tear down the neatly manicured shrubbery and carefully groomed hillsides and convert Sidley Park into a Gothic wilderness, complete with a waterfall, gloomy forest, and picturesque hermitage. He defends himself, saying simply, "It is the modern style."

The battle fought between Lady Croom and Noakes over the condition of Sidley Park's gardens is reflected in some of the play's less tangible ideas as well. In the contemporary scenes, Bernard Nightingale and Valentine Coverly line up on each side of

TOPICS FOR FURTHER STUDY

- Like many playwrights who write about ideas, Stoppard relies on symbolism to convey deeper levels of meaning. In *Arcadia,* one of the more important symbols is the landscape of Sidley Park, which undergoes several changes in the course of the play and is talked about by all the characters, past and present. Examine the ways the landscape at Sidley Park is viewed by the people who stay there and explain how it becomes an important symbol in the play.

- One of the principal themes in *Arcadia* is a collision between passion and reason, the heart and the head. The Romantic movement of the late-eighteenth and early-nineteenth centuries influenced all of Europe. Explore Romanticism by investigating some of the great Romantic literary figures of the age like Lord Byron, Percy Bysshe Shelley, Samuel Taylor Coleridge, Mary Shelley, and Victor Hugo. What are some of the great Romantic works of literature written by these artists? What is the Romantic view of the world? How do these Romantic artists express this view in their work?

- Very few plays rely on mathematics and scientific theory as essential plot elements, yet they are essential to *Arcadia.* Investigate the most important scientific theories of the play: Fermat's Last Theorem, Chaos Theory, and the Second Law of Thermodynamics (brief information about each is available in most encyclopedias). What do each of these theories suggest? How or why is each theory *symbolically* important to the events, characters, and themes of *Arcadia?*

- In *Arcadia,* Stoppard uses a technique known as *juxtaposition* to place characters and thoughts next to each other for the audience to compare and contrast. This happens each time the scene changes from the historical past to the contemporary present. It seems there are characters in Sidley Park's past (the 1809-12 scenes) who have counterparts in the modern scenes. They may share personality traits, express similar ideas, or share the same interests. Who do you suppose is Septimus's counterpart in modern day Sidley Park? How about Ezra Chater's? Does anyone in the present come close to resembling Thomasina and her powers of intuition? Compare two or three sets of character counterparts and explain how the *juxtaposition* of these characters helps your understanding of the play.

---

the debate between intellect and emotion. Bernard is acting on instinct and emotion, pursuing the unlikely theory that Lord Byron left England in 1809 because he killed a minor poet in a duel. He persists in his notion, even in the face of evidence to the contrary, because of "Gut instinct. The part of you which doesn't reason. The certainty for which there is no back-reference."

Valentine, on the other hand, is a graduate student at Oxford, studying chaos theory, and trying to find a pattern in the rise and fall of numbers in his family's centuries-old hunting books. To him, Bernard's interests are trivial. "The questions you're asking don't matter, you see," he tells the arrogant professor, "It's like arguing who got there first with the calculus. The English say Newton, the Germans say Leibnitz. But it doesn't *matter.* Personalities. What matters is the calculus. Scientific progress. Knowledge."

In the end, each combatant learns a lesson about the other's viewpoint. Bernard rushes ahead to publish and promote his theory before learning all the facts and is publicly embarrassed to discover he was completely wrong. A little more analysis and a little less gut instinct would have served him well. For his part, Valentine must admit to the existence of genius, a human impulse that surpasses science, when he works his way through Thomasina's lesson book and finds she perceived a theory for chaos long before scientists knew one existed.

Genius

A genius is someone with natural talents, possessing exceptional intelligence or creative ability. Their powers of perception may be broad and encompass many areas of study and craft, or they may be gifted in a very particular area, such as writing, math, or communications. A couple characters in *Arcadia* are referred to as geniuses while others are trying desperately to gain that status. Others doubt the existence of genius in the same way they don't believe in fate or God.

Thomasina Coverly is probably a genius. At thirteen, she is seeking proof for Fermat's Last Theorem and trying to devise a numeric formula that will describe the shape of a leaf. She perceives things others do not and can match wits with anyone at Sidley Park. When she asks Septimus, her tutor, if she is more clever than her elders, he admits: "Yes. Much." For his part, Septimus believes genius is a primal ability, existing somewhere in all human beings of every age. When Thomasina laments the loss of the historic library at Alexandria, Septimus reassures her, "You should no more grieve for the rest [of the lost Greek tragedies] than for a buckle lost from your first shoe, or for your lesson book which will be lost when you are old. We shed as we pick up, like travelers who must carry everything in their arms, and what we let fall will be picked up by those behind." Lost plays, mathematical theories, and creative inventions will all be discovered again by geniuses of the future, who will appear, Septimus believes.

Thomasina's counterpart in the present day is Gus Coverly. Like the ancient prophets, ironically struck blind by the gods in order to "see" the future, fifteen-year old Gus is a genius who can't speak and shies away from most human contact. The nature of his ability is not as apparent as Thomasina's, though he is described as someone with great powers of intuition, capable of guessing the needs of others. He found the ruined foundations of the estate's boathouse for his mother, after experts spent months searching; and he provides Hannah with her most important clue: a sketch of Septimus Hodge, the Sidley Park hermit, and his pet tortoise, Plautus.

Valentine doubts the nature of genius when it reaches beyond what he feels are ordinary limitations. After studying Thomasina's lesson books with Hannah and considering the stacks of algebraic illustrations left behind by the Sidley Park hermit, he still can't bring himself to believe someone could have imagined such a theory years before the existence of calculators. "There's an order things happen in," he insists, "You can't open the door until there's a house." Hannah has a unique definition for genius. To her, genius can be found not only in extraordinary abilities but in the rigorous pursuit of knowledge. "It's wanting to know that makes us matter," she stresses to Valentine, "Otherwise we're going out the way we came in."

STYLE

Juxtaposition

While *Arcadia* is set in only a single location, a large room in the Sidley Park manor, the action of the play occurs in two very different time periods: 1809-1812 and the present day. Setting the play in both eras allows Stoppard to use a literary device known as *juxtaposition* to cleverly compare and contrast characters and ideas. Juxtaposition occurs when two things are placed side by side, or on top of one another, and their dominant qualities are compared.

In *Arcadia,* pairs of characters are sometimes juxtaposed and compared this way. For example, Ezra Chater is a vain, would-be poet, given to fits of overreaction. In some ways, he finds his counterpart in Bernard Nightingale, the flashy, blustery Sussex don who, though he is vastly more intelligent than Chater, is still easily led astray by his pride and search for glory.

The continuation of ideas through both time periods is another effective use of juxtaposition in the play. By experimenting with primitive chaos theory, Thomasina seems to be following a natural human tendency to try to explain and bring order to her world. Though she dies before completing her work, her experiments are picked up in the present by Valentine Coverly, who feeds them into a computer and takes them leagues further than the young Thomasina could ever have done with pencil and paper. In the process, he learns a lesson about present human condition from the past.

Perhaps the greatest advantage of juxtaposition in *Arcadia* is the *dramatic irony* it provides the audience who are allowed the omnipotent ability to see events of the past take place and then watch characters in the present attempt to reconstruct them. Dramatic irony occurs when the audience of a

Scene from the1800s setting in Arcadia: *Septimus and Thomasina are joined by Jellaby the butler during one of their lessons*

play, or the reader of a novel, knows something the characters do not. Stoppard's audience knows that it is Septimus, and not Lord Byron, who was supposed to have dueled Ezra Chater in 1809. When contemporary scenes are juxtaposed on the scenes of the past, the guessing-game nature of historical studies is highlighted. The audience gets to watch Bernard and Hannah try to piece together the clues, repeatedly coming up with the wrong answers. From this, they can assume that history is often put together through such lucky (and unlucky) guesses, and that at best it is, like Thomasina's formula for chaos, only a theory.

Symbolism

In literature, a symbol is something that represents something else. Symbols are often used to communicate deeper levels of meaning. In Nathaniel Hawthorne's famous novel *The Scarlet Letter,* for example, the red letter ''A'' worn by Hester Prynne is a symbol not only of her supposed crime (adultery) but also of her neighbors' bigotry and her own courageous pride. Like many playwrights who write about important *ideas,* Stoppard relies on many symbols in his work to communicate deeper levels of meaning to his audiences.

In *Arcadia,* one of the prominent symbols is the landscape around Sidley Park, which represents, among other things, the battle between Enlightenment and Romanticism, or intellect and emotion, that is raging among the characters inside the house. Heat becomes another important symbol. Early in the play, Thomasina is considering the effects of motion and friction on the jam in her rice pudding. By the end, she has perceived the Second Law of Thermodynamics which insures that Mr. Noakes's steam engine will always take more energy to operate than it is capable of producing. Ultimately it is heat, in the form of a terrible fire, which kills Thomasina. By then, the symbolism is clear: Eventually the loss of heat will be the end of the entire universe; Thomasina perishes by that which she sought to understand.

Pastoral Poetry

While *Arcadia* is not itself a pastoral poem, the title is taken from the tradition of pastoral writing, and the play shares many of the form's best known qualities. Arcadia was a region in ancient Greece that was regarded as the ideal of rural simplicity and happiness. Pastoral poetry is a form of literature in which an author uses simple shepherds and country folk, such as those who may have dwelt in Arcadia, and presents an idyllic vision of rural life in marked contrast to the misery and corruption of life in the city. The Roman poet Virgil is known for pastoral poetry in the first century B.C., and the Italian writer Sannazzaro is credited with reviving the form during the Renaissance.

The characters in Stoppard's play, like the farmers and shepherds in pastoral poetry, live in the countryside, away from the chaos of city life. Lady Croom even brags to her daughter, " *'Et in Arcadia ego!'* 'I too have lived in Arcadia,' Thomasina.'' Whether Sidley Park is a paradise, however, is questionable. In the present day, Hannah laments that even the grounds as Lady Croom knew them were becoming unnatural: ''There's an engraving of Sidley Park in 1730 that makes you want to weep. Paradise in the age of reason. By 1760 everything had gone—the topiary, pools and terraces, fountains, an avenue of limes—the whole sublime geometry was ploughed under by Capability Brown. The grass went from the doorstep to the horizon and the best box hedge in Derbyshire was dug up for the ha-ha so that the fools could pretend they were living in God's countryside.''

In either event, the pastoral setting becomes essential if the arguments the characters make are to have their full impact. Like simple country folk, proud of the peaceful lives they lead, the characters at Sidley Park, both past and present, all seem to be searching for ideals—in mathematics, science, poetry, and love—and *Arcadia*'s rural setting, far removed from the bustle of civilization, helps magnify the importance of their quests.

HISTORICAL CONTEXT

History is practically a character itself in *Arcadia*. The play takes place in England in two different time periods, the early nineteenth century and the present day. While the scenes in the present day often seem disconnected from the world outside, other than scattered references to advancements in math and science and television as the modern day mass media of choice, they are intensely interested in the past. The entire plot, in fact, hinges on the events of 1809-1812, when, in the world of the play, a young girl was formulating theories decades ahead

of their time, Lord Byron was writing the poems that would make him famous, and Europe was transforming itself through wars, experiments in art, and the inventions of science.

The period Stoppard chose to contrast with the present has been labeled a transformative era in world history, the twilight of one age and the dawn of another; much of the creative energy and tumult of the period can be found in *Arcadia*. Three of the most important historical influences on the play are England's Industrial Revolution, European political upheaval and empire building, and Romanticism in art and literature.

Britain's Industrial Revolution

The first Industrial Revolution in Britain began late in the eighteenth century and almost immediately altered the way products were manufactured, what products were created, the location of industry, and the transportation of goods around the country and around the world. Because greater production efficiency could be achieved when the resources required by industry were centrally located, the population of Britain began a gradual shift from scattered rural dwellings to primarily urban communities.

In *England in the Nineteenth Century,* David Thomson noted: ''Most Englishmen in 1815 still worked on the land or in trades connected with agriculture, though within the next generation most Englishmen became townsmen engaged in industry: sixteen years after Waterloo probably half the population already lived under urban conditions. . . . During the first thirty years of the century Birmingham and Sheffield doubled in size, Liverpool, Leeds, Manchester, and Glasgow more than doubled. London, in 1815, was above the million mark, and five years later numbered 1,274,000.''

The people who moved to the new centers of industry found working conditions quite different from what they had known before. Individual craftsmanship was superseded by collective manufacturing efforts: Instead of handling goods from start to finish, workers were taught a particular part of the job, given the tools necessary, and placed in a factory setting where, by sheer force of numbers, they could produce greater amounts of goods than ever before (a process that came to be known as the ''production line''). Britain very quickly became the workshop of the world and a major exporter of

COMPARE
&
CONTRAST

- **1809-1812:** Britain's Industrial Revolution makes it the workshop of the world. England transforms from a primarily agricultural society to an increasingly skilled working class system built on venture capitalism. Inventions like the steam engine, patented in 1769 by Englishman James Watt, make possible industrial marvels like the locomotive, which first appears in 1804.

  Today: Another technological revolution, the "Information Age," is sweeping the globe. The work of industry is increasingly handled by automated machines run by computers. Automation and high speed information gathering, storage, retrieval, and dissemination came about through a series of technological discoveries beginning with the transistor in 1948, followed by integrated circuits in the 1960s, and the microprocessor in the 1970s. Automated machinery and sophisticated communications tools such as personal computers, cellular telephones, fax machines, and paging devices rely on more and more powerful microprocessors. By 2010 the computer industry is expected to be the largest industry on earth.

- **1809-1812:** The Romantic style dominates the literature of Europe. Authors such as William Wordsworth, Lord Byron, Samuel Taylor Coleridge, and Percy Bysshe Shelley rely on imagination, freedom of thought and expression, the creation of new forms, and an idealization of nature.

  Today: *Postmodernism* defines the literature of the late-twentieth century. These works often invoke or borrow from earlier periods, using a technique known as *pastiche.* Another technique found in postmodernist literature, music, art,

and, the postmodern medium of choice, film, is *montage.* Rather than telling a story in traditional, linear fashion, montage often presents a series of seemingly unrelated, sometimes contradictory images that defy explanation. Traditional elements like plot, character, and language are fragmented and disoriented.

- **1809-1812:** Women in England are treated as second-class citizens and widely regarded as intellectually inferior to men. They receive only limited schooling, no higher education, and have access to a limited number of vocations. They are subjected to an extremely rigid, conservative code of sexual behavior and hold almost no legal rights, especially once married.

  Today: After an arduous, sometimes violent suffrage movement, women received the right to vote in Britain in 1918 and now enjoy equal rights under the law as well as equal access to education and employment. Margaret Thatcher became the first female Prime Minister in 1979, serving until 1990.

- **1809-1812:** Although it lost its colonies in America in 1783, Britain is still building its worldwide empire. By the end of the nineteenth century the empire stretches across all seven continents, in countries as far-flung as Trinidad, Newfoundland, South Africa, and Hong Kong.

  Today: Territories in the British Empire began resisting colonial rule after World War I. Egypt, India, Malaysia, and a host of other holdings have reverted back to their citizens during the past few decades. In 1997, Britain returns control of Hong Kong, one of its last colonies, back to the Chinese.

---

all sorts of goods from furniture to textiles to fine china.

Exporting goods, of course, relied heavily on transportation, both within the country, to transfer

goods from factories to shipping centers, and without, to get goods from rail stations and ports to their foreign destinations. To accomplish this, enormous improvements and advances were made in the country's transportation system. In *England in the Eighteenth Century*, J. H. Plumb wrote:

> The canals, the roads, the ships of England were the nation's pride. Inexpensive Irish labor was used to cover Britain with a network of canals. By 1815, 2,600 miles of canal had been built in England; 500 in Scotland and Ireland. They cheapened production and lowered prices. . . . But the revolution in road transport was more vivid, more exciting, to contemporaries. Road engineering did not begin to improve until the last quarter of the century, and it was given a strong stimulus, in 1784, with the introduction of the mail coach for the rapid transport of letters and passengers. The stage coaches responded to the threat of competition and road surfaces were improved to help faster travel. In 1754 it took four and a half days to travel from London to Manchester; in 1788 the journey had been reduced to 28 hours.

At the same time, Britain's ports and shipping abilities were being improved to handle all the additional trade. By 1810 the total freight weight of ships using British ports reached 2 million tons. Between 1800 and 1810, thirty acres of new iron docks were built in London, along the Thames River, making Britain's capital the greatest port in the world.

All this industry was accompanied by equally important gains in efficient agricultural techniques. Researching and perfecting new methods of tilling, the rotation of crops, and improved stock-breeding relied on capital and returned their investments a thousandfold, which meant that England's rich were getting richer. Landed aristocrats, like the Coverlys bearing the Croom lordship title in Stoppard's play, owned more and more land, which they would let to tenant farmers or hire laborers to farm for them. Through this method, they became the "leisure class" in England, allowing their money to work for them, while they enjoyed comfortable lives in elegant country houses, such as Sidley Park.

One of the residents of Sidley Park, Lady Croom, considers herself cursed by the advancements in industry and technology, particularly by Noakes's new steam engine, which she feels is systematically ruining her garden. "If everybody had his own I would bear my portion of the agony without complaint," she wails. "But to have been singled out by the only Improved Newcomen steam pump in England, this is hard, sir, this is not to be borne."

Military Conflict in the Nineteenth Century

At the same time that they were radically improving transportation methods, agriculture, and manufacturing techniques, Britons, along with most of Europe, were embroiled in a series of wars that shaped the modern European continent. Two of history's greatest revolutions had already been fought: the American Revolution (1775-1783) and the French Revolution (1789-1799). By the following century, the fallout from these great wars was still echoing through the politics and social structure of Europe. The first fifteen years of the nineteenth century was the age of Napoleon and the infancy of America. At various times during this period England fought against the forces of the French, the Spanish, and the Americans. Some of Britain's greatest victories were achieved—such as Lord Nelson's triumph over the French-Spanish fleets in the Battle of Trafalgar in 1805 and Napolean's final defeat at Waterloo in 1815 by British general Arthur Wellesley, the first Duke of Wellington.

Although the armed conflicts of Europe do not intrude directly into the peaceful lives of the residents at Sidley Park, they are certainly aware of them. Lady Croom, upon hearing that one of her favorite house guests, the poet Lord Byron, is planning an adventure abroad warns, "The whole of Europe is in a Napoleonic fit, all the best ruins will be closed, the roads entirely occupied with the movement of armies, the lodgings turned into billets and the fashion for godless republicanism not yet arrived at its natural reversion."

The Romantic Age

Coursing throughout the action of *Arcadia*, and somehow affecting the lives of all the characters, past and present, is the spirit of the Romantic Age. Broadly speaking, Romanticism was a movement that bridged the eighteenth and nineteenth centuries, affecting the literature of most European countries, the United States, and Latin America. Romantic writing is characterized by a reliance on imagination and subjectivity of approach, freedom of thought and expression, unfettered by traditionally accepted forms of literature and an idealization of nature in its pure form—a marked contrast from the increasingly mechanized and industrial world that surrounded Romantic writers. It also contrasted severely with the preceding Enlightenment era, which stressed orderly, rational thought, strict adherence to form, and a reliance on Classical Greek and Roman models. In essence, Romanticism was, for a time, the triumph of feeling over thinking, the heart over the head.

This battle between intellect and emotion rages through *Arcadia*. Stylistically, Lady Croom contin-

ues to live in the past. She adores her well manicured gardens, steeped in the balance and order of
Classical Greece and the Enlightenment age. The
unseen Lord Croom, however, is pitching headlong
into the new age and has brought in the landscape
architect Noakes to sculpt Romanticism into the
countryside. In the present, Hannah, Valentine, and
Bernard quarrel over the efficiency of science in the
face of the intuition of genius. Bernard ''feels'' his
theory about Lord Byron is right. He advocates ''a
visceral belief in yourself. Gut instinct.''

Young Thomasina, of course, is central to the
debate, as she is central to the play. In her can be
found the best elements of both logic and emotion.
She is as comfortable seeking a solution for Fermat's
Last Theorem and plotting the shape of a leaf with
numbers on a graph as she is reveling in the poetry
of the age. She laments the loss of the library at
Alexandria and in the same breath scorns Cleopatra
for not being more sensible and logical. Like the age
in which she lives, Thomasina is filled with marvelous contradictions. In the final scene of the play,
after happening on what would one day become the
Second Law of Thermodynamics governing the
exchange of heat between objects, she quickly discards the thrill of discovery, longing only for the
pleasure of learning to waltz and her romantic love
for Septimus.

CRITICAL OVERVIEW

Arcadia premiered at the Royal National Theatre of
Great Britain in 1993, won the prestigious Olivier
Award for best play then transferred to London's
West End for a lengthy and successful run. In
London, everything about the play was praised—its
plot, characters, fascinating ideas intricately woven
into witty dialogue, the scenery, the acting, and the
directing. The play received its American debut at
New York City's Lincoln Center Theater in 1995,
where—in spite of actors who were generally considered less fit for their roles than their English
counterparts and a theatre with poor acoustics—the
play earned acclamation from excited Stoppard
aficionados. The work also earned the playwright
newfound respect from some of his severest critics.
''*Arcadia* is wonderfully inventive and funny, full
of the epigrams, puns, and verbal pyrotechnics
characteristic of this dramatist,'' wrote Anne Barton in the *New York Review*. Clive Barnes crowed in

the *New York Post*, ''It is a work shot through with
fun, passion and, yes, genius.''

Michael Feingold, a longtime critic of the playwright's work, admitted in the *Village Voice:* ''Until *Arcadia,* you couldn't have convinced me that
Tom Stoppard was a playwright. At best, I'd have
called him a sometimes diverting entertainer, whose
show-offy, cerebral houses of cards usually turned
up a few ace witticisms before collapsing into a
litter of pasteboard. *Arcadia* changes all that.''
Other critics welcomed Stoppard back into popular
consciousness. Donald Lyons suggested in the *Wall
Street Journal* that ''*Arcadia* is Mr. Stoppard's
happiest invention since 1974's *Travesties.*'' In
Variety, Jeremy Gerard said, ''*Arcadia* fulfills the
promise of Stoppard's 1983 boulevard comedy, *The
Real Thing*. In *Arcadia,* he gets everything right.''

Many reviewers remarked on *Arcadia* 's collection of eccentric characters—a schoolgirl genius
and her handsome, romantic tutor; insultingly witty
members of the aristocracy; a flamboyant, puffed-
up university professor and his antagonist, a no-
nonsense historian as comfortable in garden trench-
es as she is at her typewriter. Typical of Stoppard's
critical reception, however, even more attention
was paid to the *thoughts* of the characters and the
themes of the play.

''This is one of Stoppard's guessing game
plays,'' Howard Kissel wrote in the *Daily News,*
where the interest lies less in the characters' changing relationships than in the ideas the playwright so
adroitly juggles.'' Barnes noted, ''Nothing is safe
from the intoxicating whirl of ideas which it draws
into a vortex, be it English landscape gardening,
Newtonian physics, Byron's mysterious flight from
England in 1809, the classicism of Claude and the
Gothic romanticism of Salvator Rosa, Horace Wal-
pole and Thomas Love Peacock, the second law of
thermodynamics, the conundrum of Fermat's mathematical theorum of numbers, the lost plays of Sophocles and Aeschylus, even dwarf dahlias in the
botanically unlikely region of Mazambique.''

The way Stoppard successfully assembled such
a range of characters and ideas in one place struck
some critics as an amazing feat. John Lahr noted in
the *New Yorker:* ''The brilliance of *Arcadia* is not
so much in the wordplay as it is in the construction.'' Lahr explained Stoppard's use of two different time periods, set in the same household, and

suggested, "By crosscutting the Coverly family story and the story of the contemporaries trying to reconstruct it, Stoppard utilizes the ironies of history—the symmetries and accidents that lead, nonetheless, to a kind of order—as a way of demonstrating the outcome of chaos theory."

The *New York Review*'s Barton appreciated that, while the play is a whirlwind of ideas and emotions, Stoppard did not resort to some of the theatrical tricks employed by his previous plays. "In theatrical terms . . . *Arcadia* is muted by comparison with most of Stoppard's previous work," she wrote, "No yellow-suited gymnasts dangerously construct and implode human pyramids (*Jumpers*); nor does an entire troupe of traveling actors stow away and improbably contrive a musical performance inside three barrels (*Rosencrantz and Guildenstern Are Dead,* 1967); no drama critic gets surprised and killed by the play he is reviewing (*The Real Inspector Hound,* 1968), nor is there any equivalent to the public librarian in *Travesties,* who seems to strip on top of her desk while delivering a heartfelt panegyric on Lenin."

Despite the majority of praise, at least one critic found some major problems with *Arcadia,* mainly with the way the play pushes the boundaries of probability. Comparing Stoppard to his popular predecessor, Oscar Wilde (*The Importance of Being Earnest*), in *New York,* John Simon complained, "[Wilde] would not have an Englishman in 1809 use the Yiddishism *tush,* or have two characters—including the 13-year old Thomasina-interpret Poussin's famous *Et in Arcadia Ego* ("I too have lived in Arcadia") as being spoken by Death, i.e., the skull in the picture, a theory first proposed by Erwin Panofsky a century and a half later." Simon also regretted that some of the more interesting characters (such as Lord Byron and Mrs. Chater) never appeared on the stage while the more foolish ones (Chater and Captain Brice) did. In summary, Simon felt, "There are goodly chunks of the play that seem to have been written for the delectation of graduate students in literature and science, and you often wish Stoppard would rein in his parade."

In spite of its possible faults, the dominant opinion of *Arcadia* was that it is one of Stoppard's finest works. It is "pure entertainment—entertainment for the heart, mind, soul and all those interstices between we forget about," wrote Barnes. "It's brief candle lighting up a naughty world."

CRITICISM

Lane A. Glenn

Glenn is a Ph.D. specializing in theatre history and literature. In this essay he examines Stoppard's critical reputation as a wordsmith, and his use of language in Arcadia *as a means of creating humor, identifying characters, and exploring themes in the play.*

In his *Poetics* (c. 335 BC), Aristotle, the great Greek philosopher and literary theorist, suggested six elements that are crucial to theatre: plot, character, thought (or theme), diction, music, and spectacle. He explained each element in what he felt was its order of importance and devoted to each a corresponding amount of space in his treatise. When he arrived at "diction," the words the playwright places in the mouths of his characters, Aristotle explained the difference between common and elevated vocabulary, riddles, and jargon. He suggested: "The greatest thing by far is to have a command of metaphor. This alone cannot be imparted by another; it is the mark of genius—for to make good metaphors implies an eye for resemblances."

In more than two-thousand years of plays, playwrights, and players since Aristotle, different eras have found one or the other of his six elements to be more important than the rest. The Neo-classicists of the eighteenth century, for example, prized plot like the Greeks. Writers of "problem plays" in the late-nineteenth century, like George Bernard Shaw and Henrik Ibsen, often emphasized important themes in their work. Many twentieth century dramas are noted particularly for their characters, while modern musicals often draw crowds for the spectacle they offer audiences. From every era, however, it is the playwrights with a masterful command of *language*—the greatest gifts for metaphor—who are passed along to the generations that follow.

The Greeks gave Aristophanes to posterity—a writer of satire and wit so dexterous, politicians of his day avoided him for fear they would appear in one of his plays. In sixteenth century England, the Elizabethans loved language. They experimented with it. They played games with it ("quibbling" was a pub pastime that relied on clever wordplay). And, of course, they produced William Shakespeare, who managed to create a great deal of it.

While there are several contenders poised to represent the twentieth century as the era's great master of dialogue and dialectics, Tom Stoppard

WHAT DO I READ NEXT?

- Stoppard's *Rosencrantz and Guildenstern Are Dead* (1967) is a play about the absurdity of life as seen through the eyes of the two minor courtiers in William Shakespeare's *Hamlet*. Like *Arcadia*, the work is noted for its ferocious wordplay and lofty ideas.

- Also by Stoppard, *Travesties* (1974) is a comedy-drama that imagines three of history's quirkier characters—Vladimir Lenin, James Joyce, and Tristan Tzara—all living together in Zurich during World War I.

- Other playwrights with a distinctively British flair for characters and comedy include Alan Ayckbourn, whose series *The Norman Conquests: A Trilogy of Plays* (1988) is an hilarious family farce packed with witty one-liners, and Alan Bennett, the author of *The Madness of George III* (1992), which became a popular film a year later (retitled as *The Madness of King George*), and *Talking Heads* (1993), a collection of six unique monologues that were originally broadcast on the BBC.

- *The Selected Poems of Lord Byron*, available in a variety of editions, is a wonderful introduction to the poetry of the Romantic era. For a wider sampling, try *English Romantic Poetry: An Anthology* (1996), edited by Stanley Appelbaum, which contains poetry by six of the best-known Romantics: William Blake, William Wordsworth, Samuel Taylor Coleridge, Lord Byron, Percy Bysshe Shelley, and John Keats.

- *Foolscap: A Novel* (1991) is Michael Malone's satirical take on the research of literary history and the pursuit of academic fame. Like Bernard Nightingale in *Arcadia*, Theodore Ryan, the protagonist of *Foolscap* is out to make a name for himself in the cutthroat world of academic scholarship. Since no one will produce his play about Sir Walter Raleigh, Theodore devises a way to pass the play off as Raleigh's own work and have a forged copy "discovered" by a well-known Renaissance scholar.

---

appears at the top of many critics' lists. In *Tom Stoppard's Plays: A Study of His Life and Work*, Jim Hunter observed:

> Perhaps it is the words one notices first, in Stoppard. Later the sense of theatre, the craftsmanship, the thinking and the caring may seem more important; but at first one is dazzled—the cliché; seems accurate— by the brilliance of the verbal polish. Stoppard comes across as fluent to the point of facility, gifted with the gab of the Irish: Wilde, Shaw, Joyce, Beckett, and perhaps through these if not directly, Swift. The brilliance also seems to have an academic element: he might well be taken for a University Wit."

High praise indeed for an artist who left school at seventeen, received no university education, and is whose facility with letters is largely self-taught. Yet the praise is entirely apt. Throughout his thirty-year career as a playwright, critics and scholars have attuned themselves to the language in Stoppard's

plays. Writing about the debut of Stoppard's 1974 play *Travesties* in *Plays and Players,* Garry O'Connor observed, "Clever, all this stuff, and occasionally very funny indeed: full of acrostics, limericks, parody, absurdity; quite exhilarating: altogether a relief to be teased and dazzled by words for once."

Stoppard's unique talent for language lies in his ability to turn words upside-down and inside-out in a search for ambiguities, contradictions, double-meanings, humor, and half-hidden truths. Not since Shakespeare has an English playwright so strenuously exercised his native tongue. In an article Stoppard wrote for the *Sunday Times* early in his career, he admitted:

> [I have] an enormous love of language itself. For a lot of writers the language they use is merely a fairly efficient tool. For me the particular use of a particular word in the right place, or a group of words in the right

order, to create a particular effect is important; it gives me more pleasure than to make a point which I might consider to be profound. On the other hand, when one does concentrate mainly on the language itself, with luck this appears to have some meaning, often in a general sense and, when one is very lucky, in a universal sense.

Stoppard's love of language is extremely evident in his 1994 work, *Arcadia.* The first words of the play, in fact, are the set-up for a pun. ''Septimus, what is carnal embrace?'' the youthful genius Thomasina asks her harried tutor. ''Carnal embrace is the practice of throwing one's arms around a side of beef,'' comes the carefully chosen reply. It is a simple, clever piece of verbal humor, with layers of meaning lurking beneath the surface. As John Lahr noted in his review of the play for the *New Yorker,* ''The question mirrors the image of Paradise about to be lost, and Stoppard's play goes on to answer her question. To embrace the flesh is also to embrace all the sins that the flesh is heir to—the sins to which Stoppard's labyrinthine plot, whose ingenious twists and turns involve greed, rapacity, vainglory, skullduggery, cruelty, delusion, confusion, and genius, bears ample witness.'' All this promised, and the play has only just begun.

Each of the characters in *Arcadia* is recognizable for his or her own idiosyncratic style of speaking. In the presence of his student, the tutor Septimus Hodge is the picture of propriety, as when he delicately explains the truth about ''carnal embrace'' or scolds his young protegé for her unique take on her homework, saying, ''A fancy is not a discovery.'' For her part, Thomasina Coverly is precocious but in the very best ways. She is clever beyond her years and responds to Septimus appropriately by returning, ''A gibe is not a rebuttal.'' Their dueling dialogue escalates through the play until finally, by their final scene, Septimus is bested by his student, struck silent, and his only recourse is to dance with her.

Their present-day counterparts are Bernard Nightingale, the flamboyant university professor, and Hannah Jarvis, the best-selling, no-nonsense author. Nightingale flaunts his gift for language and, when pressed, uses it as a weapon. Upon meeting Hannah walking up from the ''ha-ha'' (a sort of scenic moat used in landscape architecture) he corrects her pronunciation as ''Ha-hah!'' and explains, ''A theory of mine. Ha-hah, not ha-ha. If you were strolling down the garden and all of a sudden the ground gave way at your feet, you're not going to go 'ha-ha', you're going to jump back and go 'ha-hah!''' Hannah is unimpressed, and later

tells Valentine Coverly that Bernard's verbal jousting is just for show. ''[His] indignation is a sort of aerobics for when he gets on television,'' she quips.

In reviewing *Arcadia,* critics found themselves praising Stoppard's use of language and comparing him to other great writers. In *Time* magazine Brad Leithauser wrote, ''It is a play that holds up beautifully not only on the stage but on the page. When Thomasina, hungry for a new mathematics, exclaims, 'If there is an equation for a curve like a bell, there must be an equation for one like a bluebell,' we might have stepped into an Auden poem. When a formidable lady [Lady Croom] silences her brother [Captain Brice] by snapping, 'Do not dabble in paradox, Edward, it puts you in danger of fortuitous wit,' we can hear Wilde whispering, 'I wish I'd said that.' As for concentrated lyricism, the scene in which Thomasina bewails the burning of the classical library of Alexandria—a doomed girl genius lamenting the conflagration of ancient genius—is absolutely stunning.''

In the *New York Post* Clive Barnes noted, ''Stoppard pays his audience the sensible compliment of assuming we know more than we do, while his language ranges from gutter-chic to epigrams that sound Wildean, but without Wilde's smug sense of gotcha-self-congratulation.'' Anne Barton wrote in the *New York Review of Books,* ''*Arcadia* is wonderfully inventive and funny, full of the epigrams, puns, and verbal pyrotechnics characteristic of this dramatist. From the interchange between thirteen-year-old Thomasina Coverly and her tutor with which the play begins . . . to the end, Stoppard's highly individual love affair with the English language never slackens . . . Stoppard's puns, far from being drearily Derridean, are something Shakespeare would have understood. He loves to demonstrate how exciting it can be when two meanings . . . lie down together irregularly in the same bed: as they do when Thomasina's 'carnal,' meaning 'sensual,' cohabits disconcertingly with its other connotation of 'meat.'''

For all the careful craftsmanship that goes into writing a play with such a marvelous flair for language, sometimes, Stoppard has admitted, his gift for metaphor and symbolism is happy circumstance. In a conversation with critic Mel Gussow, Stoppard revealed how he stumbled upon the name for Bernard Nightingale, *Arcadia*'s eccentric Sussex don, then chanced into a clever bit of character confusion ''The odd thing about these names is that they kind of detonate in a way that looks pre-

Charter recites some of his terrible poetry as Septimus and Thomasina look on in amusement

planned,'' Stoppard explained. ''In *Arcadia,* Hannah makes reference to Thomas Love Peacock. She believes Bernard's called Peacock and she says, 'Your illustrious namesake.' He says, 'Florence?' If I'd called him Thrush, God knows what he would have replied. There's a wonderful element of good luck in these things.''

Stoppard's wordplay may not be for everyone. In reviewing *Arcadia* for *New York* magazine, John Simon complained, ''Stoppard—who never went to university and has an autodidact's infatuation with his homemade erudition—overdoes it: There are goodly chunks of the play that seem to have been written for the delectation of graduate students in literature and science, and you often wish Stoppard would rein in his parade.''

For the playwright, however, there is no other way to work. ''I write plays because writing dialogue is the only respectable way of contradicting yourself,'' he once cleverly revealed to Gussow in the *New York Times.* ''I'm the kind of person who embarks on an endless leapfrog down the great moral issues. I put a position, rebut it, refute the rebuttal, and rebut the refutation. Forever. Endlessly.''

Source: Lane A. Glenn, for *Drama for Students,* Gale, 1999.

Tim Appelo

In this essay, Appelo positively reviews Arcadia, *placing the play among Stoppard's best work. Of particular note to the critic is the vibrancy and emotion of the central characters.*

In *Ulysses,* there is an Oxford don who goes around pushing a lawnmower that chuffs ''Clevercleverclever.'' Though he quit school at 17 and ran off to the circus of newspaper journalism, Tom Stoppard has always been very like Joyce's professor, forever cramming his head with arcane books and emitting their more entertaining notions in clipped, endlessly articulate, witty disputations. The question has always been whether Stoppard is anything more than cleverclevercever—is he simply a prestidigitator of prose and a joke mechanic, a whiz kid staging fantastically elaborate intellectual collisions as if they were toy-train wrecks? Or is he in it for deeper satisfactions than the transitory sparks a nice crackup tosses off?

Stoppard himself has admitted that his early play *The Real Inspector Hound* (1968) was ''a mechanical toy,'' but his work has been getting more human ever since. There's more of *him* in his later work, too; he is a recovering drama critic who began as a playwright by occupying other people's plays like a hermit crab. Pre-fame, he aped Robert Bolt and Arthur Miller; in *Rosencrantz and Guilden stern Are Dead* it was Beckett and Shakespeare; in *Hound,* Agatha Christie; in *Travesties,* Oscar Wilde. Starting with *Night and Day* (1978), he's tended to cling less to coattails and be more his own man, owning up to real emotions. He retains a perverse sense of humor akin to Beckett's; he's debate-besotted like Shaw, but he can see both sides of most questions; he's unearthly fluent and funny like Wilde, though he's grown more earnest. Yet his dramatic ideal remains what it was back in 1960, when he raved Richard Attenborough's *The Angry Silence* because it fused ''entertainment and education as completely as a row of chorus girls explaining Einstein's theory of light.'' His plays are, I think, a highly refined, mutant strain of journalism.

If all we had to go on was *Hapgood,* the 1988 faux-spy thriller that recently closed at Lincoln Center after a smash production, we might think the old rap on Stoppard still had some currency. The gratuitous beauty of the staging and the performances by David Straithairn as a droll physicist-philosopher and Stockard Channing as the eponymous spymaster heroine (whose name, according to Stoppard scholar Katherine E. Kelly, refers to turn-of-the-century Russian literature translator and *Nation* contributor Isabel Florence Hapgood) might blind us to the fact that *Hapgood* is lively without being good. Stoppard seems not to give a rip about his incomprehensibly intricate le Carré-pastiche plot, let alone his characters. (''I'm no good at character,'' he once confessed, amazingly. ''It doesn't interest me very much.'') What has interested him lately is post-Newtonian physics, and *Hapgood* is a physics essay masquerading as a play. As Updike said of Bellow's, *The Dean's December,* a novel that began as an essay, ''This book has swallowed the earlier one but has transparent sides, so that we can see the non-fiction book inside the novel and can observe how incomplete the digestion process has been.''

Incomplete intellectual digestion is a besetting sin of authors who read too much. Stoppard has been the chief of sinners in this regard, conducting his education at public expense; but he now redeems himself with *Arcadia,* at the Vivian Beaumont at Lincoln Center, his most important work since *The Real Thing* (1983). Unlike the spy-jive mac-guffins he juggles in *Hapgood,* the mystery addressed in *Arcadia* is one to which Stoppard is fully emotionally committed. If all those cigarettes kill him shortly,

> THE MYSTERY ADDRESSED IN *ARCADIA* IS ONE TO WHICH STOPPARD IS FULLY EMOTIONALLY COMMITTED. IF ALL THOSE CIGARETTES KILL HIM SHORTLY, *ARCADIA* IS ALMOST GOOD ENOUGH TO SERVE AS THE CAPSTONE TO HIS CAREER''

Arcadia is almost good enough to serve as the capstone to his career.

The setting, nicely realized by Mark Thompson, is the English country house of the Coverlys (I assume Stoppard alludes to Addison's squire Roger). There are two dueling story lines, exhilaratingly orchestrated by director Trevor Nunn, concerning the Coverlys of 1809 and of today. In the earlier frame, we are introduced to chaos theory by teenager Thomasina Coverly, who is based on its modern prophet, Benoit Mandelbrot, whose ''Mandelbrot set,'' infinitely iterated images of the order lurking within nature's seeming disorder, you have seen depicted in a million articles about chaos. Like Mandelbrot, Thomasina (fetching but conventionally so, as played by Jennifer Dundas) is no math prodigy, but she can actually see the subtle geometry of chaos in her head. Her tutor is the Newtonian college math major Septimus Hodge. (Hodge was the name of Samuel Johnson's spoiled, oyster-eating cat, and this cat, smartly portrayed by Billy Crudup, is the spoiled, horny house guest of the Coverlys.) Hodge is baffled by Thomasina's dazzling musings about how post-Newtonian physics demolishes determinism. Forget Euclid and his lovely inviolable rules, Thomasina pouts, and let's look at the real world: ''Mountains are not pyramids and trees are not cones.''

Hodge is more preoccupied with brassiere cones, and the calculations necessary to remove them while dallying with another's wife in the gazebo by night. His machinations after being discovered *inflagrante* with fellow house guest Charity Chater by her sputtering husband, Ezra, propel the Feydeau-style Restoration comedy that leavens the mathematical debate. But the sex farce isn't purely frivo-lous—in Stoppard's mind, romance is the welcome snake that saves Eden from the overdetermination of natural law. As one character puts it, illicit sex is ''the attraction that Newton left out. All the way back to the apple in the garden.''

Arcadia's twentieth-century scenes are devot-ed to two interrelated detective stories about the 1809 characters. In the first, Thomasina's mod-ern relative and fellow mathematician Valentine (the vulnerably lovely Robert Sean Leonard of *Dead Poets Society* fame) incredulously discovers Thomasina's eerily prescient equations (just as Mandelbrot rediscovered Gaston Julia's World War I-era documents in 1979), and, like Mandelbrot, uses a computer to extend and validate the earli-er work.

Thomasina's vindication is a foregone conclu-sion, because her ''New Geometry of Irregular Forms'' is simply modern physics, and because her theme is the point of the play: that determinism is false, that fate and free will are like waltzing mice, that life is messy, so eat it over the sink. A similar lesson is learned by the second set of modern-day detectives: two literary historians, Hannah Jarvis (brassy Blair Brown) and Bernard Nightingale (vain-glorious Victor Garber), who have descended on the Coverlys' Arcadia to mine the place for career advancement. Nightingale's ingeniously erroneous theory about what really happened in the house in 1809—he believes Lord Byron shot Ezra Chater dead in a duel—is the entertainment engine of *Arcadia,* a tour de force of scholarly folly that sets up Garber as the star of the show. We may have to struggle to keep the rest of the plot straight, but since we've seen what really happened in 1809, we can have great fun watching Nightingale pump up his ego until it explodes. ''Is the universe expand-ing?'' he demands. ''Is it contracting? Is it standing on one leg and singing 'When Father Painted the Parlour'? Leave me out. I can expand my universe without you.''

In making a laughingstock of Nightingale, a Euclidean type without a trace of humility in the face of nature, Stoppard is really recanting his old line about maintaining ''the courage of my lack of convictions'' through a scrupulous aestheticism. Now he seems more on the level, less distanced from his material, as the art-for-art's-sake, inflex-ibly arrogant argument loses big.

Nowhere is this clearer than in *Arcadia's* deep-ly moving final scene, where the worlds of 1809 and the present do not so much collide as coincide. It is the night before Thomasina's 17th birthday, and if she knows something about the future of physics that nobody else does, the modern Valentine and Hannah (and we in the audience) know a terri-ble secret about her future that she does not. I can't indicate on the page just how he does this, but Stoppard blends the dialogue and actions of modern and long-vanished characters in a way quite different from his usual comic convergences. He's long been the master of people talking past each other, but here their conversations embrace across the centuries. Valentine finally figures out Thomasina's immortal discovery—that she, and we, are demonstrably, mathematically, doomed—but instead of going for the sixties-style cosmic laugh, Stoppard makes the revelation a moment of rueful acceptance. The dialogue pointedly echoes Eliot's *Four Quartets,* and the vibe is that of the late Shakespearean fables, spectral but deeply charged with feeling.

David Merrick, the producer of Stoppard's first hit, *Rosencrantz and Guildenstern Are Dead,* com-plained that if you took the main characters and put them on a graph, ''they would all come out as one line.'' *Arcadia's* plots may leave the play with more characters than it can comfortably handle, but the main ones describe an elegant arabesque worthy of Mandelbrot himself.

Source: Tim Appelo, review of *Arcadia* in the *Nation,* Vol. 260, no. 17, May 1, 1995, pp. 612–13.

John Lahr

In this laudatory review of Arcadia, *Lahr calls the work Stoppard's ''best play so far,'' finding brilliance in the construction and deft wordplay. The critic ultimately termed the drama ''brave and very beautiful.''*

In Tom Stoppard's 1966 novel, *''Lord Malquist and Mr. Moon,''* Malquist remarks, ''Since we cannot hope for order, let us withdraw with style from the chaos.'' This notion has made Stoppard a very rich man. He says that his favorite line in modern English drama is from Christopher Hampton's ''The Philanthropist'': ''I'm a man of no convictions—at least, I *think* I am.'' Over the years, in twenty-one plays, Stoppard has turned his spectacular neutrality into a high-wire act of doubt. ''I write plays because dialogue is the most respectable way of contradict-ing myself,'' he once explained. The three-ring circus of Stoppard's mind pulls them in at the box office, where news of the intellect, as opposed to the emotions, is a rarity. Marvel at his marriage of Beckett and Shakespeare in the death-defying clown act of *"Rosencrantz and Guildenstern Are Dead"* (1967). Watch him play with logical positivism and the meaning of God in *"Jumpers"* (1972). See him juggle Oscar Wilde, James Joyce, and Lenin in *"Travesties"* (1974). Stoppard's mental acrobatics flatter an audience's intelligence and camouflage the avowed limits of his plotting and his heart.

In *"Arcadia,"* at the Vivian Beaumont—to my mind, his best play so far—Stoppard is serving up another intellectual stew (the recipe includes "a seasoning of chaos and a pinch of thermodynamics following a dash of quantum mechanics," he says), but with a difference. Stoppard, whose stock-in-trade is parody, which is skepticism in cap and bells, has found a metaphor that takes him beyond parody to vision. Here, despite some casting glitches, Trevor Nunn's elegant production pits the heart against the head in a subtle theatrical equation, which factors out into a moving ambiguity.

The play begins and ends with an image of Eden before the Fall. In this lush, tranquil landscape, painted onto a curtain, lit from behind, that wraps around the thrust stage like a kind of illuminated lampshade, no animals and no fear intrude on perfect pastoral harmony as Eve holds out to Adam the Apple of Knowledge. Only scudding gray clouds in the background suggest the confusion about to beset mankind once Adam takes a bite. The consequence of curiosity, once the curtain goes up, is a vaudeville of consciousness in a fallen world. "Septimus, what is carnal embrace?" the thirteen-year-old math brain truster Thomasina Coverly (the pert Jennifer Dundas) asks her handsome tutor, Septimus Hodge, in the play's first line. The question mirrors the image of Paradise about to be lost, and Stoppard's play goes on to answer her question. To embrace the flesh is also to embrace all the sins that the flesh is heir to—the sins to which Stoppard's labyrinthine plot, whose ingenious twists and turns involve greed, rapacity, vainglory, skulduggery, cruelty, delusion, confusion, and genius, bears ample witness.

The brilliance of *"Arcadia"* is not so much in the wordplay as it is in the construction. Stoppard has built his story along two time lines: life at Sidley Park, the Coverlys' country house in Derbyshire, in 1809, and life at present in the same house, where a couple of academics are picking over the bric-a-brac of Coverly family history. The action is set in a high-ceilinged room of grand Georgian design, which

is dominated by a large oblong table cluttered with books, implements of learning, and a dozy pet turtle. A fissure in the cupola of Mark Thompson's shrewdly designed interior is the only physical hint of the skewing of world views that takes place around the table as the play shuttles back and forth in a nanosecond between centuries. (Actors in one time frame exit as actors from the other enter.) By crosscutting the Coverly family story and the story of the contemporaries trying to reconstruct it, Stoppard utilizes the ironies of history—the symmetries and accidents that lead, nonetheless, to a kind of order—as a way of demonstrating the outcome of chaos theory; that is, as the program note explains to us scientific simpletons, how reality "can be both deterministic and unpredictable." This is an enormous theatrical feat—a kind of intellectual mystery story—in which Stoppard provides the audience with the exhilarating illusion of omniscience. We become cosmic detectives, outside time, solving the riddle of history from the clues and connections that we see but the characters, who are caught in time, do not. For instance, the equation that Thomasina works out to explain the asymmetry of a leaf, her "New Geometry of Irregular Forms," later turns out, with the help of computers, to undo the assumptions of Newtonian physics. She is to classical mathematics what Picasso is to art history. The spirited youngster, who shouts "Phooey to Death!" in the first scene, works out a formula that, by the last scene, prophesies the ultimate doom of the universe, which is collapsing like a chocolate soufflé from the slow loss of heat. Even Thomasina's offhand doodle on the landscape architect's plans for a Gothic vista at Sidley Park—she sketches a hermit to inhabit the planned Romantic hermitage—turns out to have been a prophecy of Septimus Hodge's destiny. The caprices of history, like the accidents that become inevitabilities in a plot, are the charms of chance that Stoppard and the audience stand in awe of.

Life's terrifying randomness is a mystery that compels mankind to impose order. Chaos is psychologically intolerable; man's need for coherence is greater than his need for truth. Landscape, like ritual, is consoling because it holds the magical promise of permanence. "English landscape was invented by gardeners imitating foreign painters who were evoking classical authors," says Hannah Jarvis (Blair Brown), a modern who is writing a book about the Sidley Park hermitage and the garden. The imaginative ideal is made into a reality; and Stoppard contrives to dramatize a moment in the life of the estate when the old illusion of reality is being adapted to fit a new one. At Sidley Park, Nature was originally tamed according to a neoclassical symmetry. The projected Romantic version, for which Stoppard supplies fascinating visual aids, is a triumph of the picturesque over the well proportioned. The planned irregularity and ''naturalness'' of the reimagined landscape capture the nineteenthcentury drift toward Romantic individualism: from formality to spontaneity, from aristocratic public space to middle-class privacy, from the balance that reflects the Enlightenment's God of Reason to the brooding Romantic freedom that makes a god of the self. ''The decline from thinking to feeling, you see,'' Hannah says. No wonder Septimus (Billy Crudup, making a persuasive Broadway debut) refers to the landscape architect who engineers the loss of this particular version of Paradise as the Devil. ''In the scheme of the garden he is as the serpent,'' Septimus says. The wildness of the picturesque style is an attempt to contain chaos by building the unpredictable into the landscape, just as Thomasina, in her algebraic equation, is unwittingly introducing chaos into the physical laws of life

Meanwhile, the lives and loves of these citizens take their apparently ordinary lustful course. The philandering Septimus cunningly evades a duel with the cuckolded poet Ezra Chater (Paul Giamatti), who enters in fury and exits in flattery, inscribing Hodge's copy of his poem ''The Couch of Eros,'' after the tutor, lying, promises to review it favorably ''Did Mrs. Chater know of this before she—before you—'' Chater sputters, seeing his wife's infidelity not as a leg over for her but as a leg up the literary ladder for him. Septimus encourages this delusion, and Chater is triumphant. ''There is nothing that woman would not do for me,'' he crows, thereby illustrating Stoppard's larger theme—that people will rationalize anything to avoid chaos.

The compulsion for coherence has its comic apotheosis in the biographical sleuthing of Bernard Nightingale, a dot from Sussex University who is a whirlwind of spurious intellectual connections. Nightingale (played with swaggering and hilarious arrogance by Victor Garber) has stumbled on the copy of Chater's ''The Couch of Eros'' that contains both the poet's inscription and an unnamed challenge to a duel, and he has traced the volume to Byron's library. A literary climber of the first order, Nightingale sniffs a mother lode of lit-crit kudos in making the connection between Byron and Chater. No one is better at this kind of academic flimflammery than

Stoppard, and he has a good time teasing the literary second-guessing that too often passes for biography. Within minutes of insinuating himself into Sidley Park, and Hannah's orbit, Nightingale is spinning his academic wheels and turning what we know to be Septimus's face saving deceit into a sensational case of adultery, literary infighting, and the death of Chater in a duel with Byron after the latter poet's devastating review of Chater's work appears in *Piccadilly Recreation*. ''Without question, Ezra Chater issued a challenge to *somebody*.'' Nightingale says, reading from his completed paper in the tour-de-force opening of Act II. ''Without question, Lord Byron, in the very season of his emergence as a literary figure, quit the country in a cloud of panic and mystery, and stayed abroad for two years at a time when Continental travel was unusual and dangerous. If we seek his reason—*do we need to look far?*'' Hellbent on literary glory, Nightingale rushes past the truth—''Is it likely that the man Chater calls his friend Septimus Hodge is the same man who screwed his wife and kicked the shit out of his last book?'' The paper is proof positive of the cynic's adage that ''history is something that never happened written by someone who was never there.''

Arcadia uses intellectual argument as a kind of riptide to pull the audience under the playful surface of romance with which the characters in both time frames fill their days and nights. In *''Arcadia's''* comic conceit, seismic intellectual shifts are treated as superficial, while superficial changes of the heart are treated as monumental. For the evening to work, the audience must feel the pull of sexuality as well as the play of knowledge. In London, with Felicity Kendal, Emma Fielding, and Harriet Walter in the major female roles, the erotic amperage was high; here, though, the American actresses can articulate the words but not the sexy twinkle beneath them. As Hannah, Blair Brown shows a sharp intelligence, but she can't give Stoppard's lines that nervy bluestocking spin which flirts with learning and turns the alarming into the charming. ''Oh, shut up,'' she tells Nightingale, when he is upbraiding her after discovering she has written a letter to the London *Times* giving the facts of Chater's death. (He was killed by a monkey bite in Martinique after discovering the dwarf dahlia.) ''It'll be very short, very dry, absolutely gloat-free,'' she says of her letter. ''Would you rather it were one of your friends?'' The strut of Stoppard's epigrams is also missed by Lisa Banes as Lady Croom, who delivers some of the most delightful *mots* without the louche aristocratic aura of entitlement that makes them properly pay off. "Do not dabble in paradox," she says to Captain Brice (David Manis). "It puts you in danger of fortuitous wit." Even the pint-size Jennifer Dundas, who has the smarts to make Thomasina a credible, if cloying, prodigy, hasn't the stature to make her a compelling object of desire. The cumulative effect is not to undermine the production but to dim it.

Still, the brilliance of Stoppard's metaphor shines through. In the final scene, Thomasina is horsing around with her brother when Septimus enters with her latest diagrams under his arm. "Order, order !" Septimus shouts to his rambunctious pupil, now nearly seventeen years old, who would rather waltz than work. By the end of the scene, when Septimus comprehends her latest equation, he sees that order—the Enlightenment notion of it—has entirely collapsed. Now the time frames merge, with the characters in the present overlapping with and commenting on the issues raised by characters in the past. "It's a diagram of heat exchange," says Valentine Coverly, a graduate student of mathematics (played expertly by Robert Sean Leonard), looking at the same diagrams that Septimus is studying. Septimus looks up. "So, we are all doomed," he says. "Yes," Thomasina answers cheerfully, not knowing that she is soon to become another integer in her equation of chaos. (She will perish the same night in a fire; and Septimus will become the hermit of Sidley Park, speaking to no one except his pet turtle.) But for the moment, with the geometry of the universe's doom in his hand, Septimus says, "When we have found all the mysteries and lost all the meaning, we will be alone, on an empty shore."

At the prospect of such an awesome, godless void, Thomasina suggests that they dance, and finally gets Septimus to his feet. The audience knows the outcome but the dancers don't: they live in the comedy of the moment, not in the tragedy of history. Hannah waltzes with Gus Coverly (John Griffin), a smitten teen-ager who has given her the final piece of the puzzle of Septimus's story. Together, the couples whirl around the old table covered with the inventory of centuries of learning. The ravishing image moves the play, in its last beats, from story to statement. The dance becomes the dance of time: one awkward, one graceful; one in celebration, one in resignation. The waltz, an act of grace in the face of gloom, is a perfect embodiment of Stoppard's spiritual standoff. Playwriting, like the dancing, is a way of giving off heat in a cooling universe: an assertion and an abdication at the same

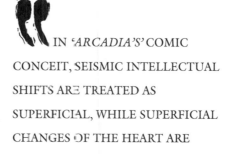

IN *'ARCADIA'S'* COMIC CONCEIT, SEISMIC INTELLECTUAL SHIFTS ARE TREATED AS SUPERFICIAL, WHILE SUPERFICIAL CHANGES OF THE HEART ARE TREATED AS MONUMENTAL"

time. It's the dance of a stoic, and, from where I sit, it is brave and very beautiful.

Source: John Lahr, "Blowing Hot and Cold" in the *New Yorker,* Vol. LXXI, no. 8, April 17, 1995, pp. 111–13.

SOURCES

Aristotle. *Poetics,* S. H. Butcher; translation in *Dramatic Theory and Criticism: Greeks to Grotowski,* edited by Bernard F. Dukore, Holt, Rinehart, and Winston, 1974, p. 50.

Barnes, Clive. Review of *Arcadia* in the *New York Post,* March 31, 1995.

Barton, Anne. "Twice around the Grounds" in the *New York Review,* June 8, 1995, pp. 28-32.

Canby, Vincent. Review of *Arcadia* in the *New York Times,* March 31, 1995.

Feingold, Michael. Review of *Arcadia* in the *Village Voice,* April 11, 1995.

Gerard, Jeremy. Review of *Arcadia* in *Variety,* April 3, 1995.

Gussow, Mel. "Stoppard Refutes Himself, Endlessly" in the *New York Times,* April 26, 1972, p. 54; reprinted in *File on Stoppard,* edited by Malcolm Page, Methuen, 1986, p. 87.

Hunter, Jim. *Tom Stoppard's Plays: A Study of His Life and Work,* Grove Press, 1982, p. 93.

Kissel, Howard. Review of *Arcadia* in the *Daily News,* March 31, 1995.

Lahr, John. Review of *Arcadia* in the *New Yorker,* April 22, 1995.

Leithauser, Brad. Review of *Arcadia* in *Time,* April 10, 1995.

Lyons, Donald. Review of *Arcadia* in the *Wall Street Journal,* March 31, 1995.

O'Connor, Garry. Review of *Travesties* in *Plays and Players,* July, 1974, p. 34; reprinted in *File on Stoppard,* edited by Malcolm Page, Methuen, 1986, p. 50.

Plumb, J. H. *England in the Eighteenth Century,* Penguin Books, 1990, p. 147.

Simon, John. Review of *Arcadia* in *New York,* April 10, 1995.

Stoppard, Tom. ''Something to Declare'' in the *Sunday Times,* February 25, 1968, p. 47; reprinted in *File on Stoppard,* edited by Malcolm Page, Methuen, 1986, p. 85.

Thomson, David. *England in the Nineteenth Century,* Penguin Books, 1991, pp. 11-12.

Winer, Linda. Review of *Arcadia* in *New York Newsday,* March 31, 1995.

FURTHER READING

Cahn, Victor L. *Beyond Absurdity: The Plays of Tom Stoppard,* Associated University Presses, 1979.
> A treatise that places Stoppard's early work in the context of the Theatre of the Absurd, a style of drama that breaks conventional forms, presents a ''comic-pathetic'' view of life, and emphasizes the chaotic nature of the universe.

Grosskurth, Phylis. *Byron: The Flawed Angel,* Houghton Mifflin, 1997.
> A biography of George Gordon (aka Lord Byron) the Romantic poet, womanizer, and soldier of freedom. The book also provides a history of the times in which the poet lived.

Gussow, Mel. *Conversations with Stoppard,* Nick Hern Books, London, 1995.
> A series of conversations between Stoppard and theatre critic Gussow between 1972 and 1995, covering many of Stoppard's plays, as well as his personal life.

Hall, Nina, editor. *Exploring Chaos: A Guide to the New Science of Disorder,* W. W. Norton, 1994.
> In scientific circles, chaos theory has been called the twentieth century's third revolution, alongside relativity and quantum mechanics. This collection of reports, complete with photographs, by the foremost researchers of chaos theory attempts to bring order to the disorder by describing all sorts of phenomena, from dripping faucets and swinging pendulums to weather patterns.

Harty III, John, editor. *Tom Stoppard: A Casebook,* Garland, 1988.
> A collection of essays about Stoppard's most important plays, accompanied by a chronology of his work and an annotated bibliography of Stoppard criticism.

Page, Malcolm. *File on Stoppard,* Methuen, 1986.
> A collection of excerpted criticism of Stoppard's plays, taken largely from theatre reviews in London and New York newspapers and magazines. Also includes a chronology of the playwright's work.

Singh, Simon. *Fermat's Enigma: The Epic Quest to Solve the World's Greatest Mathematical Problem,* Bantam Books, 1998.
> The story of Andrew Wiles, a mathematician at Princeton University who solved Fermat's Last Theorem in 1994. Also includes a 350-year history of ''Fermat's Enigma,'' and some mathematician humor.

The Birthday Party

HAROLD PINTER

1958

Harold Pinter's *The Birthday Party,* was the playwright's first commercially-produced, full-length play. He began writing the work after acting in a theatrical tour, during which, in Eastbourne, England, he had lived in "filthy insane digs." There he became acquainted with "a great bulging scrag of a woman" and a man who stayed in the seedy place. The flophouse became the model for the rundown boarding house of the play and the woman and her tenant the models, respectively, for the characters of Meg Boles and Stanley Webber.

In an earlier work, *The Room,* a one-act play, Pinter had worked on themes and motifs that he would carry over into *The Birthday Party* and some of his succeeding plays. Among these themes are the failure of language to serve as an adequate tool of communication, the use of place as a sanctum that is violated by menacing intruders, and the surrealistic confusions that obscure or distort fact.

Directed by Pinter himself, the finished full-length play premiered in Cambridge, England, at the Arts Theatre, on April 28, 1958. There and on tour in Oxford it was quite successful, but when, under the direction of Peter Wood, it moved to London and later opened, on May 19, at the Lyric Opera House in Hammersmith, it met with harsh reviews and closed down within a week. Among the reviewers, only Harold Hobson of the *Sunday Times* saw much promise in the play. He thought that Pinter had considerable originality and was "the

most disturbing and arresting talent in theatrical London.'' However, his review appeared too late to do the production any good. The show was already off the boards, done in by abysmal attendance, including one matinee audience of six, and persistently hostile reviews. Most critics opined that Pinter floundered in obscurity and suffered from the negative influence of Samuel Beckett (*Waiting for Godot*), Eugene Ionesco (*The Bald Prima Donna*), and other avant-garde writers.

Pinter would later marvel at the fact that in London the play was ''completely massacred by the critics'' but noted that it was the only maltreatment he had received from reviewers and that it never dimmed his interest in writing. The work, in fact, became the dramatist's first full-length ''comedy of menace,'' a group of plays that secured Pinter's reputation as a premier, avant-garde playwright. Subsequent productions were much better received, including the play's 1964 revival at London's Aldwych Theatre and its 1968 Broadway premier at the Booth Theatre in New York. By the mid-1960s, the burgeoning appreciation of absurdist drama and the success of other plays by Pinter, including *The Dumbwaiter* (1959) and *The Caretaker* (1960), had secured for *The Birthday Party* a reputation as a classic in the dramatic genre that literary critic Martin Esslin dubbed the Theatre of the Absurd.

AUTHOR BIOGRAPHY

Harold Pinter was born on October 10, 1930, in Hackney, a section of metropolitan London, England. His father, Hyman, and his mother, Frances Mann, were descended from Sephardic Jews from Portugal, who had, around 1900, migrated to England after an interim residence in Hungary. The family, relatively poor, lived very frugally, like the other working-class families in the area.

Between 1941 and 1947, Pinter attended the Hackney Downs Grammar School, where he began writing poetry and prose. He also took an interest in theater, taking roles as both Macbeth and Romeo in school productions of Shakespeare. His education continued in 1948, when he obtained a grant to study at the Royal Academy of Dramatic Art, but, finding the academy oppressive, he only stayed for two terms. In the same year, he tried to obtain legal status as a conscientious objector, which he was denied, and he was eventually fined when he refused to answer an army draft call.

In 1949, while he continued to write non-dramatic works as Harold Pinta, he launched a career as professional actor. His first work was as a bit actor for the British Broadcasting Corporation's (BBC) Home Service radio, from which, in 1951, he moved up to a role in Shakespeare's *Henry VIII,* a production of BBC's Third Programme. He also resumed formal training at the Central School of Speech and Drama. Thereafter, under the stage name David Baron, he acted with Shakespearean and other repertory companies in both England and Ireland. On tour, he met and worked with the actress Vivien Merchant, whom he married on September 14, 1956. The pair struggled to make ends meet, and Pinter was forced to assume a variety of odd jobs, including stints as a dance-hall bouncer or ''chucker,'' a dishwasher, a caretaker, and a salesman.

Pinter's first foray into playwriting came in 1957, when a friend asked him to write a piece for production at Bristol University. The result was *The Room,* a one-act play that earned the favorable notice of critic Harold Hobson and revealed Pinter's unique talent and technique. The work was not professionally produced until after *The Birthday Party* opened and floundered in 1958, but it was Hobson's review of *The Room*'s university production that brought Pinter to the attention of the young, new-wave producer Michael Codron, who decided to stage *The Birthday Party*.

Pinter's first major staged success was *The Caretaker,* which, in 1960, began a run in London's West End and won the playwright *The Evening Standard Award.* Along with *The Birthday Party* and *The Homecoming* (1965), *The Caretaker* established Pinter's reputation as a major absurdist playwright, and, in the opinion of some commentators, his claim to being Britain's most important dramatist since George Bernard Shaw (*Major Barbara*).

In the 1960s, Pinter proved his diversity by producing a steady stream of both stage and media works. He began an extended association with the Royal Shakespeare Company in 1962 with *The Collection* at the Aldwych Theatre, but by then he had also begun writing for cinema, adapting *The Caretaker* to film. Although his creative energy remained unabated, he devoted more and more of it to scripting plays for television and the screen. Some of these were originally written for the stage, but most were first written for specific media. Some, like *The Pumpkin Eater* (1964) and *The Quiller Memorandum* (1966), were adaptations from the fiction of other writers. Acclaim for his media works quickly rivaled that awarded his stage works and greatly expanded his creative involvement and focus.

Although some believe that Pinter's best theatrical works were his earliest pieces in the absurdist mode, the playwright has remained a major voice in the British theater since the early-1960s. If financial success and the diffusion of his creative energy have diminished his stage power, as some have claimed, there has been no real erosion in his reputation as England's premier, post-World War II playwright, his only serious rivals being John Osborne (*Look Back in Anger*) and Tom Stoppard (*Arcadia*). Nevertheless, despite some well-received plays like *One for the Road* (1984) and *Mountain Language* (1988), the playwright has met with some decline in his critical fortunes. It is has almost become a scholarly truism that none of Pinter's works written for the stage after the 1960s has superceded *The Caretaker, The Homecoming,* or *The Birthday Party* as Pinter's major contributions to modern theater.

Harold Pinter

PLOT SUMMARY

Act I

The Birthday Party opens in the living-dining area of a seedy rooming house at an unnamed seaside resort in England. Petey and Meg Boles, the proprietors, converse while she prepares his breakfast and he reads the newspaper. Their talk is inane, centering on their tenant, Stanley Webber. Petey also tells her of two strangers who might come to rent a room.

Meg decides to wake Stanley for breakfast and goes to his room. Unshaven and half dressed, Stanley comes downstairs and sits at the table to eat. After Petey goes off to work, Stanley teases Meg about her "succulent" fried bread, but when she becomes affectionate, he gets irritated and complains that her tea is "muck" and the place is a "pigsty."

Meg tells Stanley about the two men who may be new tenants. At first he is worried but then shrugs the information off as a "false alarm." Meg fends off his insistence that she obey him, getting him to speak of his musical career. He tells her that once,

after a piano concert, he had been "carved" up by persecutors identified only as "they." He then scares her by saying that the strangers will soon arrive, bringing a wheelbarrow in a van, looking to haul *her* away.

After Meg leaves to shop, Lulu enters with a package. She airs out the room, then sits at the table and chides Stanley for his unkempt appearance and anti-social behavior. He rejects her offer of going out, and she concludes that he is "a bit of a washout." When she leaves, Stanley goes to the kitchen to wash his face. Through the hatch separating the two rooms, he spies Goldberg and McCann entering through the backdoor and slips off. Goldberg advises McCann to relax and speaks of his family ties and his partnership with McCann, who responds as if Goldberg were his mentor. McCann, still uneasy, asks whether their current job will be the same as their previous ones, and Goldberg reassures him with official-sounding double talk.

Meg returns, carrying some parcels. Politely and affably, Goldberg introduces himself and McCann, then begins asking after Stanley. She says that it is Stanley's birthday, prompting Goldberg to insist that they have a party. Delighted, Meg leads the two men upstairs to their room.

Stanley returns just before Meg comes back. He grills her about the men, trying to find out if she knows who they are. He also denies that it is his birthday, but he accepts her present, left by Lulu on the sideboard. It is a toy drum. He straps it on his neck, then marches around banging on it. Just before the curtain, his beating becomes erratic and finally ''savage and possessed.''

Act II

It is evening of the same day. McCann, at the living room table, methodically tears Petey's newspaper into strips. Stanley enters and begins a polite conversation. When McCann mentions the birthday party, Stanley insists that he wants to celebrate alone, but McCann says that, as the guest of honor, Stanley cannot skip out on it.

When Stanley tries to leave, McCann blocks his path. Stanley angers him by picking up one of the strips of paper. McCann, now even more intimidating, contradicts Stanley's claim that they had met before. Unnerved, Stanley starts speaking of his plans to return home, asserting that he is the same man he was, despite his heavy drinking. Frustrated in his attempts to find out why McCann and Goldberg have intruded, he grows almost frantic. He finally grabs McCann by the arm, saying that what he has told him was a mistake. McCann observes that Stanley is in a bad state and that he is ''flabbergasted'' by Stanley's behavior. Stanley then speaks of his admiration for the Irish.

Goldberg enters with Petey, prompting a new round of introductions. Goldberg talks about his youth, confessing that he was then called ''Simey,'' while Petey explains that it is his chess night and that he will miss the party. When he and McCann exit, Stanley tries to convince Goldberg to pack up and leave, but Goldberg simply talks about celebrating life, implying that late risers, like Stanley, miss out on a lot. Stanley cuts him off and orders him to get out, but Goldberg does not budge. McCann re-enters, and he and Goldberg order Stanley to sit down. Stanley repeatedly refuses until McCann threatens physical violence. The two intruders then begin interrogating Stanley with rapid-fire questions that range from the accusatory to the ridiculous. When they tell Stanley that he is dead, he screams and tries to fight back by kicking Goldberg in the stomach and threatening McCann with a chair, but they all suddenly revert to civility when

Meg enters beating on the toy drum. She is dressed for the party, and preens under Goldberg's complements about her looks. She fetches glasses for toasting Stanley, and, prompted by Goldberg, McCann turns out the lights and shines his flashlight on Stanley's face while Meg toasts ''the birthday boy.''

With the lights back on, Lulu arrives and the celebration begins in earnest. Goldberg insists that Stanley sit down and then begins a meandering, sentimental speech. McCann turns out the lights and once more shines his flashlight in Stanley's face. When the lights are on again, Goldberg entices Lulu to sit on his lap while Meg tries to get Stanley to dance. Rejected, Meg settles for dancing by herself. While Lulu flirts with Goldberg, Meg breaks into a nostalgic reverie about her girlhood room, after which McCann talks of his heritage and sings an Irish ballad.

The characters then start playing blind man's bluff. When it is Stanley's turn to be the blind man, McCann takes his glasses from him and deliberately breaks them. He also makes Stanley trip over the toy drum, which catches on Stanley's foot. Stanley drags the drum around, then finds Meg and begins choking her. As McCann and Goldberg rush to interfere, the lights go out again. In the confusion, McCann once more shines his flashlight, but Goldberg knocks it to the floor. In the dark, Stanley picks up Lulu and deposits her, spread eagle, on the table. McCann finds the flashlight and shines it at Stanley, who appears on verge of sexually assaulting Lulu. Stanley backs away, giggling uncontrollably, and as the others advance towards him, the curtain falls.

Act III

It is early the next morning. As before, Petey sits at the table reading the newspaper. Through the hatch, Meg explains that Goldberg and McCann had eaten all the breakfast food. She enters to pour Petey some tea and spots Stanley's present, broken and discarded in the fireplace. She plans to fetch Stanley down, observing that she had gone up earlier and found him talking to McCann. Meg asks Petey about Goldberg's car and the suspicious wheelbarrow, which, he tells her, does not exist.

As Meg prepares to go shopping, Goldberg enters. She asks after Stanley and then about Goldberg's car, which he praises for its ample room. She leaves, and Petey inquires about Stanley's health. Goldberg tells him that Stanley had suffered a sudden, unexpected mental breakdown. Petey, growing suspicious, says that if Stanley does not improve, he will fetch a doctor, but Goldberg assures him that things are under control.

McCann arrives with two suitcases and tells Goldberg that he gave Stanley back his broken glasses. Petey suggests that they repair the busted frames with tape, then asks again about a doctor. Goldberg says that they will be taking Stanley to ''Monty,'' and that the doctor is not needed.

Petey goes out, and McCann begins tearing the morning paper into strips again, annoying Goldberg. The two men try to decide whether to bring Stanley down, but the matter seems to depress Goldberg. When McCann, trying to console him, calls him Simey, he explodes with anger. McCann then decides to get Stanley, but before he leaves, Goldberg makes the younger man peer into his mouth. After talking of his excellent health as the secret to his success, he instructs McCann to blow in his mouth two times.

When Lulu enters, McCann excuses himself and exits. Lulu refuses Goldberg's familiar advances, claiming that she has had enough games. The two verbally spar for a moment. She speaks of her first love, Eddie, then laments that Goldberg, during the night, taught her things that no girl should know. McCann returns and tries to get Lulu to confess to him. She is encouraged by Goldberg, who claims that McCann is an unfrocked priest. As the men advance on her, Lulu retreats through the back door.

McCann then goes off and returns with Stanley, now dressed in a suit and clean, collared shirt. He appears defeated and docile. The pair make him sit and begin another harangue about Stanley's health and necessary recuperation. He can only emit nonsensical, gagging sounds. When they begin to take Stankey away, Petey enters and tries to interfere, but they back him off with threats. The pair take Stanley out.

Meg enters and asks about Goldberg and McCann. Petey confirms their departure, but when Meg asks after Stanley, Petey tells her that he is still in bed. The pair chat briefly about the party. Meg claim to have been ''the belle of the ball,'' repeating her conviction as the final curtain falls.

CHARACTERS

Benny

See Nat Goldberg

Meg Boles

Petey's wife, Meg Boles is a good-natured woman in her sixties. If only from a lack of any reference to offspring of her own, it is implied that she and Petey are childless, thus she fills a void in her life by turning the Boles's boarding-house tenant, Stanley Webber, into a kind of surrogate child. She insists on calling him ''boy'' and mothering him. She even takes liberties appropriate to a parent—though not to the landlady of an adult roomer—by invading his privacy to fetch him down to breakfast.

At the same time, Meg flirts with Stanley, trying to fill a second void in her life. Her marriage to Petey has settled into mechanical routine, as their listless and inane dialogue that opens the play reveals. Meg tries to win Stanley's approval of her as a woman, shamelessly fishing for compliments. Stanley, in his mildly perverse manner, responds by teasing her, knowing that she is both vulnerable and gullible.

As the play progresses, it becomes clear that Meg, though a mental lightweight, is a decent woman. She is also rather sentimental. Although it is probably not even Stanley's real birthday, she insists that it is, determined to help Stanley weather his self-destructive despondency. She also seems to be his last hope, and her absence when he is taken away near the end of the play intensifies his final wretchedness.

Petey Boles

Like his wife, Petey Boles is in his sixties. He is a deck-chair attendant at the unidentified seaside resort where he and Meg own their boarding house, which, although it is ''on the list,'' has seen much better days. Petey is dull and ambitionless, no more inclined than his wife to find challenges beyond the confines of their rooming house. The pair have simply settled into a humdrum existence appropriate to their mundane minds.

Because it is his chess night, Petey is not present during the birthday party. He leaves before

MEDIA ADAPTATIONS

- On March 22, 1960, two years after its first staging, *The Birthday Party* was televised by ARD (Associated Rediffusion-TV). The work was directed by Joan Kemp-Welch and featured Richard Pearson as Stanley and Margery Withers as Meg. There has been no release of the video.

- *The Birthday Party* was adapted to film in Britain in 1968. It was produced by Max Rosenberg, Edgar J. Scherick, and Milton Subotsky, directed by William Friedkin, and adapted by Pinter. The film features Robert Shaw as Stanley, Patrick Magee as Shamus McCann, Dandy Nichols as Meg Bowles, Sidney Tafler as Nat Goldberg, Moultrie Kelsall as Pete Bowles, and Helen Fraser as Lulu. The film has not yet been released on video in the United States.

- In 1986, *The Birthday Party* was again produced for British television by Rosemary Hill. It was directed by Kenneth Ives and featured Colin Blakely as McCann, Kenneth Cranham as Stanley, Robert Lang as Petey, Harold Pinter as Goldberg, Joan Plowright as Meg, and Julie Walters as Lulu. The video has not been released in the United States.

it begins, then appears the following morning, when he makes a feeble attempt to prevent Goldberg and McCann from taking Stanley away, though he backs down when the two men suggest that they might take him as well. Petey's decency is finally as ineffectual as Meg's. At the play's conclusion, he can do nothing but slip back into vapid conversation with his wife, who reveals that she was not even aware that he had completely missed the party.

Nat Goldberg

Nat Goldberg, in his fifties, is the older of the two strangers who come to interrogate and intimidate Stanley before taking him away. He is a suave character, a gentleman in appearance and demeanor. He also seems to exude superficial good will, inclined to give kindly advice to both his henchman, McCann, and the other characters. He is nostalgic, too. He fondly and affectionately recalls his family and events in his early life. He also insists that Meg and the others honor Stanley with a birthday party.

Goldberg's softheartedness is, however, pure sham. His outward charm and polite manner mask a sadistic nature. This cruelty is first revealed in his initial interrogation of Stanley. His ugliness is fur-

ther betrayed by his unspecified carnal use of Lulu, who complains the morning after the party that Goldberg subjected her to some deviant sexual experiences inappropriate even for wives. It is this discrepancy between Goldberg's calm appearance and his vicious interior that makes him the more sinister of Webber's two persecutors.

Lulu

Described as a ''girl in her twenties,'' Lulu is a neighbor who first appears carrying Stanley's birthday present, the toy drum and drum sticks that Meg had bought for him. On the flirtatious side, she is self-conscious about her sexual appeal and can not sit still for long without taking out a compact to powder her face. To her looks are obviously important, and she sees Stanley as a ''washout'' because he seems to care nothing about his unkempt appearance.

Behind her glamour, there is some youthful innocence to Lulu. She is blind to Goldberg's predatory nature and is drawn into his charm. She sits on his lap and flirts with him, a foreshadowing of what occurs between them later that night. That she is some sort of sexual sacrifice is also suggested in the conclusion to the bizarre events that take place when the lights go out during the party. When they are restored, she is revealed "lying spread-eagle on the table," with Stanley hunched over her giggling insanely.

In the last act, Lulu seems broken by the night's experiences, but she is also angry. Goldberg, who baldly claims that he shares some of her innocence, had entered her room with a mysterious briefcase and begun sexually abusing her, using her, she complains, as "a passing fancy." She leaves angry and frightened when McCann and Goldberg threaten to exact a confession from her.

Dermont McCann

McCann, in his thirties, is Goldberg's younger associate. Unlike Goldberg, who reveals a Jewish heritage, McCann is a immoral Irish Catholic, possibly a defrocked priest. Like Goldberg, he exercises careful self control, a quality which contributes to the sinister impression of both men. He is also methodical and compulsive, as is revealed in his ritual habit of carefully tearing Petey's newspaper into strips. He differs from Goldberg in important respects, however. More reticent, he is not as superficially warm or outgoing, and when he does speak he seems more inclined to echo Goldberg than to offer new observations. He is also physically more intimidating than Goldberg, who deliberately covers his viciousness with a mask of fatherly interest in the others and disarms everyone with his nostalgia. It is McCann who shoves Stanley at the party and snaps and breaks his glasses.

When he does talk, McCann usually just adapts to the mood set by Goldberg. Usually, too, he defers to Goldberg's age and authority, even obeying the older man's peculiar request that McCann blow into his mouth. However, at times he seems more Goldberg's equal partner, especially during the interrogations of Stanley, when, just as voluble, he become Goldberg's co-inquisitor.

Simey

See Nat Goldberg

Stanley Webber

Until his nemeses Goldberg and McCann appear, Stanley is the only lodger at the Boles' run-down seaside boarding house. The basis of his relationship to Goldberg and McCann, at best hinted at, is never fully revealed, but their coming finally destroys Stanley's last vestiges of self-control. Near the play's end, when they have reduced him to idiocy, they haul him off in Goldberg's car to face the "Monty," some vague, ominous fate.

Stanley in his late-thirties, is an unemployed musician, reluctant to leave the boarding house, which has become a kind of refuge from "them," the nebulous persecutors who, in the past, destroyed his career as a concert pianist. He has grown both slovenly and desultory, and although he fantasizes about playing in great cities on a world tour, he has no real hope. Lacking a piano, he cannot even practice. As he confides in an honest moment, his only success in concert was in Lower Edmonton, a pathetic contrast to the cities he names as venues on his dream tour.

Stanley's dread of what lies beyond the boarding house traps him in a trying relationship with Meg, for whom he must act as both wayward child and surrogate husband. He is not always able to mask his disgust with this relationship and is prone to express his contempt for her in cruel verbal jibes and petty behavior. He also teases her. For example, he tells her that "they" are coming in a van with a wheelbarrow, looking for someone to haul off, presumably Meg. His hostility finally takes a more violent form when, during the birthday party, he tries to strangle her but is stopped by McCann and Goldberg.

Stanley, the nominal protagonist of *The Birthday Party*, barely struggles against his persecutors, quickly succumbing as if before some inevitable and implacable doom. Although he never evidences any guilt for his betrayal of the unspecified cause, he responds to his inquisitors as if he knows that there is nowhere to run, nowhere to hide. At the end, although unable to voice his feelings, he seems resigned to his unknown fate.

THEMES

Absurdity

As in many absurdist works, *The Birthday Party* is full of disjointed information that defies

TOPICS FOR FURTHER STUDY

- Investigate the ways in which Pinter's ethnic background and his early years growing up in a working-class section of London helped shape both his pacifism and his craft.

- Research the influence of Franz Kafka on Pinter's "comedies of menace."

- Compare the style, structure, and techniques of Pinter's *The Birthday Party* with those of Eugene Ionesco's *Bald Soprano* or Samuel Beckett's *Waiting for Godot*.

- Investigate Pinter's own observations about language and silence as concerns in his early work.

- Research the Irish Republican Army (IRA) and the possibility that it may be interpreted as the organization betrayed by Stanley Webber in *The Birthday Party*.

---

efforts to distinguish between reality and illusion. For example, despite the presentation of personal information on Stanley and his two persecutors, who or what they really are remains a mystery. Goldberg, in particular, provides all sorts of information about his background, but he offers only oblique clues as to why he has intruded upon Stanley's life.

What has Stanley done to deserve persecution? The facts of his past are so unclear that his claim to be a pianist may even be false. *The Birthday Party* influences the audience to doubt anything with certainty, which as it does in Kafka's work, intensifies the dreadful angst experienced by the protagonist. This effect is achieved through truncated dialogue, by Pinter's deliberate failure to provide conclusive or consistent information, and by his use of ambiguity and nonsense.

Alienation and Loneliness

Stanley has isolated himself from society, with only the vaguest of explanations offered as to why.

What is clear is that he has "dropped out" of everyday life. He is the sole lodger in the Boles' boarding house. He has forgone any efforts to make himself presentable, remaining depressed and sullen, half-dressed, unkempt, and unwilling to leave the womb-like comfort of his rundown digs.

Clues suggest that he is not simply hibernating. He is hiding out, fearful of some retribution if he is found. He is scared to leave the rooming house. He fends off Lulu's casual advances, and he is unwilling to look for a job as a pianist, though he fantasizes about taking a world concert tour.

While Stanley's loneliness is self-imposed, Meg's is not. She is mired in a marriage that is routine and uneventful, and she seeks to fulfill her needs by both flirting with and mothering Stanley. She is a decent but sad figure, easily tormented by Stanley, who treats her badly when he grows tired of her suffocating affection.

Lulu, too, looks to overcome her loneliness, first by trying to interest Stanley, then, at the birthday party, by flirting with the much older Goldberg. In the aftermath of the party, he goes to her room and introduces her to some sort of deviant sexual practices, aided by unidentified toys and devices carried in a mysterious briefcase. In the last act, she claims that she has been abused and abandoned by Goldberg, who dismisses her with the suggestion that she got exactly what she wanted.

Apathy and Passivity

Although anger and even violence break through Stanley's apathy at key moments, he generally appears to have given up on life. His apathy is apparent in his slovenliness. He remains unshaven, unwashed, and half dressed. He is unwilling to venture out, although he talks about dreams. He is, as Lulu says, "a bit of a washout."

In mood shifts that turn him suddenly aggressive, Stanley resists his tormentors, Goldberg and McCann, just as he sporadically lashes out at Meg. After the first interrogation conducted by his inquisitors, he kicks Goldberg in the stomach and threatens to hit McCann with a chair, and during the party he tries to choke Meg and, possibly, to rape Lulu. But at the end he is passive and docile, no longer able to resist, no longer even able to voice objections to his fate. He slumps off in the company of his two persecutors, who may or may not be his executioners.

Doubt and Ambiguity

In the sense that it conveys doubt and ambiguity, *The Birthday Party* is built on words that confuse more often than they clarify. Things that the audience or reader thinks are revealed by one snatch of dialogue may be contradicted or rendered illogical in the next, making it impossible to separate allegations from truth and fact from fiction. Even the most mundane issues are cloaked in doubt—questions for which there should be simple yes or no answers. Is it really Stanley's birthday, as Meg claims, or is it not, as Stanley insists? Has Meg really heard Stanley play the piano, as she claims, or has Stanley's situation made that an impossibility? Is he, in fact, even a pianist?

Although there are many details in the play, it is almost maddeningly free of facts that confirm anything or sufficiently explain the behavior of characters. For brief moments, some key things seem to be known, but soon they slip away like water down the drain. Most importantly, the cause that Stanley has allegedly betrayed is never really identified, and it remains as mysterious as Goldberg's sexual implements carried in his briefcase, the literalness of the Monty, or the exact nature of Stanley's approaching fate.

Guilt and Innocence

Although Goldberg and McCann's verbal assaults on Stanley defy any easy interpretation, it is clear that Stanley is somehow vulnerable, that their accusations do wound him, and that there is guilt to expose and sins to expiate. Still, until the arrival of Goldberg and McCann, Stanley's self-imposed exile in the rooming house, though depressing, at least offers a modicum of security. He seems docile initially, only flaring up at Meg, whose motherly affection he finds suffocating. His dread is dormant until he learns that two strangers may arrive on the scene. They ignite his inner fear, offering some sort of retribution for Stanley's real or imagined crimes which, in their bizarre tribunal, run the gamut of crimes against humanity. Goldberg and McCann are hardly avenging angels, however. Although outwardly warm and engaging, Goldberg is perfectly willing to defile innocence. He not only seduces

Lulu, he takes her on a journey into debauchery. It is such contradictions that obscure the intruders' true identities.

Language and Meaning

A concern of absurdists is their belief that language, rather than facilitate, may prevent genuine human communication. Meaning is more likely to be conveyed not by what is being said but by its subtext, what is left unsaid or the manner in which it is said. With Pinter's work in particular, words tend to mask the authentic self, while silence threatens to expose it and make it vulnerable. Pinter's characters seem to dread silence.

In *The Birthday Party* words are used in noncommunicative ways. For example, there are the inane exchanges between Meg and Petey, who, when they are alone, really have little or nothing to say to each other. They live in the ashes of their marriage, a condition they will not face. They evade the truth by mouthing empty and routine phrases that confirm only self-evident and insignificant facts. Their small talk both begins and ends the play.

Language for others is a tool of deceit, especially for Goldberg, who uses his insincere friendliness to torment Stanley. Using disingenuous flattery on Meg, Goldberg pushes for the birthday party, an ironic contrast to his more sinister purpose, which may well be to take Stanley off to be executed.

In *The Birthday Party,* as in many of Ionesco's plays, words are often used like physical objects. They are as palpable as clubs in Goldberg and McCann's interrogations of Stanley. In their inquisitions, their alternating lines even establish a rhythm that mimics striking blows.

In general, language is treated as an unreliable tool of human expression, which is of focal concern for Pinter. At the end of the play, it seems to fail altogether, at least for Stanley. About to be taken off by McCann and Goldberg, he is incapable of uttering anything but nonsensical syllables. It is only then that his terror is fully exposed.

Rites of Passage

Although it may be argued that interpreting the basic action of *The Birthday Party* as a rite of passage is very tenuous, some critics view Stanley as a symbol of the alienated artist who must be socially reintegrated. In this schema, Goldberg and McCann represent, respectively, the Judaic and Christian strains that impose on modern society, their "organization," various obligations. In this scheme, described by Martin Esslin in *Pinter,* "Stanley is the *artist* who society claims back from a comfortable, bohemian, 'opt-out' existence." The ritual of reintegration involves both the second-act initiation, the birthday party, and the third-act investiture, the dressing of Stanley in the habit or "uniform of respectable, bourgeois gentility."

There is also the second initiation, that of Lulu into sexual depravity, but this rite of passage is wholly secret and occurs offstage. It is one that also contributes an ironic comment on the other, for it is the fatherly Goldberg who is the ritual's high priest. The implication is that although society tries to redeem its outcasts, it also corrupts and violates its members.

Sex

The death of love is a common theme or condition in much absurdist drama. Aberrant behavior, violent aggression and sexual repression are likely to play important roles, as they do in *The Birthday Party.* In his listlessness, Stanley seems largely indifferent to Lulu, who, obviously on the prowl, tries to encourage his interest. Although momentarily hopeful at the prospect of going off with Lulu, Stanley falls back into his fatalistic despair, killing any hope of a "normal" relationship. His sexual repression finally gives way to his aborted rape of her at the end of Act II.

In the seedy rooming house, love seems either ineffectually sad or depraved. Meg, even in the face of his abuse, flirts with Stanley, though she is twice his age; and Lulu flirts with Goldberg, who introduces her to unspecified (though presumably horrible) sexual experiences. With Goldberg, sex is an empowering experience, a violent way to control or destroy and a terrible mockery of its function in a loving relationship. In Pinter's world, such a healthy relationship seems an impossibility.

Violence and Cruelty

At various points in the play, aggression gives way to verbal cruelty or physical violence, both actual and implied. Stanley is abusive towards Meg, whom he enjoys tormenting. During the party, he even tries to throttle her. Still, most of the threatened violence is directed at Stanley. Goldberg and McCann represent power that Stanley can not effectively resist, although at first he tries. He attempts to remain uncooperative, and he even kicks Goldberg in the stomach; but he is really no match for the two men. After their abusive interrogation, when the party starts, they ritually disarm Stanley, breaking his glasses and controlling his behavior. Unlike Stanley's violence, evident in his manic drum beating, choking of Meg, and aborted rape of Lulu, the violence of Goldberg and McCann is either merely threatened or is exercised offstage, as in the sexual abuse of Lulu. That they can achieve their aims with little more than veiled threats makes them a very sinister pair.

STYLE

Setting

The Birthday Party uses a single setting, the living-dining room of a seaside boarding house somewhere on the coast of England. Its anonymity contributes to a sense of place as symbol, especially in allegorical interpretations of the play.

Although doors permit characters to enter and exit the room, there are features suggesting that the room is isolated from the world outside. The wall separating the room from the kitchen has a hatch allowing characters in the kitchen to peer into the room, like jailors peering into a prison cell. There are also windows that permit characters to see into the room but give no real glimpse of what lies beyond them.

References to the outside world beyond the room offer virtually no clues to time or place. Petey reads a newspaper (which McCann later destroys), but the information he relates from it is trivial. Names and places alluded to are either of little help or simply misleading. In his fantasy concert tour, Stanley mentions Constantinople, which had become Istanbul in the fifteenth century when it fell to the Turks, and in their interrogation of Stanley, Goldberg and McCann ask him about the Blessed Oliver Plunket, an Irish-catholic martyr executed in

England in 1681, and about the medieval, Albigensian heresy. Such puzzling references help create the impression that the setting is either a microcosmic symbol or an existential, timeless vacuum.

Symbolism and Allegory

Justified or not, *The Birthday Party* has been read as a kind of modern allegory. That interpretation is partly based on the fact that there is little to anchor the play's setting in a world beyond its limits. Pinter's deliberate vagueness and use of fragmented information tend to confirm that he has a symbolic purpose. Some elements seem particularly conducive to interpretation. Among other things, the toy drum, the birthday party itself, McCann's seemingly gratuitous act of breaking Stanley's glasses, and the outfitting of Stanley in respectable clothes before he is led off.

Yet, to fit the diverse elements into some sort of consistent allegorical has proven more difficult. Is Stanley the embodiment of the modern artist who has reneged on his obligations to both his craft and society and turned to living in an inert, totally irresponsible state? Critics have remarked that the play's setting is womb-like, offering Stanley a place of comfort and security and isolating him from the world beyond. Still, while it provides a refuge, the place is dingy and depressing, and Stanley is hardly happy living in it. He obviously shoulders some sort of guilt. Goldberg and McCann tap into that, and they intimate that there will be retribution for Stanley's alleged transgressions, possibly death. However, part of what they say in the last act suggests that they are not so much his inquisitors and potential executioners as exorcists and healers who have come to make Stanley whole again. Such uncertainties make a consistent allegorical interpretation of the play difficult.

Structure

Despite its absurdist elements, *The Birthday Party* has a conventional, three-act structure and follows a straightforward chronology. The play begins the morning of Stanley's alleged birthday and concludes the following morning, after Goldberg and McCann cart him off. The first and second acts both end with strong, even manic moments: the frantic beating of the drum in Act I and the near-rape of Lulu in Act II. However, the last act, like the opening of the first, is understated in its emotional force, returning as it does to the shallow conversation of Meg and Petey. Meg, not even aware that Stanley has been removed, makes small talk about the party while Petey tries to read.

Working through some sort of causal necessity, such a structure traditionally imposes predictable patterns of behavior on character, but Pinter breaks through such strictures, at times letting his characters go amok. For example, at the birthday party in the second act, for no discernable reason, Stanley becomes very violent. There are also strange bits of stage business that border on the bizarre, as when, for example, in the last act Goldberg has McCann blow in his mouth. Such odd behavior offers a very unsettling contrast to the more predictable events that usually evolve within such a traditional structure.

Foreshadowing

In his teasing of Meg, Stanley claims that the two strangers who plan to show up at the boarding house will come in a van carrying a wheelbarrow, which they use to cart somebody off. Meg, a gullible target for Stanley, grows very nervous, fearful that she will be their victim.

Although Stanley's purpose is to frighten Meg, his description foreshadows his own fate. He is the one to be taken off. His teasing story predicts the sinister arrival of Goldberg and McCann and is an important bit of foreshadowing.

Irony

The Birthday Party has some ironic elements. There are, for example, ironic discrepancies in character, especially in Goldberg's case. On the surface, he is amiable and pleasant, a spokesman for old world values and familial loyalties, but he is also sexually abusive, even depraved. McCann, his associate, possibly a killer, is a rather taciturn, finicky sort of fellow. He sits quietly, methodically tearing newspaper into strips, an ironic bit of activity given the fact that he has a brutal purpose. Like Ben and Gus in Pinter's *The Dumbwaiter* or the hit men in Hemingway's short story "The Killers," the pair seem to be civilized and calm, not vicious or nervous. It is the ironic contrast between their normal exterior and their undisclosed but violent purpose that makes them so sinister and menacing.

Nonsense

Nonsense in Pinter's *The Birthday Party* is not as obvious as it is in Ionesco's dramas. Still, nonsensical elements are present, a fact which prompted some critics to note the influence of Ionesco on Pinter's play.

In the play, which avoids farce, the nonsense is mostly verbal. In the last act, it takes the form of Stanley's choking, unintelligible sounds. But it is also present in Act II, when Goldberg and McCann, alone with Stanley, put their victim through an incongruous and chaotic interrogation. The two henchmen ask a series of unrelated and often unanswerable questions, some of which are patently ludicrous. It is their barrage that gives hints but no firm indication of the two men's real purpose.

HISTORICAL CONTEXT

In the late-1950s, when Pinter wrote *The Birthday Party,* the developed nations of the world were deeply mired in a cold war that pitted the communist powers of the Soviet Union and Red China against the free-world nations, including both the United States and the United Kingdom. Fears of a third world war, one fought with atomic weapons, were widespread. At the beginning of the decade, war had broken out in Korea, pitting communist North Korea and its ally, Red China, against South Korea and a United Nations "police force" comprised largely of American troops. Further outbreaks of open warfare were threatened throughout the 1950s, as in 1956, when Hungarian rebels, pleading for help from the West, were crushed by Soviet troops and tanks.

In the same period, the United States and the Soviet Union began the "Space Race," an undeclared competition in which each country sought to prove itself the most technologically advanced. The Soviets launched Sputnik I in 1957, the first artificial satellite to be put into orbit, and in the following year, the United States sent up its counterpart, Explorer 1. Meanwhile, other events were setting the stage for further armed hostilities. The 1954 Geneva Accords divided Vietnam into North and South Vietnam, a division that would lead to war and the increasing involvement of the United States, while in Cuba, Fidel Castro began the rebellion that would bring down the Cuban dictator, Fulgencio

Batista, and lead to a communist takeover of the country. Abroad, other nations formed important alliances, not just for political but for economic reasons. Of major importance to Great Britain, in 1957 the democratic countries of western Europe formed the Common Market, from which, initially, England was excluded, its membership vigorously opposed by France. Also, in the next year, Egypt, Syria, and Yemen formed the United Arab States, partly in response to Israel's defeat and invasion of Egypt in 1956.

In these same years, Great Britain continued its decline as a major world power. Its influence in Africa and Asia was quickly eroding. In 1952, India, the jewel of the British Empire, gained its independence and elected its first prime minister, Jawaharial Nehru. In 1956, Egypt nationalized the Suez Canal and forced the British to surrender control of the canal and withdraw. Meanwhile, at home, the British continued to suffer from the domestic bombings and mayhem carried out by the outlawed Irish Republican Army (IRA), whose primary goal was to liberate Northern Ireland from the United Kingdom and incorporate it into the Republic of Ireland.

The decline of England's world's prestige, if not directly evident in the British plays of the late-1950s, certainly contributed to the anger and detachment that dominated the mood of many of them. For many artists, in a period of doubt, pessimism, and insecurity, rage seemed the only genuine response.

John Osborne's *Look Back in Anger* (1956) is frequently named as the seminal play in this "Angry Theater." Its protagonist, Jimmy Porter, furious at having to live in a "pusillanimous" world that he cannot change, tunes it out. However, Osborne's method, like that of most of the "Angries," is basically conventional, despite his use of contemporary speech and anti-heroic characters. However, the sense of alienation and helplessness that characterizes some of the angry plays was also conveyed in the new, unconventional drama of the absurdist playwrights, led by Beckett and Ionesco, whose works, imported from Paris, evidenced both revolutionary dramatic methods and the existential conditions of nausea and ennui. London audiences encountered this very controversial drama in 1956, when English-language versions of both Beckett's *Waiting for Godot* and Ionesco's *The Bald Soprano*

COMPARE & CONTRAST

- **1950s:** Britain's decline as a world power continues and challenges to its remaining global influence persist for decades, reaching armed conflict in 1982 in the war with Argentina over the Falkland Islands.

  Today: Although the United Kingdom still holds some far flung territories, including the Falklands, in 1998 it ceded Hong Kong, its last important Crown Colony in the Far East, to the Republic of China. The breakup of what was once the Great British Empire is now virtually complete.

- **1950s:** Popular culture is on the verge of explosion with the impact of both television and rock music, though old institutions like the English dance hall are still popular. These halls feature sentimental ballads, swing dance music, and vaudeville comedians.

  Today: Television and rock music dominate western culture. The dance-hall is long gone, having given way to large scale, arena concerts.

- **1950s:** The Irish Republican Army (IRA) tries to achieve its primary objective, an end to British rule in Northern Ireland. Its activities, although sporadic and of varying severity, constitute a continual threat. The organization employs terrorist methods, murdering British soldiers and bombing government and commercial buildings. Although inconclusive, there are hints in Pinter's *The Birthday Party* that it is the IRA that Stanley is supposed to have betrayed.

  Today: Although the radical offshoots of the IRA continue to use violence, serious efforts have been made by the British government and the political wing of the IRA to negotiate a settlement of the Irish "question." It remains difficult, partly because Protestants have a large and powerful presence in Northern Ireland. However, there is promise. Negotiators have arranged truces that both sides have tried to honor, and representatives of the IRA and British government continue to talk, something unthinkable in the 1950s.

---

were staged. To Pinter belongs some of the credit of synthesizing these new strains, for it is in his earliest plays, including *The Birthday Party,* that absurdist elements are for the first time welded to the angry mood and detachment then dominating the new wave in British theater.

CRITICAL OVERVIEW

The nearly unanimous negative reviews that assaulted the 1958 London premier of Pinter's *The Birthday Party* baffled the young playwright but never dampened his spirits. Those early reviewers, with the exception of Harold Hobson, found Pinter's play unfunny, obscure, and derivative. In the *Evening Standard,* Milton Shulman, scoffed that the work would "be best enjoyed by those who believe that obscurity is its own reward" and further complained that the play was not very funny, in part because "the fun to be derived out of the futility of language" was becoming a "cliche of its own." Meanwhile, M. M. W., the reviewer in the *Manchester Guardian,* wrote that Pinter simply obfuscated both character and action with "non-sequiturs, half-gibberish, and lunatic ravings," and suggested that the playwright might do much better if he would forget "Beckett, Ionesco, and Simpson." For the anonymous reviewer in the *Times,* the play stacked up to a discordant and opaque conundrum. Act I "sounds an offbeat note of madness;" Act II rises to "a sort of delirium;" but Act III gives "not the slightest hint of what the other two may have been about."

Even though many of the early reviewers recognized Pinter's kinship with Beckett, Ionesco, and other new wave, anti-realist dramatists, they seemed to expect his play to develop an idea in the manner of the thesis-play. Critics were unable adjust to the playwright's "shifts in aesthetic key," those lurches back and forth between psychological realism and symbolic surrealism that create a sense of dislocation and menace, Pinter's signature moods. What bothered early critics most was the play's maddening failure to authenticate experience or verify facts. As Arthur Ganz noted in *Pinter: A Collection of Critical Essays,* however, "it is the threat of meaning rather than the threat of violence that lies at the root of Pinter's menace." The disclosure of verifiable information, such as the identify of Goldberg and McCann's organization, would only help relieve the angst that arises from an inner fear of its disclosure and thereby rob the play of its forceful intensity. Only Harold Hobson, writing in the *Times* seemed to recognize this fact, noting that the play's evasiveness gives it its power, and that it is precisely in its "vagueness that its spine-chilling quality lies."

In 1960, with the London staging of *The Caretaker,* critical assessments of Pinter markedly improved. There were still nay-sayers, but many important critics began amending their initial judgments of Pinter. For example, one of England's dramatic gurus, Kenneth Tynan, wrote in the *Observer* that in *The Caretaker* Pinter had "begun to fulfill the promise" that Tynan had "signally failed to see in *The Birthday Party*" two years earlier. By that time, too, reviewers had begun adjusting their critical radar to the new theater, aided by the much publicized "London controversy" in which Ionesco intellectually squared off with Tynan over Ionesco's supposed lack of doctrinal convictions and his assault on language. The debate, if it did not create sympathy for the new drama, at least prompted a better understanding. Furthermore, *The Birthday Party,* presented on television in 1960, impressed millions of viewers, whose influence certainly helped Pinter's growing reputation by revealing that his play could communicate with ordinary folk if not with critics.

In 1961, when Martin Esslin first published *The Theatre of the Absurd,* his important seminal study of the movement, he placed Pinter among its "Parallels and Proselytes" along with such important writers as Fernando Arrabal, Max Frisch, Edward Albee, Arthur Kopit, Slawomir Mrozek, and Vaclav Havel. Just three years after the premier of *The Birthday Party,* Esslin, recognizing the playwright's genius, concluded that Pinter had "already won himself an important place among the playwrights of this century." It was an assessment that stuck and has certainly not abated.

In 1964, when *The Birthday Party* was revived at the Aldwych Theatre in London under Pinter's direction, the work garnered greater respect among the city's drama critics. There were still those who remained belligerent, like W. A. Darlington of the *Daily Telegraph,* who, although he found the play more compelling than the first time around, still felt that *The Birthday Party* should have disclosed what it was Stanley had done. By then, of course, new assessments about what Pinter was about were slowly making such questions both unanswerable and ultimately irrelevant. It had become clear that Pinter, like Ionesco, had created his unique brand of "pure theater," one deliberately cut adrift from specific current events and doctrinal adherence in its questing through human fear and anxiety. *The Birthday Party* was well on its way to being recognized as one of the greatest examples of absurdist drama.

CRITICISM

John W. Fiero

Fiero is a Ph. D., now retired, who formerly taught drama and play writing at the University of Southwestern Louisiana. In this essay he discusses The Birthday Party *as a work of anti-text, pure theater that gains great power at points where language fails or simply eludes logical analysis.*

If, as the poet Wallace Stevens maintained, there are thirteen ways of looking at a blackbird, there ought to be at least as many ways of looking at a play. There are really, however, only two essential perspectives: one which views the play as a literary text, and the other which views the play as a script to be performed. Judged strictly from the first perspective, Harold Pinter's *The Birthday Party* remains an impassable mote to trouble the critical eye, while, from the second perspective, it seems a powerful

Stanley (John Alderton) and Lulu (Paula Wilcox) meet in the first act of The Birthday Party

stage vehicle, capable, metaphorically speaking, of slicing through an eyeball like the razor in Salvador Dali's surrealistic film, *Un Chien d'Anlou.*

Yes, astute directors will try to interpret a play for production through synthesizing the two approaches, yet they must ultimately evaluate the text as a vehicle for performance, concerned not with its literary merits but with its *theatricality,* which, arguably, Pinter's play offers in abundance. The problem for him and other writers identified with the theater of the absurd is that most literary critics and scholars concentrate on the text, which, of

course, is their proper job. Unfortunately, though, they are the guardians of anthologies, the gate keepers who decide what passes into classical posterity. They cannot make their judgments on the basis of how well a play is realized, for its articulation on stage is ever-changing, subject to the individuals responsible for each production of the work. They must look almost exclusively to its printed text, which, if not just less, is certainly other than the staged play.

The texts of absurdist playwrights, like Pinter's early "comedies of menace," present such critics

WHAT DO I READ NEXT?

- Franz Kafka's novel *The Trial,* written in 1914 but not published in English until 1937, bears similarities to Pinter's play. Its anti-hero, Josef K., beset by vague guilt, is taken to his execution by polite gentlemen who are death's angelic summoners. Along with Beckett, Kafka had a major and acknowledged influence on Pinter, who, in 1993, adapted *The Trial* to the screen.

- Pinter's long one-act play, *The Dumbwaiter,* written at about the same time as *The Birthday Party,* includes parallel characters that invite contrast. In it, two hired killers, Ben and Gus, await orders from an organization which remains as mysterious as that for which Goldberg and McCann work.

- Ernest Hemingway's short story ''The Killers,'' first published in 1927, has a chilling pair of killers who appear in a small-town diner looking for their victim. Like Goldberg and McCann, they are unnervingly calm and fastidious in their manners. Critics have noted their similarity to Pinter's characters in both *The Dumb Waiter* and *The Birthday Party.*

- John Osborne's play *Look Back in Anger,* produced in 1956, is a seminal work in the Angry Theater of post-World War II Britain. Its protagonist, Jimmy Porter, offers an interesting contrast to Stanley Webber. Both are variations on the sensitive and angry young man mired in a world shorn of hope and human dignity.

---

with a special problem. Distrusting language as an adequate or sufficient tool of communication, many of these playwrights deliberately strip their dialogue of logic or sense. This is the opposite of the realists, for example, who, while using commonplace language, advance their plots in the manner of Ibsen, in traditional, action-reaction models that rely both on rational discourse and known or verifiable events. In addition to rejecting logic, the absurdist writer frequently descends into ludicrous parodies of common speech, even, finally, into incomprehensible babble. As Pinter himself claimed, his characters often use ''a torrent of language'' as a kind of silence, as speech that ''is speaking of a language locked beneath it.'' It is like so much verbal clothing, covering an emptiness that real silence might leave exposed and vulnerable.

Such an unconscious evasion of an inner fear—perhaps the fear of nothingness—is seen at the very beginning of *The Birthday Party,* in the opening dialogue of Meg and Petey Boles. Both characters confirm what is entirely self-evident, such as the fact that Petey has indeed come back and that, yes, he has his newspaper and is eating his cornflakes.

What is not said in this silence of words is that their marriage is as passionless as a wet rag. They are not a very complex pair, to be sure. They are basically free of the sort of angst that afflicts their more intriguing tenant, Stanley Webber. The inner, frustrated longings of Meg are exposed quickly because her words become transparent clues as she speaks of Stanley as if he were both the male child she never had and the lover for whom she still pines. In fact, the two characters seem disarmingly realistic, for their conversation barely exaggerates the idle breakfast banter of many average people. They even offer evidence that Pinter is at least as faithful to actual human behavior as the many ''realistic'' plays that artificially imposed order on behavior to a suit some moralizing purpose.

The opening scene of *The Birthday Party* also has a conventional resonance, for it seems like a wry variation on the old ''feather duster'' of drawing-room comedy, the type of scene in which maids and butlers or cooks prep an audience for its encounter with the major characters. In fact, *The Birthday Party* starts much like a working-class burlesque of one of those sparkling depression-era comedies, such as Noel Coward's *Private Lives,* in which, dressed and groomed to the nines, the wealthy, well-heeled society gent first appears for a late breakfast and witty repartee. Instead, in Pinter's play, the proverbial cat drags in Stanley, slovenly, half-dressed, and grunting in monosyllables.

Of course, Stanley and his persecutors, Goldberg and McCann, will soon take the audience into strange and unfamiliar territory, lurching in and out of a dreamscape in which nothing is transparent and all realistic bets are off. No key events revealed can be confirmed or verified, even the assertion that Stanley is a down-on-his-luck pianist could be a fabrication—no on stage proof is offered that he can even *play* the piano. Even the most elementary questions go unanswered, whether, for example, it is actually Stanley's birthday or whether Meg has merely said it is as an excuse to give Stanley his present, the toy drum. Nothing important is decisively disclosed, for just as soon as a fact appears solidly established it is contradicted.

What is certain is that Goldberg and McCann somehow reach into Stanley's insides and set his fear racing violently. They menace because they threaten to expose the real Stanley to the other characters. Yet, paradoxically, they are also like confessors or exorcists, attempting to cure Stanley by finding the fear's source, that which has led to his withdrawal, hermit-like, from life. The final, devastating revelation of the play is that without his fear, Stanley is pitifully anemic. It has been that inner fear that somehow both defined and sustained him. In the last act, following the ritual release of this dread in the form of violence, he is reduced to an inarticulate automaton, outfitted with respectable dress but seemingly inert in his passivity and all but brain dead. It is as if, indeed, he has become nothing.

It is in his evasiveness that Pinter has been critically maligned. His text deliberately misdirects readers and audiences, leading to the charge that his earliest work is difficult at best, opaque at worst. If we know more than we need to know about Meg and Petey, we know far less than we think we want to know about Stanley and his relationship to the two intruders. Most perplexing, the source of Stanley's fear, although hinted at, is never revealed. As indicated, it is aroused and transmuted into violence during the birthday party, but it is never simply identified or explained. This fact has frustrated many critics, even those within theater. According to Robert Brustein, writing in the *New Republic,* Pinter in his "grotesque naturalism" fails to com-

municate at all, because although he uses "authentic colloquial speech," he has "stripped it bare it of reflective or conceptual thought." But Pinter is, after all, a poet, and one who understands that a play, like a poem, as Archibald MacLeish insisted, "should not mean but be." Furthermore, as an actor and director, he knows that it can only truly "be" in performance.

Stanley's fear also simply *is* a monster within, evident from the start by his erratic and sometimes violent behavior. It does not first appear with the intrusion of Goldberg and McCann. It is latent, almost dormant, but it rises in his emotional gorge even before he learns about the two strangers. It breaks through his civil conversation with Meg, when he suddenly recoils from her in disgust and verbally assaults her for her lousy tea and poor housekeeping. When she tells him about the strangers, he is obviously shaken, and he cruelly teases her about two men in the van with a wheelbarrow who will come to the door. It is an ironic moment, for Goldberg and McCann come not to wheel Meg away but to draw out Stanley's fear and force him to confront it—though who they are and why they seek out Stanley remains an utter mystery. The result is that Stanley and the two intruders seem more symbolic than real.

That fact has led to interpretations of *The Birthday Party* as a modern "allegory on the pressures of conformity" as well as "an allegory of death," as Martin Esslin noted in *Pinter: A Study of His Plays.* But, as Esslin argued, such interpretations miss the mark, for Pinter's play, like Beckett's *Waiting for Godot,* "simply explores a situation which, in itself, is a valid poetic image that is immediately seen as relevant and true." Like the Black Death, discussed by Antinon Artaud in *The Theatre and Its Double* as a sort of ultimate theatrical and awful presence, Stanley's gnawing fear is just there, a presence that is perhaps more devastating because its origins are unknown. Arguably, Pinter's verbal misdirections were designed to increase the nerve-wracking impact of *The Birthday Party,* deliberately obscuring the root cause of Stanley's fear and thereby making it even more devastating, just as the ignorance of the great plague's origin profoundly increased the terror of its potential victims.

Much of the play's power is released precisely at times when no words are spoken, when they utterly fail to communicate, or when what they communicate lies beyond their literal sense. For example, the first act ends with Stanley marching around the room, frantically and violently beating on the toy drum. Nothing is said, but as Stanley's beating grows more terrible, Meg's smiling pleasure gives way to an alarmed expression. Despite all the noise, it is a silence in Pinter's sense, an intense moment of exposure.

Even more violent moments of exposure occur in the second act, during the party games. Blindfolded, Stanley stumbles around the room, falls over the drum, gets up, finds Meg and savagely begins to choke her, just before the lights fail. Similarly, the act ends with another violent sequence in which Stanley, who appears on the verge of raping Lulu, is exposed by McCann's flashlight and forced to back away. As he moves off, Stanley begins giggling with a mounting, nearly insane intensity as the other characters move towards him, like lions circling their intended kill.

Memorable text-bound moments, when words are plentiful, are often moments when language fails, for the simple fact is that nothing that contributes to the indelible sense of Stanley's repressed fear can be expressed in words. It emerges in Stanley's cacophonous gagging on word fragments in the last act, for example, but perhaps is even more memorable wedged into the two word-rich litanies of Goldberg and McCann, used when they are alone with Stanley in the second and final acts. In their chant-like rhythm and responsive structure, these are like dreadful incantations. They are also verbal puzzles, a mumbo-jumbo melange of nonsense and serious but unsubstantiated accusations and inactivated threats. The words are powerful, not because of what they literally mean but because of the intimidating way in which they are delivered. They seem as physical as punches delivered with violent force to the abdomen or head, and, like such brutal attacks, Stanley cringes before them.

These moments are moments of pure theater, vivid and powerful. They erupt in text-empty places or tear through the text with an intense fury that contrasts with the disquieting deliberation of Goldberg and McCann; they are memorably caught in McCann's slow and methodical tearing of strips from Petey's newspaper. And they are, of course, moments to experience, to view. They lose their power when the text is simply read; stage directions describing Stanley's maniacal beating of the drum are no match for the realization of such a disturbing scene. Therein, however, lies the critical rub, for unlike much of the time-honored, poetic drama of Western culture, to an important degree valued for

its language, an anti-text play like Pinter's *The Birthday Party* must be judged on more appropriate grounds, not just as ritual, myth, game, or symbol, but as viable theater. As well as any other modern dramatists, in *The Birthday Party* Pinter shows us why we must constantly rethink exactly what a classic work of drama should be. Until we do, we will not be at peace with the theater of the absurd or give it its proper regard.

Source: John W. Fiero, for *Drama for Students,* Gale, 1999.

Rosemary Pountney

In the following essay, Pountney provides an overview of Pinter's first full-length play, delineating the primary plot points and discussing the work's major themes.

The Birthday Party, Pinter's first full-length play, takes place at the home of Meg and Petey Boles and concerns their lodger, Stanley, whose past is obscure, though he fantasises about having been a concert pianist. Meg gives Stanley a drum for his birthday, which he plays as though possessed as the first act closes. In Act II Stanley tries to get rid of some new lodgers, Goldberg and McCann, but they respond by subjecting Stanley to rapid-fire interrogation, until he is reduced to speechlessness. The act culminates in Stanley's birthday party, in which McCann breaks Stanley's glasses during a game of blind man's buff, the lights go out and, in a sinister climax, Stanley (encumbered by the drum, into which he has stumbled) begins to strangle Meg and is bent giggling over a young girl, Lulu, when the curtain falls. Act III comes full circle with Meg and Petey at breakfast, as at the opening of the play. Stanley is brought down a changed man, still speechless (''Uhgug-ug-gug-eeehhh-gag''). Goldberg and McCann leave, taking Stanley ''to Monty'' and threaten Petey when he tries to stop them. Meg at the end of the play has understood nothing and fails to register Stanley has gone.

The initial lack of success of *The Birthday Party* in the late 1950's is not surprising. Pinter had yet to create a market for the particular brand of menace that is the signature of his early plays, such as *The Room* and *The Dumb Waiter* (also 1957), where, like Stanley, the protagonists are sequestered in a room and are threatened by intruders into their womb-like privacy. Critics, such as Milton Shulman, were puzzled: ''The world of Harold Pinter is shadowy, obsessed, guilt-ridden, claustrophobic and, above all, private. You are expected to find your way through it without signposts, clues or milestones''.

Pinter is even said to have received the following enquiry from an audience member:

> I would be obliged if you would kindly explain to me the meaning of your play *The Birthday Party*. These are the points which I do not understand. 1) Who are the two men? 2) Where did Stanley come from? 3) Were they all supposed to be normal? You will appreciate that without the answers to my questions I cannot fully understand your play.

Pinter's reputed response (''1) Who are you? 2) Where do you come from?'', etc.) naturally ignored such strictures—and audiences gradually became increasingly fascinated, hooked into the plays by their ambiguities, a technique Pinter had learned from Samuel Beckett. (Pinter warmly acknowledges a debt to Beckett since first discovering his writing in 1949.)

One of the major pleasures of Pinter's drama is his use of language, ranging from jargon used as a protective shield to prevent intruders seeing what is underneath, to a characteristic use of pauses of varying lengths, so that a work is virtually orchestrated by silence, and meaning accrues in the subtext—in what is *not* said. At the opening of *The Birthday Party* it is as though Pinter had produced a tape recording of the inanities we actually speak, as opposed to the shapely sentences often given to stage figures by earlier dramatists. In using such dialogue onstage, Pinter not only introduces a rich vein of humour, but allows an audience to recognise the realism of stating the obvious. Many a break-fast-time conversation is based on similar emptiness:

> *Meg:* Is that you Petey? (*Pause*) Petey,
>   is that you?
> *Petey:* What?
> *Meg:* Is that you?
> *Petey:* Yes, it's me.
> *Meg:* What? (*She opens the hatch and looks through.*) Are you back?
> *Petey:* Yes.

The Birthday Party also demonstrates a use of language as a weapon, as Goldberg and McCann, by their quick-fire questioning of Stanley (a known technique in brainwashing, designed to fluster and confuse) reduce him to inarticulacy:

> *Goldberg:* Which came first?
> *McCann:* Chicken? Egg? Which came first?
> *Goldberg:* Which came first? Which came first? Which came first? (*Stanley screams*)

Stanley's subsequent silence marks the disintegration of his personality. Following Goldberg and McCann's ministrations he does indeed ''need spe-

> ❝ ONE OF THE MAJOR PLEASURES OF PINTER'S DRAMA IS HIS USE OF LANGUAGE, RANGING FROM JARGON USED AS A PROTECTIVE SHIELD TO PREVENT INTRUDERS SEEING WHAT IS UNDERNEATH, TO A CHARACTERISTIC USE OF PAUSES OF VARYING LENGTHS, SO THAT A WORK IS VIRTUALLY ORCHESTRATED BY SILENCE, AND MEANING ACCRUES IN THE SUBTEXT—IN WHAT IS *NOT* SAID''

cial treatment''—for which the two men are ''taking him to Monty'' as Goldberg ominously informs Petey. Goldberg and McCann seem in a sense to be projections or manifestations of Stanley's strongly-developed sense of guilt and fear of pursuit—of which we are made aware before he encounters the two men. At the same time Goldberg and McCann are frighteningly real. The barrage of words with which they crush Stanley, their vitality and comic vulgarity, the swagger and aggression, and the rhythms of their language have a richness that comes straight out of the Jewish idiom of Pinter's family background as well as the regional influence of London's East End. For audiences unused to the Jewish idiom, the disturbing power of Pinter's writing owes a good deal to the strangeness of this mixture of the unfamiliar with the familiar.

The ambiguities in *The Birthday Party* are integral to the play's impact. We never know precisely who Goldberg and McCann are, or what (if anything) Stanley has done, that they seem to be pursuing him. We are left with a sense of genuine unease, as though indescribable evil really were stalking outside the door of even the most ordinary of homes, awaiting its chance to enter.

Source: Rosemary Pountney, ''The Birthday Party'' in *The International Dictionary of Theatre*, Volume 1: *Plays,* edited by Mark Hawkins-Dady, St. James Press, 1992, pp. 67–68.

Thomas M. Disch

In this excerpt, Disch favorably reviews a 1988 revival production of Pinter's play. In addition to affirming the power of the playwright's text, this production, in the critic's opinion, offers skilled direction and powerful performances.

Harold Pinter's *The Birthday Party* is appearing through May 22 at the C.S.C. Theatre on East Thirteenth Street. I regret being so tardy in my recommendation, for Carey Perloff's production is vivid and well marshaled. More than most plays, *The Birthday Party* depends on a director who can mold clear dramatic action from a text that is a puzzle-box of ambiguities. It was Pinter's specific inspiration to create a plot that is all event and atmosphere, where the warring tonalities of hard-boiled thriller and Beckettesque farce alternate and finally fuse. Any effort to account for the action on the basis of the characters' histories and motivations is wasted effort, nor is there any simple one-to-one symbolic schema by which the action can be interpreted. But that's not to say Pinter has evaded writing *about* anything. *The Birthday Party* is very cogently and accessibly about the ways in which people tease and terrorize each other, about the kinds of intelligence specific to prey and predator, and much else that, rendered as a maxim of psychology, might seem dull or doubtful but that *plays* very well. By unmooring his story from a basis in strict narrative logic, Pinter gives his audience the distanced perspective of an alienist who listens for the meaning of what a patient says in the inflections and cadences of his speech. All good dramatists rediscover the primacy of body English, gesture and phatic utterance, each in his own way. In this, his first full-length play, Pinter made the discovery with unusually clarifying effect, an effect that is still invigorating thirty years later.

Georgine Hall and Robert Gerringer as Meg and Petey are the incarnate spirit of English *lumpen* gentility. David Strathairn as Stanley, the cookie that all the play's machineries have been designed to crumble, is just smarmy enough that it is very hard not to identify with his gleeful tormenters, Goldberg and McCann, when they mysteriously appear and set to work on Stanley's nerves and sanity. In the latter roles, Peter Riegert and Richard Riehle steal the show, as is intended.

The only exception I take to the production is Loy Arcenas's set. More than most plays, *The Birthday Party* requires one invisible wall, not three. When the action hinges on Stanley being repeatedly prevented from exiting through an invisible door in an invisible wall, the suspense is theoretical at best.

Source: Thomas M. Disch, review of *The Birthday Party* in the *Nation,* May 21, 1988, p. 727.

SOURCES

Brustein, Robert. "A Naturalism of the Grotesque" in the *New Republic,* Volume CXLV, 1961, p. 21.

Darlington, W. A. "Enjoyable Pinter" in the *Daily Telegraph,* June 21, 1964, p. 18.

Esslin, Martin. *The Theatre of the Absurd,* revised and enlarged edition, Penguin Books, 1976.

Ganz, Arthur, editor. Introduction to *Pinter: A Collection of Critical Essays,* Prentice-Hall, 1972.

Hobson, Harold. "The Screw Turns Again" in the *Times,* May 25, 1958, p. 11.

Hollis, James. *Harold Pinter: The Poetics of Silence,* Southern Illinois University Press, 1970, p. 15.

M. M. W. "*The Birthday Party*" in the *Manchester Guardian,* May 21, 1958, p. 5.

"Puzzling Surrealism of *The Birthday Party*" in the *Times,* May 20, 1958, p. 3.

Shulman, Milton. "Sorry, Mr. Pinter, You're Just Not Funny Enough" in the *Evening Standard,* May 20, 1958, p. 6.

Tynan, Kenneth. "A Verbal Wizard in the Suburbs" in the *Observer,* June 5, 1960, p. 17.

FURTHER READING

Burkman, Katherine H. *The Dramatic World of Harold Pinter: Its Basis in Ritual,* University of Ohio Press, 1971.
    This study treats Pinter's early plays not as comedies but rather as recreations of ancient fertility myths and rituals.

Dukore, Bernard F. *Where Laughter Stops: Pinter's Tragicomedy,* University of Missouri Press, 1976.
    This brief study argues that Pinter's technique is to move from what is funny to what is unfunny and threatening, even though the source for what was comic remains the same for what has been transmuted into the tragic.

Esslin, Martin. *Pinter: A Study of His Plays,* expanded edition, W. W. Norton, 1976.

Esslin, who authored *The Theatre of the Absurd,* approaches Pinter in the fashion of that seminal work, attempting to explain the puzzling aspects of the playwright's work by examining and analyzing, among other things, influences, sources, and techniques underlying ''Pinterese.'' The work includes a useful chronology extending from 1930 through 1975.

Gabbard, Lucina Paquet. *The Dream Structure of Pinter's Plays: A Psychoanalytic Approach,* Fairleigh Dickinson University Press, 1976.

As Gabbard's title indicates, her approach is Freudian, and she relates various dramatic motifs in Pinter's early plays to the Oedipal and other subconscious wishes. For Gabbard, *The Birthday Party* is treated as ''a punishment dream'' incorporating, symbolically, ''the wish to kill.''

Gale, Steven H. *Butter's Going Up: A Critical Analysis of Harold Pinter's Work,* Duke University Press, 1977.

A stylistically direct study of Pinter's work written up to 1976, this text offers terse interpretations of each piece and several valuable aids to further study, including some chronologies and an annotated bibliography. It treats *The Birthday Party* as the thematic companion to two other ''comedies of menace:'' *The Room* and *The Dumbwaiter.*

Hinchliffe, Arnold P. *Harold Pinter,* revised edition, Twayne, 1981.

This study in is a useful bio-critical study of Pinter that provides useful aids and a good overview of the playwright's early work. Three important chapters for the study of Pinter's *The Birthday Party* are 1 (''The Pinter Problem''), 2 (''Language and Silence'') and 3 (''Comedies of Menace''). Includes a chronology and bibliography.

Kerr, Walter. *Harold Pinter,* Columbia University Press, 1967.

An important critic of British theater, Kerr approaches Pinter as an Existentialist and interprets his early plays in light of that philosophy's perception of the fundamental absurdity of the human condition and its attendant feelings of nausea and dread.

Killinger, John. *World in Collapse: The Vision of Absurd Drama,* Dell, 1961.

An important aid to understanding absurdist plays, this work identifies and discusses the origins and purpose of various motifs and techniques used by

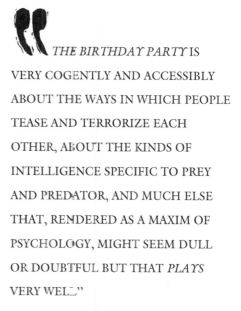

THE BIRTHDAY PARTY IS VERY COGENTLY AND ACCESSIBLY ABOUT THE WAYS IN WHICH PEOPLE TEASE AND TERRORIZE EACH OTHER, ABOUT THE KINDS OF INTELLIGENCE SPECIFIC TO PREY AND PREDATOR, AND MUCH ELSE THAT, RENDERED AS A MAXIM OF PSYCHOLOGY, MIGHT SEEM DULL OR DOUBTFUL BUT THAT *PLAYS* VERY WELL.''

Beckett, Ionesco, and other writers, including Pinter.

Knowles, Ronald. *Understanding Harold Pinter,* University of South Carolina Press, 1995.

A succinct monograph in the ''Understanding Contemporary British Literature'' series, Knowles's study offers an overview of Pinter's achievements in theater, radio, television, and film and the various influences on his craft. Knowles discusses *The Birthday Party* as an ''amalgam'' of diverse cultural undercurrents.

Taylor, John Russell. *Anger and After: A Guide to New British Drama,* revised edition, Methuen, 1969.

Appearing under the alternate title *The Angry Theatre,* this valuable study offers a critical survey of British drama from 1956 through the 1960s. It includes an important chapter on Pinter, who is identified as the most poetic writer among the new wave dramatists. He notes that Pinter deliberately employs contrary assertions by characters to thwart facile and superficial interpretation.

Edward II: The Troublesome Reign and Lamentable Death of Edward the Second, King of England, with the Tragical Fall of Proud Mortimer

CHRISTOPHER MARLOWE

1594

Christopher Marlowe's play *Edward II: The Troublesome Reign and Lamentable Death of Edward the Second, King of England, with the Tragical Fall of Proud Mortimer* is an intense and swiftly moving account of a king controlled by his basest passions, a weak man who becomes a puppet of his homosexual lover, and pays a tragic price for forsaking the governance of his country. The action takes place in early fourteenth-century England, during a period when England was surrounded by enemies in Scotland, Ireland, Denmark, and France. Edward, preoccupied by the banishment of his lover, Gaveston, barely acknowledges the nascent crises that threaten his realm; he indulges his passions and abdicates his duties, failing to recognize that his willful and persistent refusal to attend to state affairs is eroding his royal authority. It is this resulting loss of power, which he has brought upon himself by his own irresponsibility, that irks him more than the absence of his lover. He picks his battles, preferring those petty skirmishes over Gaveston's fate to those that would benefit his rule and enhance the power of the state. When a group of nobles has Gaveston executed, Edward's own execution soon follows, and the play closes by unveiling the Machiavellian vices of the would-be saviors.

Marlowe found most of his material for this play in the third volume of Raphael Holinshed's *Chronicles* (1587). He stayed close to the account, but he embellished history with the character of Lightborn (or Lucifer) as Edward's assassin. First

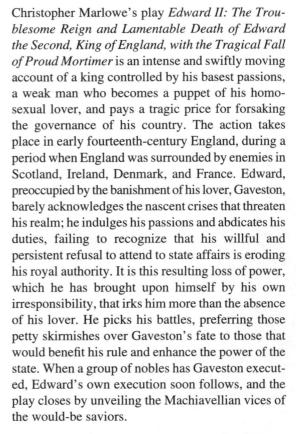

played in 1593 or 1594, *Edward II* was printed in 1594. It has played sporadically throughout the twentieth century, usually to audiences surprised by the power of a work by one of Shakespeare's contemporaries.

AUTHOR BIOGRAPHY

Born in the same year as William Shakespeare, 1564, Christopher Marlowe was the son of an affluent shoemaker in Canterbury. Like Shakespeare, Marlowe eventually migrated to London, where he became a member of an erudite social circle that included Sir Walter Raleigh, Thomas Kyd, and others; these men were regarded as freethinkers, in part because they endorsed the new and controversial "scientific" thinking. Marlowe spent six years as a Cambridge scholar, reveling in subjects such as rhetoric, logic, and philosophy; he was especially drawn to the works of Aristotle, which he approached not from the religious perspective of most of his peers, but from a more philosophical and literary angle. Marlowe probably attended numerous university productions of comedies, satires, and tragedies, many of which dealt with the lives of scholars. His own plays tended toward the philosophic, probing the limits of human knowledge and power and exploring the implications of surpassing those limits. A poetic innovator, he set a new standard for blank verse, creating lines that are lyrical, cadenced, and intellectually taut. His inclination toward the abstract and his broad academic background made his work stand in sharp contrast to that of the young Shakespeare, whose plays and poetry demonstrate a keener interest in questions of human behavior and psychology and greater familiarity with people from all walks of life. Because Marlowe's plays were in the theaters before Shakespeare's, and because he was breaking new ground in poetics, Marlowe had a profound influence on his now more famous peer; Marlowe, however, did benefit from seeing Shakespeare's early plays.

The Elizabethan period of England was a time of fervid Puritanism, and Catholics were actively persecuted. Cambridge, where Marlowe studied, produced Protestant clerics, men who would go on to take positions of power and prestige in the Protestant church. Just before taking his Master's degree, however, he mysteriously disappeared. It was rumored that he had gone to a Catholic center at Rheims to convert, secretly, to Catholicism. Upon

Marlowe's return, however, and despite the rumors, he quickly obtained the queen's endorsement for his degree. Her allusion to "matters touching the benefit of his country" indicate that he may have been spying on catholic converts for his queen, merely pretending to practice heresy; it is speculated that she employed him in her extensive espionage network on several other intelligence-gathering missions too. Other aspects of his life are equally shadowy, partly because of an attempt to defame his character after his death. We can surmise, however, that he was bold, intelligent, witty, argumentative, and irreverent.

At the age of twenty-nine, while awaiting trial for a charge of atheism, Marlowe was stabbed in the forehead by a companion. His murderer was pardoned a mere month after the event. There has been much speculation over the nature of the argument that led to his death and whether his murder was planned and politically motivated. Whatever its genesis, his early demise cut down a promising talent whose genius had barely begun to flower.

PLOT SUMMARY

Act I, scene i

The first scene opens with Gaveston reading a letter from Edward II, newly crowned sovereign of England after the death of Edward I. Gaveston had been banished from court because of his corrupting influence on the young prince Edward. Now, with the elder Edward out of the way, Edward II is inviting Gaveston to return and share the kingdom with him. In a few quick lines, Gaveston's soliloquy makes clear the homosexual nature of their relationship ("take me in thy arms") as well as the theme of power that runs throughout the play. Gaveston muses about surrounding himself and the king with all manner of pleasure-seekers: "Wanton poets, pleasant wits," and "men like satyrs" who for sport might hunt down a "lovely boy" as they would a deer. When the king and his entourage enter, Gaveston steps aside to overhear their conversation.

What he hears displeases him. Lancaster and Mortimer, two noble lords, are counseling the king to break off his relations with Gaveston and attend to affairs of state. Edward bristles at their boldness, and his brother Kent warns them that the king would be within his right to behead them for their impertinence. They exit with a final threat to take up arms

Christopher Marlowe

against Edward's "base minion." Gaveston steps forth and Edward professes that he would rather "the sea o'erwhelm [his] land" than suffer another separation from his lover. He confers several lofty titles on his lover, all of them in excess of Gaveston's station.

Now enters the Bishop of Coventry, the one directly responsible for Gaveston's banishment. Edward punishes the Bishop with exile, first performing a perverse baptism on him by stripping of his holy vestments and having him dumped into the channel. Gaveston leaves to take over the ruined man's worldly goods as the Bishop is transported to the tower.

Act I, scenes ii & iii

The Mortimers, Warwick, and Lancaster bemoan the "reign" of Gaveston. They are joined by the Bishop of Canterbury, who sees Edward's treatment of the Bishop of Coventry as violence against the Church itself. Gaveston learns of their plan to take up arms, which he announces to Kent

Act I, scene iv

In this longest scene of the play, Edward commits further consecrations against the kingship by seating Gaveston in the Chair Royal, the queen's chair. This incites to nobles to exile Gaveston once again, and he is taken away, along with the Earl of Kent. The inclusion of the latter clouds the issue somewhat, since Kent has merely acted as a faithful and sober advisor to his brother. The angry lords admonish the astounded king to "rule us better and the realm," but the king is obsessed with his lover, and he once again claims that he would let England "fleet upon the ocean / and wander to the unfrequented Ind[ia]" before he would willingly part with his lover. In a last ditch attempt to sway them, he offers each of the usurpers a new title. Alone again, the king wildly imagines slaughtering priests in revenge, then revises Gaveston's banishment by assigning him the governorship of Ireland, to which border he accompanies him. The queen, Isabella, realizes that being left alone with a mourning husband will not restore him to her, so she attempts to persuade the lords to return Gaveston. The plotters, however, decide that only Gaveston's death can break the spell he holds over their king. They enlist Isabella to pretend that Gaveston is being returned, which will facilitate his murder. The elated and unsuspecting king forgives all and heaps honors upon them as a reward. A renewed calm, as well as a reminder that other great leaders—Alexander, Hercules, and Achilles—were not impaired by their male lovers, persuades the plotters to leave this pair alone. They pronounce themselves ready, however, to rebel again the moment Gaveston flaunts his riches and power in their faces.

Act II, scene i

In this brief scene the innocent niece of the king, muses upon the affections of her avowed lover, Gaveston. She and two king's attendants, Baldock and Spenser, believe that Gaveston loves the young lady.

Act II, scene ii

A quarrelsome Edward refuses to perform his kingly duty and ransom one of his warriors, Mortimer's father, who has been caught by the Scots. The angry lords list the harms done to the realm by Edward's licentiousness: enemies from Ireland, Scotland, and Denmark have made inroads into England, and English garrisons have been routed from France. Edward's few military campaigns have made him a laughing stock. The court is a sham to which foreign countries send no worthy ambassadors. In fact, the state of affairs is so bad that Kent turns against his brother and joins Mortimer.

Alone but for his lover and Baldock and Spencer, Edward promises his niece to Gaveston in marriage.

Act II, scenes iii & iv

Kent is accepted by the rebels and they leave together to attack Gaveston and Edward. The two try to escape, but Isabella betrays them to the arriving nobles. She and Mortimer exchange admiring words, setting the stage for their liaison.

Act II, scene v

Gaveston is captured and is to be executed for the "country's cause." The king sends a message with Arundel begging for one last visit with his lover. Mortimer refuses, diabolically offering to send the lover's head instead. Both Arundel and Pembroke offer to vouch for Gaveston's return, and he is sent to await the king's visit.

Act III, scene i

While waiting for the king's visit, Gaveston is surprised by Warwick, who takes him away to be killed. The king will not see his lover again.

Act III, scene ii

Hugh Spencer senior comes to Edward with 400 men to defend him. For this display of loyalty, Edward confers a title on Spencer junior. The queen enters with bad news from France, where Edward's "slack in homage" has lost him Normandy. Edward blithely dispenses Isabella and their fourteen-year-old son to resolve this, being more interested in Gaveston's fate. Arundel arrives to announce that Gaveston is dead. This has two effects on the King, a decision to punish the nobles through war, and a transfer of his interests to Spencer. At this, the nobles once again overstep their authority and demand the removal of Spencer from "the royal vine." Edward, embracing Spencer, refuses to reply.

Act III, scene iii

The two factions meet in arms and Edward is victorious. He sends the errant nobles to the tower.

Act IV, scenes i through v

Kent proclaims the wrongs of Edward and once again joins Mortimer to meet the Queen and her son in France, where a friendly French lord offers to assist them against Edward. Back in England, the King receives news that his son has succeeded in frustrating the queen's attempts to enlist French support for their cause against him. The queen and her entourage return to England and succeed in routing King Edward, who flees for Ireland. Kent notices that Mortimer and Isabella "do kiss while they conspire," and so once again he switches sentiments; he again questions Mortimer's right to raise arms against his lawful king. The queen, perhaps sincerely, expresses sorrow for her husband.

Act IV, scene vi

The king has taken refuge at a monastery in northern England, where he is caught by Leicester. Edward resigns himself to his fate as he takes his leave of his remaining loyal nobles. A mower, the man who betrayed the king's presence at the abbey, asks for payment for his services as the scene ends.

Act V, scene i

The king is deposed, but his crown is needed to instate the new king. Edward at first refuses to give it up, knowing that it will effectively belong to Mortimer, not to his young son, who will be overruled by the powerful nobles. However, he finally relents, sending along with the crown a handkerchief, wet with his tears, to be given to his estranged wife. Berkeley comes to take him away, doing so with quiet respect for the broken king.

Act V, scene ii

Now Mortimer "makes Fortune's wheel turn as he please," as he controls the kingdom through the prince. Mortimer is content to let Edward II rot in his cell, but Isabella demands his death, so that she will not have to worry about the possibility of revenge. Mortimer complies, adding to the order that the king is to be treated harshly on his trip. The dissembling queen asks for her kind thoughts to be conveyed to her husband. Kent recognizes the grim situation and attempts to take the prince away, but Mortimer intercedes and carries Levune (the prince) off by force. Kent departs to attempt a rescue of the king.

Act V, scene iii

In a stinking dungeon, the guards shave off the king's beard with puddle water, a final insult against his sovereign person. Kent arrives and demands the king's release, saying "Oh miserable is that commonweal where lords / Keep courts, and kings are locked in prison!" Kent is bound and taken away.

Act V, scene iv

Mortimer hires Lightborn to commit the regicide (the murder of a king), planning to place the blame on the other lords if necessary. The newly crowned king enters and discovers that he will not be allowed to rule: Mortimer forces him to sentence his own uncle (Kent) to death. The queen offers to take her son hunting, to take his mind off of his sorrow.

Act V, scenes v & vi

Lightborn has the guards make ready a red-hot spit while he woos his victim into trust. Finally, the king's screams indicate that he has been impaled upon the instrument. (In Holinshed's account, the spit was thrust into the king's anus, in vicious contempt for his sexual proclivities. The guards, Matrevis and Gurney, kill Lightborn and toss his body in the moat; they carry the king's body to Mortimer. But by the time they arrive at the castle, Gurney has fled. Matrevis warns that Gurney may betray Mortimer. The queen enters to report that the young king is outraged and is busy planning retribution. The queen begs her son more urgently for mercy on Mortimer than she did for her king, but Mortimer accepts his fate—fortune's wheel simply did not stop while he was at the top. Edward III shows himself decisive and fair; he sends his mother to the tower to await a trial and orders Mortimer beheaded. When Mortimer's severed head is presented, the king orders a proper burial for his father.

CHARACTERS

Archbishop of Canterbury

The Archbishop is moved to act upon the king's immoral behavior when Edward deposes the Bishop of Coventry, sends him to the Tower, and then turns over his lands to Gaveston. He considers Edward's acts to be a form of violence against the Church itself.

Robert Baldock

Baldock is scholar who read to the king's niece when she was young and serves her.

Beaumont

A servant to King Edward.

Sir Thomas Berkeley

Berkeley is made to take the king from the abbey to his own castle. He does not keep him long,

for Mortimer has the king moved to jail, where Matrevis and Gurney are his guards.

Bishop of Coventry

It is the Bishop of Coventry who pens the order banishing Gaveston the second time, and for this he is shamefully stripped of his symbolic gown and sent to die in the Tower by Edward II.

Bishop of Winchester

The Bishop of Winchester comes to Neath Abbey in Northern England where Edward has sought refuge; his mission is to carry back the crown to Mortimer. He tells the king that "it is for England's good."

Piers de Gaveston, Earl of Cornwall

The historical Gaveston's father had loyally served Edward I, so Gaveston was, at an early age, consigned as companion to the young Prince of Wales (Edward II). It is generally believed that Gaveston was Edward's lover. When Edward I learned of Gaveston's corrupting influence, the king banished Gaveston. However, after the king's death, Edward II recalled him. Now Gaveston added insolence to depravity, accepting titles from the king far beyond his lowborn social status and influencing the king's haphazard administration of the realm. Marlowe presents a Gaveston of unctuous deceit and depravity. He dreams of turning the court into a sybaritic playland filled with "men like satyrs grazing on the lawns." He nearly succeeds in making his dream a reality, a state of affairs that infuriates the nobility. They force Edward II to banish him once again; but they soon relent and he is recalled. He secretly hides and listens in to the noble's conversations, a physical posture symbolic of his presumptuous, unwelcome, and inappropriate status in court. He relishes the idea of destroying those of whom he is envious, urging the king to banish Mortimer to the tower for daring to question the king's refusal to ransom Mortimer senior, taken hostage by the Scots. Arrogant and spiteful while in command of his king, he wheedles and begs when the tables are turned and he has been captured. His death seems an expedient and necessary action to save the king and kingdom.

Earl of March

See Roger Mortimer

King Edward, II

The historical Edward took the throne at the age of twenty-three and managed to hold it through twenty years of intrigue, intoxication, and ineptitude. He was the pawn of his advisors, Piers Gaveston and Hugh Despenser. Reputedly he was Gaveston's lover as well. His French queen, Isabella, along with her lover, Roger Mortimer, successfully deposed him in 1327, whereupon they locked him in a cold cell in Gloucester Castle, hoping he would die there of disease. Some evidence points to the possibility that in 1328 he was murdered there. In Marlowe's play, which collapses more than twenty years of his reign into a matter of days, Edward is self indulgent, a playboy with little aptitude for or interest in the governance of his country. He reveals his misguided priorities when he says he'd ''sooner the sea o'erwhelm my land / Than bear the ship that shall transport [Gaveston] hence.'' He never seems to comprehend the nobles's accusation that he has abandoned the country for his lover. It is not the king's homosexuality that bothers the nobles, but his neglect of the realm and his heaping of honors on this lowborn, manipulative man. When the nobles murder Gaveston, Edward merely transfers his interests to a new minion, Spenser. Marlowe's Edward earns no measure of respect until his imprisonment, when he recognizes what he has lost in losing the kingship. Although he fails to repent or to acknowledge the impact his folly has had on his country, he does become more human, vulnerable, and therefore a more sympathetic character; standing in the filth and mire of a cold dungeon, he asks a messenger to ''Tell Isabella the queen, I looked not thus / When for her sake I ran at tilt in France.'' He becomes no longer a wicked figure, but a pitiable one, one who seems incapable of performing the duty he had inherited. He ends a broken and destroyed man who followed his impetuous heart instead of his sovereign duty.

Prince Edward, III

The young prince does not figure in the play until his father is imprisoned. At that point he shows his filial loyalty by disobeying his mother (who is French and seeks the English throne) and bribing the French king not to take up her cause by warring with England. In this he is successful. However, he cannot prevent his father's ultimate fate, and at the tender age of fourteen he ascends to the throne. At first he allows himself to be controlled completely

MEDIA ADAPTATIONS

- British director Derek Jarman produced a film called *Eaward II* in the United Kingdom in 1991 (it is available on VHS video). Jarman uses Marlowe's text as a springboard for a gay liberation manifesto, taking lines from Marlowe, heightening the homosexual nature of the king's love interest, and encasing it in a modern context. The screenplay, with photos from the film, was published by Jarman and Malcolm Sutherland in 1991 for the Trinity Press, Worcester, under the title *Queer Edward II*.

by Mortimer. He accepts his father's overthrow, because he recognizes his father's faults. But when his innocent uncle Kent is also executed by Mortimer, the young king's resolve is galvanized—he asserts his power and, by the end of the play, shows himself poised to recover his kingship. Most importantly, he proves that his reign will differ from his father's because he won't allow his heart to betray his kingly obligations. He sends his mother to the Tower to await a proper trial, telling her that ''If you be guilty, though I be your son, / Think not to find me slack or pitiful.'' He has the right balance of heart and leadership, holding a straight course between personal and public demands.

Edmund Fitzalan, Earl of Arundel

Fitzalan, the Earl of Arundel remains loyal to the king. He is the messenger who asks if Edward may see Gaveston before he is executed. With the denial of that request, he offers to take Gaveston in his own trust, a guarantee to offer up himself if Gaveston escapes. Although Arundel is honorable, the rebel nobles decide to put Pembroke, one of their own, in charge instead.

Guards

These guards at Killingworth Castle, Sir John Matrevis and Thomas Gurney, wash the king with puddle water and shave off his beard. After Lightborn murders the king, they murder Lightborn and throw him into the moat.

Henry, Earl of Leicester

Brother to Lancaster, Leicester attends the king in his exile, where he attempts to assuage Edward's grief and fear by telling him to imagine he is in his own court. When the Bishop of Winchester arrives, Leicester advises the king to go ahead and give up the crown, so that young Edward will not be hurt. He is trusted by the king and by Mortimer.

Levune

See Prince Edward III

Isabella

Isabella, daughter of the King of France and wife of Edward II, plays a small but vicious role in her husband's destruction. At first audiences sympathize with her because Edward abandons her for Gaveston, and she seems genuinely to mourn the loss of his attentions, saying ''Witness this heart that sighing for thee breaks.'' This lack of faith in female loyalty comes straight from Holinshed's *Chronicles* and represents standard assumptions during the Renaissance about the fickle nature of women. She is accused the moment she comes on stage of being in love with Mortimer, and indeed, it comes out that they ''kiss as they conspire.'' She begs her son to spare Mortimer with more sincerity than she had shown when asking Mortimer for mercy toward her husband.

Sir John, of Hainault

A French noble who hosts the queen when she goes to France to garner support for Mortimer against King Edward.

Kent

Brother of Edward II, Kent offers sage advice to his errant sibling and provides a weathervane for the audience's sympathies. At first he is offended by the noble's questioning of his brother's command, but he soon finds himself in league with them because he cannot abide Edward's self-indulgence. Kent remains on the outside of Mortimer's ring, however, and when he sees how his brother is treated by the vengeful Mortimer, he attempts to rescue Edward. Kent, the audience's representative in the play, recognizes that political expediency has given way to vile revenge. Mortimer, for the convenience of having him out of the way, foolishly orders Kent executed—a serious political mistake given that Kent had the trust of the new king and would have made an excellent advisor.

Hugh Le Despenser, Junior

Spenser is a lesser lord who serves Gaveston until Gaveston is banished. Edward transfers his attention to Spenser after Gaveston's death. Spenser encourages the king to stand up to the nobles.

Hugh Le Despenser, Senior

Spenser arrives in the nick of time with four hundred bowmen to defend Edward against Mortimer.

Lightborn

The paid assassin who murders Edward II. He in turn is murdered and thrown into the moat to cover up the king's murder. His name is a pun on Lucifer (''Luc'' being a Latin root word for ''light''), and he represents pure evil. His name can also be understood literally as someone of low birth, perhaps someone who simply does not comprehend the intricacies of court, but can be employed to carry out its evil acts because he does not have the sense nor the inclination to question them. It is the lower-born men who are forced to commit the foul deeds designed by higher-born, more powerful men.

Roger Mortimer

The elder Mortimer, uncle of Mortimer junior, does not appear in the play except briefly in the opening scenes. Nonetheless, he figures in the plot when he is taken hostage by the Scots. Edward, ignoring duty and honor, refuses to rescue him, thus setting off a series of events that will lead to Edward's deposition.

Roger Mortimer, the younger

The historical Roger Mortimer began his association with Edward II honorably enough as a solider in the Scottish wars of 1306-1307. He acquitted himself admirably and earned an assignment in Ireland with the rank of lieutenant. However, he was disturbed by the manipulation of Edward II by Gaveston and the Despensers; thus he joined with the other barons who attempted to oust them. He was captured, then escaped, and then become the paramour of Queen Isabella, who shared his disgust with her dissolute husband. Together they succeeded in deposing the king in 1327. However, the young Edward III, whom Mortimer aided to the throne, chose to eliminate Mortimer's controlling influence by having the rebel arrested and then hanged in 1330. The character of Roger Mortimer retains all of this material, with an added twist of Machiavellian excess. At his death, he accepts that the wheel of fortune, which he had ridden to its highest point, was now taking him back down.

Nobles

These noblemen, Guy Earl of Warwick, Thomas Earl of Lancaster, and Aymer de Valence, Earl of Pembroke, join with Mortimer to remove Gaveston from court, by force. Of them, Pembroke is seen as most trustworthy and honorable.

TOPICS FOR FURTHER STUDY

- What consequences should there be for a sovereign who abandons his duties for personal pleasures?

- Contrast the rise and fall of Mortimer with the fall of King Edward II.

- Research the role of pageantry in Elizabethan England. How does Edward's interest in pageantry compare with Queen Elizabeth's?

- William Shakespeare wrote *Richard III* about a year after Christopher Marlowe's *Edward II* was first performed. Look for parallels between the two plays that indicate ways in which Shakespeare may have been influenced by Marlowe. Pay special attention to the structure of the plays, their use of contrasting characters, for example, and speeches.

THEMES

Politics: Machiavellian Style

In Elizabethan England, Niccolo Machiavelli's *Il Principe* (*The Prince*, 1505) was considered a treatise on the science of evil statesmanship because it outlined how a cunning tyrant could, through brutal and forceful measures, take and maintain control over a region and a people. In fact, it seemed a veritable handbook for tyranny, with its exhortation that "It is necessary for a prince wishing to hold his own to know how to do wrong, and to make use of it or not according to necessity." Although *The Prince* advocates morality in a prince, it also urges the ambitious prince to use whatever means necessary to keep the state intact, and that could mean resorting to evil behavior, supposedly in the name of good. Use of force is an art, the most important one the prince has at his disposal: "A prince ought to have no other aim or thought . . . than war and its rules and discipline; for this is the sole art that

belongs to him who rules." Marlowe's *Edward II* explores two aspects of Machiavelli's theory: the misuse of power, and the neglect of power. Edward breaks a Machiavellian cardinal rule when he lets go the royal reins in order to indulge his private desires; *The Prince* warns, "When princes have thought more of ease than of arms, they have lost their states." Edward abdicates his responsibility as head of state, and he pays a dear price for it because the nobles do not tolerate his neglect of power. Mortimer, on the other hand, does not let love interfere with his quest for power; in fact, his love for Isabella serves his larger purpose to take over the state. Thus, at first he seems the epitome of Machiavellian leadership because he does not shirk at using all available means, including executing the king's lover, to restore order to the kingdom. However, Mortimer becomes a Machiavellian despot when he misuses his power in overriding the young King Edward III and executing Kent, who could have become an important and trustworthy advisor to the king. Machiavelli emphasizes that it is always necessary to portray as much "liberty" and fairness as possible, in order to keep the people's trust. Mortimer betrays this trust by stepping beyond the line of decency and political expediency, for his murder of Kent alienates him from the young king, who decides to gather forces against him.

Duty and Responsibility

Edward's preoccupation with Gaveston would not be a matter of concern to the nobles if it did not threaten the state. It is Edward's lack of interest in pressing matters, such as France's takeover of Normandy and the battle in Scotland, that drives them to the treasonable point of questioning their king. Edward's first order of business as king seems to have been to mail a letter to Gaveston, releasing him from banishment and offering to share the kingdom with him. This act of selfish interest would have been harmless in itself, but Mortimer junior and senior had sworn to Edward I on his deathbed to prevent the return of Gaveston at any cost. The dying king knew that his son's plaything would prevent him from ruling England properly. The titles Edward bestows on his lover shock even Kent, who says ''Brother, the least of these may well suffice / For one of greater birth than Gaveston.'' Edward admits that he cares for nothing but Gaveston, and when the nobles force him to sign a new banishment order, he tries to bribe them with lands and titles, desiring only to hold back ''some nook or corner . . . to frolic with [his] dearest Gaveston.'' He is over-liberal in all of his gifts, not using them strategically to advance the state, but squandering them drunkenly. This lavishness and his constant reveling run the treasury dry, putting the entire country at risk, for he will not be able to conscript, feed, and arm a fighting force without money. Twice he acknowledges, using the same metaphor, that he'd rather England were overwhelmed by the sea than give up his minion; his carelessness nearly drowns his realm. Because of his behavior, honored peers and ambassadors have left his court, and his enemies in Scotland, France, Denmark, and Ireland have taken advantage of his weakness to make inroads into his territory.

STYLE

Blank Verse

Blank verse, unrhymed lines with a measured rhythm, was not invented by Christopher Marlowe,

but he is credited with having instituted its use in English drama. The rhythm usually takes the form of iambic pentameter, ten syllables with the accent falling on every other syllable. Marlowe's blank verse demonstrates how the measure can be varied, using slight variations in accenting or in the placement of pauses (*caesura*) to retain the freshness of normal speech, while maintaining the formality of poetry. Because of its great flexibility, it is a medium that lends itself perfectly to the expression of natural sentences: ''Here, take my crown, the life of Edward too, / Two kings in England cannot reign at once.'' Although balanced by the rhythm, these two lines also contain the spontaneity of unrehearsed speech. In the hands of Shakespeare, the same form became even more elastic: ''For God's sake, let us sit upon the ground / And tell sad stories of the deaths of kings . . .'' (*Richard II*). Marlowe freed dramatic lyrics from the constraints of rhyming lines, thus paving the way for further lyric innovations. By taking greater liberties with the stresses but holding to the overall rhythm of iambic pentameter, Shakespeare produced his psychologically realistic plays, as he let his characters express even more realistic utterances than Marlowe was able to achieve.

Imagery

The images conveyed in the language of a play usually suggest or subtly foreshadow the general themes of the play. Also, whether it's purely linguistic or in the form of actual items on stage, imagery can serve to remind the audience of the settings and paraphernalia that accompany a person's status. Images of the external marks of status appear over and over again throughout *Edward II,* such as the crown, battle ensigns (flags), ceremonial robes, jewelry, hats, and so on. In many cases, the intended function of these items is perverted by the king, in his mania for entertainment and self-indulgence. For example, when the Bishop of Coventry angers him for having signed the order banishing Gaveston from court the first time, Edward punishes the holy man by stripping away his vestments. A priest's vestments hold symbolic importance, and to lay hands upon them is a form of sacrilege that to the Bishop of Canterbury—as well as Elizabethan audiences—represents an act of violence against the Church itself. This scene is essentially repeated with Edward as the victim at the end of the play when he is dressed in tatters in the dungeon, stripped of his crown. He tells Lightborn to convey a message to Isabella saying that he "looked not thus" when he "ran at tilt in France / And there unhorsed the Duke of Cleremont." His appearance is an integral part of his status. The tournament was a popular Renaissance pageant where the players dressed in their finest to perform mock battles with each other. Renaissance audiences were particularly attuned to the differences between real war and play war, both of which required the players to dress up. That Edward was willing to "undress" a priest marks him as dangerously irreverent. He is also depicted as overly concerned with pageants and show. His nobles complain that he only once went to battle, at the Battle of Bannockburn, and there he was so garishly dressed that he made himself a laughingstock. Significantly, he lost the battle. His attention to show, rather than substance, led him to ruin. In another case, he asks the nobles to tell him what "device" or design they have put on their ensigns, or battle flags. Each of the nobles in turn describes a scene that can be read as a symbolical threat to the king, and one of their devices contains the Latin phrase *Undique mors est,* which means "surrounded by death." Edward is thus surrounded by subtle visual images that symbolize the danger of his own obsession with image.

HISTORICAL CONTEXT

The Reigns of Edward I & II

The historical Edward I (1239-1307) was an effective king, although he made excessive demands on Wales, Scotland, and Ireland. He began the process of building an administration capable of taxing the people through a body called the Commons, adjunct to the Great Council (the king's advisors). The Commons consisted of locally elected representatives, who would be more inclined to collect much-needed taxes for the king if they had loyalties both to the throne and to their constituents. It would take another 500 years for this body to take on the democratic form of representation it has today. The Commons also served as a funnel for petitions requesting national statutes; this process resulted in the growing body of laws that steadily eroded the jurisdiction and power of the baronry and other local landowners and began the scaffolding of

nationalism. The final blow to the nobility would be an act that made illegal the conscription of armed forces by any one other than the king himself.

Edward II was apparently as dissolute as Marlowe's play presents him. He lost the faith of the nobles and was imprisoned and probably murdered by them. He lost Normandy to France and his defeat at Bannockburn led inexorably to Scottish Independence. Edward II's deposition, at the hands of his wife and her lover Roger Mortimer, constituted the first deposition of a king since the instatement of William the Conqueror in 1066, but was in line with the slow path toward democracy begun by Edward I. The kingship was no longer seen as inviolable; a precedent was thus set for questioning the king's moral worth, and for taking steps against a king deemed unworthy.

Scottish War of Independence— Bannockburn, 1314

In Marlowe's play, the only reference to Bannockburn comes in Act II, scene ii, when Lancaster mocks King Edward with a gibing song about his defeat there in 1314. Historically, the defeat was devastating for England because it led to the end of its rule of Scotland fourteen years later. In a way, Edward had no business losing the battle. He arrived with 16,000 men and a twenty-mile supply line. Robert the Bruce had only a band of 6,500 desperate but clever men. Edward had superior forces and armaments, but he lacked the drive of Robert the Bruce, a national hero in Scotland to this day. The immediate object of the battle was to assist the English-held Stirling Castle which was under siege by the Scots. English governor Philip Mowbray was about to surrender when Edward arrived. Edward made some strategic mistakes and led his men into a trap, a bog-filled area that was difficult to maneuver in. A handful of Scots were then able to herd them into a nearby river and slaughter them. Edward called a retreat that was so panicked that many English soldiers were shot by their own bowmen who couldn't tell who they were firing at. Edward and 500 men fled to Stirling Castle, only to be rebuffed by Mowbrey, who foresaw that Robert would win. Edward headed elsewhere and ultimately returned home, leaving behind scores of dead, prisoners and hostages, plus a fortune's worth of equipment. It was a great triumph for the Scots and a devastating blow to Edward's military credibility.

COMPARE & CONTRAST

- **14th century:** Homosexuality was a fairly common practice in the upper-classes and among courtiers. However, sodomy was officially considered anti-Christian and was punishable by law.

  16th century: Homosexuality was not openly tolerated in Elizabeth's time, although it was common at the university and elsewhere. The many derogatory terms—sodomite, buggerer, and so on—attest to the negative stigma homosexual activity had in numerous circles of society; and, as in the 14th century, sodomy was punishable by fines, arrest, and placement in the pillory. The act of sodomy was widely considered a vile import from the continent, specifically from Turkey and Italy.

  Today: More tolerant values tend to prevail in today's culture. A few states retain laws against sodomy, and though they are rarely enforced, they represent sites of legal and moral controversy for many people. Those who believe that society has progressed beyond such official intolerance and prejudice feel that these laws should be struck down; they also argue that existing laws and rights should be amended to explicitly protect homosexuals. Others, people who are more conservative and perhaps fearful, assert that such laws, and the moralism behind them, represent a kind of corrective for what they see as a lack of morality and discipline in society.

- **14th century:** The King enjoyed god-like status, and his power was thought to be bestowed by heaven. No one dared question him openly for fear of being accused of treason, the punishment for which was death. It was even unlawful to express the thought that the king might die.

  16th century: Queen Elizabeth I also reigned under this precept, and she acted upon treasonous activities by imprisoning or executing offenders.

  Today: Leaders, of course, are no longer associated with godliness, and it is perfectly legitimate in a democracy like the United State to criticize the president's work (it is somewhat less legitimate, although very popular, to also criticize his life). Threats against a president or other world leader are nevertheless taken very seriously and quickly investigated.

- **14th century:** Kings were expected to be warriors who would defend their territory using all of the means—men, money, arms—at his disposal. It would not be possible to remain king without a show of power, because many nobles could muster enough men, money, and arms to usurp the crown.

  16th century: Queen Elizabeth I had to make use of all of her diplomatic skills to maintain her sovereignty in a world dominated by men. She established a veritable cult of herself in order to make her reign seem inviolable. A master strategist, she also used her wiles to keep a bevy of powerful men loyal to her so that she could count on their armed support against the Spanish Armada, among other enemies.

  Today: Modern leaders are not necessarily expected to participate in wars; the popular belief is that they should use diplomatic and other nonviolent means to avoid such conflicts. However, the taking of military action is still considered a sign of strong leadership.

CRITICAL OVERVIEW

Edward II first opened in 1594, played by the Earl of Pembroke's Men. The next record of its performance indicates that it was played at the Red Bull in 1617 by Queen Elizabeth's acting troupe. The innovative blank verse (unrhymed iambic pentameter) of *Edward II* led Marlowe's contemporary George

WHAT DO I READ NEXT?

- William Shakespeare's play *Richard II* depicts another deposed king who laments his loss of status and power. Written just one year after Marlowe's play, *Richard II* reveals the influence that Marlowe had on his contemporary; notice especially the similarities between the speeches of the two kings as they surrender the crown.

- The Renaissance play *Edward III*—which may have been written by Shakespeare, by Marlowe, or by both (scholars disagree)—takes the story through the next generation, as young Edward III, known as the Confessor, reigns during the Black Plague.

- The 1995 film *Braveheart*, directed by and starring Mel Gibson, portrays the conflict between England and Scotland just prior to the action of *Edward II*. In *Braveheart*, Scottish commoner William Wallace unites Scotland in rebellion against the father of Edward II, Edward I (Longshanks), who demands the ancient right of *Prima Nocta*, the "right" to be the first to sleep with a new bride. The film includes realistic (and gory) depictions of Medieval battle.

- Niccolo Machiavelli's *Il Principe* (*The Prince*, 1505) influenced Marlowe's development of Mortimer's character. It is a work that has been interpreted to suit widely differing values, and it makes fascinating reading.

Peele to dub Marlowe the "Muse's darling." When Puritanism closed the theaters in 1642, Marlowe's plays were all but forgotten, although his reputation as a poet (for *Hero and Leander*) survived. Not even Marlowe's *Dr. Faustus* earned the attention of dramatists for two centuries. Marlowe the man, however, captured the interest of the nineteenth-century Romantics, who saw him as the unfettered genius of the Renaissance, partly because of the perpetuated myth that he had died in a brawl. It would not be until an American discovered the identity of Marlowe's murderer (Ingram Frizer) and the account of the crime, that Marlowe's reputation would be even partially restored. Nowhere near as popular as the Shakespeare histories, *Edward II* has appeared sporadically at theaters in England and the United States throughout the early twentieth century. Bertold Brecht produced his own inimitable Marxist interpretation of the play in 1924, soon to be followed by other reinterpretations of Western canonical plays with the typical Brechtian spin. Brecht's *Edward II* features a pared-down text, which focuses on the conflict between selfish interests and political obligations, and several ballads, a Brecht dramatic signature; a 1987 restaging of Brecht's version in Chicago was appreciated for its

social commentary, with its emphasis on "the common suffering," and its sparse staging. An especially brilliant performance in the summer of 1958 in London brought wide acclaim and a rekindled interest in the play. It reached American theaters the same year, when it played at the Theatre de Lys in New York, directed by Toby Robertson. Then, in 1969, Ian McKellan's Edward in a production at the Edinburgh International Festival elicited rave reviews for his portrayal of "this weakest of kings" because, according to Clive Barnes's *New York Times* review, Mr. McKellan "induces pity and understanding . . . even though he never once plays for our sympathy." The play lay dormant in America for some time, even though director John Houseman recognized that the relaxation of sexual mores of the 1970s would enable him to de-emphasize the play's moral implications and focus on it's intense portrayal of psychological deterioration. In 1974 Houseman said that "With the fading of sexual inhibitions of our contemporary stage, it has become possible to realize a production [of *Edward II*] that I have been dreaming of for more than a dozen years." Although Houseman never realized this dream, a 1992 production at the Yale Repertory Theatre did create a play that focuses not on "Edward's sexual orientation, but his lack of political and social discrimination in choosing the distinctly foreign and unworthy Gaveston.'' The success of the production led the *New Yorker* reviewer, Randall Louis Anderson, to predict that ''the decade of *Edward II* is now upon us.'' Perhaps this play about intense and selfish personal gratification at the expense of probity in the affairs of state, with its depiction of the brutal consequences that await a leader when he or she tries to evade the demands of an indignant group of officials, will soon find an audience in the United States, where in 1998 the president was impeached for lying under oath to avoid the legal consequences of covering up his illicit liaisons.

CRITICISM

Carole Hamilton

Hamilton is a Humanities teacher at Cary Academy, an innovative private school in Cary, North Carolina. In this essay, she discusses Marlowe's use of a particular image as the structuring device that organizes the play's action.

The details of a play's descriptive lines can often seem unrelated to the story being told; they are thus all too easy to dismiss as curious but rather outdated examples of the parlance of the day. Renaissance writers like Marlowe were well versed in the themes and stories of classical writers such as Ovid, Virgil, and Homer; it is not surprising then that the names of Greek and Roman gods and goddesses appear in their literary works. For example, in *Edward II,* Edward speaks of his heart beating like ''Cyclop's hammer'' and Gaveston is likened to Phaeton, who was unable to control his father's chariot and thus serves to intimate that Gaveston will not be able to control the chaos he causes. Certain images and allusions, however, carry more significance than others, and uncracking the code of these images can cast a revealing light on the entire play.

In *Edward II,* images of pageants and masques, jousts and tournaments, sports and pleasures abound; this is apt given that one of the play's themes is Edward's excessive fondness for entertainment and regalia at the expense of statecraft. The first pageant image, however, occurs oddly out of context, before we know of Edward's tastes. It comes at the very beginning of the play, when Gaveston receives a

letter from Edward inviting him to come and share his realm. Gaveston is delighted and begins to daydream about the kinds of court entertainment— comedies and Italian masques—he will plan for his king. One game he describes in detail, with a great deal of relish. He envisions ''men like satyrs'' who lounge about the palace lawns watching a young boy adorned in pearls and hiding his genitals with a laurel branch. This young boy he likens to Actaeon, a character from Ovid's *Metamorphosis* who is turned into a hart (deer) as punishment for having seen Diana bathing. In Gaveston's daydream the young-man-cum-hart is brought down by ''yelping hounds'' and seems to die. Gaveston is quite pleased with his imagined entertainment, for ''such things as these best please his majesty.'' His gruesome vision is interrupted by the arrival of the King, Mortimer, and the lords, and is never alluded to again. However, the brief image has set the scene for the action of the play to come, for it will be the king himself who will be brought to ground while he frolics in foolish games on the palace grounds.

Before the king is set upon, however, another man is made prey to the nobles. The nobles have Gaveston banished, but when they realize that he might raise an army in Ireland, they invite him back so that they can ambush him. It is an unfair hunt, one in which the prey does not know the rules of the game and blindly steps into a trap. While the king and nobles await Gaveston's return, Edward is in a jolly mood and the nobles are feeling more at ease with him than ever before. To bide the time, he inquires of them what device, or flag, they have designed for their battle insignia. To the king, the visible signs of status are more important than the reality. According to David Zucker, ''His idea of royal dignity rests exclusively on such forms, which for him define what he is, both as a private and as public man.'' The king listens as the two nobles relate their designs. Mortimer's, depicting a ''canker'' climbing the bark of a tree in which an eagle perches, clearly corresponds to his usurping actions against the king (the eagle is a common symbol for a king). Lancaster admits that his is ''more obscure.'' On his flag, a flying fish ''takes the air'' and is brought down by a fowl. Lancaster's also bears the Latin motto *Undique mors est,* which translates to ''death is on all sides''; his device portrays a creature leaving its natural element, water in this case, and being seized by a predator it would not normally encounter. Hearing of these symbolically threatening images, the king angrily confronts the two lords for their impertinence; he sees the threat in

A London production of Marlowe's play, depicting King Edward (Ian McKellan) with the object of his affection, Piers de Gaveston

their symbolic representations, but he fails to respond to them on anything more than a superficial level. It will not be by granting titles to these men that their concerns will be abated. He will find out later that both images foreshadowed his own end: being set upon by social climbers then hunted and devoured by predators (courtiers) that would not normally threaten a king. Immediately upon Gaveston's return, Mortimer wounds Gaveston in the presence of the king, thus enacting the attacks symbolized on the flags. When Gaveston is next seen on stage, he is running from the nobles, "fly-

ing" to and fro, again enacting the metaphor in the image. Gaveston taunts his pursuers, saying he has escaped their "hot pursuits"; but his last words as they take him captive echo the Latin motto of Lancaster's ensign—he says "And death is all." He encounters his death not in his imagined Elysian palace grounds, but in a trench. The king threatens war, exclaiming that he will not allow them to "appoint their sovereign / His sports, his pleasures, and his company." In other words, he once again focuses not on the substance of the problem but on the surface, because his main concern is that they denied him the right to pursue his private sport. Ironically, he will become their public sport, and the play presents this as a pageant for an Elizabethan audience.

Images and allusions to sport and game abound in this play; this is a staged masque with real-life consequences. When Mortimer escapes to France, he, the queen, and Sir John of Hainault (a French lord) speak of their upcoming confrontation with King Edward as a game. Sir John asks the young prince what he thinks of the "match" and likens it to a game called prisoner's base ("to bid the English king a base"). The scene of their arrival (Act IV, scene v) finds Edward and his cohorts "flying about the stage." Edward moans, "What, was I born to fly and run away?" He acts like the flying fish of Lancaster's insignia. When he escapes to Ireland, Mortimer says of him "he shall be started thence"; the word "started," in hunting terminology, refers to routing a wild animal from its hiding place. Edward has become nothing more than a wild animal being hunted for sport. Even Kent sees the king in this position, albeit with more sympathy: "Unhappy Edward, chased from England's bounds." Edward too casts himself in the position of a caught animal, defeatedly telling Leicester to "rip up this panting breast of mine." The motif of hunting appears overtly when, in Act V, scene iv, Isabella suggests it as a way of taking young Edward's mind off of his uncle's beheading. Poignantly, the young man asks, "and shall my uncle Edmund ride with us?" knowing full well that his uncle would not be going. This scene underscores the human devastation of the nobles' game of hunting a sovereign. Such games can lead to the death of worthy individuals.

In the last Act, Edward draws a direct parallel between himself and the hunted beast, comparing his state to that of the "the forest deer [that] being struck / Runs to an herb that closes up the wounds." Edward, however, cannot obtain the succor of nature, but instead must "rend and tear" his gored lion's flesh, "scorning that the lowly earth / Should drink his blood." He must make of himself a formal sacrifice. Again he likens himself to "a lamb encompassed by wolves" and accuses his jailers of having been "nursed with tiger's milk" and Mortimer of having "tiger's jaws." Following the theme of the hunted animal, Mortimer tells Isabella that they have the "old wolf by the ears." Mortimer torments his prey by sending him from one foul prison to another and commanding that the jailers treat him roughly, as one would an animal. Edward

feels "vexed like a nightly bird / whose sight is loathesome" and asks when Mortimer's appetite "for blood" will be satisfied. Edward has been hunted down like an animal, toyed with mercilessly, stripped of the symbolic crown that made him greater than human, and left to rot in filth; a piece of meat is tossed at him now and again for sustenance. His demise is in some ways a contorted and perverse manifestation of Gaveston's imagined scene of a hunted man turned into prey and brought down by his own courtiers. It is also a tragic reversal of the sport, pageantry, and erotic pleasure-seeking that was Edward's sole interest. He plays the central, sacrificial figure in his final pageant, instead of playing pageant-maker and royal audience, as he would have done.

How might an Elizabethan audience judge this play about the hunting-down of a king? Depicting an act of violation against a monarch bordered on treason in Marlowe's day, because such a depiction would have been seen as, in a way, inviting the questioning Elizabeth herself, and she actively suppressed such "treasonous" acts. In "Marlowe, *Edward II,* and the Cult of Elizabeth," Dennis Kay proposes that "Edward is a negative exemplum of Elizabeth." That is, Edward represented the antithesis of Elizabeth, and his character and the plot represent a kind of extreme "what if" situation: Elizabethans feared that their queen—as a woman—might fall prey to various temptations, like love. Although the play demonstrates the possible outcome of such a situation, the intent was not to incite the audience to "hunt" Elizabeth, but rather to assuage its fears with an exaggerated depiction of her opposite. She would not allow her love life to interfere with her rule, and her pageants were not the fulsome games of satyrs but legitimate demonstrations of her sovereignty.

Thus, Edward's cruel punishment at the hands of Mortimer serves as a catharsis for the audience, who had real worries about the consequences of Elizabeth's love life but no avenue to express any misgivings (for fear of being charged with treason). Viewing a play such as *Edward II* allowed the public to explore "treasonous" thoughts—thoughts about sovereigns who do not perform their duties and are therefore punished—and to explore these thoughts in the safe, external, performative space of the theatre. Furthermore, the courtiers portrayed in the play exhibit a variety of ways of working out "conflicts of loyalty implicit in the courtier's life"; models range from Spenser, who follows his king to the abyss, to Arundel, who maintains his integrity throughout. These characters would have had their counterparts in Elizabeth's court, and the play offers a means to assess their contributions as well as the justness of their rewards.

Edward II, then, served at least two purposes: it was a window through which one could view and appraise Elizabeth's court, and it was a means to stage a carnivalesque pageant that celebrated Queen Elizabeth's qualities through an intentionally and extreme opposite depiction.

Source: Carole Hamilton, *Drama for Students,* Gale, 1999.

Janet Clare

In this essay, Clare provides an overview of Marlowe's play, contrasting its comparatively sparse narrative style to the playwright's other works, notably Tamburlaine *and* Doctor Faustus.

In *Edward II,* arguably his last play, Marlowe departs from the foreign and exotic landscapes of earlier drama and turns to English history to write a *de casibus* political tragedy. The King's infatuation with the young Piers de Gaveston leads to growing opposition from the barons, spearheaded by the Earls of Lancaster and Warwick, Mortimer, and his nephew, young Mortimer, who becomes the principal antagonist. Resentment of Edward's culpable neglect is fuelled by Gaveston's lowly origins; he is dismissed scornfully by Mortimer as ''one so base and obscure''. Edward greets such hostility with defiance but the barons are powerful enough to coerce the King into agreeing to Gaveston's banishment. However, they then work to have him recalled so that they can discredit Edward further in the eyes of the House of Commons. Gaveston returns and is treated contemptuously by the earls, who blame Edward's infatuation for the deterioration in national morale and in international status. This erosion of royal authority, coupled with the Mortimers' personal grievance at Edward's refusal to ransom their kinsman, leads to threats of rebellion and deposition. Gaveston tries to escape, but is captured and eventually executed. Edward's expression of grief— ''O shall I speak or shall I sigh and die?''—is followed by avowals of revenge and the adoption of a new favourite, Young Spencer. The ambitious Mortimer is imprisoned in the Tower, but he escapes to France and creates a faction around the Queen and her son, the young Prince Edward.

As Mortimer gains ascendancy, Edward's fall appears imminent. The Queen and Mortimer, now lovers, land in England and gather support. Edward

> *EDWARD II* EXPLORES THE TRAGIC EFFECTS OF INFATUATION; IN THIS CONTEXT EDWARD IS TYPICAL OF THE INTEMPERATE MARLOVIAN FIGURE CONSUMED BY AN OVERRIDING DESIRE"

is taken captive and, having relinquished his power and craving death, he is passed between jailers until he arrives at Kenilworth Castle. In a scene of hideous cruelty, he is pierced with a burning spit and murdered by Mortimer's agent, Lightborn. Mortimer's triumph is short-lived: the newly crowned Edward III accuses him of treason and orders his death. The final tableau reveals Mortimer's head proffered to Edward's hearse as the young King dons his mourning robes.

Edward II explores the tragic effects of infatuation; in this context Edward is typical of the intemperate Marlovian figure consumed by an overriding desire. But there is little evidence of nobility in the wilful king who squanders his Kingdom because Gaveston is more important to him: ''Ere my sweet Gaveston shall part from me/This isle shall fleet upon the ocean/And wander to the unfrequented Inde''. The barons, however, do not act from moral outrage, but because they see in Gaveston a threat to their privileges. They loathe Gaveston because of his lowly birth and because of his foreign and effeminate ways. Gaveston, for his part, despises their uncouthness and hereditary privileges: ''Base leaden earls, that glory in your birth,/Go sit at home and eat your tenants' beef''. Edward can only respond to this conflict by helplessly following his self-destructive passion, steadfastly believing that Gaveston loves him ''more than all the world''. Whether this trust is justly founded, or whether Gaveston is motivated by social ambition, remains uncertain.

The play is structured as a series of careers of individuals who scale the summit of their ambition and are destroyed by it. Baldock reminds his friend Spencer that ''all rise to fall''. Spencer's career as the King's favourite does, indeed, mirror (albeit less spectacularly) that of Gaveston. But it is Mortimer

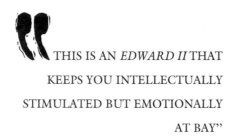

THIS IS AN *EDWARD II* THAT
KEEPS YOU INTELLECTUALLY
STIMULATED BUT EMOTIONALLY
AT BAY"

whose ambitions exemplify most fully the *de casibus* motif. He boasts of his authority which he believes to be unassailable, only to realize that it is unwise to presume upon Fortune's perpetual goodwill: "Base Fortune/now I see that in thy wheel/There is a point to which when men aspire/They tumble headlong down; that point I touched,/and seeing there was no place to mount up higher''.

Marlowe's language in *Edward II* is uncharacteristically lean, pared of most of the evocative imagery and sensuousness of *Tamburlaine* and *Doctor Faustus*. This comparative austerity is relieved by Gaveston's expressions of sensual hedonism and by Edward's pitiful laments, which must have influenced Shakespeare in his portrayal of the deposition of Richard II. In the early scenes Isabella's language too is emotionally affecting, but as she aligns with Mortimer it acquires a plainness and loses the passion which underscored her earlier distress.

Source: Janet Clare, "*Edward II; The Troublesome Reign and Lamentable Death of Edward II*" in the *International Dictionary of Theatre,* Volume 1: *Plays,* edited by Mark Hawkins-Dady, St. James Press, 1992, pp. 213–15.

John Simon

Simon is a well-known drama critic. In this excerpt, he reviews an unconventional production of Edward II *that was staged in 1991. While the critic has mixed feelings regarding the production's heavy emphasis of Marlowe's homosexual themes, he feels that, overall, the new interpretation is worthwhile.*

Back at the Pit, We get Marlowe's *Edward II* staged by Gerard Murphy as camp tragedy. Can you imagine a Charles Ludlam or Charles Busch putting all his extravagance—not to mention overexplicit homosexual acts—into a basically somber, almost unrelievedly grief-filled text? It is an eerie affair, by no means ineffectual, but its sensationalism out-

weighs its tragic dignity. This Edward's historic death—anal impalement with a white-hot poker—is acted out in full gory detail, but it is preceded by Lightborn, the murderer, stripping to the waist and mounting the muckcovered king in his nightgown in a quasicopulation scene, which the script nowise calls for.

On the other hand, the heavy kissing between Edward and his favorite, Piers Gaveston—as well as, later, between Edward and young Spencer—seems appropriate and dramatically helpful. But I cannot condone a floor show by three not very acrobatic young men simulating sex à *trois* by way of a royal entertainment. And though there is some sort of desperate honesty in making every character in the play both physically and morally unprepossessing, if not repellent, it ends up being as unreal and unconvincing as the old Hollywood's overcosmeticized blanket glamour. Thus Ciaran Hinds, as young Mortimer, . . . *Troilus,* Queen Isabella and Lady Margaret are both on the overweight and frumpy side, and so on.

Simon Russell Beale, the RSC's rising star, is uncompelling of face, squat of body, acrid of voice. Yet he is a consummate actor, and his Edward is not lacking in a grating, pitiful humanity. His passion for Grant Thatcher's pretty and effeminate—yet in some ways also boyishly loutish—Gaveston is credible enough, and his pathos as a starved and sleepless prisoner knee-deep in filth is as palpable as any stage can make it. But Beale finally lacks the charisma that would explain his queen's passionate yearning for him despite constant, brutal rejection and the flaunting of his affair with Gaveston. Perhaps the most satisfying performance comes from Callum Dixon as young Prince Edward, who makes the transition from boy to boy-king to full-fledged monarch authentic and compelling.

The other unqualified success here is Ilona Sekacz's score for violin, viola, and cello, some of it live, some of it electronically amplified, which whips up a storm of feelings but is confined to transitions between scenes and never allowed to become a nuisance. There is much to be said for the simple set by Sandy Powell and Paul Minter: a neutral cloth artfully draped over a few poles, and brought to colored life by Wayne Dowdeswell's impassioned lighting. The designers' costumes have an aptly brooding color scheme: mostly black, some gold, Gaveston in white, and, here and there, some sea green flooding the black. But the mixing of exaggerated period elements (e.g., overassertive codpieces further enhanced in some cases with rubbery studs) and contemporary touches (e.g., sneakers for Gaveston) may be too much of a muchness. This is an *Edward II* that keeps you intellectually stimulated but emotionally at bay—almost as if the RSC were performing Brecht's adaptation rather than Marlowe's original.

Source: John Simon, ''London, Part I'' in *New York,* Vol. 24, no. 34, September 2, 1991, pp. 49–50.

S. F. Johnson

In this brief essay, Johnson focuses on the theme of music in Marlowe's play, particularly as it applies to the dialogue.

Gaveston's speech reflects the medieval and Renaissance conception of the power of music, which was thought to be capable of inducing specific psychological effects (see James Hutton, ''Some English Poems in Praise of Music,'' *English Miscellany,* II [1951], 1–63, and the exchange of letter between Hutton and the present author, ''Spenser's *Shepherds' Calendar,*'' *TLS,* March 30 [p. 197], May 11 [p. 293], and Sept. 7 [p. 565], 1951). Gaveston does not wish to retain the poor men who have just sued to enter his service; instead, in order to maintain his power over Edward, he will employ poets and musicians to stir Edward's less kingly desires. The pliancy of Edward accords with his unsympathetic characterization in the first half of the play, and his first ''musical'' image (of the noise of the Cyclops' forge) further rebuffs sympathy, since it serves to express his ignobly passionate harping upon his minion's enforced exile.

Both of these references, however, together with less significant allusions to the drums and trumpets of the battle field (lines 1494, 1526, 1569; xi, 185, 217, 259) and to Pluto's bells (line 1956; xvii, 88), lend added force to Edward's speech just before his murder. He has been characterized increasingly sympathetically since Gaveston's murder and his Queen's seduction. He is no longer the ''pliant king''; one of his keepers remarks. ''He hath a body able to endure More then we can enflict, and therefore now, Let us assaile his minde another while.'' Just as Richard II is at his most sympathetic in the dungeon scene in Shakespeare's play, so Edward II is in Marlowe's; and just as Richard hears ''broken music'' (and moralizes on the topic concord vs. discord, for which there is no parallel in Marlowe's play), so Edward hears the drum beats that ironically realize his own earlier fantasy of the

> THE MUSICAL IMAGES AND ALLUSIONS ARE HARDLY CENTRAL TO THE MEANING AND POWER OF MARLOWE'S PLAY, BUT THEY SERVE TO REINFORCE MORE OBVIOUS ELEMENTS IN ITS STRUCTURE''

Cyclops' forge and grotesquely parody the effects of Gaveston's music. The final irony is that Edward, unlike Richard II, again becomes a ''pliant king'' at the point of death: ''I am too weake and feeble to resist'' (line 2556; xxii, 106).

The musical images and allusions are hardly central to the meaning and power of Marlowe's play, but they serve to reinforce more obvious elements in its structure and are all too likely to be missed by contemporary readers who are unaware of the Elizabethan significance of Gaveston's ''Musitians.''

Source: S. F. Johnson, ''Marlowe's *Edward II*'' in the *Explicator,* Vol. X, no. 8, June, 1952, p. 53.

FURTHER READING

Bredbeck, Gregory W. *Sodomy and Interpretation: Marlowe to Milton,* Cornell University Press, 1991.
>   Explores the history and literary representations of homosexuality in the Renaissance.

Deats, Sara Munson. *Sex, Gender, and Desire in the Plays of Christopher Marlowe,* University of Delaware Press, 1997.
>   Finds instances of role reversals and androgynous characters in Marlowe's plays.

Gill, Roma. ''Christopher Marlowe'' in *Dictionary of Literary Biography,* Volume 62: *Elizabethan Dramatists,* Gale Research, 1987, pp. 212-31.
>   A fairly broad representation of critical theory applied to Marlowe's plays.

Godshalk, W. L. *The Marlovian World Picture,* Mouton, 1974.
>   A standard analysis of Marlowe's plays.

Grantley, Darryll, and Peter Roberts, editors. *Christopher Marlowe and English Renaissance Culture,* Scolar Press, 1996.

Describes the historical context of Marlowe's plays and speculates on aspects of the political cultures that find their way into his plots.

Kay, Dennis. "Marlowe, *Edward II,* and the Cult of Elizabeth," *Early Modern Literary Studies,* Vol. 3, No. 2 (September, 1997): 1-30.
Considers *Edward II* a negative exemplum of Elizabeth's monarchy, and thus a tribute to her style of reign.

Kuriyama, Constance Brown. *Hammer or Anvil: Psychological Patterns in Christopher Marlowe's Plays,* Rutgers University Press, 1980.
Attempts to demonstrate that Marlowe's plays show his awareness of the destructive nature of his own egotism.

Levin, Harry. "Marlowe Today," *The Tulane Drama Review,* Vol. 8, No. 4 (Summer, 1964): 22-31.
Argues that Marlowe's characters, with their intensely personal struggles, are a good fit with the modern *Theatre of the Absurd.*

McAdam, Ian. "*Edward II* and the Illusion of Integrity," *Study of Philology,* Vol. 92 (Spring, 1995): 203-29.
Analyzes 300 years of commentaries on Marlowe and his plays, beginning with his contemporaries and ending with a George Bernard Shaw essay of 1896.

MacLure, Millar, editor. *Christopher Marlowe: The Critical Heritage,* Routledge, 1995.
Three hundred years of commentaries on Marlowe and his plays, beginning with his contemporaries and ending with a George Bernard Shaw essay of 1896.

Meehan, Virginia M. *Christopher Marlowe: Poet and Playwright,* Mouton, 1974.

A study of the aptness and musicality of Marlowe's poetic diction and metaphors.

O'Neill, Judith, editor. *Critics on Marlowe: Readings in Literary Criticism,* George Allen and Unwin, Ltd., 1969.
Three hundred years of commentaries on Marlowe and his plays, beginning with his contemporaries and ending with a George Bernard Shaw essay of 1896.

Pincess, Gerald. *Chistopher Marlowe,* Frederick Ungar Publishing Co., 1975.
Brief biography and analysis of Marlowe's major plays.

Ribner, Irving. *"Edward II": Text and Major Criticism,* the Odyssey Press, 1970.
Includes nine essays on the play, plus the text.

Rowse, A. L. *Christopher Marlowe: His Life and Work,* the Universal Library, 1966.
The famed biographer of William Shakespeare turns his attention to Christopher Marlowe.

Sales, Roger. *Christopher Marlowe,* St. Martin's Press, 1991.
A study of Marlowe's major plays in light of the concept of the "theatre of hell" and the Elizabethan obsession with pageantry.

Thomas, Vivien, and William Tydeman, editors. *Christopher Marlowe: The Plays and Their Sources,* Routledge, 1994.
The three main histories used by Marlowe to compile his play—Holinshed's *Chronicles,* Stow's *Annals,* and Fabyan's *Chronicles*—are generously excerpted.

Zucker, David Hard. *Stage and Image in the Plays of Christopher Marlowe,* University of Salzburg, 1972.
A study of the impact of Marlowe's imagery and stage directions on the meaning of his major plays.

Equus

PETER SHAFFER
1973

Peter Shaffer was inspired to write *Equus* by the chance remark of a friend at the British Broadcasting Corporation (BBC). The friend recounted to Shaffer a news story about a British youth who blinded twenty-six horses in a stable, seemingly without cause. Shaffer never confirmed the event or discovered more of the details, but the story fascinated him, provoking him ''to interpret it in some entirely personal way.'' His dramatic goal, he wrote in a note to the play, was ''to create a mental world in which the deed could be made comprehensible.''

Equus depicts the state of mind of Alan Strang, the imaginative, emotionally-troubled stableboy who serves as the play's protagonist. In relating his themes, Shaffer combines psychological realism with expressionistic theatrical techniques, employing such devices as masks, mime, and dance. The ongoing dialogue between Alan and Dr. Martin Dysart, the boy's analyst, illustrates Shaffer's theme of contrary human impulses toward rationality and irrationality. Curing Alan, making the boy socially acceptable and more ''normal,'' Dysart frets, will at the same time squelch an important spark of passionate creativity in the youth.

Equus, which some critics labeled a ''psychodrama,'' premiered in London at the Old Vic Theatre on July 26, 1973. The production was a huge success, impressing both audiences and critics alike and securing Shaffer's reputation as an important contemporary dramatist. *Equus* had its American

premiere at New York's Plymouth Theatre on October 24, 1974, and later received the Antoinette Perry (Tony) Award, the Outer Critics Circle Award, and the New York Drama Critics Circle Award. The play was adapted into a film in 1977.

AUTHOR BIOGRAPHY

Peter Shaffer and his twin brother Anthony (also a playwright and novelist) were born May 15, 1926, in Liverpool, England. Peter attended St. Paul's School in London, graduating in 1944, near the end of World War II. For the remainder of the war, he was conscripted to work as a coal miner; because a large number of England's adult male workforce were off fighting the war, many labor positions were filled by women, children, and young adults.

After the war Shaffer attended Trinity College, Cambridge, from which he received a degree in 1950. Following graduation he moved to New York City, where he worked in a book store and the New York Public Library. He returned to London in 1954, working for music publishers Bosey & Hawkes. He began writing scripts for radio and television during this period as well as serving as literary critic for the journal *Truth* from 1956-57.

Shaffer's first stage play, *Five Finger Exercise,* was produced in 1958. He followed it with the paired one-acts *The Private Ear* and *The Public Eye* in 1962. In 1963 Shaffer cowrote, with noted stage director Peter Brook (*Marat/Sade*), the screenplay for Brook's film adaptation of William Golding's novel *Lord of the Flies.*

Shaffer's reputation as an accomplished dramatist was secured by the 1964 premiere of his full-length work *Royal Hunt of the Sun: A Play Concerning the Conquest of Peru.* The play—which creatively blends ritual, dance, music, and drama—reenacts the sixteenth-century Spanish conquest, by Francisco Pizarro, of the Incan empire. The Incas dominated the culture of western South America in the fifteenth and sixteenth centuries; the center of their empire lay in what is now Peru, a country founded by Pizarro. Shaffer's plays of subsequent years include the one-act *Black Comedy* (1965), a piece based on a device borrowed from Chinese theatre in which actors pretend to be in total darkness although the stage is lit.

Shaffer's 1970 full-length *The Battle of Shrivings* was widely considered a disappointment, but the playwright followed it with *Equus* (1973), a play that is generally considered his greatest achievement to date. *Equus* received the Antoinette Perry (Tony) Award for best play as well as the New York Drama Critics Circle Award. Shaffer also wrote the screenplay for the film adaptation of *Equus* in 1977.

In 1979, Shaffer produced what is generally considered his best-known work, *Amadeus,* which he has described as ''a fantasia on events in [18th century composer Wolfgang Amadeus] Mozart's life.'' Like *Equus, Amadeus* is a probing exploration of the human psyche, centering on the royal court composer Antonio Salieri and his jealousy of Mozart's seemingly effortless brilliance. Mozart is portrayed as a vulgar, self-centered genius, a sort of prototypical rock star. The play won the 1980 Tony award, and the 1984 film adaptation won Academy Awards for best picture and best screenplay adaptation (for Shaffer's script). Shaffer's plays since *Amadeus* include *Yonadab: The Watcher* (1985) and the popular comedy *Lettice and Lovage* (1987).

With a long-standing reputation for craftsmanship, Shaffer's career is marked by theatrical success and prestigious honors. In addition to his many popular successes in drama, he is a fellow of the Royal Society of Literature, a member of the Dramatists Guild, and was granted the title Commander of the British Empire in 1987.

PLOT SUMMARY

Act I

The play opens on two scenes: Alan Strang fondles the head of a horse, who in turn nuzzles the boy's neck; subsequently, Dr. Martin Dysart addresses a lecture audience about the case of Alan Strang, a troubled boy of seventeen who blinded six horses. Dysart begins his narrative with the visit by his friend Hesther Salomon, a magistrate who managed to persuade the court to put Alan in a psychiatric hospital rather than in prison. As the action on the stage enacts this recollection, Salomon tells the doctor that she feels something very special about the boy. Dysart agrees to see Alan, although he is already overworked.

In their first session, Alan is evasive, singing advertising jingles in response to Dysart's questions. Alan is clearly startled when the psychiatrist coolly responds to the jingles as if Alan were speaking normally. Upon conclusion of the meeting, the boy is reluctant to leave the doctor's office, and, as he is finally ushered out, he makes a point of passing "dangerously close" to Dysart.

Returning to the lecture format, Dysart reveals to his audience that he is suffering nightmares in which he is a ancient priest sacrificing children, on whom he sees the face of Alan. At the same time, however, Dysart feels he has achieved a breakthrough with his patient, who is beginning to open up. Dysart pays a visit to Alan's parents in the hopes of learning something of the boy's background. The father, Frank, is still at work, but his wife Dora informs the doctor that Alan was always captivated by horses, particularly a story about a talking horse called Prince, who could only be ridden by one special boy. Alan also memorized a Biblical passage about horses in the Book of Job; he was particularly taken with the Latin word *Equus.* When Frank returns home, he tells the doctor that he blames Alan's problems on the Biblical passages about the death of Jesus, which Dora read to the boy night after night. Frank shares his belief that religion is only so much "bad sex."

Dysart must discover the reason behind Alan's screams of "Ek!" in the night. Although Alan has grown more communicative, he still resists interviewing, making the doctor answer his own queries for each question Dysart poses. Question follows question, but when Dysart asks Alan directly why he cries out at night, the boy reverts to singing television jingles. Dysart dismisses Alan, and this reverse psychology causes Alan to begin talking about his first experience with a horse. At the beach, a man let Alan join him on his horse and ride as fast as the boy liked. Alan's parents saw him, became worried, and caused him to fall. Alan claims this was the last time he ever rode a horse.

In three unexpected visits, Dysart acquires a great deal of new information. From Dora Strang, he learns about a particularly graphic image of Christ, "loaded down with chains," on his way to crucifixion, which used to hang above Alan's bed. It was torn down by Frank after one of their frequent fights about religion and replaced with a photograph of a horse that pleased Alan immensely. In the second visit, Mr. Dalton, the stable owner, informs Dysart that Alan was introduced to the stables by a young employee of his, Jill Mason. Dalton com-

Peter Shaffer

ments that Alan was always a terrific worker before the blinding incident but that for some time he suspected the boy may have been taking the horses out at night to ride them. Finally, Frank Strang pays Dysart a visit, describing with great difficulty how he once discovered Alan reciting a parody of a Biblical genealogy and then kneeling reverently in front of the photograph of the horse and beating himself with a coat hanger. Frank also reveals that Alan was out with a girl the night he blinded the horses.

In their next conversation, Dysart asks Alan more directly about Jill. The boy calls the doctor "Bloody Nosey Parker!" and in turn asks about Dysart's relationship with his wife, suspecting that the couple never has sex. Startled that Alan so quickly discovered his "area of maximum vulnerability," Dysart orders the boy out of his office. Speaking later with Hesther, Dysart laments his sterile marriage. Hesther reminds Dysart that it is his job to make Alan normal again, but Dysart questions the value of what society views as normal. When Alan next comes before the doctor he is more subdued, and Dysart succeeds in hypnotizing him through a game he calls "Blink." In this state, Alan is persuaded to discuss in detail his ritualistic and ecstatic midnight rides. An expressionistic, theatrical enactment of one of these rides brings the first act to a close.

Act II

In another monologue, Dysart continues to question rhetorically the value of his profession. The speech is interrupted by the entrance of a nurse, who reports that Mrs. Strang has slapped Alan after violently refusing the lunch she brought for him. Dysart confronts Mrs. Strang and orders her to leave. She expresses to the doctor the frustration she feels as a mother, wanting Dysart to understand that what is wrong with Alan is not a result of anything she or Frank did to him. "I only know he was my little Alan," she mourns, "and then the Devil came."

In a subsequent discussion with Dysart, Alan denies anything that he said under hypnosis. At the same time, however, the boy suggests that he would take a "truth drug," to make him reveal things he is withholding.

Talking again with Hesther, Dysart reveals further reluctance to cure Alan, especially if it means denying him the worship which is central to his life. The doctor envies the boy's passion. Alan later apologizes for having denied what he said under hypnosis and acknowledges that he understands why he is in the hospital. Dysart is extremely pleased. Sending for Alan in the middle of the night, he gives the boy a placebo—an aspirin that he tells Alan is a truth drug—and with encouragement Alan begins to speak freely about his relationship with Jill Mason.

Jill started talking to Alan one night after work, commenting how she noticed his beautiful eyes and obvious affection for the horses. She suspected that, like her, Alan found horses, especially their eyes, very sexy. Jill encouraged Alan to go to a pornographic film with her, and in the cinema, seeing a woman naked for the first time, Alan was mesmerized. Suddenly noticing his father in the audience of the film, however, Alan was ashamed to be caught at a "dirty" movie (though he was more shaken to discover his father there). Alan refused to go home with Frank, insisting it was proper to see Jill home first.

On their walk home, Alan made two important discoveries: first, he finally saw his father as man just like any other, and second, he realized he wanted very much to be with Jill, to see her naked and to touch her. Alan eagerly accepted when Jill suggested that they go off together but was disturbed to learn that her destination was the stables.

The young couple undressed, but Alan found himself unable to touch Jill, "hearing" the disapproval of Equus. Furious, Alan ordered Jill out of the stables, took up a pick, and put out the eyes of Dalton's horses.

With the repressed pain of Alan's angry and destructive act now brought to the surface, Dysart feels he can relieve the boy of his nightmares and other mental anguish. But Dysart's monologue that ends the play is the strongest indictment yet of the work he is doing. Dysart laments that in treating Alan, he will relieve the boy not only of his pain but of all feeling, inspiration, and imagination. As for himself, the lesson of Alan has showed him how lost he truly is: "There is now, in my mouth, this sharp chain," Dysart concludes. "And it never comes out."

CHARACTERS

Harry Dalton

A stable owner. He is bitter about Alan's blinding of his horses and feels the boy should be in prison, not "in a hospital at the tax-payers' expense." Before the blinding incident, however, Dalton was extremely friendly and supportive of Alan when the boy came to work at his stable; he told Alan, "the main rule is: enjoy yourself."

Martin Dysart

A psychiatrist in his mid-forties. He reluctantly accepts Alan as a patient, persuaded by his lawyer friend Hester Salomon that there is something special about the boy. While Dysart is able to help the young man face his problems, the experience of analyzing Alan has a profound effect on Dysart's view of his own life as well. Alan's probing questions about Dysart's relationship with his wife—a Scottish dentist named Margaret—causes the Doctor to reflect upon how estranged they have become as a couple. They have no children and share minimal, if any, sexual intimacy. Dysart regrets how "briskly" he and his wife have lived their lives together.

When he compares himself to the boy he is treating for insanity, Dysart questions himself. He can cure Alan and make the boy more "normal," but he regrets that the cost of this process may be Alan losing his unique passion and creativity. Dysart comes to doubt the value of his own work and, perhaps as a result, suffers nightmares. In these dreams he sees himself as a high priest killing children in ritual sacrifice rather than healing them.

Horseman

The Horseman, who Alan describes as "a college chap," and Frank later calls "upper class riff-raff," provides six-year-old Alan his first experience riding a horse. Alan's parents are frightened for Alan's safety, and Frank pulls his son violently from the horse, causing Alan to fall. The Horseman is incredulous at the anger of Alan's parents. He flippantly calls Frank a "stupid fart" and makes a point of starting his horse so that its hooves cover the family with sand and water as he rides away. The same actor who plays the Horseman also plays Nugget, one of Dalton's horses that Alan takes for his midnight rides. This actor is among the chorus of six actors who depict horses.

Jill Mason

In her early twenties, "pretty and middle class." Jill introduced Alan to Harry Dalton, helping the boy get a job in Dalton's stables. Jill is attracted to Alan and encourages him to take her to a pornographic film, where they run into Alan's father. Later, in the stable, Jill and Alan have a failed sexual encounter. In his shame, Alan sends Jill away and blinds the horses, a deed which catalyzes the play's dramatic action. Dalton reports that Jill had a nervous breakdown after hearing of Alan's act.

Hesther Salomon

A magistrate. She brings Alan to Dysart after pleading with the court to allow the boy a psychiatric evaluation. She is a friend to Dysart and hears him out as he relates his personal problems—many of which he has been forced to face as a result of treating Alan. She tries to persuade Dysart that his psychiatric work has value and that curing Alan is an important task: "The boy's in pain, Martin," she observes. "That's all I see. In the end."

Alan Strang

A "lean boy of seventeen," who is arrested after blinding six horses at Harry Dalton's stable where he works. He appears very troubled; in his first session with psychiatrist Martin Dysart, Alan will only respond by singing advertising jingles. Alan has developed a complex ritual of devotion to the god Equus, which he practices through ecstatic

MEDIA ADAPTATIONS

- *Equus* was adapted into a film in 1977 by United Artists and directed by Sidney Lumet. Shaffer's script received an Academy Award nomination for best screenplay based on material from another medium. The film also received Academy Award nominations for best actor (Richard Burton portraying Dr. Dysart) and best supporting actor (Peter Firth as Alan).

- A BBC sound recording of *Equus* was made in 1984 (distributed in the United States by Audio-Forum).

midnight rides on Dalton's horses. Alan's pagan ritual transfers much of his mother's Christian faith onto the image of the horse, which Alan associates with the forbidden since the disaster of his first riding experience. Frustrated and ashamed following his sexual failure with Jill, Alan blinds the horses to protect himself from the vengeance of Equus, who "saw" the boy in disgrace.

After resisting Dysart's initial attempts to help him, Alan gradually grows more comfortable with the psychiatrist. Although Dysart regrets that curing the boy might give him a life as devoid of real passion as the doctor's own, professional considerations prevail. Alan purges a great deal of pain in his later sessions with Dysart, and the play concludes with the implication that the doctor will continue to heal the boy's mental anguish.

Dora Strang

Alan's mother, a former school teacher (Alan declares proudly to Dysart, "She knows more than you"). She is religious, frequently talking to Alan about the Bible (much to the frustration of her atheist husband, Frank). Dora also feels she married beneath herself socially, a regret that shows itself in various ways. She comes from a "horsey family," while Frank finds riding to be an affectation of "upper class riff-raff." She did not want Alan to work in a shop because "shops are common."

Dora visits Alan in the hospital, and when the boy throws his lunch at her, she slaps him. She regret this act of violence but expresses to Dysart the level of her frustration under the present circumstances. She is incredulous that Dysart would view Alan's violence as a product of his upbringing. ''I only know he was my little Alan,'' she mourns, ''and then the Devil came.''

Frank Strang

Alan's father, a printer by trade. He is a self-declared atheist, which goes hand-in-hand with his political beliefs (Dysart calls him an ''old-type Socialist. Relentlessly self-improving''). He frequently quotes Karl Marx's adage, ''Religion is the opium of the people'' in response to his wife's religious beliefs. As an atheist, he sees religion as ''just bad sex,'' holding his wife responsible for Alan's psychological condition.

Frank comes alone to Dysart's office to describe to the doctor how he once discovered Alan reciting a parody of a Biblical genealogy and then kneeling reverently in front of a photograph of a horse and beating himself with a coat hanger. Frank also reveals to Dysart that Alan was out with a girl the night he blinded the horses, neglecting to mention that he knows this because he encountered the couple in a pornographic cinema.

THEMES

Freedom

There is an ethical ambiguity explored in *Equus,* the conflict between two ideas of right. The freedom of the individual to do whatever he or she wants must always be balanced with the social need to limit this freedom when a person's actions are harmful to others. This is certainly the case with Alan's shocking crime; society's highest priority in this case is to put Alan away, or to cure his psychological distress so that, hopefully, he will not again cause such harm. Dysart recognizes that he cannot simply allow Alan to act entirely of his own will, but at the same time he is loathe to administer a cure that will most likely quell or kill the boy's imagination and passion. The doctor also worries that the force driving Alan's actions is something closer to instinct rather than a simple mental problem. He is concerned that squelching such impulses will essentially rob Alan of all identity. Yet the concerns of society as a whole prevail in this case; Alan's actions, if left unchecked, will ultimately hinder the freedom and happiness of others.

God and Religion

Not only is religion a significant theme in *Equus,* it has shown itself important to Shaffer's writing throughout his long career. Shaffer is fascinated by the human need to believe in a god, to discover a suitable form of worship. In this play the primary theological distinction is between Christianity and paganism (in the form of a horse-god). Alan has been brought up in a Christian faith by his mother, but the horrific tales of Christ's crucifixion disturbed him. He creates his own religion, channeling Christian beliefs and practices into his worship of the god Equus, a horse figure that is far more comforting to him than the bloodied Jesus. Dr. Dysart, with his passion for classical culture, makes associations between Alan's beliefs and the ancient, pagan Greek society which is viewed as so influential upon Western civilizations (Greek culture embraced many gods who they believed influenced various facets of their lives; they built a system of arts and social government that is often cited as a model for modern society). Dysart understands intellectually (and begins to feel genuinely) that, as he says, ''life is only comprehensible through a thousand local gods.''

Growth and Development

Horse figures play an enormous role in Alan's development. Images of the horse pervade the play, appropriate for a near archetypal figure which has such important historical and cultural associations. Dora Strang relates how Alan was fascinated as a boy with a historical fact regarding the conquest of the Americas: when Christian cavalry arrived in the new world, the indigenous people often mistook horse and rider for one creature, a four-legged animal with the powers of a god. This anecdote greatly influences the development of Alan's personal mythology of Equus; as he matures and begins his naked midnight rides, this mythos incorporates sexual elements as well. This is depicted in the last scene of Act One. In a near sexual/religious frenzy, Alan rides the horse, crying, ''Bear me away! Make us One Person!''

Other encounters with horse images, or actual horses, were also important to Alan's development—the storybook his mother read to him over and over, the odd photograph of a horse which

TOPICS FOR FURTHER STUDY

- Compare and contrast the beliefs that Alan's mother and father have on concepts such as class, religion, sex, and, of course, horses. What effect have each of the parents had on Alan's development?

- Dora Strang describes the religious picture which hung above Alan's bed as "a little extreme" in its depiction of Christ "loaded down with chains," being beaten by Roman soldiers on his way to crucifixion. Research the figure of Christ in the history of Western art, analyzing some of the different ways in which he has been depicted. What do you think disturbed Alan about Jesus and the Christian religion as a whole? What prompted him to start his own religion?

- Discuss whether *Equus* ultimately seems to be supportive or critical of the value of psychoanalysis.

- Research the theories of Carl Jung, who Shaffer has called "one of the greatest minds of the twentieth century." Drawing on Jung's concept of archetypal images and other aspects of his philosophy, discuss the importance of the horse (and the centaur) as a symbol in *Equus*.

- Research the mythology and religious practice of Classical Greece. Discuss the significance of this pagan culture to the themes and characters of *Equus*. In particular, how does Shaffer's play enact the philosophical clash between the Apollonian, or rational, and the Dionysian, or instinctive?

- Research Sigmund Freud's theories of human psychology, including such concepts as Id/Ego/Superego, transference, repression, and defense mechanisms. Use as many of the concepts as seem applicable to provide a Freudian analysis of Alan's childhood development and how he came to commit his particular act of violence.

---

replaced the portrait of Christ's crucifixion, and the traumatic experience of being pulled from a horse by his father after a thrilling oceanfront ride. Other cultural associations with horses—their speed and power, their majestic carriage—make plausible to a contemporary audience the idea that a boy could find divinity in the equestrian image.

Memory and Reminiscence

A form of reminiscence—the replaying of scenes from the past—provides *Equus* with a dramatic structure. Memory, especially repressed memory that must be brought to light, is additionally an important thematic component in the play. In a classic Freudian formula, Alan has repressed certain memories in his subconscious and as a result suffers nightmares and other forms of mental unrest. Dr. Dysart uses techniques such as hypnosis and a "truth drug" placebo to lower Alan's psychic defenses and allow these repressed memories to rise to the surface, where they can be confronted and treated by the psychiatrist. There is an abreaction, a venting of psychic pain, which takes the form of theatrical performance and provides each act with an expressionistic conclusion (Alan on one of his midnight rides at the end of Act One; his recollection of blinding the horses near the end of Act Two).

Sanity and Insanity

Like the theme of religion, this theme operates on many levels in the play. Dysart is confronted, on the one hand, with a boy who is psychologically troubled, has committed a violent act society views as insane, and whose pain can be removed by treatment. The play unfolds dramatically, in fact, precisely because of Dysart's success in uncovering Alan's repressed memories, and it concludes with the implication that Dysart can cure Alan's distress. But in treating Alan, Dysart begins to view these labels of sanity and insanity as social constructions, values which appear fixed but actually change greatly over time and across cultures. Dysart is scared that by curing Alan, making the boy sane in a socially-accepted manner, he might take away from Alan a passion for life which most people never feel (and which Dysart admits he envies).

Sex

Sex and religion are probably the two most significant, and closely intertwined themes, in the play. Both are crucial factors in Alan's childhood development; in both instances, Alan makes a transference of what society views as "normal" forms of sex and worship onto his pagan, equine religion. The play hints at the sexual undertones of many events in Alan's childhood. Frank Strang's comment that Christianity to him "is just bad sex," and his reference to a particularly graphic depiction of Christ's crucifixion as "kinky," imply connections between sexual desire and religious ecstasy which the father may have instilled in Alan as a youth. Alan's ride with the Horseman is also given sexual undertones, a pleasure he is clearly attempting to replicate on his naked, midnight rides with Equus. (Alan has essentially made a religious practice out of a masturbatory act.) At the play's climax, Alan is confused when he finds himself sexually aroused by Jill Mason. He feels great shame as a result both of his "infidelity" in the presence of Equus and his inability to actually have intercourse with Jill. Sex is thus a major factor both in Alan's development, and in the violent act which initiates the dramatic action of the play.

STYLE

Dramatic Genre

Equus closely resembles a suspense thriller in form and structure, revealing Shaffer's fondness for detective stories. Dysart is much like a classic sleuth solving a crime; he painstakingly tracks down the factors that led Alan to blind the six horses. Shaffer has worked in many dramatic genres, including domestic tragedy, farce, and historical drama. Many critics have noted that what makes *Equus* a unique theatrical experience is its seamless incorporation of several dramatic genres. In addition to being a serviceable suspense tale, the play has also been credited for its intriguing examination of the roots of mental illness as well as its canny updating of Greek tragedy. The play's popularity among audiences and critics has been attributed to its ability to

appeal to numerous tastes. Likewise, not linked to any one dramatic school of thought, Shaffer has demonstrated his versatility with each new play.

Point of View

In *Equus*—as he has in other plays such as *Amadeus*—Shaffer uses the dramatic device of the *raisonneur,* a kind of "color commentator" who directly addresses the audience, providing details that assist the viewer in understanding the play's action. Thus, the point of view of *Equus* is largely that of Dysart (the play's *raisonneur*), who provides the context in which the story unfolds. However, certain elements in the play are clearly presented from Alan's perspective: the flashbacks are a theatrical reenactment of Alan's memories.

Staging

The set for *Equus,* rather than being realistic, is flexible and allows for numerous different performing spaces. The almost cinematic structure of the play—multiple, brief scenes in numerous locations—requires rapid changes in staging. This effect is achieved through a rotating turntable as well as other set techniques such as spot lighting and sparse use of props. For example, Alan picks up benches at one point and moves them, forming three stalls for a scene at Dalton's stables. The use of mimed objects and actions is also significant to the play's theatrical technique. Clive Barnes wrote in the *New York Times* that Shaffer "has his theatre set up here as a kind of bullring with a section of the audience actually sitting on stage." In addition to members of the audience, all the actors are seated on stage, rising to perform in scenes and then being seated, still in view of the audience. Thus, there is little separation between stage and audience, creating an intimacy which underscores the intensity of the drama. Irving Wardle wrote in the London *Times* that the stage "combines the elements of rodeo, stable, and Greek amphitheatre."

Temporal Organization

Rather than moving forward in strictly linear time, *Equus* combines a main plot unfolding in the present with repeated flashbacks to past events. Dysart's opening monologue in each act, and some of the therapy sessions with Alan, take place in the present. Incidents involving Alan's childhood and the night of his crime are in flashback, as are the sequences in Dysart's life that lead up to his treating the boy. The different temporal threads are woven together, with overlapping elements providing points of transition.

For example, the Nurse's comments to Dysart about Alan's condition are melded with Dysart later relating the same details to Hesther. By staging both events on stage at the same time, Shaffer achieves a kind of cinematic edit that allows the same topic to be simultaneously discussed in two distinct settings. The Nurse tells Dysart that Alan has been having nightmares during which he repeatedly screams "Ek!" Hesther, however, not Dysart, asks "Ek?" but the Nurse continues, "Yes, Doctor. Ek." The past is revealed in glimpses, usually an acting out of what one character is telling another in the present. As these memories are recalled in the present, lighting and set placement allow the actors to slip to another part of the stage and enact the past event being described.

Catharsis

Many critics have called *Equus* a "modern tragedy," some evoking Aristotle's principles of tragedy (as he outlines in his *Poetics*) to discuss the manner in which the play operates. While *Equus* does not truly follow the formula for tragedy, it does contain many of the genre's important components. One of the most closely related is that of catharsis: the purgation of feelings of pity and fear, which Aristotle identified as the social function of tragedy. Parallel to the concept of catharsis is that of abreaction, the discharge of the emotional energy supposed to be attached to a repressed idea, especially by the conscious verbalization of that idea in the presence of a therapist. Thus, the staging of Alan's repressed memories has a therapeutic purpose that mirrors the potential cathartic effect of the play upon an audience.

Philosophical Content

The 1964 full-length play *Royal Hunt of the Sun: A Play Concerning the Conquest of Peru* introduced Shaffer's characteristic technique of opposing two central figures (in that play's case, the Inca king Atahualpa and the Spanish conquistador Francisco Pizarro) whose actions establish a dialectic on complex philosophical questions. This technique revealed itself again in the pairing of Dr. Dysart and Alan and would later resurface with the characters of Mozart and Salieri in Shaffer's 1979 play, *Amadeus*. Dysart and Alan stand, respectively, as philosophical representatives for subdued rationalism and passionate instinct. As the factors under-

lying Alan's violent act are revealed, Dysart discovers a dilemma of his own. Ridding Alan of his mental conflicts only succeeds in transferring them onto Dysart himself.

The Horse Chorus

In Greek theatre, the masked chorus serves to comment on the action of the play. Shaffer has a similar concept in mind with his chorus, although they make equine noises of humming, thumping, and stamping rather than speaking. In the early scenes concerning Alan's interaction with horses, the choral noises intensify the emotional content, making a connection between the early scenes and the foreshadowing of the act Alan will later commit. This non-realistic technique allows the audience a glimpse into Alan's state of mind—for the noise, as Shaffer comments, "heralds or illustrates the presence of Equus the God."

Among the chorus are six actors who represent Nugget and the other horses in the play. No attempt is made to make them appear realistic; they wear horse-like masks of wire and leather beneath which the heads of the actors are visible. Barnes observed that while "is not easy to present men playing horses on stage without provoking giggles . . . here the horses live up to their reputed godhead." Mollie Panter-Downes commented in the *New Yorker* that "these masked presences standing in the shadows of the stable manage to suggest the eeriness and power of . . . the old hoofed god."

When Alan mounts Nugget for the first time, all the other horses lean forward to create a visual picture that highlights Alan's belief that his god Equus resides in all horses. By having the same actor play the Horseman and Nugget, a visual connection is established which suggests Alan's transference of emotions from humans onto horses.

HISTORICAL CONTEXT

Equus premiered in 1973, near the beginning of a decade largely characterized in Britain by crisis and economic decline. Recovering from the ruins of World War II, Britain slowly built prosperity on a moderately socialist model. Many private institutions were nationalized, but the foreign debt tripled. The Labour government of the late-1960s lost ground due to the eroding economic situation, especially

An example of how the horse chorus is represented in Equus; *Alan's therapy provokes him to recall one of his encounters with the horse*

the monetary devaluation crisis of 1967, in which the country's currency dropped precipitously against other world markets.

Although the economy improved slightly in 1969, the Conservative Party rose to power in the election of 1970. Regarding foreign policy, the disastrous Suez Crisis of 1956, in which England lost control of the vital Suez Canal shipping passage, suggested strongly that Britain was no longer a major world power. Since the height of the British Empire in the early twentieth century, important possessions had been surrendered (most significant-

ly, independence was granted to India, one of the Empire's colonial jewels, in 1947). Beginning in the late 1950s, the British government followed a deliberate policy of decolonization, one that systematically dismantled the country's once vast system of colonies.

In the early 1970s the British government continued to struggle with inflation. Violence plagued Northern Ireland, as battles between Protestant and Catholic factions continued to erupt. Both problems would dog British governments throughout the decade. In early 1974, Conservatives lost the general

COMPARE
&
CONTRAST

- **1973:** Children are widely viewed as innocent, and an act of violence like that committed by Alan is considered especially perplexing. As Hesther observes of Alan's actions in *Equus,* even psychiatric professionals "are going to be disgusted by the whole thing."

Today: Rates of violent crime committed by children have skyrocketed in the latter decades of the twentieth century. While the U.S. has been shocked by a rash adolescent violence—notably a series of shootings at schools in 1998—violent crimes by children are less a factor of life in Britain. Through isolated incidents and exposure to international media, however, British society has been made aware of the propensity for violence among troubled youth.

- **1973:** While the Conservative Party controls Parliament, the British Labour party is developing strength and will win important elections in the following year. After several more years of recession and other economic problems, however, voters will usher in a new Conservative government in 1979, led by Prime Minister Margaret Thatcher.

Today: Ending eighteen years of Conservative Party control of the Parliament, the Labour Party achieves an overwhelming national election victory in 1997. Tony Blair becomes Prime Minister, but many feel that "New Labour" has abandoned so many of its traditionally leftist policies

that the election is not so much a victory for working class people in Britain as it might appear.

- **1973:** Britain, like many nations in the industrialized West, is in the midst of an economic crisis characterized by wild inflation and labor unrest.

Today: The economy has largely stabilized. Conservative governments held down inflation in the 1980s and early-1990s and privatized many national industries. The social cost of these policies, however, was a widening of the gap between rich and poor in Britain, cause for even more class resentment like that expressed by Frank Strang in *Equus.*

- **1973:** The British are a people known for their love of animals and are especially reverent toward horses. Shaffer must carefully tailor his depiction of Alan's crime so that *Equus* will startle audiences without sickening and outraging them. The 1977 film adaptation of the play depicts the blinding of the horses in a realistic and bloody fashion, drawing protests from animal-rights activists and criticism from Shaffer himself.

Today: The British, like every culture so heavily exposed to the media, have been forced to adjust to ubiquitous images of violence. The welfare of animals, however, continues to be of great concern in Britain, where animals-rights activism is much more common than in other countries.

---

elections in the midst of a coal miners' strike. The government's refusal to capitulate to the miners' demands forced energy rationing and a fuel-conserving three-day work week. Although victorious, the Labour party lacked a full majority in Parliament, significantly limiting their power to enact policies in support of working people. Labour won a full majority of Parliamentary seats in October, 1974, but Britain continued to be plagued by inflation and economic decline. Widespread economic

discontent led eventually to the victory of the Conservatives in 1979, and the election of Prime Minister Margaret Thatcher, whose term in office would be riddled with controversy, partisan battles, and wildly fluctuating public support.

On October 6, 1973, Egypt and Syria attacked Israel, both sides blaming the other for having initiated the new aggression (Israel had shot down two Syrian jets). The Yom Kippur War (named for the Jewish Holy Day of Atonement on which the conflict began) was the fourth Arab-Israeli war since 1948. The Soviet union gave military support to the Arabs in response to U.S. support of Israel. Thus, the war had a distinctly Cold War context in which Britain was also implicated.

The greatest impact of the Arab-Israeli war on the West, however, was the resulting oil embargo by Arab members of the Organization of Petroleum Exporting Countries (OPEC). The oil embargo exacerbated an energy crisis that was already gripping the world. Connected to the energy crisis and other factors, the West additionally experienced an inflation crisis; annual double-digit inflation became a reality for the first time for most industrial nations. The oil shock and soaring grain prices precipitated a world monetary crisis and then a worldwide economic recession, the worst since the Great Depression of the 1930s. In Britain, these economic contractions contributed to an increasing sense of social hopelessness.

The Bahamas gained full independence July 10, 1973, after 256 years as a British crown colony. The British Empire continued its inexorable progress toward decolonization. As British control was waning in far-flung parts of the world they once dominated, so British independence was challenged by the growing movement toward union among Western European nations. In 1973, Britain joined the European Community after a decade of controversy, agreeing to participate in common decisions on trade, agriculture, industry, the environment, foreign policy, and defense. In 1993, the European Union (E.U.) was created following ratification of the Maastricht Treaty. Britain is today an uneasy member of the E.U.; they would not take part, for example, in the creation of a common currency, the euro, which debuted on world markets on January 4, 1999.

Across the Atlantic, 1973 was also a tumultuous year in American society. American troops were withdrawn from the war in Vietnam but bombing raids on that country continued. The U.S. launched *Skylab,* its first space station. The U.S. Supreme Court legalized abortion in their landmark decision *Roe v. Wade.* Public approval for President Richard Nixon continued to plummet, as accusations and evidence continued to support the fact that he had granted approval for the June 17, 1972, burglary of Democratic National Committee offices at the Watergate complex in Washington. Like public opinion over Vietnam, Watergate was an important symbol both of stark divisions in American society and a growing disillusionment with the integrity of national leaders. In late 1973, Vice President Spiro Agnew resigned under pressure, pleading no contest (*no lo contendre*) to charges of income tax evasion and consequently setting the tone for scandals that would continue to rock the executive branch (Nixon himself, under threat of impeachment and removal from office, resigned the following year; other cabinet members, such as Nixon's Attorney General, John Mitchell, and Chief of Staff, H. R. Haldeman, would also be implicated in the crime).

Culturally, London had in the 1960s become a world capital of theatre, fashion, and popular music, but this image was tarnished somewhat by ongoing the economic decline. Save some notable exceptions, 1973 was not a banner year for the London theatre: Alan Ayckbourn's *Absurd Person Singular* and David Storey's *Cromwell* being two of the few works to share acclaim with Shaffer's *Equus.* On the American stage, 1973 saw the premier of Lanford Wilson's *Hot l Baltimore,* Neil Simon's *The Good Doctor,* and the blockbuster musical *A Little Night Music* by Stephen Sondheim.

CRITICAL OVERVIEW

When *Equus* premiered on July 26, 1973, it provoked strong reactions from critics, as might be expected given the play's startling topic and innovative production. Many reviews praised the philosophical and theatrical complexity of the work, heralding it as the high point of Shaffer's dramatic career. Dissenting reviews called the play pretentious or contrived; few writers, however, failed to observe that the play was a major theatrical event of the 1973 London season. Michael Billington of the Manchester *Guardian* described the play as "sensationally good." Billington observed that Shaffer continued to explore a theme common to his earlier works but judged *Equus* superior to its predecessors because in it, "the intellectual argument and the poetic imagery are virtually indivisible." Harold Hobson of the *Sunday Times* similarly raved about the play.

Taking an opposing view, Ian Christie of the *Daily Express* called the script "pretentious, philosophical claptrap.'' Irving Wardle of the daily London *Times,* meanwhile, was among the critics who expressed a mixed opinion. Wardle thought some of Dysart's speeches were excellently written and found the central image of the horse ''poetically inexhaustible,'' but he found much of Shaffer's writing contrived. ''There is very little real dialogue,'' Wardle wrote. ''Even the interviews consist of solo turns introduced with wary parleys on both sides.'' Wardle faulted Shaffer's dramatic creations as heavy handed, calling his characters ''schematic automaton[s].''

While many critics, even those who appreciate Shaffer's work, have pointed out the many similarities between his plays (Wardle called *Equus* a ''variation on a theme''), Clive Barnes saluted the originality of this play. *Equus,* he wrote in the *New York Times,* ''is quite different from anything Mr. Shaffer has written before, and has, to my mind, a quite new sense of seriousness to it.'' Although still intended as a popular play, *Equus* ''has a most refreshing and mind-opening intellectualism.'' Writing about the New York production (which opened October 24, 1974), Barnes commented that *Equus* ''adds immeasurably to the fresh hopes we have for Broadway's future.'' Walter Kerr, in another *New York Times* review, similarly found Shaffer's play to be of great stature. ''*Equus,*'' he wrote, ''is one of the most remarkable examples of stagecraft, as well as of sustained and multifaceted sensibility, the contemporary theatre has given us.'' Building on such acclaim, the Broadway production of *Equus* enjoyed an exceptionally long run of 1209 performances.

Initial criticism of *Equus* focused on such questions as whether the intellectual content of the play melded well with its dramatic form and content and whether or not Peter Shaffer's dialogue was up to par with the play's theatrical production, which was widely viewed as ingenious. In more extended analyses of the work, critics began to delve deeply into the psychological complexity of *Equus,* drawing out a number of interrelated themes. As intellectual touchstones, critics have elucidated elements of *Equus* by referring to the work of Sigmund Freud and Carl Jung as well as the philosopher Friedrich Nietzsche. Articles have variously drawn upon Freud's theories of childhood development and the human subconscious, Jung's philosophies of archetypal images, and Nietzsche's concept of tragedy (based upon the human failure to transcend individuation).

Starting with Freudian principles, critics have analyzed the structure of the play as a therapeutic reenactment, or abreaction, of memories repressed in Alan's subconscious. Many articles have illustrated how the play functions primarily as a study of human sexual development. ''Here,'' wrote John Weightman in *Encounter,* ''was a new and interesting example of the way sex can get mixed up with religion, or *vice versa.*''

Additionally, many critics have focused on the play's religious themes independent of their relationship with sexual development. In such an analysis, Alan is a product of conflicting religious impulses, one Christian, one pagan. More broadly, many critics see an ongoing process of theological introspection as a fundamental element of Shaffer's drama. James R. Stacy, in *Peter Shaffer: A Casebook,* observed that Shaffer has been engaged on a ''search for worship.'' John M. Clum, meanwhile, commented in the *South Atlantic Quarterly* that Shaffer has been ''fascinated with the impulse toward faith. For him the adversary of the man of faith is not a cosmic void or universal chaos; it is rationality. . . . Shaffer is not concerned with existence of a god: he is fascinated with man's need for religion, for transcendence, for passionate submission.''

Wardle, J. W. Lambert, Frank Lawrence, and Doyle W. Walls are among critics who have evoked the cultural associations with the Greek gods Apollo and Dionysus as a way of contextualizing the play's intellectual conflict between subdued rationalism (widely viewed as normality) and passionate instinct (viewed as insanity). Lambert wrote in *Drama* that in this, *Equus* focuses on ''a theme constant throughout human history, never resolved, always relevant, and very much in the air today.''

Equus continues to attract critical inquiry because of its psychological complexity, its theatrical innovation, and its enduring philosophical weight. Writing in *Peter Shaffer: A Casebook,* Dennis Klein marveled that Shaffer ''has so carefully constructed it that there are no loose ends left for the audience to tie together; and yet the play has inspired such diverse interpretations.'' Recent critics, reviewing more than four active decades of writing by Shaffer, still consider the success of *Equus* an important benchmark in the playwright's artistic development. C. J. Gianakaris wrote in *Peter Shaffer* that ''*Five Finger Exercise* and *The Royal Hunt of the Sun* signaled the arrival on the scene of a new, innovative voice in the theatre; *Equus* confirmed it.''

CRITICISM

Christopher G. Busiel

In this essay, Busiel discusses the element of memory in Shaffer's play. Developed in collaboration with director John Dexter, the playwright's depiction of Alan Strang's repressed memories is, in the critic's opinion, the most stunning element of Equus. *As Busiel writes, the scenes of abreaction, in which the past is represented theatrically rather than discussed verbally, lend the play a delicate balance, creating moments where the past collides with the present, sexual desire with religious practice, and realism with abstraction.*

Equus is a play in which present and past collide and intertwine in spectacular and thematically significant ways. Psychoanalysis (a process of evaluating mental health that was developed by Sigmund Freud) drives the plot forward, as the psychiatrist Martin Dysart succeeds in drawing out of Alan Strang a series of repressed memories. His intention is to achieve abreaction, which is the discharge of the emotional energy attached to a repressed idea. Theatrically, the past events in the plot of *Equus* are strikingly represented, diverging from analytical and expository dialogue; rather than related verbally, these memories are acted out in flashback.

By staging the past rather than revealing it through exposition (analysis usually being a process of *verbalization*), Shaffer takes great advantage of the visual power of the theatre. In the staging of Alan's memories, he allows himself a more lyrical tone, a more ritualistic style than that employed in the realistic dialogues between Dysart and the other characters in the play. In his book *Peter Shaffer,* critic C. J. Gianakaris observed: "What will be best remembered about *Equus* is its brilliant dramatising of man's attempt to reconcile the personal and the metaphysical aspects of his universe." As Gianakaris wrote, with the "immeasurable help" of director John Dexter, Shaffer "strikingly fused realism with mimetic ritual," achieving a "daring stylisation" which is crucial to the success of the play.

Ultimately, the abstract scenes in *Equus* powerfully reveal the relationship between sex and religion—the two most significant, and closely intertwined, themes in the play. Both sex and religion are crucial factors in Alan's childhood development: in both arenas, Alan transfers "normal" social views of sex and worship onto his pagan, equine religion. The play hints at the sexual undertones in many events in Alan's childhood. Frank Strang's comment that Christianity "is just bad sex" implies connections between sexual desire and religious ecstasy which run through the play. Frank observes of Alan:

> A boy spends night after night having this stuff read into him: an innocent man tortured to death—thorns driven into his head—nails into his hands—a spear jammed through his ribs. It can mark anyone for life, that kind of thing. I'm not joking. The boy was absolutely fascinated by all that. He was always mooning over religious pictures. I mean real kinky ones, if you receive my meaning.

Alan's ride with the Horseman is also given sexual meaning; it is a pleasure he clearly attempts to duplicate on his naked, midnight rides with Equus. (Alan has essentially ritualized a masturbatory act into a religious practice.) At the play's climax, Alan is confused when he finds himself sexually aroused by Jill Mason. He feels great shame as a result both of his "infidelity" in the presence of Equus and his impotence with Jill. Sex is a major catalyst, both in Alan's development and in the violent blinding of the horses.

The thematic connection between sexual identity and religious practice is cemented in the details of the play's staging. *Equus* is a play of thematic complexity and depth, and Shaffer's writing of dialogue is, by and large, up to the task of expressing this complexity (although some critics have disagreed on this point). The true novelty and genius of *Equus,* however, may rest in the manner in which Shaffer utilizes theatrical techniques to enact powerfully the psychological and religious dimensions of the play. Past and present collide in theatrical spectacle, as the dialogue of Alan's sessions with Dysart is given a larger, visual dimension, powerfully underscoring the play's psychological themes. Gianakaris comments:

> The flexibility of the stage design permits striking variations in the way the action is presented. Straightforward realism alternates with imaginative stylised scenes of mime. Dysart's is the cool, detached world of science where clinical evidence determines one's actions. His dealings with others are consequently portrayed realistically, with narrated interjections. But Alan Strang's ritual worship is especially well suited to abstract staging.

The most stunning moments of reenactment (the abreaction) are the extended scenes which conclude each act of *Equus.* The first act ends with Alan riding horseback to the point of orgasm, with images culled from passages in the Book of Job from the Old Testament. The second act contains an equally dramatic nude scene of attempted inter-

WHAT DO I READ NEXT?

- *Amadeus,* often regarded as Shaffer's greatest dramatic achievement. The 1979 play is a probing exploration of the human psyche, centering on the court composer Antonio Salieri and his jealousy for fellow composer Wolfgang Amadeus Mozart, who is portrayed as a vulgar, self-centered musical genius. The play won the 1980 Antoinette (Tony) Perry Award. In 1984, the film adaptation won Academy Awards for best picture and best screenplay adaptation, which Shaffer composed from his original text.

- *The Royal Hunt of the Sun,* a 1964 play which secured Shaffer's reputation as an accomplished dramatist. The play—which creatively blends ritual, dance, music, and drama—reenacts the sixteenth-century Spanish conquest of the Incan empire. Like *Equus* and *Amadeus,* this play employs two opposing central characters to create not only dramatic tension but also a philosophical dialectic on central themes.

- *One Flew over the Cuckoo's Nest,* by Ken Kesey (Viking, 1962). Set in a mental institution and told through from the perspective of Chief Bromden, a Native American patient, Kesey's book was adapted for the stage and made into one of the most successful films of all time. The novel depicts the struggle between the wild and free-spirited Randal McMurphy and the autocratic Nurse Ratched, offering an unqualified criticism of the treatment of individuals at the hands of the psychiatric institution.

- *The Butcher Boy,* by Patrick McCabe (Fromm, 1993). This novel (recently adapted into a film by Neil Jordan) explores the descent into madness of a boy who has experienced a harsh upbringing in a small Irish town. Like Alan in *Equus,* Francie Brady inhabits a world largely of his own imagination. Francie's growing antagonism toward the society around him culminates with an act of startling violence.

- *The Myth of Mental Illness: Foundations of a Theory of Personal Conduct* by Thomas Szasz, M.D. (revised edition, Harper Row, 1974). Szasz is the author of dozens of iconoclastic books challenging the fundamental principles of the psychiatric industry. In this ground breaking work, he argues that human behavior has reasons rather than causes, dissects what he views as flaws in the medical model of mental illness, and challenges the notion of psychiatrists as beneficent healers.

---

course (between Alan and Jill), the blinding of the horses, and words from the New Testament's Book of Revelation. The themes of religion and sex are repeatedly linked

In the first case, having hypnotized Alan through a game he calls "Blink," Dysart encourages his patient not merely to talk about his ritualistic worship of Equus but to act out the process as well. Dysart's prompts provide an important encouragement, but gradually the voice of the doctor fades out and the theatrical reenactment subsumes the dramatic action. With a hum from the chorus, the actors depicting horses slowly rotate a turntable, on which Alan and his mount are fixed in a bright spotlight.

Alan's "ride" becomes more and more frenzied, and as the choral humming increases in volume, Alan shouts powerfully:

> WEE!. . .WAA!. . .WONDERFUL!. . . I'm stiff! Stiff in the wind! *My* mane, stiff in the wind! *My* flanks! *My* hooves! Mane on my legs, on my flanks, like whips! Raw! Raw! *I'm raw! Raw!* Feel me on you! *On* you! *On* you! *On* you! I want to be *in* you! I want to BE you forever and ever!—*Equus, I love you!* Now!— Bear me away! Make us One Person!

Alan rides ever more frantically, chanting ritualistically "One Person!" and then, simply, "HA-HA!" With Alan's body twisting like a flame, the chorus gradually brings the turning square to a stop. Alan drops off the horse, kisses his hoof and cries up to him: "AMEN!" The act concludes completely within the framework of this reenactment without returning to Dysart for commentary or further dialogue between doctor and patient.

The conclusion of the play is given a similarly startling theatrical dimension. Dysart has prompted Alan through the process of reenactment, even taking on the voice of Equus himself as he says: "The Lord thy God is a Jealous God! He sees you." But as in the first act abreaction, Dysart gradually retreats to the background as the reenactment of Alan's repressed memory takes over the stage:

> ALAN: Thou— God— Seest— NOTHING! *(He stabs out Nugget's eyes. The horse stamps in agony. A great screaming begins to fill the theater, growing ever louder. ALAN dashes at the other two horses and blinds them too, stabbing over the rails. Their metal hooves join in the stamping. Relentlessly, as this happens, three more horses appear in cones of light: not naturalistic animals like the first three but dreadful creatures out of nightmare. Their eyes flare—their nostrils flare—their mouths flare, they are archetypal images—judging, punishing, pitiless. They do not halt at the rail but invade the square. As they trample at him, the boy leaps desperately at them, jumping high and naked in the dark, slashing at their heads with arms upraised, and shouting "Nothing!" savagely with each blow. The screams increase.)*

The scale of the reenactment—an exceptional bit of theatricality—suggests the monumental importance of the blinding, both as it originally occurred and in its retelling. Building upon the tremendous sense of release Alan will feel from this abreaction, Dysart hopes he will be able to cure the boy of his mental anguish. John Weightman wrote in *Encounter* that the stabbing out of the horses' eyes "gives another fine frenzy when the scene is re-enacted as psychodrama."

Through such reenactments there is an important mirroring of revelation in the play; the audience makes important discoveries just as Dysart is making them. Past and present are folded into one another as theatrical representation takes the place of expository dialogue. During the flashback scenes, the lights turn warm in color and intensity, investing the remembered action with a great deal of theatricality. The staging of the events allows the audience a glimpse into Alan's mind; he views the world with a passionate sense of wonder few people possess. The purposefully non-realistic depiction of the horses, for instance, allows the animals to "evoke the essence of horses as we recognize them in daily life" but also, crucially, gives them "the regal bearing of transcendent beings as Alan perceived them," noted Gianakaris. Shaffer notes that in the depiction of the horses, "great care must also be taken that the masks are put on before the audience with very precise timing—the actors watching each other so that the masking has an exact and ceremonial effect."

While audiences marveled at the theatrical power of *Equus,* critics have differed in their assessments of Shaffer's writing and his success at integrating a variety of complex themes and theatrical styles. Reviewing the play in the Manchester *Guardian,* Michael Billington judged *Equus* superior to Shaffer's earlier work because in this play, "the intellectual argument and the poetic imagery are virtually indivisible." While some critics have found considerable merit in the unity of the work, others argue that the real strength of *Equus* lies only in its theatricality. Henry Hewes commented in the *Saturday Review* that "the play's statement is less impressive than is Shaffer's skillful theatrical fabrication, which deftly finds layers of comic relief as he inexorably drills deeper into the hard rock of tragedy." *America*'s Catherine Hughes similarly focused on the staging, arguing that "on the level of theatricality . . . *Equus* is stunning. . . . Although Shaffer's philosophizing is too shallow, sometimes to the point of glibness, to be entirely convincing, one in the end forgives it in the wake of the play's brilliantly rendered imagery."

A few critics have argued against even the theatrical power of the concluding scene, although such harsh criticism is rare. J. W. Lambert, for one, commented in *Drama* that "Mr. Shaffer has not made [Alan's] course of action seem inevitable. The act of gouging out the horses eyes, when it comes, seems if not arbitrary then hardly less perverse than it would have done had we been given no reasons for it at all. And after all the purpose of the play's exposition is to offer us some reason for the irrational."

Shaffer has observed that theatre "is, or has to be, an ecstatic and alarming experience. And a beautiful one. That doesn't mean it's one continuous shout-out; it also must have great spaces of tranquillity and lyricism in it." The powerful scenes of abreaction in *Equus* lend the play *both* lyricism and ecstasy. Further, they offer a glimpse into Alan's mind, which is crucial given the philosophical importance lent to the passionate instinct with which the boy has led his life. While *Equus* is cleverly constructed from top to bottom, the enduring power of the play may still rest in the skill with which Shaffer and director John Dexter chose to depict the memories repressed deep within the subconscious of its primary character.

Source: Christopher G. Busiel, for *Drama for Students*, Gale, 1999.

Barry B. Witham

Witham examines Shaffer's play, finding it to be neither "great theatre nor bad psychology." The critic does, however, find Equus *to be "an exhilarating play" that succeeds in being simultaneously thought-provoking and melodramatic. In his discussion of anger in the play, Witham compares Shaffer's play to John Osborne's* Look Back in Anger.

Peter Shaffer's *Equus* is neither great theatre nor bad psychology, but it has elements of both. It is an exhilarating play: a remarkable blend of delayed exposition and theatrical effect, of melodrama and circus, which has inspired huge ticket sales and adoring critical reviews. And it is that increasingly rare serious drama which capitalizes on lurid events while maintaining a devotion to "ideas." Yet, in spite of its wide popular acclaim, *Equus* is difficult to sort out even when all the clues have been discovered. Why does Alan make his slightly sadomasochistic leap from Jesus to horses? What specifically does the scene in the porno theatre have to do with Alan's confrontation with Jill and the horses? Is the climactic nude scene an organic part of the play's structure or simply a gratuitous bow to contemporary fashion?

These questions—and a variety of others—have been raised in the aftermath of the play's initial sensation. Sanford Gifford has criticized the drama for its faulty psychology and for its deceptive views of the patient-psychiatrist relationship. And John Simon has indicted it as a trumped-up plea for a homosexual life style. James Lee, on the other hand, has praised *Equus* for the fullness of its dramatic experience, and James Stacy has pointed out the strength of its religious passion, particularly in relation to Shaffer's earlier *Royal Hunt of the Sun*. What we are confronted with, then, is a major work of serious drama which continues to enthrall sophisticated (and not so sophisticated) audiences, but which leaves many viewers uneasy because they are uncertain what they are so enthusiastically applauding. Robert Brustein, for instance, has written about his surprise at seeing Broadway audiences heartily endorsing sodomy. It is probable that the controversy will continue, and the purpose of this essay is to shed some light on the traditions which have given

EQUUS IS THAT INCREASINGLY RARE SERIOUS DRAMA WHICH CAPITALIZES ON LURID EVENTS WHILE MAINTAINING A DEVOTION TO 'IDEAS'"

us *Equus* nearly twenty years after a similar work—*Look Back in Anger*—began changing the face of the contemporary English theatre.

The comparison is not so surprising as might be initially assumed. In its subject matter, its dramatic tradition, *Equus* is still infused with the same philosophical outlook which was so popular and controversial in 1956. And in spite of a variety of dramatic viewpoints carefully exhibited by two generations of English playwrights, we seem to be back almost where we began. Thus, being truly alive is synonymous with suffering an intensity of experience which frequently borders on the abnormal and which is repeatedly glamorized as "passion." Alison Porter in *Look Back in Anger* can only be "saved," after all—as she herself comes to realize—if she grovels and suffers. (This despite the fact that she confides to Helena that she was very happy for the first twenty years of her life.) Jimmy Porter, whose passions we are sometimes invited to admire in much the same way that we are Alan Strang's, tells his wife that there is hope for her if she "could have a child and it would die." Indeed, Jimmy accuses everyone of wanting to avoid the discomfort of being alive, and he describes the process of living as a realization that you must wade in and "mess up your nice, clean soul." Routine is the enemy for Jimmy Porter, and those who are not willing to take part in his crusade of suffering are forced to desert him.

The same points and counterpoints are echoed in Shaffer's drama. Dr. Dysart's bland and colorless life is endlessly exhibited and catalogued. Like Alison and her brother, Nigel, Dysart is not a participant but a spectator. He has never ridden a horse. He experiences passion only vicariously. He is married to an antiseptic dentist whom he no longer even kisses. He travels to romantic climes with his suitcases stuffed with Kao-Pectate. And because he is acutely conscious of his normality, he feels accused by Alan just as Alison is attacked by Jimmy.

Alan Strang, on the other hand, experiences passion in its extremity; a passion which Dysart not only lacks but envies. Like Jimmy Porter, Alan has made a pain which is uniquely his, and uniquely part of his being alive.

> DYSART. His pain. His own. He made it. Look . . . to go through life and call it yours—your life—you first have to get your own pain. Pain that's unique to you. You can't just dip into the common bin and say, "That's enough!"

Dysart's description of Alan recalls Jimmy's complaint that, "They all want to escape from the pain of being alive," as well as Alison's cry, "Oh, don't try and take his suffering away from him—he'd be lost without it."

The pain that defines both Jimmy and Alan, of course, is always contrasted with the commonplace, the normal experiences of everyday life. Both of these plays explore, without ever resolving, the conflict between the abnormal and the ordinary events of our existence. Jimmy wants Alison to show some enthusiasm in order to experience the emotions of being alive. But it is always life by his terms, and his terms are demanding. He wants to "stand up in her tears." And ultimately he wins. "I was wrong," she admits. "I want to be a lost cause. I want to be corrupt and futile." She becomes a kind of victim-healer, because she is willing to give him his pain and reaffirm his vision of a world where "plundering" is equated with being alive.

Shaffer covers much of the same ground. Instead of Jimmy Porter, we now have the tormented Alan, whose horrible acts are translated by Dysart into a kind of enviable pain. The extremity of Alan's passions is what Dysart covets, and he is reluctant to remove Alan's pain because (like Alison) Dysart sees in the pain the source of a passionate life.

> You won't gallop any more, Alan. Horses will be quite safe. You'll save your pennies every week, till you can change that scooter in for a car, and put the odd fifty P on the gee-gees, quite forgetting that they were ever anything more to you than bearers of little profits and losses. You will, however, be without pain. More or less completely without pain.

Dysart finally accepts his part as healer because any other alternatives are simply unacceptable. Alan's extremity—the blinding of the horses—is a shocking dramatic device, but no amount of theatrical trickery can enable Shaffer to equate barbarism with an enviable passion for life.

But what are we to make of all this? Is this stern indictment of the commonplace what is so compelling about *Equus?* Is it the core "idea" at the center of the drama? Or is it a metaphor for a more complex statement?

John Simon has examined the thematic issues in *Equus* and discovered a thinly disguised homosexual play beneath the surface of Shaffer's pseudo-psychology. Simon claims that the depiction of Dysart's wife and marriage, the sexual imagery associated with the horses, and the inability of Alan to perform with Jill are all clear indications of a viewpoint which rejects heterosexuality—the ordinary—in favor of a homosexual world view. Simon additionally points out that the marriage of Jill's parents is also painted in a bad light, and that Jill, herself, is presented as a naughty seductress tempting Alan away from his Horse-Eden. Thus, for Simon the play abounds with dishonesty: ". . .toward its avowed purpose, the explication of 'a dreadful event,' by making that dreadfulness seem fascinating and even admirable. Dishonesty to the audiences, by trying to smuggle subliminal but virulent homosexual propaganda into them. Dishonesty toward the present state of the theatre, in which homosexuality can and has been discussed openly and maturely."

This point of view is particularly interesting in light of the comparison with *Look Back in Anger,* because Osborne's play has also been analyzed in terms of its strong homosexual overtones. Indeed, psychiatric criticism of the play addressed the *ménage à trois* implications of the Porter household two decades ago. How else, some critics believed, could you account for the characters' behavior? Writing in *Modern Drama,* E. G. Bierhaus, Jr. has argued that the real lovers in the play are Jimmy and Cliff, and that while both of the women pursue Jimmy, he pursues only Cliff. "That Alison loses her baby and Cliff keeps his ulcers is symbolic: neither can give Jimmy what he needs."

Uncovering homosexuality in literature, however, is often a shell game, and the degree of sleight of hand frequently vitiates the worth of the results. Once certain premises are established, almost anything is fair game. Perhaps Simon is accurate, and Bierhaus too, but there may be a more obvious answer to the apparent disdain with the ordinary which seems to infuse both *Look Back in Anger* and *Equus.*

Certainly the "angry young men" of the 1950's did not require a homosexual world view in order to see the failures of the welfare state, the outdated monarchy and the vanishing empire. Assaulting the commonplace was for Osborne and his contemporaries a thematic way of rejuvenating the English drama as well as tapping the *angst* that was so compelling in the surrealistic experiments of Beckett and Ionesco. And the normal represented everything from the inequalities of the class system to the blunders at Suez. In its world view, then, *Equus* is an extension not only of *Look Back in Anger,* but also of John Arden's *Live Like Pigs,* Arnold Wesker's *Roots,* Harold Pinter's *The Lover,* and numerous other dramatic ventures which contrasted the passion of the abnormal with the drabness of the postwar English world, and which, consequently, have led to an often misplaced admiration of violence and aberration.

In the final analysis, the thematic issues in *Equus* sometimes seem muddled and confused not because the play is disguised homosexuality, but because it is part of an ongoing fascination with life as "passion," a fascination which also has its counterparts in English films and popular music. The current extremity termed "punk rock," for example, owes its lineage to the grittiness of the early Rolling Stones just as much as *Equus* descends from *Look Back in Anger* . Iconoclasm has become institutionalized. The original "causes" are somewhat shrouded, but the rebellion goes on. Life as "passion" continues to be dramatic and highly theatrical, but after twenty years somewhat unsatisfactory as "IDEA."

Fortunately, like so many other English plays of the past two decades, *Equus* lives not by what it says but by the sparks that it ignites in its attempts to be articulate. And while Shaffer's dramatic traditions go back to *Look Back in Anger,* his theatrical tradition is closely linked to the experiments of a decade ago in the modes of Brecht and Artaud. For what is ultimately applauded in *Equus* is not its message but its packaging. Like spectators of *Marat-Sade,* audiences at Shaffer's play are frequently carried headlong into a vague kind of catharsis without a very clear knowledge of what they are experiencing or applauding. This is not, and has not been, an unusual occurrence in the contemporary theatre. It would be interesting to know, for instance, how many audience members have come away from *Marat-Sade* confused by the complex arguments of Peter Weiss's dialectic on revolution, yet enormously moved by the grotesque images in the play: the deranged inmates, the club-swinging nuns, the saliva, semen and revolutionary songs.

The "total theatre" of a decade ago was an exciting theatre. And it did play a large part in replacing a poetry of words with what Artaud called a poetry of the senses. *Marat-Sade* is the most famous of the total theatre experiments, because of the publicity surrounding its creation and its huge popular success outside the United Kingdom. But there were others of the same ilk. John Whiting's *The Devils* is a wonderfully theatrical play which rambles in its structure, avoids an obvious obligatory scene, and strains for "meaning" on a variety of levels. Ultimately, however, it works—or does not work—in terms of its theatrical effects: the possessed sisters, Jeanne's sexual obsessions, Grandier's torture. (Interestingly, Ken Russell focused on these very elements in filming Whiting's script.) In varying degrees, the same may be said of Edward Bond's *Narrow Road to the Deep North,* John Arden's *Serjeant Musgrave's Dance,* Shaffer's own *Royal Hunt of the Sun,* and others.

It is from this theatrical tradition that *Equus* also draws, and it is this tradition which frequently convinces us that we are seeing and hearing something *important* because the images which bombard us are so exciting. *Equus* is an exciting play. The eerie music and equus noise are provocative and foreboding. The men as horses serve as a compelling theatrical invention which helps to intensify both the act-one curtain and the blinding sequence near the end of the play. The nude encounter between Jill and Alan is strikingly theatrical, as is the physical setting of the drama which allows one scene to flow rapidly into the next.

But ultimately *Equus* is a schizophrenic play, because its theatrical fireworks cannot mask its muddled logic and tired philosophy. After sorting through what Shaffer has to say, it is tempting to dispense with the intellectual straining and experience the play on a more visceral level. After all, Alan *will* be better once he is cured. And Dysart, too, may yet survive his menopause and move on to a time and place where he can admire his own great gifts as much as his patients' horrifying illnesses.

Source: Barry B. Witham, "The Anger in *Equus*" in *Modern Drama,* Volume XXII, no. 1, March, 1979, pp. 61–66.

Henry Hewes

In this review, Hewes praises Shaffer's play for its powerful portrayal of anger at society. In addition to the originality of the text, the critic commends the quality of the actors and the staging in the production he viewed.

In this remarkable season when the majority of new theatrical attractions on Broadway have been imported from abroad, the most strikingly successful entry appears to be Peter Shaffer's *Equus.*

Equus locks together the ordeals of two very different protagonists. One, Martin Dysart, is a quietly unhappy psychiatrist, who has a longing for a Greek civilization where myths and rituals were based on instinctively experienced truths, but who has accepted a frigid marriage and package tours to Greece as a safe substitute for a more passionate and more fully realized existence. Martin's way of non-life is suddenly challenged when he is asked to treat the play's second protagonist, Alan Strang. Alan is a teenage psychopath, who has committed the incredibly horrible act of blinding all of the horses in a stable with a spike.

With insistent theatricality *Equus* follows the psychiatrist, as by means of various tricks and devices he uncovers the pertinent factors that have caused his young patient to go berserk. It is revealed that an incompatibility between Alan's mother and father has led Alan to acquire a religious fixation, which, when blocked, is transferred to a fixation on horses. Thus his ultimately unsuccessful attempt at lovemaking with a girl in a stable brings Alan a double wave of shame. Not only has he failed as a man among men, but also he has desecrated his temple of horses, whose staring eyes become unbearable. Quite superbly the action builds to a violent and naked climax in which Alan relives for us the terrible moment. This reliving is, we are told, the healthy process of abreaction that will cure Alan of his obsession with horses. However, we are also told that Alan had found, in the fierceness and nobility of the horse, an object worthy of worship in a world where true worship had become most difficult. And Martin concludes with a final lament that his cure will reconcile Alan to a smaller, worshipless living-out of his years.

Some American critics have found in Martin's situation a disguised statement of the plight of the timid homosexual, who lacks the courage to pursue the dangerous consummation of his desires. However, Shaffer has strongly denied any such intention, and the play works quite well if Martin is taken to represent the apparently ingrained tendency of many modern Britons to accept, without passion or anger, a well-ordered but watered-down existence. Yet the play's statement is less impressive than is Shaffer's skillful theatrical fabrication, which deftly finds layers of comic relief as he inexorably drills deeper into the hard rock of tragedy. Indeed, *Equus* emerges as a surprisingly painless modern tragedy, which accounts for both its popularity and the reservations some serious critics have expressed about its significance.

Certainly a great part of the play's success comes from its boldly inventive staging, by John Dexter, and the dedication its performers bring to their nightly ritual. Using a stage arrangement similar to the one Ingmar Bergman developed for his Stockholm production of *Wozzeck,* Dexter creates all the play's action in an empty space between two opposing groups of theatergoers. Everything is simple and exact, with no scenery and all actors and props always onstage. When horses are required, some of the actors simply put on horses' heads, made of sculpted wire, and elevated iron hooves. Similarly, when a character must participate in a scene, the performers just rise from their onstage benches and beautifully manage their instant transformations into the characters they must play. Most spectacular is Peter Firth, who makes the furtive and insolent Alan into an ultimately sympathetic victim. And, as the troubled psychiatrist, Anthony Hopkins is frequently electrifying in quick flashes of deeply felt anger. And Marian Seldes, Roberta Maxwell, Michael Higgins, and Frances Sternhagen all suggest hidden depths in characters whose functions are primarily supportive.

All in all, one suspects *Equus* is at its truest when it is reflecting its author's anger at his own civilization.

Source: Henry Hewes, "The Crime of Dispassion" in the *Saturday Review,* Volume 2, no. 9, January 25, 1975, p. 54.

SOURCES

Barnes, Clive. "*Equus* a New Success on Broadway" in the *New York Times,* October 25, 1974, p. 26.

Billington, Michael. Review of *Equus* in the Manchester *Guardian,* July 27, 1973, p. 12.

Christie, Ian. Review of *Equus* in the *Daily Express* (London), July 27, 1973, p. 10.

Clum, John M. "Religion and Five Contemporary Plays: The Quest for God in a Godless World" in the *South Atlantic Quarterly,* Vol. 77, no. 4, 1978, pp. 418-32.

Hewes, Henry. "The Crime of Dispassion" in the *Saturday Review,* January 25, 1975, p. 54.

Hughes, Catherine. "London's Stars Come Out" in *America,* December 8, 1973, pp. 443-44.

Kerr, Walter. "*Equus:* A Play That Takes Risks and Emerges Victorious" in the *New York Times,* November 3, 1974, p. 11.

Klein, Dennis A. "Game-Playing in Four Plays by Peter Shaffer" in *Peter Shaffer: A Casebook,* edited by C. J. Gianakaris, Garland (New York), 1991, pp. 95-113.

Lambert, J. W. Review of *Equus* in *Drama* (London), Vol. 111, 1973, pp. 14-16.

Lawrence, Frank. "The *Equus* Aesthetic: The Doctor's Dilemma" in *Four Quarters,* Vol. 29, no. 2, 1980, pp. 13-18.

Panter-Downes, Mollie. "Letter from London" in the *New Yorker,* November 12, 1973, pp. 181-84.

Peter Shaffer ("English Authors Series," Vol. 261, revised edition), Twayne, 1993.

Shaffer, Peter. "*Equus:* Playwright Peter Shaffer Interprets Its Ritual" in *Vogue,* February, 1975, p. 136.

Stacy, James R. "The Sun and the Horse: Peter Shaffer's Search for Worship" in *Peter Shaffer: A Casebook,* edited by C. J. Gianakaris, Garland, 1991, pp. 95-113.

Walls, Doyle W. "*Equus:* Shaffer, Nietzsche, and the Neuroses of Health" in *Modern Drama,* Vol. 27, no. 3, 1984, pp. 314-23.

Wardle, Irving. "Shaffer's Variation on a Theme" in the *Times* (London), July 27, 1973, p. 15.

Weightman, John. "Christ As Man and Horse" in *Encounter,* Vol. 44, no. 3, 1975, pp. 44-46.

FURTHER READING

Contemporary Literary Criticism, Gale: Volume 5, Volume 14, Volume 18, Volume 37, Volume 60.

This resource compiles selections of criticism; it is an excellent starting point for a research paper about Shaffer. The selections in these five volumes span Shaffer's career. For an overview of Shaffer's life, see the entry on him in Volume 13 of the *Dictionary of Literary Biography.* Also see Volume 7 of Gale's *Drama Criticism.*

Cooke, Virginia, and Malcom Page, compilers. *File on Shaffer,* Methuen, 1987.

This slim but excellent resource reprints excerpts from a wide variety of sources (reviews, interviews, etc.). It also includes a chronology of works, production, and publication data as well as information on Shaffer's non-theatrical works.

Eberle, Thomas. *Peter Shaffer: An Annotated Bibliography,* Garland, 1991.

A resource intended to serve the needs of both teachers/students of dramatic literature and theatre professionals. Organized with each major play as a separate

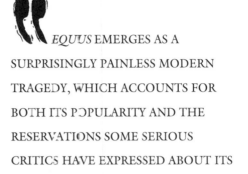

"*EQUUS* EMERGES AS A SURPRISINGLY PAINLESS MODERN TRAGEDY, WHICH ACCOUNTS FOR BOTH ITS POPULARITY AND THE RESERVATIONS SOME SERIOUS CRITICS HAVE EXPRESSED ABOUT ITS SIGNIFICANCE"

chapter. The bibliographic entries are subdivided as follows: editions of the text, play reviews, news reports and feature stories, scholarly essays, and (where applicable) film adaptations and reviews. The span of this work is from March, 1956, to May, 1990 (through *Lettice and Lovage*). It also contains a complete chronology of Shaffer's plays and additional chapters covering general works (biographies and works analyzing more than one play), interviews, and Shaffer's early works (prior to *Five Finger Exercise*).

Gianakaris, C. J *Peter Shaffer,* Macmillan (New York), 1992. A book-length study of Shaffer and his works. Gianakaris writes of Shaffer, "*Five Finger Exercise* and *The Royal Hunt of the Sun* signaled the arrival on the scene of a new, innovative voice in the theatre; *Equus* confirmed it." In his analysis of specific plays, Gianakaris defines the common threads of theme and technique which run through many of Shaffer's theatrical works.

Gianakaris, C. J., editor. *Peter Shaffer: A Casebook* ("Casebook on Modern Dramatists" series, Vol. 10), Garland, 1991. This collection includes ten essays on Shaffer and a 1990 interview with the playwright. Many of the selections offer comparative readings of Shaffer's major works. Also included are a comprehensive index of opening dates for Shaffer's plays and an abbreviated bibliography.

Klein, Dennis A. *Peter Shaffer,* revised edition, Twayne, 1993. A general study of Shaffer's works by a critic who has also published on *Equus* in particular ("Peter Shaffer's *Equus* as a Modern Aristotelian Tragedy" in *Studies in Iconography,* Vol. 9, 1983). The opening section provides an outline of Shaffer's life and discusses his early and minor works. Each chapter on one of the major plays provides sections on the plot; the major characters; sources, symbols, and themes; structure and stagecraft; and critical appraisal.

The Heidi Chronicles

WENDY WASSERSTEIN

1988

Wendy Wasserstein's *The Heidi Chronicles* is her best-known play. It was first produced Off-Broadway at Playwrights Horizons, December 11, 1988, running for three sold-out months, before moving to the Plymouth Theater on Broadway on March 9, 1989. The play averaged 90% full houses during its run and, in 1989, garnered numerous awards, including the Pulitzer Prize for drama as well as the Antoinette Perry (Tony) and New York Drama Critics' Circle awards for best play. Other honors include the Outer Critics Circle Award, the Dramatists Guild's Hull-Warriner Award, and the Susan Smith Blackburn Award for women playwrights.

Following its debut, critical reaction to *The Heidi Chronicles* was mixed. Many praised Wasserstein for her unflinching portrayal of the Baby Boom generation's coming of age. Heidi is a character typical of many women born in the post-World War II era: she is intelligent, well-educated, and attempting to make it in a society dominated by men. While many critics admired the events Wasserstein depicts, some faulted her for undermining the play's serious issues with sitcom humor, half-baked characters like the indecisive Susan Johnston, and a contrived ending.

Many feminists also found fault with *The Heidi Chronicles*. While some were happy that a play with strong feminist themes was a mainstream success, they were displeased with Wasserstein's negative comments (primarily through the voices of her male

characters) on the woman's movement. The title character Heidi is often a mute observer, dominated by her two male friends, Scoop and Peter. Feminists believed that Wasserstein blames the women's movement for the fact that women are trivial and men more serious.

Despite such complaints, *The Heidi Chronicles* is largely seen as a success in the subgenre of feminist theatre. The play distinguished Wasserstein as a significant dramatic voice of the Baby Boom generation. Political/gender issues aside, most critics and viewers found the play to be entertaining and few could deny Wasserstein's facility with comedic dialogue. Moreover, many women *did* relate to Heidi's search for her own identity and the anguish she suffers as a woman in modern society.

Wendy Wasserstein

AUTHOR BIOGRAPHY

Wendy Wasserstein was born in Brooklyn, New York, on October 18, 1950. Her parents were Jewish immigrants who came to America from Central Europe as children. Her father, Morris, was a prosperous textile manufacturer. Her mother, Lola, was a homemaker and a nonprofessional dancer. To compete for attention in her large family Wasserstein developed a sharp, unique sense of humor that would later become a hallmark of her writing. Her mother, described by the playwright as a flamboyant, larger-than-life figure, introduced her to the theater as a child, and Wasserstein recognized the dramatic genre as an outlet for her creativity. While her colorful family served as inspiration for many of her plays, especially *The Sisters Rosensweig* (1992) Wasserstein also felt she could never meet their high expectations. When the family moved to Manhattan, the thirteen-year-old Wasserstein experienced feelings of alienation at school as well.

Wasserstein pursued higher education at Mount Holyoke College, taking her first playwriting class at nearby Smith College. Though her instructor encouraged her gifts, she still searched for an identity. Wasserstein's talents are widely thought to have come of age in the late-1960s, when she discovered the women's movement, a key aspect of *The Heidi Chronicles* (1988) and a concept that has informed all of her work.

Following her graduation in 1971, Wasserstein moved back to New York City. There, she earned an

M.A. from the City College of New York, studying under such literary notables as playwright Israel Horovitz (*The Indian Wants the Bronx*) and novelist Joseph Heller (*Catch-22*). Still uncertain of what course to take in life, Wasserstein applied to both the Yale School of Drama and the Columbia Business School. After being accepted by both, Wasserstein decided to go to Yale. Though she initially felt isolated and lost as the only woman among a dozen men in the program, Wasserstein eventually came to recognize her own place and the unique manner in which she could theatrically give voice to women's issues.

At Yale, Wasserstein studied the plays of Anton Chekhov (*The Cherry Orchard, Uncle Vanya*). She was impressed with the Russian playwright's balance between sympathy and ridicule for his characters. Inspired by Chekhov, Wasserstein modeled several of her early plays on his style. Other great playwrights she studied, however, offered stereotypical women, female characters greatly removed from Wasserstein and her peers. At Yale, Wasserstein began work on the one-act *Uncommon Women and Others* (1975), a comedic social commentary based on her experiences at Mount Holyoke. The play received significant praise when a revised and enlarged (Wasserstein expanded the original text to a two-act) version of the play was produced Off-Broadway in 1977.

During the 1980s Wasserstein worked to establish herself as a professional playwright, achieving moderate success. In 1988, she wrote *The Heidi Chronicles,* a work that is generally considered a high water mark and one of her most challenging plays. The play was first produced in a workshop at the Seattle Repertory Theater in 1988 and subsequently premiered Off-Broadway at the Playwrights Horizon that same year. *The Heidi Chronicles* debuted on Broadway at the Plymouth Theater in 1989 and received numerous awards and honors, including the Pulitzer Prize, a Drama Desk Award, and the Antionette (''Tony'') Perry Award for best play of the year.

While *The Heidi Chronicles* cemented Wasserstein's dramatic reputation, she has had continued success with plays such as *The Sisters Rosensweig* and 1997's *An American Daughter.* She also wrote the screenplay for the film adaptation of Stephen McCauley's novel *The Object of My Affection,* starring Jennifer Aniston. Like Heidi Holland in *The Heidi Chronicles,* Wasserstein has considered adopting a child as a single parent.

PLOT SUMMARY

Act I, prologue

The Heidi Chronicles opens in a lecture hall at Columbia University in 1989. Heidi Holland, a forty-year-old art history professor, delivers a lecture on three women artists, Sofonisba Anguissola, Clara Peeters, and Lilly Martin Spencer. She points out that while these women were either highly regarded in their time and/or extremely talented, they are virtually unknown today.

Act I, scene 1

The year is 1965, the setting a high school in Chicago. Sixteen-year-old Heidi attends a dance with her friend Susan Johnston. When the scene begins, Heidi and Susan look out at the dance floor singing along to ''The Shoop Shoop Song.'' A boy, Chris Boxer, asks Heidi to dance, but she declines, telling him she doesn't want to leave her friend. When a ladies' choice dance is called, Susan hikes up her skirt and runs out on the floor to ask a boy she likes to dance, leaving Heidi alone. Heidi sits down

and pulls out a book, *Death Not Be Proud.* A boy named Peter Patrone approaches her, complimenting her with ''You look so bored you must be bright.'' They talk, and Peter teaches her a dance.

Act I, scene 2

It is now 1968, and Heidi attends a dance in Manchester, New Hampshire, for the volunteers and supporters of presidential candidate Eugene McCarthy. Heidi lingers near the food table and is approached by Scoop Rosenbaum. Scoop is overbearing, cutting down her every opinion. Heidi tries to evade him by saying her name is Susan Johnston, until he points out that she is wearing a nametag. Scoop tries to impress her with his intelligence, his work as a journalist, and his well-read opinions. Although he is derogatory toward her, he admits that he wants to have sex with Heidi. At the end of the scene, they passionately kiss.

Act I, scene 3

This scene takes place in 1970 in a church basement in Ann Arbor, Michigan. Jill, a forty-year-old mother of four and Fran, a thirty-year-old lesbian feminist, lead a women's consciousness-raising group. Among the attendees are Becky, a seventeen-year-old abandoned by her parents and living with an abusive boyfriend, Heidi, and Susan. Susan is now a law student, while Heidi attends graduate school at Yale. The group is concerned with empowering themselves. As they sit in a circle and talk, Heidi tries to not make waves by keeping her opinions and feelings to herself. Heidi finds herself drawn into their dialogue, and she talks about her relationship with Scoop. She reveals that she drops everything to see him, realizing that she lets him define how she feels about herself. The scene ends with the group singing a camp song.

Act I, scene 4

Heidi and Debbie, a new friend, protest the lack of women artists included in exhibits at the Chicago Art Institute in 1974. They plan to march on the curator's office. Peter enters and chants sarcastically, making fun of the protestors. Debbie leaves to look for other supporters. Peter, now doing his medical internship, chides Heidi for not visiting him while she is in Chicago. The two friends share their sexual secrets: Heidi stills sees Scoop but only to sleep with him; Peter reveals is he is homosexual. Their discussion is interrupted by Debbie, who will not let Peter accompany them inside to talk to the curator. Debbie goes ahead, and Heidi and Peter eventually go in together.

Act I, scene 5

It is 1977, and Heidi, Peter, Susan, and Molly attend Scoop's wedding to Lisa Friedlander at the Pierre Hotel. Having abandoned her law career and a prestigious Supreme Court clerkship, Susan now lives with a women's collective in Montana, and Molly is a friend from there. Scoop and Heidi discuss their lives. Heidi reveals that she is seeing an editor. Scoop says that he is going to give up practicing law to start a magazine called *Boomer*. Scoop also explains that he could not have married Heidi because she would have been competing with him. However, he says that he still loves her. The scene closes with them dancing to "You Send Me."

Act II, prologue

A return to the same lecture hall from the first act's prologue. Heidi lectures on Lilla Cabot Perry and compares her to Lily Martin Spencer. Heidi points out that the women in both artists' paintings are separate from the situations in which they are depicted: outsiders in their own pictures.

Act II, scene 1

Heidi attends a baby shower for Lisa in 1980. Susan is also present as well as Lisa's sister Denise. Susan has been attending business school in New York and announces that she has just accepted a vice president position at a Hollywood production company.

Heidi has just returned from England, where she almost married, to accept a position as an art historian at Columbia. Before coming to the shower, she had been in Central Park, mourning the death of John Lennon. When Lisa leaves the room for a moment, Heidi tells the others about seeing Scoop with another woman there; he told Lisa he was at a conference in Princeton.

Denise works as a production assistant on a show called *Hello New York,* and invites Heidi to appear on the show to talk about her book about women and art, *And the Light Floods in from the Left.*

Act II, scene 2

Two years later, in 1982, Heidi appears on the show with Scoop and Peter, who is now an immensely successful pediatrician. Before the taping,

Denise instructs them on the topics—ranging from turning forty to sex and relationships. April Lambert, the host, is extremely perky, and while she directs questions to Heidi, Peter and Scoop continually interrupt with their own opinions before she can get more than a few words in. After the taping, Heidi fumes. Scoop uses the opportunity to invite April to lunch because her husband owns a significant chunk of Manhattan real estate.

Act II, scene 3

Heidi meets Susan for lunch at a trendy New York restaurant in 1984. Heidi and Susan talk a bit about Heidi's life—she was dating a lawyer for a while. Heidi reveals she called Susan to talk, but Susan turns the lunch into a business meeting.

Denise joins them because she now works as a story editor for Susan. Susan and Denise want to develop a television show about single women in the art world in Houston, and they want to hire Heidi as a consultant. In the course of the conversation, Susan disavows her feminist political past. Heidi grows uncomfortable throughout the lunch, and tells Susan she cannot help them.

Act II, scene 4

Heidi addresses a high school alumnae luncheon at the Plaza Hotel in 1986. Heidi tells the audience she is doing her speech off the cuff. The topic was supposed to be "Women, Where Are We Going?," but Heidi talks about something that happened to her the day before. After teaching, she went to an exercise class and found herself totally out of sync with the other women in the locker room. Their concerns did not relate to hers yet she found herself envying them. Just when she was about to leave the locker room, she tripped and fell into the group of other women. She imagined what they must think of her, and she told the exercise instructor she could not go to class because she was too unhappy. Referring to the women's movement, she tells the audience: "I thought we were all in this together." Shaken and clearly disturbed, she quickly exits the stage.

Act II, scene 5

It is nearly midnight, Christmas Eve, 1987. Heidi shows up at a hospital children's ward carrying boxes of donations. Peter cannot believe she has showed up out of the blue with such gifts. He tells her he does not want to hear about her problems. She tells him that she's moving to Minnesota tomorrow and has come to say good-bye. He becomes angry because many of his friends are dying of AIDS, and he regards her unhappiness as trivial and a "luxury." He tells her that he feels his life growing smaller. She decides to stay for him.

Act II, scene 6

Heidi has just moved into a new, still empty apartment. It is 1989. Scoop enters, and tells her that he just sold his magazine. He expresses anxiety towards his uncertain future. Heidi tells him that she is not always going lend a sympathetic ear to his troubles; she has her own life to lead. After discussing their past, Scoop reveals that he knows about her adopting an infant from Panama. Heidi has named the baby Judy. Scoop gives Heidi a silver spoon for the baby. Heidi brings her out. After Scoop leaves, Heidi sings "You Send Me" to her. The last image of the play is a photo of Heidi and the baby in front of a banner announcing a retrospective of Georgia O'Keefe, a significant female artist.

CHARACTERS

Denise Friedlander

Denise is Lisa's sister. She works as a production assistant on a show called *Hello, New York.* Susan Johnston hires her as her assistant when she becomes a Hollywood executive.

Lisa Friedlander

Lisa Freidlander marries Scoop Rosenbaum and works as an illustrator of children's books. She accepts the role of housewife and mother to Scoop's children. She is always cheery and sweet, despite the fact that her husband is cheating on her. She and Scoop have two children, Maggie and Pierre.

Heidi Holland

Heidi is the woman around whom *The Heidi Chronicles* is constructed. Over the course of the play, episodes of Heidi's life are depicted, from the 1960s to the 1980s, from ages 16 to 40. As an adult, she is an art historian; it is through a series of art lectures that her story unfolds. Two of her lectures describe overlooked female artists who remained on the periphery of the art world, artists whose works are notable for their observational nature.

Like the artists she describes, Heidi is often a spectator in her own world. As the play advances chronologically, she becomes increasingly disillusioned with her role in the world. She also becomes disenchanted with the women's movement, the men in her life, and her own quest for happiness; she laments her lack of identity. Despite attaining independence and professional distinction she finds her life empty. At the end of the play, she hopes to find fulfillment when she adopts a baby from Panama.

Huron Street Ann Arbor Women's Consciousness-raising Rap Group

This women's group includes Jill, a housewife with four children; Fran, a lesbian physicist friend of Susan's; and Becky Groves, a seventeen-year-old high school student who live with an abusive boyfriend. The group is influential in Heidi's emergence as a feminist.

Susan Johnston

Susan is Heidi's best female friend. She changes careers and political leanings as the times dictate. She goes to law school only to quit a Supreme Court clerkship to move to a woman's collective in Montana. She then goes to business school, ostensibly for the collective, but, upon graduation, is offered a job in Hollywood as an executive for a new production company that wants to target a young, female audience. She rationalizes that she is taking the job for the good of all women, so that someone who isn't sensitive to women's issues won't take the job. Yet she turns into a stereotypical dealmaker, bent on greed and power. She turns a lunch in which Heidi wants to talk about personal matters into a business deal.

April Lambert

April hosts *Hello, New York,* the show on which Peter, Scoop, and Heidi appear to talk about their generation. She is married to an important real estate magnet, David Lambert, with whom Scoop wants to do business.

Peter Patrone

Peter is one of Heidi's best friends, a caustic cynic. He meets her at a high school dance and is impressed by her boredom. Over the course of the play, Peter reveals to Heidi that he is homosexual. Following college, he becomes a successful pediatrician living in New York City. When Heidi complains about her unhappiness, he tells her that he is tired of his friends dying of AIDS and that her boredom and discontent are luxuries. When she announces her intentions to leave New York City, Peter talks Heidi into to staying for him.

Scoop Rosenbaum

Scoop Rosenbaum is another friend of Heidi's and her former lover. They first meet at a political fundraiser for Eugene McCarthy. From the beginning, he is arrogant, glib, and self-assured, though not without charm. He is Heidi's intellectual equal. He has a habit of grading or assigning points to everything, from cookies to songs to experiences.

Scoop works primarily as a journalist, starting his own newspaper after dropping out of Princeton. He briefly becomes a lawyer before starting a magazine targeted at Baby Boomers titled *Boomer.* Scoop marries Lisa, who he knows will stay home, have his children, and be a devoted wife—he cheats on her while she is pregnant. Though she is essentially his soul mate, he does not marry Heidi because she would compete with and challenge him.

THEMES

Success and Failure

Underlying much of the tension of *The Heidi Chronicles* is how success differs for men and women. Though it is known from the prologue of the first act that Heidi has a successful career as an art historian, the play focuses more on her success as a feminist and autonomous person; unlike the male characters, career success for Heidi does not equal a fulfilled life.

As Heidi's generation demanded, she became an independent woman in a male-dominated world. Yet this success seems hollow to Heidi near the end of the play. She hoped that feminism would provide solidarity with her fellow women and offer significance in society, but her reality has proven this false. Her women friends have bought into superficial happiness and material success: Susan Johnston changes identities frequently, going from an idealistic law student to a feminist to a Hollywood power broker; she ultimately becomes disenchanted with the feminist cause and insensitive to her friend's problems. Heidi also has little luck with men, sustaining no real lasting relationships and ultimately having her life choices shaped by them. Only in her decision to adopt a child does Heidi achieve an independent success.

MEDIA ADAPTATIONS

- *The Heidi Chronicles* was adapted into a television movie for Turner Television Network (TNT) in 1995. The production stars Jamie Lee Curtis as Heidi, Peter Reigert as Scoop, and Tom Hulce as Peter.

From the play's male perspective, Scoop and Peter are successful in a more traditional sense. Scoop has a long-term marriage, two children, a promising career as a lawyer and later as a publisher. The magazine he starts is wildly prosperous. Though by the end Peter finds many of his friends dying, he is a highly regarded pediatrician in New York City who has successful relationships with men. Because society is male-dominated, the standards by which these men are judged are far less strict than those applied to women. To exemplify themselves, women in Wasserstein's world (as well as the real world) must often work twice as hard as men.

Identity

One primary theme that Heidi is concerned with is the search for her own identity. In the first two scenes of the play, she is young, sixteen- and nineteen-years-old, but she is sure of her intellect and her belief in women's causes. Her allegiance to feminism is illustrated in the women's consciousness-raising group scene. Heidi commits to other women, promoting their equality in art and in life.

Yet this identity undergoes rigorous tests, such as Scoop's wedding reception, during which he tells Heidi that he could not have married her because she would have wanted to be his equal. His statement is a harbinger for future disappointment in her life. Throughout the second act, she finds herself out of step with other women, at a baby shower, at the gym, and even at a friendly lunch gathering. Her friend Susan reflects these changes. Susan begins as a feminist lawyer but ultimately renounces her ideals. Near the end of the second act, Heidi decides

TOPICS FOR FURTHER STUDY

- Research the paintings that Wasserstein mentions in *The Heidi Chronicles*. Discuss the parallels between them and the events depicted in the play.

- What is the role of feminism and other women in Heidi's life? Are her male friends ultimately more important? Is *The Heidi Chronicles* truly a feminist play?

- Compare and contrast *The Heidi Chronicles* and *The Big Chill,* a movie about the same generation. Do both groups of characters share similar problems and concerns?

- In *The Heidi Chronicles,* Heidi says "Have you ever noticed that what makes you a person keeps you from being a person?" What do you think Wasserstein meant by this comment?

---

to go to Minnesota to reinvent herself, but Peter convinces her to stay because *he* needs her near. Until she chooses motherhood, Heidi's identity is pushed and pulled by those around her.

Coming of Age

The Heidi Chronicles shows the evolution of its title character, depicting her awkward teen years through her adult life. The backdrop is the mid-1960s to the late-1980s, when the United States underwent profound political and social changes such as the Vietnam War, the rise of feminism, and the threat of the AIDS virus. As she matures, Heidi finds herself caught up in the politics of the moment, first in the Eugene McCarthy for President movement ("clean for Eugene"), then the burgeoning feminist movement. While the latter gives her an identity and purpose—Heidi protests the lack of women artists exhibited at the Chicago Art Institute—it is not everything she expected. When Heidi realizes how out of step she is with other women—a feeling personified by Susan—and unexpectedly announces it to a roomful of fellow alumnae from her high school, she has accepted her

reality. Near the play's conclusion, she decides to move to Minnesota but ends up staying in New York City and adopting a child. While the other events in her life have shaped her maturity, it is her individual decision to care for another life, the choice of motherhood, that ultimately reflects her coming of age.

Friendship

Almost every relationship depicted in *The Heidi Chronicles* is a friendship. Friendships sustain each of the major characters. Heidi's closest friendships are with two men, Peter and Scoop, who, for a time, also functions as her lover. While Susan is a close friend in the first act—she takes Heidi to the Eugene McCarthy party and the women's consciousness-raising group—her defection to traditional society and values alienates Heidi. Women's solidarity is supposed to be the point, in Heidi's mind, and this betrayal upsets Heidi's sense of the world.

Heidi's friendship with Scoop is also troubled. Scoop flirts with her at the McCarthy party, while simultaneously undermining her beliefs; he reveals his belief that women exist for the pleasure of men, not as intellectual equals. When they are sexually involved, she puts aside everything to see him. Heidi and Scoop's breaking point comes at his wedding, when he admits he could not marry her because she would compete with him. After that, they remain friends but are no longer close. In the last scene, he reflects on this fact and is jealous of the closeness that she and Peter share.

Peter and Heidi are friends from the first scene. Though they bicker—and he frequently trivializes her concerns—they are devoted to and respect each other. Heidi stays in New York City for him in the second-to-the-last scene, instead of moving to Minnesota as she had planned. While Peter and Scoop are similar characters, the large distinction is Peter's homosexuality, which allows his friendship with Heidi to function on a level removed from the sexual tensions that exist between her and Scoop. Peter also accepts Heidi as a complete person and a relative equal, status that Scoop's worldview prohibits him from bestowing.

STYLE

Setting

The Heidi Chronicles is a comedic drama that spans the years 1965 to 1989 and employs numerous locations for its setting. The play is framed by two scenes that open each of the acts. These are set in the present in a lecture hall at New York City's Columbia University where Heidi teaches. While these scenes frame and define the action, the main body of the play is told through a series of flashbacks that span Heidi's adult life.

In Act I, locales include a high school dance at Miss Crane's School in Chicago in 1965; a party for Eugene McCarthy in Manchester, New Hampshire, in 1968; a church basement in Ann Arbor, Michigan, where the women's group meets, in 1970; outside of the Chicago Art Institute in 1974; and the anteroom to the Pierre Hotel in New York City where Scoop has married Lisa Friedlander in 1977.

Act II takes place entirely in New York City. The first scene occurs in Scoop and Lisa's apartment in 1980. The next scene shifts to 1982 and a television studio where the show *Hello, New York* is taped. Susan, Denise, and Heidi have lunch in a trendy restaurant in 1984, and two years later, Heidi gives an address to a luncheon at the Plaza Hotel. Heidi visits Peter in the children's ward at a hospital in 1987. The final scene takes place in Heidi's new, unfurnished apartment in 1989.

By spreading the play across some twenty-five years, Wasserstein is able to illustrate the development of her protagonist. The time span and the often shifting locations lend the play an epic feel that recalls such classic works as Homer's *The Odyssey*, in which the exploits of a heroic character are charted over a great period of time. While *The Heidi Chronicles* is not a narrative on the scale of Homer's work, it is presented as a sort of epic for modern women. By taking Heidi through several eras and social/political movements, Wasserstein attempts to illustrate the life of a typical late-twentieth century woman.

Point of View and Narrative Structure

The Heidi Chronicles is told from the point of view of Heidi Holland, primarily in episodic flashback. In three scenes, Heidi directly addresses the audience with monologues: a prologue opens each act while in Act II, scene 4, Heidi addresses a group at a luncheon. In the rest of the play, Heidi is present in every scene, primarily reacting to the characters and events around her. Such a technique enables Wasserstein to direct the audiences' attention to what is occurring in Heidi's life. By showing the various struggles and triumphs from the point of view of her lead character, Wasserstein is able to

show the audience what a feminist might go through in attempting to build an independent life.

Symbolism and Imagery

Wasserstein uses symbolism in several ways in *The Heidi Chronicles*. She frequently uses popular songs to link scenes, emphasizing their symbolic meaning. For example, the tone for the women's group scene is set by Aretha Franklin's "Respect," a song about a woman demanding better, equal treatment from her man. Heidi admits her relationship with Scoop is not good for her, and she, in fact, deserves respect. The women's solidarity is solidified when they sing a campfire song together. To emphasize the point, the scene closes with a reprise of "Respect."

At the end of Act I, Heidi dances with Scoop to the romantic song "You Send Me," which speaks of a love that elevates a person, taking them above the trivial concerns of the world. In this context the song is bittersweet. Scoop and Heidi still love each other, but they know they cannot have a lasting relationship. At the end of Act II, Heidi's life changes again when she adopts a daughter and moves into a new apartment. She rocks her daughter, singing "You Send Me" to her. In this scene, the song represents Heidi's love for her new baby; the song now symbolizes a much purer love, one that is based in nurture rather than romance.

More literal symbolism is found in the art Heidi describes in the lecture scenes. The women artists she discusses are ignored by much of the mainstream art world. Heidi sees their value, describing two works in particular, Lilla Cabot Perry's "Lady in Evening Dress" and Lily Martin Spencer's "We Both Must Fade." Heidi sees that the women in both paintings are spectators in their own pictures, helping others ease in. Heidi's life is similarly spent reacting to others and aiding them. This comes to a head in the television interview scene, when Heidi sits crunched between Peter and Scoop, unable to speak more than a few words. Her thoughts are never complete but merely give the men a point from which to expound on their own opinions.

The art symbolism also extends to Lisa, Scoop's wife. She is an under-appreciated artist like the women Heidi discusses, an award-winning illustrator of children's books. Only Peter recognizes the value of her art because he is a pediatrician and his patients like it. Scoop approves of his wife's career because she does not compete with him—in fact, he chooses to think of it as more of a hobby than a career.

HISTORICAL CONTEXT

Women's Issues

As the 1980s came to a close, conservative forces remained in control of the White House and other aspects of American society. Republican George Bush assumed the presidential office in 1989, following eight years of conservative rule under President Ronald Reagan. The largely conservative U.S. Supreme Court upheld state restrictions on access to abortions. Though this ruling did not overturn Roe v. Wade, the case which legalized abortion in America, the ruling was seen as a victory for pro-life activists. Another victory came when President Bush vetoed a bill that would allow the federally-funded Medicaid to pay for abortions for women who were victims of rape or incest.

It seemed that the pro-life movement, often regarded as the antithesis to the women's movement, was gaining in power and prestige because of these important political victories. Still, the women's movement, which was primarily pro-choice, did not take this assault on what they regarded as a woman's fundamental right without a fight. They also demonstrated and supported political candidates that were pro-choice. One of the largest rallies they held was in Washington, D.C., in 1989, when approximately 600,000 women marched on the Capitol.

Despite such activity, feminism and the women's movement was on the decline in the late-1980s. After the Equal Rights Amendment, a proposed addition to the Constitution that would have barred discrimination based on sex, was defeated in 1982, feminism lost much of its former power. Many felt that what remained of the women's movement was out of touch with the lives of most women in the United States.

Instead of having it all—something the female characters in *The Heidi Chronicles* discuss—an article in the *Harvard Business Review* claimed that women in managerial positions have two choices: career and family (also known as the mommy track) or career-primary. Some women claimed that raising children and staying at home were legitimate career choices. The number of single parents also rose throughout the 1980s. Wasserstein seems to

endorse these choices when Heidi adopts a child at the end of the play. Many women still worked while raising a family, however, and day care became an important issue.

Art in America

Of the major art exhibits that opened in 1989, none were centered around female painters. This inequality is central to Heidi's career as an art historian. The arts came under fire, in part because of controversy over an exhibit, partially funded by the National Endowment for the Arts (NEA), of work by Robert Mappelthorpe, whose photography was thought by many conservatives to be pornographic. Legislation was proposed in Congress to prevent funding of "obscene" art by the federally-funded NEA.

Health Crises and the Rise of AIDS

The number of AIDS cases was on the rise in 1989, and only one drug, AZT (zidovudine or retrovir), was approved for treatment of the disease in the United States. There was no cure or vaccine. While knowledge about the disease increased, nearly 2.5 million people in the Western Hemisphere (approximately 1 to 1.5 million Americans) became infected with HIV, the virus that causes AIDS. AZT was also being used, somewhat successfully, to delay development of full-blown AIDS in people with few or no symptoms of the disease. Many of Peter's friends died of this disease, and the overwhelming grief associated with the constant lost affects him deeply in the play's later scenes.

CRITICAL OVERVIEW

Critical reaction to *The Heidi Chronicles* has been mixed since its debut in 1988. Many feminists critics applauded the fact that a play about women and women's issues was such a smashing success. The depiction of a modern woman living an anxiety-filled life was a concept with which many women identified. But some such critics believed this success came at a price, complaining that Heidi and the other female characters are not as well-rounded as they could be. Heidi merely reacts to what is going on around her, while the male characters tend to dominate the action. Gerald Weales wrote in *Commonweal* that "Heidi is so muted in her behavior that she serves as a little more than a foil for the

COMPARE
&
CONTRAST

- **1989:** There are many unknowns about the AIDS disease, its causes and cures. The number of deaths from AIDS is on the rise.

  Today: The number of deaths from AIDS has stabilized. Much is known about the disease and there are a number of drugs to treat symptoms of AIDS on the market. While there is still no cure, these new treatments have proven to retard or halt the disease's progress and thus prolong and improve victims' lives.

- **1989:** George Bush enters the White House, following the two-term reign of Ronald Reagan, insuring twelve years of Republican rule in America. The Democratic control of Congress makes for considerable gridlock in the legislative process.

  Today: Democrats control the White House, in the form of two-term President Bill Clinton. The Republicans now control Congress and partisan politics still make for lethargic policymaking.

- **1989:** The Women's Movement is on the decline in the United States as many find the goals and ideals of feminism out of step with their reality.

  Today: In a post-feminist society, women's organizations regroup to address concerns of many women. The National Council of Women's Organizations (representing 6 million women) draft potential legislation for the National Women's Equality Act, calling for the end of sex discrimination, in 1998. The threat of losing abortion rights has also galvanized many women (and men) into political action.

- **1989:** Pro-life activists win important political victories in restricting access to abortion.

  Today: President Clinton refuses to sign legislation banning partial-birth abortions, a controversial procedure whose abolition is a cornerstone of the pro-life movement.

---

more animated characters—a kind of wall on which Wasserstein can hang her snapshots.''

Many critics debated the strength of the characters in *The Heidi Chronicles,* with criticism focusing on the fact that they are at once complex and oversimplified. They have a self-depreciating sense of humor and are aware of their faults, yet can question others. Some critics felt that Heidi is too self-aware and unbelievable. Other critics disliked the way Heidi's friend Susan is little more than a recurring punchline, an indecisive wanderer who drifts toward whatever trend is in vogue at the time. A feminist critic, Gayle Austin writing in *Theatre Journal,* stated: ''Wasserstein portrays Heidi's women friends as trivial and her men friends as serious and has Heidi blame the women's movement for that situation.'' Indeed, Wasserstein's chiding of the women's movement is not always appreciated, especially by feminist critics. Still, Moira Hodgson in the *Nation,* commented, ''The most moving insight comes when Heidi, who feels betrayed by the women's movement, says, 'I was a true believer who didn't understand it was just a phase.'''

Wasserstein often plays such differences for their humor, which many regard as her strong point. But some critics argued that her humor in *The Heidi Chronicles* can be ill-timed and is not up to the standards of her previous work. They believed that her humor weakens the potency of the timely topics she addresses. While Robert Brustein, writing in the *New Republic,* said, ''Wasserstein has a wry, self-depreciating humor that helps her avoid self-righteousness without losing her sting,'' later in his review he stated ''Their [the characters'] weakness for wisecracks makes them seem shallower than intended and undercuts the seriousness of the work.''

Another facet of the play that was received with mixed praise are the scenes in which Heidi directly addresses the audience, lecturing about lost women artists. Several reviewers pointed out that Heidi's unprofessional behavior, especially her titters and

The art museum protest scene, in which Heidi and her friends demand that the gallery display more works by female artists

jokes, perform a disservice to the message. They argued that Wasserstein makes fun of such lectures when their point is highly relevant to her play.

The construction of the play itself also came under critical fire. Some critics believed that the episodic nature of the plot weakens the impact of *The Heidi Chronicles*. Some also argued that the ending seems contrived and does not fit with the tone of the rest of the play. Feminist critics, especially, saw Wasserstein's conclusion as a cop-out rather than true closure because Heidi's adoption of a baby girl seems to replace all her other relationships, especially with women. Still, Cathleen McGuigan in *Newseek* wrote: ''Wasserstein sometimes can't balance savagery and heart, but her satire is never empty; she has a strong point to make about lost values.''

CRITICISM

A. Petrusso

In this essay, Petrusso discusses the weakness of the female characters and the dominant role of the male characters in Wasserstein's play; this

unbalanced power structure is reflective of traditional views of male/female roles in society.

Despite its reputation as a feminist play, the male characters and their values dominate *The Heidi Chronicles*. In a review of the original Broadway production, Cathleen McGuigan said in *Newsweek:* ''The men in Heidi's life are more interesting [than her female friends].'' Another critic, Gayle Austin from the *Theatre Journal* called Heidi passive and claimed the play ''gives them [men] all the best lines.'' Many of Heidi's choices are made for and defined by men. Indeed, her role in many scenes is limited to a reactive one; she responds to the sentiments of her male counterparts. Save Heidi, the women in the play are reduced to stereotypes: aggressive businesswomen, single-minded feminists, doting wife and mother. They are often regarded as the weakest part of the play.

The problem with the female characters is embodied in Susan, Heidi's best female friend. Susan has no real depth, none of the heart and self-awareness that Scoop and Peter frequently display. Wasserstein emphasizes Susan's shallowness by having her change careers and attitudes with the trends of the times. She goes from being a law

WHAT DO I READ NEXT?

- *Eastern Standard* is a play by Richard Greenberg written in 1989. The play concerns several professionals living in the 1980s and finding their Yuppie lives meaningless. One character, a writer, suffers from AIDS.

- *Isn't It Romantic,* written by Wasserstein in 1984. Like *The Heidi Chronicles,* it employs an episodic structure and music to set the tone of the play. The plot centers around two women and the choices they make for personal fulfillment.

- *In the Company of Woman: Voices from the Women's Movement* (1998), edited by Bonnie Watkins and Nina Rothchild, is a collection of essays. They tell the stories of eighty-three women and their experiences in the women's movement from the 1960s to the present.

- *The AIDS Crisis: A Documentary* (1998), edited by Douglas Feldman and Julia Wang Miller, is a comprehensive study charting the history of the disease.

- *The Guerilla Girls' Bedside Companion to the History of Western Art,* published by The Guerilla Girls (a group of women artists). This book is a feminist history of art and includes many women artists.

---

student to a feminist collective member to a business school grad working as a power-hungry Hollywood executive. In her last appearance on stage, Susan even states: "By now I've been so many people, I don't know who I am. And I don't care."

Susan also shows disregard for the well-being of her fellow woman in two key scenes. In Act One, scene one, the teenaged Heidi and Susan attend a high school dance. Susan abandons Heidi to dance with a boy who can twist and smoke at the same time (a superficial attraction that reveals much about Susan's attractions later in life). This occurs after Heidi has refused to dance with a boy because she didn't want Susan to feel left out. In Act Two, scene three, when Heidi invites Susan to lunch to talk about personal matters, Susan, in her Hollywood dealmaker persona, turns the friendly get-together into a business meeting and tries to convince Heidi to help her with the development of a television series. She pitches it as a project that will benefit Heidi, but it is clear that Susan cares little for her friend's well-being; her intentions are only for her own success.

In Heidi's climactic monologue, Act Two, scene four, Heidi sighs, "I thought the point was that we were all in this together," the "we" meaning women. This is clearly not the case with Susan and Heidi's relationship. Even Heidi's own support of other women is, at times, questionable. When Heidi and her colleague Debbie stage a protest outside of the Chicago Art Institute lamenting the lack of women artists, Heidi abandons Debbie to be with Peter. Debbie says, "God, I despise manipulative men." Peter can't resist responding, "Me, too." He should know. Both Peter and Scoop undermine Heidi's relationships with women—and her feminist allegiances—from the first scene of *The Heidi Chronicles.*

As the primary male characters in Wasserstein's play, Peter Patrone and Scoop Rosenbaum are portrayed as opposite sides of the same coin. Peter is a gay pediatrician with a ready wit. He practices a traditional, hallowed profession, which gives him a certain status in society. Scoop also has a pithy sense of humor and makes commonly accepted choices. He is a lawyer and a journalist. He marries well, expecting his wife to have a career that is not as important as his so that she can rear their children (Lisa's career as an illustrator of children's books is portrayed as more of a hobby than an occupation; she is primarily Scoop's wife and the mother of his children). These male characters are shown to have lives beyond their careers, they are not ruled by

Heidi meets Scoop, one of the two men in her life, at a Eugene McCarthy Fundraiser. Scoop is shown to be a far more rounded character than Heidi

trends. In contrast, Susan is nowhere near as well-rounded as either man. But there are similarities in the way these three characters respond to Heidi's needs. While both Scoop and Peter can be supportive, they, like Susan, show little regard for Heidi and her choices.

Peter regularly insults Heidi's female friends. Heidi meets Peter at the same high school dance that she attended with Susan. After Susan leaves her, Heidi pulls out a book and begins to read. Peter approaches Heidi, complimenting her by saying: "You look so bored you must be very bright." Peter proceeds to cut down Susan, sarcastically calling her an "unfortunate wench." He then teaches Heidi a dance. Heidi learns something from him, not another woman. A few scenes later, during the protest, Peter also insults Debbie's name and her feminist attitude. Such comments, while presented as humor, undermine Heidi's relationships with women, they erode her respect for feminist ideals. Peter can be an equal opportunity prig, however. He also insults Scoop and his overbearing personality.

Peter also makes Heidi feel guilty in a number of scenes. In the protest scene, Peter berates her for not calling him while she was in Chicago. He

happens across her because he is meeting someone. But when she tries to express what she is feeling, Peter turns the tables and says that she made him feel guilty about his homosexuality. In the second to the last scene of the play, Heidi visits Peter at his hospital ward late at night on Christmas. She has been, unsuccessfully, trying to reach Peter all week. She intends to say goodbye to him and move to Minnesota the next day. But Peter dismisses her problems and the unhappiness that has prompted her decision to relocate, calling her "insane." When the discussion is about Peter—especially the overwhelming emotional pain he feels as many of his friends die of AIDS—Heidi is supportive. Having turned the focus from Heidi to himself, Peter convinces her she is a bad friend for leaving him in his hour of need. Heidi decides to stay in New York for Peter, saying "I could become someone else next year." For the most part, however, her feelings are of little interest to Peter.

While he is in many ways her soul mate, Scoop is even more manipulative of Heidi and repeatedly illustrates his insensitivity to her needs—and those of all women. While Peter does show his support for Heidi at key moments (at Scoop's wedding reception, for example), Scoop is too self-absorbed to notice when he is hurting her. Scoop tells Heidi at one point: "Why should you like me? I'm arrogant and difficult. But I'm very smart. So you'll put up with me." And she does. Like Peter, Scoop insults Susan. At the time of the wedding reception, Susan is living in a women's collective in Montana after abandoning a prestigious Supreme Court clerkship. Of this choice, Scoop says: "She could have been brilliant," implying that an allegiance to the women's collective somehow diminishes Susan's intelligence. Heidi defends her friend, who is standing right there, but Scoop gets away with it. When Susan walks away, he further ridicules her beliefs, calling her "a fanatic" and "crazy."

In comparison to Scoop's treatment of Heidi, however, Susan gets off relatively easy; Scoop continually undermines Heidi's sense of herself. At their initial meeting, a dance for college students working for the Eugene McCarthy presidential campaign, Scoop questions everything Heidi does or says in a manner that makes him seem intelligent and reduces her to a stereotypical woman with little social merit. Heidi tries to be polite, asking him questions about himself. He responds with "Did they teach you at Vassar to ask so many inane questions in order to keep the conversation going?" He scorns her career choice of art historian as "suburban."

Scoop's final affront, the one that rings throughout the play, is a condemnation of Heidi's feminist ideals. He dismissively tells her: "You'll be one of those true believers who didn't understand it was all just a phase." In Wasserstein's world, a female character like Susan is never this insightful about herself or another woman. At the end of the scene, Scoop admits he is trying to "go to bed" with Heidi. Heidi allows him to passionately kiss her before he leaves, and they eventually become romantically involved.

Scoop eventually marries Lisa because she fits his ideals for wife and mother. Still, he manipulates Heidi's emotions at his own wedding reception, telling her he couldn't marry her because of her ambition and her need to be an equal partner in a marriage. While Scoop talks about his own unhappiness to Heidi, he chooses not to be his wife's partner for her first dance at their wedding. Scoop wreaks havoc on these two women's lives, then has the impudence to ask Heidi "Why did you let me do this?," implying that Heidi somehow is responsible for his decision.

Wasserstein allows men to have a measure of control over Heidi's life and emotions. Scoop goes on to be right about the women of Heidi's generation—especially Heidi, telling her, "you 'quality time' girls are going to be one generation of disappointed women. Interesting, exemplary, even sexy, but basically unhappy." Scoop does attempt a half-hearted apology by the end of the wedding scene, however.

Heidi stands up to Scoop in the last scene, after she has adopted her baby. Scoop continues to ridicule her, calling her "prissy" but then says she's important to him. He is in turmoil because he has sold his magazine and is uncertain about his future; he looks to Heidi for comfort and assurance. Heidi tells him, "Don't look at me with those doe eyes and tell me how spoiled you are. Next thing I know, you'll tell me how you never meant to hurt me." This is a small victory and an encouraging show of independence. It is noteworthy that Heidi's new resolve occurs following her adoption of a child, a life-changing choice.

The depth of male dominance in *The Heidi Chronicles* is exemplified by the two scenes in which no men appear. In the women's consciousness raising group in Ann Arbor, Heidi admits she will drop everything just to be with her then-boyfriend, Scoop. She does not say that he drops everything to see her, but she admits he is really only attentive when she tries to leave him. Heidi calls him "a creep," qualifying her insult by adding: "But he's a charismatic creep." Though the women bond over her breakthrough, it only emphasizes the relative importance of the men in *The Heidi Chronicles*. The same thing happens during Lisa's baby shower scene. Much of the conversation revolves around Scoop, Peter, and other men. Lisa believes her husband is at a conference in New Jersey. But Heidi has seen him in Central Park with another, younger woman who works at his magazine.

Heidi makes only two significant choices for herself in the course of *The Heidi Chronicles*: her career choice and adopting the baby. Nearly every other action is influenced by or dictated to her by the other characters. And, almost always, these other characters are Scoop and Peter. To say that *The Heidi Chronicles* is a feminist play is incorrect. While Heidi has a career, Heidi becomes exactly what traditional (male-dominated) society defines as the ultimate female role: a mother.

Source: A. Petrusso, for *Drama for Students,* Gale, 1999.

Gerald Weales

In this mixed review of The Heidi Chronicles, *Weales praises the performances but complains that the play "has no dramatic center" in its title character. He criticizes Wasserstein for providing a protagonist who is little more than a foil for the supporting characters.*

Wendy Wasserstein's *The Heidi Chronicles* began as a workshop production at the Seattle Repertory Theatre; then, shepher ded by the Seattle Rep's Daniel Sullivan, it moved to a well-received off-Broadway debut and then to Broadway; it has now been blessed by the Pulitzer Prize committee. It is a typical American-theater success story of the 1980s, but I have trouble working up much enthusiasm for its triumphant journey.

The Heidi of the title is an art historian, a presumably intelligent and sensitive woman who moves from 1965 to 1989, picking her way through the ideational thickets of those years, only to find that the goal of her generation, to become an independent woman in a male world, brings emptiness with it. The audience follows Heidi's progress in brief scenes that teeter on the edge of broad satire and sometimes, as in the consciousness-raising meeting, fall over completely. Heidi remains pretty much the same throughout the fifteen years—concerned, but a little cold, a little distant, her involvement tinged with self-irony. On her stroll down memory lane, she is accompanied by the two men closest to her—a homosexual doctor who remains her best friend (and incidentally provides an excuse to bring in AIDS as an item in Wasserstein's cultural catalogue) and a fast-talking charmer, sometimes her lover, an intellectual conman who plays the main chance and persists in confusing the fashionable with the significant. Heidi's oldest woman friend, the only other important character in the play, is a Wasserstein joke, a chameleon who becomes whatever the moment requires: a ditsy sexpot, a jargonesque feminist, a member of an ecological commune, a power-lunch paragon in the entertainment business.

The chief weakness of the play is that it has no dramatic center. Heidi is so muted in her behavior that she serves as little more than a foil for the more animated characters—a kind of wall on which Wasserstein can hang her snapshots. Joan Allen is one of the finest reactors among American performers (consider last year's Tony-winning performance in *Burn This*), but however fascinating it is to watch Allen work, Heidi remains flaccid. We are supposed to understand the distress within the character, which surfaces primarily in runs of nervousness and in one unlikely overt moment in which she turns a speech at an alumnae gathering into a high whine of generational regret. At the end of the play, she has adopted a child and the suggestion is that she has found a certain solidity as a single mother, but nothing in the play or the character makes motherhood look like anything but an occasion for Heidi's next disappointment. The ending is as arbitrary as that of Wasserstein's earlier hit, *Isn't It Romantic,* in which the heroine decides for no very clear reason not to marry the man she loves; perhaps she had been to see *My Brilliant Career* at her local moviehouse.

If Heidi as activist and Heidi as unrealized lover are a bit difficult to accept in her *Chronicles,* Heidi as art historian is impossible. She is supposes to be an expert on female artists, correcting the sexual imbalance in the history of art, and we see her in lectures at the beginning of each act. Her manner is oddly frothy, her disclosure decorated with what I think of as wee academic jokies. The wee academic jokie, of which there are far too many on campuses, is not funny if it sounds as though it were written into the lecture, if it is taken out of the classroom context, if it makes the speaker sound as though she were apologizing for her subject matter. So it is with all of Heidi's jokies. Her lectures diminish the whole enterprise of rethinking the female presence in art. In part, that is a product of the unanchored Heidi described in the paragraph above. In part, it grows out of the play's tendency to trivialize the genuine concerns of women in particular, radicals in general, by emphasizing the fashionable patina on social change. As a comic writer, Wasserstein can see what is ludicrous in the convoluted social history of the last fifteen years. On the serious side, *The Heidi Chronicles* is one of those gee-it-didn't-turn-out-the-way-we-expected plays, another offspring of *The Big Chill.*

Source: Gerald Weales, "Prize Problems" in *Commonweal,* Vol. CXVI, no. 9, May 5, 1989 , pp. 279–80.

John Simon

In this review of The Heidi Chronicles's *Broadway debut, Simon finds that the play is more effective than it had been in its previous, Off-Broadway setting. While he still has complaints about certain aspects of the plot—notably the title character's unconvincing career—he finds the production to have considerable merit.*

Having been less enthusiastic than other critics about Wendy Wasserstein's *The Heidi Chronicles* Off Broadway, I hasten to point out that, reversing the pattern, it looks and plays better on. Thomas Lynch has skillfully adapted his tongue-in-cheek scenery, Pat Collins has made her good lighting even more evocative, and the bigger space allows more room for the play's grand ambition to portray two decades of change in our society. A school dance looks more like a school dance, a pediatrics ward is more up to the old pediatrics, etc. And it's nice to bask in oversized slide projections in the hall where Heidi Holland—Wendy Wasserstein transmuted into a feminist art historian—lectures on women in art, even if the splendid Joan Allen mispronounces Sofonisba Anguissola as no art historian should.

The play chronicles Heidi's progress from a frightened but fast-quipping wallflower at a 1965 Chicago high-school dance, through becoming a timid onlooker at a New Hampshire Eugene McCarthy rally (1968), to being a Yale grad student in fine arts visiting a friend in Ann Arbor and shyly observing her consciousness-raising group in session (1970), then to a women-in-art protest march on the Chicago Art Institute (1974), and so on through thirteen scenes—all the way to 1989, when Heidi moves into a commodious New York apartment and adopts a baby girl. Cautiously, she does not name her Sofonisba, Artemisia, or even Angelica, after one of her beloved women artists.

Here the first problem surfaces: the inconsistencies in Heidi's character. In contrast to her feminist and postfeminist friends, Heidi remains an almost Candide-like innocent, despite one of the sharpest and fastest tongues this side of the Pecos. When she lectures, however, her humor changes from vertiginous epigrams to patronizing down-home jokiness. Further, she seems to have an ample and diversified offstage sex life with one editor or another, yet is involved on stage with only a couple of unlikely men throughout.

There is Scoop Rosenbaum, a dazzling opportunist who goes from liberal journalism to putting out *Boomer,* the slickest of slickly upward-mobile magazines, and thence (as I understand it) into politics. Heidi has an off-and-on affair with him, but he wenches around and finally marries an intellectual 6 (instead of her 10)—a wealthy young woman who becomes a leading book illustrator, which is not bad for a 6. And there is Peter Patrone, as

> HEIDI IS SO MUTED IN HER BEHAVIOR THAT SHE SERVES AS LITTLE MORE THAN A FOIL FOR THE MORE ANIMATED CHARACTERS—A KIND OF WALL ON WHICH WASSERSTEIN CAN HANG HER SNAPSHOTS"

cynically scintillating at repartee as Scoop; he, however, becomes an earnest and distinguished young pediatrician. We follow him, a homosexual, through a number of liaisons with men; as far as I can tell, he never sleeps with Heidi. But she is, for obscure reasons, enormously important to him as, in the end, we see him bitterly grappling with AIDS among both his special friends and his child patients.

Now, there are in life beautiful women who have weird problems with men, and witty women who are nevertheless shy; but to make them credible on stage takes a heap more than we are accorded here. When Miss W. had herself portrayed on stage by the portly, ethnic Alma Cuervo, she automatically spoke a good part of the truth; belief boggles at the elegant, glamorous Joan Allen in that role. Equally hard to take are the smart-aleck rapid-fire epigrams from almost everyone; this fits into the unrealistic, stylized milieus of Wilde, Coward, and Orton, but clashes with W.W.'s naturalistic ambience. Finally, the play is a mite too much of a survey course in women's studies; or, to put it bluntly, a check, or even laundry, list. All the same, it is clever and funny and sometimes even wise, and there is, under Daniel Sullivan's direction, good acting from all, and much more than that from the subtly complex Miss Allen, the trenchantly ebullient Peter Friedman and Boyd Gaines, and the especially cherishable Joanne Camp.

Source: John Simon, review of *The Heidi Chronicles* in *New York,* Vol. 22, no. 13, March 27, 1989, pp. 66–67.

Mimi Kramer

Characterizing The Heidi Chronicles *as Wasserstein's "best work to date," Kramer offers a*

HEIDI REMAINS AN ALMOST CANDIDE-LIKE INNOCENT, DESPITE ONE OF THE SHARPEST AND FASTEST TONGUES THIS SIDE OF THE PECOS"

positive review of the play's Off-Broadway debut. Praising the playwright for avoiding moralizing in her work, the critic assesses that "Wasserstein's portrait of womanhood always remains complex."

At the emotional turning point of "*The Heidi Chronicles,*" Wendy Wasserstein's manless heroine Heidi Holland (Joan Allen), an essayist and art-history professor, is supposed to deliver a speech at the Plaza Hotel. The occasion for the speech is an alumnae luncheon, the topic "Women, Where Are We Going?" We've seen Heidi speak in public before—in the classroom sequences that, prologue-like, begin each act—and we've grown familiar with the mock girls'-school bonhomie she exhibits toward the women painters who constitute her particular area of expertise. Ordinarily, the public Dr. Holland is a model of wry composure. On this occasion, however, instead of giving a speech (she hasn't prepared one) Wasserstein's heroine gets up and extemporizes. She begins by sketching a fictional portrait of herself as an "exemplary" New Woman, whose busy and full life—complete with ideal husband and children—would excuse her showing up speechless at a luncheon where she herself was the featured event. Then, in an apparent non sequitur, she tells a story about going to the health club and being too much affected by the other women in the locker room to go through with the exercise class she had planned to attend. Wasserstein never makes the connection between the two halves of the speech; she leaves it to us to infer that Dr. Holland was "too sad" to produce a speech for the Miss Crain's School luncheon, just as she had been "too sad to exercise" that day. Moreover, the cause of Heidi's depression—her manlessness—is never alluded to. Instead, Wasserstein duplicates that feeling in us by having Heidi describe the women in the locker room: two girls discussing "the reading program at Marymount nursery school"; a woman her mother's age complaining about her daughter-

in-law; another older woman "extolling the virtues of brown rice and women's fiction." She imagines the young mothers thinking that women like her "chose the wrong road": "'A pity they made such a mistake, that empty generation.' Well, I really don't want to be feeling this way about all of them. . . . It's just that I feel stranded. And I thought the whole point was that we wouldn't feel stranded, I thought the point was we were all in this together."

"*The Heidi Chronicles,* " which opened last week at Playwrights Horizon in a bangup production directed by Daniel Sullivan, is actually a very funny play. The scene at the Plaza is a tour de force: it justifies the whole play, yet nothing in the play has prepared us for it. We have never been told that the heroine is to make a speech; we have never heard of the Miss Crain's School. We arrive at the Plaza not by any dramaturgical route but by a device of Thomas Lynch, the set designer. That we are able to feel, once we're there, that this scene is where Wasserstein's play has been leading all along is a mark of her artistry.

"*The Heidi Chronicles*" is probably Wasserstein's best work to date. What distinguishes it from her earlier plays is that it actually says something. It's one thing to be able to record an experience or capture the spirit of a time—to write bittersweet autobiography about the bright, promising people one knew in college ("*Uncommon Women and Others*") or how hard it is to grow up and break free of overprotective parents ("*Isn't It Romantic*")—and quite another to send us out of a theatre feeling that we see something in a different light. "*The Heidi Chronicles*" is autobiographical only in the most interesting way: Wasserstein's heroine is, like Wasserstein herself, a student of other women—particularly women engaged in creating images of womanhood. It's significant that the women we see Heidi lecturing on belong to another time: it suggests that Wasserstein's subjects—the young men and women who came of age in the sixties and dropped out to work on radical newspapers or in women's collectives—stand somehow outside the purview of her own and her heroine's experience. Wasserstein wants Heidi to be not an advocate of the women's movement but one of its victims—a vessel carrying around the ideals and experiences of her time. Throughout the play, Heidi remains mostly mute and passive, aloof from the proceedings. That's one of the reasons it's so good to see Miss Allen in the role—of all our younger actresses the most eloquent in silence or repose. "You're the one whose life this will all change significantly,'' warns a charismatic pseudo-radical young man Heidi meets at a McCarthy rally in Manchester, New Hampshire, in 1967, and we see his prophecy fulfilled. At a consciousness-raising session in Ann Arbor in 1970, Heidi is an interloper, forced by feelings and circumstances into ''sharing'' with the other women and surrounded by them, at the end of the scene, in an uncomfortable embrace. We witness Heidi's seduction by the women's movement just as we witnessed her seduction by Scoop, the charismatic young man in the scene before—one of that horde of clever, intense young men who knew how to badger women into profound conversations and shallow beds by making astute personal remarks. It's one of the clevernesses of Wasserstein's play that she makes Scoop (Peter Friedman) a *pseudo*-radical. ''You'll be one of those true believers who didn't understand it was just a phase,'' she has him say. Twenty years later, a routine philanderer and the editor of his own lifestyle magazine, Scoop will be thinking of going into politics, and Heidi will be adopting a baby. We'll never find out exactly what makes Heidi tick, but then we never really find out what makes Isabel Archer tick.

This moving-snapshot style of theatre, in which the progress of a particular character is charted through a succession of years in different towns and cities, is popular among playwrights of Wendy Wasserstein's generation and is most often used to chronicle their disillusionments and disappointments, as Wasserstein uses it here. The danger inherent in such an approach—one that has to go so far afield in space and time in order to make a point—is that what the playwright has to say may turn out to be either trivial, as in the case of Michael Weller's ''Loose Ends,'' or untrue, as in the case of David Hare's ''Plenty.'' Freed from the necessity of discerning some *pattern* of truth in human action, one can, after all, say anything.

Like the health-club speech, Wasserstein's entire play is a tour de force: it mimics the faults of her generation's style of theatre yet manages to transcend them. It spans twenty-three years and rockets us back and forth in time and place. And though it tracks the main characters from the sixties to the present there isn't a single scene in which anything that anyone does has consequences in a later scene. That the play manages to seem economical can only be attributed to some alchemical combination of graceful-mindedness and good writing; the Chekhovian fabric of the dialogue—the degree to

> WASSERSTEIN WANTS HEIDI TO BE NOT AN ADVOCATE OF THE WOMEN'S MOVEMENT BUT ONE OF ITS VICTIMS—A VESSEL CARRYING AROUND THE IDEALS AND EXPERIENCES OF HER TIME''

which characters' ways of talking differ from one another or change over time—creates a Stanislavskian offstage life, so that to witness one conversation between Scoop and Heidi is to know what their subsequent relationship as lovers will be like. Wasserstein never states anything that can be inferred; it's one of the ways she keeps her heroine free of righteousness and self-pity. We aren't shown Heidi's disappointment when her charming, self-effacing friend Peter (Boyd Gaines) announces that he is gay, just at the moment when we're wondering why Heidi doesn't settle down with him (the way we keep wondering why Isabel doesn't settle down with one of the nice young men in ''Portrait of a Lady''); instead, we feel disappointed ourselves.

There's generosity in the writing, toward the characters, certainly, not one of whom is made to seem ludicrous or dismissible, but also toward the performers, who get to engage in a delicious brand of highly specific character acting: Mr. Gaines and Mr. Friedman, irresistible as the two principal men; Drew McVety, making frequent cameo appearances (as a preppie, a bullied waiter, a pediatric resident); Ellen Parker, Anne Lange, Joanne Camp, and Sarah Jessica Parker, playing a host of different women of such varying degrees of liberatedness and niceness that Wasserstein's portrait of womanhood always remains complex. She is herself too much a lady to moralize. She condemns these young men and women by simply capturing them in all their charm and complexity, without rhetoric or exaggeration. They are measured and found wanting. Her final comment on the me generation is contained in Heidi's wish for her daughter: that no man should ever make her feel she is worthless unless she demands to have it all.

Source: Mimi Kramer, ''Portrait of a Lady'' in the *New Yorker,* December 26, 1988, pp. 81–82.

SOURCES

Austin, Gayle. Review of *The Heidi Chronicles* in *Theatre Journal,* March 1990, pp. 107-08.

Brustein, Robert. Review of *The Heidi Chronicles* in the *New Republic,* April 17, 1989, pp. 32-35.

Hodgson, Moira. Review of *The Heidi Chronicles* in the *Nation,* May 1, 1989, pp. 605-06.

McGuigan, Catherine. "The Uncommon Wasserstein Goes to Broadway" in *Newsweek,* March 29, 1989, pp. 76-77.

Wasserstein, Wendy. *The Heidi Chronicles* in *The Heidi Chronicles and Other Plays,* Harcourt Brace Jovanovich, 1990, pp. 155-249.

FURTHER READING

Ciociola, Gail. *Wendy Wasserstein: Dramatizing Women, Their Choices, and Their Boundaries,* McFarland, 1998.

This book discusses several of Wasserstein's plays in depth, including *The Heidi Chronicles.* Ciociola often relies on a feminist perspective.

Franklin, Nancy. "The Time of Her Life" in the *New Yorker,* April 14, 1997, pp. 63-71.

This article discusses Wasserstein's life and background, as well as the subjects that inform her plays.

Keyssar, Helene. "Drama and the Dialogic Imagination: *The Heidi Chronicles* and *Fefu and Her Friends*" in *Modern Drama,* March 1991, p. 88.

This academic article discusses *The Heidi Chronicles* in terms of the theories of Mikhail Bakhtin, a philosopher-critic.

Shapio, Walter. "Chronicler of Frayed Feminism" in *Time,* March 27, 1989, pp. 90-93.

This article discusses Wasserstein's background, family, and career.

"Wendy Wasserstein: The Art of Theater XIII" in *Paris Review,* Spring, 1997, pp. 164-88.

The article provides a brief overview of Wasserstein's life and an in-depth interview with the playwright. She discusses her career, inspirations, and plays.

The Iceman Cometh

EUGENE O'NEILL

1946

Written in 1939, Eugene O'Neill's *The Iceman Cometh* was not produced until seven years later, largely because O'Neill was concerned that America was not ready for the play's dark vision. When it was staged in 1946, the play received mixed reviews. By that time, O'Neill was already an internationally-known playwright. In addition, the 1946 production marked the end, for O'Neill, of a twelve year absence from Broadway. Critics praised the play's passion, suspense, and well-drawn characters but complained about its prosaic language, redundancy, and excessive length—the play runs for almost four hours. In 1956, *The Iceman Cometh* was revived and this time, widely acclaimed as a masterpiece that would ensure for O'Neill a place among the greatest of modern dramatists. There have been numerous revivals of the play since.

The Iceman Cometh is noted for its dark realism; its setting and characters closely resemble real life. The world of the play is a cruel place. Despair is a constant presence, love only an illusion, and death something to which one looks forward. Relief comes in alcohol and pipe dreams—groundless hopes for a future that will never arrive. Some critics find hope in the characters' camaraderie and endurance. Others consider such a reading too optimistic, believing O'Neill's vision to be unremittingly dark.

In spite of critical disagreement, however, the importance of *The Iceman Cometh* to twentieth-century theater is undisputed. It is truly a modern

classic, considered by many to be the greatest play by one of America's greatest playwrights.

AUTHOR BIOGRAPHY

On October 16, 1888, Eugene O'Neill was born in a hotel on Broadway in New York City. His father was a professional actor, and O'Neill lived on the road with his parents until he began attending boarding school at the age of eight. O'Neill's mother, born into an affluent family, was unhappy with the nomadic theatre life, which she considered less than respectable. In part because of O'Neill's difficult birth, she became addicted to drugs. In 1903, she attempted suicide, and O'Neill, at the age of fifteen, learned for the first time of her addiction. That same year, he himself began drinking heavily in a pattern that would persist for most of his life.

O'Neill attended Princeton University, but a drunken prank resulted in his expulsion in 1907 after only nine months of study. Two years later, O'Neill married Kathleen Jenkins. The two had one child, a son, Eugene, Jr. O'Neill and Jenkins did not officially divorce until 1912, but within days of the marriage, O'Neill went to sea, traveling to Honduras and Buenos Aires, where he experienced first-hand the life of a penniless drifter. In 1911, O'Neill returned to New York, where he lived at Jimmy the Priest's, a saloon populated by drunkards, has-beens, and outcasts. Later in his life, O'Neill called Jimmy the Priest's "a hell hole" and said of the establishment, "One couldn't go any lower." It was Jimmy the Priest's, with its atmosphere of failure, hopelessness, dashed dreams, and despair that, together with its miserable clientele, eventually became the model for Harry Hope's saloon in O'Neill's 1946 play, *The Iceman Cometh.*

In 1912, O'Neill developed tuberculosis, an event that became a turning point in his life. During the five months he spent in a sanatorium, he decided to become a playwright. He began reading modern dramatists and was particularly affected by the dark work of August Strindberg (*Miss Julie*), whom he later cited as one of his greatest influences. O'Neill studied playwriting at Harvard for one year. He then moved to Greenwich Village, New York, where he became involved with an avant-garde group of artists and radicals. A number of these people later formed the Provincetown Players, the first group to produce a play of O'Neill's, *Bound East for Cardiff,* in 1916.

In 1918, O'Neill married Agnes Boulton, with whom he had two children, Shane, in 1919, and Oona, in 1925; the marriage ended in divorce in 1929. In 1920, O'Neill's first full commercial success, *Beyond the Horizon,* was produced, resulting in the first of four Pulitzer Prizes for its author. That year also saw the production of *The Emperor Jones,* which focuses on the violence in human nature. In 1924, *Desire under the Elms,* which reflected O'Neill's interest in Freudian psychology, was produced. Other important plays in the O'Neill canon include the trilogy *Mourning Becomes Electra* (1931), modeled on the ancient Greek playwright Aeschylus's *Oresteia;* the autobiographical *Long Day's Journey into Night,* probably written around 1939 but produced and published after O'Neill's death (per his decree, given the intensely personal nature of the play); and *The Iceman Cometh,* written in 1939, produced in 1946, and considered by many to be O'Neill's greatest work. In 1936, O'Neill won the Nobel Prize for Literature.

During the last ten years of his life, O'Neill was in ill health, suffering from tremors in his hands, which eventually rendered him unable to write. He died of pneumonia November 27, 1953. He is considered by many to be America's greatest playwright.

PLOT SUMMARY

Act I

The first act of *The Iceman Cometh* opens in Harry Hope's saloon in the early morning of the day before Hope's annual birthday party. The room is occupied by an assortment of disheveled ne'er-do-wells—most in their fifties and sixties. Also present are Rocky, the night bartender, and Harry Hope himself. All of the men sleep except for Larry Slade, a former anarchist. As the curtain opens, Rocky sneaks Larry a free drink. Larry says he'll pay "tomorrow," then remarks that all of the men have great plans for a tomorrow that will never come, that all are given hope only by "the lie of the pipe dream." Larry claims to be the exception; he believes he has no pipe dream. He only waits for death.

Rocky and Larry then speak of Hickey, who comes in every year for Hope's birthday on one of his two annual drinking binges. He's known for buying everyone drinks but also for the joking and laughter he brings to Hope's saloon, particularly his running gag about finding his wife, Evelyn, in bed with the iceman. As Larry and Rocky talk, the others awaken from their drunken slumber. All lead existences built on drunkenness, poverty, and despair, but they also speak continually of their grand pasts and their ambitions for tomorrow.

Parritt, a young man who claims to be a friend of Larry's, enters. Larry continually stresses that Parritt means nothing to him. He was only a friend of the boy's mother when he was still a committed anarchist, dedicated to what he and Parritt now call "the Movement." Now Parritt's mother has been arrested in the wake of a political bombing. Parritt escaped arrest, and as the young man talks, indications that he betrayed his mother to the police become evident.

One by one, the men in the bar talk about their plans for the future, but all are equally obsessed with getting their next drink. The prostitutes Margie and Pearl enter followed by Cora, another prostitute, and Chuck, the day bartender. These characters reveal their own pipe dreams of respectability. The much-anticipated Hickey arrives, jovial and generous to everyone. He soon reveals, however, that he has stopped drinking. As he explains, he no longer needs alcohol because he has given up his pipe dream and found peace. He wants Hope's roomers to do the same, including Larry, who is offended by Hickey's suggestion that the ex-anarchist has a pipe dream. Hickey falls asleep, and the roomers express their disappointment at the change in his personality.

Act II

The saloon is now decorated for Hope's birthday festivities. The time is around midnight of the same day. Chuck, Rocky, and the three prostitutes are making further preparations for the party, while complaining about Hickey trying to control not only the party but also the roomers' lives, insisting that each give up his or her pipe dream. Hickey enters and renews his attempts to bring the others the peace he's found. Hickey tells Larry that once he gives up his view of himself as a man who merely observes life, waiting for death, he'll also find peace. The others enter, all determined to prove to Hickey that their plans for the future are not pipe dreams. Parritt enters and tries to speak to Larry about his mother, but Larry does not want to listen, even when Parritt admits that he betrayed his mother to the police for a reward.

As the roomers speak among themselves, it becomes clear that the camaraderie that once existed is unraveling. Where they had once supported

Eugene O'Neill

each other's pipe dreams, fights now break out as they see each other through Hickey's eyes. The party begins, but the celebration is dampened by Hickey's continual appraisals regarding the dark truth of each person's situation. As anger at Hickey grows, Larry asks Hickey if this time he really did find his wife in bed with the iceman. Hickey tells them Evelyn is dead. All are immediately sorry for their anger, but Hickey says he is not sad. His wife is finally rid of him, and she is at peace.

Act III

Hope's saloon, the next morning. Larry, Rocky, Parritt, and a number of the roomers are present. Rocky and Larry discuss the previous night's party, which broke up early because of Hickey's constant badgering. Parritt persists in his attempt to forge a relationship with Larry. While he had previously told Larry that he ratted his mother out for ideological reasons, he now admits that he did it so he could use the reward money on a prostitute. Larry hints that if Parritt has any sense of honor he should end his life. As some of the regulars arrive, it becomes clear that Hickey has turned former friends against each other. Each, while still hanging onto the promise of his own pipe dream, now accuses the others of fooling themselves. Some of the regulars come in with clean clothes, ready to go out into the world, proving to Hickey that their dreams can come true. Most turn in the keys to their rooms, proclaiming that they will never return to Hope's saloon.

Hickey enters and says that all will return when they realize that nothing will ever come of their pipe dreams. And Hickey says that Larry will finally face the fact that he is also kidding himself. Hickey characterizes Larry as an old man afraid to die. Hope, who has not left the saloon since the death of his wife twenty years earlier, now walks outside to prove that he can go out into the world again, but he soon returns, depressed and miserable, just as Hickey claims that Hope can now be at peace. Larry tells Hickey that all that he's brought Hope is the peace of death, then confronts Hickey with his own belief that Hickey drove his wife to suicide. Hickey tells Larry that his wife was murdered, that the police don't know who did it but that they soon will. Parritt, meanwhile, becomes agitated at the talk of murder and proclaims that he did not kill his mother. The act ends with Hickey expressing concern that the death of Hope's pipe dream has not made him happy.

Act IV

Hope's saloon at 1:30 a.m. All of the roomers are sitting at tables, drinking. They have returned from their failed attempts to realize their pipe dreams. Parritt claims that while Larry now realizes that he does not have the courage to die, Larry believes that Parritt should kill himself. Hickey has left to make a phone call but returns and hears Larry contending that Hickey now realizes that the peace he proclaims is false. Hickey denies this but then says he doesn't understand why the roomers, now that their dreams are dashed, have not found contentment. Larry accuses Hickey of killing his wife because he found her in bed with the iceman. Hickey admits that he killed his wife, that he had to because he loved her. If he had killed himself, it would have broken her heart; she would have believed she was to blame. Larry tells Hickey to be quiet, that he does not want to know; he doesn't want to be responsible for Hickey going to the electric chair.

Two policeman, Moran and Lieb, enter, asking for Hickey; they received a call that Evelyn's murderer could be found in Hope's saloon. Hickey then tells the others why he killed Evelyn. As a young man, he was considered wild, reviled by his hometown. Only Evelyn believed in him and loved her, and she was the only person he loved. During their marriage, he drank and went to prostitutes, but Evelyn continued to believe his pipe dream—that

he would someday straighten up and become a good husband to her. Because of her continuing belief in him, he felt intensely guilty. One night while she was asleep, he concluded that the only way to bring her peace was to keep her from ever waking up, and so he shot her. Hickey's confession brings Parritt to admit that he turned his mother in because he hated her.

Remembering his last words to Evelyn, ''Well, you know what you can do with your pipe dream now, you damned bitch,'' Hickey denies that he could ever have hated Evelyn and concludes that he must have been insane to kill her and call her a bitch. The roomers seize on that statement, claiming that they knew Hickey must have been crazy but acted otherwise to humor him. The police take Hickey away.

Parritt sees his situation as a parallel to Hickey's, except that he cannot claim his mother is at peace; for someone who loves freedom as she does, prison is worse than death. Larry finally tells Parritt that the only thing he can do is to kill himself. Parritt leaves as the roomers continue to claim prior knowledge of Hickey's insanity. As they gradually resume their good-natured banter, Larry becomes more and more disturbed. He finally hears Parritt jump off of the fire escape and is horrified. He realizes that Hickey converted him. He is no longer just an observer; by telling Parritt to kill himself, Larry has become an active participant in life. As the others, who do not know of Parritt's death, begin to sing, celebrating Hope's birthday in earnest, Larry stares out of the window, oblivious to the noise.

CHARACTERS

James Cameron
See Jimmy Tomorrow

The Captain
See Cecil Lewis

Cora
Cora is a prostitute. Chuck Morello is her pimp, but the two of them fantasize about someday getting married and moving to the country. After Hickey's arrival, she and Chuck leave to get married but are ultimately unable to do so. She believes that Chuck will hold her past against her, and he wonders why he should marry her when he can get her money

anyway. At the end of the play, she and Chuck return to their pipe dream of a future marriage.

The General

See Piet Wetjoen

Hickey

Hickey is a hardware salesman who comes to Harry's Hope's saloon twice a year for a drinking binge. The roomers look forward to his arrival. He buys them drinks, tells them jokes, and allows them to forget the bleakness of their lives. They especially like the running gag in which he says he has left his wife, Evelyn, in bed with the iceman. When Hickey arrives this time, however, he has changed. He claims to have finally found peace, having let go of his pipe dream. He wants the roomers to find peace the same way. To that end, he harasses the roomers, endlessly nagging them, eventually persuading them to realize their pipe dreams. His belief is that they will recognize that they can never achieve these dreams, give them up, and be happier.

The roomers do as Hickey advises, but to his surprise, they become even more miserable. After prodding from Larry to reveal the reason for his change, Hickey first says only that his wife has died. Finally, however, he admits that he has killed his wife, whom he describes as the perfect loving and forgiving woman. She believed that he would one day be a good and faithful husband to her. He initially claims he killed her to end her pipe dream and bring her peace. While describing the murder, however, Hickey calls her a bitch and is horrified at his words. His real pipe dream, unbeknownst to him, is that he truly loved his wife. Rather than face his hatred of Evelyn, however, Hickey says that he must have been insane to call her a bitch and that everything he has said to the roomers since he arrived was the result of his insanity. Thus Hickey, who tried so hard to force the roomers to face their illusions, cannot face his own. Like the others, he returns to the safety of his pipe dream.

Theodore Hickman

See Hickey

Harry Hope

Harry Hope is the proprietor of Harry Hope's Saloon, the setting for *The Iceman Cometh*. Although he has a gruff manner and tries to act tough, he is a softhearted sort, and the roomers depend on his kindness when they can't pay their bills or afford

MEDIA ADAPTATIONS

- *The Iceman Cometh* was adapted as a film in 1973. This version was directed by John Frankenheimer (*The Manchurian Candidate*). It stars Lee Marvin as Hickey, Robert Ryan as Larry, and Jeff Bridges as Parritt.

---

another drink. He has not left the bar since the death of his wife, Bessie, whom he idealizes as the perfect wife. The truth is that she was a terrible nag. Hope's pipe dream is that he will one day leave the safety of the bar and go out into the world again, but his effort to do so ends in failure.

Hugo Kalmar

Kalmar was once the editor of anarchist periodicals. He knew Parritt's mother and recognizes Parritt when he sees him. Kalmar spent ten years in prison for the Movement, but he is now lost in an alcoholic haze.

Cecil Lewis

Lewis was once a Captain in the British Army. He fought in the Boer War, in which the Boers, South Africans of Dutch ancestry, fought for an end to British occupation.

Lieb

Lieb is one of the two policemen who come for Hickey at the end of the play.

Margie

Margie is a prostitute, with Rocky as her pimp, but she calls herself a "tart," not a whore, before Hickey's arrival. Hickey initially convinces her that she is indeed a whore, but at the end of the play, she returns to her pipe dream.

Pat McGloin

McGloin is a former Police Lieutenant who was thrown off the force for corruption. His pipe dream is to return to his old position with the force, but his efforts to be reinstated are met with rejection.

Moran

Moran is one of the two policemen who come for Hickey at the end of the play.

Chuck Morello

Morello is the day bartender at Harry Hope's. He is actually Cora's pimp, but the two of them dream of someday marrying and moving to the country. After Hickey's arrival, the two leave to get married, though they soon realize that their plans to marry are a pipe dream. When Hickey leaves, the two return to their whimsical wedding plans.

Ed Mosher

Mosher is the brother of Harry Hope's deceased wife, Bessie. He is a former circus man and petty swindler. His pipe dream is that he will someday return to his position with the circus, but his attempt to return to that occupation fails.

Joe Mott

Mott, the only Black character in the play, was once the proprietor of a Negro gambling house. Before Hickey's appearance, he continually refers to himself as someone who is ''white,'' meaning he has risen above the other members of his race. After Hickey comes, he justly accuses the white roomers of looking down on him because of his color. He no longer believes he can be one of them.

Willie Oban

Born to a wealthy but corrupt businessman, Oban graduated from Harvard Law School but is now a hopeless alcoholic whose family has rejected him. Oban's pipe dream is that he will some day quit drinking and practice law, but he will never be able to do either.

Don Parritt

A stranger at Harry Hope's saloon, Parritt arrives looking for Larry Slade, whom he remembers as his mother's friend—the only one of her friends that ever paid attention to him. Although he initially claims that he is running from the law following his anarchist mother's arrest—and his own involvement with radical politics—it soon becomes clear that Parritt is hiding something. Eventually he reveals that he betrayed his mother and her friends to the police, though he initially claims to have done so

because of his own ideological beliefs. He then claims that he betrayed her for money, which he wanted to spend on a prostitute. Finally, however, Parritt admits that he betrayed his mother simply because he hated her. Throughout the play, Parritt attempts to convince Larry to help him, but Larry rejects his entreaties. After Parritt admits the true reason for his betrayal, however, Larry tells him what he wants to hear—that suicide is the only solution for him. Parritt jumps from the fire escape as the roomers, having returned to their pipe dreams, celebrate Harry Hope's birthday.

Pearl

Pearl is one of the three prostitutes in the play. Rocky is her pimp, but she says he is not, and, like Margie, she is careful to refer to herself as a ''tart,'' not a ''whore.'' After Hickey arrives, she finally sees herself as a whore, but returns to her pipe dream by the end of the play.

Rocky Pioggi

Rocky is the good-natured night bartender. Although he is clearly a pimp for the prostitutes Margie and Pearl, he deludes himself into thinking he is above such a lowly profession. He refers to himself instead as the women's ''manager.'' He claims that a pimp would not have a job and that he takes the women's money because they wouldn't know what to do with it anyway. After Hickey arrives, Rocky briefly admits to being a pimp, but once Hickey is considered to be insane, Rocky returns to his pipe dream.

Larry Slade

Slade is considered by many to be the protagonist in *The Iceman Cometh*. He is a former anarchist who became disillusioned with the Movement and abandoned it after years of involvement. He sees himself as having no pipe dreams. He simply sits in the grandstand, observing life and waiting for death. Parritt and Hickey, however, prove him wrong. He was once friends with Parritt's mother and may be the young man's father, but when Parritt arrives, Larry insists that the troubled man means nothing to him. As Parritt exposes more and more about himself, slowly revealing that he betrayed his mother, Larry's continued insistence in his lack of interest in Parritt seems more and more desperate, suggesting that Larry is involved in spite of himself.

Eventually it is Larry who tells Parritt that suicide is his only choice and thus becomes Parritt's executioner. Hickey's belief that Larry's vision of himself as an observer, no longer involved in life, is a pipe dream is shown to be true. At the end of the play, Larry is the only one of the roomers who is truly changed by Hickey's anti-pipe dream campaign. Larry calls himself "the only real convert to death Hickey made." Deprived of his illusion as a mere observer, for the first time, Larry truly does wait for death.

Jimmy Tomorrow

Jimmy Tomorrow is a former Boer War correspondent. He was dismissed from his position as a reporter because of his heavy drinking. He claims that he began drinking because his wife, Marjorie, was unfaithful to him. The truth is that he began drinking long before that, however, and was grateful to his wife for giving him an excuse to drink. He is called Jimmy Tomorrow because he repeatedly speaks of how he will return to the newspaper and get his job back "tomorrow." This is his pipe dream. After he leaves the bar in his attempt to return to his job, a policeman finds him by the river. Other characters conclude that he wanted to jump in the river but didn't have the nerve.

Piet Wetjoen

Wetjoen is the former leader of a Boer commando. The Boers, now called Afrikaners, are South Africans of Dutch ancestry. They fought against British occupation in the Boer War. Wetjoen is friends with Cecil Lewis, who fought on the British side in that war.

THEMES

Hope and the American Dream

The promise of the American Dream, a goal of material prosperity and success, has long been regarded as a crucial element of American culture. For many, it is the possibility of this dream that separates America from other nations. It is the hope of the downtrodden. The faith Americans have in the dream, that, given enough ambition and determination, absolutely anyone can "make it" is almost religious in nature.

For the inhabitants of Harry Hope's Saloon, however, faith has led to despair; the dream has soured. O'Neill populates Hope's with characters from diverse backgrounds. Some, such as Willie Oban, a Harvard Law School graduate, and Jimmy Tomorrow, a former war correspondent, have come close to success—though it ultimately eluded their grasp. Others, such as Joe Mott, the former proprietor of a Negro gambling house, and Ed Mosher, a former circus man, have lived on the edge of respectability. Still others, such as the prostitutes, have always lived lives of petty crime. What unites all but Larry and Parritt, however, is a need to retain their dream, for if the dream is attainable, there is no hope for them. Each sees their failure as a personal issue, not a deficiency in the system. Jimmy Tomorrow rationalizes that as long as he *believes* that he can quit drinking, get his job back, and resume his former place in society, he can live with his despair.

The former anarchists, however, represent a different perspective. For anarchists, the American Dream is a lie and good can only come when all government is eliminated. Although this too is a dream, it flies in the face of the traditional American belief of individual success within the system. In the early decades of this century, anarchy and socialism were regarded as viable alternatives to an American social system many viewed as flawed. Alternative political beliefs were seen by many as a new hope for America. But in *The Iceman Cometh,* O'Neill shows that this hope is no more attainable than the roomers' elusive dreams. Even those who believe that the American dream is an illusion have nothing to offer in its stead.

Death

Harry Hope's saloon, Larry notes at the beginning of the play, is "harmless as a graveyard." In a sense, however, Hope's saloon *is* a graveyard— "The End of the Line Café," as Larry calls it. The saloon's inhabitants cling to their pipe dreams, but their lives are essentially over. Death is the next stop. Larry claims to hope for death. He welcomes it as "a fine long sleep, and I'm damned tired, and it can't come too soon for me."

As long as the roomers have their pipe dreams, they believe they can hold death at bay, but Hickey's arrival brings the reality of death. Hickey first brings a spiritual death, telling the roomers that their pipe dreams are empty. Later, Hickey brings literal death into the world of Hope's Saloon; not only is the news of Evelyn's murder shattering, it ultimately paves the way for Parritt's death. Larry, who tells Parritt that his only solution is suicide, becomes Larry's executioner. After Parritt's death, Larry says, "By God, I'm the only real convert to death Hickey made here." No longer a mere observer, Larry's desire for death is now a reality.

TOPICS FOR FURTHER STUDY

- Research the anarchist movement of the early-twentieth century, particularly the life of Emma Goldman. What do you feel might have led people like Larry Slade in *The Iceman Cometh* to first embrace and then abandon the anarchist movement?

- Compare and contrast the roomers in *The Iceman Cometh* with the tramps Didi and Gogo in Samuel Beckett's *Waiting for Godot.* To what extent do the roomers and the tramps control their respective fates?

- Research the physical and social effects of alcoholism. What part does alcohol play in the lives of O'Neill's roomers? What social circumstances contribute to their drinking?

- Discuss the women in O'Neill's play, considering both those onstage and those who are only spoken of. Why are so few of the women onstage? What does the play suggest about relationships between women and men?

- Compare and contrast *The Iceman Cometh* with Maxim Gorky's *The Lower Depths.* What differences do you think might be attributed to the fact that Gorky is a Russian writer while O'Neill is an American? How are the playwrights' views of dreams and illusions similar? How are they different?

Numerous critics have pointed out that the "iceman" of O'Neill's title is in fact Death, the Grim Reaper. It is Death that has come to Evelyn, sent by Hickey into the arms of the iceman at last. And it is Death that Hickey brings to Hope's saloon. However, as the play ends, the roomers are able to resume their pipe dreams, denying Death access. Even Parritt's suicide is unnoticed by all but Larry. Hickey is able to return to his own pipe dream, to deny his hatred of Evelyn as well as his responsibility for her death. He believes that he must have been insane. Only Larry realizes that Death has truly come to Hope's. For him, that has changed everything.

Isolation

The characters in *The Iceman Cometh* are isolated from mainstream society. This is evident from the beginning, when the curtain opens on the drunken, sleeping men alone in the literal world of their dreams. As the play progresses, the essential isolation of the characters becomes clear. Even awake, each character remains caught in his or her own dream. There is a sort of camaraderie among O'Neill's roomers, but this small sense of community is revealed as a thin veneer following Hickey's arrival; his proclamations of false dreams reveal an underlying animosity. Forced to face their hopeless realities, the roomers fight among themselves until Hickey's departure allows them to return to their pipe dreams.

Parritt arrives at Hope's bar searching for Larry, hoping to end his own isolation. He comes to the ex-anarchist because he recalls Larry being kind to him. Larry, however, rejects Parritt's appeal for friendship. He believes himself to be in the grandstand, an isolated observer rather than a participant in life, and he intends to remain, isolated, uninvolved.

Hickey also seeks an end to his isolation. In past visits, he was satisfied with his superficial friendship with the roomers. Now, however, he claims to have given up on his pipe dream and is not content with just changing his own life. In his search for relief from isolation, Hickey wants the roomers to come to his realization. His story about murdering Evelyn is an attempt to understand his pain he has felt, but the roomers make it clear that they don't want to hear him. Only when he declares that he must have been insane, when he is willing to return to superficial relationships, is he once more accepted by the roomers.

Larry, despite his efforts, develops a brief but real connection with Parritt. That connection, however, only brings him pain. As the play closes, the roomers return to their thin sense of camaraderie, but O'Neill reveals the depth of their isolation. When the roomers begin to sing in celebration of Hope's birthday, each sings a completely different song. Larry, meanwhile, is spiritually as well as physically isolated from the group. Each of the characters ends the play alone.

STYLE

Setting

The Iceman Cometh is set in the summer of 1912 in Harry Hope's saloon, a seedy establishment on the downtown West Side of New York. All of the play's action takes place either in the bar or the back room of the saloon, visually affirming O'Neill's intention that the bar is a world unto itself. The condition of the bar reflects the hopeless squalor of the roomers' lives. O'Neill describes the walls and ceiling as once white but "now so splotched, peeled, stained and dusty that their color can best be described as dirty." Adding to the play's themes of alienation and isolation, the windows are so filthy that it is impossible to see the outside world through them. The bar is crowded with tables and chairs "so close together that it is a difficult squeeze to pass between them." This crowded condition adds to the suffocating nature of the bar, its atmosphere of hopelessness and despair. Because the setting changes little throughout the play, the audience gains a gradual sense of the saloon's oppressiveness.

The only major change in the setting occurs in Act II, when the saloon is decorated for Hope's birthday party. The room has been cleaned, and a space has been cleared for dancing. Added props, such as a piano, presents, and the birthday cake, contribute to the festive atmosphere. But this lighter setting stands in sharp contrast to the anger and accusations that evolve later in the act, as the camaraderie is destroyed by Hickey's proselytizing. In this case, the party setting heightens the effect of the stage action with a visual contrast to the dark emotions that present themselves. In the final two acts, the saloon resumes its atmosphere of dirt and

despair. In fact, in the final act, when the roomers have come full circle and returned to their pipe dreams, the set is once more as it appeared in Act I, heightening the sense that—save Larry's situation—little has really changed.

Time and the Theater

A recurring criticism of *The Iceman Cometh* is that, at nearly four hours running time, the play is simply too long. This begs the question: Is it proper to fault a play for its length? Such a criticism may seem petty and is rarely leveled at novels or poems. It is this sort of criticism, in fact, that brings into relief an important difference between drama and other forms of literature. Unlike other genres, a written drama is not the play's finished form. The final work is the production (resulting from the work of actors, directors, set dressers, and others involved with the staging) that emerges from the text. A play exists *in time* in a way that other forms of literature do not. A production of *The Iceman Cometh* cannot be set aside like a paperback novel, to be picked up later at the viewer's leisure. An audience's ability to focus on the play over a continuous time period is a factor that must be taken into consideration.

Directors do consider attention spans. It is not at all uncommon for a director to provide his own "criticism" by cutting the playwright's dialogue. One director, in fact, managed to shave the running time of *The Iceman Cometh* by one hour through extensive script edits. It is important, however, that the student of drama not arbitrarily set an "ideal" length for a play. It is more useful to consider the ultimate effect of the play's length. Does that length serve a useful purpose? In *The Iceman Cometh* the length of the play adds to the feeling of oppressiveness and hopelessness. The continued repetition in O'Neill's dialogue, which is sometimes cut by directors who fail to grasp the meaning in its iterations, emphasizes the redundant, looping quality of the characters' lives. The extreme length of the play contributes to the suffocating atmosphere of Hope's saloon.

Symbolism

A symbol is something that stands for or suggests something other than itself. In *The Iceman Cometh* the iceman is a symbol of death. In the time period of the play, before there were electric refrigerators, people owned iceboxes which kept food cold by keeping it in an enclosed space with large blocks of ice. The ice was delivered by the iceman, who traveled from door to door.

From the beginning of the play, the roomers look forward to Hickey's running gag about leaving his wife in bed with the iceman. When they discover how much Hickey has changed, some begin to suspect that he did find his wife with the iceman. The figure of the iceman is easily associated with death. In western culture, death is traditionally associated with cold. In addition, it was once customary to use ice to preserve corpses until they could be buried. From this practice comes the slang expressions ''to put someone on ice'' or ''to ice someone,'' both of which mean ''to kill'' that ''someone.'' The iceman Hickey left Evelyn with is Death. When used in the title with the word ''cometh,'' the implication is that Death comes in the present tense—it is always arriving for someone. At the end of the play, Death comes for Parritt. Larry expresses a longing for Death, the iceman, who will eventually come for everyone in the bar.

The Unities

The unities are the three rules that govern classical drama. They are unity of time, unity of place, and unity of action. Unity of time generally means that the action of a play should take place within a twenty-four-hour period. Unity of place means that the action of the play should take place in one location. Unity of action means that events must follow logically from one another.

The concept of the unities originated in the writings of the ancient Greek philosopher Aristotle, in his treatise *Poetics.* Many, however, consider Aristotle's discussion of the unities descriptive; he is simply describing the dramatic style of his own time. During the Renaissance, however, the unities became prescriptive—rules for playwrights to follow—particularly in Italy and France. Following the rule of the unities was supposed to make a play more believable for the audience.

In *The Iceman Cometh* O'Neill adheres to the three unities. The play takes place in one location, within a relatively short period of time, and with events following logically from one another. O'Neill, greatly influenced by classical drama, may have used the unities in order to create an association between *The Iceman Cometh* and classic Greek tragedy. The unities can contribute to a sense of realism. The audience lives the events as the charac-

ters live them and thus experiences the stagnation and despair of Hope's saloon as if it were real.

HISTORICAL CONTEXT

Anarchy in the U.S.

During the late-1800s, anarchy, the belief that all systems of government are immoral and unnecessary, was a serious political movement in the United States. Following the assassination of President William McKinley by an anarchist in 1901, anarchists were banned from entering the country; nonetheless, the movement remained viable. Emma Goldman, perhaps the best remembered of the anarchists of this period, may have served as a model for Parritt's mother. Goldman was still quite active in 1912, the year in which *The Iceman Cometh* is set. But by the time O'Neill wrote *The Iceman Cometh* in 1939, Goldman had been deported to the Soviet Union and, in 1938, the House of Representatives had set up a committee to investigate so-called un-American activities. The major movements of the radical left—anarchism, socialism, and communism—were not as strong as they had been in previous years.

During the early-1930s, the first years of the Depression, with its worsening economic conditions, led many to turn to the radical left for solutions. But by the 1939, when O'Neill wrote *The Iceman Cometh,* the increasing success of labor unions, the reforms of President Franklin Delano Roosevelt's New Deal, and the 1938 passage of the Fair Labor Standards Act (which set a minimum wage of forty cents an hour and a maximum work-week of 44 hours) made radical change seem less necessary. In addition, increasing military tension in Europe had begun to command the time and attention of Americans. German leader Adolf Hitler's 1939 invasion of Poland marked the beginning of World War II.

Although Americans now tend to romanticize World War II as a justifiable war that enjoyed popular support from the beginning, this was not the case in 1939. The radical left opposed U.S. involvement in what they considered an imperialist war. But it was not only the left that had qualms about American involvement. Shortly after Hitler's invasion of Poland, President Roosevelt announced in a radio broadcast, ''This nation remains a neutral nation.'' It was not until the United States itself was attacked by Japan two years later—the December 7,

COMPARE
&
CONTRAST

- **1912:** Temperance groups work toward the goal of complete prohibition of the manufacture and sale of alcoholic beverages. Eight years later Prohibition becomes the law of the land.

  1939: Six years after Prohibition ends in failure, alcoholism continues to be a major social problem. The fledgling group Alcoholics Anonymous, founded in 1935, works to help people overcome what is perceived as a personal failing.

  Today: Alcoholism is now generally viewed as a disease that often has a strong genetic component, but the problem of alcoholism is far from solved. Approximately 18 million Americans are alcoholics and teen drinking is a serious problem.

- **1912:** In spite of a 1901 law prohibiting anarchists from entering the country, the anarchist movement is close to the peak of its popularity in the United States. Socialism and communism are also considered by many to be serious alternatives to capitalism.

  1939: The increasing success of labor unions, the reforms of the New Deal, and laws designed to protect workers make the radical left's criticism of government seem less potent.

  Today: The dismantling of the Berlin Wall and the fall of the Soviet Union result in a general sense in America that what the radical left offers is no longer a viable alternative. The movements of the radical left still exist, but within the United States, anarchism, communism, and socialism have virtually no popular support.

- **1912:** The women's movement fights for suffrage (the right to vote) and the right to birth control. Social discrimination and discrimination in employment and education remain strongly in force.

  1939: Having won the right to vote and the right to birth control, many believe the women's movement is no longer necessary. National attention is focused on the economy and the war in Europe.

  Today: Women have earned legal rights equal to those of men, but in actual practice, women still face discrimination. Feminists are particularly concerned about the rights of women in non-Western nations.

- **1912:** Discrimination against African Americans is widespread. Many southern Blacks move North but continue to endure poverty and racism.

  1939: Some of the reforms of the New Deal benefit African Americans but social and legal discrimination remain.

  Today: Discrimination against African Americans is no longer legal or socially acceptable, but many more Blacks than whites suffer from poverty and a lack of education. Affirmative action programs, which have aimed at providing more opportunities for non-whites, are under attack by conservative politicians.

1941, bombing of Pearl Harbor—that America entered the war.

Civil Rights in the Early-Twentieth Century

In 1912, the primary issue for women's groups was that of suffrage, the right to vote. Women were actively engaged in social issues, particularly in assisting the poor and fighting for temperance, the prohibition of alcoholism. In order to achieve the reforms they desired, however, women realized that they needed to be able to vote. Another important issue for women was birth control. In 1912, the distribution of birth control information was illegal in the United States. The anarchist Emma Goldman was active in the fight for birth control, which had the potential of giving women the same sexual freedom allowed to men. In 1920, women won the right to vote, and in the decade following that victory, doctors were legally allowed to dispense birth control information. With these successes, many women assumed that their movement was no longer necessary. That and the economic troubles of the Depression made women's rights much less of an issue by 1939.

In 1912, discrimination against African Americans was widespread. In every southern state, African Americans were denied the right of suffrage. In some states, blacks were prohibited from opening businesses of any kind. In 1909, white northerners and blacks joined together and formed the National Association for the Advancement of Colored People (NAACP), which fought for racial equality. Nonetheless, tremendous discrimination continued, especially in the South. Many southern African Americans moved North but could often only work as laborers or servants, if they could find work at all. In addition, many whites in the North and South continued to consider blacks as their intellectual and social inferiors. Joe Mott, the only black character in *The Iceman Cometh,* has himself absorbed this attitude and continually speaks of himself as being white or acting white. He and the other roomers consider this high praise and a superior social position than that afforded to blacks.

By 1939, many blacks had benefited from the reforms of the New Deal. Employment and social discrimination continued, however. In 1939, the Daughters of the American Revolution (DAR) denied the singer Marian Anderson permission to sing in Constitution Hall in Washington, D.C., solely because she was black. First Lady Eleanor Roosevelt resigned from the DAR in protest, then assisted in making arrangements for Anderson to sing at the Lincoln Memorial instead. This incident helped to cement African American support for the president and first lady, which translated into support for the Democratic Party.

1930s Culture

While Americans of the late-1930s were dealing with the harsh realities of the Depression and the approaching war, much of the popular culture of the time provided a means of escape from the bleak reality of daily life. This is perhaps best exemplified by the films of the era. Light entertainers such as Shirley Temple, the Marx Brothers, W. C. Fields, and Mae West were all popular in the 1930s. In 1937, the first full-length animated film, Walt

Disney's *Snow White and the Seven Dwarfs,* was produced. The year 1939 saw the production of the fantasy film *The Wizard of Oz.* The movie version of Margaret Mitchell's romantic *Gone with the Wind,* the most popular novel of the decade, was also produced in 1939. At first, this focus on escapism seems quite at odds with the bleak world of *The Iceman Cometh.* But the pipe dreams of the roomers in O'Neill's dark world reflect nothing so much as the decade's need for an escape from reality.

CRITICAL OVERVIEW

Although *The Iceman Cometh* is now considered a masterpiece of twentieth-century drama, when the play first appeared on Broadway in 1946, its critical reception was mixed. By the time of the play's production, O'Neill was a well-established playwright, a recipient of the Nobel Prize, and *The Iceman Cometh* marked the end of his twelve-year absence from Broadway. Rosamond Gilder, whose review for *Theatre Arts* is reprinted in *O'Neill and his Plays: Four Decades of Criticism,* noted "O'Neill's return has done more than give the new season a fillip of interest; it has restored to the theatre something of its intrinsic stature." Of the play itself, Gilder wrote, "*The Iceman Cometh* is made of good theatre substance—meaty material for actors, racy dialogue, variety of character, suspense and passion." In his book *Eugene O'Neill,* Normand Berlin quoted George Jean Nathan, who remarked in his review of this production that *The Iceman Cometh* made other American plays seem "like so much damp tissue paper."

Yet the play was not free from negative commentary. As Berlin noted, "Those who faulted the play mentioned its prosaic language, its schematic arrangements and, most often, its excessive length." It is the latter criticism that has continued to haunt the play even as it has received greater and greater acclaim in the decades since its debut. Repeatedly, critics have complained that a full production of *The Iceman Cometh,* which takes nearly five hours, is simply too long.

Gilder noted in her review that the play "could readily be compressed into a more reasonable running time." A shorter version, she wrote, "would have brought into sharper focus the conflicting and merging elements of the three chief figures of the fable. The subsidiary characters are not sufficiently important or rounded to demand the time and atten-

A scene from the original 1946 Broadway production, featuring James Barton as Hickey and Dudley Diggs as saloon owner Harry Hope

tion they absorb.'' Critic Brooks Atkinson, whose review of the 1956 revival is also reprinted in Cargill's book, disagreed. Atkinson allowed that the play "could be cut and compressed without destroying anything essential." "But," he continued, "as a creative work by a powerful writer, it is entitled to its excesses, which, in fact, may account for the monumental feeling of doom that it pulls down over the heads of the audience."

As director of the German-language premiere, Eric Bentley, whose writing on the matter also appears in Cargill's book, clarified his own position on the matter of length. By cutting O'Neill's dialogue, Bentley managed to shave one hour off the length of his production. "Not wishing to cut out whole characters," he wrote, "we mutilated some till they had, I'm afraid, no effective existence." The result, Bentley claimed, was a "shortened, crisper version." In his book *O'Neill's Scenic Images,* however, Timo Tiusanen wrote that Bentley in his production "apparently cut away part of the spontaneity of the play." Tiusanen suggested that "It is conceivable that the criterion of those most eager to shorten O'Neill has been a play with a tightly knit plot. *The Iceman Cometh* is a play of another kind."

Berlin agreed that extensive cutting does a disservice to the play. In *O'Neill's Shakespeare,* he wrote of O'Neill's roomers, "We live with them for four hours; a long time—a time that is necessary because O'Neill wants us to feel the sheer survival quality of these creatures who have come to the 'last harbor.'" The play is long, according to Berlin and many other critics, because it needs to be long. Its length is intrinsic to O'Neill's purpose.

Another important issue that arises in the play's criticism is the question of which character in the play is O'Neill's protagonist. Bentley argued that "Larry is . . . the center of the play." But that is so because the stories of Parritt and Hickey "are brought together through Larry Slade whose destiny . . . is to extract the secret of both protagonists." In other words, Larry is central only because he serves the purpose of drawing together the primary characters. Berlin remarked in *O'Neill's Shakespeare* that he saw Larry as "the play's central character, certainly the most haunting character."

Though he is central, however, for Berlin, Larry functions as the Fool, a traditional character, particularly in Renaissance comedy and tragedy, described by Berlin as "seemingly set apart, looking at the others in the play, commenting on them, allowing us to see the world through his eyes, which are clear and awake and contain a gleam of sardonic humor.'' For Berlin, Larry, like the Fool in William Shakespeare's *King Lear,* provides a crucial commentary on what happens onstage but is not really a part of the play's action. In *The Haunted Heroes of Eugene O'Neill,* Edwin A. Engel described Larry as the protagonist but noted that Larry serves ''a choral function as he comments upon the action and interprets the motives of the numerous other characters.'' Although Engel compared Larry to the chorus of ancient Greek drama, rather than the Fool, he too saw Larry's centrality as related to his commentary, not his participation in the action.

Tiusanen also believed that *The Iceman Cometh* functions with what is essentially a Greek chorus, but for him, that chorus was not Larry but the roomers at Hope's saloon. For Tiusanen, Larry was ''a pivotal character,'' but the play's protagonist is Hickey. Tiusanen quoted Tom F. Driver, who wrote that ''The play might be diagrammed with three concentric circles.'' For Driver, the outermost circle is occupied by Harry and the roomers, the second by Larry and Parritt. Hickey, however, ''occupies the play's innermost circle.'' The story Hickey tells ''is virtually a play within the play and . . . the core of the entire business.''

A more uncommon view of the protagonist's identity was expressed by Rolf Scheibler in his book *The Late Plays of Eugene O'Neill.* For Scheibler, Harry Hope ''is the centre of this little world, and if we are to speak of a protagonist at all, it is he who is the main character.'' It is Hope who ''enables the outcasts to lead the kind of life they want.'' He gives them ''food, drink, and rooms, and thus grants them the shelter they need.'' Hope's name is also significant for Scheibler. ''The only hope for man to gain his soul lies in adopting the tolerant attitude of the saloon owner.'' For Scheibler, the ''simple message'' of *The Iceman Cometh* is that ''if we are tolerant, we shall not lose our spirituality even if we are subject to the laws of nature. And then, by doing what is possible to-day, perhaps there will be a better tomorrow.'' Because Hope embodies this attitude, Scheibler saw him as the play's protagonist. It should be noted, however, that Scheibler remains in the minority in this view. Most critics see either Larry or Hickey as the play's central figure.

The question of the identity of the play's protagonist, or whether the play even has a real protagonist, will doubtless remain a subject of disagreement among critics. In spite of differences of interpretation, however, and consideration of possible flaws, such as the play's length, most critics now agree on one point: *The Iceman Cometh* is a play of major importance among O'Neill's work as well as in the history of twentieth-century American drama.

CRITICISM

Clare Cross

Cross is a Ph.D. candidate specializing in modern drama. In this essay she discusses Hickey's wife and Parritt's mother in terms of sexual stereotypes.

In Eugene O'Neill's play *The Iceman Cometh,* the two most significant female characters never appear onstage. These women, Parritt's mother, Rosa, and Hickey's wife, Evelyn, although physically absent throughout the play, are nonetheless powerfully present in the lives of the men who know them. Indeed, Rosa and Evelyn are absolutely essential to the action of the play. Yet O'Neill chose to give these women no voices of their own; the audience sees them exclusively through the eyes of the men who hated and ultimately destroyed them. The result is an incomplete picture of who Rosa and Evelyn really are. An examination of these women and their places in the play must therefore take into consideration the distortion of the lens through which the audience views them.

Edwin A. Engel wrote in his book *The Haunted Heroes of Eugene O'Neill:* ''Hickey's wife and Parritt's other represent antithetical aspects of love— the former an excess of love and forgiveness, the latter a deficiency. Both generate hate in the men who are closely associated with them.'' By framing the love of Evelyn and Rosa in terms of ''excess'' and ''deficiency,'' Engel essentially faults them for not adhering to some sort of ideal degree of love. His comment that the women ''generate hate'' suggests that they are to blame for the hatred the men feel, and by extension, are at least partly responsible for their own downfall. The women are essentially destroyed, however, because they are not what the men want or expect them to be. While this can certainly be framed in terms of how much love Evelyn and Rosa are supposed to have for Hickey and Parritt, perhaps a clearer and more telling way to consider this issue is in terms of sexual stereotypes.

WHAT DO I READ NEXT?

- *The Lower Depths,* a 1902 play by Maxim Gorky, is also concerned with the lives of a group of outcasts and their desire to use illusion to shield themselves from the pain of life.

- *Waiting for Godot,* a play by Samuel Beckett written in 1952, focuses on two tramps who wait vainly for the arrival of the mysterious figure Godot to give meaning and purpose to their lives.

- *Living My Life* is the 1934 autobiography of famed anarchist Emma Goldman, who may have served as a model for Parritt's mother Rosa. Goldman's story provides useful context for Larry and Parritt's discussions regarding the Movement.

- *The Lost Weekend* is a 1944 novel by Charles Jackson. It is the story of an alcoholic who attempts to resist drinking but finds he is helpless before his addiction. The film version, which was produced in 1946, the year of the first production of *The Iceman Cometh,* adds an optimistic ending not warranted by Jackson's dark novel.

- *Long Day's Journey into Night,* an O'Neill play produced in 1956, is an autobiographical domestic tragedy dealing with addiction and dysfunctional relationships. The play is widely considered to offer insight into O'Neill's personal life.

In the time in which O'Neill was writing, the ideal, traditional woman was absolutely selfless and, although willing to accommodate her husband's sexual needs, was without any sexual desire of her own. If married, she put her husband's needs before her own. If a mother, she sacrificed everything for her children. Published in *The Conscious Reader,* Virginia Woolf described such an ideal in her 1942 essay, "The Angel in the House," named for the heroine of a Victorian poem:

> She was intensely sympathetic. She was immensely charming. She was utterly unselfish. She excelled in the difficult arts of family life. She sacrificed herself daily. If there was chicken, she took the leg; if there was a draught she sat in it—in short she was so constituted that she never had a mind or a wish of her own, but preferred to sympathize always with the minds and wishes of others. Above—I need not say it—she was pure. Her purity was supposed to be her chief beauty—her blushes, her great grace.

The life of Rosa Parritt is antithetical to that of this "ideal" woman, the angel in the house. Rosa is therefore seen as a selfish and unloving mother, and her son hates her. Evelyn, on the other hand, is an angel in the house in every way. Still, because of her selflessness and love, Hickey grows to hate her as much as Parritt hates his mother. In *The Iceman*

Cometh, these women are, as the saying goes, damned if they do/damned if they don't. Whether or not they fix themselves to the model of the angel in the house, Rosa Parritt and Evelyn Hickman are condemned, hated, and ultimately destroyed by the primary men in their lives.

Rosa is a political activist, a sexual being, and a parent. In all three roles she rejects traditional femininity and is, in turn, rejected by her son, who finds her mothering skills lacking. The first time the audience hears of Rosa it is in regard to her political actions. Larry reports that she has been arrested for her participation in an anarchist bombing that resulted in several deaths. The action of the play occurs in 1912, eight years before women even had the right to vote. In a time when women have no political voice at all and are expected to accept the system run by men, Rosa is dedicated not simply to a change in government but to the abolition of government itself; where women are supposed to be passive, the "gentle sex," Rosa takes violent action; when women are supposed to live for their families, Rosa is dedicated to the Movement.

Even in radical political movements, women have often been expected to stand on the sidelines, supporting the men. The American women's movement of the 1970s, in fact, partly grew out of women's frustration with the way they were treated within the radical student movements of the late-1960s and early-1970s. Female students felt that they were expected to subordinate themselves to men. But Rosa takes a back seat to no one. In essence, Rosa acts like a man, and her dedication to her lifestyle, which would probably be acceptable, even admirable, in a man, is part of the reason for Parritt's hatred.

Speaking to Larry of his mother, Parritt says, "To hear her go on sometimes, you'd think she was the Movement." Larry immediately recognizes the hostility of this comment. He is "puzzled and repelled" and tells Parritt, "That's a hell of a way for you to talk, after what happened to her!" Parritt quickly backtracks: "Don't get me wrong. I wasn't sneering Larry, only kidding." It is clear, however, that even if said in jest, Parritt's comment is still hostile. Elsewhere Parritt shows that his hostility regarding his mother's political involvement stems from his own feeling that, largely because of Rosa's dedication to the Movement, she was not the good mother for which he longed. He tells Larry, "You were the only friend of Mother's who ever paid attention to me. . . . All the others were too busy with the Movement. Even Mother."

Parritt recognizes that, for Rosa, the Movement took precedence over all personal relationships and is therefore puzzled that Rosa continued to write Larry after he left the Movement. Parritt says that, in regard to the Movement, his mother is "Like a revivalist preacher about religion. Anyone who loses faith in it is more than dead to her; he's a Judas who ought to be boiled in oil." Parritt knows that the bond between mother and child is not as sacred to Rosa as her political beliefs. Just before he commits suicide at the end of the play, Parritt anticipates Rosa's reaction to his death. "It'll give her the chance to play the great incorruptible Mother of the Revolution, whose only child is the Proletariat. She'll be able to say: 'Justice is done! So may all traitors die!. . . I am glad he's dead! Long live the Revolution!'" While very few would admire this level of fanaticism in men or women, such sentiment is especially intolerable in a mother, who, by stereotypical definition, is supposed to be selfless and forgiving, to always put her children's needs before her own.

The angel in the house does not allow herself sexual freedom—or even sexual feeling. Rosa Parritt,

however, does. "You've always acted the free woman," Parritt tells her when she complains about his keeping company with prostitutes. The word "free" in this context means sexually free. Rosa does not play the part of the ideal wife, who has sex to please her husband, or the prostitute, who at first glance may seem more free. In fact, the prostitute is not free at all. She too has sex to please men; the sex act is not gratifying to her. When Hickey talks about joking with prostitutes, making them laugh, Cora responds, "Jees, all de lousy jokes I've had to listen to and pretend was funny!" Rosa's sexual relationships are for her own pleasure. She even uses men in the way men have traditionally used women.

Parritt tells Larry that Rosa still respected Larry because he left her before she left him. "She got sick of the others before they did of her. I don't think she ever cared about them anyway. She just had to keep on having lovers to prove to herself how free she was." The possibility that Rosa had sexual relations for her own pleasure is unthinkable to Parritt. Rosa's sexual freedom is offensive to her son. "Living at home," he says, "was like living in a whorehouse—only worse, because she didn't have to make her living." As Parritt recalls, even the tolerant Larry objected to Rosa's sexual freedom. "I remember her putting on her high-and-mighty free-woman stuff, saying you were still a slave to bourgeois morality and jealousy and you thought a woman you loved was a piece of private property you owned. I remember that you got mad and told her, 'I don't like living with a whore, if that's what you mean!'" Rosa's sexual freedom would be more acceptable in a man, but because she is a woman who has sex without being a wife or a prostitute she is condemnable. To Parritt and, if Parritt's story is accurate, to Larry, Rosa is even worse than a whore, fit neither to be a good wife nor a good mother, unwilling to sacrifice her own feelings to the desires of men.

If Rosa Parritt's life is a repudiation of the "traditional woman" concept, Evelyn Hickman *is* the angel in the house. She is so selfless, loving, and forgiving that she seems to be more of a fantasy ideal than a real woman. When Hickey drinks or goes to prostitutes, Evelyn forgives him. When he gives her venereal disease, she pretends to believe he got it from sharing drinking cups on trains and again forgives her husband. When Hickey doesn't come home from a drinking binge for more than a month, she never expresses anger when he returns. When he promises to change, she believes him. And when he inevitably returns to his old ways, Evelyn, as always, forgives him.

In his book *The Late Plays of Eugene O'Neill,* Rolf Scheibler called Evelyn ''an unattainable ideal,'' but she is an ideal only when seen in terms of her adherence to the role of the angel in the house. A man who behaved the same way would be considered a ''sucker,'' a ''pushover,'' a ''sap.'' Scheibler also stated that Evelyn ''finds that happiness can be achieved by giving and forgiving.'' In reality, however, the audience never knows whether or not Evelyn is happy, whether or not she believes her husband's empty promises, and whether or not she ever truly forgives his trespasses. She is, after all, seen only through Hickey's eyes, and it is convenient for him to believe in her happiness. For the angel in the house, however, the question of personal happiness does not even arise; she is required to always place others' needs and feelings above her own. Acceptance of such a duty, however, should not be construed as happiness.

Evelyn completely embraces the role of the angel in the house, yet Hickey is no more satisfied with her than Parritt is with Rosa. Hickey cannot tolerate the guilt he feels at Evelyn's love and forgiveness. ''That's what made me feel such a rotten skunk,'' Hickey tells the roomers, ''her always forgiving me.'' According to Hickey, it is not his own actions that make him feel guilty; Evelyn's forgiveness is to blame. ''Sometimes,'' he says, ''I couldn't forgive her for forgiving me. I even caught myself hating her for making me hate myself so much.'' In contrast to Parritt, Hickey wants Evelyn to act less like a traditional woman and more like a man. He believes it would be better if she committed adultery as he had.

Hickey's belief is reinforced by Jimmy Tomorrow, whose wife did respond to his drinking by sleeping with other men. ''I was glad to be free,'' Jimmy says, ''even grateful to her, I think, for giving me such a good tragic excuse to drink as much as I damned well pleased.'' Evelyn, however, gives Hickey no such excuse. So he turns his disgust with himself into hatred for Evelyn. He finally murders her because, in comparison to himself, she is too perfect, too good.

Hickey kills Evelyn for her attainment of the feminine ideal, while Parritt betrays his mother to a fate he says is worse than death for her rejection of that ideal. Both women are ultimately destroyed because of the way they choose to live. Rosa's scorn for the role of the traditional female displeases

her son; Evelyn's acceptance of that role—and her perfection of its ideals—confronts her husband with his own inadequacies. Both women pay with their lives.

Source: Clare Cross, for *Drama for Students,* Gale, 1999.

Robert Brustein

Brustein is a noted literary critic as well as a respected director of drama. In this essay he reviews a 1985 revival of The Iceman Cometh *that features the 1956 Circle in the Square production's star and director—Jason Robards and Jose Quintero. The critic finds that both the play and the creative talents behind its staging have aged well.*

When *The Iceman Cometh* was first produced by the Theater Guild in the mid-1940s, hostile intellectual critics invidiously compared it with Ibsen's *The Wild Duck* and Gorky's *The Lower Depths.* After it was successfully revived ten years later by Circle in the Square, commentators began to recognize that, for all its clumsy dialogue, repetitiveness, and schematic plotting, the play was a great work that surpassed even those distinguished influences in depth and power. Today, almost 40 years after its initial appearance with James Barton and Dudley Digges, *The Iceman Cometh* has been restaged at the Lunt-Fontanne Theatre by the original director of the Circle in the Square revival (Jose Quintero) with the same Hickey (Jason Robards) and, despite arthritic moments in the production, emerges not only richer than ever but as the inspiration for much that has been written for the stage since.

The play resonates. It is at the same time familiar and strange. One is caught in its potent grip as by a gnarled and crippled hand. Robards, with his past history of alcoholism and air of personal suffering, has always been the American actor who shows the greatest personal affinity with O'Neill's spiritual pain, and this blood kinship, coupled with a valiant heart, carries him through the handicaps of playing Hickey in his late 60s. Hair darkened, face rouged, mouth dentured, energy flagging, Robards would now appear to be too old for the part, and there are times when he seems less to be living his role than remembering it. Still, if the performance is a bit of an overpainting, Robards has belonged to Hickey for many years, and when this remarkable actor makes his first entrance in a boater and off-the-rack pin-striped suit, throwing his bankroll at Rocky the bartender and exhorting the inmates of Harry Hope's saloon in his slurred whiskey bass, there is a thrill of simultaneous immediacy and recognition.

The Iceman Cometh resonates. It is at the same time familiar and strange. One is caught in its potent grip as by a gnarled and crippled hand. Age has given Robards an extraordinary translucency—pallid skin, transparent eyes. His Hickey continually promises his drunken friends the reward of spiritual peace (each act but the last ends on the word ''happy''), but for all his drummer's energy, finger snapping, vaudeville physicality, and carny shill delivery, he is a ghost from the moment he walks on stage. Robards is continually undermining his character's professed optimism, as when he gets ''sleepy all of a sudden,'' trips over a chair, and falls into a faint; Robards's face goes slack as though he's had a minor stroke. For while Hickey has the remorseless cheeriness of an American evangelist (he was no doubt inspired by Billy Sunday or by Bruce Barton's characterization of Jesus as the world's greatest salesman), only Larry Slade looks as deeply into the abyss of life without hope or redemption.

Robards is surrounded by a fine cast, the one weakness being Paul McCrane's rather flaccid Parritt. Barnard Hughes is a roistering Harry Hope, John Christopher Jones an intellectually degenerate Willie Oban, James Greene a gaunt Jimmy Tomorrow, and Donald Moffat a dignified Larry Slade, while most of the smaller roles are played with strength. Still, Robards's realism, even when unfulfilled, is of such intensity that it sometimes makes the others seem a little ''classical.'' Take Barnard Hughes, so ingratiating and roguish when holding court in his saloon but not quite anguished enough when his ''pipe dream'' is exposed, or Donald Moffat, quietly eloquent and detached throughout the play, yet resorting to languorous legato cadences in his time of agonizing self-recognition.

And I wish that Quintero had been a little bolder in his approach. Ben Edwards's bar setting is selectively seedy, and Jane Greenwood's costumes really look like secondhand clothes that have been rotting on the bodies of the characters. But apart from the opening scene, with the stubble-bearded living-dead derelicts sleeping open-mouthed under Thomas R. Skelton's pasty light, there has been little effort to suggest that this is a world at the bottom of the sea or that *The Iceman Cometh* has a reverberant symbolic interior as well as a naturalist facade. Quintero acknowledges O'Neill's hints (in his archaic title and elsewhere) that Hickey and his 12 companions bear a strong resemblance to Christ

and his disciples—Parritt being Judas and Larry being Peter, the rock on which he builds his church—and that Harry Hope's birthday party is based on the Last Supper (his actors fall into poses inspired by Leonardo da Vinci's painting, Hickey hovering over them with his palms outstretched).

But otherwise the production is a retread of the one staged in 1956, as if nothing had happened to the theater in 30 years. Even the exits and entrances seem designed for Broadway applause. I don't mean this version is old-fashioned—it has too much life for that—and I admit that a more imaginative interpretation might very well have obscured the play's intentions. Still, O'Neill was a very reluctant convert to Ibsenite realism (''holding the family Kodak up to ill-nature,'' as he called it) and never truly abandoned his devotion to symbolic substructures. A play as thickly faceted (and familiar) as this one deserves more audacious treatment.

Even conventionally staged, however, *The Iceman Cometh* has lost none of its consuming power. The play is long—it lasts almost five hours—and sometimes painfully repetitious, since each character is identified by a single obsession that he continually restates. Thus, each act offers a single variation on the theme of illusion. The action never bursts into spontaneous life; and the characters rarely escape O'Neill's rigid control, as, say, Falstaff escapes Shakespeare's or Mother Courage escapes Brecht's. Still, one must recognize that the work consists not of one but of 13 plays, each with its own story; O'Neill has multiplied his antagonists in order to illuminate every possible aspect of his theme, and every rationalization, whether religious, racial, political, sexual, psychological, or philosophical, with which humankind labors to escape the truths of raw existence. And in some crazy inexplicable way, the very length of the play contributes to its impact, as if we had to be exposed to virtually every aspect of universal suffering in order to feel its full force.

This exhaustiveness of design probably accounts for the influence of *The Iceman Cometh* on so much subsequent work; seeing the play today is like reading the family tree of modern drama. Surely, *Death of a Salesman,* also recently revived (superbly) as a film for television, owes a strong debt to *The Iceman Cometh,* with its O'Neillian theme of an illusory tomorrow embodied in another philandering drummer cheating on another saintly wife in out-of-town hotels. (The name Willy Loman even unconsciously echoes O'Neill's character Willie

Oban.) Hickey's long-delayed entrance ("Would that Hickey or Death would come") may have inspired a similar long-awaited figure, Beckett's Godot, who, like Hickey, stands in an almost supernatural punitive relationship to hapless derelicts. And there is no question that Jack Gelber's dazed junkies in *The Connection* owe a great deal to O'Neill's drunks in Harry Hope's "End of the Line Cafe," just as it is likely that if the play were written today, the characters would have been drug addicts.

I cite this partial list of influences not to swell the secondary reading list of the dramatic lit syllabus but to suggest how a great play over time becomes a seedbed of riches. And *The Iceman Cometh* is as great a play as the modern theater has produced. The current production brings no new insights. It is occasionally badly paced and laborious, especially in the overly schematic third act; and the actors, gifted as they are, sometimes draw back from the precipice. But by the conclusion of this long evening, this masterwork has managed to cut to the bone, and that makes the production a signal event in any Broadway season.

Source: Robert Brustein, "Souls on Ice" in the *New Republic,* Vol. 193, no. 18, October 28, 1985, pp. 41–43.

Stark Young

In this review Stark appraises the 1946 Broadway production of O'Neill's play. In his positive assessment of the staging, the critic labels the work "beautiful, luminous, filled with the witty and the poetic together mingled."

"The Iceman Cometh" marks the return of Eugene O'Neill to Broadway after an absence of twelve years. The performance of the play runs into two sessions, of about an hour and a quarter before the dinner intermission, and two and three-quarters after. The Theatre Guild, by its own lights, has brought the highest intentions to its production, a large company mostly of experienced actors, plus the décor by Robert Edmond Jones and the directing by Eddie Dowling.

The scene of "*The Iceman Cometh* " is Harry Hope's, a saloon with a back room curtained off, which can pass as a restaurant and run Sundays as well as week days, and with lodgers upstairs, which turns it into a Raines Law hotel that can stay open night and day. Among the guests are a former Harvard man; a one-time editor of Anarchist periodicals; a one-time police lieutenant; a Negro, one-time proprietor of a Negro gambling house; a one-

> **HICKEY GETS THE ROOMERS ALL OUT, ONE BY ONE; HE KNOWS THEY WILL COME BACK AGAIN, BEATEN BUT FREE OF THEIR PIPE-DREAMS, AND SO WILL FIND PEACE"**

time leader of a Boer commando; a one-time Boer War correspondent; a one-time captain of British infantry; a onetime Anarchist; a one-time circus man; a young man from the West Coast, who has squealed on his Anarchist mother; a hardware salesman; the day and night bartenders; and three tarts. They have, the majority of them, fallen from what they once were and live in a kind of whiskey-sodden dream of getting back: tomorrow will make everything right. The first session of "*The Iceman Cometh*"—absorbing and in the early O'Neill manner—is taken up with the revelation of the various characters as they wait for the arrival of Hickey, the hardware salesman, who joins them every year at this time to celebrate Harry's birthday with a big drunk. Hickey arrives, greets them with the old affection and surprises them with the announcement that he has left off drink and that he has come to save them not from booze but from pipe-dreams. It is these, he says, that poison and ruin a guy's life and keep him from finding any peace; he is free and contented now, like a new man, all you need is honesty with yourself, to stop lying about yourself and kidding yourself about tomorrow. He hands out a $10 bill to start the party and falls asleep from fatigue.

In the next act Hickey's effect is seen. Harry must go out on the street for the first time in twenty years and see his friends in the ward about the alderman's post they had once offered him; the short-change expert must go back to the circus; the various others back to their old positions in life; the day bartender and one of the tarts must go on and marry instead of always talking about it, et cetera. But now the friendly backwater of sots and wrecks and whores turns into hate, violent rows and imminent fights. Hickey gets them all out, one by one; he knows they will come back again, beaten but free of their pipe-dreams, and so will find peace. They all return, everything has gone wrong, even the whiskey has lost its kick. Hickey, who has confessed to killing his beloved and loving wife, to free her and free himself from a torturing pipe-dream of his reform, turns out to be insane, and this at last, and this only, frees them. All but two, for whom death is the end, go back to their dreams, somewhat gloriously, and the whiskey works again.

Eddie Dowling has directed ''The Iceman Cometh'' in his by now well known style. His is a method sure to be admired: it consists largely in a certain smooth security, an effect of competence, of keeping things professional and steady, and often of doing pretty much nothing at all. To this he adds in ''The Iceman Cometh'' a considerable degree of stylized performance, actors sitting motionless while another character or other groups take the stage. Since there is a good deal of stylization in the structure of ''The Iceman Cometh'' this may well be justified. But in my opinion the usual Dowling method brought to the directing of this O'Neill play would gain greatly by more pressure, more intensity and a far darker and richer texture.

The same remark applies to the acting. It is a relief to see so many expert actors instead of the usual run of technically indifferent players we so often get on Broadway nowadays. The three actresses who have the tart roles belong, alas, to this latter indifferent rank; otherwise the acting is notable for its excellence, especially E.G. Marshall, Nicholas Joy, Frank Tweddel, Carl Benton Reid and Russell Collins, plus fair enough performances by Paul Crabtree, John Morriott and Tom Pedi. James Barton as Hickey, a most central character in the entire motivation and movement of the play, prays the part very much, I should imagine, as Eddie Dowling would have played it, judging from his performance in ''The Glass Menagerie'' and elsewhere, and from his directing. Which means a sort of playing that is competent, wholly at ease and with a something that appears to settle the matter, to close the subject as it were, so that for the moment at least you are prevented from thinking of anything else that could be done about it. Only afterward do you keep realizing what might have been there and was not. Russell Collins could have played the role of Hickey with much more inner concentration, depth, projection and unbroken emotional fluency.

It was these qualities that appeared in Dudley Digges's performance. His Harry, the proprietor, was on a different plane from every other to be seen on the stage at the Martin Beck. It was exact, with

the exactness that belongs to all fine art; and full of the constant surprise that appears in all first-rate art whatever, as it does in whatever is alive in our life. It was beautiful, luminous, filled with the witty and the poetic together mingled. 'Twere to consider too curiously to consider so, as Horatio says, and most unfair, perhaps, to wonder what would happen to ''The Iceman Cometh'' if more of the players could do the same by it. But that would imply no doubt a condition equal to that of the Moscow Art Theatre in Gorky's ''The Lower Depths.'' How much the play could be cut or not cut then would remain to be seen. As ''The Iceman Cometh'' now stands, it is a remarkable play but could certainly be cut.

Robert Edmond Jones's setting for ''The Iceman Cometh'' seems to me one of those impalpable evocations of his in the medium of décor, austere, elegant and elusively poetic, and uncannily right for the realistic-poetic quality of this O'Neill drama. It suggests, too, the same passionate undercurrent of feeling that lies within the play throughout.

Source: Stark Young, ''O'Neill and Rostand'' in the *New Republic,* Vol. 115, no. 16, October 21, 1946, pp. 517–18.

SOURCES

Atkinson, Brooks. Review of *The Iceman Cometh* in *O'Neill and His Plays: Four Decades of Criticism,* edited by Oscar Cargill, N. Bryllion Fagin, and William J. Fisher, New York University Press, 1961, pp. 212-13.

Bentley, Eric. ''Trying to Like O'Neill'' in *O'Neill and His Plays: Four Decades of Criticism,* edited by Oscar Cargill, N. Bryllion Fagin, and William J. Fisher, New York University Press, 1961, pp. 331-45.

Berlin, Normand. *O'Neill's Shakespeare,* University of Michigan Press, 1993, pp. 176-77.

Engel, Edwin A. *The Haunted Heroes of Eugene O'Neill,* Harvard University Press, 1953, pp. 283-86.

Gilder, Rosamond. Review of *The Iceman Cometh* in *O'Neill and His Plays: Four Decades of Criticism,* edited by Oscar Cargill, N. Bryllion Fagin, and William J. Fisher, New York University Press, 1961, pp. 203-08.

Tiusanen, Timo. *O'Neill's Scenic Images,* Princeton University Press, 1968, pp. 265-73.

Woolf, Virginia. ''The Angel in the House'' in *The Conscious Reader,* edited by Caroline Shrodes, Harry Finestone, and Michael Shugrue, Macmillan, 1988, pp. 264-68.

FURTHER READING

Berlin, Normand. *Eugene O'Neill,* Macmillan, 1982.
  This book provides a brief biography of O'Neill and a general introduction to his plays.

Gelb, Arthur and Barbara Gelb. *O'Neill,* Harper, 1960.
  This is a more extensive, in-depth biography of O'Neill.

Scheibler, Rolf. *The Late Plays of Eugene O'Neill,* Francke Verlag, 1970.
  This book provides a careful analysis of *The Iceman Cometh* as well several of O'Neill's later plays.

Zinn, Howard. *The Twentieth Century: A People's History,* Harper & Row, 1984.
  This book presents a history of twentieth-century America from a leftist political perspective.

The Member of the Wedding

CARSON MCCULLERS

1950

Carson McCullers's *The Member of the Wedding* is only one of two plays written by the author and by far the most successful. Adapted from her 1946 novel of the same name, *Member* was first produced at the Empire Theatre on Broadway in 1950. McCullers had only seen several professional theatrical productions—two on Broadway (Arthur Miller's *Death of a Salesman* and Tennessee Williams's *The Glass Menagerie*)—prior to her attempt at adapting her work for the stage. McCullers undertook the task when encouraged by Williams, who had read the novel and was greatly impressed with its potential for the stage. The veteran playwright invited McCullers and her husband to his home in Nantucket, where he offered his advice on the novel's adaptation (later, he was also instrumental in obtaining financial backing and production staff for the play's bow).

Though personal obstacles prevented a speedy transformation from page to stage, *Member*'s 1950 debut was an immediate success, running for 501 performances on Broadway. It won several prestigious awards for McCullers, including the New York Dramatics Circle Award for best play, two Donaldson Awards (for best play and best first play by an author) and the Theatre Club, Inc.'s gold medal for best playwright of the year. After its Broadway run, the play was produced for a national tour and a feature film. This is one of the few instances in which an author successfully adapted their own work to the stage, and it led to

McCullers's membership in the National Institute of Arts and Letters.

Though McCullers is primarily known as a novelist, critics praised her dramatic interpretation of *The Member of the Wedding,* in great part due to the stylistic chances the play takes. Critics lauded her imaginative emphasis on character, emotion, and mood over the more traditional dramatic elements of plot and staging. In an unconventional move, almost all of the play's dramatic action takes place off stage (including the wedding of the title). Some critics found this lack of plot to be a great weakness. Others, however, found the author's focus on such an unusual protagonist (Frankie) and the play's overwhelming theme of loneliness to be a breath of fresh air and a unique perspective. Even McCullers was said to be surprised by the acclaim. *The Member of the Wedding* proved that mainstream dramatic productions could focus on emotional states in favor of narrative thrust. That so many viewers were able to identify with the plights of Frankie, Berenice, and John Henry testified to this fact. While late-twentieth century appraisals of the play have tended to focus on the racial aspects of the play—particularly the second-class citizenship of Berenice and Honey—McCullers's work is still highly regarded for its sensitive examination of adolescent alienation.

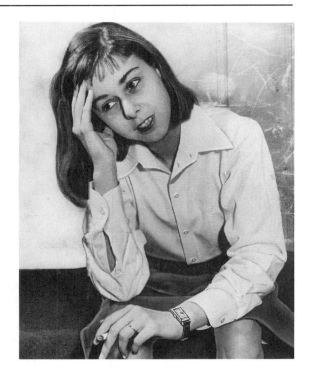

Carson McCullers

AUTHOR BIOGRAPHY

Carson McCullers was born Lula Carson Smith on February 19, 1917, in the small mill town of Columbus, Georgia. She was the daughter of Lamar Smith, a jeweler, and his wife Marguerite Waters Smith. McCullers's mother reportedly had premonitions during her pregnancy that Lula would be artistically inclined. Her hunch proved correct, and McCullers was given every advantage, sometimes to the exclusion of her younger sister, Margarita, and younger brother, Lamar, Jr. As a child, McCullers often wrote and staged plays with family and friends, just as the central character Frankie does in the author's 1950 play (and 1946 novel) *The Member of the Wedding.* McCullers also studied piano intensely. She had a complicated relationship with the family of her piano teacher, Mary Tucker, that bears a striking resemblance to the extra-familial relationships depicted in *Member.*

In 1934, McCullers's family sold a piece of family jewelry so that she could study piano and writing in New York City. McCullers lost the money upon her arrival and was forced to work a variety of odd jobs to support herself while she studied writing at both Columbia and New York University. She met Reeves McCullers, an aspiring novelist such as herself, in 1936. They married the next year, and moved to North Carolina, where they lived for several years. It was during this period that McCullers produced some of her most notable work, including the novels *The Heart Is a Lonely Hunter* (1940) and *Reflections in a Golden Eye* (1941).

The McCullers moved back to New York City in 1940, where each was involved in several complicated love affairs; the couple divorced later that year. In 1941, McCullers suffered her first stroke (attacks of varying severity would plague most of her adult life) but continued to work on her next novel, *The Ballad of the Sad Café.* The novel was published in 1943, and McCullers garnered wide critical and popular acclaim for the work. Having enlisted to fight in World War II following their divorce, Reeves was wounded in combat in 1944 and returned stateside later that year. He and McCullers remarried in 1945.

The next year, McCullers published *The Member of the Wedding* as a novel. It is arguably her most popular work. She began work on the dramatization of the novel in 1946, at the urging of noted playwright Tennessee Williams (*A Streetcar Named Desire*), who also assisted with the adaptation and subsequent production of the work. Despite such impetus, the project was delayed for several years due to personal crises. McCullers and her husband moved to Paris in 1946, and Reeves subsequently began an excessive indulgence with alcohol. McCullers then suffered three severe strokes in 1947, leaving her paralyzed on her left side. Despite these setbacks, she managed to complete the play, which opened to wide acclaim on Broadway in 1950. It won numerous awards, including the New York Drama Critics Circle Award and a Theatre Club gold medal.

This success allowed McCullers to buy a home in Paris in 1952. She continued to write, but Reeves's alcoholism was exerting a tremendous strain on their relationship; he committed suicide in France in 1953. McCullers wrote only one more play, *The Square Root of Wonderful,* which was inspired by the deaths of Reeves and her mother. The play was a moderate success, lasting only forty-five performances. McCullers's health continued to decline throughout the 1950s. She published one other novel, *Clock without Hands* (1961), and a book of children's poems before succumbing to her final stroke on September 29, 1967.

PLOT SUMMARY

Act I

The setting is the kitchen and yard of a house in a small southern town in August, 1945. It is late afternoon. Berenice, the black cook, serves drinks to her employer, Mr. Addams; his son, Jarvis; Jarvis's fiancée, Janice; and his daughter, Frankie, a twelve-year-old girl with short-cropped hair. Also present is Frankie's seven-year-old cousin John Henry. Jarvis has brought Janice home to meet his family. Mr. Addams tells them that Frankie has been talking non-stop about the wedding since Jarvis announced the engagement. Taking a sip of lemonade with liquor in it, Frankie awkwardly tries to get attention by imitating a drunk. Janice notices music coming from a nearby clubhouse and, when she asks Frankie about it, the girl tells her she is not yet a member of that group.

After everyone leaves, Berenice accuses Frankie of being jealous of Jarvis and Janice. Berenice, Frankie, and John Henry play a game of three-handed bridge. Frankie talks about her mixed feelings regarding the wedding. The bridge game takes an odd turn when Frankie and Berenice realize that John Henry has cut out the pictures of the jacks and queens. Frankie gets frustrated with him and sweeps the cards from the table. She laments her life, how she wants to leave the family home. It is revealed that Frankie gave John Henry the doll that Jarvis brought for her. Sounds of neighborhood children are heard. John Henry wants Frankie to join him outside with the other children. She refuses, but she goes out when a group of older girls enter the yard. The girls inform Frankie that she was not elected to their club—Mary Littlejohn was. Frankie becomes angry. Berenice suggests she start her own club with the neighborhood children, but Frankie does not want to lead "those little young left-over people."

Frankie decides that she wants to be called F. Jasmine Addams. She worries that she is too tall for her age and a freak. She wants to improve herself before the wedding, then she wants to die. When John Henry gets on her nerves, she makes him go home. Frankie starts to get a splinter out of her foot with a knife. She laments that her best friend has moved away. Frankie repeats something Janice said about her earlier, that Frankie wouldn't grow much more, then embellishes it. Berenice points this out, and the fact that Frankie is very jealous. The cook says that Frankie has a crush on the wedding and teases the girl. Frankie gets so angry that she throws the knife at the wall. She swears that she is going to leave town as soon as the wedding is over.

Berenice's beau, T. T. Williams, and her foster brother, Honey Camden Brown, come by to pick up Berenice. T. T. tells the cook that her brother got in a fight with a soldier and the military police beat him. The threesome depart, leaving Frankie alone. Frankie decides that she's going to go with Jarvis and Janice after the wedding, so that she can belong to something, so that she can be a part of a "we."

Act II

It is the following day, the same kitchen/yard setting. Berenice is cooking and John Henry is blowing soap bubbles when Frankie enters. The cook is angry at Frankie because she has been gone all day. Frankie tells Berenice that she bought her outfit for the wedding, and then went all over town telling everyone she is leaving with Jarvis and Janice after the wedding. She says that she will kill herself if they do not take her. Berenice changes the subject as she serves Frankie and John Henry supper. She thinks that Frankie needs a boyfriend and suggests Barney MacKean, who lives next door. Frankie calls Berenice crazy. The racket of the piano tuner chimes in, making Berenice tense. Frankie finds something Berenice says funny and starts to shadow box. Silence falls as the girls in the club pass through the Addams's yard. Frankie yells at them.

T. T. and Honey come in the back door, informing Berenice that Sis Laura, an old vegetable seller, has died. Frankie changes into her dress for the wedding to show Berenice. It is an orange satin evening dress inappropriate for a young girl. Frankie asks Berenice for her honest opinion, and the cook tells her she does not like it. The others basically agree. Mr. Addams comes in and yells at his daughter for being late. He asks T. T. and Honey if they would like to work for him next week at his jewelry store. T. T. politely tells him he cannot work on that day, but Honey is less polite in his gruff, negative response. Mr. Addams insults him, then goes back to the store. Honey and T. T. leave soon after.

Frankie reflects on death for a while, and Berenice talks about each of her four husbands. She says she loved only the first one, Ludie; she only married each of the subsequent ones because, in some way, they reminded her of Ludie. Berenice tells Frankie she knows of the young girl's intentions. Berenice warns the girl to be careful about her preoccupation with the wedding. Still, a few moments later, Frankie begins rhapsodizing about the places she, Jarvis, and Janice will visit and the many adventures they will have together. Berenice pulls Frankie onto her lap and calms her down. Frankie says she does not understand much of the world. The scene ends with Frankie, Berenice, and John Henry singing a hymn.

Act III, scene 1

It is just after the wedding ceremony the next day. In the kitchen, Berenice and T. T. arrange the refreshments for the reception. Berenice and T. T. watch the wedding from inside the door. It is revealed that Honey is in trouble again, having pulled a knife on a white bartender who refused to serve him; the young man is now wanted by the police and has disappeared. Frankie enters and says that she has not yet told Jarvis and Janice about her plans to live with them. She could not get the words out, and she is embarrassed about her dress. Frankie leaves and John Henry enters. He tells T. T. and Berenice that Frankie gave him lots of her stuff while she packed. Frankie returns and Berenice tries to dissuade her from her plan. The bride and groom

are ready to leave, and Frankie says goodbye to the group in the kitchen. She leaves, and the sound of an argument immediately ensues offstage. John Henry returns to tell Berenice and T. T. that Frankie is in the newlyweds' car and won't get out.

Moments later, Mr. Addams pulls Frankie into the kitchen and asks her what is wrong. Jarvis and Janice follow. They try to console her, but Frankie cannot accept that she is not a part of the couple. The young girl is very upset, and Berenice tries to comfort her. John Henry tells Berenice he is sick, but she does not believe him. Frankie continues to cry. Mr. Addams tries to help, but Frankie declares that she is tired of her existence, picks up her suitcase, and runs away. T. T. and Mr. Addams run after her, while the sounds of a storm rumble in the background. John Henry gets scared and again says that he has a headache. The power goes out. Berenice admits that she is scared as well.

Act III, scene 2

It is the following morning, about four o'clock. Mr. Addams and Berenice are in the kitchen together. Frankie is still missing, and John Henry has become quite ill; it is revealed that he has meningitis. Mr. Addams goes to find out about his condition, and, after he leaves, Frankie returns. Berenice shakes her, and Frankie says that she has run all over town. She says that she decided to kill herself and had her father's pistol out. But at the last second, she decided not to pull the trigger. As Berenice marches her off to bed, Honey arrives. Honey tells Berenice that the police are after him. Berenice gives him money to leave town.

Act III, scene 3

The scene opens in the Addams's kitchen, several months later. The kitchen is bare, and Berenice is the only one on stage. There is a suitcase at her feet. Frankie enters. Berenice has quit because Frankie and her father are moving into a new house with her aunt and uncle, the Wests. Frankie wants Berenice to come with them, but the cook refuses. Frankie reveals that she has new friends, Mary Littlejohn and Barney. Berenice reveals that Honey hung himself in jail and that she nursed John Henry through his illness until he, too, died. Frankie talks about Barney, but Berenice finds she can no longer relate to the young girl. Frankie states that Jarvis and Janice are in Germany now. She talks about the around-the-world trip she and Mary will make together. Barney and Frankie leave. The lights go down on Berenice, who is left alone on the stage.

She hums the hymn that she, Frankie, and John Henry sang together at the end of Act II.

CHARACTERS

Frankie Addams

Frankie is the character around whom *The Member of the Wedding* revolves; her moody discourses form much of the play's dialogue. She is a twelve-year-old struggling with the early stages of adolescence and feels very out of place in her world. The only daughter of a widower (her mother died giving birth to her), she longs to be accepted as a vital member of a group. Frankie is a tomboy and has recently chopped her hair off in a crew cut. She is tall and gangly, caught between childhood and adulthood. Though Frankie has Berenice and her neighbor/cousin John Henry as faithful, loving companions, she longs for a deeper sense of kinship with people more like herself. She decides that she wants to live with her brother and his new wife after they marry—including accompanying the couple on their honeymoon. She begins to see the impending wedding as an emblem of the family life for which she yearns. Ultimately, she is not allowed to go with the newlyweds, and she runs away. She returns, and she and her father move in with her aunt and uncle. By the last scene, which takes place several months after the rest of the play, she has begun to accept the family that she has, realizing that she is a member of that group.

Jarvis Addams

Jarvis is Frankie's twenty-one-year-old brother. He is a soldier in the army stationed at Winter Haven, Georgia, and has served in Europe. It is his impending wedding that has set Frankie's familial aspirations in motion. He is affectionate towards his sister but does not have any real understanding of her problems or needs. For example, when he comes to announce his engagement, he brings the tomboyish Frankie a doll. Like his father, he is more than a little put off by his sister's need for attention and kinship.

F. Jasmine Addams

See Frankie Addams

Mr. Royal Addams

Frankie's father, Mr. Addams is a jeweler who has been a widow since his wife died giving birth their daughter. He is old-fashioned and conserva-

tive. Like Jarvis, he does not understand Frankie and her needs. While he loves his daughter, he is unable to connect with her, failing to provide her with a sense of belonging. Uncomfortable confronting his troubled child, he spends much of his time at work.

Berenice Sadie Brown

Berenice is a middle-aged African-American cook in the Addams's household. She has been married four times but admits to only loving her first husband. The rest, drunks and crooks, all had something that reminded her of the first one. Her only living relative is Honey Camden Brown, her foster brother. Berenice is a mother figure to Frankie. She nurtures the young girl and tries to help her, yet the depth of her actions is hindered by her race and position. Though Frankie frequently disregards Berenice's advice, she does look to the maid for some measure of love and support. Berenice is also very fond of John Henry, often calling him "Candy." While she offers the children a great deal of love, they do not return her affection with the same intensity.

Berenice is the most controversial character of McCullers's play. Late-twentieth century critics have justifiably complained that the playwright's portrayal of the maid (as well as those of her brother and boyfriend) is, while allowing for a vastly different racial climate when the work was created, is ultimately racist. Despite this, Berenice is also commonly regarded as the heart and soul of the play. While the narrative action is driven by Frankie's troubles, it is Berenice's sensibility and nurturing ways that ground the drama in human emotion. It has been labeled as curious (and possibly racially-motivated) then that, of all the surviving characters, it is Berenice's happiness that appears the most unsure. By the end of play, Honey has been killed, John Henry has died, and the disillusioned maid decides not to move with Frankie's family to their new house. Having failed to find satisfactory relationships with the Addams, she chooses to find her future elsewhere.

Honey Camden Brown

Honey is Berenice's foster brother. He is about twenty years-old. He dresses in loud clothes and challenges the racially unequal status quo for African Americans. He refuses to address Mr. Addams as "sir" and, later in the play, assaults a white bartender who refuses to serve him—an act which results in his arrest. In many ways, he is the polar opposite of T. T. Williams, who bows to and operates within the era's unbalanced racial environment. Honey ultimately hangs himself in jail.

Candy

> *See* John Henry West

Janice

Janice is Jarvis Addams's young fianceé. She is young, only eighteen or nineteen years-old. She tells Frankie she is excited by the prospect of having a little sister. She is pretty but not very realistic or sensitive to other people's feelings and needs.

John Henry West

John Henry is Frankie's seven-year-old cousin and neighbor. He is a solemn, delicate young boy, who wears wire-rimmed glasses. In the time before the play begins, he was often Frankie's playmate. Now that she is struggling through early adolescence, however, she treats him with disdain. Still, he loves Frankie and her family and spends much of his time in Berenice's kitchen, sweetly commenting on events as they happen. He develops meningitis by the end of the play and dies a short time after the wedding. His death contributes to Berenice's decision to quit her job. John Henry's innocence and unjust death drive home a point that life is not always fair nor as one would hope.

T. T. Williams

T. T. is Berenice's current boyfriend. He is a middle-aged African American, about fifty years of age. He wears the clothes of a church deacon. He is a good, proper man who is given to occasional moments of pomposity. He defers to Mr. Addams and other white men as the times dictate, but he is also shown to have a strong sense of self. His decency towards his fellow man is illustrated when he searches for Honey and Frankie when both are missing.

THEMES

Alienation and Loneliness

Both Frankie and Berenice suffer from alienation and loneliness. Frankie, a twelve-year-old on the verge of adolescence, does not feel like she belongs to any peer group. She considers children, like her seven-year-old cousin John Henry, too

MEDIA ADAPTATIONS

- *The Member of the Wedding* was adapted into a film in 1952 by Columbia. It features many of the actors from the original Broadway production, including Julie Harris as Frankie, Ethel Waters as Berenice, and Brandon de Wilde as John Henry.

- A made-for-television version was filmed in 1982. Directed by Delbert Mann, it features Dana Hill as Frankie and Pearl Bailey as Berenice.

- Another made-for-television adaptation was filmed for the USA Network in 1997. It stars Anna Paquin as Frankie and Alfre Woodward as Berenice.

young, and she feels no more at ease within her own age group. Frankie's best friend, Evelyn Couch, has moved away, and she feels like an outsider among other twelve-year-olds. The members of the girls' club are a year or two older, and they reject Frankie. Yet much of Frankie's alienation is by her own design. When Berenice suggests she befriend a neighbor boy named Barney, Frankie scoffs at the suggestion. The young girl's isolation is compounded by her family situation: her mother died in childbirth; her widowed father spends most of his time at work; and her older brother, Jarvis, does not understand or really know Frankie (he brings the young tomboy a doll). The answer to her isolation, Frankie reasons, is to live with Jarvis and Janice after their wedding. The couple comes to represent a group to which she can finally belong. Though this solution proves unrealistic, by the end of the play, Frankie has learned to live within her own world. She has made friends with Barney and Mary Littlejohn, a new girl in the neighborhood.

Berenice also lives an alienated life on several levels. She has no family, save her foster brother, Honey, and he is dead by the play's conclusion. Berenice only loved her first husband, but after his death, she married three other men whose compan-

TOPICS FOR FURTHER STUDY

- Compare the drama *The Member of the Wedding* to McCullers's 1946 novel. What elements did McCullers retain in the transition from page to stage? Why do you think she discarded the elements that she did?

- Compare Frankie to a character in one of Judy Blume's young adult novels such as *Blubber, Then Again, Maybe I Won't,* or *Are You There God, It's Me Margaret.* How has the literary portrayal of the transition from childhood to adolescence changed since the 1940s? Discuss the differences.

- Research racism in the American South of the 1940s. How is it embodied in the play? Does it manifest itself differently in adults and children?

- Compare *The Member of the Wedding* to McCullers's 1943 novel *The Ballad of the Sad Café,* exploring the psychological implications of being an outsider.

---

ionship was ultimately disappointing. Her current boyfriend, T. T. Williams is a good, decent man, but she does not love him. Berenice is also African American, a fact that leads Frankie to believe that the cook is part of a tight-knit racial group. While it is true that Berenice mentions her involvement with her church and other African-American groups, the black community is also portrayed as distinctly separate from the white society in *Member.* Berenice is employed as a cook in the Addams's household, and spends most of her days with white children, which is also an alienating situation. At the end of the play, she has quit her job because the Addams are moving in with the Wests. Her brother is dead and the family to which she nominally belonged is moving on without her. As the final curtain goes down, she is literally left alone.

Coming of Age

Much of *The Member of the Wedding* deals with Frankie's awkward transition from childhood to adolescence. The dialogue, especially, shows Frankie's difficulty in navigating this stage of life. She acts like a child one moment (shamelessly mugging for attention) and the next putting on adult airs (insisting that her name is now F. Jasmine Addams, buying an inappropriate evening gown for the wedding). Frankie feels too tall and gangly to be considered a child, yet she still finds comfort sitting on Berenice's lap. The young girl is beginning to realize that there is more to the world than the town in which she lives. She wants to see and experience this world, but she does not know how to go about discovering it. She feels helpless in her situation, unable to make the right choices. In the last scene of *Member,* however, Frankie is more sure of herself. She has experienced disappointment and disillusionment, witnessed the death of someone close to her (John Henry), and realized that there still may be happiness in the world. She is learning that part of being an adult means compromise, accepting that sometimes things don't work out as planned.

Race and Racism

An underlying theme of *The Member of the Wedding* is race. Berenice is a black servant in a white household. She is primarily concerned with domestic duties, taking care of Frankie and constant visitor John Henry. Other African Americans visit Berenice at the Addams house and represent two prevalent black stances in Postwar America. T. T. Williams is a pleasant man who calls Mr. Addams "sir" and is unfailingly polite, even when he is treated unfairly. Honey, however, is not so accommodating. He is representative of the rising dissatisfaction among blacks that will evolve into the Civil Rights Movement of the coming decades. Honey has had trouble with the law because he refuses to tolerate racial slights. Mr. Addams does not like him because the young man refuses to address him as "sir." Honey pulls a knife on a white bartender who will not serve him, which leads to his arrest and eventual suicide.

While the racial theme is not overt, McCullers makes an effort to show contemporary racial attitudes. This effort on the playwright's part has earned *Member* some scorn from critics in the latter half of the twentieth century. Because McCullers accurately portrays the manner in which whites treated blacks, the second-class citizenry to which they were consigned, many deem the play as racist. Still other critics note the depiction as a strength, praising the play as an historical record of the injustices of the past. These scribes further note that had McCullers truly wished to degrade African Americans, she would not have taken such pains to make Berenice a strong, intelligent character who functions as the soul and conscience of the play.

Death

Those already deceased and the characters who die during *The Member of the Wedding* affect the plot deeply. Frankie's mother died in childbirth, leaving the girl motherless, a situation that plays a large part in her feelings of alienation. Similarly, Berenice has no family save Honey, and the only man she loved, her first husband, is long dead. McCullers emphasizes the rapidity of change and Berenice's loneliness by having both Honey and John Henry die by the end of the play. These deaths also act in contrast to Frankie's emergence as an adolescent. She successfully makes the transition, even though she also considered suicide. While both Berenice and Frankie are survivors, Frankie has a future ahead of her. The deaths that play upon the young girl's life act as an ultimately positive experience that makes her smarter and stronger. Berenice is middle-aged and part of disenfranchised minority; she does not have as many options as the young white girl. The deaths affecting her represent closed doors; they are further proof of her estrangement.

STYLE

Setting

The Member of the Wedding is set in a small town in Georgia during fours days in August, 1945; the conclusion takes place one day in November of that same year. The action of the play takes place exclusively in the back yard and kitchen of the Addams's household. There is an arbor attached to the back yard. Most of the action takes place in the kitchen itself, where Berenice cooks and tends to Frankie and John Henry. McCullers's use of one setting emphasizes the static nature of life, particularly as Frankie sees it. It also underlines the isolation of both Frankie and Berenice. Frankie sees members of the girls' club, who represent the outside world from which Frankie feels estranged, walking through her yard from inside the kitchen. As she is depicted in the play, Berenice never leaves the kitchen; as with Frankie, the room represents her isolation from the mainstream—although in the

cook's case, her segregation stems from a racist climate rather than the young girl's growing pains.

Costumes, Lighting, and Music

Although the set remains static, McCullers employs other elements to engage the dramatic action. A significant tool in this endeavor is the appearance the playwright designates for her protagonist. It is revealed that Frankie cut her hair off before the play began. This haircut is but one example of Frankie's status as a tomboy. She also favors short pants and a sombrero early on; both items emphasize her height and discomfort with her age. After Frankie decides she wants to be known as F. Jasmine, a more adult name in her opinion, she buys an orange satin evening gown for the wedding. The dress is clearly intended for an adult woman and looks ridiculous on Frankie's still maturing frame, but its inappropriateness underscores her struggle. To show the difference between T. T. and Honey, McCullers calls for T. T. to wear conservative, acceptable (at least to the white community) clothes (like "a church deacon") while Honey favors "loud-colored, snappy clothes" that illustrate his conscious efforts to be different and separate from whites.

McCullers also employs lighting to similar end. The stage directions of *Member* call for dim lighting to open the play and gradually reveal the characters. The stage goes to black during the storm at the end of Act III, scene one, when Frankie runs away after learning that she cannot live with Jarvis. Dim lighting cues are again called for in Act III, scene two when Frankie and Honey are in trouble. The murky lighting foreshadows Honey's impending death and Frankie's ultimate struggle with her surroundings. While the darkness signals Honey's end, it also represents an obstacle that Frankie will surmount.

Music also emphasizes thematic concerns and underscores much of the dramatic action in the play. In Act I, music comes from the girls' clubhouse. Frankie notices the music but its sound is distant, out of reach, symbolizing the distance between the young girl and her peers. Tense situations are underscored several times by trumpet music (in Acts I and II) and a piano being tuned in Act II (the dissonant sounds emanating from the piano add tension to the dialogue between Berenice and Frankie). Act II ends with Frankie, Berenice, and John Henry signing a hymn that is truncated by the end of the scene. At the end of the play, in Act III, Berenice's loneliness is emphasized by her singing, solo, a few lines from that hymn as the final curtain goes down.

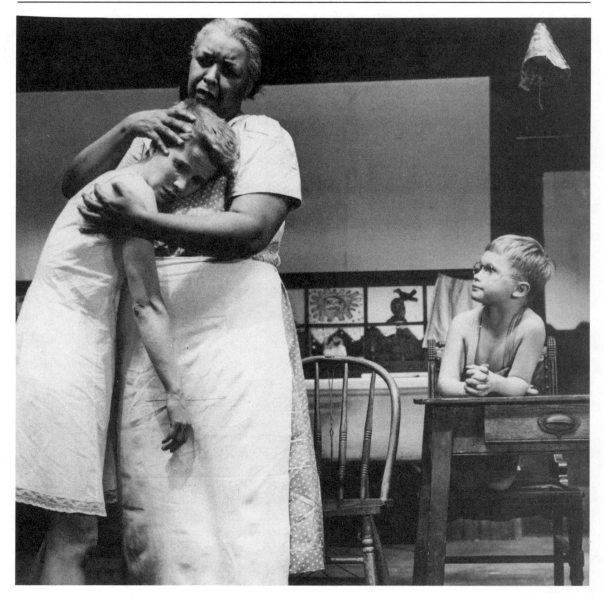

Despite the racial barrier that exists between them, Frankie (Julie Harris) is still able to take comfort from Berenice (Ethel Waters) as John Henry (Brandon de Wilde) looks on

Structure

The Member of the Wedding is episodic in structure and there is little in the way of traditional plot. Most of the major dramatic events of the play—including the titular wedding, Frankie's attempt to leave with the newlyweds, and the deaths—occur offstage. The play itself consists primarily of conversations between Frankie, Berenice, and John Henry. This dialogue relates key events and reveals the characters' feelings. Frankie dominates such proceedings, with her dark moods of isolation hov-

ering over the whole of the play. This static approach allows the themes of the play to emerge in an untraditional, evocative manner.

HISTORICAL CONTEXT

The last years of World War II were difficult ones which transformed the American cultural landscape.

COMPARE & CONTRAST

- **1940s:** In August, 1945, the United States drops two atomic bombs, nicknamed Fat Man and Little Boy, on the Japanese cities of Hiroshima and Nagasaki, effectively ending World War II in the Pacific theater.

  Today: The United States leads efforts to reduce the number of active nuclear warheads in the arsenals of the world.

- **1940s:** Public schools, especially in the South, are often segregated between black and white students.

  Today: After years of bussing students to integrate schools, some parents and school districts are challenging this policy in court.

- **1940s:** The word ''teenager'' becomes commonly used, and the looks, behavior, and rituals of these young people form a significant part of American culture.

Today: The concept of the teenager is firmly entrenched in society. Capturing the support of the ''youth market'' is a valued goal for advertisers and marketers; teenagers spend billions of dollars each year to maintain their appearance, entertain themselves, and impress their peers.

- **1940s:** During World War II, many consumer items are scarce. These include plastic and metal for children's toys, basic baking goods such as flour and sugar, and the rubber used to produce a wide variety of products such as automobile tires.

  Today: The only limitation on the consumer market is demand. There are hundreds of new toys introduced each year, an abundance of affordable foodstuffs, and numerous manufacturers of rubber goods.

The uncertain future created by war had altered people's decision-making processes. People often married quickly, perhaps looking for stability in a chaotic world. Jarvis Addams's wedding is the event that drives the action of *The Member of the Wedding.* Jarvis is a young army soldier who marries a girl from the town where he is stationed, much to the surprise of his family. In addition to the security that the event represents for the couple, Frankie, too, looks to the wedding as a symbol of belonging and safety within an unsure world. While her angst is not directly war-related, in Frankie's eyes, Jarvis's status as soldier offers a way to see the world and escape her life.

While many American citizens became more worldly due to their wartime experiences, those on the homefront suffered shortages and frequent rationing of such basic consumer items as gasoline, chewing gum, and cotton fabrics. Despite such hardship the industrial thrust of the war effort created a plethora of employment opportunities for

many disenfranchised groups, including women who were called upon to assume the workforce roles previously held by the men now fighting the war. The need for war materials to be produced quickly and cheaply forced American industries to rethink their processes. The refinement resulted in a golden economic age for many Americans. The Postwar years saw a boom in both technological advances and sheer production numbers, with items such as automobiles and new homes becoming abundant and affordable. The expanding infrastructure created numerous new jobs for the men returning from the war.

Although times were good for these men, the women who had made significant contributions to America's industrial evolution were, by the war's end, stripped of their wartime jobs and told that it was time for them to return to their kitchens and support their men. While some women were happy to return to their domestic roles, many others relished the independence and satisfaction that came from being a productive member of a workforce. The Postwar years showed significant growth in the number of women striking out on their own, joining the male-dominated workforce on many levels, and fighting for equality in the workplace. As a young woman coming of age in this era, an individualist such as Frankie would have benefited greatly from the efforts of these women.

Another group that was called upon to contribute both fighting men and members of the wartime workforce were African Americans. Their contributions to both arenas were invaluable to America's victories in each endeavor. Yet, as with the female workforce, when the war ended, these people were once again returned to the second-class status that had plagued them for years. But the war years gave them a taste of autonomy, and the Postwar years saw significant growth of the struggle that would become the Civil Rights Movement. In the coming decades, organized protests would take the form of both peaceful demonstrations such as sit-ins and the full-blown violence of the race riots that rocked Detroit, Michigan, and the Watts section of Los Angeles as blacks protested their unsatisfactory social status. The New York State Commission Against Discrimination, the first governmental organization of its kind, was organized to fight racial and other forms of discrimination.

Though many African Americans questioned the status quo, little real progress was made in the movement's early years. Schools and other public institutions were largely segregated, especially in the South. The phrase ''separate but equal'' entered the lexicon, but the situation was anything but equal. The funding for black schools was grossly below the budgets allotted to white institutions and the public facilities provided for blacks were substandard. Many universities refused to admit black people. The National Association for the Advancement of Colored People (NAACP) became a significant force in the fight to equalize the racial issue. By the 1950s, the group had attained key victories in the Civil Rights Movement, notably the Brown vs. Board of Education court case that overturned the legality of segregated schools. The military was also segregated until 1948.

Southern whites fought the civil rights victories at every turn, often with murderous violence against African Americans. Many blacks of this era were afraid to rock the boat, fearing the very real threat of violence from white-dominated society. Yet a great many others, like Honey, were fed up with the prejudice and economic hardship thrust upon them. They chose to challenge the system, despite, as Honey did, often paying with their lives.

CRITICAL OVERVIEW

Critics have generally regarded *The Member of the Wedding* favorably since its Broadway debut on January 5, 1950. Contemporary critics mostly praised McCullers's realistic characterizations and keen depiction of loneliness. Many found her dialogue to be extremely believable, noting that she used the southern vernacular to good effect. If nothing else, the play was seen as moving and absorbing, emotionally deep and well-timed.

John Mason Brown, from the *Saturday Review of Literature,* found Frankie to be an overwhelming and fascinating character. He argued that that the play was successful from the start in large part because of the high quality of the original Broadway cast. Along similar lines, a critic in *Newsweek* wrote, ''In lesser hands, the wonder and the torment of the girl's obsession and her hysterical bitterness in rejection inevitably would seem tenuous stuff for a full-bodied drama. That here is has emotional substance and depth stems almost as much from the acting as the writing.''

Other critics faulted McCullers with a lack of focus. An anonymous critic writing in the *New Yorker* found the racial theme, as embodied by T. T. Williams and Honey Camden Brown, ''contrived'' and claimed that it only detracted from the play. This sentiment would find support, along with complaints of outright racism from critics in later years.

In the play's initial assessment, however, the biggest point of controversy concerned the drama's lack of a traditional plot in favor of character development and extensive dialogue. While many acknowledged that *Member* is stylistically innovative, they did not know what to make of this unconventional play. Brown, writing in the *Saturday Review of Literature,* discussed the difference between plot and story, pointing out that McCullers was obviously influenced by Russian playwright Anton Chekhov (*The Cherry Orchard*), whose plays are noteworthy more for their characters and concepts than actual narrative. While Brown found much to praise about the production, writing that ''it is felt, observed, and phrased with exceptional sensitivity,'' he ultimately deemed the play as static. The critic for the *New Yorker* concurred, calling *The Member of the Wedding* ''a curiously uneven work—sometimes funny, sometimes moving, but also, unfortunately, sometimes just a trifle incoherent and shapeless.''

Some critics have argued that *The Member of the Wedding* might not be a play at all because of its untraditional structure and lack of action. Margaret Marshall of the *Nation* wrote, ''it is not so much a play as it is whatever in the theater corresponds to the tone poem in music.'' But she noted, ''The audience cheered at the end. I *think* for the right reasons.'' The theater critic in *Time* magazine was not as kind, writing that *Member* ''suffers after a while from being so much less a play than a mere picture of people. It would make an ideal long one-acter.''

Like Marshall, many critics who found fault with the play's structure nevertheless believed that it was ultimately art in some form. Brown called *Member* ''the work of an artist,'' while the theater critic in the *New Yorker* called the play ''poetry.'' Since the original production, critics have come to realize the power its non-traditional structure. In 1975, Francis B. Dedmond, writing in the *South Atlantic Bulletin,* said: ''The structure is rather a psychological one, the pattern of which Mrs. McCullers hints at in her stage directions preceding Act One.'' Dedmond complimented McCullers's ''ability to dramatize the abstract values of the play.''

Other noteworthy critics such as Clive Barnes have continued to compare *The Member of the Wedding* to the works of Chekhov. The play is now considered historically significant for what it tried, and many argue, succeeded in accomplishing.

CRITICISM

A. Petrusso

In this essay, Petrusso discusses the racial aspects of The Member of the Wedding *and how they enrich the themes of the play.*

In a review of the original Broadway production of Carson McCullers's *The Member of the Wedding,* a critic writing in the *New Yorker* argued,

''The racial subplot . . . seems to me only to confuse and diminish the play.'' On the contrary, the African American characters and the dilemmas they face underscore Frankie's actions and concerns as well as the play's greater themes. The issue also adds realism to the play, offering a snapshot of the racial climate of the South in 1945. By examining the contributions Berenice and Honey (and, to a lesser extent, T. T.) make to *The Member of the Wedding,* it becomes clear that they are vital to the play, particularly in reference to its themes of loneliness, isolation, and rebellion.

Arguably, the most important person in Frankie Addams's world is the family's black cook, Berenice. Berenice acts as Frankie's confessor, nursemaid, storyteller, and surrogate mother. She is Frankie's primary female and adult role model. Berenice shares several key characteristics with Frankie. Frankie has few friends, and her blood family has little or no time for her. Her mother is dead, her father works all the time, and her brother is a soldier stationed in another town. Berenice is also lonely in her personal relationships. She has no family, save her foster brother, and though she was married four times, she only loved her first husband, Ludie Maxell Freeman.

Like Frankie, Berenice lives a limited, seemingly unchanging life, confined primarily to the Addams's kitchen. White adults pay her little mind because she is black and a domestic. They regard Frankie the same way, dismissing her as a child. Their essential isolation from their immediate surroundings, as well as their loneliness, draw the two together. Yet this is clearly a temporary alliance. Though Berenice is the mature adult in the relationship, the era in which she lives and her race limit her opportunities. Frankie has the potential to change, grow, and move forward. Frankie will outgrow her relationship with Berenice. McCullers uses this fact to increase dramatic tension in *Member.*

Frankie, a self-absorbed twelve-year-old on the verge of adolescence, can rarely see the world beyond herself. She is ignorant of Berenice's problems. In a telling passage at the end of Act I, Frankie tells her young cousin, John Henry: ''The trouble with me is that for a long time I have just been an 'I' person. All other people can say 'we.' When Berenice says 'we' she means her lodge and church and colored people. . . . All people belong to a 'we' except me.'' A few lines later, Frankie reveals that she plans to join her brother Jarvis and his new wife

WHAT DO I READ NEXT?

- The 1946 novel by Carson McCullers of the same name, on which *Member* is based. The novel delves deeper into the psychology of the characters and issues, providing a more complete picture of Frankie's pain and struggle.

- Eudora Welty's short story "A Memory," originally published in the *Southern Review* of Autumn, 1937. Like McCuller's tale, the story focuses on a young girl's coming of age in the South.

- *The Square Root of Wonderful* is the only other stage play McCullers wrote. First performed in 1957, the drama centers around Mollie Lovejoy and her tumultuous relationship with her ex-husband, Phillip, and his family. The play was largely inspired by McCullers's relationship with her husband Reeves. The melancholy tone of the play is largely thought to have been influenced by Reeves's death.

- *Racism Matters,* published by William D. Wright, in 1998, discusses the history of race and race relations in the United States. The book provides good historical background on the environment in which Berenice, T. T., and Honey lived.

- *The Heart Is a Lonely Hunter* is McCullers's 1940 novel. One of its main characters, Mick, is an adolescent girl like Frankie Addams who suffers from isolation and loneliness.

---

after the wedding, for "they are the *we* of me." While Berenice may "belong" to a church and a lodge, we never see nor hear of them during the course of the play, except on one point. Yet the "colored people" to whom the cook belongs are only manifested in three individuals—Berenice's boyfriend, T. T. Williams; her foster brother, Honey Camden Brown; and an old vegetable vendor—who each appear for only a few moments on stage. No full-fledged community is depicted for Berenice, except in the kitchen of the Addams's house.

Berenice spends almost all of her time with Frankie and John Henry in the kitchen. She is a black woman working, essentially living, in a white world. Though her skin color identifies her membership in a racial group, that group is so rarely present that Berenice's isolation rivals—even exceeds—Frankie's. Frankie does not once consider that the kitchen community might be a "we" for her as well as Berenice; she fails to see the comfort that can be given and received between them. Her loneliness is absolute (and somewhat unrealistic) because of her age (it is common for adolescents to feel that they don't belong to any particular group). Despite the different roots of Frankie's pain, Berenice's own existence allows her to understand them. The theme of loneliness manifests itself maturely in Berenice.

Francis B. Dedmond, writing in the *South Atlantic Bulletin,* claimed that Berenice is "persistent in trying to get Frankie to look at life through adult eyes—to face the demands of reality—but Frankie's world of fantasy, always near the surface, will not long stay submerged." In many ways, Berenice is an adult version of Frankie, trying to guide the girl's growth and avoid the pitfalls of her own life. Excited by the prospect of her brother's forthcoming union, Frankie looks to Berenice for information about weddings. She tells Frankie about her four marriages, hoping to make the girl realize that a new wedding is about two people, not three. Yet Frankie persists in her ideal of a "family" with Jarvis and Janice.

By the end of *Member,* Frankie has accepted the fact that she cannot live with her brother and his new wife; she begins to adjust to being an adolescent. She and her father are moving in with her aunt and uncle into a new house. She has also made some new friends. Frankie now belongs to several groups, yet none of them include Berenice. For Berenice, life has gotten worse rather than better. Since the "we" of the kitchen is irrevocably broken with John Henry's death, Berenice is more alone than before. Honey is also dead. She has decided not to move with the family. The play ends with her alone in the empty kitchen. This contrast again emphasizes the different manifestations of loneliness and belonging relative to age. McCullers also uses this to make a statement about African Americans and their unchanging status in this time period. It is noteworthy that the white characters come through their troubles with a sense of optimism while the black characters' futures remain bleak.

To further emphasize this point, McCullers contrasts Frankie with Berenice's foster brother, Honey. Frankie refuses to accept her status as a young woman. She has shorn off her hair, favors shorts and other boyish outfits, and acts in a frustrated, rebellious manner. Though Honey is a black man about twenty years-old, he shares many of Frankie's traits. McCullers describes him as "very high-strung and volatile." She dresses him in "loud-colored, snappy clothes." Like Frankie, he constantly challenges the status quo, unwilling to accept the role society has dictated for him. Unlike Frankie, however, he suffers physical harm for his nonconformity. When he is first introduced, he has a lump on his head because he was hit by an MP (military policeman) for pushing a white soldier who pushed him.

Both Honey and Frankie run away when rejected, and both are miserable in their existences. The day before the wedding, in Act II, Berenice gives Honey enough money for two beers. It is later revealed that, at the bar, Honey drew a knife on a white bartender who refused to serve him (this action takes place off-stage). During the wedding, Berenice and T. T. talk about Honey's flight from the police. When Frankie is rejected by Jarvis, she too runs away. Inside her suitcase is her father's pistol. She spends the night in the alley behind her father's jewelry story. When she returns home, she tells Berenice that she had the gun in her hand and that she contemplated shooting herself.

Honey comes to Berenice at nearly the same time, and she gives him money to run away. Honey tells her: "I know now all my days have been leading up to this minute. No more 'boy this-boy that'—no bowing, no scraping. For the first time, I'm free and it makes me happy." Honey does not get far, however. In the last scene of the play, Frankie and Berenice discuss his untimely death.

He was caught by the police and put in jail, where he later hung himself.

The differences between the rebellions of Frankie and Honey are telling. Frankie's is, by its very nature, short-lived. She is a child trying to find her place within a family (though not necessarily one of blood). While Honey also desires his own place, his struggle involves the whole of American society. Frankie just has to grow up and find a place where she can belong. While she realizes that it may be a difficult struggle, she also discovers that it is not a grave, life or death issue. Frankie can become part of some aspect of white society but Honey cannot. For him, death is preferable to bending his will to the dictates of others. Honey, like Berenice, puts Frankie's problems in perspective. The play does not belittle the young girl's dilemma but shows how similar problems can take different forms with different people.

While many contemporary critics have complained that McCullers's play is racist, depicting its black characters as inferior to its white. Others, while conceding certain distasteful racist elements, find the play to be an accurate picture of America at that time. They further view the playwright's take on blacks as a sympathetic one. The fact that the play hinges on the interaction between Frankie and Berenice says a great deal about what McCullers thought of black people. *The Member of the Wedding* is greatly enriched, not diminished, by its racial content. McCullers expertly uses the status of southern blacks to complement and underscore Frankie's conflict. The stories of Berenice and Honey balance the play, giving it deeper significance. *Member of the Wedding* illustrates that the same emotions can result in vastly different destinies for different people. Yet McCullers demonstrates that loneliness and rebellion are universal human concerns, not ones unique to a specific race or social strata.

Source: A. Petrusso, for *Drama for Students,* Gale, 1999.

Moira Hodgson

Hodgson reviews a 1989 production of McCullers drama. While finding much to praise in the play's cast and crew, the critic is dismayed at the "sorry picture it presents of race relations."

Twelve-year-old Frankie Addams, the heroine of Carson McCullers's *The Member of the Wedding,* is also on a quest for discovery of self. She longs to

> I FIND IT HARD TO IMAGINE THAT ANYONE, EVEN IN 1950, COULD SIT THROUGH THIS PLAY, THE PINNACLE OF SOUTHERN GOTHIC, WITHOUT FLINCHING AT THE SORRY PICTURE IT PRESENTS OF RACE RELATIONS"

escape the confines of the "ugly old kitchen" which is her world, and discover the larger world outside. But that world, as we see from the adults around her, is in many ways even more confining.

Harold Clurman, who directed the original production in 1950—starring Ethel Waters, Julie Harris and Brandon de Wilde—saw the action of the play as springing from Frankie's dream of becoming "a member of the whole world" and saw the other characters of the play as variants of her struggle for connection. Harold Scott, who directs the present revival at the Roundabout Theatre, has been quoted as saying that Clurman directed the play from a white point of view, regarding Berenice as a "mammy." But, says Scott, "I'm directing it as a black man who has been through the 1960s."

I did not see the original version or the subsequent film, so I can't compare them with Scott's production. But I find it hard to imagine that anyone, even in 1950, could sit through this play, the pinnacle of Southern Gothic, without flinching at the sorry picture it presents of race relations. Looking at it now, in the light of all that has gone on since then, Frankie's struggle seems minor compared with the hopelessness of the struggle facing the black characters. In the South of 1945 a white child could, as in the play, feel closest to her "mammy." But by the end of the play, Frankie is ready to become part of the white world. Berenice, the housekeeper, meanwhile, is left with nothing. John Henry, Frankie's young cousin and a frequent visitor to the kitchen, has died of meningitis. Berenice's only son, arrested for an attack on a white man who refused to serve him, has hanged himself in his cell.

Scott has drawn excellent performances from Esther Rolle, who is a dignified and restrained

Berenice; Calvin Lennon Armitage as John Henry; and Amelia Campbell, who is exceedingly convincing if at times a little too fidgety as she pushes her adolescent being, as Clurman put it, "like a sharp plant struggling upward through the resistant soil."

The Member of the Wedding has its flaws, but the saddest part of seeing this play nearly forty years later is the realization that in the interim so little has been accomplished.

Source: Moira Hodgson, review of *Member of the Wedding* in the *Nation,* Vol. 248, no. 23, June 12, 1989, p. 825.

John Simon

In this review, Simon appraises a 1989 revival production of Member of the Wedding. *He discusses the extant problems the play has with its controversial racial issues, as well as the difficulty in casting the lead role of Frankie. He concludes that this production meets with mixed success.*

"I dislike intensely the work of Carson McCullers," wrote Flannery O'Connor, one of America's greatest and still undervalued writers, about her fellow Georgian, one of America's most overrated mediocrities. McCullers, along with Truman Capote, was most responsible for putting the "thick" in Southern Gothick. Though I find all her works precious and achingly elucubrated, her 1950 stage adaptation of her novel *The Member of the Wedding* is by far her most acceptable work, being also the most nearly autobiographical and, as dictated by dramatic necessity, the most structured. As many people know, at least from the movie, it is the story of Frankie Addams, a twelve-year-old, motherless, small-town southern tomboy whose shopkeeper father neglects her and whose education takes place in the kitchen.

The Addams kitchen is the stronghold of Berenice Sadie Brown, one of those archetypal powerful black female retainers. Four times married and thrice burned, Berenice exudes calm, somewhat caustic, worldly and motherly wisdom. Sharing the kitchen with her and Frankie is John Henry, Frankie's tiny, blond, bespectacled cousin, one of those precocious innocents destined for early death— McCullers cannot resist putting him in angel's costume the last time we see him. Frankie, a lonely and wildly imaginative girl, develops a crush on a couple: her soldier brother, Jarvis (the time is 1945), and Janice, whom he is about to marry. Rich in fantasy lives, Frankie dreams that the young couple—"the we of me," she calls them—will take her along on their honeymoon and keep her with them forever. The inevitable and fierce disappointment, the wisdom of Berenice (and her own concurrent bereavement), and John Henry's death constitute Frankie's rites of passage.

The play is a trio for three superb players, the other characters chiming in with a mere obbligato. In the original production, under Harold Clurman's direction, Ethel Waters, Julie Harris, and Brandon De Wilde gave extraordinary performances both individually and in concert, whose memory subsequent mountings have not been able to efface— something a wholly successful revival would have to do. The Harris—Waters—De Wilde team was so good that you forgot the feyness and tenuousness of the material and thought you were witnessing some vital statement about adolescence, such as *Huckleberry Finn* or *Le Grand Meaulnes.*

In the Roundabout revival, none of the trio is bad, but none of the performances falls into place with either the click of inevitability or the music of genius. Esther Rolle is a fine actress and a commanding presence, and she conveys the skepticism and irony of Berenice handsomely, but the passion with which she loved Ludie, her first husband, and her sensuous nature, which establishes a bond with Frankie's impetuous yearnings, are shortchanged by an excessively measured delivery, a too muted interpretation. As a result, Berenice's final transformation into a chastened, defeated person does not register strongly and tragically.

Frankie is always a problem, requiring an actress of histrionic and existential maturity who can yet embody a sexually ambivalent twelve-year-old in looks and personality. This was Miss Harris's forte; Amelia Campbell, the incumbent, though in many ways right for the part, works too hard at it: A leg or an arm is always twitching or flailing; there is too much throwing of oneself around as if in the throes of St. Vitus' dance. Here the director, Harold Scott, must share in the blame. Calvin Lennon Armitage, as John Henry, is a sweet, natural actor, but acoustics at the Roundabout are poor, and Scott has him facing upstage too much; the six-year-old's diction, though appealing, is not that good.

The supporting cast is uniformly undistinguished or worse, with the exception of Jeri Leer, whose Janice couldn't be more authentic. Thomas Cariello's

> THE MEMBER OF THE
> WEDDING IS BY FAR MCCULLER'S
> MOST ACCEPTABLE WORK, BEING
> ALSO THE MOST NEARLY
> AUTOBIOGRAPHICAL AND, AS
> DICTATED BY DRAMATIC NECESSITY,
> THE MOST STRUCTURED"

set, though adequate in its culinary aspects, comes to grief outdoors, e.g., with Spanish moss that looks neither mossy nor Spanish. Scott's direction, however competent in its broad outlines, lacks the fine dynamic shadings this sort of chamber music requires. A *Wedding,* then, you can drop in on but would not especially want membership in.

Source: John Simon, "Wedding Nells" in *New York,* Vol. 22, no. 15, April 10, 1989 , p. 100.

Isaac Rosenfeld

In this review of McCullers's original novel, which she later adapted for the stage, Rosenfeld finds Member of the Wedding *a somewhat engrossing story, though one that is ultimately hindered by McCullers's self-centered point of view.*

Southern writers have produced the nearest thing in America to a genuine, contemporary folk art. Other regions have their spokesmen, but only the South has stood still long enough for the best writers to catch up with it. The ingredients of a folk art are there, still undisturbed by the progressive industrialization of the country. The South has legend, history and tradition, a relatively primitive folk culture among the Negroes and poor whites, a bourgeois culture in the cities and the trappings of a decrepit but still pretentious agrarian aristocracy; all of which elements put the Southern writer in a position somewhat similar to that of the Russian novelists of the nineteenth century. It is no accident that the South has produced the leading regional writers.

Eudora Welty and Carson McCullers are surely among the finest of their generation of Southern writers. But it is curious to see how each in her own

"IN RELATION TO THE SOUTH AND TO THE FOLK MATERIAL THAT IS SO LIBERALLY USED, *THE MEMBER OF THE WEDDING* IS OBLIQUE AND SELF-CENTERED. IT PRESENTS NOT SO MUCH SOUTHERN LIFE, AS A PARABLE ON THE LIFE OF THE WRITER IN THE SOUTH, THE ALIENATION AND WITHDRAWAL THE SENSITIVE SOUTHERNER MUST FEEL"

way makes what one might call an attempt to escape from the South. I don't mean arbitrarily to assign to Miss Welty and Miss McCullers the intention of achieving folk art, only to call the absence of a true folk quality in their writing an "escape." Each has her own distinctive aims as a writer, which it would be foolish to surrender to folk demands. I do, however, mean to point out that Miss Welty and Miss McCullers cannot utilize all the resources of their native regions; the reasons for this may have some bearing on American regionalism and folk literature in general. . . .

Carson McCullers' novella, *The Member of the Wedding,* stands in more or less the same oblique relation to the South. It is the story of Frankie, or F. Jasmine Addams, in her thirteenth year, cut off from her girlhood friends and from the life around her. Frankie is a member of nothing and belongs to nothing ; she is insanely bored. When her brother returns on furlough from Alaska to marry a local girl, Frankie gets the idea that he will invite her to accompany them on the honeymoon. This notion fills the great gap in her life, and the novella shows how she enlarges on her fancies, building them up out of nothing, until the inevitable disappointment. The interest here is more readily maintained than in Eudora Welty's novel; the dramatic line is stronger and more clearly drawn, the anticipation mounts in spite of some padding with which Miss McCullers has filled out her slender story, and there is an overall irony and detachment that reinforces the emo-

tional quality of the writing. But in relation to the South and to the folk material that is so liberally used, *The Member of the Wedding* is also oblique and self-centered. It presents not so much Southern life, as a parable on the life of the writer in the South, the alienation and withdrawal the sensitive Southerner must feel.

It is this aspect which these two books, otherwise dissimilar, have in common, and I think it is of some significance. In both novels, as in much of Southern writing, there is an unavowed double standard which divides the material used from the personal uses to which the author puts it. The subject matter, the color, the speech, the characters are all taken at first hand, from a deep social involvement; but the meanings that the author wishes to express are not so closely related to the Southern environment and share little more than its surface values. At the level of personal expression, the author withdraws, turns inward to the sensibility, as Eudora Welty does, or to the theme of alienation, as with Carson McCullers. Though both have taken a wedding as their theme of symbolic unification, it does not unite them with a folk or traditional society, as such a symbol might be expected to do, but serves rather to indicate their degree of withdrawal—which, in terms of the values involved, is solipsistic in relation to the South. It is an inevitable withdrawal, for the serious American writer cannot but be alienated from American society, close though he may be to it, and much though he may wish to belong. And it is this, I think, which is responsible for the fact that though we have regionalism in abundance, it will never attain its goal of folk art. This contradiction is all the more clearly seen in the South, where the folk material is richest and the folk appeal strongest. But the social contradictions of the South are also the greatest you will find in this country; and they are such that the whole society may be called the antithesis of art. I do not see how a serious Southern artist can really and truly feel at home in his home.

Source: Isaac Rosenfeld, "Double Standard" in the *New Republic,* Vol. 114, no. 17, April 29, 1946, pp. 633–34.

SOURCES

Brown, John Mason. "Plot Me No Plots" in the *Saturday Review of Literature,* January 28, 1950, pp. 27-29.

"Brook and River" in the *New Yorker,* January 14, 1950, p. 46-47.

Dedmond, Francis B. "Doing Her Own Thing: Carson McCullers's Dramatization of *The Member of the Wedding* in the *South Atlantic Bulletin,* May 1975, p. 47-52.

Marshall, Margaret. Review of *The Member of the Wedding,* in the *Nation,* January 14, 1950, p. 44.

McCullers, Carson. *The Member of the Wedding,* New Directions, 1951.

"New Play in Manhattan" in *Time,* January 16, 1950, p. 45.

Review of *The Member of the Wedding* in *Newsweek,* January 16, 1950, p. 74.

FURTHER READING

Carr, Virginia Spencer. *The Lonely Hunter: A Biography of Carson McCullers,* Doubleday, 1975.
  A complete biography of McCullers's personal and professional life. Features significant discussion of *The Member of the Wedding.*

Clark, Betsey Lyon and Melvin Friedman, Editors. *Critical Essays on Carson McCullers,* G. K. Hall, 1996.
  Critical reflections on McCullers's writing, including good overviews and assessments of *The Member of the Wedding*

James, Judith Giblin. *Wunderkind: The Reputation of Carson McCullers, 1950-90,* Camden House, 1995.
  This volume discusses the critical response to McCullers and her influence on American letters. Includes an assessment of *Member.*

McCullers, Carson. *The Flowering Dream: Notes on Writing,* Esquire, 1965.
  In this professional autobiography, McCullers discusses her technique, influences, and motivations for writing. Includes an essay on *The Member of the Wedding.*

McDowell, Margaret B. *Carson McCullers,* Twayne, 1980.
  A biography of McCullers, focusing on her career as a writer.

Wikborg, Eleanor. *Carson McCullers's The Member of the Wedding: Aspects of Structure and Style,* Acta Universitatis Gothoburgensis, 1975.
  An in-depth analysis and critical study of *The Member of the Wedding,* focusing on the play's unconventional structure and character emphasis.

Mother Courage and Her Children

BERTOLT BRECHT

1939

First produced in Zurich, Switzerland, in 1939, Bertolt Brecht's *Mother Courage and Her Children* is considered by many to be among the playwright's best work and one of the most powerful anti-war dramas in history. The play is based on two works by Hans Jacob Christoffel von Grimmelshausen: his 1669 novel, *Simplicissimus* and his 1670 play, *Courage: An Adventuress*. Many critics believe *Mother Courage* to be the masterwork of Brecht's concept of Epic Theater. This dramatic subgenre, pioneered by Brecht sought to present theatre that could be viewed with complete detachment. Through such techniques as short, self-contained scenes that prevent cathartic climax, songs and card slogans that interrupts and explains forthcoming action, and detached acting that wards off audience identification—techniques that came to be known as "alienation effects"—the playwright sought to present a cerebral theatrical experience unmarred by emotional judgement. Brecht wanted audiences to think critically and objectively about the play's message, to assess the effects of war on an empirical level.

Much to Brecht's chagrin, however, audiences identified with the play on a deeply emotional level, drawing immediate parallels between the Thirty Years' War that the characters face and the horrors of World War II. *Mother Courage* was written in 1938-39, just as World War II was breaking out in Europe. Brecht completed the play while living in exile, having fled his native country in the face of a rising fascist government. It would not be until 1949

that *Mother Courage* would debut in Brecht's home-land, with a production in East Berlin, East Germany. Brecht set the play during the monumental Thirty Years' War, which occurred three centuries earlier, instead of the contemporary conflict. Brecht hoped that, because the events depicted were removed in time, audiences would be more objective when they viewed the play. But many of the European viewers and critics had first-hand experience with the horrors of war. They easily found personal meaning in the play's setting and story. Brecht rewrote the play for the 1949 East German production, hoping to minimize an emotional response from the audience, but *Mother Courage* still proved a powerful experience. In the decades since its debut, the play has grown to be regarded as one of the twentieth century's landmark dramas and a potent condemnation of war.

AUTHOR BIOGRAPHY

Brecht was born Eugen Bertolt Friedrich Brecht on February 10, 1898, in Augsburg, Bavaria, Germany. He was the son of a Catholic father, Friedrich Brecht, who worked as a salesman for a paper factory, and a Protestant mother, Sofie. Brecht grew up in a middle-class household and was precociously intelligent in school. He began writing poems while still in secondary school and had several published by 1914. By the time Brecht graduated, he was also interested in the theatre. Instead of continuing on this path, however, he studied science and medicine at university to avoid the draft. It did not work, and he was drafted in 1918 at the end of World War I. He served as an orderly in the military hospital in Augsburg.

Both his upbringing and his experience in the military profoundly affected Brecht and his writing. He rejected the bourgeois values of his youth and also developed a keen understanding of religion, largely informed by the conflicting influences of his parents' respective faiths. The wartime horrors that Brecht experienced firsthand in the military hospital led to his life-long pacifist views. He expressed these beliefs in his depiction of the horrific Thirty Years' War in his 1949 play *Mother Courage and Her Children.*

Brecht began writing plays as early as 1922, with the production of his first work *Baal*. Concurrent with his artistic work, his anti-war beliefs led him to sympathize with communist politics; he

Bertolt Brecht

began a long affiliation with communist organizations in 1919, following the end of World War I. After finally abandoning his sporadic university studies, Brecht became the dramaturg (''drama specialist'' or writer in residence) at a theater in Munich and began writing full time by 1920.

Over the next thirteen years, Brecht published several short stories and poems and successfully staged many of his own plays. He collaborated with composer Kurt Weill on several musical plays, including one of his best known works, 1929's *The Threepenny Opera*. By 1930, Brecht's plays had become highly political, espousing his belief that communism would solve many of the world's social inequalities and political problems. When the National Socialist Party (the Nazis) came to power in Germany in the early 1930s, Brecht and his works were essentially banned. He and his family fled the increasingly hostile environment in 1933; the playwright essentially went into exile for the next fifteen years.

Brecht continued to write in exile, hopping between European countries and the United States. In addition to a novelization of *The Threepenny Opera,* he produced numerous plays that were specifically critical of the Nazi regime and, in general, the world's political situation. Of these plays, the anti-war *Mother Courage and Her Children* became one of his best-known and critically acclaimed works.

The end of World War II found the defeated Germany divided into East and West factions. With the animosity of the Nazi party dispelled, Brecht was invited home. He decided to settle in the communist controlled East Germany, in part because they offered him a theatre and funding. Brecht formed the Berliner Ensemble, which debuted in 1949. That same year Brecht wrote his last original play, *The Days of the Commune* (though the work would not see production until 1957), as he devoted all his time to running the theater and working as its stage manager. He continued to write poetry and adapt other playwright's work for his theater, however. By the mid-1950s, the importance of Brecht's plays had been realized and they became popularly recognized. Brecht died on August 14, 1956, in East Berlin, from a coronary thrombosis.

PLOT SUMMARY

Scene 1

Mother Courage and Her Children opens on a highway outside of town in Dalarna, Sweden, in 1624. A recruiting officer and his sergeant are scouting for men to enlist for the Swedish Army's upcoming campaign in Poland. They discuss the fact that they are having trouble finding soldiers when Mother Courage, her children, and her canteen roll by. The military men stop the canteen, demanding Mother Courage's papers and asking about her children. She tells them how each child has a different father. The soldiers attempt to recruit the boys, especially Eilif, but Mother Courage interferes.

To distract the soldiers, Mother Courage has them draw slips of paper from the sergeant's helmet. One of them has a cross symbolizing their early death. The Sergeant feigns interest in a belt buckle Mother Courage has for sale. While she is distracted, the officer convinces Eilif to enlist, and he leaves with the soldiers. The family workforce now reduced, Kattrin joins her brother Swiss Cheese in pulling the wagon.

Scene 2

Several years later, Mother Courage is still following the Swedish Army through its Polish campaign. When the scene opens outside of the Swedish commander's tent, Mother Courage is negotiating with the Cook over the price of a chicken, eventually convincing him to buy the fowl. She plucks the chicken for him as they listen to the action inside the tent. The Commander is with the Chaplain and Eilif, who is being hailed as a hero. Eilif led his troops into a skirmish with peasants which resulted in the capture of a number of cattle. Eilif and his mother reunite.

Scene 3

Three years later, Mother Courage, Swiss Cheese, and Kattrin are with their canteen near another camp in Poland. Swiss Cheese is now a paymaster with the regiment. Yvette, a young woman who follows the camp as a prostitute, laments that all soldiers are liars. Yvette leaves, and the Chaplain and the Cook enter. They talk about politics surrounding the war. Their conversation is interrupted when the Catholic forces stage a surprise attack. In the ensuing chaos, Yvette leaves, the Chaplain hides his identity, and Swiss Cheese returns with the cash box containing the regiment's payroll. His mother wants him to throw it away, but he will not. They hide the money in their wagon.

Three days later, Mother Courage, Kattrin, Swiss Cheese, and the Chaplain sit at the canteen, prisoners of the Catholics. Swiss Cheese worries about his responsibility for the Swedish Army's money. Mother Courage and the Chaplain leave to buy a Catholic flag and meat. She tells Swiss Cheese not to get rid of the box now because there are spies. Swiss Cheese decides to take the money and bury it by the river. Kattrin tries to warn him that the spies are watching him, but she is unsuccessful. Mother Courage and the Chaplain return. Two Catholic soldiers enter with Swiss Cheese, who has been arrested. Swiss Cheese denies that he knows anyone at the canteen, saying he just ate a meal there. Mother Courage also pretends to not know her son.

Later that evening, Mother Courage tries to come up with the ransom for Swiss Cheese. She hopes to sell her wagon to an old colonel who is involved with Yvette. When the colonel and prostitute arrive, Mother Courage tells them that she only wants to pawn the canteen, buying it back from them once she raises enough money. They negotiate a price. Mother Courage hesitates, trying to negotiate a lower ransom. Her deal making is too slow, however, and Swiss Cheese is executed. Soldiers bring the body by the canteen for identification, but Mother Courage again denies knowing him.

Scene 4

Mother Courage waits outside an officer's tent. She wants to make a complaint about damage done to her merchandise. As she waits, two soldiers approach. The younger one wants to make a complaint because he was not given a reward for saving a colonel's horse, and he has not been given enough food. The older soldier tries to dissuade him from complaining. Mother Courage empathizes with the younger soldier's situation, but she tells him if his rage is not enduring, it is not worth it. After Mother Courage sings ''The Song of Great Capitulation,'' both she and the young soldier decide not to register their complaints.

Scene 5

It is 1631, and Mother Courage's canteen wagon is in Bavaria, outside a war-torn village. The Chaplain enters, needing linen to bandage some peasants whose farmhouse has been destroyed. Kattrin wants to give him some shirts from the wagon, but Mother Courage refuses to give up the clothing, stating that the peasants have no money for her goods. Kattrin threatens her mother with a board, and the Chaplain takes the shirts anyway. A child's cry is heard from a burning farmhouse. Kattrin runs into the building and rescues the child.

Scene 6

A year later, the canteen is outside of Ingolstadt, where the funeral of a fallen commander is taking place. Mother Courage serves drinks to soldiers who are not at the funeral. While waiting on her customers and taking inventory, Mother Courage and the Chaplain discuss how long the war will last. She wonders if she should buy more goods while they are cheap. Each states their belief that the war will never end.

Mother Courage decides to buy more supplies, sending Kattrin into town to pick them up. The Chaplain reveals that he would like a relationship with Mother Courage, but she turns him down. Kattrin returns with a large cut on her forehead. Mother Courage tries to give her Yvette's red boots, but the clearly upset girl is uninterested in the boots that she once coveted.

Scene 7

Mother Courage, Kattrin, and the Chaplain pull the wagon down a highway. Mother Courage sings a song about the profitability of war over peace and the need for constant movement.

Scene 8

It is still 1632, and the canteen is parked outside of a camp. A peace is unexpectedly brokered. Mother Courage is pleased because she might see Eilif again. The Cook arrives. The Chaplain decides to put on his pastor's clothing now that the Catholics no longer pose a threat to him. The Cook and the Chaplain bicker over Mother Courage. Mother Courage decides that she must get rid of her goods.

While Mother Courage is in town, Yvette shows up looking for her. She sees the Cook there and realizes that he is an old boyfriend who abandoned her years ago. A soldier stops by with Eilif in chains. He has been arrested for murdering a peasant and stealing cattle. The Chaplain leaves with Eilif and the soldier. It is implied that Eilif will be executed. Mother Courage returns with news that the war has resumed. The Cook stays with Mother Courage and Kattrin.

Scene 9

It is 1634 and Mother Courage and her canteen are again traveling behind the Swedish Army. Business is bad. The Cook gets a letter that his mother has left him an inn in Utrecht. He invites Mother Courage to come and run it with him. She refuses when she learns the invitation does not extend to Kattrin. The Cook exits for a moment, and Kattrin and Mother pull the canteen away, leaving him behind.

Scene 10

Kattrin and Mother Courage stop and listen to someone singing in a farmhouse. The song concerns their prosperity in the house.

Scene 11

Near Halle, a Protestant village, the canteen is outside of a small farmhouse for the night. Mother Courage is in town getting supplies. Three Catholic soldiers come out of the woods and hold the peasants captive, including Kattrin. One of the peasant boys is taken by the soldiers. He shows them the path to town. An older peasant man climbs to the roof and sees a Catholic regiment moving through the forest toward the unsuspecting town. There will be no warning, they believe, because the watchman must have been killed. Kattrin hears them talk of the children that might be harmed in the surprise attack. She climbs onto the roof with her drum and begins pounding out a warning on it. The soldiers come back. They shoot her when she refuses to stop making noise. Kattrin dies.

Scene 12

It is the following morning. Mother Courage sits by Kattrin's body. She expresses her disbelief that Kattrin is dead. The peasants bury Kattrin while Mother Courage departs to follow the army. She pushes the wagon by herself.

CHARACTERS

The Chaplain

When the Chaplain is introduced, he works for the Swedish Army. He is attached to the same unit as the Cook and Eilif. In scene three, when the Catholics attack and imprison the unit, Mother Courage helps him hide his true identity. He travels with Mother Courage and Kattrin for several years as they follow the Catholics. He chops wood and helps out as he much as he can. When there is a temporary peace, he returns to his clerical life.

The Cook

When the Cook is first introduced, he is in the employ of the Swedish Army, working for the Commander. Mother Courage sells him a chicken for an exorbitant price. He is a blond Dutchman who smokes a special pipe. He was a one-time boyfriend of Yvette, and she thinks he is a scoundrel. He is attracted to Mother Courage. When the Cook's mother dies, he inherits an inn in Utrecht. He asks Mother Courage to come with him to run it, but she refuses because he will not let Kattrin come along.

Mother Courage

Mother Courage is the woman around whom the play is constructed. She is middle-aged and has three children by three different men: two sons named Eilif and Swiss Cheese and a daughter named Kattrin. Mother Courage runs a mobile canteen which sells food and goods. She is a cutthroat businesswoman and follows the war, and the commerce it provides, wherever it goes. Formerly known as Anna Fierling, Mother Courage got her name from an incident in Riga in which she drove her canteen through a bombardment to sell her bread and came out alive.

Throughout the play, Mother Courage continually demonstrates that the preservation of her business is the most important thing in her life. She tries to avoid having her sons recruited for the war, not because she fears for their safety but because their help is needed pushing the wagon. When she fails to do so and Swiss Cheese is captured and sentenced to death, she haggles over the price of his ransom until it is too late. Still, she has a soft spot for her daughter, Kattrin, who is simple-minded and cannot speak. Mother Courage refuses the Cook's offer to run an inn with him because he will not allow Kattrin to accompany them. By the end of the play, all three children have died, and Mother Courage pulls the canteen alone.

Feyos

See Swiss Cheese

Anna Fierling

See Mother Courage

Kattrin Haupt

Kattrin is Mother Courage's only daughter. The product of a relationship that Mother Courage had with a German man, Kattrin is a mute, due to an incident that occurred when she was little: a soldier stuck something in her mouth. She does a great deal of work for her mother, washing dishes and cleaning up the canteen wagon. Mother Courage promises that she will get Kattrin a husband when there is peace.

Like her half-brother Swiss Cheese, Kattrin is sensitive and simple. She likes children and pretty things. For example, she covets Yvette's red boots. When Kattrin hears that a family of peasants needs linen for bandages, she gives the Chaplain shirts behind her mother's back. She also runs into a burning house to save a child despite her mother's protests. Sometime later, Kattrin runs an errand into town for her mother and comes back with a gash across her forehead. It is implied that she has been assaulted and raped. At the end of the play, Kattrin sacrifices her own life to save her mother and the people in a town; she overhears about a surprise attack and bangs a drum from a rooftop to warn the townspeople. Soldiers shoot her to keep her quiet.

Eilif Noyocki

Eilif is Mother Courage's eldest son and the result of her union with an intelligent soldier. Protective of his mother, he is a hotheaded young man who is sure of his prowess with firearms and knives. He is recruited by Swedish officers at the beginning of the play to fight on the side of the Protestants. When Mother Courage sees him again several years later, he is regarded as a hero for a successful attack he has led. He stole a large number of cattle from a group of peasants. Several scenes and years later, a temporary peace has been achieved, and Eilif is arrested for stealing cattle. It is implied that he is executed for the crime, but the actual act is not shown.

Eilif's story is a prime example of Brecht's hatred of war. His rise and fall are used as an example to illustrate the playwright's belief that war creates confused values and a skewed reality. When Eilif steals the herd of cattle during wartime, he is hailed as a hero. Yet when a peace comes, he is arrested and executed for that very act.

Peter Piper

See The Cook

Yvette Pottier

Yvette is a young woman who also follows the war and the soldiers for business reasons; she is a prostitute. She was led into this life when she became involved with the Cook as a young girl in Flanders. He abandoned her, and she ran after him. She becomes involved with a colonel and tries to help save Swiss Cheese from execution. Yvette eventually marries the colonel's brother. He dies, but she is apparently left enough money to survive.

Madame Colonel Sarhemberg

See Yvette Pottier

Swiss Cheese

Swiss Cheese is Mother Courage's younger boy. He is the son of a Swiss military engineer who was also a drunkard. Like his brother Eilif, Swiss Cheese is protective of his mother, but, unlike his ruthless brother, he is a more sensitive, honest

MEDIA ADAPTATIONS

- *Mother Courage and Her Children* was filmed in 1960, featuring much of the cast of the 1949 German stage production, including Helene Weigel as Mother Courage. It was directed by Peter Palitzsch and Manfred Wekwerth.

- The play was also adapted into a television production by the British Broadcasting Corporation (BBC) in 1959.

person. His mother says that he is simple and good at pulling wagons. After Eilif is recruited into the army, Swiss Cheese works as a paymaster for the Swedish Second Regiment. During an attack by the Catholics, he tries to protect the cashbox by hiding it, first in the canteen and then in a mole hole by the river. He is caught by two Catholic officers. When the officers bring him by, Swiss Cheese pretends like he does not know Mother Courage, hoping to protect both himself and his family. He is later executed while his mother haggles over the price of his ransom. When his body is brought to her for identification, she claims to not know him. Swiss Cheese is buried in an anonymous mass grave.

THEMES

War and Peace

Mother Courage and Her Children takes place during the Thirty Years' War, a religious war (Catholic versus Protestant) which ravaged Europe in the seventeenth century (1618-48). Every event, attitude, and emotion felt in this play is affected by the circumstances of war. Mother Courage's livelihood is based on a canteen wagon through which she sells food and various goods to soldiers. She and her children pull the wagon, following the Swedish regiments to wherever the war takes them.

Each of Mother Courage's children suffer the consequences of war and are eventually destroyed

TOPICS FOR FURTHER STUDY

- The character of Mother Courage is often compared to Niobe, a character in Greek mythology. Research Niobe and compare and contrast her with Mother Courage.

- Research the effect of war on the psyche of the common man. Is there a psychological explanation for Mother Courage's actions?

- Compare the histories of the Thirty Years' War and World War II. How do events in World War II parallel what is portrayed in *Mother Courage and Her Children?*

- Playwright Brecht was a communist. How do the tenets of communism manifest themselves in the themes and events of *Mother Courage?*

by it. Eilif is recruited when soldiers are needed for the Swedish Protestant army. He becomes a brutal soldier, losing his humanity, his sense of right and wrong, and, ultimately his life. Swiss Cheese joins the same army as a paymaster for a Protestant regiment—he takes the clerical position so that he will not have to fight in the war. Still, his position leads to his death. Kattrin loses her life when she tries to warn a town of a surprise attack by Catholics.

Other characters' lives are also affected profoundly by war. Yvette became a camp follower when her soldier boyfriend abandoned her. She started following regiments looking for him and eventually became a prostitute to support herself. Numerous common folk are depicted throughout the play, many of whom see their homes and land destroyed by the fighting.

Despite the loss of her children to the war, Mother Courage does quite well financially. Though business does go bad several times—notably during a short peace—Mother Courage survives every calamity that befalls her. Eilif is not so lucky. He attacks peasants and steals cattle during wartime and is considered a hero. He does the same thing during the short peace—though he does not know

there is a truce—and is arrested. By the end of the play, Mother Courage has to pull the canteen wagon by herself, but her business drive motivates her to persevere. She has to survive. Through his protagonist's actions, Brecht shows war as a never-ending commercial opportunity, but he also highlights its affects on the common man and woman. He shows peace being less prosperous, a state in which finances are less assured.

Choices and Consequences: Commerce versus Family

Though Mother Courage runs her canteen to support herself and her children, she often makes choices that put her commerce before her family. Each of her children are adversely affected while she is brokering business deals: Eilif is recruited by the Swedish army officer while Mother Courage tries to sell a belt buckle; Swiss Cheese is executed by the Catholics while she haggles over the price of his ransom; Kattrin dies while Mother Courage is in town buying goods.

Mother Courage also makes choices in support of her children, however, especially Kattrin. The Cook likes Mother Courage and travels with the canteen briefly; he asks her to run an inn with him. Mother Courage eagerly accepts, telling Kattrin that she will finally fulfill the many promises she has made to her mute daughter. Yet when she learns that Kattrin is unwelcome at the inn, Mother Courage refuses to go and abandons the Cook by the side of the road. Ultimately, Mother Courage is capable of doing right by her children but not at the expense of her business.

STYLE

Epic Theater

Mother Courage and Her Children is a prime example of Brecht's concept of Epic Theater. Instead of following a traditional Aristotelian model of theater, which calls for directly linked action and an emotional climax at the end of the play, Brecht constructs the play more like an epic poem. Each scene is only loosely linked, though there is something of a plot. The play also has an ambiguous, open ending; it is not clear where the remaining years of the war will take Mother Courage. Further,

Brecht tries to distance the audience from the action of the play with what he calls alienation effects. He does this to limit the audience's emotional involvement with the play and its characters. This distancing is performed in the hopes that the viewer can concentrate on the meaning of the action and its inherent social criticism.

These ideas take several forms in *Mother Courage*. Before each scene, a summary of the events to come are projected to the audience. Thus, they know what will happen and can focus on the meaning of the action. Most every action that could provoke an emotional response—the execution of Swiss Cheese, for example—is not shown onstage, and its emotional aftermath—the grieving—is never shown. Such choices direct the audience's attention to Brecht's intellectual antiwar message. There are also songs that emphasize the themes of the play while undercutting its reality by interrupting the action. Black comedic elements, especially in the dialogue of Mother Courage, add to the dramatic tension, being intellectual rather than emotional in nature.

Setting

Mother Courage and Her Children is an antiwar drama set in Europe during the Thirty Years' War, specifically covering the years 1624-1636. The action takes place in a number of locales in Europe, including (in order) Darlana, Poland, Bavaria, Fichtelgebirge, central Germany, and Halle. Almost every scene is set in the outdoors, on roads and highways, next to camps or peasants' farms, or inside tents. This represents the constant change and flux of a wartime environment. The settings illustrate the impermanence in Mother Courage's life. There are only two constants in each scene of the play: Mother Courage and her canteen wagon, and these items are notable for their mobility; they are capable of moving quickly as the war progresses.

Foreshadowing

Though *Mother Courage and Her Children* is a factually straightforward drama that, through Brecht's alienation effects, informs the audience of forthcoming events, the playwright does employ some elements of foreshadowing to more subtly intimate future developments. One event in the first scene foreshadows the deaths of Mother Courage's children as well as others. Mother Courage claims to have ''second sight.'' When the recruiters try to

Brecht's titular character, Mother Courage (Diana Rigg), in a 1995 production staged at the National Theatre in London

take Eilif away, she has them all draw lots. She tears up a piece of paper into four slips and draws a cross one of them. Everyone who draws, the three children as well as the Swedish sergeant, picks the piece of paper with the cross on it. The cross symbolizes that death is coming to these characters.

Irony

Irony is defined as incongruity between the actual result of a sequence of events and the expected result of those events. There is an underlying irony that drives the plot of *Mother Courage*. Mother Courage engages in her trade to support herself and her family in the unstable economy of war. The expectation is that she will earn enough for her family's survival. But this very enterprise—and Mother Courage's all-consuming focus on it—contributes to the death of her three children. Mother Courage focuses on preventing Eilif's recruitment by two Swedish soldiers until an opportunity for a sale presents itself. She haggles over the amount she should pay for Swiss Cheese's ransom to prevent his execution. Though she wants to save her son, she does not want to compromise her finances. Mother

Courage is in a village trying to buy up low-priced goods from scared citizens when Kattrin is gunned down by Catholic soldiers preparing to make a surprise attack. Though this last death might not have been preventable by Mother Courage, her absence ensures no intercession on her child's behalf. It is ironic that Mother Courage's goal is the survival of her family but the means for that survival becomes the instrument of the children's demise.

HISTORICAL CONTEXT

The years just before and at the outbreak of World War II were tense and uncertain ones for much of Europe. Adolf Hitler, the leader of the National Socialist (also known as Nazi) party, became dictator of Germany in 1933. Hitler secretly armed Germany in violation of the Versailles Treaty which ended World War I and allied himself with Italy and Japan. In 1938, Germany occupied Austria and annexed most of Czechoslovakia in 1939. Hitler continued to invade and occupy many nations in Europe in 1940, adding Denmark, a number of Norwegian port cities, The Netherlands, Belgium, and much of France to his empire. Though Great Britain stopped Hitler's planned invasion across the British Channel in 1940, the dictator continued his march across Europe. Great Britain and other countries tried to fight back, but it was not until the United States was drawn in to the war by Japan's bombing of Peal Harbor at the end of 1941, that their efforts had success. World War II did not end in Europe until 1945.

Though *Mother Courage and Her Children* is set during the Thirty Years' War of the seventeenth century, Brecht draws several parallels between that war and the events that were unfolding in Europe as he wrote the play. Uncertainty was a way of life in both eras. Men of all ages were conscripted to fight in the war. In 1930s Germany, every man between the ages of nineteen and forty-five were deemed fit for military service, amounting to more than eight million people in the army alone.

Just as Mother Courage looks to the Thirty Years' War as a business arena, so too was World War II a commercial enterprise. The United States, as well as Germany and other European countries, converted almost all their national infrastructure to service the war; industry became focused on turning out war goods at ever-increasing rates. In the United States, the federal government spent $370 billion on World War II. Even before the U.S. entered the war, however, the American economy geared up to produce goods for war-torn Europe. This boom in production fostered a new age of industrial technology in the U.S. and would pave the way for the prosperity of the postwar years. Despite the frenzied production, which in the United States meant around the clock shifts in factories, there were shortages of consumer items all around the world. This was partially due to the scarcity of some raw materials, again because of the war. In occupied countries, shortages were the most acute. Small-time entrepreneurs such as Mother Courage were able to supply in-demand items and carve a profitable niche for themselves.

Individuals in every country, directly involved or not, suffered during World War II and not just because of the wartime economic realities. In Germany, Hitler and his Nazi party held a tight ideological grip on the populace. In addition to their anti-Semitic policies, the Nazis did not allow freedom of the press or other forms of free expression. People who did not agree with government ideology and expressed those beliefs were dealt with in a harsh manner; many were imprisoned, tortured, and murdered. A great number of Jewish scientists and artists, as well as every-day citizens, fled the country if they were able. Though Brecht was not Jewish, he professed communist beliefs and was critical of the Nazi party. Many of his plays were banned. He escaped, his family fleeing Germany in 1936. He spent almost all of the next decade moving around Europe and the United States, avoiding the Nazi occupation. His story is typical of many people in wartime Germany. Such refugees usually had only one focus: survival, just like Mother Courage.

CRITICAL OVERVIEW

From its earliest productions, critics praised the power and complexity of *Mother Courage and Her Children,* especially its main character. Though *Mother Courage* was written in the late-1930s, it was not produced until April 19, 1941. The play debuted in Zurich, Switzerland, at the Schauspielhaus

COMPARE
&
CONTRAST

- **1600s:** The Thirty Years' War rages in Europe from 1618 to 1648.

  1930s-40s: World War II ravages Europe and the Pacific from 1939-45.

  Today: There is no widespread warfare in the world. Global or continent-wide wars have given way to small pockets of geographically contained conflict such as the Persian Gulf War of the early-1990s.

- **1600s:** The Thirty Years' War begins as a conflict of religious ideology, Catholic versus Protestant.

  1930s-40s: World War II is a tactical war fought for geographic gain. A religious element still persists, however, in Nazi Germany's persecution of European Jews as well as other ethnic minorities who do not fit Adolf Hitler's Aryan ideal.

  Today: Religion plays a role in several regional conflicts in the world. In Northern Ireland, it is Catholic versus Protestant; in the Middle East, it is Jewish versus Muslim.

- **1600s:** Because the Thirty Years' War drags on for so many years, armies have a difficult time replenishing their fighting forces.

  1930s-40s: Germany has mandatory military service for men aged eighteen to forty-five. The United States has a similar policy.

  Today: The United States has an all-volunteer army and has a hard time recruiting enough personnel. However, eighteen-year-old men are required to register for the draft in the event of a war.

- **1600s:** The population of Europe, especially in Germany, becomes severely depleted because of the long war and unchecked disease. For example, in the Wuttemberg, the population drops from 450 000 in 1634, to 100,000 in 1638.

  1930s-40s: World War II leads to widespread death of both civilian and military personnel, though not nearly as bad as the Thirty Years' World. Still, as a result of the atomic bomb dropped on Hiroshima in 1945, 50,000 people immediately die.

  Today: The peacetime population booms. Diseases such as AIDS, cancer, and other health concerns are the primary causes of death.

Zurich, a major theater, and was immediately successful—despite the fact that the country was surrounded by Nazis and invasion was always a possibility. (Brecht was regarded as a leftist and his plays were banned by the Nazis in German.) One critic, for the major Swiss newspaper, compared Mother Courage to a Shakespearean character. Another critic, Victor Wittner, writing in *Theatre Arts,* found powerful commentary on World War II in Brecht's story of the Thirty Years' War: "With all its cynicism, *Mutter Courage* is a compelling portrait, often with subtle humor, often with diabolical undercurrents of meaning, often with a certain fatalism, but also often with pure human simplicity and tenderness. And what moves us even more than that is the parallel with today's events, the actual recognition that one war is like another, one misery yields nothing to another in gruesomeness."

Following World War II, Brecht directed the first production of *Mother Courage* in Germany in 1949. Eric Bentley, writing in *Theater Arts,* wrote that this production was "The big Berlin theatrical event of the past few months, if not of the whole post-war period so far." Bentley continued: "This story of the ravages of the Thirty Years' War is fearfully apt in the ruined cities of present day Germany." Some audiences were said to be moved to tears. Other productions in postwar Europe were also well-received.

The first American productions of *Mother Courage* were not as highly acclaimed as their European counterparts. The first performance, in San Francisco in 1956, received tepid reviews. The critic for the *San Francisco Chronicle* wrote that the play "lacked suspense," assessing that "There have been many plays that are sharper weapons against war." The first Broadway production in 1963 was a box office bomb, lasting for only fifty-two performances. The critic for *Variety* called the play "sophomorically obvious, cynical, self-consciously drab and tiresome." While other critics found much to praise in *Mother Courage,* most agreed that the play was not typical commercial theater, and the production was not true to Brecht's intentions of an emotionally detached, epic theatrical presentation.

The character of Mother Courage, and what she represents, has been a major point of critical discussion. Many critics, especially of the first production in Zurich, argued that she is a tragic character. In several articles, she is compared to the tragic figure of Niobe, a character from Greek mythology who suffers greatly and turns to stone after all her children are killed. Noted theatre critic Robert Brustein, in his essay "Bertolt Brecht" in his *The Theatre of Revolt: An Approach to the Modern Drama,* said: "Mother Courage is no Niobe, all tears, but the author of her own destruction." Other critics, citing Mother Courage's numerous contradictions, find her to have more complexity than the often one-dimensional characters of classic tragedy. One scholar, Ronald Gray in his book *Brecht the Dramatist,* appraised Mother Courage as "adept at turning every situation to her own advantage, conforming with and adapting herself to it."

Another critical debate surrounds the themes of *Mother Courage.* Brecht, as well as many critics and scholars, asserted that the play is about the link between war and commerce, as epitomized in Mother Courage and her love-hate relationship with war and the money it brings her. Charles R. Lyons in his *Bertolt Brecht: The Despair and the Polemic,* argued that "Anna Fierling, Mother Courage, does not resist the war, she accommodates and uses it. It is this accommodation which Brecht decries." Ronald Gray disagreed with this assessment in *Brecht the Dramatist,* arguing that "if we look at the occasion on which she curses war, we see that she is not perceiving the commercial nature of war at all. She curses it because her daughter has been assault-

ed . . . because her daughter has been dumb since a soldier stuffed something into her mouth . . . because both of her sons have disappeared, and one of them has been killed." Gray went on to say that "Peace horrifies her." He stated that the play's real theme is "the possibility and the desirability of virtue in a corrupt world. To this question, Brecht gives, as always, an ambiguous answer."

CRITICISM

A. Petrusso

In this essay, Petrusso discusses the character of Mother Courage as both a hero and an antihero.

The title character of Bertolt Brecht's *Mother Courage and Her Children* has been the subject of much critical debate. Critics have agreed that Mother Courage's choices have been hard because of the demands of war-time life. Yet opinions vary widely on the nature of her true character. Some have labeled her a greedy coward; some call her a callous, practical businesswoman; still others deem her courageous. In this essay, Mother Courage is examined as both a hero and an antihero. For every heroic action she takes, she balances it with an antiheroic gesture. By definition, a hero is courageous and noble, distinguished by bravery and admired by others. An antihero is the exact opposite, someone who wallows in negative actions. By looking at Mother Courage in this bifocal fashion, a greater understanding of her motives—specifically the choices she makes—will be reached.

Mother Courage has two goals: for her family to survive the seemingly endless Thirty Years' War and to make a profit while doing so. The origin of her nickname "Mother Courage" is telling. During a battle in Riga, the former Anna Fierling drove her canteen wagon through a ferocious bomb attack so she could sell fifty loaves of bread before they went moldy. She claims she needed to sell the bread to feed her children, but by doing so, she put herself and everyone in the wagon at risk. How necessary a risk this was is not stated, but the act is illustrative of Mother Courage's nature as a businesswoman: she is willing to risk death to earn her profit. As a hero, she wants to survive the war and support her children. As an anti-hero, she puts that very intention at risk to earn money.

Mother Courage's canteen fulfills a need in the Thirty Years' War. Armies relied on such canteens

WHAT DO I READ NEXT?

- *The Private Life of the Master Race,* written by Brecht in 1944, is his interpretation of Hitler's New Order policies.

- Hans Jacob Christoffel von Grimmelshausen's *Courage: The Adventuress,* a novel written in 1670, is centered around a character much like Mother Courage. It is one of the sources Brecht used for *Mother Courage.*

- *King Lear,* a play by William Shakespeare written around 1605, concerns a family in which the tension between greed and caring plays a role in their destruction.

- *The Thirty Years' War,* a nonfiction book published by C. V. Wedgewood in 1938, is a history of the war, focusing on its effects in Germany.

- *Germany, Hitler, and World War II: Essays in Modern German and World History,* is a collection published in 1995 and edited by Gerhard Weinberg. The topics include Hitler and German history, including events leading up to and including World War II.

to provide food, alcohol, and goods, as many such items were not provided for the soldiers. For an unmarried woman with three children and no place to call home, the canteen wagon offers a decent livelihood for Mother Courage's family. With few alternatives, it is definitely more appealing than prostitution. Instead of begging for a living or abandoning her children, Mother Courage is responsible for her family. Her canteen allows her to take care of her children while fulfilling a basic need for the soldiers. Yet Mother Courage takes advantage of her heroic situation, looking to the war as a potential for profit and her children as a means to that end. She charges outrageous prices for her goods and refuses charity to those in need. She is called greedy several times and regularly puts profit before people.

While Mother Courage does take care of her children, keeping them fed and clothed, and tries to protect them from direct participation in the war, she loses each of them in her quest for profit. She spends much of the first scene trying to keep Eilif from being recruited to a Swedish army regiment. He ends up joining when Mother Courage's attention is diverted by two soldiers who represent a potential sale. The officer takes Eilif aside and convinces him to sign up while the sergeant haggles with Mother Courage over the price of a belt buckle.

If she had not been so concerned with profit, Eilif would not have been recruited (and subsequently executed for a crime).

Mother Courage's overwhelming concern for money also leads directly to the death of her other son, Swiss Cheese. When he is captured by Catholic soldiers, she haggles over the amount of a ransom that is offered to save him from the firing squad. Her greed prolongs the transaction, and Swiss Cheese is killed before a price is settled. Kattrin suffers a similar fate due to her mother's negligence. The mute daughter is left with a peasant family overnight while Mother Courage is in a town purchasing goods. When Kattrin learns of a surprise attack on the town, she climbs to a rooftop and drums out a warning. Her selfless act saves her mother and the town, but she is killed by soldiers. Once again, Mother Courage's preoccupation with her business (securing materials to sell), has prevented her from properly protecting her offspring. In these situations, Mother Courage's antiheroic nature outweighs her heroic actions.

Yet this is not a black and white issue: Mother Courage does make some sacrifices for her children and others as well. Her outfit has followed the Protestant armies, namely the Swedish, for most of the war. During an attack by the Catholics and a

An example of one of Brecht's best-known alienation effects, Mother Courage (Diana Rigg) and her two sons break into song. Such techniques disrupt the narrative action of the play, preventing the audience from forming emotional attachments to the characters

revealing itself). Similarly, when the Swedish army Cook catches up to them and has nowhere to stay, Mother Courage lets him travel with them—though on the same work-for-shelter terms as the Chaplain.

Mother Courage and the Cook share a mutual affection for one another. When the Cook gets an offer to run an inn in Utrecht, he invites Mother Courage to assist him. She declines this opportunity to get away from the war. The Cook will not let Kattrin, Mother Courage's only surviving child at this point, accompany them. This act shows the title character taking responsibility for her child, though some have argued that Mother Courage is not interested in working *for* the Cook and simply needs Kattrin to carry on her independent business.

In scene five, the canteen wagon is located at Magdeburg, where a recent battle has taken place. In a nearby farmhouse, several peasants are suffering from injuries and their home is partially destroyed. The Chaplain begs Mother Courage for some linen to bandage their wounds. Mother Courage says that she has already sold all the bandages she has, and she will not give him officer's shirts, which are made of linen, for this purpose. The Chaplain begs her, but she replies, ''They have nothing and they pay nothing!'' It is not until Kattrin threatens Mother Courage with a board and the Chaplain bodily moves her from the wagon that he gets the needed linen. This incident is one of the best examples of Mother Courage's antiheroic nature.

Despite such selfish actions there is evidence that Brecht's title character has redeemable qualities which she has imparted to her offspring. Of her three children, two perform heroic acts, which says something positive about how she raised them. After Swiss Cheese is arrested by the Catholics, he protects his mother and sister by denying he is related to them (he tells his captors that he was merely eating a meal at Mother Courage's canteen). This action probably saves their lives.

The mute Kattrin pursues her heroism to much greater lengths, taking great personal risks to help others. Kattrin tries to warn Swiss Cheese about the spies that are following him before his arrest to no avail. When Kattrin overhears the Cook telling Mother Courage that Kattrin is not part of the offer, Kattrin makes ready to leave so that her mother can have a better life. Mother Courage refuses to abandon her daughter, however, and they move on together. The mute girl care also shows great concern for the wellbeing of those outside her family,

subsequent detention, Mother Courage does her best to hide the Protestant Chaplain who had been visiting her. She makes him take off his cleric's coat and put on a generic beggar's cloak. As the canteen follows the Catholic armies around, she shelters the Chaplain's identity, though she insists that he do work to earn his keep (her antiheroic nature again forcing her mother to surrender the linen for bandages and risking her life to save children from a fire. At the end of the play, Kattrin does give her life to save a town from a surprise attack. The upbringing of these two children is implicitly heroic for Mother Courage.

Yet, in keeping with the duality of the character, Mother Courage's remaining child displays the influence of her darker side. After Eilif is recruited, he becomes a cutthroat soldier. He is lauded by his commander for his skill as a killer and for pillaging a peasant village, including the clever theft of a herd of oxen. Later, he is arrested for the same crime during peacetime. It is implied that he is executed for this. Eilif's actions are antiheroic, directly contributing to the death and destruction of war. His behavior counters his siblings' bravery, balancing the heroic with antiheroic actions.

Mother Courage and Her Children is play full of such balances and contradictions. Mother Courage continually curses war yet embraces its circumstances for profit and survival. Peace means uncertainty to her, and there is no profit in uncertainty. Of her two goals, preserving her family through the war and turning a profit, she achieves neither by the play's end. All her children are dead, the canteen wagon is nearly empty, and she has little money. She is now resigned to hauling the wagon by herself.

Mother Courage is both hero and antihero, each of her positive actions has a negative counterpart. Brecht shows this duality as a negative consequence of war. It is an unnatural perverse state in which common values are challenged at every turn; people are forced to act on both their good and bad impulses, in the hopes that a balance of the two forces will insure success. Mother Courage's behavior is driven by a need to survive during wartime, yet by the time the action in the play begins, it is clear her priorities on this matter have become skewed. She has equated the relentless pursuit of profit (her antiheroic side) with success and survival; she comes to believe that if she is profitable, it will allow her family to survive the war. She has allowed this side of her to rule each situation, despite what her heroic nature might dictate. Yet in the end her pragmatism and devotion to commerce leaves her emotionally and financially bankrupt. It is this last point that hammers home Brecht's primary theme in the play: war is pointless, it robs people of their humanity, and, ultimately, everyone involved loses. While gains may be made in geographic terms, humanity is left poorer for the experience.

Source: A. Petrusso, for *Drama for Students,* Gale, 1999.

Ronald S. Woodland

In the following critical essay, Woodland discusses the manner in which audiences identify with Mother Courage's continual suffering, examining Brecht's dramatic technique and the ways in which it, quite contrary to the playwright's intentions, serves to make his title character such a sympathetic one.

It is by now a critical commonplace that Brecht's *Mother Courage and her Children* owes its success, if indeed it has any, not so much to the author's implementation of his many theories of playwriting as to his inability, in spite of himself, to put these theories into full practice in his own work. Thus, it is claimed, we respond not to the story of Mother Courage but to the character herself. We are inspired by the woman's courage and sent home from the theater admiring her fortitude, ourselves encouraged to emulate her ineffably good qualities. We respond to the play in terms of our response to its title character. In short, we identify with Mother Courage, make her character our own, and turn her survival into an encouraging affirmation of our own human will to survive. Mother Courage is, ultimately, truly courageous, and her courage sees her through all her tribulations: so we, as audience to her courage, take comfort and gain succor through seeing ourselves in Mother Courage. We are better able to face with internal valor the hardships of our own existence, better able to bear the burdens placed upon us by our society. The ultimate nobility of Mother Courage is the play's success, whether Brecht wished it so or not—as indeed his constant revisions and reworkings, all with a view toward making the title character less sympathetic, clearly indicate. Even the more pervid admirers of Brecht's theories and practices of dramatic art seem to insist that the play's success arises from its strength of characterization and its affirmation of human will. Martin Esslin writes that audiences at *Mother Courage* are ''moved to tears by the sufferings of a poor woman who, having lost her three children, heroically continued her brave struggle and refused to give in, an embodiment of the eternal virtues of the common people.'' (*Brecht: The Man and His Work,* Anchor, 1961.) Similarly, Eric Bentley finds in *Mother Courage* an affirmation and admiration for a certain kind of courage. ''This is, to borrow a phrase from Paul Tillich, 'the courage to be'—in this case, the courage to exist in the face of a world that so powerfully recommends non-existence.'' (*Seven Plays of Bertolt Brecht,* Grave, 1961.)

If critics have made of Mother Courage primarily a play of character and attributed its success to the empathy audiences feel for the title character, producers and actors have been quick to respond to this challenge. The recent New York production, under, as a matter of fact, Bentley's supervision, is reported to have ended with Mother Courage's having drawn the wagon twice around the stage—the extra turn being obviously a play for a final upheaval of sympathy from the theater party sentimentalists in the audience. And what actress can really be impervious to the temptation of playing for this empathy. Even Helene Weigel, once Brecht was gone, seemed in the eyes of at least one observer, to be playing for more empathy than the playwright might have wished. ''Weigel's performance [is] more winning, coy, and less distant than the depths other voice and the worldliness of her character lead one to expect. . . . She did not so much underplay, I felt, as overstate, taking a good deal more time to cool things (if that was it) than she needed.'' (*Tulane Drama Review,* Vol.3.)

This is all very fine—one supposes. But it is not the play Brecht wrote. Nor is it as good or as important a play as the one Brecht wrote. As a play of character, *Mother Courage* is an insignificant portrait. if we as audience identify with Mother Courage as character and believe her to triumph, then her triumph is ours and we are left only with a rather narcissistic satisfaction. We learn nothing. Our consciousness of human existence is no more broadened than when we entered the theater. If, on the other hand, we are unable to identify with Mother Courage, unable to feel empathy for such an unsavory heroine, we are able to see the causes and roots of the evil she represents. We then share not in Mother Courage's humanity, but in Brecht's anger at the evil her story portrays. Realizing further that this evil is a result of the nature of society, we, as parts of society, share in the guilt for that evil. Without empathy we see ourselves not as Mother Courages preyed upon by a hostile society, but rather, as members of that predatory and hostile society. Where our critics, actors, and producers — and ourselves as playgoers, no doubt—have made of *Mother Courage* a play that is in the long run comforting, Brecht wrote a play that is highly disturbing, a play that brands us all with a collective guilt for the evils of the world.

One reason, probably, for the misdirection which analyses and productions of *Mother Courage* have taken is that most of the playwrights of the last hundred years at least have accustomed us to viewing plays primarily in terms of character. The psychological complexities of a Willie Loman, a Hedda Gabler, or a Henry IV are meant to give us valuable insight into our own psychologies. If we accept a system of belief in which behavior is controlled by individual psychology, then indeed those plays do accomplish their task. Brecht, however, we must remember, was, whether or not he was an orthodox Soviet Communist, a thoroughly conditioned and fully believing Marxist. For him, the primary determinant of human behavior was external. Individual behavior, to any Marxist, is the product of the social and economic structure in which that individual lives. Individual psychology is merely a superstructure built upon a pre-established socio-economic foundation. Given this presupposition, Brecht, when he wrote plays dealing with individual human beings, had to find a way of showing the action of these individuals in relation to its social foundations. To do this, he turned from the individually oriented drama of character to the drama of action or narrative. In the drama of narrative, we are to be concerned not so much with the individual character's psychology as with the relationship between one incident in the narrative and another. We are to see the progress from event to event, to see how one event causes or leads to another. In Brecht's plays, we are to see also how this progression of events is caused by conditions external to the characters, how those characters are at the mercy of the relentless logic of universal socio-economic-historical law. All the devices of Brecht's much eulogized but little analyzed ''Epic theatre'' are aimed at making the audience see more clearly the relation of events both to each other and to the laws under which they take place. The alienation effect in acting, the rejection of suspense by announcing to the audience what is about to happen in a scene, the non-realistic scenic devices, are all calculated to take the audience's mind away from individual character and to concentrate it upon the action or narrative itself.

That *Mother Courage* is to be regarded as a narrative play is clear from its subtitle: *A Chronicle of the Thirty Years' War.* The action of the play is Mother courage's fight for survival during that war. Survival, for Brecht, is the first instinct of the human race, and to assure that survival the first principle of all behavior. When other instincts run contrary to the instinct to survive, they will be sacrificed. Thus, Mother Courage, when faced with the loss of her children as the price of survival, has no choice in the matter. In the haggling scene, for instance, the price of Swiss Cheese's life will be the selling of Mother Courage's wagon, the means of her livelihood. She has no choice but to haggle until it is too late. Similarly, she has no choice but to deny recognition of her son and leave him without ministration. The same lack of choice is evident in the death of Kattrin. In order to provide for her livelihood Mother Courage must leave her daughter unwatched, where she can bring harm upon herself. Again, Mother Courage must deny her daughter any last ministrations in order to catch up with the marching soldiers from whom she gains her living.

In each major episode of the narrative, Mother Courage, to assure her economic survival, has to deny some good instinct that threatens by ramification that survival. The narrative of her struggle for survival thus becomes also the narrative of the loss of whatever goodness Mother Courage might once have had within her. Her mother love, a symbol Brecht uses repeatedly in his plays to stand for pure, instinctive, and uncomplicated goodness, must finally be sacrificed to the need for survival. As the narrative goes on, Mother Courage is driven to increasingly desperate measures, and this desperation leaves her little time for her children. At each new point in the play, it becomes more inevitable that she will have to give up her motherhood in order to survive. At the end, she has lost all her children and all her instinctive goodness. She has left at this point only the basic animal need to survive. Leaving the body of her daughter behind her in the end, she leaves only a ''little'' of the great deal of money she has made in the town. Physically she is reduced from the human being riding on the wagon to the animal pulling it. From a human being with some instinctive goodness at the beginning of the play, she is reduced to an animal with the instinct only to survive. Another indication of the progressive dehumanization of Mother Courage is that each of the children represents some aspect of the goodness that is, at first, instinctive to Mother Courage. Eilif is courage, Swiss Cheese honesty, Kattrin unreasoning love. As each of the children is sacrificed to the need for survival Mother Courage loses the human aspect represented by that child. With the children gone, Mother Courage's humanity is gone. She remains only with animal instinct.

The thought behind this action is that the condition of human society makes necessary the sacrifice of innate human goodness to the exigencies of

MOTHER COURAGE IS, ULTIMATELY, TRULY COURAGEOUS, AND HER COURAGE SEES HER THROUGH ALL HER TRIBULATIONS: SO WE, AS AUDIENCE TO HER COURAGE, TAKE COMFORT AND GAIN SUCCOR THROUGH SEEING OURSELVES IN MOTHER COURAGE"

economic subsistence in the world. In setting the play during the Thirty Years' War, Brecht has chosen a time in which war is not exceptional but routine. Thus, metaphorically, he characterizes the routine life of capitalistic society as a life of constant warfare. In a society where trading and bargaining are necessary to survival, goodness does not have a chance. It even defeats itself. Mother Courage refuses to leave Kattrin for the Cook only to bring herself to the necessity of leaving Kattrin unprotected at the peasants' farm. The greatest act of goodness Mother Courage tries to perform leads to the final deprivation of her humanity. In the action of Mother Courage's fight for survival, we see the sacrifice of humanity which that fight requires. We see also that it is the constant warfare state of capitalist economy that makes these sacrifices necessary.

As written, as a play of narrative exposing the social causes of Mother Courage's inhumanity, this is anything but an inspiring and comforting affirmation of the human will to live. It is, instead, a condemnation of each of us who contributes to the society in which the requirement of such sacrifice becomes inevitable. Just as Mother Courage shares in her guilt by living according to the laws of that society, so we share in her guilt by assenting to those laws. *Mother Courage* as Brecht wrote it is not an easy play for Western audiences to take; the truth, someone once said, always hurts. But it is a much our critics, producers, and actors have been representing Brecht as having written.

Source: Ronald S. Woodland, ''The Danger of Empathy in *Mother Courage*'' in *Modern Drama,* Vol. XV, no. 2, September, 1972, pp. 125–29.

> COURAGE MAY CURSE THE WAR AS A MOTHER, BUT AS A BUSINESSWOMAN, SHE IS IDENTIFIED WITH IT. A 'HYENA OF THE BATTLEFIELD,' SHE SPECULATES ON THE LIVES OF MEN. AND SINCE HER CANTEEN WAGON IS HER ONLY MEANS OF SURVIVAL, SHE TREATS IT AS A FOURTH CHILD, TIED TO HER BY A COMMERCIAL UMBILICAL—THE THREE CHILDREN OF HER FLESH, SIGNIFICANTLY, ARE ALL TAKEN OFF WHILE SHE IS HAGGLING"

Robert Brustein

In this 1963 essay, Brustein examines Brecht's political motivations in creating Mother Courage and Her Children. *Finding the play to be a prime example of the playwright's pacifist views, the critic asserts that the work is a "Marxist indictment of the economic motives behind international aggression."*

Brecht's masterly chronicle of the Thirty Years War, *Mother Courage and Her Children,* is often interpreted as a straightforward pacifist document, but it is not simply that. It is also a relentless Marxist indictment of the economic motives behind international aggression. If property is theft in *The Threepenny Opera,* it is rape, pillage, and murder in *Mother Courage*—war, in short, is an extension not of diplomacy but of free enterprise. As for the financier, he is no longer a gangster, like Macheath. He is now a cynical warlord—like the Swedish King Gustavus, who pretends to be animated by religious zeal but who is actually seeking personal gain and territorial aggrandizement. In this atmosphere, where Protestants and Catholics slaughter each other for fun and profit, all human ideals degenerate into hypocritical cant, while heroism shatters into splinters of cruelty, madness, or greed. Brecht works these grim sardonic ironies, however, without bringing a single military adventurer center

stage. Like the invisible bourgeoisie of *Threepenny,* the kings and commanders of *Mother Courage* remain in the background of the play, as well as in the rear of the battles. The external conflict is narrated, like newspaper headlines, in legends preceding each scene; but the dramatic action focuses on the lives of the war's subordinates and noncombatants, playing local commerce. "The war is just the same as trading," and "General Tilley's victory at Leipzig" has significance only insofar as it "costs Mother Courage four shirts."

Mother Courage, to be sure, is a pathetic victim of this war—she sacrifices three children to it. She is not, however, simply a passive sufferer, she is also an active agent in her own destruction. Precariously suspended between her maternal and commercial instincts. Courage may curse the war as a mother, but as a businesswoman, she is identified with it. A "hyena of the battlefield," she speculates on the lives of men. And since her canteen wagon is her only means of survival, she treats it as a fourth child, tied to her by a commercial umbilical—the three children of her flesh, significantly, are all taken off while she is haggling. Thus, Mother Courage is another of Brecht's split characters, a compound of good and evil—but one which adds up to more than the sum of its parts. For Courage achieves a third dimension beyond her ideological function. Like Falstaff (her Shakespearean prototype), she is an escaped character who baffles the author's original intentions. Salty, shrewd, hardbitten, and skeptical, Courage is a full-blooded personification of the anti-heroic view of life. In a moving lyric, "The Song of the Great Capitulation," she traces her progress from a youthful Romantic idealist to a cautions compromiser, marching in time with the band, and, throughout the play, she remains faithful to the doctrine of number one. What she preaches is that the Ten Commandments are a mug's game, and that virtues like bravery, honesty, and unselfishness will invariably bring you low—as indeed such virtues flatten foolhardy Eilif, simpleminded Swiss Cheese, and, finally, kindly Kattrin. Restraining her motherly feelings, Courage survives; yielding to hers, Kattrin dies. But in the world of the play, death and survival are equally dismal alternatives. At the end, childless and desolate, Courage straps herself to her battered wagon and continues to follow the soldiers, having learned nothing except that man's capacity for suffering is limitless. But this knowledge is the tragic perception; and Brecht, for all his ideologizing, has recreated a tragic universe in which the cruelty of men, the venality of society, and the indifference of the gods seem immutable conditions of life.

The ideological structure, however, provides the intellectual spine of the drama; and I have stressed its importance because the current production is intellectually spineless. It is difficult to say why, since it is totally free from the usual Broadway hokum or cynicism. Eric Bentley's idiomatic translation preserves the bite of the German, Paul Dessau's score is sharp and wheedling, and Jerome Robbins' direction proceeds, in all externals, with almost reverential fidelity to the text. Still, the only episode which works is the emotionally charged Drum Scene (virtually stage-proof anyway). The rest of the evening is too often static and labored, and the ironies very rarely register. Certainly, the affluent Broadway audience is partly to blame. Lacking either the wit or the inclination to respond to Marxist mockery, it has a Yahoo's appetite only for blunt obscenities (a soldier's ''Kiss my ass,'' for example, brought the opening night house down)—and no actor is going to press for unappreciated subtleties. Then, again, Mr. Robbins, for all his good intentions, is not enough of a director for a play of this scope, mounted in a four-week rehearsal period. Taking place on a clean bare stage, dressed only with Courage's wagon and occasional set pieces, the action itself seems peculiarly clean and bare. One misses stage business, directorial detail, the bustle of life; the actors do not seem sufficiently at home with their props and costumes; and underneath the surface scruffiness, a hint of American wholesomeness still sneaks through. One of Robbins' effective devices is to project, on a burlap cyclorama, photographs of twentieth-century soldiers and civilians in dusty retreat—but this merely emphasizes the play's anti-war implications, which are already rather obvious.

Even this scheme could have been partially compatible with Brecht's design; but the central role of Mother Courage is disastrously miscast. Ann Bancroft should probably be commended for undertaking a character beyond her years, training, and talents—but like the bravery of Courage's son, Eilif, this often strikes one as mere foolhardiness. Miss Bancroft's impersonation of age is particularly unconvincing, partly because of flat make-up and a form-fitting waist, partly because of her own inexperience. In order to overcome these handicaps, she has been forced into monotonous vocal intonations, which, along with her aphoristic inflections, account for much of the evening's tedium. Beyond this, the part of Mother Courage demands intelli-

gence and a capacity for being unpleasant; Miss Bancroft is an exclusively emotional actress who cannot resist playing for sympathy. Her best moments, apart from her rendering of the songs, come in climaxes of grief, and the final scene, where Courage painfully pulls at her wagon, her mouth agape like a wounded animal, is truly harrowing. For the balance of the play, however, Miss Bancroft has the sound and gestures of a tired Jewish housewife, with no more cutting edge than Molly Goldberg. Zohra Lampert, on the other hand, is expressive, lovely, and poignant as the mute Kattrin (though perhaps too spastic in her movements). And though Barbara Harris lapses into Second City vocal mannerisms as the whore Yvette, Mike Kellin and Gene Wilder contribute moments of crisp humor as the Cook and the Chaplain, and Eugene Roche and John Harkins are vigorous in lesser roles. I have harped on the failures of the production; but there are still sufficient virtues in it to make this an important theatrical occasion. A Brecht masterpiece has been produced with all the care, respect, and expertise that our professional theatre can muster. If this is still not quite enough, we must locate the inadequacy in the nature of the American theatre itself.

Source: Robert Brustein, ''Brecht versus Broadway'' in his *Seasons of Discontent: Dramatic Opinions, 1959–1965* , Simon & Schuster, 1965, pp. 152–55.

SOURCES

Bentley. Eric ''A Traveler's Report . . .'' in *Theatre Arts,* June, 1949, pp. 26-30, 94.

Brecht, Bertolt. *Mother Courage and Her Children* in *Bertolt Brecht: Plays, Volume II,* translated by Eric Bentley, Methuen, 1955, pp. 1-81.

Brustein, Robert. ''Bertolt Brecht'' in his *The Theatre of Revolt: An Approach to the Modern Drama,* Little, Brown, 1964, pp. 229-78.

Gray, Ronald. *Brecht: The Dramatist,* Cambridge University Press, 1976.

Lyons, Charles R. ''Mother Courage: Instinctive Compassion and 'The Great Capitulation''' in his *Berltolt Brecht: The Despair and the Polemic,* Southern Illinois University Press, 1968, pp. 89-109.

Schoeps, Karl H. *World Dramatists: Bertolt Brecht,* Frederick Ungar, 1977.

Wittner, Victor. ''Premieres in Zurich'' in *Theatre Arts,* April, 1942, pp. 250-52.

FURTHER READING

Bentley, Eric. ''Bertolt Brecht and His Work'' in *Theatre Arts,* September 1944, p. 509-12.
    This journal article gives an overview of Brecht's career and writing through 1944.

Brecht, Bertolt. *Brecht on Theatre: The Development of an Aesthetic,* translated by John Willet, Methuen, 1963.
    This nonfiction book discusses Brecht's theories of writing and theater, including epic theater.

Demetz, Peter, editor. *Brecht: A Collection of Critical Essays,* Prentice Hall, 1972.
    This includes a number of essays on many aspects of Brecht's work, including one solely concerned with *Mother Courage and Her Children.*

Ewen, Frederic. *Bertolt Brecht: His Life, His Art, and His Times,* Citadel, 1967.
    This biography concerns Brecht's life as well as the context in which his work was written.

Speirs, Ronald. *Bertolt Brecht,* St. Martin's, 1987.
    This work discusses all of Brecht's works, including an in-depth analysis of *Mother Courage and Her Children.*

No Exit

JEAN-PAUL SARTRE

1944

Jean-Paul Sartre's *No Exit* is considered by many to be the author's best play and most accessible dramatization of his philosophy of existentialism. Sartre wrote the original draft in two weeks at the Café Flore in Paris. Titled *Huis clos* in the original French, it was first produced in Paris's Vieux-Colombier Theater. At the time, during World War II, this part of France was occupied by Nazi Germany. Sartre deliberately wrote *No Exit* as a one-act play so that theater-goers would not be kept past the German-imposed curfew. Many forms of entertainment, including plays, had to be approved by German censors. During rehearsals, clearance to perform the play was given and taken away several times. Despite such setbacks, *No Exit* opened in the spring of 1944, and it was an immediate success. The original production played in Paris for several years, even after the war ended and Paris was liberated. Parisian audiences appreciated Sartre's subtle message of resistance and implied subversiveness. Critics, however, gave it mixed reviews, mostly because of the social and political climate of the time. The fact that Inez was a lesbian was an extremely controversial point for both audiences and critics alike.

No Exit was translated into English (and is sometimes known as *Behind Closed Doors*), and made its Broadway debut in 1947. In general, American audiences were not as appreciative as their European counterparts. Some critics did not know what to make of the play and its themes.

Others thought that the play stretched the fundamental concept to its breaking point. Still, most appreciated the clever concept: three people confined to a drawing room as their punishment in hell. Despite these mixed reviews, *No Exit* was voted the Best Foreign Play in New York in 1946.

AUTHOR BIOGRAPHY

Jean-Paul Sartre was born on June 21, 1905, in Paris, France. He was the only son of Jean-Baptist Sartre, a French naval officer, and his wife, Anne Marie. Sartre's father died when he was only 15 months old, and Sartre and his mother moved in with her parents in Paris. His grandfather, Charles Schweitzer, doted on him and instilled a love of literature. Sartre did not attend school; instead, his grandfather, a language professor, taught him and arranged for tutors. Sartre began writing stories during this time. Religion played a key role in his education; his grandfather was a staunch Protestant while his grandmother was Catholic. An atheist, Sartre did not believe in either religion, but retained some of the ideals of both. This influence is felt in *No Exit,* which is set in Hell.

After his mother remarried in 1916, Sartre began attending school and excelled in his studies. He studied philosophy at the University of Paris where he met his life-long companion, Simone de Beauvoir, an author and scholar. After graduation, Sartre served in the army for two years, then taught at lycées (French high schools) for several more. While teaching, Sartre continued to study philosophy and develop his own. In 1938, Sartre published his first novel, a largely autobiographical book titled *Nausea* (published as *La Nausée* in French). The success of this book brought him some notoriety in France. Like many of his fictional works, including *No Exit, Nausea* explores Sartre's philosophical and political ideas in a fictional setting.

When World War II broke out in Europe in 1939, Sartre again served in the French army and was taken as a German prisoner of war (POW) for several months in 1940-41. After his release, Sartre returned to Paris and participated in the Resistance, a French underground movement that worked against the Germans occupying the country. Sartre continued to study philosophy, and in 1943 he published *Being and Nothingness* (known in French as *L'Être et le néant*). In this book, Sartre develops his philosophy of existentialism, arguing that each human is alone in the world and thus totally free to make his or her own choices to define and re-define himself or herself, but is ultimately morally responsible for his or her actions. They do not have to stay in the roles society has defined for them. These aspects of existentialism are also explored in *No Exit,* written in 1944.

In addition to *No Exit,* the second play written by Sartre, he also wrote a handful of other dramatic works, several screenplays, short stories, and novels. The bulk of Sartre's writing after the end of World War II is nonfiction. Many of these works reflect Sartre's refinement of existentialism as well as his increasingly Marxist political views. Sartre refused both the Nobel Prize for literature and the French Legion of Honor for his writings. His output decreased due to failing health in the late-1970s, and Sartre died in Paris on April 15, 1980, of uremia.

PLOT SUMMARY

No Exit opens with a valet leading Joseph Garcin into a drawing room. The small room has three couches and a mantelpiece with a bronze statue on it. Garcin is surprised by the room and its contents. He expected instruments of torture, not a windowless room. The room upsets him and he asks why they did not leave him at least a toothbrush. The valet finds his concerns silly, like the concerns of all the other guests, because they have no need for such human concerns. Garcin guesses that they will never sleep in this room, and notices that the valet never blinks. Garcin becomes further upset when he finds out that the lights are always on. Before the valet goes, Garcin asks if the bell works. The valet tells him it works only intermittently, then exits.

Garcin is left alone for a few minutes, then the valet returns with Inez. After the valet leaves again, Inez thinks that Garcin is to be her torturer. Garcin is amused, and assures her that he is not. Garcin notices that there are no mirrors in the room. Garcin suggests they be polite to each other so that they can survive in the small space, but Inez refuses. They are silent for a moment, and Garcin twists his mouth around. This annoys Inez, who is curt with the man. They both agree that they have not yet begun to suffer. Inez paces while Garcin sits down. His mouth twitches again and he covers it with his hands.

The valet enters again with Estelle. Garcin looks up and is about to uncover his mouth when

Jean-Paul Sartre

Estelle begs him not to. She has mistaken him momentarily for someone whose face had been mangled. After the valet tells her that no else is coming, Estelle comments on the colors of the sofas. She insists on taking the couch that Garcin is sitting on because it better matches her dress. Inez immediately tries to get Estelle's attention, telling her that she wishes that she had some flowers to give her. Estelle has died yesterday and she can see her funeral. She tells them that she died of pneumonia, Inez died from the fumes of gas stove, and that Garcin was shot with twelve bullets in his chest. Estelle is uncomfortable with the word ''dead'' and insists that they use the term ''absentees.''

Garcin shares that he is from Rio, and he describes what he sees. His wife is waiting for word about him in front of a barracks. Garcin becomes rather warm and begins to remove his jacket. Estelle stops him, saying she cannot stand a man in shirtsleeves. She asks Inez's opinion, and Inez replies that she does not care much for men, period. Estelle believes a mistake has been made in putting the three of them together, but Inez believes that everything, including the room, was planned to the last detail.

Garcin believes they should talk about why they are there, and Inez seconds the idea. Estelle is reluctant, but tells the others that she married an older man for the sake of her younger brother. Then she met a younger man with whom she fell in love. She does not believe this is a sin. Garcin asks if a man should stand by his principles. He tells them about the pacifist newspaper he ran, and that they shot him for believing in this. Inez implies that she does not believe that Garcin and Estelle are telling the whole truth, and they are in hell because they are damned. She believes that they are each other's torturers.

Garcin suggests that they remain silent to counteract this, and work out their own means of salvation. After they agree to this and there is silence for at least a few moments, Inez begins to sing. Estelle tries to fix her makeup, but she realizes that there is no mirror for her to look in. Inez says that she will act as Estelle's mirror for her, and does so. Inez's forthrightness embarrasses Estelle, and she asks for Garcin's help. Garcin ignores them for awhile, until it becomes intolerable. He begs them to be silent, but they will not. Estelle tries to get his attention as a man, and Inez wants Estelle's attention. Inez points out they cannot ignore each other.

Garcin sees the wisdom in Inez's words, and begins to fondle Estelle's neck. This makes Estelle uncomfortable. Garcin believes that each of them should be totally honest about why they are there, for this might save them. Garcin admits he was mean and abusive to his wife. Inez describes her affair with a woman named Florence. Inez lived with her cousin and his wife, Florence. Inez seduced her away from her cousin, and he died in a tram accident. Inez told Florence that they killed him, and eventually Florence turned on the gas stove one night and killed them both. Inez admits she is a very cruel person.

Estelle still says that she has no idea what she has done. After some goading by the other two, Estelle admits she had a baby with her lover that she did not want. She murdered the infant in front of him and he killed himself over the incident. Estelle's husband knew nothing of the baby or the lover, and she returned to his side after the suicide. She tries to cry, but finds that tears do not flow in hell.

Inez tries to comfort Estelle. In her grief, Estelle allows Garcin to take off his coat. Garcin thinks the next step is to try to help each other for that is the only way they can save themselves. Inez does not want Garcin's help. She starts to have her own vision of the room where she died. Someone is looking at it. When the vision is over, she refuses to try to help him because she is too rotten. She says she cannot even feel sorry for herself. Still, she agrees not to harm him if he will leave her and Estelle alone. But Estelle wants his help. Inez says that she will be Estelle's forever, but Estelle ignores her. Estelle asks Garcin to take her in his arms, but Inez signals for him not to do that. Garcin complies, but Estelle rejects Inez, spitting in her face. Inez threatens Garcin.

Garcin seizes the opportunity to approach Estelle. Estelle fawns on him, taking him for what he is. They nearly kiss. Garcin begs Estelle to trust him, but she is evasive. Garcin admits he ran away to Mexico to evade military service. He asks if Estelle thinks he is a coward, but she says he must decide that for himself. Garcin begs for Estelle to have faith in him, but she laughs at him. She loves him because he is a man; his cowardice is immaterial to her. This upsets Garcin, and he says he is disgusted by both of them.

Garcin goes to the door and rings the bell. He pounds on the door, while Estelle begs him not to leave. Estelle says that if the door opens, she is leaving, too, rather than stay with Inez. The door suddenly opens, and Garcin is immediately afraid. He will not leave, nor will he help Estelle push Inez out of the room. After shutting the door, he further explains that Inez understands cowardice, and he must convince her that he is not a coward. Estelle and Garcin align themselves together, and Inez is hurt. She calls him a coward, reminding him of the power she has. Garcin moves away, saying he cannot be with Estelle while Inez is watching. Estelle tries to stab Inez with a paper knife, but it does nothing. Inez says they are dead and stuck there forever. The three of them laugh, and as it ends, Garcin says, "Well, well, let's get on with it."

CHARACTERS

Joseph Garcin

Garcin is the first of the three dead people to enter the drawing room. Prior to his death, he was a newspaperman in Rio de Janeiro, Brazil. He was shot twelve times because he tried to avoid serving in the military. He is a pacifist, and he tells Inez and Estelle that is why he was condemned. Garcin is polite, keeping his coat in on the stuffy room because Estelle cannot stand a man in shirtsleeves. Garcin tries to make the situation tolerable, suggesting that they all keep quiet. This does not work, however, as the three continue to hound each other. He reveals that the real reason he is in hell is that he abused his wife and fled to Mexico to avoid military service. His former friends in Rio are now calling him a coward. Garcin desperately wants Inez to see him as a hero and strives to change her opinion of him. In contrast, Estelle seeks his attention and he continually rebuffs her. When the door to the drawing room opens, he has the opportunity to leave, but he is afraid of the unknown and he still has not proven himself to Inez. His inability to act on the opportunity of the open door represents his inability to change or to learn from his mistakes, one of the reasons why he is in the room in the first place.

Estelle Rigault

Estelle is the last of the "absentees" (her preferred term for their deceased state) to enter the room. Before her death, she was a beautiful young society woman married to a rich older man. Estelle is demanding, insisting on taking the sofa that best matches her dress. At first, Estelle says she does not know why she is in hell. She believes it is an error. Estelle is superficial, concerned with her makeup and her appearance and almost immediately discovers that the room has no mirrors. Though Estelle died from pneumonia, it is revealed that she is in hell because she drowned her newborn daughter in front of the man with whom she was having an illicit affair. The lover subsequently killed himself over the incident, and Estelle returned to her husband. Though Inez tries to console Estelle, Estelle is repulsed by Inez and concerned only with Garcin, ingratiating herself to him and trying to seduce him. When Inez pushes her too far, Estelle tries unsuccessfully to stab her with a paper knife. This incident makes Estelle realize that she is indeed stuck in hell for eternity.

Inez Serrano

Inez is the second person to enter the drawing room. Before her death, she worked as postal clerk in Paris. When Inez first comes in, she thinks that Garcin is to be her torturer. He dispels her fears immediately, but she remains hostile to him throughout the play. On the other hand, Inez is attracted to Estelle from the moment she enters the room. She tries to win Estelle's favor several times but to no avail. Garcin tries to win Inez's favor, but she thinks he is a coward. Unlike the other two, Inez is realistic about her reasons for being in hell. She lived with her cousin and his wife, Florence, and Inez seduced Florence away from her husband. Florence's husband died in an accident, and Inez tortured Florence by claiming they had killed him. Inez died when Florence turned on the gas stove, consciously committing a murder/suicide. Inez knows she is sadistic and acknowledges that she received pleasure from making Florence and her husband suffer. Unlike Garcin and Estelle, there is no one left in life who is thinking about her. The only vision she has from her life is the empty room where she died. Inez is the first to realize that they are each other's torturers, and relishes the role from the first.

Valet

The valet escorts each of the characters into the drawing room. It is unclear what he is; more than likely he is a demon. He is amused by the others' preconceived notions of hell as well as their need to cling to their humanity. He does not blink, which is Garcin's first realization about the nature of his new

MEDIA ADAPTATIONS

- *No Exit* was filmed in French as *Huis Clos* in 1954. It starred Arletty, Nicole Courcel, Louis De Furies, and Jean Debucourt.

- The play was adapted for film again in 1962, starring Rita Gam as Estelle and Viveca Lindfors as Inez.

existence, and possibly symbolic of the fact that in hell, one is not able to close one's eyes or turn away from the truth anymore. The valet tells Garcin that the bell used to summon the servants only works sporadically. This fact may indicate that one crucial element of hell, in Sartre's definition, is not being heard by others.

THEMES

Choices and Consequences

Though nothing will change for any of the characters in *No Exit,* the choices they made while they were living are directly responsible for their sentence in hell. Each one of them made irresponsible and immoral choices during his or her lifetime. Garcin teased and abused his wife. He also brought home another woman and slept with her while his wife was in the house. She served them coffee in bed. While married, Estelle ran away with her young lover. She bore him a child, then murdered it in front of him. He later committed suicide because of the incident. Inez was a sadist. She lived with her cousin and his wife, Florence, and seduced her away from him. When her cousin died in a tram accident, she tortured the wife by saying that their affair led to his death. Inez's actions led the wife to turn on the gas stove during the night, murdering them both. Each character chose to commit theses crimes, and

TOPICS FOR FURTHER STUDY

- Research Sartre's philosophy of existentialism. Discuss *No Exit* in terms of this theory.

- Explore the history of the time and place in which *No Exit* was written—German-occupied Paris during World War II. How do you think these conditions influenced Sartre when he wrote *No Exit*?

- Compare *No Exit* to other depictions of hell in art, music, literature, and other plays. One possible book is Dante's *Inferno*.

- Compare *No Exit* to *The Victors,* another play by Sartre that takes place in a single room and concerns the torture of others. Discuss possible reasons why *No Exit* has retained its popularity and *The Victors* has not.

for these crimes they were condemned. Consequently, they will torture each other over their weaknesses for eternity.

Appearances vs. Reality

Two of the characters in *No Exit* hide behind façades for much of the play, unwilling to admit the real reason they are condemned to hell. Only Inez is willing to acknowledge from the start that she is a cruel person. Though Garcin worries about his cowardice from the first moments of the play, he says that he is unsure why he is in hell. He rationalizes that he stood up for his pacifist principles and that is the reason he was put to death by his government. In reality, Garcin was trying to escape to Mexico to avoid serving in the war, and he was extremely mean to his wife. He admits these two incidents only after goaded. Estelle does not understand why she is in hell at all, at least at first. She thinks it is some sort of error since she died from pneumonia. Like Garcin, she only acknowledges the truth—that she murdered her baby and drove a man to suicide—when pressed by the other two. Reality, in this play, is facing up to the truth about oneself.

Self-defininition and Interpersonal Relationships

Throughout the rounds of conversation that comprise *No Exit,* the characters are forced to define themselves through their relationships with each other. Their eyes are constantly open (there is no blinking in hell). The lights are always on. There are no mirrors. They are stuck in the same, small, stuffy room together. These conditions force each person to interact with the other two, and look for some acknowledgement about who they are. Garcin wants Inez to believe he is not a coward. Estelle wants Garcin to be a man for her. Inez wants Estelle to be attracted to her. Since no one will get what they want from another without conflict from the third, their interlinking desires ensure an eternity of torture. Garcin believes that if they work together, there might be some kind of redemption. But their conflicting personalities ensure that this will be impossible.

Death and Permanence

What makes the situation in *No Exit* so desperate is the fact that Garcin, Inez, and Estelle are dead. They are permanently in hell, and permanently in the drawing room with each other. During the play, they are afforded an opportunity to leave when the door opens unexpectedly. However, they are too afraid of the consequences to leave. Similarly, they cannot change or grow as people because they are dead. They are forced throughout eternity to "live" with the choices they made in their lives. They will forever rationalize these choices to each other.

STYLE

Setting

No Exit can be called an existentialist play and a philosophical drama. The action takes place in hell, which is represented as a hot and stuffy drawing room, with the only entrance a door that is locked. There is a bell to ring for servants, but it works only intermittently. The room is decorated in Second Empire style. A heavy bronze statue sits on a mantle, but it is too heavy to move. There are three sofas of different colors for the three characters to sit on. There is also a paper knife next to the statue, but no books. There are also no mirrors or windows. This tight setting forces the characters to constantly see each other, and thus engage in torture.

Furthermore, the drawing room is somewhat unremarkable, except that it is in hell. In depicting hell as a familiar setting, Sartre suggests that hell is more of a state of mind than a place. There is nothing particularly hellish about the drawing room itself; instead, it is the combination of personalities in the room that makes the experience so hellish for Garcin, Estelle, and Inez.

Symbolic Props

The few objects in the room have symbolic meaning, especially in defining the characters. The sofas are of different colors—wine-colored, blue, and green—and Estelle insists on taking the blue one because it best matches her dress. This symbolizes her superficiality. Estelle also uses the paper knife to stab Inez. This is ineffective and leads to Estelle's acceptance that she is truly dead and in hell. The bronze statue serves a similar purpose for Garcin. The statue represents how escape is futile because it is too heavy to move. Garcin is also concerned about the bell, and if it works, more than the other characters. The bell symbolizes a link with the outside world, but it does not always ring.

Visions

The characters all have visions about what is going in the world they left. Though these visions are unseen by the audience, they represent the last links to the living world for the characters. Garcin sees two different parts of his former life. He has visions of the newsroom where he worked. His co-workers are calling him a coward, which upsets him greatly. Garcin also sees the wife he mistreated. She stands outside the prison, awaiting word of his fate, then learns that he has died. Later, she dies. Estelle's visions always include her friend Olga. Estelle sees her own funeral and burial, where Olga escorts Estelle's sister, who can only manage a few tears. She later sees Olga with Peter, a young man who admired Estelle in life. Olga tells Peter about the crimes that Estelle has committed, and he is shocked. Unlike Garcin and Estelle, there is no living person who cares about Inez. The only vision she sees is of the room where she and Florence died. She views it twice: once when it is empty and dark, and a second

time, when potential renters come in to look the place over.

Three Unities of French Drama

No Exit follows the classical rules of unity of action, time, and place. The play takes place in the length of time it takes to perform it. There is only one course of action, and everything in the setting works towards that one end. The action is also confined to one place, the drawing room. There is nothing extraneous about any aspect of the play; it is focused to one purpose.

HISTORICAL CONTEXT

Occupation of France Influences Philosophy

World War II engulfed Europe beginning in 1939. Nazi leader Adolf Hitler took power in Germany and embarked on an aggressive military campaign as early as 1936. He began annexing European states by 1938. France declared war on Germany in 1939, and Hitler invaded and conquered France by 1940. The war in Europe ended in the spring of 1945, and Paris was finally liberated.

Daily life was difficult in France during World War II. A large part of France was occupied by Nazi Germany, including Paris, where Sartre lived. Because France was an occupied country, life, in many ways, was at a standstill. In Sartre's hell, too, life was very static. France's occupation also led to shortages of everything, including heat and electricity. Sartre makes an ironic comment on this situation by having an overabundance of heat and light available in hell. German censors controlled the plays performed in the theater and the movies shown in the cinema.

During the occupation, France was ruled by the Vichy government. It was ostensibly semi-independent but still under Nazi control. French people who worked with the Nazis were called Collaborators. The prewar pacifists Garcin talks about were often considered Collaborators. Many French citizens fought the Nazi control by participating in the Resistance. The Resistance was an underground

COMPARE
&
CONTRAST

- **1944:** In occupied France, German censors must approve plays before they are allowed to be performed.

  Today: A controversial rating system has been put in place on television programming in the United States. The labels are primarily for parents, to inform them of content that may not be appropriate for children.

- **1944:** Many plays and movies are concerned with World War II and its effects on society, either explicitly or implicitly.

  Today: World War II continues to be a popular theme in television, movies, and literature. One of the biggest box office successes in the United

  States in 1998 is *Saving Private Ryan,* which re-enacts the D-Day invasion at Normandy, France.

- **1944:** The philosophy of existentialism develops in France, which has been devastated by two world wars, as a way of dealing with the nature of good and evil and one's responsibility in life and as an explanation of the nature of being in general.

  Today: Existentialism continues to be influential in literature and the arts, mainly as its ideas have been co-opted by more recent movements, such as the Beats, who believe that one is responsible only to oneself.

movement that began soon after the Nazis took over Paris. Charles de Gaulle, a government official in the French government before the occupation, organized a French government in exile in Great Britain. In 1940, he called for French citizens to resist the Germans via a radio broadcast. Though only a few people in France heard him speak, a Resistance was formed.

The Resistance was not formally organized, but it took on many forms. It worked to block delivery of supplies and men to Germany. French citizens were conscripted by the Germans when they needed people to work in factories and the like. Many such draftees took to the hills in France and worked against the Germans. Other French citizens passed military intelligence to Great Britain and other Allies, helped British pilots who were shot down by the Germans escape, and wrote and distributed anti-German pamphlets. Sartre was active in the Resistance. At the end of World War II, it was thought that the Resistance contributed to the liberation of Paris.

The wartime atmosphere also created a change in the intellectual climate. The reality of war forced intellectuals to make political choices. This was

reflected in the literature of the day. A poetry of the Resistance was developed with a direct language, and Paul Valéry was regarded as the best of these. Sartre was influential in the literary scene, and his philosophy of existentialism became the theory of the Resistance. Existentialists believed in the liberty of humankind and that everyone is endowed with a certain responsibility for their lives. *No Exit,* an existentialist play, is regarded as a symbol of the liberation of Paris.

CRITICAL OVERVIEW

When *No Exit* was first produced in Paris in 1944, the critical response was mixed, due in part to the political climate of the time. Much of France was occupied by Germany. Sartre was identified with the Resistance, the French underground movement that sought to overthrow the German occupation. *No Exit* was regarded by many as subversive, full of in-jokes and subtle wartime criticism. Critics might have been afraid to openly praise such a play for fear

Sartre's three doomed protagonists, Inez (Wendy Wright), Garcin (Troy F. Sill), and Estelle (Nancy Wright).

of repercussions, though *No Exit* was produced by permission of German censors. Those critics who favored the Germans or collaborated with them would not have wanted to praise something this controversial. Several critics, including André Castelot, called for censoring the play.

Numerous French critics, regardless of their political views, agreed that the core idea of the play was brilliant. But there was controversy among critics and audiences alike over the brutality of the crimes committed by the characters as well as the character of Inez herself. Openly lesbian characters were unusual at the time.

No Exit was first produced in the United States on Broadway in December, 1946. American critics and audiences shared some of the French concerns over the characters, but many did not know what to make of the play as a whole. Wolcott Gibb, writing in *The New Yorker,* attributed the play's success in Europe (the play was also a hit in London) to the Europeans' "temperament." Gibb dismissed *No Exit* as "little more than a one-act drama of unusual monotony and often quite remarkable foolishness." The critic for *Newsweek* was not as negative, calling the play "weird and fascinating." Like their Euro-

pean counterparts, many American critics were intrigued by Sartre's concept of hell, but many Americans thought the play became repetitious near the end. Joseph Wood Krutch of *The Nation* took this view. He wrote, "Chief among the virtues is a genuinely macabre quality which makes itself felt most effectively during the first fifteen minutes. Unfortunately, like most plays based upon a conception which can be effectively stated in a few words, *No Exit* suffers from the fact that the interest tends to decline steadily from the moment the conception has been grasped."

One point that the American critics of the time debated was the nature of existentialism, since *No Exit* was regarded as an existentialist play. The philosophy was relatively new and not completely understood in the United States. Since its original productions, existentialism has become widely studied and discussed by scholars. The play has been debated in these terms. *No Exit* and its themes are now better understood, and the play is generally regarded as a classic. Unlike most of Sartre's other plays, *No Exit* has retained an accessibility because it is not rooted in a specific time and place.

There has been an extensive critical debate over the meaning of the play's most famous line, "Hell is other people." Many believe it means that interpersonal relationships are inevitably hellish. Others, including Sartre, disagree, arguing that it means people are too dependent on other people's opinions of them. Critics and scholars also have debated the meaning and nature of Sartre's hell, comparing it to other literary depictions. In an essay Jacques Guicharnaud contributed to *Sartre: A Collection of Critical Essays,* he wrote, "the play is not a metaphor of Hell but that the image of Hell is a metaphor of the hopeless suffering of individuals in search of their definitions in the eyes of others, yet constantly brought back to themselves."

CRITICISM

A. Petrusso

In this essay, Petrusso discusses the theme of cowardice and how it affects the plot of Sartre's play.

The three characters that are condemned to the hell in *No Exit* all have one thing in common: each of them displays cowardice. Cowardice means they lack courage. Joseph Garcin, the pacifist newspaper reporter, and Estelle, the young socialite, both lacked courage in their lives, and in hell, they cannot face the truth about themselves. Inez is at once a more complex yet more simple character. She believes she is a sadist, and her actions more than prove that. But a sadist needs others to torture, and Inez cowers from aloneness. No matter what their differences, all three of them share one act of cowardice at a key moment in the play. The door to the drawing room opens, offering an unknown opportunity, but none of them is brave enough to leave. In understanding each character, and what hell does for them as a whole, the reason why they make that decision becomes clearer.

Garcin's cowardice is the most obvious of the three and takes several forms. When he was alive, he was an editor at a newspaper in Rio de Janeiro in Brazil. Garcin was a pacifist, and he was put to death for his convictions. These are the first two facts Garcin presents about himself to the women in hell. Garcin agrees with Estelle at first; they do not know why they wound up in hell. He thinks it's a fluke. Garcin asks at one point early in the play, "do

you think it's a crime to stand by your principles?" But Garcin is ultimately forced to admit the truth about himself. He was cruel to his wife, going as far to bring another woman into their home and sleeping with her while his wife was upstairs. To make matters worse, his wife served Garcin and his lover coffee in bed.

The other truth about Garcin is his most literal cowardice. Though Garcin was indeed a pacifist, he acted on his beliefs in a spineless manner. Instead of staying and exclaiming his pacifist beliefs in Brazil, Garcin jumped on a train to Mexico, where he intended to start a pacifist paper. He was caught by officials near the border, imprisoned and shot by a firing squad for trying to run away from military service. But even in his cell while he awaited his fate, Garcin rationalized that "If I face death courageously, I'll prove I am no coward." Inez asks him how he faced it, and Garcin admits, "Miserably. Rottenly." This is compounded by the fact that from hell, Garcin can hear his colleagues at the paper talking about him and calling him a coward. Garcin did not have enough time in life to correct this image of himself, and he regrets it.

Estelle's cowardice takes on similar forms. In her life, she married a rich older man because she was poor and needed help taking care of her younger brother. Roger, an impoverished young man, became enamored with her, and she fell in love with him. They carried on an affair, and Roger wanted to have children with Estelle. She became pregnant by him and delivered a baby without her husband's knowledge. But Estelle did not want the baby, so in one cowardly act, she murdered the infant in front of its father. Roger was so distraught that he committed suicide. Estelle cannot admit her cowardice had a suicidal effect on him. She claimed "It was absurd of him, really, my husband never suspected anything." Instead of facing her crime, she chose to be superficial and cowardly. She eventually died from an unrelated illness, pneumonia.

Even more than Garcin, Estelle is in denial about her reasons for being in hell. She even cowers from the word "dead," insisting on the phrase "absentee." She thinks there has been some sort of clerical error that led to her being in this room with the others. "Just think of the number of people who—who become absentees every day . . . probably they're sorted out by—by understrappers, you know what I mean. Stupid employees who don't

WHAT DO I READ NEXT?

- *Being and Nothingness,* a nonfiction book published by Sartre in 1956 in translation, explicates his early theories on existentialism. It was originally published as *L'Être et le néant* in French in 1943.

- *Man and Superman* is a play published by George Bernard Shaw in 1904. It is set in hell.

- *Devils, Demons, Death, and Damnation,* is a book published in 1971 by Ernst and Johanna Lehner. It features images of hell throughout history.

- *The Victors,* another play published by Sartre in 1948, also concerns a small group of people confined to a small room. They are French Resistance fighters who must decide the meaning of their own deaths. It was originally published in French as *Les Morts sans sépulture,* c. 1946.

- *Old Times,* a play by Harold Pinter published in 1971, is centered around three characters. In a relatively unadorned set, the three engage in a sexual power struggle.

- *The History of Hell,* published by Alice K. Turner in 1993, discusses images of hell in art and literature throughout history.

---

know their job. So they're bound to make mistakes sometimes.'' She does not have the courage to face truth in either life or death but is forced to by Garcin and Inez. This is reinforced by Estelle's vision of her friend Olga, who is still alive. Olga tells Peter, another young man who admired Estelle in life, about Estelle's indiscretions.

Inez does not show cowardice in the same way as the other two. From the first, she accepts her fate in hell. She believes that she deserves to be there. She says that she was not human, even when she was alive. When Garcin asks for her aid in defeating ''their devilish tricks'' by helping him, she replies, ''Human feeling. That's beyond my range. I'm rotten to the core.'' In life, Inez was a self-described sadist. She lived with her cousin and his wife, with whom she began a lesbian affair. The cousin was distraught and eventually died in a tram accident. Inez tortured Florence by telling her that they killed him together. Florence eventually killed both herself and Inez by turning on the gas stove during the night.

Inez's sadism is the core of her cowardice. She needs someone else to torture to be sadistic. Though she despises Garcin and desires Estelle, she needs both of them to be recipients of her sadism. Inez wants to control Estelle as she did Florence, and use her to punish Garcin. Garcin puts himself at the mercy of Inez, wanting her confirmation that he is not a coward. Inez needs these kinds of relationships. She engineers them in the course of the play. Though it is never explicitly stated, Inez is afraid to be alone. Without others, she cannot exist. This comes into focus late in the play when Garcin and Estelle try to ignore Inez and kiss. Inez squeals in agony, saying anything to break them up, just so she can be part of the action. She does not have to be at its center, but she must control it in some way.

The three characters' cowardices come to a head during a moment of crisis for Garcin. He decides to accept Estelle's advances towards him, but only if she has faith in him that he is not really a coward. Inez forces Estelle to admit that she likes him simply because he is a man. She cannot assure him he is not a coward, because she does not understand what he wants from her. Garcin is appalled and starts banging on the door to escape from the two women. While Inez tries again to seduce Estelle, Estelle says she will leave with Garcin. All of a sudden, the door flings open and Garcin nearly falls into the passageway. Garcin and Estelle hesitate, but then do not leave. Inez finds the situation outrageously funny, and starts to laugh. Estelle tries to push Inez out, and Inez cries, ''Estelle! I beg you let me stay. I won't go, I won't go! Not into the passage.'' Garcin says that he is staying in the room for Inez's approval, and shuts the door.

This exchange shows how each of the characters cowers from the unknown. Garcin needs Inez to confirm he is not a coward. Estelle will not leave without Garcin. And Inez resists going out into the passageway where there might not be anyone for her to torture. They would rather be in a small, stuffy, overheated room with people they do not like or trust than to be caught in the passageways of hell. There is more certainty in a room that is always alight, where they can never blink or rest, than in the unknown of the hallway. They accept at that moment that their eternal fates are linked together. They can face the truth about themselves, but they cannot face the unknown. Their cowardice has a new dimension.

For most of the play, the threesome come to grips with who they are and why they are in hell. They learn that they can only face the truth with each other. Their fates, as Inez points out, are intertwined. There are no mirrors in which to see themselves. They can see who they are only through the eyes of another. Such self-realization combined with the circle of tension will occupy them for eternity because they can do nothing about their crimes. Growth is impossible because they are already dead. Inez says, ''One always dies too soon—or too late. And yet one's whole life is complete at that moment, with a line drawn neatly under it, ready for the summing up. You are your life, and nothing else.'' Their punishment is to see their lives and their crimes judged by the others forever. To live the life of a coward is bad enough, but to ''live'' as one for eternity is even worse.

Source: A. Petrusso, for *Drama for Students,* Gale, 1999.

John Mason Brown

Brown reviews the English translation of No Exit, *discussing Sartre's portrayal of Hell and how it compares to modern perceptions and those presented in classic literature.*

As if the contemporary world were not reason enough, there is also *No Exit,* a new play by Jean-Paul Sartre, to make hell highly topical as a subject just now. M. Sartre's hell is quite a different place either from the hell to which life of recent years has exposed people everywhere, or that to which literature and the drama have accustomed us.

Tantalus, old and withered, standing in a pool up to his chin, and in his terrible thirst lapping at the water which disappears eternally just as he is about to moisten his parched lips. Sisyphus, his body arched everlastingly against a rock which he must push up a hill, only to find at the crest that it rolls down again and he must recommence his labors. Tityos, stretched on the earth, his giant hands powerless to move, as vultures on either side of him plunge their beaks into his flesh and pluck at his liver. These are among the classic images of the punishments of the damned. Ever since Odysseus looked upon them, they or their kind have haunted men's minds.

Dante added to these images his own longer catalogue of horrors in ''The Divine Comedy.'' What is more, most of us are brought up even now to picture a Christian hell in terms of variations of these themes. Stoke the furnaces of Gehenna; add demons, pitchforks, and brimstone; but, above all, let the flames roar and include the agonies of eternal roasting, and you have some approximation of that hell of physical suffering in describing which hosts of ministers have not only exercised but demonstrated their fictional talents.

Why fictional talents? Because, as we are tempted to forget, the hell which the Thunderers of the Sawdust Trail have always loved to depict in every lurid detail as if they were travelers just returned from there, is hard to find in the Bible. Apparently as a notion, fearsome and corrective, it shared one, and only one, trait with Topsy. It ''jes' growed.''

It grew out of man's natural fears, out of his knowledge of pain, out of his conviction that Satan in his great power must exceed even man's inventiveness at cruelty. It came as an inheritance from, and an extension of, mythology. It blossomed by association, because Gehenna was a valley near Jerusalem used for the disposal of garbage.

To prevent disease, this refuse was burned, and constant flames flared there. The intellectual step connecting the disposal of garbage with the disposal of humans who, so to speak, were also refuse, was a simple one. The belief in purification through fire must be as old as fire itself. Hence the nostril-choking flames of Gehenna became almost inevitably for the imaginative the sulphurous flames of hell. But hell as it is usually pictured—hell as many people envisage it—is apochryphal. One of the most terrible reflections on man's nature is the torture he has been able to imagine in God's name.

No punishments known to Hades or "The Inferno," or dear to the traditionalists of the "Old-time Religion," are worse than the tortures to which the lost souls in M. Sartre's *No Exit* are condemned. M. Sartre's is a very special, post-Freudian, post-Briffault hell. In its choice of inmates and range of torments, it is French. It is French in its flavor, too; French in its intellectual agility; French because even in such sulphurous surroundings neither the eternal triangle nor "La Garçonne" has been forgotten. They have merely gone underground.

Yet Gallic as it is, it is more than that. It casts its oblique light on the thinking of a Europe wearied and ravaged by these past years. For this very reason it is comparable in its interest to a book so dubious in its detail, though evidently so valid in its general tone, as Curzio Malaparte's "Kaputt."

"The mind is its own place, and in itself / Can make a heaven of hell, a hell of heaven," says Milton's Satan. M. Sartre's hell is free of active physical cruelties. It gets along without scourges, flames, or furnaces. No devils intrude, pitchforking the damned into the gaping bicuspids of a smoking "Hell-Mouth" as they did in the old Mystery plays. They do not have to. Beelzebub is already in full possession of the brains of the three lost souls in this intellectual guignol. The punishments with which M. Sartre appalls and intrigues us are all mental, a fact which does not lessen their pain.

The first misery suffered in his House of the Dead is claustrophobia. Hell, says one of his characters, is other people. It is also ourselves, because, in spite of what M. Sartre may preach as an Existentialist, as a dramatist he holds individuals accountable for their own doom. His hell is likewise the fearsome fate of being compelled to live with two other unbearable persons in a small windowless room. Not only this, but also of seeking help in vain from these companions, and then being engulfed all over again in the same pattern of repeated meannesses.

The room into which M. Sartre's condemned are led by a satanic bellboy is a forbidding place. Had the devil been a stage designer, he could not have done a better job at exercising his spell than Frederick Kiesler has done for him. Mr. Kiesler's setting is an interior, ugly and out of joint. Yet it is

"SARTRE'S HELL IS QUITE A DIFFERENT PLACE EITHER FROM THE HELL TO WHICH LIFE OF RECENT YEARS HAS EXPOSED PEOPLE EVERYWHERE, OR THAT TO WHICH LITERATURE AND THE DRAMA HAVE ACCUSTOMED US"

more than this. Palpably it is meant to make self-destruction impossible. Though it is not one, it has the feeling of a padded cell and is as constricting as a straitjacket.

It is a tawdry living room seen in nightmarish terms. But it is also a dungeon, made the more unendurable because its furnishings do not confess its function. In spite of being lighted, there is in it something of that "darkness visible" which was seen after the Fall by Milton's Satan. This makes itself felt terribly, for example, at the moment when we learn that behind the curtains which promise a window, a view, and even some hope of escape, there are only imprisoning bricks where there should be glass.

The three people M. Sartre sentences to torturing one another with their obsessions and their memories are not a pretty trio. One of them is a Lesbian because of whom a girl has committed suicide. The second is an American nymphomaniac who has betrayed her husband and her lover. The third is not only a collaborationist, at one moment swaggering, at the next sniveling, but a sadist who has brought misery to his wife. What they undergo for an hour and a half in their shifting antagonisms and relationships is an anguish macabre and terrible, though nonetheless absorbing.

George Jean Nathan has wisely pointed out how much half-baked Wedekind and Strindberg there is in M. Sartre's script. Almost everyone who has seen *No Exit* has realized that during the last ten minutes the play drags and the attention wanders. Certainly, M. Sartre's play is not all it might and should be as a drama. For me, at least, it suffers, in addition to its own insufficiencies, because of the intermittent colloquialisms of Paul Bowles's translation.

Even so, I found *No Exit* one of the most interesting of the season's offerings. I, for one, would rather sit before it than a monthful of such shopworn fables as "The Fatal Weakness," "Happy Birthday," or "Present Laughter." At least it abandons the familiar stencils and grapples with an unusual idea. A mind is at work in it; a mind, alert, audacious and original, which has been touched by the agony of the modern world.

The evening *No Exit* affords is not designed for those whose only demand of the theatre is that it take over where the soap operas leave off; that it bolt its doors on the unpleasant; or that it function as a public nursery where adult kiddies can be left untroubled for an hour or so to play with toys which cannot hurt them. In spite of what is too special in them for the play's good, the sinners in *No Exit* can claim one radiant virtue. They shatter the ordinary formula. They supply playgoers with escape *from* escape, rather than escape itself. In the words of a man who, though royal, was not a Prince of Darkness, this is "a consummation devoutly to be wish'd."

Moreover, as adult theatre, M. Sartre's play has been given an adult production here. A certain fear of inviting the baneful siren of the Black Maria may at times inhibit the acting (as apparently it did not either in Paris or London). But the production has been sensitively and, for the most part, unflinchingly directed by John Huston. It is admirably acted by Peter Kass as the bellboy, Claude Dauphin as the collaborationist, and Annabella as the homosexual. As the frenzied American Ruth Ford has her excellent moments, too, though she lacks the fire Tallulah Bankhead would have brought to the part without any stoking.

Source: John Mason Brown, "The Beautiful and the Damned, in the *Saturday Review,* Volume 29, no. 52, December 28, 1946, pp. 26–29.

Joseph Wood Krutch

In this excerpt, Krutch discusses the worldwide popularity of Sartre's play, affirming its appeal as both an intellectual treatise and an entertaining work of theatre. Of the work's virtues in the latter category, Krutch praises the play for a "genuinely macabre quality."

No Exit (Biltmore Theater) is the English version of a phenomenally successful French play by Jean-Paul Sartre, high priest of existentialism. The scene is hell, the running time only a little over an hour and a quarter, and the total effect that of a rather ingenious shocker of a sort which would not have been out of place on the program at the Grand Guignol a generation ago. Three people—a Lesbian, a male collaborationist, and an American playgirl who murdered her child—find themselves after death shut up together in a hotel room. They enter at once upon a brief cycle of disputation in the course of which each manages to torture the other; then, as the cycle begins to repeat itself exactly, the curtain goes down. The three, it is evident, will pass eternity going over the same painful ground again, and again, and again. Since they will never sleep, hell, as one of them says, is merely life with no time off.

Of existentialism I know only what I read in the papers—including *The Nation.* It is, I have been told on various occasions, the theology of Kirkegaard with God left out; the conviction that though the world is both evil and without meaning nothing much can be done about it; and, finally, the determination to reject society while acting as an atomic individual. So far as I can see, it neatly combines the disadvantages of religious faith with those of nihilistic atheism. It seems, in other words, to assert moral responsibility while at the same time insisting that virtue has no reward, and it thus enables M. Sartre to revive the ancient proclamation, "There is no God and I am his prophet." But if this summary is inadequate, the fact is of no great importance at the moment, since no more—indeed hardly that much—could be deduced from the present play, whose virtues and limitations are obvious enough even to a spectator who has received no previous indoctrination.

Chief among the virtues is a genuinely macabre quality which makes itself felt most effectively during the first fifteen minutes, when the central conception is being presented and the atmosphere of horror being established. The ugly room, furnished in rather expensive bad taste and hideously lit by an unshielded chandelier in the ceiling, is just small enough to generate in the spectator a disconcerting claustrophobia, and as the victims are introduced one after another we share to some real extent both their nervous apprehension and the horror with which they realize the implications of their situation. Baudelaire talked about the *frisson nouveau,* and though it is no longer exactly new the shiver or thrill can still be provoked. Unfortunately, like most plays based upon a conception which can be effectively stated in a few words, *No Exit* suffers from the fact that the interest tends to decline steadily from the moment when the conception has been grasped and the playwright begins to try to fill in with sufficient material to stretch the action out beyond playlet length. In the present instance the revelation at the very end that the action is to repeat itself exactly through all eternity does provide an effective curtain, but up to that moment the tension has been going down rather than up, and there is no very good reason why the whole should not have been presented in half the short time now given it.

The popular French actor Claude Dauphin, who has been brought over to undertake the leading male role, gives a very effective if necessarily unpleasant performance as the bad-tempered, cowardly, neurotic, and self-despising collaborationist. Indeed, he seems to feel and transmit the emotions called for to a degree never-approached by Annabella and Ruth Ford, who play competently enough the other two principal parts. But not even the genuineness of his performance can conceal the fact that the main action itself is not very different from that of a sensational triangle play as, let us say, Bourdet or even Bernstein might have written it. It is one thing to say that hell will merely be life lived eternally and without respite. It is another to illustrate that statement by an action not essentially different from one which has been presented many times by dramatists who were saying merely that life is sometimes hell, not—what is really quite different—that hell is life.

To compare the reaction of an American audience with what is said to be the reaction of Parisians is to realize how much the success of the play in France must be the result of the special state of the post-war mind. Here it was being discussed during the one brief intermission merely as a *tour de force,* a sensational novelty; there it obviously means something to a population whose pessimism has become not so much an intellectual conviction as a neurotic derangement. Existentialism would appear to be less a philosophy than a state of mind, and less a state of mind than a state of nerves. "Hell," said Shelley, "is a city much like London," but that does not make Shelley an existentialist, for the simple reason that he was neither cold, nor hungry, nor defeated. And the difference makes the artistic as well as philosophical difference between "Peter Bell, III," and *No Exit.*

Source: Joseph Wood Krutch, review of *No Exit* in the *Nation,* Volume 163, no. 24, December 14, 1946, p. 708.

EXISTENTIALISM WOULD APPEAR TO BE LESS A PHILOSOPHY THAN A STATE OF MIND, AND LESS A STATE OF MIND THAN A STATE OF NERVES"

SOURCES

Gibb, Wolcott. 'Dream Boy," *The New Yorker,* December 7, 1946, pp. 61-64.

Guicharnaud, Jacques. "Man and His Acts," in *Sartre: A Collection of Critical Essays,* Prentice-Hall, 1962, pp. 62-72.

Krutch, Joseph Wood. A review of *No Exit* in *The Nation,* December 14, 1946, p. 708.

Sartre, Jean-Paul. *No Exit* in *No Exit and Three Other Plays,* Vintage, 1976, pp.1-47.

"Three in a Room," *Newsweek,* December 9, 1946, p. 92.

FURTHER READING

Barnes, Hazel E. *Sartre,* J.B. Lippincott Company, 1973.
     This is a critical overview Sartre's life and work.

Champignay, Robert. *Sartre and Drama,* Summa Publications, 1982.
     A comprehensive analysis of Sartre's work in the theater, including *No Exit.*

Cohn, Ruby. "No Exit (Huis Clos)," in *From "Desire" to "Godot": Pocket Theater of Postwar Paris,* University of California Press, 1987, pp. 36-51.
     This book discusses the background of plays and their productions. The essay on *No Exit* includes details on the writing, casting, and critical reception.

Contat, Michel, and Michel Rybalka, editors. *Sartre on Theatre,* Pantheon Books, 1976.
     This is a collection of documents written by Sartre on theater, including his own plays.

Picnic

WILLIAM INGE
1953

Picnic is based on an earlier short play by William Inge, *Front Porch,* written in 1952. This predecessor was a fragmented character study of several women. In using *Front Porch* as the basis of *Picnic,* Inge expanded upon the female characters to include several male figures and a more developed plot.

Picnic was a success with audiences when it opened on Broadway in February, 1953. It also earned significant praise from critics, winning the Pulitzer Prize for Drama, the Outer Circle Award, the New York Drama Critics Award, and a Donaldson Award. The movie adaptation in 1955 expanded the story's appeal and garnered two Academy Awards, a Golden Globe Award, and a listing as one of the ten best films of 1955. Inge's exploration of small town life, his focus on family relationships, and his depiction of the loneliness that permeates so many peoples' lives struck a chord with 1950s audiences and has continued to do so in the decades since *Picnic*'s debut.

Because he was writing about subjects with which he was familiar, Inge's plays deliver an authentic tone. The role of alcohol and sexual impropriety is a common theme in his work, which serves as a contrast to the American Dream image so familiar to 1950s audiences—that of white picket fences surrounding perfect people leading perfect lives. The women in *Picnic* are all looking for a way to escape the boredom and loneliness of their lives, and the men of the play are confused and unsure of

what they want. While embraced by mass audiences for its superficial charms, critics lauded Inge's play for its much darker themes. *Picnic* has come to be regarded as a pioneering drama for its frank depiction of sexuality and its subliminally cynical take on the "love conquers all" hypothesis.

AUTHOR BIOGRAPHY

William Inge, born May 3, 1913, was the fifth and last child of Maude and Luther Inge. He was raised in Independence, Kansas, by his mother; his father was a salesman and was rarely at home. After graduating from the University of Kansas in 1935, Inge attended the George Peabody College for Teachers but left before completing a master of arts degree. After a brief period teaching English at a local high school, Inge returned to college to complete his master's program. He also worked as a drama critic, and it was during this period that he met renowned playwright Tennessee Williams (*A Streetcar Named Desire*), who encouraged him to write. Inge completed his first play that year, and with the help of Williams, *Farther off from Heaven* was produced two years later, in 1947.

Plagued by depression and substance dependencies, Inge joined Alcoholics Anonymous in 1948, having already begun Freudian analysis in an attempt to alleviate his psychological problems. In 1949, he wrote *Come Back, Little Sheba,* which was produced on Broadway in 1950 and earned Inge the George Jean Nathan and Theatre Time Awards. Three years later, Inge scored another hit with *Picnic,* which won the Pulitzer Prize in Drama, the Outer Circle Award, the New York Drama Critics Circle Award, and the Donaldson Award. Inge had two more hits on Broadway in quick succession: *Bus Stop* (1955) and *The Dark At the Top of the Stairs* (1957; an earlier version was staged in 1947). After this success, Inge's next plays, *A Loss of Roses* (1959), *Natural Affection* (1963), and *Where's Daddy?* (1965) were commercial failures, each closing after only a few performances.

Despite these theatrical failures, Inge had great success with his 1961 foray into screenwriting. *Splender in the Grass* earned him the Academy Award for best original screenplay in 1961. Following this success, he moved to Los Angeles to concentrate on cinematic writing, but he never

William Inge

repeated his early success. Inge was deeply affected by negative reviews of his work. He struggled with depression and alcoholism much of his life. Many of his plays focus on the complexity of family relationships and deal with characters who struggle with failed expectations, depression, and addiction. His death in 1973 from carbon monoxide poisoning was ruled a suicide.

PLOT SUMMARY

Act I

As *Picnic* opens, Millie is sneaking a cigarette outside, while Hal and Mrs. Potts have just finished breakfast next door. It is the last day before school starts and everyone is getting ready for a Labor Day picnic to be held that evening. The main characters are introduced, and the tomboyish Millie, while pretending not to care, is shown to be envious of her older sister Madge's beauty but contemptuous of her intellect.

Madge enters. Hal, a drifter recently arrived in town and employed doing odd jobs for Mrs. Potts, is immediately attracted to her, and Madge is clearly attracted to him. When Flo enters, her wariness indicates that she perceives Hal as a threat to her plans, mainly marrying Madge off to the wealthy Alan. Flo warns Madge that a pretty girl does not have much time before her beauty begins to fade, urging her daughter to seize the moment and secure Alan's interest. Madge enjoys Alan's company but is not in love with him. Instead, she is fixated on the train whistle in the distance which, to her, symbolizes the prospect of freedom from the small town.

The Owens' roomer, Rosemary, enters the scene and attempts to convince the other women that she is not interested in men or in marrying. But her tone indicates that marriage is the one thing she does desire. She leaves with two other single teachers. Alan arrives and embraces Hal as an old friend from college. The two reminisce, and Hal relates his most recent activities. Alan's acceptance of Hal eases Flo's worries about the drifter and validates Mrs. Potts's fondness for her new handyman. Hal is asked to escort Millie to the picnic that evening, and the act ends with Hal, Alan, and Millie leaving to spend the day swimming.

Act II

It is late afternoon, and Madge has spent the day helping her mother prepare the food for the picnic that evening. Rosemary is getting ready for her date with Howard, who soon arrives. Hal and Alan have also arrived in two separate cars. After Alan goes inside the house to help Flo, Millie sits down to draw Hal's picture. Howard leaves to get something from his car, returning with a bottle of whiskey. After initially pretending that she is unfamiliar with alcohol, Rosemary has several drinks, as does Hal and Howard.

When Rosemary walks to the other side of the yard, both Hal and Howard step back to admire Madge, who they can see primping in the window. Rosemary returns and wants to dance to the music everyone can now hear coming from the park. Although Howard has told Rosemary that he cannot dance, he makes an attempt to please her after she begins dancing with Millie. Hal attempts to teach Millie some new steps; Rosemary is fixated on him as he swoons to the music. When Madge enters, and she and Hal begin to dance, Rosemary, already very drunk, begins a verbal attack on Hal, who has refused to dance with her. Rosemary correctly assesses Hal's social skills and his insecurities. Her attack leaves him defeated, and when Madge tries to comfort him, he embraces her, carrying her offstage.

Act III, scene 1

It is very late, after midnight, when Rosemary and Howard return. They have had sex and Rosemary expects Howard to marry her. Howard's attempt to escape, by repeatedly promising that they will talk about their future at another time, is not acceptable to Rosemary. She makes it clear that even one more day of the loneliness and emptiness of her life is unsuitable. Although he has claimed to be set in his ways and unwilling to marry, Howard is no match for the determined Rosemary. She pleads and begs until he promises to return in the morning to discuss the issue. A few moments later, Madge and Hal enter. They have also had sex, and both are feeling very ashamed at their betrayal of Alan. The scene ends with Madge running into her house in tears.

Act III, scene 2

It is early the next morning. Everyone is carefully discussing the events of the evening before. Alan arrives and asks to speak to Madge. While he waits, Millie tells him that she has always liked him. As they are waiting for Madge to come outside, Howard arrives to speak to Rosemary, who has packed her bags and is prepared for an immediate wedding. Using the presence of her friends and the Owens, whom she has certainly told of her wedding plans, Rosemary effectively traps Howard into agreeing to an immediate wedding.

Madge comes outside to speak to Alan, who tells her that Hal has left town. But Hal has been hiding nearby, and his entrance provokes a fight between the two young men. Hal easily defeats Alan, who says he is leaving town with his father. Hal is being pursued by the police and must also leave town. He tries to convince Madge to go with him, but she is frightened. He leaves to catch the train to Tulsa without her. After Hal leaves, Madge enters the house crying. She emerges in a few moments with her packed bag and announces that she, too, is going to catch the train and join Hal. In spite of her mother's pleadings, Madge walks offstage.

CHARACTERS

Howard Bevans

Howard is Rosemary's suitor. He is his forties and reluctant to marry. He brings a bottle of whisky to a gathering and this leads to several serious problems. Millie drinks and becomes ill. Hal drinks and engages in a sexual encounter with Madge. Rosemary and Howard also drink and this, too, leads to a sexual encounter. When Howard tries to take Rosemary back to the Owens' home early the following morning, she pleads with him to marry her. In spite of his reluctance, he agrees.

Bomber

Bomber is the teenage newsboy. His role is small, primarily to comment upon Madge's beauty and to leer at her.

Hal Carter

Hal is young and very handsome. He has no ties and frequently moves from town to town, changing jobs as he goes. While he qualifies as a drifter, his charm and good looks raise him above the typical transient. Hal has led a colorful life. He was a football hero in college and was promised a Hollywood movie career, but when that did not work out, he worked as a cowboy. Hitchhiking to Texas, he was picked up by two women and robbed. He is in town, hoping that his college buddy Alan and his father can get him a job.

Despite his past popularity, Hal reveals that he does not know how to act around socially refined young women and has not engaged in even the most typical of social functions; he has never been on a picnic. His childhood was spent in near-misses with the law, his father died from alcohol abuse, and he is estranged from his mother. Although he belonged to a fraternity in college, it was only his football heroism that paved the way for social acceptance. In reality, Hal is insecure, socially inept, and frightened that others will see through his bravado. When he has too much to drink, he seduces a willing Madge. Alan's father has him pursued on a trumped up charge of auto theft, and Hal must leave town. Before he goes, however, he stops to see Madge one final time. To Madge, the freewheeling Hal represents the opportunity for which she has been longing: a means out of the small town in which she has spent her entire life. She agrees to leave with him.

Irma Kronkite

Irma, is a teacher and a friend of Rosemary's. She has been to New York during the summer and returns in the fall to teach.

MEDIA ADAPTATIONS

- *Picnic* was adapted to film in 1955. The film, starring William Holden as Hal, Kim Novak as Madge, and Cliff Robertson as Alan, was very successful, winning two academy awards for art direction and editing; it also won a Golden Globe for the director, Joshua Logan.

Mrs. Flo Owens

Mrs. Owens is a widow of about forty. She thinks that a marriage between wealthy Alan and her oldest girl, Madge, would improve the family's status and guarantee a better life for her daughter. Flo pushes Madge to encourage Alan, telling her daughter that youthful beauty will not last and another opportunity for marriage may not come her way. Flo is especially afraid that Madge will end up struggling and poor just as she did. She is nervous about Hal's intrusion into their lives, recognizing in him a threat to Madge's future with Alan. Although it is never stated, it is implied that when she was young, Flo succumbed to an inappropriate love affair. This explains her disapproval of Madge's involvement with Hal.

Madge Owens

Flo's oldest daughter is eighteen and exceptionally beautiful. She works part-time as a store clerk but is sensitive about this occupation; she is hoping for better. But Madge also understands that it is her beauty that men admire and not her intelligence. Her mother, Flo, has trained Madge to cook and sew—attributes considered essential for a "good," domestic wife, and she is the daughter who stays home to cook, while the other young people go off to swim. The train whistle in the distance represents freedom for Madge, who wants to travel and experience life away from the small town in which she was born and raised. Her opportunity for escape occurs after a night spent with Hal. After he leaves, she realizes that she loves him, and although she also understands that he may amount to little in life, she wants to take the chance of being with him. The play ends when she leaves with her few belongings packed in a small suitcase.

Millie Owens

Millie is one of Flo's daughters. She is sixteen, shy but boisterous, and assertive in an effort to appear confident. She is not as attractive as Madge, but she is a better student. Millie is something of a tomboy, preferring sports and the company of boys to staying home and learning how to perform domestic chores. Millie wants to go to college, become a writer, and escape to a life in New York.

Helen Potts

Mrs. Potts is a widow, almost sixty years old. She and her mother share a house. She hires Hal to do some chores and in doing so, sets in motion the events that will change all their lives. Mrs. Potts's mother is demanding; it is clear that she has kept her daughter from ever having a real life with a man. The rumor is that after Helen married Mr. Potts, her mother had the marriage annulled. Helen kept his name just to remind her mother of those few hours of freedom. She encourages Hal because she is attracted to him and wants him to find the happiness in life that was denied her.

Christine Schoenwalder

Christine is a new teacher who has just moved to town. She socializes with Rosemary and Irma.

Alan Seymour

Alan is a wealthy young man and Madge's steady boyfriend. He and Hal are acquainted from their college days together. When Alan realizes that Hal is working next door, he is overjoyed to find his friend. Alan's father is sending him back to college, probably to get him away from Madge, who is from the wrong side of town. Alan loves Madge and turns on Hal when he realizes the two are attracted to one another. He leaves town after it becomes clear that Madge loves Hal.

Rosemary Sydney

Rosemary is a roomer in the Owens' household. She is an unmarried school teacher who assumes an attitude of indifference to what happens around her. She pretends to be uninterested in men, and she also implies that she is younger, although she is close to Flo's age. The reality is that Rosemary wants very badly to marry. After alcohol

loosens her inhibitions, she has sex with Howard and then pleads with him to marry her.

THEMES

Beauty

Beauty is important to the play, as it is the initial quality by which both Madge and Hal are judged, the same quality that Millie and Rosemary desire. Madge is afraid that her beauty is all that she has, and her fear is affirmed by her mother, whose lectures on *carpe diem,* seizing the day, reinforce the idea that she will be worth nothing once her beauty has faded. That a rich man desires her—Alan states that he is so overwhelmed by her beauty that he can scarcely believe that she notices him—only serves to convince Madge that she has no other attributes or at least any that are equal to her looks. Hal's beauty has always offered him a means to survive. He has used his attractiveness to help him succeed with women, and it is their mutual good-looks that first attract Madge and Hal to one another. In addition, Hal's appearance, along with his athletic prowess, has enabled people to overlook his social shortcomings. Millie is envious of her sister's beauty, but she also appears to realize that it is ultimately intellect, not superficial beauty, that will lead to success. Millie has set her sights on college and a career. For Rosemary, it is faded youth and beauty that are her greatest enemies. She is desperate to marry Howard before her last opportunity for marriage escapes.

Choices and Consequences

When Howard brings the bottle of whisky into the Owens' yard, he sets in motion a series of events that will change all the character's lives. Rosemary's drinking loosens her inhibitions enough that when she is rejected by Hal, she responds with a vehement attack on his insecurities and his fears. Although Rosemary's sexual encounter with Howard occurs offstage, it is implied that the alcohol led to her willingness to have sex with him. Her insistence that Howard pay the consequence, marriage, is a product of a long-standing realization that he may be her last chance to marry. If she wants marriage, Rosemary has no choice but to convince Howard to marry her; she seizes on the opportunity to use their sexual encounter as leverage in coercing Howard into marriage.

The choice that Hal and Madge make to have sex will also have unanticipated consequences. Hal's friendship with Alan will be destroyed; Madge will choose to leave her home; and her mother's dreams of a better life (elevated status by marrying into Alan's wealthy family) will be lost.

Freedom

The train whistle in the background represents freedom to Madge—when she hears it, she yearns to be on that train, heading to a new, exciting future. The small town offers no new opportunities for her. Madge is the prettiest girl in town, but no one will give her the chance to be anything else. It is not clear if she can be more than a small-town beauty, but she wants to try. Hal, with his wanderings and exciting stories, represents freedom from such a repressive, small town life. Although she is eighteen years old, Madge needs Hal to stimulate her escape into another world. If she does not take this step, Madge might end up like Mrs. Potts—tied to lost dreams and her elderly mother.

Love and Passion

When Madge and Hal first see one another, there is an instant attraction. This passion contrasts with Madge's relationship with Alan, which seems to consist of hesitant, passionless kisses. The quickly ignited fire between Madge and Hal leaves little doubt that their passion will be consummated. It is only when Hal is forced to leave, however, that Madge is able to admit that what she feels for him is love.

Loneliness

Loneliness is an important theme for several characters in *Picnic*. All of the women are lonely in one way or another. Mrs. Potts and Flo Owens are lonely and filled with regret at missed opportunities. Both are alone, but Mrs. Potts appears as an especially sad victim of her mother's interference. She is described as a sixty-year-old woman who was married only briefly before her mother had the marriage annulled. It's not clear what happened to Flo's husband, but her biggest concern is in protecting her daughters, for whom Flo has been both father and mother for ten years. Millie feels isolated by her lack of beauty and the image of an older sister, whose beauty she cannot match. However, Madge is isolated by the very beauty that too many people envy but are afraid to touch. And finally, Rosemary is lonely. Although she has friends with whom she

TOPICS FOR FURTHER STUDY

- Research the economic future of small town America in the period immediately after World War II. Consider the importance of agriculture, as well as job opportunities for young men and women. Why do so many of the young people in *Picnic* seek to escape?

- Explore the overt sexuality of *Picnic* and Inge's 1949 play *Come Back, Little Sheba*. Compare and contrast how this topic is handled in each play.

- Compare Madge and Millie. In their common desire to escape, they appear very alike, and yet, each seems to have different plans for their respective futures. Discuss their similarities and differences and argue for each young woman's chances for success in achieving their goals.

- Research the role of alcohol in Inge's plays. Consider its function as a catalyst for change. Is alcohol portrayed positively or negatively in these works?

can spend time, Rosemary is lonely for the companionship of marriage and love. Hal's arrival amidst this group of lonely women provides the center for the drama that occurs.

STYLE

Act

An act is a major division in a drama. In Greek plays the sections of the drama were signified by the appearance of the chorus and were usually divided into five acts. This is the formula for most serious drama from the Greeks to the Romans and to Elizabethan playwrights like William Shakespeare. The five acts denote the structure of dramatic action. They are exposition, complication, climax, falling action, and catastrophe. The five act structure was followed until the nineteenth century when

Henrik Ibsen combined some of the acts. *Picnic* is a three-act play. The exposition and complication are combined in the first act when the audience first learns of Madge and Hal's attraction. The climax occurs in the second act when Hal is verbally attacked by Rosemary and Madge is attracted by his vulnerability. This leads to their sexual encounter later that evening. Rosemary and Howard also have a sexual encounter, and these trysts provide the falling action. The catastrophe occurs in the third act when their deception is revealed to Alan and when Madge realizes that she loves Hal and chooses to run away with him.

Scene

Scenes are subdivisions of an act. A scene may change when all of the main characters either enter or exit the stage. But a change of scene may also indicate a change of time. In *Picnic,* the second scene of Act II occurs later on the same day, and thus, indicates the passage of time in the play.

Character

A person in a dramatic work. The actions of each character are what constitute the story. Character can also include the idea of a particular individual's morality. Characters can range from simple, stereotypical figures (the jock, the damsel in distress, the fool) to more complex multi-faceted ones. ''Characterization'' is the process of creating a life-like person from an author's imagination. To accomplish this the author provides the character with personality traits that help define who he will be and how he will behave in a given situation. For instance, in the beginning of the play, Madge answers her mother's questions about Alan in a manner that hints that her attraction for him is not as intense as her mother hopes. With the introduction of Hal, Madge begins to realize that what she feels for Hal is love. All the passion that was missing from her relationship with Alan is present with Hal.

Drama

A drama is often defined as any work designed to be presented on the stage. It consists of a story, of actors portraying characters, and of action. But historically, drama can also consist of tragedy, comedy, religious pageant, and spectacle. In modern usage, the term drama is also used to describe a type of play (or film) that explores serious topics and themes yet does not achieve the same level as tragedy.

Plot

This term refers to the pattern of events in a play or story. Generally plots should have a beginning, a middle, and a conclusion, but they may also be a series of episodes that are thematically connected together. Basically, the plot provides the author with the means to explore primary themes. Students are often confused between the two terms; but themes explore ideas, and plots simply relate what happens in a very obvious manner. Thus the plot of *Picnic* is the story of how a drifter passing through town changed the lives of five lonely women. But the themes are those of loneliness, lost opportunities, and passion.

Setting

The time, place, and culture in which the action of the play takes place is called the setting. The elements of setting may include geographic location, physical or mental environments, prevailing cultural attitudes, or the historical time in which the action takes place. The location for Inge's play is the porch and yard of two homes in a midwestern city. The action occurs over a period of twenty-four hours.

Symbolism

Symbolism is the use of one object to replace another. Symbolism has been an important force in literature for most of the twentieth century. The symbol is an object or image that implies a reality beyond its original meaning. This is different from a metaphor, which summons forth an object in order to describe an idea or a quality; the motorcycle that Hal refers to is a metaphor for freedom, representing the means to travel and explore new places. Hal is a symbol of sexual opportunity and the latent sexual desire that several of the women feel but do not recognize. He is also a symbol of freedom to Madge.

HISTORICAL CONTEXT

When *Picnic* debuted in February of 1953, the United States was still embroiled in the Korean Conflict half a world away. Josef Stalin, having ruled the Soviet Union, since 1928, was nearing the end of his life, but communism appeared stronger

COMPARE & CONTRAST

- **1953:** The article "Cancer by the Carton" is published in *Reader's Digest*. It warns the public of the health hazards of smoking cigarettes.

   Today: Evidence surfaces that tobacco companies have known for many years about both the health risks and addictive nature of cigarettes. Many states sue tobacco manufacturers for heath care costs incurred in treating sick smokers. A settlement that will reach into the billions of dollars is reached.

- **1953:** *Playboy* magazine begins publication with a nude photograph of Marilyn Monroe. Conservative groups are shocked by this wanton display and predict the end of traditional American values.

   Today: Nudity and sex are no longer topics that generate much controversy. Magazines, such as *Playboy* have been eclipsed by nudity in film and on the internet. Many conservatives still contend that the quality of American life has been reduced by such open displays of sexuality.

- **1953:** On January 22, *The Crucible* opens at New York's Martin Beck Theatre. The play's historical witch hunt parallels the persecution of innocent people by the McCarthy Hearings in the senate.

   Today: Many refer to independent prosecutor Kenneth Starr's investigation of President Clinton as a "witch Hunt," a reference to both Miller's play and the McCarthy Hearings of the 1950s.

- **1953:** Drought plagues much of the Midwest. Parts of thirteen states are declared disaster areas.

   Today: The summer and fall of 1998 have seen several extremes of weather, from flooding and tornadoes to hurricanes. Damage to crops, livestock, property, and citizens of small towns reaches record highs.

- **1953:** Frozen TV dinners are introduced by C. A. Swanson & Son. They sell for ninety-eight cents and prove to be extremely popular among people who don't have time to prepare a meal.

   Today: American lifestyles have become more frenetic and busy; many still embrace frozen meals for their convenience. They prove to be particularly popular with single people.

---

than ever and seemed ready to expand into many of the world's developing nations. There were rumblings in Vietnam, then a French colony, and requests by the French for American assistance in maintaining order marked the beginning of America's long involvement with that Asian nation.

In the United States, fears of spreading communism and apprehensions regarding atomic weapons (the first such devices were used eight years earlier on Nagasaki and Hiroshima, Japan) lead to the persecution of many people from suspected spies to common citizens with only the most tenuous of ties to communist politics. Feeding on the public's communist paranoia, Senator Joseph McCarthy and his House Committee on Un-American Activities were able to ruin the lives of many people suspected of having communist sympathies. While on the surface, television and film tried to maintain the illusion of quiet perfection in America, political unrest was beginning to make itself felt. Arthur Miller's 1953 play *The Crucible* used the Salem Witch Trials to demonstrate the parallels between the hysteria of that seventeenth century persecution of innocent women and the McCarthy hearings into communism that cost many people their careers and families.

While horrifying, Miller's play could not capture the reality of the paranoia, tension, and fear that swept across America during this period. In 1953, Hollywood stars such as Charlie Chaplin were banned from entering the United States, based on their politics. The U.S. government also convicted spies Ethel and Julius Rosenberg, who were tried for giving plans for the atomic bomb to the Soviet Union. They awaited execution in 1953.

In America's small towns, this political unrest seemed a long distance away, at least on the surface. But it revealed itself in the growing unrest among young men and women, who, moved by a growing dissatisfaction with small town life, began to search for the happiness and promise of the American Dream. While music from the opening years of the 1950s is barely distinguishable from that of the late-1940s, within a year or two, rock 'n roll would prove to be a social catalyst, turning the dissatisfaction and unrest of youth into a motivated, focused force. Parents in the 1950s blamed personalities such as Elvis Presley and James Dean for their children's rejection of traditional values, but it was really a culmination of political and social events that led young adults, such as Madge Owens and Hal Carter, to look to the open road and large urban areas for excitement. Even a fifteen-year-old, like Millie, is already planning ahead to the day when she can leave for the big city and a more exciting life. This burgeoning sense of wanderlust and thirst for new experiences would pave the way for one of America's most experimental and significant decades, the 1960s.

Picnic begins with Millie sneaking outside to smoke. The 1950s was notable as a decade in which the earliest warnings about the dangers of smoking surfaced. One of the first messages to reach the public was a *Reader's Digest* article, "Cancer by the Carton," which warned about the risks of smoking. Cigarette manufacturers responded with the introduction of filter cigarettes, which they promised would reduce many of the risk factors. Now, after forty-five years of health warnings, the audience of 1998 would view Millie's opening cigarette very differently from the 1953 audience. During World War II, smoking was so acceptable that cigarettes were airlifted to the troops, even behind enemy lines. Cigarettes were also included in the food packets (c-rations) that were provided to each soldier in Korea. But in those cases, cigarettes were intended for men; women smoked, but there was still an element of disrepute attached to young women smoking. That would soon change. Although women had always smoked less frequently than men, Hollywood films showing glamorous stars smoking had helped to change the idea of smoking into a more respectable image for women. Thus, Millie, who begins each day with a cigarette,

reaffirms the message sent by Hollywood films, but she also signals the change toward a greater acceptability for young women smoking.

CRITICAL OVERVIEW

Picnic was very popular with theatre critics when it debuted in 1953, with special notice given to the theme of ordinary people living ordinary lives in small town America. Brooks Atkinson, writing for the *New York Times,* observed that "Inge has made a rich and fundamental play" from these "commonplace people." Atkinson found the female characters particularly well drawn and praised the way that Hal effortlessly brings all the women to life. Calling *Picnic* an "original, honest play with an awareness of people," Atkinson, also noted that while most of the characters may not demonstrate an awareness of what they are doing, "Mr. Inge does, for he is an artist."

In a review for *New York Journal American,* John McClain stated that Inge's characters "are easily recognizable from anybody's youth, and if the author has not chosen to bring them to grips with any problems of cosmic importance, he can certainly be credited with making them powerfully human." Although McClain argued that *Picnic* lacks the depth of Inge's earlier work he did note that "it succeeds wonderfully well in bringing a small theme to a high level."

An even more glowing review appeared in the *New York Post.* Richard Watts, Jr. singled out the work of Inge's director, Joshua Logan, for special praise, referring to *Picnic* as "excellently acted and sympathetically staged by Mr. Logan." Watts's greatest praise, however, was reserved for Inge, who he said, "revealed the power, insight, compassion, observation and gift for looking into the human heart that we all expected of him." Watt argued that Inge's writing has "great emotional impact" and that it is Inge's "capacity for looking into the human heart" that gives *Picnic* its major claim to distinction. As did so many other reviewers, Watt also focused on the characters, especially the women, who he said are "depicted with enormous understanding and compassion, so that they are not only striking as theatrical characters but moving and genuine as human beings." Watts argued that there is no "figure in the play that Mr. Inge doesn't seem to understand and see into." Concluding that Inge "is a dramatist who knows

A scene from the 1958 Broadway production; Madge (Janice Rule) is seated on the porch while Flo (Peggy Conklin) talks with Hal (Ralph Meeker), Millie (Kim Stanley) is in the foreground

how to set down how people behave and think and talk,'' Watts stated that the playwright is ''able to write dramatic scenes that have vitality, emotional power and heartbreak. There is a true sense of the sadness and wonder of life in this new dramatist.''

A few critics focused on the comedy of *Picnic* in their reviews. John Chapman's review, which ran in the *Daily News,* called Inge's play ''an absorbing comedy of sex as sex is admired and practiced in a small town somewhere in Kansas.'' Although, Chapman found the romance between Hal and Madge

''pitiful'' and ''shabby,'' he did find that ''Inge has created his characters so well and they are so persuasively acted that they become fascinating.'' This occurs because ''Inge looks upon them all with understanding, humor and affection.'' The *Daily Mirror*'s Robert Coleman, agreed, calling *Picnic,* a ''stirring, hilarious click.'' Coleman, citing Inge's ''admirable skill,'' declared that ''it is amazing how well rounded and real all the people are in his play.''

Negative responses to *Picnic* were centered on the direction, which William Hawkins referred to as too slick and professional. Hawkins noted in a review for the *New York World-Telegram* that Logan's work "sometimes detracts from the heart of it." Walter Kerr, writing for the *Herald Tribune,* was even more critical of the director. Kerr called Logan's direction "strident," arguing that "characters pose, prance, pause, and writhe with alarming mathematical efficiency. Every effort is carefully calculated, planned for the great big boff. Comedy lines are slapped down noisily; the pathos is always conscious of its style." Having reserved brief praise for the setting, Kerr concluded that the performance of Inge's play is "hopped-up Broadway." Kerr was in the minority among Broadway critics, however, as the majority of them embraced Inge's play, lauding it as a model of modern playwriting.

CRITICISM

Sheri E. Metzger

Metzger is a Ph.D. specializing in literature and drama at the University of New Mexico. In this essay, she discusses the manner in which Inge's play forecasted future trends in sexuality, particularly with regard to women in the entertainment world.

At the end of *Picnic,* Madge packs her bags and leaves town to follow Hal. But this was not the ending that Inge originally envisioned when he wrote the play. The playwright's initial view of love was much darker and not so easily reconciled, and he left Madge to continue much as she had before Hal's arrival—minus the security of her relationship with Alan. The 1953 stage director, Joshua Logan, wanted, and received, a happier ending, but Inge's original conclusion reappeared in a rewrite of *Picnic,* published in 1962 as *Summer Brave.* Inge's desire to portray young love as sexually charged and rebellious revealed an America hidden behind the perfect world so often depicted in 1950s entertainment, a world that would further reveal itself in the films, music, and plays of the coming decades.

While ignoring the realities of the Cold War, the Korean Conflict, and other prevalent threats of the era, television and film generally tried to convey American life as romantic, carefree, and lighthearted, subscribing to an unwritten code of conduct. As depicted on Broadway in the 1950s, *Picnic* suitably reflected those ideals. When Madge leaves for a life with Hal, she bolsters the idea that sexuality, though wrong in a premarital situation, is a prelude to marriage. The ending that Inge initially envisioned, however, more accurately reflected the America of the late-1960s, a country where women did not always fulfill society's expectations of proper behavior. In *Summer Brave,* Inge implies that Madge is no worse for having spent a night with Hal, and that her experience does not lead to promiscuity or a lower station in life. But in the early-1950s, single women who engaged in sex were expected to marry their lover or face a life of social damnation.

Inge first challenged this restrictive social edict three years earlier in *Come Back, Little Sheba.* In that play, the character Marie uses a boy named Turk solely as a sexual partner, a plaything, one whom she has no interest in marrying. Turk does not represent Marie's future, but he is an interesting diversion while she waits for the marriage with the man she truly desires. In this instance, sex is divorced from both love and marriage. The idea that sex might not lead naturally to marriage resurfaces in the original *Picnic,* when Madge chooses to remain behind after Hal leaves. Had director Logan left that last act intact, the audience would have seen two very different endings evolve from similar experiences. Instead, the conventions of sexuality and marriage are maintained for both couples; Rosemary and Howard will marry and an eventual union is implied for Hal and Madge.

Inge uses Rosemary's story to provide the conventional ending in *Picnic,* the one expected by a 1950s audience. After she and Howard engage in drunken sex, Rosemary insists that Howard do the honorable thing and marry her. Her entrapment of the reluctant suitor provides much of the comedy in the play. With that couple's romantic plot, Inge is using the comedic formula adapted by William Shakespeare in so many of his comedies, when, after a suggestion of sexual misconduct, the woman and man are wed in the play's happy conclusion. Rosemary and Howard are unconventional lovers, both older and yet both naively expecting a different outcome from their tryst: Rosemary expects a more romantic Howard, one who wants to marry her while Howard expects that nothing has changed and that Rosemary will simply continue dating him. Instead, Rosemary seizes upon Howard as the only opportunity she will have for marriage.

R. Baird Shuman stated in *William Inge* that Rosemary reaches out "pitifully toward Howard, not because she really loves him, but because she fears she will continue to live her life 'till I'm ready

WHAT DO I READ NEXT?

- Andrew Marvell's "To His Coy Mistress," published in 1681, is an early poem that argues that time is fleeting and that young lovers should seize the opportunity to be happy together, especially with respect to sexual intimacy; and "To the Virgins to Make Much of Time," a short poem written by Robert Herrick in 1648, that warns young women to marry quickly rather than wait for the perfect mate

- *Splendor in the Grass* is a film written by Inge. Released in 1961, the film focuses on the love affair between a young teenage couple who

cannot deal well with the sexual pressure and family interference that beset them.

- Theodore Dreiser's *An American Tragedy,* published in 1925, explores the tragedy of young love when social status and economic gain push a young man to commit a horrible crime.

- *Bus Stop,* written by Inge in 1955, is considered by many to be the playwright's finest comedy. In the play the young lovers' theme takes on a new twist when a naive young man attempts to force a reluctant young woman to be his wife.

---

for the grave and don't have anyone to take me there.''' Howard underestimates Rosemary's desperation for marriage and the fact that he is her sole marital target. While funny, this element of comedy is also tragic, in that it reveals all of Rosemary's insecurities and fears and makes clear the stereotype that she represents: the spinster schoolteacher, too unattractive to marry and resigned to a lifetime of devotion to her students. Their romance contrasts with the Madge/Hal relationship, which deviated from the expected in Inge's original ending. When the playwright changed the ending to fit Logan's vision, he not only reaffirmed traditional expectations of conventional comedic theatre but also rendered *Picnic* as a non-threatening social commentary.

Jane Courant argued in *Studies in American Drama, 1945-Present* that these romances represent much more than "faithful renderings of cliches of culture, language, and behavior during a period characterized by extreme social conformity." She reminded readers that Inge's plays almost predicts the changes that would come in film and music in the next few years. The advent of films depicting freedom-craving bad boys like Marlon Brando, James Dean, and Peter Fonda seems to echo Hal's observations about his theft of a motorcycle. Hal stole the motorcycle because he "wanted to get on the damn thing and go so far away, so fast, that no

one'd ever catch up with me." The motorcycle is a symbol of freedom, a means for escape, rebellion, and adventure—all things that Hal needs to survive. These are the same elements that motivate the film rebels of Brando's *The Wild One* (1954), Dean's *Rebel without A Cause* (1955), and Fonda's *Easy Rider* (1969). Just as importantly, they are the same needs that appeal to Madge, who finds Hal's story romantically exciting. When she says, "I think— lots of boys feel that way at times," she is also silently adding—and girls, too.

The sexuality of music and dance that Inge incorporates into Act II establishes the mood for the sexual encounters that follow. When Hal begins to dance with Madge, the act is seductive, as Inge intended it to be. His stage directions refer to their dance as a "primitive rite that would mate the two young people." Inge is confirming that music and dance can serve as a prelude to physical love, planting the seed of fear that would flower in many parents' suspicions of teenagers and rock and roll. Courant wrote that a year after *Picnic* opened in 1953, the first volley of rock and roll songs, by such artists as Bill Haley and the Comets, would shake the world of popular music; Elvis Presley's subsequent arrival would herald a new era of sexuality in music. Hal's appropriation of music and dance as foreplay is a prologue to the pattern that would be established in the "teenybopper" films of such entertainers as Presley, Frankie Avalon, and Annette Funicello. In these films, young people were brought together through music and dance, and while these movies are chaste in comparison to the explicit films of later decades, the implication of sex was very clear. Inge used Madge and Hal to establish a picture of youthful love and sexuality that was just on the horizon.

In an interview that he gave to writer Walter Wager in *The Playwrights Speak,* Inge said that he was not a social activist and that he thought very little in political terms. Yet later, in the same interview, he stated that he saw a new generation of American youth "challenging the cliches of the established culture ... [and] creating cliches of their own." It is this questioning of convention that Inge tries to capture in his play. Madge rejects the image of beauty that encapsulates her life. She wants to be noticed and admired for qualities that have nothing to do with her appearance. She also wants more than the American Dream marriage ideal that her mother envisions in a union with Alan. She recognizes her intellectual limitations and laments her future as a clerk; it is her jealousy of Millie's academic achievements that creates much of the sisterly conflict in the play. But while Madge may be less intellectual than her younger sister, she is pragmatic. At the play's ending, when Madge is challenged by her mother, Madge tells her that she does not believe that loving Hal will provide all the answers. She acknowledges Hal's poor record with women and his lack of economic prospects.

Madge's awareness of the love's limitations contradicts critic Gerald Weales's appraisal of *Picnic* in *American Drama since World War II.* Weales argued that "the prevailing message of the play is that love is a solution to all social, economic, and psychological problems." Certainly this is not true of the original ending that Inge intended for his play, but even the sanitized Broadway version permits Madge to raise doubts about her future, serving up a cynical view of love and its power to solve problems. When Flo tells Madge that Hal "will never be able to support you ... he'll spend all his money on booze. After a while there'll be other women," Madge replies, "I've thought of all those things." Isolated in this last scene, these words indicate that Madge is rejecting reality in favor of romance, but that perception ignores Madge's earlier expressions, her stated desire to leave town and find freedom. It ignores her longing glances toward the train and her fear that all the town has to offer is a

lifetime of clerking in a small store. This information makes Madge's decision to follow Hal far more plausible. To her, Hal represents the best opportunity for escape from the nothingness of small town life, from an existence based solely on beauty. At the beginning of the play, Madge is, indeed, "marking time," as Ima Honaker Herron noted in the *Southwest Review,* she is waiting for something better to come along. By the end of the third act, she has found that something. In leaving she is taking a chance, but she is also hoping to insure that she will not end up one of the lonely, aimless women of this small Kansas town. She has escaped.

Source: Sheri E. Metzger, for *Drama for Students,* Gale, 1999.

John Simon

In this review of a 1994 revival of Picnic, *Simon finds that several decades have not diminished the theatrical power of Inge's 1953 play. The critic praises the work for both its sharply drawn characters and its tangible sense of place, which he feels delivers "a sense of something pent-up longing to break out."*

When is a classic born? When a once highly successful commercial play, revived several decades later, is found to be speaking just as strongly to the time of its revival. At that point you exclaim, "Damn it, this is art, after all!" That has now happened to *Picnic,* thanks to the Roundabout Theatre revival, and one only wishes that the playwright, William Inge, a lonely suicide in 1973 who would have turned 81 this year, could have lived to see it.

Picnic (1953), Inge's second hit after *Come Back, Little Sheba,* ran for two years in sold-out houses, but the one person it never made happy was its author. Inge had originally written a much bleaker play, *Front Porch,* which Joshua Logan helped him rewrite less hopelessly as *Picnic,* and which he later rewrote again, gloomily and unsuccessfully, as *Summer Brave.* What Logan correctly perceived is that a happy ending need not be sappy. When the beautiful but very ordinary Madge leaves her rich boyfriend Alan to run after the handsome, likable, but shiftless Hal, a romantic yearning in the audience is satisfied. But whether the resultant union will be a fulfillment or a fiasco is anybody's guess. Similarly, when the homely schoolteacher Rosemary begs, bullies, and wheedles the bibulous shopkeeper Howard into converting their affair into a marriage, there is no sense of triumph in it. Over all hangs the shadow of

Flo, whose husband died young, and who had to raise Madge and her younger sister, Millie, a tomboy with artistic leanings, all by her weary, lonesome self.

Hal, a college chum of Alan's, dropped out and became a drifter. He returns to their Kansas town in the hope of employment, which Alan warmly offers him. In the end, he doesn't take the job but gets Madge, Alan's girl, leaving his would-be benefactor shaken. Ditto Flo, who so wanted her pretty daughter to marry up, not down. Hal also brings early sorrow to Millie, who forsook her tomboyish ways and put on a dress for a date with him for the Labor Day picnic. That eponymous bucolic romp, which we never actually see, also eludes the hero and heroine, who find a fiercer, less innocent, joy. A happy ending? Sort of, but with shadows lurking all around.

Scott Ellis, who directed, has made small, helpful changes in the text, mostly cutting out the ''Baby''s that Hal keeps hurling at Madge. He also set the action in the thirties to achieve a sense of distance. And he has done wonders with train whistles that weave their siren calls around these hinterland-locked characters. He has called on his (and our) favorite choreographer, Susan Stroman, to devise the crucial dance in which Hal and Madge first make contact. And he has eliminated the two act breaks, thus allowing the hot, clotted atmosphere of Indian summer to hold uninterrupted sway. From Louis Rosen, he got the right, ingenuous music.

Ashley Judd is not so beautiful a Madge as was Janice Rule (''Pre-Raphaelite,'' Logan called her), yet she gives a slow-building, implication-laden, almost too intelligent performance that prevails. Kyle Chandler does not have the animal magnetism of Ralph Meeker's 1953 Hal but brings to the role a sinewy, idiosyncratic presence that gradually scores. Polly Holliday is a touchingly oversolicitous Flo, and Debra Monk a rendingly desperate Rosemary, while Larry Bryggman makes Howard into a splendidly tragicomic figure. The others all contribute handsomely, but none more so than Tony Walton's spot-on scenery, William Ivey Long's canny costuming, or Peter Kaczorowski's lyrical lighting. The true protagonist, though, is the atmosphere: a sense of something pent-up longing to break out. Some escape, others resign themselves; hard to tell the winners from the losers.

Source: John Simon, ''Hairy Fairy Tale'' in *New York,* Vol. 27, no. 18, May 2, 1994.

Richard Hayes

Hayes reviews the original 1953 production of Inge's play, labeling it a powerful work of drama. The critic praises the playwright's fictional world, finding it to have ''more energy and vitality than that of any American dramatist of his generation.''

It is the supreme distinction of Mr. William Inge's world to exist solidly, as an imaginative fact, with more energy and vitality than that of any American dramatist of his generation. Neither deliquescent, as is that of Tennessee Williams, nor shaped by Arthur Miller's blurt polemic rage, it is a world existing solely by virtue of its perceived manners—a perception which, as Mr. Lionel Trilling observed in another connection, is really only a function of love. The poetry, in Mr. Inge's plays, is all in the pity; he gives us the hard naturalistic surface, but with a kind of interior incandescence. What Elizabeth Bowen said of Lawrence defines Mr. Inge also: in his art, every bush burns.

At the center of ''*Picnic*'' is a sexual situation, common and gross, but orchestrated by the playwright with a subtlety of detail and a breadth of reference dazzling in their sensibility; the form, then, is that of a theme with variations. Into a community of women—widowed, single, adolescent, virgin—comes an aggressively virile young man. What the play studies, in all its disturbing ramifications is exclusively his sexual impact on them: the initial movements of distaste and scorn, then a kind of musky stirring of memory and desire, followed by passion and willful hatred, subsiding in quiescence and resignation. It is a graph of emotion most beautifully and skillfully described, issuing in the simple wisdom of Mr. Inge's old spectator who, after this savage eruption of ''life,'' can still see that ''he was a man, and I was a woman, and it was good.''

I have done the fine articulation of Mr. Inge's play the injustice of paraphrase. But nothing in ''*Picnic*'' lacks the sting of truth. All of its observation springs from some point of hard personal knowledge, some perception to which Mr. Inge has come by pain His characters are small, but genuine in their pathos, most moving in their naked impotence before life. The script has, moreover, the benefit of a remarkable production, somewhat coarsened perhaps by Joshua Logan's strident direction, but otherwise limpid, sensual, grateful to the eye and ear.

Its second act concludes with a sustained, complex scene that is among the more notable achieve-

> THE POETRY, IN MR. INGE'S PLAYS, IS ALL IN THE PITY; HE GIVES US THE HARD NATURALISTIC SURFACE, BUT WITH A KIND OF INTERIOR INCANDESCENCE"

ments of the American theatre. It is a kind of ritual dance, involving the boy and girl only as sexual objects, but merciless in its exposure of the skein of envy, desire and psychic desolation which surround them.

Having committed myself to this degree, I feel ungrateful at expressing some fears as to the limitation of Mr. Inge's talent. He seems to me, at this juncture, an artist whose sensibility still exceeds the dispositions of his intellect—that is, his power to order and clarify experience is inadequate to his imaginative apprehension of it. Mr. Inge's "detachment," of which we hear so much, may be esthetically desirable, but I suspect a deeper search might reveal it as the characteristic attitude of a mind stunned, numbed by life. How else account for the curious inertia of Mr. Inge's plays, their lack of moral reverberation, their acquiescence in disaster? I offer these observations not as a reproach, but only as points of departure for an inquiry into the mysterious blemishes which mar this most remarkable American talent.

Source: Richard Hayes, review of *Picnic* in *Commonweal*, Vol. LVII, no. 24, March 20, 1953, p. 603.

Harold Clurman

One of the most respected critics of drama, Clurman reviews the 1953 production of Inge's play. He finds the acting and staging to be substandard, failing to do justice to the playwright's written text.

The young girl in William Inge's new play, "*Picnic*" (Music Box Theater), like Shaw's "ingenue," is waiting for something to happen. But the environment of the American play—specifically Kansas— is a place where nothing can happen to anybody. The women are all frustrated by fearful, jerky men; the men are ignorant, without objective, ideals, or direction—except for their spasmodic sexual impulses. There is no broad horizon for anyone, and a suppressed yammer of desire emanates from every stick and stone of this dry cosmos, in which the futile people burn to cinders.

If you read my description and then see the play you will be either vastly relieved or shockingly disappointed. For though what I have said may still be implicit in the words, it is hardly present on the stage. I happen to have read the playscript before it was put into rehearsal, and I saw in it a laconic delineation of a milieu seen with humor and an intelligent sympathy that was not far from compassion. What is on the stage now is a rather coarse boy-and-girl story with a leeringly sentimental emphasis on naked limbs and "well-stacked" females. It is as if a good Sherwood Anderson novel were skilfully converted into a prurient popular magazine story on its way to screen adaptation.

In this vein the play is extremely well done. It is certainly effective. Joshua Logan, who is a crackerjack craftsman, has done a meticulous, shrewd, thoroughly knowledgeable job of staging. He has made sharply explicit everything which the audience already understands and is sure to enjoy in the "sexy" plot, and has fobbed off everything less obvious to which the audience ought to be made sensitive.

All pain has been removed from the proceedings. The boy in the script who was a rather pathetic, confused, morbidly explosive and bitter character is now a big goof of a he-man whom the audience can laugh at or lust after. The adolescent sister who was a kind of embryo artist waiting to be born has become a comic grotesque who talks as if she suffered from a hare-lip; the drained and repressed mother is presented as a sweet hen almost indistinguishable from her chicks; the tense school teacher bursting with unused vitality is foreshortened as a character and serves chiefly as a utility figure to push the plot. Even the setting, which—for the purposes of the theme—might have suggested the dreary sunniness of the Midwestern flatlands, has been given a romantically golden glow and made almost tropically inviting.

Having seen the play with this bifocal vision— script and production—I cannot be sure exactly what the audience gets from the combination. Lyric realism in the sound 1920 tradition of the prairie novelists is being offered here as the best Broadway corn. In the attempt to make the author's particular kind of sensibility thoroughly acceptable, the play has been vulgarized.

The cast is good—Kim Stanley is particularly talented, though I disliked the characterization imposed on her—and it follows the director with devoted fidelity. There is a new leading lady, Janice Rule, who besides having a lovely voice is unquestionably the most beautiful young woman on our stage today.

Here at any rate is a solid success. But I am not sure whether the author should get down on his knees to thank the director for having made it one or punch him in the nose for having altered the play's values. It is a question of taste.

Source: Harold Clurman, review of *Picnic* in the *Nation*, Vol. 176, no. 10, March 7, 1953, p. 213.

> THE ENVIRONMENT OF THE AMERICAN PLAY—SPECIFICALLY KANSAS—IS A PLACE WHERE NOTHING CAN HAPPEN TO ANYBODY"

Weales, Gerald. "The New Pineros" in *American Drama since World War II,* Harcourt Brace Jovanovich, 1962, pp. 40-56.

SOURCES

Atkinson, Brooks. Review of *Picnic* in the *New York Times,* February 20, 1953.

Chapman, John. Review of *Picnic* in the *Daily News,* February 20, 1953.

Coleman, Robert. Review of *Picnic* in the *Daily Mirror,* February 20, 1953.

Courant, Jane. "Social and Cultural Prophecy in the Works of William Inge" in *Studies in American Drama, 1945-Present,* Volume 6, no. 2, 1991, pp. 135-51.

Hawkins, William. Review of *Picnic* in the *New York World-Telegram* and the *Sun,* February 20, 1953.

Herron, Ima Honaker. "Our Vanishing Towns: Modern Broadway Versions" in the *Southwest Review,* Volume LI, no. 3, Summer, 1966, pp. 209-20.

Kerr, Walter F. Review of *Picnic* in the *New York Herald Tribune,* February 20, 1953.

McClain, John. Review of *Picnic* in the *New York Journal American,* February 20, 1953.

Watts, Richard, Jr. Review of *Picnic* in the *New York Post,* February 20, 1953.

FURTHER READING

Leeson, Richard M. *William Inge: A Research and Production Sourcebook,* Greenwood, 1994.
This is a thorough critical overview of Inge's plays with information about reviews and critical studies.

McClure, Arthur F. *Memories of Splendor: The Midwestern World of William Inge,* Kansas State Historical Society, 1989.
This book contains production information and photographs of Inge and his work.

Shuman, R. Baird. *William Inge,* Twayne, 1996.
This book is primarily a biography of Inge. It also contains a detailed discussion of each of his works.

Voss, Ralph F. *A Life of William Inge: The Strains of Triumph,* University of Kansas Press, 1989.
This is a critical biography of Inge's life.

Wager, Walter. "William Inge" in *The Playwrights Speak,* Delacorte, 1967.
Wagner presents interviews with several contemporary playwrights. This book presents an opportunity to "hear" each writer express his or her thoughts about the art of writing.

Prometheus Bound

AESCHYLUS

456 B.C.

Aeschylus, considered by many scholars as the founder of Greek tragedy, wrote during a period destined to become the Greek Renaissance or Golden Age. Born in 525 B.C. about fourteen miles from Athens into a wealthy, aristocratic family, Aeschylus came of age as his homeland, which had been ruled by the tyrannical dictator Pisistratus and his sons, emerged to become a republic ruled democratically but by the elite. Aeschylus saw battle when Athens had fought against the powerful Persian empire, winning victories at Marathon (490 B.C.) and Salamis (480 B.C.), which have become legendary because of the skill with which the outnumbered Athenians defeated far superior forces.

Athens's role in the Persian wars led it to become the capital of the Dalian League, a collective of Greek city-states, and peace and prosperity led to a cultural flowering rarely equaled in history. In addition to Aeschylus, the century that followed saw such dramatists as Sophocles and Aristophanes, as well as philosophers like Socrates, Plato, and Aristotle. The importance of Aeschylus lies in his position at the beginning of this exciting period in the development of Western culture. His plays and ideas influenced much of what followed.

Aeschylus's importance in theatre history stems from his dramatic innovations which changed Greek tragedy. Traditionally, Greek tragedy consisted of a performance by one actor and the chorus. Aristotle credits Aeschylus as the first playwright to intro-

duce a second actor, thereby allowing true dialogue to create powerful dramatic conflict. Though *Prometheus Bound* contains almost no physical action, extensive character development and emotionally charged psychological action make this a dynamic drama of ideas.

A minority of scholars debate Aeschylus's authorship of *Prometheus Bound*. Because of positions the play presents on various religious and cultural issues, as well as because of certain poetic peculiarities, some believe it written by another author. Most scholars do believe Aeschylus wrote *Prometheus Bound*, however, and in any event, the authorship debate does not detract from the play's powerful drama.

AUTHOR BIOGRAPHY

Aeschylus was born in 525 B.C. in Eleusis, Greece. His father, Euphorion, headed a wealthy, aristocratic family. Little is known about Aeschylus's childhood. Growing up during the Persian Wars, he fought in the battle of Marathon (490 B.C.), in which a citizen army of Athenians proved victorious against the numerically superior invading army. His brother, Cynegirus, died at Marathon, though Aeschylus fought on. Many scholars believe the playwright also participated in the battle at Salamis (480 B.C.), among other engagements.

Following Greek resistance of the Persian Empire, Athens established its independence as a democracy of the elite and intellectual. Aeschylus came of age during this exciting time, when Athens became the headquarters of the Dalian League of Greek city-states. This brought prosperity to the city and made Athens the center of the Greek cultural world. Critics point to the relationship between the problems and challenges facing the emerging Attic republic and the themes Aeschylus treats in his plays: crime and punishment, law and revenge, tyranny and revolution.

Although scholars credit Aeschylus with writing more than ninety tragedies and satyr plays, only seven exist today in their entirety. They are: *The Persians* (first presented in 472 B.C.); *Seven against Thebes* (467 B.C.); *The Suppliant Maidens* (463 B.C.); the *Oresteia* trilogy, comprised of *Agamemnon*, the *Choephoroe* (also known as *The Libation Bearers*), and the *Eumenides* (also known as *The Kindly Ones*), which was first presented in

Aeschylus

458 B.C.); and *Prometheus Bound* (probably written in the 450s B.C. but first produced after Aeschylus's death in 456 B.C.). These plays were presented during the dramatic competitions held during religious festivals for Dionysus. Aeschylus first competition was around 500 B.C., and he won first prize thirteen times.

Scholars believe that tragedy, which had a complex social and religious function in Greek society, grew out of ritualized recitations. Such readings, like those of Homer's *Iliad* or *Odyssey*, might be social, while others conducted at temples on feast days might be religious. Early drama, such as that presented by Thespis, included only one actor and the chorus. Aristotle credits Aeschylus as the first to introduce a second actor, reduce the significance of the chorus, and highlight the role of dialogue. This accounts for why many scholars consider Aeschylus the founder of Greek tragedy because the actor he added enabled true dialogue and dramatic conflict to take place.

Aeschylus died in 456 B.C., in the Greek colony of Gela, Sicily. According to legend, he met his death when an eagle, trying to crack a tortoise's shell, dropped it on the playwright's head. Aeschylus wrote the epitaph for his own tombstone, which underscores his military activities but makes no mention of his plays. Some critics interpret this to suggest that Aeschylus believed his plays contributed to Attic religious and political culture, and in that sense, that he regarded the role of playwright itself as patriotic.

PLOT SUMMARY

A peak in the Caucasus Mountains. Force and Violence have conveyed Prometheus to the mountain, where Hephestus, the god of fire, binds Prometheus to the mountain, expressing pity and reluctance. Force, the pragmatic agent of Zeus, urges Hephestus on, condemning his sympathy for the rebellious Titan as useless and threatening reprisals from Zeus. Force declares that suffering will make Prometheus accept Zeus's authority, and Hephestus states that in time, Zeus's tyranny may moderate. Throughout their exchange, Violence says nothing.

Force, Violence, and Hephestus exit. Prometheus speaks a soliloquy which begs sympathy from his mother Earth, condemns Zeus's tyranny, and identifies the cause of his predicament, that he "loved man too well." Prometheus indicates that he realized the consequences of his actions before he intervened to save humanity, saying "All, all I knew before, all that should be." This shows Prometheus's foresight, which is the meaning of his name. His foresight proves ambiguous, however, for later in the play, the Titan will express surprise at the intensity of his punishment. Here, though, he stoically councils himself to "Bear without struggle what must be. Necessity is strong and ends our strife." This statement also proves important later, for while Force has claimed that "No one is free but Zeus," the play shows that everyone, even Zeus, must bow to Necessity (i.e. destiny and justice). For Prometheus, this realization proves a revelation.

The Chorus of sea nymphs, the Oceanides, enters, riding in a winged car. The Oceanides sympathize with Prometheus, their kinsman, informing him that "By new laws Zeus is ruling without law," for he has cast the defeated Titans into Tarturus. Prometheus indicates his knowledge of the way by which Zeus will fall from power and his refusal to reconcile with the tyrant. This and similar statements undermine the audience's faith in Prometheus's foreknowledge, as the Athenian audience knew that

Zeus would not fall. The Titan has knowledge of future events, but in some ways his insight remains incomplete and ambiguous. Prometheus himself contributes to this ambiguity when he says, hopefully, "yet some time he [Zeus] shall be mild of mood . . . and run to meet me. Then peace will come and love between us two."

The rebel Titan then explains how he came to this predicament, his support for Zeus's rebellion, his pity for humanity, and his subsequent punishment for stealing fire from heaven and giving it to people. With fire, he gave humanity knowledge of medicine, astronomy, agriculture, and other things, as well as "blind hopes."

Ocean enters, riding on a four-footed bird, an image that would appear ridiculous to the audience and thus identifies this as a comic interlude. As Prometheus's kinsman, Ocean feels sympathy, but primarily a pompous wind-bag, he mostly expresses self-importance. Ocean, believing that Zeus respects him, offers to intercede for Prometheus with the tyrant, if only the rebel will control his temper and moderate his behavior. Prometheus thanks Ocean for his wisdom, which, ironically, allowed him to escape the punishment Zeus inflicted on the other Titans. Prometheus expresses his pity for his brother Atlas, who now shoulders the world, and for Typhon, a dragon, both punished by Zeus. He then advises Ocean to leave, suggesting that Zeus might punish him for trying to help Prometheus. Driven primarily by fear and self-interest, Ocean departs.

The Chorus speaks of Zeus's tyranny, while Prometheus tells of human suffering and his attempt to alleviate it. The Chorus claims that "Zeus orders all things," but Prometheus corrects them, indicating that even Zeus must be subordinate to Necessity. The sinner's destiny results from "Retribution" for a past wrong which "unforgetting . . . Fate" never fails to punish. This dialogue also reveals that Prometheus, like the human race he aided, has "blind hope" that justice will be victorious and that his situation will improve.

Io enters, telling her tragic history. The half-mortal daughter of the sea god, she is romantically pursued by Zeus. Zeus's wife, Hera, has discovered her husband's love for Io and punished the innocent girl, having her followed first by Argos, whose thousand eyes watch her constantly, and then by a gadfly. Through no fault of her own, Io falls victim to Zeus's lust and Hera's jealousy. Prometheus tells Io about her future revenge, which is tied with his own. Prometheus reveals that he knows the circumstances surrounding Zeus's ultimate fall: Zeus will impregnate Io, and one of her distant descendants, Hercules, will destroy the tyrant. As Normand Berlin observed in *The Secret Cause: A Discussion of Tragedy,* the "meeting of Io and Prometheus is the central episode of the play. It tells us of the future; it reminds us of the past; it covers the geography of the known world." Io's tale moves the Chorus, and, as she exits, they express sympathy for her and fear of finding themselves in a similar situation.

Hermes enters, telling Prometheus that Zeus has heard his boasts of knowing about his downfall. Hermes demands to know the name of the sexual liaison which will lead to Zeus's destruction. Prometheus mocks Hermes as a child and refuses to tell him anything. Hermes threatens additional punishment and predicts future torments.

The Chorus remains with Prometheus as Hermes departs, and his prediction comes true. Amid thunder and lightening, the earth cracks, ready to swallow up the rebel Titan. As the play ends, Prometheus cries out, "I am wronged."

CHARACTERS

Chorus of Oceanids

Earth and Sky are the parents of Oceanus and Tethys, who are the parents of the Oceanids. Aeschylus's mythology, which names Prometheus's mother as Earth, makes the Titan uncle to the Oceanids. Like their father Oceanus, they sympathize with Prometheus, but more bravely. Partially out of fear of Zeus, however, they disapprove of Prometheus's behavior, urging him to attempt a reconciliation. Fear of Zeus strikes the Oceanids when they learn of Io's suffering, but still they remain with Prometheus at the end of the play, when he is cast into Tartarus.

Force and Violence

As the play opens, Force and Violence accompany Hephestus as he impales Prometheus to a peak in the Caucasus mountains. Force remains blindly obedient to Zeus, showing no pity for the Titan and respecting only Zeus's pure power. Force's attitude is realistic. When Hephestus laments that it was his skill at metallurgy that led Zeus to select him for the task of fastening Prometheus to the mountain, Force admonishes him, "Why blame your skill? These troubles here were never caused by it." Force's reverence for Zeus's power leads him to error, however, when he states that "No one is free but Zeus." As the drama unfolds, it is revealed that even Zeus remains subject to Necessity. Note that Force and Violence, who does not speak, travel together, one symbolizing power and the other the way power manifests itself. In spite of their power, Force, Violence, and even Zeus require the intelligence and foresight of Prometheus to understand the cosmos truly.

Hephestus

The god of fire, Hephestus has a distant relation with Prometheus through Uranos. As the god of fire, he is directly affected by Prometheus's theft of fire and his subsequent gift of the element to humanity. Despite this challenge to his jurisdiction and power, however, Hephestus remains sympathetic to Prometheus's suffering. Associated with the forge and volcanos, Hephestus pities Prometheus but does his duty, mostly because he fears Zeus.

Hermes

Child of Zeus and Maia, Hermes is the messenger of the gods. He enters at the play's end, trying to convince Prometheus to reveal the secret that will lead to Zeus's downfall, but the Titan refuses. Hermes taunts Prometheus and threatens him with further punishment, but the Titan ridicules him. Young and inexperienced, Hermes proves a poor mediator between Zeus and Prometheus, ultimately appearing juvenile and intemperate

Io

Niece of the Chorus, Io is the half-human daughter of a river god. Through no fault of her own, she finds herself desired by Zeus and therefore persecuted by his jealous wife Hera. She has been pursued and watched, first by Argos, whose thousand eyes never close, and then by a gadfly which seems Argos's spirit. Like Prometheus, she too suffers the injustice of Zeus's tyranny, though she is completely innocent of any transgression. Prometheus predicts that one of Io's decedents, Hercules, will revenge her by overcoming Zeus and killing the eagle that daily feeds on Prometheus's liver. This prediction becomes partially true: Hercules does kill the eagle, but Prometheus and Zeus reconcile, leaving Zeus ruler. Thematically, Io's movement contrasts with Prometheus's stasis. Physically, Io appears to be half woman-half cow.

Ocean

A titan who rules the watery elements, he is brother to Earth, Prometheus's mother, and so the rebel's uncle and father to the Oceanid chorus. Pretentious and foppish, Ocean offers to intervene with Zeus on Prometheus's behalf, showing off an influence with Zeus which he does not have. He advises reconciliation, but he cowers before Zeus's authority. Some critics see him as comic relief. In his role as the foolish advisor, he is reminiscent of Polonius in Shakespeare's *Hamlet.*

Prometheus

Greek cosmology describes three generations of gods, (1) Heaven (Earth and Sky) and the Titans, (2) Kronos, and (3) Zeus and his Olympian hierarchy. Prometheus was the son of Iapetus, a Titan, and Clymene, an ocean nymph.

Prometheus helped Zeus defeat the Titans and helped eliminate conflicts among the gods by assigning each specific jurisdictions.

During this time, humanity, created, according to some versions of the myth, by Prometheus, lived a primitive existence without hope. Zeus decided to let humanity perish, so he could create a new race himself, but Prometheus pitied people and gave them fire stolen from heaven. Fire, as Prometheus explains in his monologue, brought with it technology and astronomy, mathematics and language, agriculture and medicine, but most of all, hope. Zeus, angered by Prometheus's interference in his plans, punishes the Titan by impaling him on a mountain peak, where he is partially devoured by an eagle each day. Prometheus knows but refuses to tell how Zeus will fall. In time, Zeus gains sympathy and Prometheus humility. They reconcile. Zeus forgives the Titans and Prometheus. Acknowledging Zeus's power, the rebel exchanges a chain of flowers for the metal chain he wore.

THEMES

Guilt and Innocence

Aeschylus believed that the gods punished those guilty of human pride (hubris) by trapping them in a web of crime and revenge, from which only the gods could free them. While the reasons behind the gods' actions remain mysterious, for Aeschylus, humanity must subordinate itself to divine will, which ultimately achieves justice. In *Prometheus Bound,* this notion of inherited guilt emerges during the Titan's discussion of Necessity.

Love and Passion

Zeus feels lust for Io and follows her, hoping to seduce her. Although Io wants nothing to do with Zeus, he infects her dreams, causes her to be driven from her family and home, and sees her tormented by his jealous wife, Hera. His lust makes him behave unreasonably and Io, an innocent person, suffers because of him. According to classical ethics, as exemplified by Aristotle's *Nichomachean Ethics,* for example, moderate, reasonable behavior best suits one for a happy and ethical life.

Jealousy

Io's suffering stems from the jealousy of Zeus's wife, Hera. Suspecting Zeus of desiring this innocent woman, Hera has her followed by Argos, whose thousand eyes never entirely close and then tormented by a gadfly. Io has committed no offense, however, and suffers unjust punishment. Jealousy, like lust, interferes with a person's judgement and makes them behave unreasonably.

Rebellion

Although the reasons for Prometheus's rebellion may provoke sympathy, such behavior can disrupt social order. At the same time, Zeus's tyrannical behavior deserves, even requires, resistance. Significantly, the play presents the conflict between two value systems personified by two powerful individuals. In *Prometheus Bound,* rebellion seems justified, though within what is known of the *Prometheia* trilogy, mercy and patience in the end become the order of the day.

Parent-Child Relations

To some degree, every generation of children finds themselves in conflict with their parents' value system. Parents require obedience, children independence. Parents see their children in a specific way and act toward them according to that image. The children themselves may have outgrown that image, though, and see themselves differently. In any event, children must make a place for them-

TOPICS FOR FURTHER STUDY

- One of the questions raised by *Prometheus Bound* pertains to the meaning of justice and the power to make and enforce laws. Most readers would agree that Prometheus does no wrong in helping a suffering humanity which Zeus seems prepared to allow to perish. From Zeus's point of view, though, Prometheus seems a rebel, going behind his ruler's back and against his wishes. Have you encountered a similar situation in literature, a story from the news, or an episode from your life, one in which two different value systems compete to create an ethical dilemma? How would you make such a decision? More specifically, what criteria would you use to help you arrive at an ethical decision?

- Consider the issue of gender in Greek mythology and the ways it presents images of men and women. For example, both Prometheus and Io suffer because of Zeus, but the Titan, active, suffers as a consequence of his action, while Io, passive, suffers because Zeus finds her sexually attractive. Compare Io to Earth, who seems knowing and sympathetic. Or research other versions of the Prometheus myth. Based on further research into classical culture, how do Greek myths represent women? Men?

- In addition to fire, *Prometheus Bound* says that the Titan brought many gifts to humanity, including mathematics, language, medicine, and agriculture. Myths like this serve to explain the origins of a society, how it began and evolved. Study the role of mythology in creating social and cultural identity and as a vehicle of history and spirituality.

- Consider the the tale of *Prometheus Bound* from Zeus's point of view. How might he view Prometheus's rebellion, his interference with humanity, his threats? Can you present an image of Zeus that justifies Prometheus's imprisonment?

---

selves in the world and do so with some degree of independence. *Prometheus Bound* presents a variety of parent-child relationships, from Kronos patricide to Zeus's rebellion to the positive connection between Prometheus and his mother, Earth. Further reading in Classical mythology will reveal additional examples of fond and problematic family relations.

Atonement and Forgiveness

Most viewers see Prometheus, particularly as he appears in this first play of the *Prometheia* trilogy, as a benevolent rebel struggling against tyranny, suffering because of his love of humanity. In this respect, he resembles Jesus, who according to Christian theology suffered to save humanity. In art and religion, such struggle and pain is often linked with spirituality and redemption. A final element—forgiveness—also commonly occurs, as seen when Christ forgives his murderers (''Father forgive them for they know not what they do'') and,

in what is known of the now lost *Prometheus Unbound*, when the rebellious Titan reconciles with Zeus.

Law and Order

On one level, *Prometheus Bound* presents a conflict between two models of law, one, Zeus's, aligned with Power and another, Prometheus's, identified with sympathy. From Zeus's perspective, his monarchy requires obedience and Prometheus, by helping humanity, has broken the law and deserves punishment. Prometheus, however, has to negotiate between two codes of law, Zeus's rule in which might makes right and his own, motivated by his pity for humanity. The play explores the relationships among law, justice, and mercy, the latter a theme of greater significance in the context of the three play trilogy, the *Prometheia*. From fragments of the now lost sequels, it is known that Prometheus does acknowledge Zeus's law, exchanging his chains of steel for chains of flowers, and Zeus learns to show mercy, freeing the imprisoned Titans, including Prometheus.

STYLE

Chorus

In Greek tragedy, a dozen or so men comprise the chorus, who comment on and interpret the action unfolding on stage and underscore the play's themes and conflicts. In many ways, they stand in for the audience. For example, the Oceanides react to Prometheus and Io much as the audience would; they ask the questions and express the emotions likely to arise during an audience's viewing of the play. The Chorus performed their lyrics in song and dance, though the music and choreography have been lost.

Tragedy

According to Aristotle's *Poetics,* a drama about an elevated hero who, because of some tragic character flaw or misdeed (a hamartia), brings ruin on himself. While not exactly a flaw, Prometheus's love for humanity can be seen as the element of his character which precipitates his imprisonment, for it leads him to go against Zeus will and challenge his authority. Prometheus exhibits an element of pride (hubris) in his belief that he knows better than Zeus (even if it is agreed that, in his sympathetic attitude toward humanity, he does) and his desire for revenge against Zeus.

Hamartia

In a tragedy, the event or act that causes the hero's or heroine's downfall is known as hamartia. In *Prometheus Bound,* the Titan's rebellion against Zeus in giving fire to humanity sets the tragedy in motion and leads to his imprisonment.

Catharsis

At the end of a successful tragedy, the spectators experience a release of energy, catharsis, because they have felt pity and fear, pity for the person suffering the tragic fate, then fear that a similar fate might befall them. Viewers might feel this toward Prometheus, afraid that they might find themselves facing an ethical dilemma on a grand scale. On the other hand, audiences might more generally experience catharsis in regard to Io, an innocent person who suffers through no fault of her own—the viewer hopes that such a capricious fate never strikes them.

Tetralogy

During dramatic competition in Athens, held annually to celebrate the god Dionysus, called the Dionysia, winning playwrights presented a tetralogy of four related dramatic works, which usually consisted of three tragedies and a satyr play.

Satyr Play

A broad comedy performed with three tragedies that usually burlesqued the same legend dramatized by the tragedies.

HISTORICAL CONTEXT

When Aeschylus was born in 525 B.C. outside Athens, the city could be characterized as an unimportant polis (i.e. city-state) ruled by the tyrant Hippias. In 510 B.C., a political reformer, Clisthenes, overthrew the tyrant and developed the government into a republic ruled democratically by the elite. Reforms lessened the power of the nobility and allowed non-noble landowners to participate in government. Though conflicts between the nobility and commoners (known as the demos, hence the word democracy) remained, Athens developed into a well governed city-state led by a vital, informed citizenry.

Those citizens proved to be competent soldiers as well and fought bravely against invasion by the Persian empire. Athens and the Greeks defeated the Persians, winning land and sea victories at Marathon (490 B.C.) and Salamis (480 B.C.), respectively, against numerically superior forces.

Athens's victorious role in the Persian wars led to its selection as capital of the Dalian League, a collective of Greek city-states, and peace and prosperity led to a cultural flowering rarely equaled in

COMPARE & CONTRAST

- **525-456 B.C.:** In 510 B.C., a political reformer named Clisthenes overthrows the tyrant Hippias and establishes in Athens a republic ruled by popular democracy.

  Today: Democracy in its various forms remains one of the most important philosophies of world government. While democracy today takes various forms—direct, representative, presidential, parliamentary—all these concepts have their genesis with the Attic republic.

- **525-456 B.C.:** As the capital of the Dalian League, Athens evolves into a commercial and cultural center, with visitors and residents from throughout the known world. Teachers, artists, philosophers, and religious leaders gather at public forums to discuss their ideas and opinions.

  Today: American society mirrors Athens in its emphasis on freedom of speech and religion, and its belief in the strength of diversity and multiculturalism.

- **525-456 B.C.:** Theatre in Athens is largely

comprised of a religious festival celebrating the god Dionysus. Very large outdoor theatres hold as many as 15,000 people in festivals which last several days.

  Today: Theatre is a mostly secular form of entertainment. Plays are viewed in theatres much smaller than those of the Greeks. Festivals that celebrate drama still exist, though they pale in size to similar events featuring musical performers.

- **525-456 B.C.:** In classical Greece, only the upper- and upper middle-classes of men receive an education. Generally, they study with tutors at home and then attend an academy such as the ones run by Plato and Aristotle.

  Today: In America, compulsory education for all citizens through high school presents opportunities for men and women, as does the possibility of pursuing one's studies by attending college.

---

history. Athens evolved into one of the most important cultural and trading centers in the world. The next century was considered a Greek Golden Age, which saw such dramatists as Sophocles and Aristophanes, as well as philosophers like Socrates, Plato, and Aristotle.

Greek tragedies like those of Aeschylus were performed in Athens as part of the Great Dionysia, an annual religious festival dedicated to the god Dionysus held in early Spring. First, a statue of Dionysus was removed from his temple within sight of the theatre, carried in procession to the country, and returned to Athens. Next followed four days of performances, three of tragedies and one of comedies. The tragedies were selected in a contest among competing dramatists, a contest which Aeschylus won thirteen times. Each winning dramatist then presented a tetralogy of three tragedies and a satyr

play, in performances which began in the morning and lasted most of the day.

All of Athens became involved in the celebration. A local magistrate organized the procession and selected playwrights for the competition. He identified wealthy citizens to pay for masks and costumes and to select a chorus. Sponsors also may have had some input into selection of the contest judges and the plays selected for competition, though the playwright retained responsibility for his cast. Citizen judges swore to remain impartial and authorities severely punished misconduct of any kind during the celebration.

In Athens, performances took place outdoors in a huge theatre constructed on the hillside of the Acropolis. To imagine the theatre, picture a large, semi-circular fan. The orchestra, where the actors performed, and an altar, stood in the middle of the semi-circle. A stage building called a skene, in which actors donned masks and costumes, stood behind the orchestra. Stage sets of temples or landscapes could be displayed on the front of the skene. Benches for seating an audience of as many as 15,000 people radiated out around the orchestra. Women and children could attend, though they may have been seated apart from the men.

These theatre festivals began during the sixth century with displays of individual and choral songs and dancing. Credit for the first tragedy goes to Thespis in 536-533 B.C.; the play featured a Chorus of perhaps a dozen men and a single actor. Tragic theatre evolved under Aeschylus, who introduced the second actor, and developed further under Sophocles, who introduced the third. Actors wore masks and tunics, which may have been colored to indicate their roles (e.g. mourners in black, priests in white, kings in purple). Actors needed strong voices to make themselves heard in the large theatre and the ability to impersonate, since each actor played several characters in each play.

As the center of the Dalian League, Athens fast became the most important city in Greece, an intellectual and cultural as well as commercial and mercantile center. The Great Dionysia festival drew audiences from throughout the Mediterranean, and everyone from commoners to nobles, from merchants to ambassadors attended.

CRITICAL OVERVIEW

The title character of *Prometheus Bound,* perhaps more than any other hero, serves scholars as a sort of critical mirror. Reformers, for example, consider Prometheus a revolutionary hero, like Satan, a principled rebel who sacrifices himself for others, like Jesus, or an ethical individual who suffers in the face of absolute power, like Job. Authoritarian critics, on the other hand, understand Prometheus's urge to save humanity but condemn his disregard for hierarchical authority in doing so. Freudian and psychoanalytic critics discuss the play's complicated parent-child relations (e.g. Zeus's overthrow of his father, Kronos; Prometheus's connection with

his mother). Historical and cultural critics discuss the play in terms of contemporary events, analyzing, for example, Aeschylus's use of medical terminology in character dialogue and considering what this tells scholars about scientific knowledge at the time.

What may account for the popularity of Prometheus as a character is that fact that all these opinions seem right, if not in *Prometheus Bound* itself, then in the context of the *Prometheia* trilogy. Though two of the three plays have been lost, there exist enough fragments and commentary to understand how the story would have been resolved. The result is a rich and complex symbolic narrative of ideas.

Of foremost consideration is what the play tells audiences about Aeschylus's thinking on the human condition and tragedy. Because Prometheus's intervention to minimize human suffering comes from pity, Normand Berlin saw him as "a creature of feeling." As Berlin wrote in *The Secret Cause: A Discussion of Tragedy, Prometheus Bound* offers "the tragic condition, here encompassing god and man, macrocosm and microcosm, and brilliantly displaying the contradictory perspective of tragedy, whereby the victorious tyrant is the victim of destiny and his defeated, suffering victim is victorious in possessing knowledge of that destiny—while intelligent mankind victoriously piercing through layer and after layer of ignorance and chaos, progressing in the course of time to mastery of his world, remains helpless beneath the arbitrary and dark control of both Zeus and destiny."

On the other hand, some critics believe that present circumstance did play a role in Aeschylus's choice and treatment of subject matter. They discuss the play's exploration of themes like tyranny and revolution in the context of Athens's evolution from tyranny to democracy which accompanied its defeat of the Persian Empire. As the play opens, Zeus's cosmic government appears as brutal despotism. He acts, according to George Thomson, as a complete tyrant: ruling without laws, contemplating the murder of humanity, seducing female subjects, and suspicious even of his allies. For James Scully, Prometheus's predicament resembles that of any political prisoner being brainwashed; he has been isolated by Zeus, tortured by Hephaistos and Force, and interrogated and brow-beaten by Hermes, an official of the police state.

A depiction of Prometheus bringing fire down from the heavens to bestow on suffering humanity

Although *Prometheus Bound* dramatizes a righteous rebellion against a tyrant, Philo M. Buck, Jr. pointed out that it tells only part of the story. As the first part in a trilogy, much of which has been lost, the viewer must turn to existing fragments of the sequels to learn of Prometheus's ultimate reconciliation with Zeus.

Buck believed that Zeus's actions result from his inexperience as a leader and his unstable grasp on power. Zeus's goal, to establish order after overthrowing the anarchy of the earlier divine rulers, seems laudable, and requires, at least initially, a strong ruler. Zeus must punish the disobedient Prometheus, despite his noble reasons for revolt. Still, according to fragments of the second and third plays in the *Prometheia,* Zeus later moderates his tyranny and learns mercy, forgiving the Titans and ultimately reconciling himself with Prometheus. Justice, according to Buck, must never be arbitrary but rather human and reasonable. If Prometheus, like Socrates, has been unjustly convicted, ''he must wait for justice to release him. And this was done in the last and lost play, where allegorically the mutual claims of justice and mercy are reconciled in the reign of intelligent law.'' *Prometheus Bound,* which explores such themes as justice, ''the tyranny of the majority, the caprice of misdirected reformers,'' conveys an important social message to ''Athens, now embarked after the anarchy of the wars and the Tyrants in an effort to build a just constitution and establish human law.''

Finally, space and time, movement and stasis, memory and history all prove important motifs in *Prometheus Bound.* Almost no physical action takes place during the play, where the drama focuses on character. Consequently, stasis becomes thematically important. Central to the play are the conversations between Prometheus, doomed to remain trapped on a rock, and Io, a wanderer doomed to wander still farther. She tells Prometheus about her journeys and past, then Prometheus foretells her journeys and future. That prediction includes the story of Hercules, Io's distant relation and avenger, whose life also consists of journeys and sufferings. According to myth, Prometheus aids Hercules by helping him accomplish his labors, after which Hercules kills the eagle which feeds on the Titan's liver.

Zeus has victimized both Prometheus, who remains stationary, and Io, who seems doomed to wander. As Berlin pointed out, Io's experiences ''span the ages, while her wanderings which seem to take in the known world of the time, widen the canvas—so that Aeschylus's *Prometheus,* having already presented the progress of human consciousness through the years, seems to gather all time and all space to itself, thereby making the mood of fatalism pervasive and extensive.'' Thus, memory and foreknowledge—movement in time— connect with Io's and Hercules's journeying—movement in space. Together, their stories (and that of the *Promethia*) comprise a history that reaches from the rise of human civilization to the fifth century present, and takes in every country from one end of the known world to the other. Memory becomes history, while geography becomes empire.

In the end, regardless of which critic's argument readers find most persuasive, *Prometheus Bound* remains a moving text that leaves everyone with plenty to think about. And ultimately, its story remains optimistic. As Scully observed in a translation of *Prometheus Bound,* the ''general drift of the trilogy . . . [is] a universal progress from confusion and torment, at all levels of the universe, toward peace and joy.''

CRITICISM

Arnold Schmidt

Schmidt is a professor of English at California State University, Stanislaus. In this essay he examines the myth of Prometheus, discussing the missing plays of the trilogy that concluded the Titan's tale and also appraising Aeschylus's play as a psychodrama—a struggle in personality and ethics between the title character and Zeus.

Poets and scholars have traditionally read the tale of Prometheus as a lesson in revolution, seeing the imprisoned Titan as an emblem of the lone individual in heroic rebellion against mindless tyranny. This view became more common during the French Revolution and Napoleonic periods of the nineteenth century, when Prometheus became a symbol first of freedom, and later, of the leader Napoleon himself. We encounter this image of Prometheus in poems by various Romantic era poets, in particular Lord Byron and Percy Bysshe Shelley. Shelley, himself an accomplished classical scholar who translated works by Plato and the other notable Greek dramatists, wrote *Prometheus Unbound,* his version of Aeschylus's work that speculates what might have occurred when the Titan became free.

Remember that *Prometheus Bound* forms only the first part of Aeschylus's trilogy—commonly known as the *Prometheia*—whose other plays have been lost. We know, for example that the story of *Prometheus Bound* continued in *Prometheus Unbound* and *Prometheus the Fire-Bearer.* Significantly, Shelley's version ends with Zeus defeated, dragged down into darkness by Demogorgon, a figure of Necessity. Everything we know about Aeschylus's version of the play, however, tells another tale, that of reconciliation between the rebel and the tyrant. While the romantic version retains a certain appeal in its representation of heroic individualism and its vision of redemptive love leading to an earthly utopia, Aeschylus's version raises a different set of intriguing themes and questions. Enough fragments of the lost *Prometheia* plays remain to provide an outline of Aeschylus's conclusion, indicating that after thousands of years, Zeus and Prometheus reconciled, the tyrant learning mercy and the rebel obedience.

If we consider *Prometheus Bound* in the context of themes laid out in the trilogy, the *Prometheia*

WHAT DO I READ NEXT?

- Some have compared Prometheus with the figure of Satan, particularly the way Milton presents him in *Paradise Lost,* where his rebellion has political overtones. Students might consider what it means to be a hero and compare Satan with Milton's version of the story. *Samson Agonestes* offers another tale in which a proud individual suffers, learns a lesson in humility and inner strength, and sacrifices himself for what seems a worthy cause.

- *Prometheus Bound* offers themes of law and justice that are familiar to many of William Shakespeare's plays. *Merchant of Venice* explores the relationship between justice and mercy while *Measure for Measure,* treats the same themes from the perspective of the ideal ruler.

- The myth of Prometheus became tremendously popular during the nineteenth century. Two well-known retellings of the myth come from a husband and wife, Mary Shelley and Percy Bysshe Shelley. Mary Shelley's version of the myth, her

Frankenstein: The Modern Prometheus, is considered a masterpiece of horror fiction and has been adapted into numerous plays and films. Based on his study of Greek literature and philosophy, Percy Shelley composed what he believed might be a conclusion for *Prometheus Bound,* entitled *Prometheus Unbound.* Written in verse, many consider this his finest composition.

- After the French Revolution, the rebel Prometheus became synonymous with Napoleon and such romantic poets as Byron and Shelley wrote poems on this theme. For the historically minded, many good biographies tell the story of the Corsican who rose from artillery officer to Emperor of the French empire, though J. Christopher Herold's *The Age of Napoleon* may be one place to begin. Several twentieth century figures take on Promethean dimensions, suffering individual pain while struggling against tyranny for the good of humanity, including Mahatma Ghandi and Martin Luther King.

---

can be read as a psychological and political allegory, representing the human microcosm (i.e. the mind) and macrocosm (i.e. society). Arguably, the play suggests that freedom and authority must be balanced in any ethical person, leader, and/or society. We might see this as a shift in the notion of the hero, evolving from that of Homer's Odysseus, a wily trickster given to spontaneity and temper, to the moderate, reasonable individual validated in Aristotle's *Nichomachean Ethics.* Since Homer comes before Aeschylus and Aristotle afterward, the *Prometheia* may mark a transition between these two models of the hero. After all, the Prometheus of *Prometheus Bound* resembles Odysseus in many ways, and what we know about the reconciled Prometheus of *Prometheus Unbound* exhibits many of the characteristics Aristotle applauds. This contradicts those wanting to read the Prometheus myth as solely a struggle between two

absolutes: tyranny and freedom. Instead, being an ethical, individual ruler or society requires balance.

Prometheus faces a classic ethical dilemma, in which he must choose between two mutually exclusive systems of law. From the Olympian point of view, Prometheus wrongly disobeys authority, given classical society's need and respect for hierarchy, but he acts with noble purpose, to save humanity from destruction. Like Antigone (who defied her ruler by performing a forbidden funeral ritual for her slain brother), Prometheus commits the lesser wrong—disobeying a tyrant—and prevents the greater wrong—the destruction of the helpless human race. Seen from the human perspective, Prometheus's actions seem heroic, while seen from the vantage point of Olympus, they seem like betrayal.

So far, we have discussed what the *Prometheia* says about society, about the ruler and the ruled. By

---

reading this play as a psychodrama, we can see that Zeus and Prometheus can represent two sides of a single personality. After all, their personalities share much in common: pride, temper, stubbornness, vengefulness. If at first this seems a stretch, consider that in many ways, Prometheus's character and behavior appear ambiguous. He presents himself as the sympathetic champion of humanity, but he aided Zeus in overturning his father Kronos and the Titans. That means Prometheus also overturned the authority of his own father, the Titan Iapetus, who with the others ends up imprisoned in Tarturus.

This raises the question: why does Prometheus help humanity? He claims he feels pity for peoples' suffering, but might part of his motive to be to challenge Zeus? After all, Prometheus, having already seen the overthrow of two dynasties, now participates in the founding of a third. Remember that Zeus cannot win without the help of Prometheus, who explains that Zeus will win, not by force, but by strategy, by freeing some giants who will fight against the Titans. Thus intelligence and not physical power alone allows the overthrow of Kronos and the rise of Zeus.

Hesiod's *Theogony* describes three generations of gods, (1) Heaven (i.e. Earth and Sky [Uranus]) and the Titans, (2) Kronos, and (3) Zeus and his Olympian hierarchy. Kronos overturned his father Uranus just as Zeus overthrew him, so these first two dynasties prove violent and chaotic. Zeus's reign eliminated the anarchy that existed among the Titans and earlier gods. His success cannot be viewed as a solitary success, however. Zeus created a sense of order because Prometheus assigned different jurisdictions to the various Olympian gods. Good social order comes from a balance between Zeus's power and Prometheus's intelligence. Neither can succeed entirely without the other. Given his importance to helping Zeus gain power, might not Prometheus feel too proud to be subservient?

If this accurately characterizes the struggle between the tyrant and the Titan, what makes Zeus change his mind? Much time has passed since Prometheus's original offense, and Zeus has begun to soften—according to the *Prometheia,* in part because he pities Hercules, the mortal child he fathered with Io's descendent Alcmene.

James Scully's edition of *Prometheus Bound* contains several fragments from the lost trilogy. According to book four of his *Geography,* the Greek geographer Strabo (64 B.C. to 21 A.D.) quoted from the now lost version of *Prometheus*

Unbound. Hercules, threatened during his Labor to retrieve the golden apples from the Hesperides. Prometheus predicts that Zeus will help Hercules, saying, ''You'll come upon / the Ligyes, a horde / that doesn't know what fear is . . . / As fate has it: you'll run out of weapons,. . . / But Zeus will see you / bewildered there / and pity you.'' Zeus thus comes to Hercules's aid and saves his life.

Zeus's reconciliation with Prometheus involves a compromise on both their parts, with Zeus learning to feel pity and the Titan learning submission. Zeus indicates his victory gently, however. The *Deipnosophistae,* written about 200 A.D. by the Greco-Egyptian scholar Athenaeus, explained that in *Prometheus Unbound,* when Zeus frees Prometheus, the Titan agrees to substitute a chain of flowers for his chain of steel. Prometheus would wear the garland as painless punishment for his resistance to Zeus and as a symbol of his submission to his law and authority.

Love factors into the reconciliation, as illustrated by two predictions, Prometheus's to Io and Hermes's to Prometheus. Io, the half-mortal daughter of the sea god, has been pursued by Zeus. Zeus's wife, Hera, has discovered his adulterous love for Io and punishes the innocent girl, having her followed first by Argos, whose thousand eyes watch her constantly, and then by a gadfly. Thus, through no fault of her own, Io falls victim to Zeus's lust and Hera's jealousy. In her conversation with Prometheus, he reveals that she will have a role in Zeus's eventual fall.

Zeus will impregnate her, and one of her decedents will arrive in the Egyptian city of Canopus, where after five generations, fifty sisters will resist marriage with their ''near of kin'' and will murder the men. ''One girl, bound by love's spell, will change / her purpose, and she will not kill the man she lay beside,'' and in time, ''she will bear a kingly child'' whose descendent, Hercules, will set the Titan free. After Hermes tells Prometheus about the eagle which will daily consume his liver, the messenger says the Titan will find ''no ending to this agony / until a god will freely suffer for you, will take on him your pain, and in your stead / descend to where the sun is turned to darkness, / the black depths of death.'' This occurs when Chiron, the immortal centaur renowned for his wisdom and virtue, agrees to die in Prometheus's place.

According to E. A. Havelock, *Prometheus Bound* differs from most tragedies in which the hero fails and dies, because Prometheus triumphs and lives.

Both Zeus and Prometheus have learned and grown in the process. As R. D. Murry pointed out in *The Motif of Io in Aeschylus's "Suppliants,"* the "release of Io from her woes is to provide the initial indication of the increasing wisdom of Zeus and the concomitant sowing of the seeds of compassion for humanity." Hercules's freeing of Prometheus "marks the coming of age of the divine wisdom and the synthesis of Promethean knowledge and humanitarianism with the effective Jovian power. The trilogy is a paean in honor of the Greek mind, but above all an affirmation of the dignity of man and wise majesty of god, qualities attained through the perfecting course of evolution. Zeus the tyrant and Prometheus the forethinker coalesce" in a process of "learning through suffering."

As we have seen, the *Prometheia*'s dramatic struggles between law and justice, mercy and punishment resonate with both individuals and society. Reading *Prometheus Bound* less as an object lesson about revolution and more as a resolution of ethical dilemmas becomes more meaningful if we situate the play within the context of Aeschylus's historical moment. He wrote after the political reformer Clisthenes overthrew the tyrant Hippias and developed a republican government. Reforms lessened the power of the nobility and allowed non-noble landowners to participate in government. Conflicts between the nobility and commoners remained, however, and Athens had to develop an attitude of compromise and cooperation.

Thus, the same problems and challenges facing the characters in the *Prometheia*—crime and revenge, tyranny and revolution—also faced the young Attic republic. The citizens and rulers of Athens had to come to terms with these issues, and achieve balance freedom and authority, in themselves individually and in their society. This is in keeping with the way Scully described the "general drift of the trilogy . . . [as showing] a universal progress from confusion and torment, at all levels of the universe, toward peace and joy."

Source: Arnold Schmidt for *Drama for Students,* Gale, 1999.

J. M. Mossman

In this excerpt, Mossman discusses the imagery in Prometheus Bound, *illustrating the large role it plays in relating the drama.*

Very little to do with the exact context of *Prometheus Bound* can be proved, because of the poor state of the evidence, but several scholars, most recently Griffith, have argued convincingly that there was a trilogy by someone consisting of *Prometheus Firebearer (Pyrphoros), Prometheus Bound,* and *Prometheus Unbound* in that order, and in what follows it is assumed that that was the case. There are some fragments which suggest that images familiar from *Prometheus Bound* appeared in the other two plays as well; to these I shall return, but first the imagery within the play we actually have should be considered in some detail.

The major interest of *Prometheus Bound* is the characterization of the relationship between Zeus and Prometheus, and the tracing of Prometheus' emotional movement from despair to renewed self-respect. After the opening binding scene, where the brutal treatment he receives is graphically described and carried out on stage, Prometheus is in a pitiful state, frightened even by the rushing wings of the gentle chorus. But their sympathy, and his account of his wrongs, restore some of his spirit, as his dialogue with Ocean shows, and his great central speeches about his benefactions to mankind help him further and embolden him to mention that he knows a secret which he can hold over Zeus. The Io scene, where his gift of prophecy comes into its own, increases his confidence still further; he threatens Zeus, and remains steadfast even in the face of Hermes and a yet more terrible punishment. The imagery of the play has an important role to play in underlining the characterization of Zeus and Prometheus, and in characterizing Zeus further by means of delineating his treatment of Io. Io is linked to Prometheus by images of horse-breaking or domestication of animals, and of sickness and disease. . . .

Prometheus' bonds are described with technical terms from horse-breaking; the effect of this is to show how Zeus' regime attempts to reduce him to animal status: it adds an edge to the brutality of the binding scene. This is a relatively non-figurative use of the metaphor, since although Prometheus is not a real animal, the bonds are solid enough. The metaphor . . . used to describe the methods which Zeus uses to force Inachus to drive out Io, is obviously a more figurative one, since there is no indication that real bonds are involved. But it still makes sense to see it in the context of the bonds of Prometheus, since Zeus' treatment of Inachus is similarly violent and harsh. Harder to place is the more elaborate metaphor in Hermes' words to Prometheus [near the play's end]. . . . Here the stress is on Prometheus' activity rather than on the

> THE MAJOR INTEREST OF *PROMETHEUS BOUND* IS THE CHARACTERIZATION OF THE RELATIONSHIP BETWEEN ZEUS AND PROMETHEUS, AND THE TRACING OF PROMETHEUS' EMOTIONAL MOVEMENT FROM DESPAIR TO RENEWED SELF-RESPECT"

nature of the bonds, as in the earlier passages, and this reflects Prometheus' greater self-confidence (or unruliness, from Hermes' point of view) at this later stage in the play. Are the bit and reins against which he struggles actually his bonds, or are they more figuratively metaphorical? Hermes leaves it delicately uncertain.

The use of such images to portray Io covers a wider register of figurative and non-figurative. Imagery from domestication and horse-breaking is regularly used in sexual, nuptial, and sometimes sacrificial contexts, of young girls in early lyric poetry and in tragedy; but here, because Io is in dramatic reality half-cow, half-human, the passages which describe her as bovine are ambiguous: they can be understood simultaneously directly and as metaphors. . . . All this metaphorical domestication should be compared to the domestication of real animals as taught by Prometheus to mortals. . . . There it is one of Prometheus' benefactions, used to the benefit of civilization, but in the metaphors it represents Zeus' outrages. . . .

Less complex, with a more discernible range of figurative and non-figurative forming a more discernible pattern, is the metaphor of binding; from the actual binding instantiated on stage in the first scene, we then find a series of images of binding and entanglement, culminating in the chorus's being entangled in the net of disaster. . . . This is of course often combined with the images from horsebreaking which have just been discussed, and the two should probably not be separated out as clearly as they have been here. The real binding of Prometheus remains a dramatic fact throughout the play, but from the first scene on there are lines where the metaphoric

dimension of binding is used to describe features of that real binding. . . .

The images which represent what is wrong with Zeus' rule, domestication and sickness . . . have their most literal expression in the speeches of Prometheus, and Zeus' actions are thus characterized as perverting the benefits which Prometheus conferred on mortals, and which Zeus should be conferring and is not. Io and Prometheus are linked as victims of Zeus' cruelty by these images, and by using the cow imagery previously used of Io of the earth at the very end of the play, it may be implied that the whole earth is Zeus' victim too. . . .

In suggesting the perversion of Prometheus' gifts by Zeus, the sickness and domestication images behave in a parallel way to the other gifts he has given mankind: fire and prophecy. The fire which Prometheus stole to benefit mankind is used to punish him . . . and the emphasis on the fiery nature of the thunderbolt. . . . Zeus' coercion of Inachus by means of oracles may also imply that he is perverting another of Prometheus' gifts, namely prophecy: but in general this is the one gift of Prometheus that Zeus cannot control or pervert, and it is this which will provide the means of escape . . . which initially seems so far out of reach. And it is supremely appropriate that in giving the benefit of his prophetic skill to an individual mortal, Io, a representative of the mortals he describes himself as helping, Prometheus should work out his own salvation too, both in the short term spiritually, by giving himself courage to threaten Zeus, and in the long term by using prophecy as a weapon and causing his predictions to become self-fulfilling. . . .

Source: J. M. Mossman, ''Chains of Imagery in *Prometheus Bound*,'' in *Classical Quarterly,* Volume 46, no. i, June, 1996 , pp. 58–67.

Sallie Goetsch

Goetsch discusses the techniques necessary for the staging of Prometheus Bound, *while also addressing the debate over the play's authorship. She concludes that it was possible for the play to have been written and performed during Aeschylus's time (although she notes that someone other than Aeschylus could have been its author), discussing several key elements of the play and how they could have been staged.*

Prometheus Bound is a peculiarly controversial play. Scholars continue to debate both its authorship and its date—not to mention its quality—with considerable passion and not inconsiderable arguments. The major reason for dating the play late in the fifth century B.C.E. and thereby denying Aeschylus's authorship stems from the apparent demands for elaborate mechanical devices that were unavailable earlier in the century. A close examination, however, yields the opposite conclusion: performance of *Prometheus* does not require stage equipment or technology beyond what was available to Aeschylus in the early-mid fifth century B.C.E. In fact, within the performance traditions of Athens, *Prometheus* would have been easiest to produce before the *skene* was introduced into the Theater of Dionysus. Since the *skene* had to be in existence by the year 458, when Aeschylus produced the *Oresteia,* we have a *terminus ante quem* of about 460 B.C.E.

The idea of *Prometheus* as a play best enacted without a permanent scene-building in place has been with us at least since the time of Margarete Bieber, who pointed out that if Prometheus was to seem to disappear into the earth, it would be easiest to have the actor fall off the edge of the retaining wall at the back of the *orchestra.* Even this argument betrays the prejudices of a theatergoer accustomed to blackouts and curtains which allow actors to appear and disappear suddenly, an expectation that Prometheus must indeed be seen to be swallowed into the earth at the end of the play. Audiences, who had never known anything but outdoor performances in broad daylight and who were capable of accepting the convention of actually seeing actors waiting for hours or days at a certain place onstage suddenly take up positions and become characters, would not necessarily have required the same kind of realism. Conventions of representation in and out of the theater evolved over the course of the fifth century and down into the fourth, and *Prometheus* is a play written for the conventions belonging to the theater Aeschylus grew up with in the first half of the fifth century.

The most notable difficulties that *Prometheus* poses to a would-be producer are as follows: first, the binding of Prometheus to the rock; second, the entry of the chorus in their winged chariots; third, the entry of Okeanos on his four-footed bird; and fourth, the final cataclysm which engulfs Prometheus and the chorus. Each of these points has subsidiary problems, such as the fact that Okeanos and the chorus make no mention of or address to one another. The basic challenge involved in staging *Prometheus* can be expressed in fairly simple terms: how are all these flying characters to fly and how is the cataclysm to be effected?

> "THE MAJOR REASON FOR DATING THE PLAY LATE IN THE FIFTH CENTURY B.C.E. AND THEREBY DENYING AESCHYLUS'S AUTHORSHIP STEMS FROM THE APPARENT DEMANDS FOR ELABORATE MECHANICAL DEVICES THAT WERE UNAVAILABLE EARLIER IN THE CENTURY"

Aeschylus scholars have taxed their imaginations to the fullest over these points and provided a great number of possible solutions, most of them a considerable strain on fifth-century technology. (Indeed, most of them would be a considerable strain on twentieth-century technology.) Most of them also assume the existence of both *skene* and *mechane,* except for N.G.L. Hammond, who holds out for a natural outcropping of rock at the edge of the *orchestra* as the site of Prometheus's binding and prefers rolling mechanisms to flying mechanisms for the winged conveyances of Okeanos and his daughters. One of the biggest difficulties with this suggestion is that the cars would have to be propelled by their riders, and the scooter or skateboard type constructions which Hammond envisions would not only have been beyond the mechanical capability of fifth-century Athenians but would also have been useless on an unpaved surface. Donald Mastronarde suggests cars rolled onto the roof of the *skene;* others have claimed that all twelve or fifteen choreuts were swung from one or several cranes.

The problem with these proposed stagings goes beyond the purely practical issue of whether the stage equipment was up to it. As Oliver Taplin said in *The Stagecraft of Aeschylus,* "What on earth would be the point of this abnormal scenic technique?" Perhaps Aeschylus or one of his contemporaries or successors could have done it, but why bother?

Yet Taplin dismisses the simplest and most elegant solution, that the various spectacular flying effects were achieved by means of dance, almost as soon as he raises it. For how, he asks, could the chorus mime chariots and then step down from them? And how could Okeanos provide a "four-footed bird" by dancing alone?

These objections are trivial compared with the difficulties of any of the other proposals, and a more systematic examination of the possibilities of mimetic dance demonstrates that this simple and elegant solution is a viable one, perhaps the *only* viable one if we look at certain other indications of the text.

The very first lines of *Prometheus* stress the complete barrenness of the scene: "We are come to the farthest boundaries of earth, to the Scythian land, to a desert empty of mortal things" (1–2). Not much further on, Hephaistos refers to the "crag apart from humanity, where [Prometheus] will perceive neither voice nor body of mortals" (20–22). Both of these statements argue against the presence of a *skene*. No extant play which was written after the advent of the *skene* ignores its existence. Even in Euripides's *Suppliants,* where no one goes inside the *skene,* it is important: Evadne commits suicide by jumping off of it. Sophocles transforms the *skene* into caves and groves, and Aristophanes into all manner of things, but all plays from the *Oresteia* onwards use it. Even though *Eumenides* ignores the *skene* in its latter half, the building is necessary to that play's prologue and parodos. It is therefore hard to see where the *skene* would fit into the barren setting of *Prometheus Bound.*

The only thing referred to in the text of *Prometheus* which might conceivably be identified as the *skene* is the rock to which Prometheus is chained. And while a *skene* might be a sheer-cliffed crag as easily as a cave, pinioning Prometheus to it would make it difficult for the chorus to remain so long out of his sight. A real rock would be a more convincing rock than a wooden building would, and there was in fact no reason not to use one. The Persian sack of the Acropolis in 480/79 had left debris all over the Acropolis and Agora, and the process of clearing and rebuilding lasted late into the 440s. Although the floor of the *orchestra* was graded earth and not bedrock, it could easily have supported the weight of a rock the size of a column drum.

An actual rock has advantages besides visual verisimiltude. It would be solid enough to stand up to a good deal of lunging and struggling on Prometheus's part, and to support real metal chains. It would make striking ringing noises when Hephaistos hammered it, providing the clangor to which the Oceanids respond. The noise would also contribute to the illusion, if such is necessary, that Prometheus's very flesh is pierced during the binding process. The chains could in actuality be fixed to a single spike at the rear of the plinth so as to be easy to remove for the final exit. (Actual rocks and chains might not have been a problem for fifth-century theater technicians, but actual binding would have posed a severe difficulty to the actor playing Prometheus!)

So where in our *skene*-free performance space would this rock have been placed? A position at the center of the *orchestra* would be most convenient for the actor playing Prometheus, for both visual focus and acoustic clarity. Kratos, Bia, and Hephaistos could then drag Prometheus on from the stage-left *eisodos,* that is, the hostile side of the stage, and affix him to it, emphasizing by crossing that space the isolation to which they are leaving him. They are coming to Scythia from the known world, the Greek world, and are therefore traveling east, reinforcing the probability of a stage-left entrance.

This positioning would also place Prometheus far enough downstage that the chorus, Okeanos, Io, and Hermes could enter out of his sight, emphasizing his vulnerability by putting his back to the door, so to speak, as well as explaining the fact that he hears and smells the chorus before he sees them and that Io spots him long before he does her.

We come then to the second problem, the entry of the chorus. We have Prometheus, thoroughly, visibly bound, completely static, standing and obviously able to breathe well enough to sing, since he embarks on what he imagines will be a lonely lament. In this, however, he is mistaken. "What sound, what smell, comes to me without sight?" Prometheus asks at 115, and then indulges in a lengthy bout of speculation. At line 128, apparently still outside of Prometheus's line of sight, the chorus assures him of its friendly intent.

An arrival by means of the *mechane,* if such were feasible, would at least account for the chorus's being out of Prometheus's line of sight. But while such an entrance might bring the Oceanids on the scene in motion, they would have to hover afterwards, creating a very still tableau. The point of choosing barefoot nymphs in winged vehicles for the chorus must surely have been to contrast their constant and rapid movement with Prometheus's utter immobility, an effect which would have been completely lost if they had to hover on the crane or crowd together on the *skene* roof.

The freedom implicit in dancing, however, is entirely consistent with maintaining this contrast conceptually and visually. The racing contest of the chorus's entry could begin just before Prometheus's "What sound," which itself could as easily refer to the playing of the musician who always accompanied the chorus as to running feet and fluttering wings. Athenian audiences were clearly willing to accept dancing as a representation of flying at least as late as the production of Aristophanes's *Birds* in 414, when the chorus of birds appears at ground-level in the *orchestra*. If Prometheus is downstage center the chorus can enter via the stage-right *eisodos* (since they are friendly to Prometheus), "flying," and remain out of Prometheus's sight.

The wings themselves are a problem easily solved by means of long scarves or streamers like those used in Chinese dances of the Han period or the draperies of Loie Fuller. They would provide a spectacular visual effect and probably a rippling sound effect as well, which the chorus would need constant motion to maintain. (One reason the choral odes of *Prometheus* are so short may be the physical demands of the dancing.) And while we have no evidence for this particular technique in Greece, long strips of cloth were a common enough product of fifth-century Athens. Choruses of flying creatures had been in existence in Athens since at least the sixth century, so the representation of wings on stage was not an unusual problem for the fifth-century equivalent of a costume designer.

The objection which Taplin raises to the dance theory is, as previously mentioned, that the wings on which the Oceanids are flying are not their own: they claim to be carried on "winged chariots" (135). A streamer held in the hand is more obviously a separate object than one attached directly to a costume, but the fact that the chorus has to *tell* the audience that they are in chariots implies that the visual distinction was not immediately obvious. (In *Agamemnon,* for instance, Agamemnon does not make an explicit statement that his chariot is pulled by a horse, as the fact is unmistakable.) To "dismount" from the chariots, the choreuts would need only to set their streamers aside. In doing so they would most likely move to the edges of the *orchestra* so as not to risk tripping over the streamers in their later odes.

It is important in reconstructing the staging to get the chorus out of the way before Okeanos enters, and not only because they take no part in that scene. Even with a winged steed, Okeanos's entrance would not have been very dramatic if the chorus was still flying around the *orchestra*. If the crane existed and he were on it, he might have managed to draw attention to himself despite their movement, but why should he be flying on a higher plane, and via a different scenic convention, than the chorus? And the motion/immobility dichotomy, the fact that his departing lines (393–6) indicate he has never dismounted or touched the ground, argue strongly for constant movement from Okeanos which would have been impossible if the actor were suspended in midair.

How, then, does Okeanos accomplish mimetic dance of his four-legged bird? By using another dancer, of course. Chinese lion-dancers and the Balinese Barong are both four-footed creatures animated by two dancers apiece, and provide obvious visual parallels to Okeanos's mount? Neither one, however, supports a rider; and Athens's own tradition appears to have allowed a single person to enact the role of a four-footed animal and dance while being ridden. Having a human being in the role of the gryphon certainly explains Okeanos's ability to control it without reins.

Since Okeanos returns to his own home, he exits by the same route he entered. Io enters, like Okeanos and the chorus, from the known world, that is, from the West, but Prometheus specifically directs her to go *East*, toward the rising sun (707), so she exits by the opposite *eisodos*. Hermes will enter from the same direction to predict further doom.

We come then to the final challenge, the cataclysm which swallows Prometheus and the chorus. Dance again provides the simplest solution to the challenge of presenting an earthquake. Twelve choreuts, especially if accompanied by a drum, could very easily have produced a sound of the earth shaking and indeed an accompanying whirlwind, and could have swept Prometheus off in their midst when making a final exit—through, of course, the stage-left, eastern *eisodos*. (Simply unhooking the chains from the back of the rock would suffice to free him.)

I should add that those who live in earthquake prone areas readily believe that there is a tremor in progress: any rumbling noise can be mistaken for an earthquake. Modern lighting effects would be nice for the lightnings which Prometheus sees, but since lighting effects were totally impossible in fifth-century Athens, no one in the audience would have expected or missed them.

So we come to the end of the play and discover that it is perfectly possible to stage *Prometheus* with pre-*skene* technology, and far easier and less expensive than it would have been to try to use the *mechane*. On the basis of its staging alone, *Prometheus Bound* could be very early indeed. The language, however, continues to point to a later date of composition and performance. The brevity of the choral odes may be accounted for by the strenuousness of the dances, which would not leave the choreuts with enormous amounts of breath, but the other stylistic elements which Michael Griffith and others point out are not quite so easy to dismiss. For that reason I think that *Prometheus* is only just a pre-*skene* play, and dates to the late 460s. As for its authorship, I leave that to others to debate.

Source: Sallie Goetsch, ''Staging and Date of *Prometheus Bound*,'' in *Theatre History Studies,* Volume XV, June, 1995, pp. 219–24.

SOURCES

Berlin, Normand. *The Secret Cause: A Discussion of Tragedy,* University of Massachusetts Press, 1981.

FURTHER READING

Bullfinch, Thomas. *Bullfinch's Mythology,* Avenel, 1979.
    One of the best—if a bit old fashioned—collections of information on classical mythology, as well as on Arthurian legend and many other myths and legends.

Fitts, Dudley, editor. *Greek Plays in Modern Translation,* Dial, 1947.
    Contains a selection of Greek plays, including *King Oedipus* translated by William Butler Yeats, and *Prometheus Bound.* It closes with insightful, though brief, comments on the various plays.

Havelock, E. A. *The Crucifixion of Intellectual Man,* Beacon, 1951.
    Breezy discussion of Aeschylus's tragedy, though concluding with a particularly useful appendix on Hesiod's *Theogony,* Aeschylus's mythology, and the lost plays of the Prometheus cycle.

Herington, John. *Aeschylus,* Yale University Press, 1986.
    This offers substantial background on Aeschylus's worldview, his historical moment, and Greek theatrical conventions, as well as a chapter on each of the existing plays, including one on *Prometheus Bound.*

Hogan, James C. *A Commentary on the Complete Greek Tragedies: Aeschylus,* University of Chicago Press, 1984.
    In addition to a solid introduction about Aeschylus and the Attic theatrical tradition, this book contains an almost line-by-line commentary on Aeschylus's plays, including *Prometheus Bound.* Hogan clarifies vocabulary and mythology, and summarizes many commentators views on various crucial textual and critical issues.

McCall, Marsh H. Jr., editor. *Aeschylus: A Collection of Critical Essays,* Prentice-Hall, 1972.
    This fine essay collection discusses Aeschylus's major plays as well as his tragic vision, though only one essay deals entirely with *Prometheus Bound.*

Scodel, Ruth. *Aeschylus,* Twayne, 1982.
    With substantial material covering the playwright's biography and Greek culture, it includes discussion of all the plays, with a chapter on *Prometheus Bound.* Of particular interest is the brief analysis of contemporary Greek scientific medical knowledge and Prometheus's ''condition.''

Scully, James and C. J. Herington. *Aeschylus's* Prometheus Bound, Oxford University Press, 1975.
    Along with a translation of the play, this boasts a good introduction and most important, an appendix containing existing fragments of the lost sequels to *Prometheus Bound.*

Thomson, George. ''Prometheia'' in *Aeschylus: A Collection of Critical Essays,* Prentice-Hall, 1972, pp. 124-47.
    Offers important background about Hesiod's version of the Prometheus myth and the changes Aeschylus made in his dramatic adaptation. Also contains extensive material regarding the Prometheus cycle and discusses *Prometheus Bound*'s meaning in the context of those lost plays.

Thomson, George. *Prometheus Bound,* Cambridge University Press, 1932.
    In addition to an edition of play, Thomson's background and reference material situates the play in the context of Greek history and philosophy.

Uncle Vanya

ANTON CHEKHOV
1897

Uncle Vanya, Anton Chekhov's masterpiece of frustrated longing and wasted lives, was originally a much more conventional drama in its earlier incarnation. Previously known as *The Wood Demon,* the play was rejected by two theaters before premiering in Moscow in December of 1889 to a very poor reception (it closed after three performances). Sometime between that date and 1896, Chekhov revised the play, altering it radically. Although the work that emerged is more static than the original—in terms of narrative events, far less happens—it is considered one of the most poignant evocations of thwarted desire ever written. Vanya is literally haunted by the man he might have been: "Day and night like a fiend at my throat is the thought that my life is hopelessly lost."

Uncle Vanya was scheduled to premiere at the Maly Theater in Moscow, but the Theatrical and Literary Committee overseeing it and other imperial theaters asked Chekhov to make substantial revisions to the play. Instead of making the suggested changes, he withdrew the play and submitted it to the Moscow Art Theater, where *Uncle Vanya* was first performed on October 26, 1899, under the direction Konstantin Stanislavsky. It was well received.

With *Uncle Vanya* and Chekhov's three other dramatic masterpieces—*The Sea Gull, The Three Sisters,* and *The Cherry Orchard*—Chekhov demonstrated that a production could be riveting with-

out conforming to traditional notions of drama. In *Critical Essays on Anton Chekhov,* Russian author Vladimir Nabokov (*Lolita*) noted that Chekhov's plays are not overtly political or freighted with a social message: "What mattered was that this typical Chekhovian hero was the unfortunate bearer of a vague but beautiful human truth, a burden which he could neither get rid of nor carry." Today, Chekhov stakes a double claim in the world of literature: he is equally acclaimed as a master of the short story and of the dramatic form. *Uncle Vanya* is widely considered to be his greatest achievement in the latter genre and a masterpiece of modern drama.

AUTHOR BIOGRAPHY

Born on January 29, 1860, in the port village of Taganrog in the Ukraine, Anton Chekhov was the third son of Pavel Yegorovitch and Yevgeniya Yakovlevna (Morozov) Chekhov. Though the family was descended from Russian peasants, Chekhov's grandfather purchased the family's freedom, allowing Chekhov's father to run a small grocery store. The family's fortunes took a sudden turn for the worse, however, when his father's store went bankrupt in 1876. Following that disaster, his parents moved to Moscow, leaving Chekhov in Taganrog to complete his education.

In 1879, Chekhov reunited with his family in Moscow, where he began studying for a degree in medicine at Moscow University. In 1884, he completed his studies, began to practice medicine, and started publishing short, humorous sketches in popular magazines. In 1886 these collected sketches were published as a book, entitled *Motley Stories.* According to his biographers, Chekhov only began to take his writing seriously after he moved to St. Petersburg in 1885 and befriended an influential editor named A. S. Suvorin. During the late-1880s, Chekhov wrote some of his most famous short stories, including *"The Kiss"* and *"The Steppe."*

Chekhov had attended plays by Nikolai Gogol and William Shakespeare growing up in Taganrog, as well as appearing as an actor on the amateur and professional stage. In the 1880s, Chekhov began to write one-act and full-length plays. Many of his dramatic efforts were poorly received; the 1896 premier of *The Sea Gull* at the Imperial Alexander Theater in St. Petersburg was drowned out by whispering and derisive laughter. Chekhov's fortunes as a playwright improved after he met Konstantin Stanislavsky, who produced *The Sea Gull* at the Moscow Art Theater in 1898. In fact, the Moscow Art Theater was so indebted to Chekhov that an ideogram of a sea gull—from Chekhov's play of that title—still adorns the theater's curtain. In 1899, the Moscow Art Theater presented *Uncle Vanya,* a revised version of Chekhov's one-act play *The Wood Demon.* Chekhov's reputation as an innovative and influential dramatist rests with *Uncle Vanya* and his two subsequent plays, *The Three Sisters* (1901) and *The Cherry Orchard (1904).*

Even as his literary fortunes grew, Chekhov continued to work as a doctor, often refusing payment for the care he dispensed because he earned a good living from writing. In the summer of 1901 Chekhov married Olga Leonardovna Knipper, an actress from the Moscow Art Theater. Ill with tuberculosis, he spent much of his last years traveling to health spas in Europe. He died on July 2, 1904, in Badenweiler, a German health resort, and was buried in Moscow. Chekhov was a highly regarded short story writer and dramatist in his own lifetime and recognition and appreciation for his unique literary gifts have continued to grow throughout the twentieth century.

PLOT SUMMARY

Act I

The play opens on a cloudy afternoon in a garden behind the family estate of Serebryakov. Marina, the old nurse, is knitting a stocking, while Astrov, the doctor who has been called to tend to one of Professor Serebryakov's ailments, is pacing nearby. Astrov laments that he's aged tending the sick and that life "itself is boring, stupid, dirty." Having no one to love, he complains that his emotions have grown numb. When he worries that people won't remember him, Marina answers: "People won't remember but God will remember."

When Vanya enters, yawning from a nap, the three complain about how all order has been disrupted since the professor and his wife, Yelena, arrived. As they're talking, Serebryakov, Yelena, Sonya, and Telegin return from a walk. Vanya calls the professor "a learned old dried mackerel," criticizing him for his pomposity and the smallness of his achievements. Vanya's mother, Maria Vasilyevna, objects to her son's derogatory comments. Vanya also praises the professor's wife,

Yelena, for her beauty, arguing that faithfulness to an old man like Serebryakov means silencing youth and emotions—an immoral waste of vitality. Act I closes with Yelena becoming exasperated as Vanya declares his love for her.

Act II

It is evening and this act is set in Serebryakov's dining room. Before going to bed, Serebryakov complains of being in pain and of old age. After he is asleep, Yelena and Vanya talk. She speaks of the discord in the house, and Vanya speaks of dashed hopes. He feels he's misspent his youth, and he associates his unrequited love for Yelena with the devastation of his life. Not only is Vanya distraught about his own life, but he tells Yelena her life is dying, too. "What are you waiting for?" he asks her. "What curst philosophy stands in your way?"

Alone, Vanya speaks of how he loved Yelena ten years before, when it would have been possible for the two to have married and had a happy life together. At that time, Vanya believed in Serebryakov's greatness and loved him; now those beliefs are gone and his life feels empty. As Vanya agonizes over his past, Astrov returns and the two talk together, drunk. Sonya chides Vanya for his drinking, and he answers: "When one has no real life, one lives in illusions. After all, that's better than nothing." Sonya responds pragmatically: "All our hay is mowed, it rains every day, everything is rotting and you occupy yourself with illusions."

Outside, a storm is gathering and Astrov talks with Sonya about the suffocating atmosphere in the house; Astrov says Serebryakov is difficult, Vanya is a hypochondriac, and Yelena is charming but idle. He laments that it's a long time since he loved anyone. Sonya begs Astrov to stop drinking, telling him he is beautiful and should create rather than simply destroying himself. The two speak obliquely, though inconclusively, of love.

When the doctor leaves, Yelena enters and makes peace with Sonya, after an apparently long period of mutual anger and antagonism. Trying to resolve their past difficulties, Yelena reassures Sonya that she had strong feelings for her father when she married him, though the love proved false. The two women converse at cross purposes, with Yelena confessing her unhappiness and Sonya gushing about the doctor's virtues. Yelena is generous in her assessment of Astrov, describing him as a genius—

Anton Chekhov

a rare individual who is brave and free and imagines the future happiness of mankind.

Act III

Vanya, Sonya, and Yelena are in the living room of Serebryakov's house, having gathered to hear Serebryakov's announcement. Vanya calls Yelena a water nymph and urges her, once again, to break free, saying playfully: "Let yourself go if only for once in your life, hurry and fall in love with some River God." Sonya complains that she has loved Astrov for six years and that because she is not beautiful, he doesn't notice her. Yelena volunteers to question Astrov and find out if he's in love with Sonya. Sonya is pleased, but before agreeing she wonders whether uncertainty is better because then, at least, there is hope.

When Yelena asks Astrov about his feelings for Sonya, he says he has none and concludes that Yelena has brought up the subject of love to encourage him to confess his own emotions for her. Astrov kisses Yelena, and Vanya witnesses the embrace. Upset, Yelena begs Vanya to use his influence so that she and the professor can leave immediately. Before Serebryakov can make his announcement, Yelena conveys to Sonya the message that Astrov doesn't love her by saying he won't be coming to the estate in the future.

Serebryakov proposes that he solve the family's financial problems by selling the estate, using the proceeds to invest in interest-bearing paper and buy a villa for himself and Yelena in Finland. Angrily, Vanya asks where he, Sonya, and his mother would live. He protests that the estate belongs to Sonya and that Vanya has never been appreciated for the self-sacrifice it took to rid the property of debt. As Vanya's anger mounts, Yelena shouts: "I'm going away from this hell! I can't bear it any longer." Vanya, clearly in despair, announces: "My life is lost to me! I am talented, intelligent, brave.... Had I lived a normal life, there might have come out of me a Schopenhauer, a Dostoyevsky.... I am through with keeping accounts, making reports. I am losing my mind.... Mother, I am in despair! Mother!" Instead of comforting her son, Maria insists that Vanya listen to the professor. And Sonya pleads with her father: "One must be merciful, Papa! Uncle Vanya and I are so miserable!" Vanya leaves but then returns moments later with a gun. He fires the pistol point blank at Serebryakov but misses.

Act IV

As the final act opens, Marina and Telegin wind wool and discuss the planned departure of Serebryakov and Yelena. When Vanya and Astrov enter, Astrov says that in this district only he and Vanya were "decent, cultured men" and that ten years of "narrow-minded life" have made them vulgar. Vanya has stolen a vial of Astrov's morphine, presumably to commit suicide; Sonya and Astrov beg him to return the narcotic. "Give it back, Uncle Vanya!," says Sonya. "I am just as unhappy as you are, maybe, but I don't despair. I bear it and I will bear it till the end of my life. Then you bear it, too." Vanya returns the vial.

Yelena and Serebryakov bid everyone farewell. When Yelena says goodbye to Astrov, she admits to having been carried away by him, embraces him, and takes one of his pencils as a souvenir. Serebryakov and Vanya make their peace, agreeing all will be as it was before. Once the outsiders have departed, Sonya and Vanya pay bills, Maria works on a pamphlet, and Marina knits. Vanya complains of the heaviness of his heart, and Sonya speaks of living, working, and the rewards of the afterlife: "We shall hear the angels, we shall see the whole sky all diamonds, we shall see how all earthly evil, all our sufferings, are drowned in the mercy that will fill the whole world. And our life will grow peaceful, tender, sweet as a caress.... In your life you haven't known what joy was; but wait, Uncle Vanya, wait.... We shall rest."

CHARACTERS

Sofia Alexandrovna

Sonya is Serebryakov's daughter by his first marriage and Vanya's niece. Hard-working and plain in appearance, Sonya is twenty-four and has been in love with Astrov for six years. When Yelena offers to ask Astrov about his feelings for Sonya, she wavers, saying, "Uncertainty is better.... After all, there is hope—" Like the others, Sonya confesses to deep unhappiness but is more pragmatic. It is Sonya who holds the family together. When Vanya complains of how heavy his burdens are, she says: "What can we do, we must live!" The play closes with her soliloquy about the value of hard work in this lifetime and rest and beauty in the next.

Yelena Andreevna

A twenty-seven-year-old beauty and charmer, Yelena is married to the already elderly professor Serebryakov. Like her namesake Helen of Troy, Yelena is a woman whose beauty stirs men to action though she herself suffers from inertia. She freely admits that she's idle and bored, and she believes that any type of useful activity, such as nursing or teaching, is beyond her. Astrov jokes, "Both of you, he [Serebryakov] and you—infected us with your idleness." Yelena admits that she married out of true feeling, but that she no longer loves her husband and is now very unhappy. She dismisses Vanya's affections but is clearly attracted to Astrov. Directors disagree about Yelena's character. Sometimes she is portrayed as beautiful and vapid, flirtatious and cruel. Others see her as a vibrant life force that woos men away from their goals and therefore brings about their unintentional destruction, an idea that's supported by Astrov's statement, "It's strange how I am convinced that if you should stay on, there would be an enormous devastation."

Dr. Mikhail Lvovich Astrov

As Act I opens, Astrov, the village doctor, is lamenting that he's grown old and has not had a single day off in more than ten years. At times, Astrov appears to be close to desperation: "I work harder than anyone in the district, fate strikes me one blow after another and there are times when I suffer unbearably—but for me there is no light shining in the distance." In addition to his other frustrations, Astrov is haunted by the death of one of his patients, a railroad switchman, who died of typhus under his care. Yelena describes Astrov as having a tired, nervous, interesting face; he is a vegetarian who's passionate about nature and interested in the conservation of the woods, but he also drinks heavily and is curiously oblivious to Sonya's love for him. Many parallels exist between Vanya and Astrov; both feel beaten down by life, both are attracted to Yelena, and both believe they've squandered their talents and are now living lives of vulgarity and frustration.

Professor Alexander Vladimirovich Serebryakov

A retired professor who was regarded as a Don Juan in his younger days, Serebryakov is now married to the beautiful Yelena Andreevna. Serebryakov is Sonya's father and was married to Vanya's sister, Vera, who has since died. The professor has settled on the estate of his first wife because he can't afford to live anywhere else. Vanya criticizes him for striding around like a god, yet having achieved nothing of significance in his field (art history). Serebryakov is idolized by his mother-in-law, Maria, but Vanya despises him, having come to view him as an old fraud who's sapped everyone of their vitality. Serebryakov sets off a firestorm by suggesting that the estate, which belongs to Sonya, be sold so that he and Yelena can buy a villa in Finland.

Sonya

See Sofia Alexandrovna

Ilya Ilich Telegin

An impoverished landowner, Telegin lives on the estate and dines regularly with the family. Chekhov describes his speech as high-pitched and pretentious. Nicknamed "Waffles" because of his pockmarked face, Telegin argues for faithfulness, describing how his wife left him the day after their wedding because of his appearance, yet he remained loyal to her, supporting the children she had with her lover.

MEDIA ADAPTATIONS

- In 1994, Louis Malle directed a film version of *Uncle Vanya,* entitled *Vanya on 42nd Street.* The film takes an usual approach to Chekhov's text in that it portrays a theatre company rehearsing the play for production. The lives of the actors mirror the action within the playwright's script. Playwright David Mamet (*Speed the Plow*) wrote the adaptation of the play, Grammy nominee Joshua Redman created the jazz score, and Julianne Moore, Wallace Shawn (as Vanya), and Andre Gregory starred in the production.

- In 1962, Stuart Burge filmed and directed a film adaptation of *Uncle Vanya,* which starred Laurence Olivier, Joan Plowright, Rosemary Harris, and Michael Redgrave. The onstage version of the play was directed by Olivier at the Chichester Drama Festival.

Marina Timofeevna

Chekhov describes Marina, the old nurse, as a plain, small woman; she is a soothing presence among the frustrated, lovelorn, and angry characters on the estate. Overtly nurturing, she is often associated with food or drink ("A cup of lime-flower tea or tea with raspberry jam and it will all pass," she says in an attempt to console Sonya).

Uncle Vanya

The Uncle Vanya of the title, Voynitsky is forty-seven years old, stylishly dressed, and yawning when he first appears in Act I. A year before the play opens, he realized that he'd wasted his life by working to support the professor, whose great genius turned out to have been illusory. Vanya is in love with Yelena, whom he urges to take better advantage of her youth than he did. Discontented and angry, Vanya is derailed by his own impotence and anger; he continually makes nasty jabs at Serebryakov. After months of grumbling, Vanya erupts into violence when the professor proposes that the estate be sold so that he and Yelena can purchase a villa in Finland. Vanya shoots at the professor but misses. Having wasted his talents and squandered his life, Voynitsky has become a peripheral figure who supports his sister's family, rather than living his own life. Even his designation in the title of the play—he's known as someone else's uncle—suggests how far from the center of the action his life is lived.

Maria Vasilevna Voinitskaya

Maria Vasilevna is the widow of a privy councillor, Vanya's mother, and Serebryakov's mother-in-law. A liberal with an unwavering commitment to women's rights, she adores the professor and is content to spend her life furthering his work. As Vanya describes her: "My old magpie *Maman* is still babbling about the emancipation of women; with one eye she looks into the grave and with the other she rummages through her learned books for the dawn of a new life." Throughout most of the play, Maria reads or writes without looking up, lost in thought.

Ivan Petrovich Voynitsky

See Uncle Vanya

Waffles

See Ilya Ilich Telegin

THEMES

Anger and Hatred

Recognizing that he has wasted his life furthering the professor's scholarship, Vanya responds in anger, a new and unaccustomed emotion for him. Although Vanya's displeasure simmers throughout the play, it erupts into violence after Serebryakov announces his plan to sell the estate so that he and Yelena can buy a villa in Finland. Vanya then attempts to shoot the professor, only to miss, emphasizing the futility of his rebellion. Vanya's full name, Voynitsky, hints at his potential for belligerence (the Russian word for "war" is "voyna").

Appearances and Reality

Vanya rails against Serebryakov's intellectual posturing, knowing that the professors's claims of intelligence are a fraud. "You were to us a creature of the highest order and your articles we knew by heart," says Vanya. "But now my eyes are open! I see everything! You write about art, but you understand nothing of art! All your works, that I used to love, are not worth a brass penny! You fooled us!" Although some of Vanya's charges have merit, Chekhov's message is more complex. Serebryakov is not as bad and false as Vanya makes him out to be, but he is a self-absorbed, sick old man who has come to fear Vanya and his outbursts of indignation.

Choices and Consequences

Vanya's mother, Maria Vasilyevna, chides her son for railing against his fate, when he's taken so few steps to change the course of his life. "It looks as if you are challenging your former convictions," she says to Vanya. "But they are not guilty, it's you are guilty. You keep forgetting that a conviction in itself is nothing, it's a dead letter. . . . You should have been doing something." Serebryakov echoes the same sentiments when he departs, saying, "One must, ladies and gentlemen, do something." Although his remarks are ironic given his own barren efforts, they also contain some element of truth.

Deception

Vanya claims that he has been deceived by Serebryakov, but Chekhov also suggests that Vanya has deceived himself. After all, if Vanya has read the professor's articles for twenty-five years, why does it take him so long to notice that the professor's scholarship is empty and the man is "a soap bubble"? In many scenes, Vanya deceives himself. When Vanya exhorts Yelena to have an affair, he is, in part, motivated by self interest. He says, "Faithfulness like this is false from beginning to end; it has a fine sound but no logic." One could argue that the case Vanya makes for adultery is equally suspect.

Duty and Responsibility

Work is one of the major themes of *Uncle Vanya*. Vanya, Sonya, and Astrov all complain that Yelena's idleness has infected them, luring them from their responsibilities to loaf with her. When Sonya suggests that Yelena work, she responds: "It is only in sociological novels they teach and cure sick peasants, and how can I suddenly for no reason go to curing and teaching them?" Sonya answers: "And in the same way I don't understand how not to go and not to teach." Chekhov may be critiquing

TOPICS FOR FURTHER STUDY

- It has been suggested that Astrov's initial conversation with the nurse acts as an overture to the play, hinting at the important issues that Vanya and others will later elaborate upon, just as a musical overture introduces certain melodic themes. How might Astrov's speech be viewed as an overture? Also, discuss how Sonya's concluding speech might be viewed as the play's finale.

- Research the lives of peasants in Russia in the late-nineteenth century. What are the similarities and differences between the enslavement of African Americans in the U. S. and serfdom in Russia? Examine Marina and Telegin in *Uncle Vanya* and consider what Chekhov might be saying about the various classes in Russian society.

- The characters in *Uncle Vanya* often discuss work and idleness. For instance, Astrov, in parting from Yelena, says: "You infected us with your slothfulness. I have lazed away a whole month, while the people have grown sicker . . ." What is Chekhov saying about the value of

honest work? Be sure to discuss each character's attitude toward work, including the views set forth by Serebryakov and Maria Vasilyevna.

- Chekhov was a practicing doctor, and doctors often appear in his plays. Analyze how Astrov's profession makes him like—or unlike—the other characters in the play. Compare and contrast Astrov with the doctor characters in other Chekhov plays, such as Dorn in *The Sea Gull* or Tchebutykin in *The Three Sisters*.

- Astrov is admired by Sonya and Yelena for his love of nature and his commitment to conservation. Sonya praises him for believing that "forests adorn the earth, that they teach a man to understand the beautiful and inspire him to lofty moods." And Yelena describes Astrov's passion for the woods this way: "When he plants a little tree, he is already imagining what it will be like in a thousand years, he is already dreaming of the happiness of mankind. Such people are rare, one must love them." How does Astrov compare to ecologists of today?

---

idleness, but he also takes a dim view of meaningless work: Serebryakov's empty efforts at intellect provide an excuse for him to be demanding and pompous; and Maria Vasilyevna's work is a form of escapism, allowing her to shut out the emotional needs of her family.

Human Condition

Throughout his plays, Chekhov is concerned with the human condition and how people endure great unhappiness and personal frustration. Many of the sorrows the characters experience are inevitable. When Astrov says goodbye to Yelena, the farewell is tinged by an awareness that human life is sad: "It's odd somehow," he says, "We have known each other, and suddenly for some reason— we will never see each other again. And that's how it is in this world." The clearest evocation of how

the frustrations of the characters are simply part of the human condition comes in Sonya's final speech. "What can we do," she says, "we must live!. . . We'll live through a long, long line of days, endless evenings; we'll bear patiently the trials fate sends us; we'll work for others now and in our old age without ever knowing any rest, and when our hour comes, we'll die humbly."

Limitations and Opportunities

Vanya sees his life as circumscribed by the sacrifices he made for the professor. In a rage, he shouts, "I'm gifted, intelligent, courageous. If I'd had a normal life I might have been a Schopenhauer or a Dostoyevsky." However, even Vanya recognizes that his own possibilities may not have been so great as he sometimes claims. When his mother laments that Vanya was once a man of strong convictions and a bright personality, he responds sarcastically, ''Oh, yes! I used to be a bright personality that didn't give light to anybody.''

Love and Passion

Vanya and Astrov both adore Yelena, Yelena is captivated by Astrov, and Sonya is in love with Astrov. Sonya tells Yelena: ''I have loved him now for six years, loved him more than my own mother; every minute I hear his voice, feel the touch of his hand; and I watch the door, waiting; it always seems to me that he will be coming in.'' Passion in *Uncle Vanya* seems like an avenue for suffering, not salvation. Yelena attributes her great unhappiness to having been mistaken in her love for Serebryakov. She also compares love for a woman to the reckless devastation of the woods and criticizes men for possessing ''the demon of destruction'' in their dealings with the opposite sex.

Return to Nature

Astrov speaks eloquently of the beauty of the woods, and his love of nature is one reason why Sonya and Yelena are drawn to him. Passionate about the need to conserve forests, he says that the woods are being destroyed ''because lazy man hasn't sense enough to bend down and pick up fuel from the ground.'' Astrov also laments, ''Forests are fewer and fewer, rivers dry up, game becomes extinct, the climate is ruined, and every day the earth gets poorer and uglier.'' Man's wanton destruction of nature has parallels to the unhappiness of the members of Serebryakov's family, who feel their lives are unfulfilled and ruined. Astrov says, ''He must be a reckless barbarian to burn this beauty in his stove, destroy what we cannot create again.''

Success and Failure

The dramatic action of *Uncle Vanya* occurs within a few months time, when Voynitsky stops accepting a secondary role in life, as family provider, uncle, and dutiful son, and instead rails against the injustices of his life. For Vanya, the recognition of personal failure briefly spurs him to declare his love for Yelena, to assert his frustration, and to draw attention to Serebryakov's sense of unbridled entitlement. However, Vanya is doomed to fail, even as he fails in his attempt to avenge himself and murder Serebryakov.

Wealth and Poverty

Money matters in *Uncle Vanya*. Serebryakov and Yelena are staying at the estate because they can't afford to live elsewhere; Telegin dines with the family because he is too impoverished to have his own home. Most importantly, it is Serebryakov's proposal to sell the estate and convert the proceeds into interest-bearing paper that sets off Vanya's wrath. The dramatic climax of *Uncle Vanya,* when Vanya confronts Serebryakov, consists of an accounting of debts, past and present. Among Vanya's grievances is the pittance he's been paid, wages ''fit for a beggar.'' Wealth has been squandered, as well as youth and time.

STYLE

Revision

One way to understand the construction of *Uncle Vanya* is to contrast it with its earlier incarnation, *The Wood Demon.* Eric Bentley, in *Critical Essays on Anton Chekhov,* called *The Wood Demon* ''a farce spiced with melodrama.'' In that version, Chekhov emphasizes the romantic interests of the characters and the play concludes with the coupling of Astrov and Sonya. No one is successfully paired up in *Uncle Vanya.* In *The Wood Demon* Vanya commits suicide. In *Uncle Vanya* Vanya survives only to have his bleakest fears about life confirmed. Wrote Bentley: ''To the Broadway script-writer, also concerned with the rewriting of plays (especially if in an early version a likable character shoots himself), these alterations of Chekhov's would presumably seem unaccountable. They would look like a deliberate elimination of the dramatic element.'' *Uncle Vanya* is constructed in a purposefully unconventional way, one that illustrates certain ideas about how individuals bear up and continue to live in the midst of considerable suffering.

Setting

Uncle Vanya is set entirely within Serebryakov's estate. Although the play opens in the garden behind the estate, most of the action takes place inside the rambling, twenty-six-room estate that Vanya and Sonya have managed and Sonya presumably owns. Many of the characters find the atmosphere stifling. Yelena describes the house as a crypt, a place of exile, and later, as hell, while Serebryakov says he feels like he's ''fallen from the earth on to some foreign planet'' and he calls the estate ''a labyrinth'' and ''a morgue.'' Vanya describes the monastic life he's lived, working inside the estate to further Serebryakov's career, as sitting ''like a mole inside these four walls,'' and Astrov says he couldn't

Konstantin Stanislavsky, the director of the Moscow Art Theatre, portrays Astrov in a scene from Uncle Vanya; *Olga Knipper, playwright Chekhov's wife, is in the role of Yelena*

survive a month in the house, "I'd suffocate in this air." The setting is intentionally static and claustrophobic. One of the hallmarks of a Chekhov play is that it takes place within a single setting. The fact that every scene takes place on the estate heightens the sense of desolation and futility experienced by the characters.

Point of View

One of Chekhov's innovations was to write plays without a single clear hero or heroine. In *Uncle Vanya* and Chekhov's other major plays, several characters are of nearly equal dramatic stature. Here, Vanya, Astrov, Sonya, and Yelena are the main characters and each experiences similar frustrations. The audience comes to understand each of the four characters' unique point of view through his or her speeches when alone and the confidences he or she shares with the other characters.

Realism

Realism is an artistic movement in which authors or artists attempted to depict human beings as they actually appear in life. Begun in the 1840s in Europe and Russia, realism was a response to the highly subjective art and literature produced by the Romantic movement. Chekhov—a preeminent realist—builds up a sense of character through physical description in his stage directions and through the characters' descriptions of one another. His characters are not larger than life but have recognizable foibles. Marina is a realist heroine; she clucks at the chickens and offers tea to the characters at inappropriate moments. Vanya also appears realistically—rather than a dignified, dramatic entrance, he makes his first appearance yawning. And Serebryakov complains of mundane matters like gout and other aches and pains.

HISTORICAL CONTEXT

In 1861, one year after Chekhov was born, Czar Alexander II abolished serfdom in Russia. Serfs were essentially slaves and were forced to work for their owners unless they could purchase their own freedom. Once peasants were no longer owned by

COMPARE & CONTRAST

- **1897:** Marxist Vladimir Ilich Ulyanov is exiled to Siberia for three years for smuggling illegal literature from Europe into Russia, organizing strikes, and printing anti-government leaflets and manifestoes. Ulyanov was the older brother of Lenin, the father of Russia's communist revolution.

  Today: Soviet president Boris Yeltsin regularly meets with world leaders, including U. S. President Bill Clinton, to exchange ideas.

- **1897:** Regard for conservation of natural resources is low, with most not considering the impact of the vast depletion of forests. In *Uncle Vanya,* Astrov is concerned with the devastation of the forests. He proposes that instead of wood, peat could be used for heat and stones for building houses.

  Today: Conservation of natural resources is a primary concern. About 655 million acres—or approximately 29% of the land area of the United States—has been designated forestland and is under the jurisdiction of the United States Department of Agriculture. The state with the largest national forest area is Alaska (22.2 million acres), followed by California (20.6 million acres).

- **1897:** In *Uncle Vanya* Sonya and Vanya become distracted by the arrival of Serebryakov and Yelena, allowing the crops to remain untended. Food shortages are a regular occurrence in Europe and Russia. In 1891 and 1892, Russia was crippled by famine after the country's crops failed. Millions were reduced to starvation and others, they were not necessarily free because most of them had no possessions and were enslaved through indebtedness. In the 1860s, peasants constituted eighty percent of the population of Russia.

the rural peasants raided towns looking for food. The famine was partially relieved by a shipment of some three million barrels of flour from the United States.

  Today: Each year, the United States produces approximately 59.5 million metric tons of wheat, 7.9 million metric tons of rice, and 187 million metric tons of corn. In 1995, the U. S. exported $55.8 billion worth of agricultural products.

- **1897:** Money is an important theme in *Uncle Vanya.* In Russia, Finance Minister Sergei Yulievich Witte introduces the gold standard. World gold production reaches nearly 11.5 million ounces, up from 5 to 6 million ounces per year between 1860 and 1890.

  Today: The U.S. produced roughly 320 metric tons of gold in 1995.

- **1897:** In *Uncle Vanya* Astrov is haunted by the death of one of his patients from typhus. In 1854, an epidemic of typhus devastated the Russian army, and the disease continues to be a threat throughout the century.

  Today: Typhus is no longer a problem; in 1930, Harvard bacteriology professor Hans Zinsser—with help from John Franklin Enders of Children's Hospital, Boston—developed the first anti-typhus vaccine. Today, AIDS is the most serious epidemic in the U. S. and other industrialized nations. By 1995, more than half a million people had died of AIDS.

Once serfdom was abolished, Russia underwent a period of social unrest, characterized by student rebellion and protests by political radicals.

In 1872, Karl Marx's *Das Kapital* was translated into Russian and the Russian people were introduced to the basic tenets of communism. In 1881, Czar Alexander II was assassinated by terrorists. Alexander III assumed rule of the country, and what followed was a time of mass arrests and deportations. Alexander III ruled until his death in 1894, when Czar Nicholas assumed power.

Although Chekhov's plays and stories aren't overtly political, the writer was the grandson of a serf and throughout his lifetime he came into frequent contact with the peasants and other poverty-stricken members of Russian society because of his work as a physician. In 1890, Chekhov visited the prison of Sakhalin, to care for the sick and record the conditions of the prisoners. Despite an awareness of the plight of others, Chekhov was not among the university radicals or dissidents who pressed for reform through public demonstrations. The peasants may play prominent roles in his work, but Chekhov was not an artist who was particularly concerned with politics.

The narrowness, vulgarity, and isolation of life in Russia are part of the fabric of the characters' lives. Astrov says, "I'm fond of life as a whole, but this petty, provincial life of ours in Russia—that I can't stand, I despise it utterly." What Chekhov takes exception to is the spiritual bankruptcy of life in Russia, more than the corruptness of the country's politics. Harvey Pitcher pointed out in *The Chekhov Play* that the plight of the Russian intelligentsia was hardly an original subject when Chekhov embraced it. In fact, the talented man for whom there's no place in society was already a literary cliche by the time Chekhov wrote his plays.

In *Uncle Vanya* Chekhov is concerned with class distinctions. Marina, the old nurse, is a sterling character, and she is the only individual on the estate who seems truly at peace. Characters like Astrov are ground down by hard work and poor conditions; their freedom is curtailed by the sudden demands of well-to-do hypochondriacs like Serebryakov, who capriciously summons Astrov and then refuses to see him. Vanya's charges against Serebryakov center around the sacrifices of time and effort he's made, but he's also aggrieved by the poor wages he's earned. "For twenty-five years," says Vanya, "I have managed this estate, worked, sent you money, like a most conscientious clerk, and during all that time you not once thanked me. All the time—both in my youth and now—you paid me five hundred roubles a year for wages—fit for a beggar—and you never once thought of increasing it by even one rouble!"

Artistically, Chekhov was also a man of his times. A proponent of realism, he pays careful attention to how people actually act or live, not to some highly subjective or romantic vision of life. Thus, some of the finest dialogue of *Uncle Vanya* closely resembles real conversations, where indi-viduals talk at cross purposes or misinterpret one another. For instance, when Sonya confesses her love for Astrov to Yelena, Yelena praises the doctor for his industry and bravery, but then begins to speak of her own feelings: "There's no happiness for me in this world." Instead of responding to her heartfelt admission, Sonya laughs from pleasure at her recent conversation with the doctor: "I am so happy . . . so happy!" she exclaims. In his realism, Chekhov is akin to other great nineteenth-century writers like George Eliot, Emile Zola, and Gustave Flaubert

CRITICAL OVERVIEW

Uncle Vanya was first published in 1897 but was not performed by the Moscow Art Theater, where it premiered, until October 26, 1899. Well received by audiences, *Uncle Vanya* was not entirely a success in Chekhov's own estimation. The directors at the Moscow Art Theater—Konstantin Stanislavsky and V. I. Nemirovich-Danchenko—did not understand Chekhov's artistic vision, and Chekhov, sick with tuberculosis by the time *Uncle Vanya* was produced, could not intervene. Nemirovich-Danchenko wrote, "Chekhov was incapable of advising actors. . . . Everything appeared so comprehensible to him: 'Why, I have written it all down,' he would answer." Stanislavsky admitted to being slightly confounded by Chekhov's plays; he said that when he went to produce *The Sea Gull,* he didn't know how to proceed, the words were too simple.

Even if Stanislavsky and Nemirovich-Danchenko failed to fully appreciate Chekhov's vision, *Uncle Vanya* was much better received than its earlier incarnation, *The Wood Demon.* Chekhov's second full-length play, *The Wood Demon* was rejected by two theaters before premiering in Moscow in December 1889; it played for only three performances before closing. Chekhov insisted that *The Wood Demon* never be staged again, and he would not permit it to be included in his *Collected Works.*

Although Chekhov quickly gained fame for his short stories, his plays puzzled many Russian audiences and even other Russian writers. When Chekhov met Leo Tolstoy, the *War and Peace* author said to him: "But I still can't stand your plays. Shakespeare's are terrible, but yours are even worse!" Tolstoy was harsh in his critique of *Uncle Vanya,* which he saw performed by the Moscow Art Theater on January 24, 1900. The novelist berated Chekhov for having done nothing to support Astrov's contention that he and Vanya are the only decent and intelligent men in the district. Why, asked Tolstoy, should the audience have such a high opinion of these two men? Pitcher quoted Tolstoy as having said that Vanya and Astrov "had always been bad and mediocre, and that is why their sufferings cannot be worthy of interest."

However, some critics point out that Tolstoy's public statements may not have been entirely accurate. Pitcher noted that Tolstoy sketched out the plan for his own play, *The Living Corpse,* after having seen *Uncle Vanya.* As Pitcher stated: "Although Tolstoy, the rational thinker, could not help finding Chekhov's play inadequate, Tolstoy, the man of feeling, seems to have responded more positively to *Uncle Vanya* than he was willing to admit."

Thomas A. Eekman, in his introduction to *Critical Essays on Anton Chekhov,* said that Chekhov was not a darling of early critics, including the traditional Russian populists. Eekman cited Nikolai K. Mikhailovsky, who blamed Chekhov for writing without social concern and for failing to adequately portray the peasants. Socialists, noted Eekman, thought Chekhov lacked political and revolutionary spirit. Vladimir Nabokov, in *Critical Essays on Anton Chekhov,* commented on this exact point: "What rather irritated his politically minded critics was that nowhere does the author assign this type to any definite party or give him any definite political program. But that is the whole point. Chekhov's inefficient idealists were neither terrorists, nor Social Democrats, nor budding Bolsheviks, nor any of the numberless members of numberless revolutionary parties in Russia."

Those critics who have not viewed Chekhov through a political lens have proven more generous. One prevailing opinion is that Chekhov gave expression to the loss and hopelessness of the Russian intelligentsia and landowners in the years leading up to the Russian Revolution. In the Soviet Union after the Revolution, a country radically different from old Russia, critics tended to dismiss Chekhov as a representative of bygone times.

Nabokov hailed Chekhov as a true artist, but he found that his artistry did not lie in his word choice. Wrote Nabokov: "Russian critics have noted that Chekhov's style, his choice of words and so on, did not reveal any of those special artistic preoccupa-

tions that obsessed, for instance, Gogol or Flaubert or Henry James. His dictionary is poor ... his literary style goes to parties clad in its everyday suit. . . . The magical part of it is that in spite of his tolerating flaws which a bright beginner would have avoided ... Chekhov managed to convey an impression of artistic beauty far surpassing that of many writers who thought they knew what rich beautiful prose was. . . . The variety of his moods, the flicker of his charming wit, the deeply artistic economy of characterization, the vivid detail, and the fade-out of human life—all the peculiar Chekhovian features—are enhanced by being suffused and surrounded by a faintly iridescent verbal haziness."

Chekhov has always been highly regarded in Great Britain and the United States. In Great Britain in the 1920s, writers like Virginia Woolf and John Galsworthy embraced him, and Chekhov is revered in the United States today; his plays are frequently revived in both countries. Some critics have noted that this is odd, since Chekhov's plays—with their overriding sense of helplessness and their plotlessness—are not what usually constitutes a theatrical success. Eric Bentley wrote in *Critical Essays on Anton Chekhov:* "Why is it that scarcely a year passes without a major Broadway or West end production of a Chekhov play? Chekhov's plays—at least by reputation, which in commercial theater is the important thing—are plotless, monotonous, drab, and intellectual: find the opposite of these four adjectives and you have a recipe for a smash hit." Performing Chekhov, Bentley suggested, is an act of rebellion against the system: "It is as if the theater remembers Chekhov when it remembers its conscience."

CRITICISM

Elizabeth Judd

Judd is a writer and book reviewer with an M.F.A. in English from the University of Michigan and a B.A. from Yale. In this essay, she discusses various the methods of indirect action employed by Chekhov in Uncle Vanya.

About suffering they were never wrong/ The Old Masters: how well they understood/ Its human position; how it takes place/ While someone else is eating

WHAT DO I READ NEXT?

- *The Three Sisters,* a Chekhov play first produced at the Moscow Art Theater in 1901, is the story of a wealthy Russian family who longs to move to Moscow, but the three sisters find themselves mired in provincial life. Like *Uncle Vanya, The Three Sisters* is a play of thwarted desires and indirect action.

- In *The Cherry Orchard,* Chekhov's characters long to preserve an orchard that holds fond memories rather than allowing it to be chopped down and turned into a subdivision.

- Chekhov was deeply influenced by Leo Tolstoy. There are parallels between Tolstoy's treatment of the peasants and of religious faith in *An-*

na Karenina and Chekhov's treatment of the same subjects in *Uncle Vanya.* However, *Anna Karenina* is also considered one of the world's great, tragic love stories.

- Like Chekhov, George Eliot was a proponent of realism in literature. Her masterpiece—*Middlemarch*—is the story of Dorothea Brooke, a woman who wants to make a worthwhile contribution to society but is thwarted by a tragically misbegotten marriage.

- Henry James's *Portrait of a Lady* is one of the world's finest novels about deception and frustrated desires.

---

or opening a window or just walking dully along. . . .
—*"Musee des Beaux Arts,"* W. H. Auden

When it comes to portraying the anguish of the human condition, no other dramatist, past or present, equals Chekhov, especially in *Uncle Vanya,* his classic of thwarted desire. In practically every scene of the play, the characters give voice to their boredom, pain, and despair, yet *Uncle Vanya* is also filled with moments of lightness and comedy. Chekhov examines frustration and loss of hope indirectly, placing nearly all the climactic moments off stage, many of them in the distant past.

Chekhov is known for pioneering a dramatic technique—indirect action—which concentrates on subtleties of characterization and the interactions between individuals, instead of on flashy revelations or unexpected plot twists. In this play, "Everything," as Vanya says, "is an old story." Vanya has been editing Serebryakov's work for twenty-five years; Sonya has spent six years loving Astrov without her affections being returned; and Astrov has slaved away as a country doctor for the past eleven years. Emotional scenes have been played out and the characters are exhausted and cranky. When Maria Voinitskaya begins to describe a letter she's received, Vanya interrupts her: "But for fifty

years now we talk and talk, and read pamphlets. It's high time to stop."

If *Uncle Vanya* were a more conventional drama, Chekhov would have begun the play with the arrival of the professor and Yelena. Instead, the characters are already bored with one another by the time the curtain rises, and the first glimpse the audience catches of Vanya highlights the sense of malaise: he is yawning after an afternoon nap. In a less innovative play, Chekhov would have shown Vanya's growing disillusionment with the professor as it unfolded, rather than presenting it as an accomplished fact. In fact, the central drama of the play—Vanya's realization that he's squandered his own talents in serving the professor—occurs a year before the play begins.

When Vanya's mother observes that he's changed beyond recognition, he says: "Up to last year, I deliberately tried just as you do to blind my eyes with this pedantry of yours and not to see real life—and I thought I was doing well. And now, if you only knew! I don't sleep nights because of disappointment, and anger that I so stupidly let time slip by, when now I could have had everything that my old age denies me!" Strikingly, Chekhov is not

---

content to let the drama of such an impassioned speech pass without a moment of deflation. Sonya chides: "Uncle Vanya, that's boring," withholding even the most meager comfort.

Love is also denied, again and again, in *Uncle Vanya.* Except for two hurried embraces between Astrov and Yelena, the only romantic consummation occurs in Vanya's daydream of proposing to Yelena ten years prior, before she'd married Serebryakov. "It was so possible," says Vanya. "Now we both would have been awakened by the storm; she would have been frightened by the thunder and I would have held her in my arms and whispered: 'Don't be afraid, I am here.' Oh, beautiful thoughts, how wonderful, I am even smiling." Vanya is so demoralized that he can't even bring himself to fantasize in the present tense.

More telling is the fact Vanya doesn't sustain the thought of a romance with Yelena but launches immediately into another mental harangue about the piteous state of his life. "Why am I old?" cries Vanya, who then give voice to his real passion: how he has been deceived by the professor: "I adored that Professor, that pitiful, gouty creature, I worked for him like an ox!" For Vanya, the self-deception of his love for Serebryakov is far more painful than his unrequited love for the professor's wife.

Many critics have observed that Chekhov's three great plays—*Uncle Vanya, The Three Sisters,* and *The Cherry Orchard*—are difficult to describe because so little happens. Yet a lack of dramatic action is central to Chekhov's design. Articulating his artistic approach in a critique of a performance of *Uncle Vanya,* Chekhov faulted the actress who played Sonya for having thrown herself at Serebryakov's feet in Act III. "That's quite wrong," said Chekhov, "after all, it isn't a drama. The whole meaning, the whole drama of a person's life are contained within, not in outward manifestations. . . . A shot, after all, is not a drama, but an incident." In other words, what matters to Chekhov is the individual's emotions and motivations, not the activities that occupy his or her days. True to his convictions, Chekhov portrays the gun shot in *Uncle Vanya* as a ludicrous non-event, with Vanya firing at point-blank range only to miss the mark. Underscoring the absurdity of this act of untutored violence, Chekhov has the beautiful and bored Yelena struggle with Vanya, preventing him from firing again.

Although a conspicuous absence of drama is certainly a form of indirection, Chekhov's penchant for inserting humor into the most gloomy pronouncements or situations is an even more radical, anti-dramatic strategy. In *Uncle Vanya* heartbreakingly sad moments are undercut by incongruous details or moments of outright silliness. In some ways, Chekhov works like a magician, using the misdirection of humor to divert the audience from the sadness that engulfs Vanya, Astrov, Yelena, and Sonya. No matter how great the misery of the characters, Marina offers the same, simplistic cure—linden tea, vodka, or some noodle soup. The old nurse is unruffled by the accusations family members hurl at one another, reducing passion to the nonsense sounds made by animals. "It's all right, my child," Marina tells Sonya. "The geese will cackle—and then stop . . . cackle—and stop." And when Marina believes that Vanya has shot Serebryakov, she says, "Ough! Botheration take them!" and goes right on knitting.

Despair itself takes on its own black humor in *Uncle Vanya.* When Yelena makes the casual observation, "And fine weather today. . . . Not hot. . . ." Vanya responds: "It's fine weather to hang yourself." The intense self-pity of Vanya's pronouncement is so inappropriate that it catches the audience off guard in much the way the physical comedy of a pratfall does. In Chekhov's plays, even pleasantries are subverted. The humor of Vanya's relentless gloominess is heightened by the nonchalance of those around him. For the characters in *Uncle Vanya,* talk of suicide is so unexceptional that no one bothers to ask Vanya what's wrong or even to respond to his noisy despair. At times, the play possesses the deadpan humor of an Addams Family cartoon, where dark statements are viewed as too banal, too commonplace, to warrant acknowledgment or comment.

Writing in *Anton Chekhov's Plays,* Charles B. Timmer maintained that elements of incongruity, which he termed "the bizarre," have been overlooked in Chekhov's work, and he described the dramatist's approach this way: "The *bizarre* is not necessarily absurd: it is, as it were, a statement, or a situation, which has no logical place in the context or in the sequence of events, the resulting effect being one of sudden bewilderment; the bizarre brings about a kind of mental 'airpocket': one gasps for breath, until the tension is relieved by laughter."

To illustrate, Timmer pointed to the moment in Act IV when Astrov is about to take leave of Vanya and Sonya. In a scene that should be highly emotional, Chekhov flouts expectations by having Astrov

A scene from the Moscow Art Theatre production of Chekhov's play

observe a meaningless detail—a map of Africa hanging on the wall. "I suppose down there the heat in Africa must be terrific now!" exclaims the doctor as Sonya and Vanya pay bills. According to Timmer, "this element of restraint, applied in a scene that is charged with emotions, greatly intensifies the impression on the spectator. The element of the bizarre as a technique to retard the action and restrain the emotions is used frequently by Chekhov in his plays."

Why would Chekhov write about the frustration and sadness of the human condition, only to undercut these emotions time and again with a noticeable lack of drama and eruptions of humor? In many ways, the lack of drama *is* Chekhov's point. Many critics have observed that *Uncle Vanya* is, in some sense, an anti-play, one where the characters try to strike out and change their lives, only to fail miserably. At the end of the final act, when Marina invites Astrov to drink some vodka, the audience is reminded of the very first scene of the play when she makes the exact same offer to him. Chekhov further underscores that old patterns have been re-established by having Vanya tell Serebryakov at their parting, "You will receive what you used to receive accurately. Everything will be as always."

Imprisoned in static lives, Vanya, Sonya, and Astrov make a bid for something larger and grand-

er—for love or for an acknowledgment of how they've suffered—but nothing comes of their tired rebellion. The action of the play is indirect because it's internal, the plotting of a break that fails to materialize. As Eric Bentley wrote in *Critical Essays on Anton Chekhov:* "In *Uncle Vanya,* recognition means that what all these years seemed to be so, though one hesitated to believe it, really is so and will remain so."

In *Uncle Vanya* there is no way out of misery, no light at the end of the tunnel. "You know," says Astrov, "when you walk through a forest on a dark night, if you see a small light gleaming in the distance, you don't notice your fatigue, the darkness, the thorny branches lashing your face . . . but for me there is no small light in the distance." Vanya is also without hope: "Here they are: my life and my love: where shall I put them, what shall I do with them? This feeling of mine is dying in vain, like a ray of sunlight that has strayed into a pit, and I myself am dying." Such a bleak message can hardly be contemplated directly. Nor can Chekhov provide an answer beyond the half-hearted suggestion that the only way to live with such pain is to practice indirection.

When Astrov asks why Vanya isn't seeing Yelena and Serebryakov off, he answers: "Let them go, and I . . . I can't. I feel very low, I must busy myself quickly with something. . . . Work, work!'' Ultimately, in a world where there's no hope that the frustration will end, when there is no light and the characters' own sparks have been extinguished in a pit of engulfing darkness, all there can be is indirection and distraction—moments of humor, oases and panaceas like hard work and Marina's cup of linden tea.

Source: Elizabeth Judd, for *Drama for Students,* Gale, 1999.

Donald Rayfield

Rayfield provides an overview of Uncle Vanya, *discussing the manner in which Chekhov was able resurrect one of his biggest flops,* The Wood Demon, *as a new play that would come to be regarded as one of his masterworks.*

Uncle Vanya (Diadia Vania) can be seen as the last of Chekhov's earlier plays, all based on a problematic, male antihero. It was published in 1897 and first performed in 1899, after *The Seagull,* and was written, or reconstituted, out of the wreck of *The Wood Demon,* between 1892 and 1896. It is thus, also, the second of Chekhov's mature plays, its acts not broken into scenes, its Act IV an anti-climax of embarrassed departure, its tone hovering between cruel comedy and pathos. The basic plot, two thirds of the text, and the characters are carried over from *The Wood Demon:* comparing the two plays is a lesson on how a flop may be turned into a great play.

The core of both plays is the arrival of the professor and his young second wife, disrupting the life, and threatening the livelihood, of his daughter Sonya and of Uncle Vanya. The differences in *Uncle Vanya* are, firstly, that the Uncle turns the gun against the professor, not himself, but farcically fails to alter anything; secondly, that a new Act IV makes a mockery of reconciliation and instead leaves the old professor in full charge while the remaining characters are abandoned to their desolate future; and thirdly, that the catalyst of the action—the ecological idealist, the doctor—is also a lecherous alcoholic. Thus the inverted principles of Chekhovian comedy are established: age triumphs over youth, the servants rule their masters, and the normal world has crumbled. The subtitle—*Scenes from Country Life* —is deliberately ironic.

Like many other Chekhov plays, *Uncle Vanya* incorporates material from his stories which certainly would have guided a contemporary audience's interpretation. Dr. Astrov's impassioned

(though comically pedantic) laments for the ravaged environment recapitulate the lyrical complaints of the story *Panpipes (Svirel)* of 1887; the professor, terrified of death and torturing his wife and daughter with his hypochondria through a stormy summer night, is parodying the impressive professor, the narrator of *A Dreary Story (Skuchnaia istoriia)* of 1889. But once this material is in a dramatic framework, comic absurdity evaporates the authorial presence; the residual lyricism is to be found in the non-verbal elements—the storm winds, the nightwatchman's banging of a rail, the reproachfully silent piano, Telegin's tentative strumming of a guitar, Marina's knitting, or the starling in a cage.

The play was first offered to the state Maly theatre in Moscow. After the failure of *The Seagull* the Maly prevaricated and Chekhov ceded *Uncle Vanya* to the Moscow Arts Theatre, which had made a success of *The Seagull.* Stanislavsky was persuaded to take the role of Dr. Astrov under Nemirovich-Danchenko's direction. As always, Stanislavsky saw social comment and pathos in the ruin of the sensitive provincials, Uncle Vanya and Astrov, by the ruthless professorial careerist from the capital; Chekhov's laconic comments, however, stressed the dry comedy. Nevertheless, *Uncle Vanya* has a little of the autobiographical input that made *The Seagull* so shocking a play: the self-sacrificing Sonya, doomed to spinsterhood, was clearly recognisable as Chekhov's sister Marya, while the play's impoverished and diseased landscape was specified as the Serpukhov district around Chekhov's estate, Melikhovo.

By 1900 *Uncle Vanya* was acclaimed: for the first time Chekhov could consider himself a playwright by vocation and not renounce the theatre, although the play's success embarrassed him as much as earlier plays' failures: literati and their wives wept, while country doctors saw it as an expression of their grievances. Russian critics felt it was ''an exercise in thought, in working out life and finding a way out''.

The one resistant spectator was Tolstoy: ''I went to see *Uncle Vanya* and I was appalled. . . Where's the drama? The play treads water''. In fact, in refusing to let actions have their usual dramatic consequences—nobody arrests Uncle Vanya for firing at the professor—Chekhov shows his genius for unprecedented dramatic compression. Yelena doesn't have to compare herself to a caged bird: the starling is there in its cage. The forests don't catch fire (as they do in *The Wood Demon*): Astrov looks at the map of Africa and remarks how hot it must be there. The clothes are vestimentary markers of the character's neuroses: the professor in his galoshes and overcoat, Uncle Vanya in his flashy tie. The climaxes are built up as carefully as Ibsen's: Act III's announcement of the professor's plan to appropriate the entire estate for himself starts a long crescendo that culminates in gunshots. But the tension is constantly broken by apparent parody: Uncle Vanya goes over the top, claiming he "could have been Dostoevsky or Schopenhauer", reverting to infantile tantrums at his mother's knee. A modern audience reacts as Chekhov intended—they cannot weep at farce, but take their lead from Marina, the imperturbable servant, for whom all this row is "ganders cackling".

The key to *Uncle Vanya,* as to *The Cherry Orchard,* is in the doomed trees. Astrov's passionate defence of them is comic because it bores and puzzles his listener, Yelena; but it switches the audience's concern from the disrupted family to nature off-stage, which desperately signals its distress to the uncaring characters. Uncle Vanya, unlike Platonov or Ivanov in earlier plays, is thus out of focus, for all his eponymous status: his irrelevance makes him, in the last analysis, comic. What Chekhov shows happening to the Voinitsky family is only a symptom of a more fatal convulsion in the outside world—among the epidemics and dried-up rivers of the Russian landscape.

Source: Donald Rayfield, "*Uncle Vanya*" in *The International Dictionary of Theatre,* Volume 1: *Plays,* edited by Mark Hawkins-Dady, St. James Press, 1992, pp. 850–51.

Desmond MacCarthy

In this review of Uncle Vanya, *MacCarthy appraises Chekhov's work as a unique dramatic achievement in the sense that, while its subject matter is not sensational or thrilling, it is nevertheless a griping, "violently interesting" example of theatrical craft.*

Uncle Vanya was called by Tchekov "scenes from country life." He wished to make it perfectly clear from the outset that he was not writing a Scribe, a Sardou, or even an Alexandre Dumas *fils* play. He was writing a *Middlemarch,* only he was writing it for the theatre. He went so far as to steal one of George Eliot's characters (*vide Landmarks of Russian Literature*), Mr. Casaubon, who appeared in the flesh in this play. It is not undramatic because it is violently interesting; and it is dramatic, not be-

UNCLE VANYA CAN BE SEEN AS THE LAST OF CHEKHOV'S EARLIER PLAYS, ALL BASED ON A PROBLEMATIC, MALE ANTIHERO"

cause there is any sustained plot or any dexterity of move and countermove between the characters, but because the glimpses of ordinary everyday life which Tchekov gives us remind us poignantly of what we have seen in our everyday life. In fact, Tchekov meets the need of the Russian gentleman who said: "Je vais au théâtre pour voir ce que vois tous les jours." If that is your need, Tchekov does more than meet it, he fulfils it. If, on the other hand, you aspire to see just those very things which are lacking in your everyday life, that is to say, a spy killing Lord Kitchener, or M. Clemenceau throttling M. Poincaré on the cornice of the Arc de Triomphe, then Tchekov will disappoint you. Imagine Tchekov's *Uncle Vanya* being offered to an ordinary successful manager, and supposing, as was not long ago the case, no one had heard of Tchekov, he would at once say, "When is this play going to begin?"; and at its close, "why has it ended?"

The first act introduces us to a group of characters. In the second act the same group of characters have abounded in their own sense, abounded but not bounded, for they have not made one step forward. In the third act, one of the characters, Uncle Vanya himself, exasperated beyond human endurance, lets off a pistol at Professor Casaubon and misses him. That is all the action, properly speaking, there is in the play. In the fourth act, some of the characters leave the house where the conversation has been proceeding, and Uncle Vanya and Sonia, his niece, remain behind. That is all that happened. Yet the juxtaposition of these characters in these peculiar circumstances and the conversation which they make between them, open out vistas of thought and feeling. After seeing this play we know the whole lives of the seven or eight characters. We know their past, although they have told us little of it; we can guess their future. Moreover, although they belong to Russia, and to a distinct and marked epoch of Russian history, the period of stagnation preceding the Russo-Japanese war, during which, as a Russian

> UNCLE VANYA IS DRAMATIC, NOT BECAUSE THERE IS ANY SUSTAINED PLOT OR ANY DEXTERITY OF MOVE AND COUNTERMOVE BETWEEN THE CHARACTERS, BUT BECAUSE THE GLIMPSES OF ORDINARY EVERYDAY LIFE WHICH TCHEKOV GIVES US REMIND US POIGNANTLY OF WHAT WE HAVE SEEN IN OUR EVERYDAY LIFE"

once said, "Russia was dying of playing Vindt" (which is about the same as auction-bridge), we have met these characters in every other country. They swarm in London; not a few were in the audience when the play was being acted. We have each of us met Uncle Vanya full of good intentions and ideals turned slightly sour, brave in words, feeble in action, easily reduced to despair and tears, who, if exasperated sufficiently, can fire off a pistol which will never hit anyone. We have known Professor Casaubon's young wife, Elena, sensuous, non-moral, the would-be guardian angel, the harmless Circe so much more fatal to people like Dr. Astrov and Uncle Vanya than Circe herself, with all her paraphernalia of golden looms and grunting swine. We all of us have known Sonia, the plain, unattractive, good niece, who loves in vain and remains behind to do the accounts for her uncle. But, the reader will say, if we know all these people by heart, if the characters of George Eliot, and many other novelists, are being paraded before us, where is the originality of Tchekov as a dramatist. His originality lies in this; not only has he put real people on the stage—dramatists have done that from the days of Aristophanes to those of St. John Hankin—but what Tchekov has done and what nobody else has ever attempted, is to put on the stage that which in all other plays happens during the *entr'actes.* That is to say, when you see a drama, when the passionate lovers say good-bye, when all is over, you know that the ordinary life of the people concerned must, in spite of everything, go on; that they must change their clothes, have breakfast, tea

and supper, and that after the last good-bye has been said there will come a moment when someone will say, "The carriage is at the door," and the carriage will drive up and the guests will get into it and go, and the host will remain at home. Tchekov shows you all this; he shows you the guests going and the other people remaining at home. You hear the dull machinery of everyday once more creaking in its customary groove. This experience is novel and indescribably moving when it is presented on the stage with discretion. Of course, a great deal depends upon the acting. You cannot act a Tchekov play in the same way that you act a Pinero play, not even with the starriest of casts. Tchekov learnt this himself by bitter experience. When one of his first plays, *The Sea Gull,* was first produced at Petrograd at the State-paid theatre, the Comédie Française of Russia, full of tradition and competence, the play did not get across the footlights. But when it was gently treated by the Art Theatre at Moscow, and the play was allowed to act itself, the effect was tremendous.

So it was at the Court Theatre on Sunday and Monday. The play was produced by M. Theodore Komisarjevsky, late producer and art director at the Moscow State Theatre. It was one of the best performances the Stage Society has given, immensely superior to their last performance of the play just before the war. I missed, however, Miss Gillian Scaife as Sonia, and in some respects I preferred Mr. Guy Rathbone's Uncle Vanya to Mr. Leon Quartermaine's. Mr. Leon Quartermaine made him a little too harsh; he was neither sympathetically weak nor hysterically weak enough. In that last scene, when Uncle Vanya and Sonia sit down at the neglected writing table to work again—the only cure for their disappointments—and she makes her dim little speech about the world beyond the grave where they will forget the stale ache of them, Mr. Quartermaine did not give with equal poignancy the sense of suffering passively, such as only the weak and empty know. He ought, too, to have been made-up to look older. Miss Rathbone was perhaps a little too much the good schoolgirl, and hardly woman enough. I think in that last scene it would have been better if she had made a subtle distinction between the first part of her speech when she is repeating sincerely, yet, in a way, by rote, those consolations in which she believes, and the last few words when she puts her arms round his neck. She was excellent in all the scenes with Dr. Astrov and with Elena, excellent indeed in her bearing throughout. Miss Cathleen Nesbitt was an admirable Elena; her walk and gestures were perfect, with their suggestion of indolence and restlessness, as of an unsatisfied woman, neither cold nor passionate, a torment to herself, who tantalises others and leads them on to torment her. Her acting made it quite clear how exasperating Vanya's passion for her was, how impossible it was for her to be even decently kind to him sometimes; if only Mr. Quartermaine had made us sympathise, too, as much with Vanya in these scenes, the scenes between them would have been perfect, but he could not be utterly, helplessly emotional. Though Elena longs to be rid of her pestering lovers, she really is only interested in love. Miss Nesbitt acted the scene in which Astrov tries to interest Elena in his ideas extraordinarily well; her boredom, her inability to keep her mind on anything but the man who is talking to her she expressed to perfection.

I have a great respect for Mr. Franklin Dyall as an actor. I have never seen him fail, and I have seen him succeed where success is rare. He can give as well as anyone (and how few such actors there are) an impression of an intense character somehow bedevilled, run-to-seed, spoilt. He would make an admirable Rolling in The Wild Duck, or a good Larry in John Bull's Other Island. This characteristic suits the part of Astrov. To Sonia, Astrov, in spite of his coarseness and drunkenness, seems so fine in himself, and he even moves Elena a little. To her, too, he seems superior to the others, and she thinks of that superiority in characteristically feminine terms as "a streak of genius." The idealist gone wrong is often attractive to women; he is a person to be saved, too, which is an extra attraction, while the sense of a conflict within him suggests to them possibilities of passion. Mr. Hignett as the professor was duly empty and fatuous, yet, as he should be, a man of imposing exterior. He has written rows of books and stacks of articles on art and literature, saying in them what all clever people knew before and others take no interest in at all. We know him well. The minor parts—the old nurse (Miss Iné Cameron), the amiable tame cat of the house, Telyegen (Mr. Dodd), Vanya's old mother (Miss Agnes Thomas)—were beautifully played. When you have a good producer, one of the first effects noticeable is that everybody in the play becomes conscious of the importance of their parts. It was an admirable production, and it was borne in on one again what all clever people know and others, alas ! take no interest in—namely, that it is not talent but the art of production that our stage lacks at the present time.

Source: Desmond MacCarthy, "Tchekov and the Stage Society" in the *New Statesman,* Vol. XVIII, no. 451, December 3, 1921, pp. 254–55.

SOURCES

Bentley, Eric. "Craftsmanship in *Uncle Vanya*" in *Critical Essays on Anton Chekhov,* G. K. Hall, 1989, pp. 169-85.

Eekman, Thomas A. Introduction to *Critical Essays on Anton Chekhov,* G. K. Hall, 1989, pp. 1-7.

Nabokov, Vladimir. "Chekhov's Prose" in *Critical Essays on Anton Chekhov,* G. K. Hall, 1989, pp. 26-33.

Pitcher, Harvey. *The Chekhov Play,* University of California Press, 1985.

Timmer, Charles B. "The Bizarre Element in Chekhov's Art" in *Anton Chekhov's Plays,* W. W. Norton, 1977, pp. 272-85.

FURTHER READING

Bordinat, Philip. "Dramatic Structure in Chekhov's *Uncle Vanya* " in *Chekhov's Great Plays,* New York University Press, 1981, pp. 47-60.
    A discussion of how Chekhov's plays are structured.

Gilman, Richard *Chekhov's Plays: An Opening into Eternity,* Yale University Press, 1997.
    An examination of each of Chekhov's full-length plays, placing them in the context of Russian and European drama and of the artist's own life.

Koteliansky, S. S., editor and translator. *Anton Tchekhov: Literary and Theatrical Reminiscences,* Benjamin Blom, 1965.
    A collection of literary and theatrical reminiscences of Chekhov from writers Leo Tolstoy and Maxim Gorky and from directors V. I. Nemirovich-Danchenko and Konstantin Stanislavsky, as well as excerpts from Chekhov's diary.

Magarshack, David. "Purpose and Structure in Chekhov's Plays" in *Anton Chekhov's Plays,* W. W. Norton, 1977, pp. 259-71.
    An essay that discusses how Chekhov's plays were interpreted by the Moscow Art Theater and how his plays are constructed.

Melchinger, Siegfried. *Anton Chekhov,* Frederick Ungar, 1972.
    This book provides a biographical essay and discussions of all Chekhov's major plays.

Rayfield, Donald. *Anton Chekhov: A Life,* Henry Holt, 1998.
    A well-structured and comprehensive biography of the writer. Rayfield is a noted Chekhov scholar.

Vitins, Ieva. "Uncle Vanya's Predicament" in *Chekhov's Great Plays,* New York University Press, 1981, pp. 35-46.
    An essay on *Uncle Vanya.*

Zoot Suit

LUIS VALDEZ

1978

Zoot Suit brings to life a racially-charged trial of the 1940s, in which a group of *pachucos,* Mexican-American gang members, are charged and sentenced with the murder of another Mexican American. Playwright Luis Valdez depicts the trial of the Sleepy Lagoon Murder and the related Zoot Suit Riots of 1943 in a combination of docudrama, myth, and musical. *Zoot Suit* was designed to reach a larger audience than those targeted by the improvisational skits, or *actos,* he had produced for *El Teatro Campesino,* a theater troupe he founded to support Hispanic labor leader Cesar Chavez's efforts to unionize California farm workers during the Delano Grape Strike of 1965. Although he reached back into history for a specific Mexican-American incident, Valdez's play concerns the problems of all ethnic minorities in America.

Opening in 1978, *Zoot Suit* sold out every time it played in Los Angeles, though it met with less enthusiasm from critics in New York when it debuted on Broadway. In the play, the mythical character El Pachuco cajoles Henry Reyna to resist the social injustices of an unfair trial and fight for his community; he does so, but the play ends without resolving his future. With its Brechtian-style protest against social injustice and defamiliarization techniques, such that the action is controlled and re-directed by one of the characters, *Zoot Suit* set a new standard for Chicano theater and Valdez was recognized as a leader in American drama. A film version produced in 1981 starring Edward James Olmos and Daniel

Valdez (the playwright's brother, who had played Henry in the stage production as well) brought this vivid portrayal of social injustice to movie theaters.

AUTHOR BIOGRAPHY

Luis Valdez was born June 26, 1940, to migrant farm workers in Delano, California; he was one of ten children. His interest in drama began early: a schoolteacher introduced him to puppetry, and in high school he appeared on a local television station. He also periodically helped his family in the fields, as they moved from farm to farm, following the planting and harvest schedule. He received his Bachelor Arts in English from the San Jose State University, where he produced his first play. Later, his alma mater awarded him an honorary Doctorate of Arts degree.

Valdez worked with the San Francisco Mime Troupe for a year before helping Hispanic labor leader César Chávez organize workers during the Great Delano Grape Strike of 1965. To support this effort, Valdez founded El Teatro Campesino (The Farmworkers' Theater), serving as its Artistic Director for many years. This small theater group began performing *actos*—brief theatrical "sketches"—to communicate the need for unionization among farmworkers and to educate the public about the migrant workers' plight. Eventually, the troupe took a more artistic turn, producing plays in San Franscico and elsewhere. In 1968, El Teatro won an Obie (a distinguished off-Broadway award) for "demonstrating the politics of survival."

Valdez began writing *mitos* or "myths," such as his 1967 *Dark Root of a Scream,* a condemnation of the Vietnam War, and his 1973 *La carpa de los Rasquachis,* a story of the Mexican immigrant experience. His unique combination of *acto* (sketch), *mito,* and *corrido* (musical), along with his personal brand of Brechtian self-consciousness, combined with his goal of socio-political change quickly brought Valdez to the forefront of Chicano theater, and he enjoyed success with nationwide tours of his works. *Zoot Suit* (1978) was produced with the Center Theatre Group of Los Angeles, while he continued his leadership role at El Teatro Campesino.

Although *Zoot Suit* received mixed reviews during its New York debut, Valdez had the honor of being the first Chicano director to have a play

Luis Valdez.

produced on Broadway, and popular enthusiasm for the play encouraged him to take it on a successful national tour. This accomplishment marked the beginning of his rise as an individual artist, and he produced a well-received film version of *Zoot Suit* in 1981. In 1987, he directed the hit film *La Bamba,* which chronicled the short life of Hispanic rock star Richie Valens, and created several performances for the Public Broadcasting Service (PBS). In the 1990s, Valdez divided his time between screenwriting and teaching at California State University, Monterey Bay.

PLOT SUMMARY

Prologue

A backdrop of a giant newspaper headlines announces an invasion of "zoot-suiters," or *pachucos,* young Mexican-American men who wear slicked-down hair and suits with long, exaggerated coattails; armed forces are called in to handle the problem.

A switchblade rips through the newspaper to reveal El Pachuco, the epitome of a zoot-suiter, assuming the usual posture of defiant coolness. He begins speaking in Spanish, then switches to perfect English. In a cocky beat, he describes the Pachuco style. He exits, swinging a long watch chain.

Act I, scene i

The scene is a dance floor in the barrio, or Spanish-speaking neighborhood, in the 1940s. Couples from the 38th Street Gang dance, led by Henry Reyna with his girlfriend, Della Barrios. A few Anglo sailors dance nearby, as El Pachuco sings. The rival Downey gang enters and the dance turns violent when the rival gang leader, Rafas, shoves Henry's brother Rudy.

Act I, scene ii

The dance/brawl is interrupted by sirens, detectives with drawn guns, and a reporter snapping pictures. Sergeant Smith and Lieutenant Edwards make arrests, but they let the Anglos go. The scene dissolves into a lineup.

Act I, scene iii

El Pachuco comes forward to the pacing Henry and gives him a dose of reality: innocent or not, he will go to jail. He also tells Henry that his plans to join the Navy will not come to fruition. Henry's war is in the barrio, not overseas.

Act I, scene iv

The ever-present Press continues to update the headlines: twenty-two members of the 38th Street Gang held on "various charges," including the murder of Jose Williams. The policeman Smith beats Henry, trying to get him to talk. The stubborn Henry only passes out. As Dolores, Henry's mother, enters, time slips back to the Saturday before the gang fight. Dolores and husband Enrique quibble with Henry over his tachuche, his zoot suit, or "drapes," but they let him wear the outfit because he is a man ("es hombre"), whereas they refuse to let Henry's sister, Lupe, wear a short skirt to the dance. Enrique announces a Navy send-off party for Henry next weekend. The family bids a respectful and affectionate adieu as the young people leave for the dance.

The scene shifts to the dance floor, where El Pachuco sings and the 38th Street Gang members dance.

Act I, scene v

Back in the present, the public reads newspapers and litter the streets with them. All exit, except for one figure, a street sweeper. It is Enrique. When he has finished cleaning up, he pauses to read the news.

Act I, scene vi

The gang nervously awaits the outcome of their arrest. Joey has been beaten but hasn't told anything, and Smiley realizes, too late, that he is too old for all of this: he'd rather be with his wife and child. A "People's lawyer," George Shearer, meets his new clients and wins their trust.

Act I, scene vii: "The Saturday Night Dance"

As the boys recount the story of the dance/brawl to George, the events are portrayed on stage. Henry takes Della to Sleepy Lagoon to tell her "something." The Downey Gang is there, but the groups co-exist peacefully until Rafas, the Downey leader, pushes Rudy to the floor. Henry and Rafas are instantly in a knife fight, which El Pachuco magically interrupts, saying to the audience, "That's exactly what the play needs right now. Two more Mexicans killing each other." Henry lets Rafas go. The Downey gang leaves and the dance continues.

Act I, scene viii: "El Dia de la Raza" (The Day of the Knife)

The Press enters, building a jail of newspaper piles, while the couples recite headlines of the War and the zoot suit "crime wave." A friend of George's, Alice Bloomfield, surprises Henry with her interest in his case. George discovers that the boys have been denied the right to change their clothes or wash, an infraction of their civil rights. El Pachuco refuses to let Henry be as optimistic as his two Anglo defenders, but Henry insists he is not the "classic social victim" and will be freed.

Act I, scene ix

The "largest mass trial in the history of Los Angeles County" opens "to put an end to Mexican baby gangsterism." George raises his objection against the clothing restriction, but the Judge overrules him, saying it is a useful way to identify the witnesses. Furthermore, each time a defendant's name is mentioned, he is required to stand up. El

Pachuco encourages the boys at least to sit up straight. Della takes the stand.

Act I, scene x

The lights change to create a reflection like a lagoon on the floor. Henry and Della enact their walk along the reservoir listening to the music of a party at the Williams ranch in the distance; Della narrates. Henry is promising Della a big Pachuco wedding upon his return from the War when the Downey gang suddenly appears and proceeds to smash up Henry's car. Della cannot prevent Henry from confronting them and getting beaten senseless. When he comes to, Henry's organizes eight cars of his gang members to retaliate, but finding no Downey boys, they crash the Williams Ranch party. They don't know that Rafas and his gang have already terrorized the party. The party members react violently when they perceive a fresh attack. As Henry's gang retreats, Della vaguely sees someone brutally hitting a man on the ground with a stick. The victim is presumably Jose Williams, who will die from the attack.

Act I, scene xi

In an unfair trial, the whole gang is committed to life imprisonment at San Quentin. George vows to appeal the decision.

Act II, scenes i through v

The gang members are in prison, where they receive letters from loved ones. Alice visits Henry and they form a tense relationship that is veering toward romance. George's announcement that he has been drafted devastates the boys, even though he assures them that other competent lawyers are handling their case. Henry's temper lands him in solitary confinement. When El Pachuco tries to console him, Henry lashes out at his alter ego, sending him away.

Act II, scene vi

In Los Angeles, the Zoot Suit Riots take place between marines and zoot suiters. Rudy is being terrorized by a gang of marines when El Pachuco takes his place. Swabbie accuses him of trying to "outdo the white man" with his clothes, and then El Pachuco is overpowered and stripped down to a loincloth. Henry watches in shock as El Pachuco exits humbled but maintaining his dignity.

Act II, scene vii

Alice and Henry's attraction intensifies, but Alice recognizes it as a culmination of cultural forces as well as chemistry. She intends to get the court decision overturned, although Henry has given up hope.

Act II, scene viii

Rudy enlists, and then the Press announces a turning point in World War II, as the Pachuco boys gain their freedom.

Act II, scene ix

The boys and Rudy return to the barrio, amidst much celebration. The lights dim and the play seems to end on this happy note, but El Pachuco flicks his wrist and the lights come back up. The barrio still has its problems, and Henry must decide between Alice and Della. Surrounded by a cacophany of voices and demands, he chooses Della. Rudy and Joey get into a fight, then Rudy emotionally relates the horrors of being stripped in the zoot suit riots. In the meantime, the police are busy arresting Joey for stealing a car that actually belongs to George. Enrique restrains Henry from protecting Joey, and the entire family embraces. The Press, Rudy, Alice, and others narrate various possible futures for Henry, finishing with El Pachuco's announcement that the myth of Henry Reyna—El Pachuco—lives on.

CHARACTERS

Adella

See Della Barrios

Della Barrios

Henry's twenty-year-old current girlfriend, who sports a mini-skirt and fingertip-length coat, is prettier than Henry's last girlfriend. At Sleepy Lagoon, he proposes to marry her after he returns from his Naval duty. Although Della does not write to Henry while he is in prison, she herself serves a jail term for her involvement in the gang fight and would have had time to write. When her parents ask her to choose between home and Henry, she chooses to move into Henry's place and wait for him. Even so, she does not pressure Henry into the marriage the gang expects but lets him make his own choice.

MEDIA ADAPTATIONS

- *Zoot Suit* was filmed on stage in 1981 by Universal Pictures at the Aquarius Theatre in Hollywood with segments of cinematic material interspersed, lending occasional moments of realism. It is widely available on VHS.

Alice Bloomfield

A reporter for the *Daily People's World* newspaper, Alice heads the campaign for the gang's release. As a Jew, she insists that she understands their predicament, and that she fights for them because of the oppression of her people. Her temporary passion for Henry emanates as much from the intensity of their shared political goals as it does from the chemistry between them.

Judge F. W. Charles

Judge Charles conducts a biased case, overruling justified objections by the gang's lawyer and imposing unfair restrictions, such as not allowing the boys to cut their hair or change clothing and seating them apart from their attorney.

Cholo

Cholo, a younger member of the gang, gets left behind after the arrests. He and Rudy get into their own brawls with the Anglos one night, in which Rudy does the fighting while Cholo escorts the women out of harm's way.

Downey Gang

A rival gang who go to the dance, start fights, and later join Rafas in terrorizing the party at the Williams Ranch.

Lieutenant Edwards

Lt. Edwards is the tough cop who tells the press he refuses to "mollycoddle these youngsters any-more" as he puts the gang under arrest. He tries—and fails—to bribe Henry into squealing on the other gang members. He does so by offering to let Henry off in time to report for Navy service.

Guard

The Guard at San Quentin calls the gang "greaseballs" and puts Henry in solitary confinement for calling him a "bastard." He pantomimes reading the letters the boys receive while the writers narrate them. He is not so much an individual character as a part of the system that oppresses the pachucos.

Ismael

See Smiley Torres

Newsboy

The newsboy hawks the papers whose headlines move the plot along. He provides the voice of the media.

El Pachuco

El Pachuco (pah-choo-ko) presides over the entire play, acting as Henry's alter ego. In the plays Brechtian moments, Pachuco interrupts the action or speaks to the audience directly, and he also sings accompaniment to the action. El Pachuco is the consummate Mexican-American *pachuco* figure, a zoot-suiter who is tough, cool, slick, and defiant. He tells it like it is and is meticulous and vain about his appearance.

In a 1988 interview with David Savran, Valdez explained the role of El Pachuco: "The Pachuco is the Jungian self-image, the superego if you will, the power inside every individual that's greater than any human institution. . . . I dressed the Pachuco in the colors of Testatipoka, the Aztec god of education, the dean of the school of hard knocks." El Pachuco achieves mythic proportions when he is stripped of his zoot suit by the Anglo rioters. Dressed only in a loincloth, he adopts a regal majesty as he exits, walking backward, from the stage. When he returns, he is not content to accept the Press's damning prediction that Henry will return to prison. At his prompting, the other characters recite alternative futures for Henry. He controls the action of the play and embroiders the events of Henry's life.

Press

The Press plays the role of an antagonist in the play, as it is the headlines that inflame the Anglos to riot and biases the public's perception of the gang's innocence. When the sailors taunt Rudy and the gang members left after the arrest, the Press eggs them on, calling the zoot suiters, ''gamin' dandies.'' The Press also plays the unprecedented role of prosecutor in the trial, further emphasizing the damaging effect of the media.

Rafas

The leader of the Downey gang, Rafas pushes Rudy down at the dance and gets into a knife fight with Henry. Henry gets the upper hand, but El Pachuco prevents him from killing Rafas. Humiliated, Rafas takes his Downey Gang to the Williams Ranch and terrorizes the people holding a party there.

Dolores Reyna

Henry's mother is a traditional Mexican mother who lovingly teases Henry about his zoot suit but allows him wear it. She refuses, however, to let her daughter leave the house in a short skirt because it makes her look like a *puta* (whore). The trial is devastating to her, and she is elated when her two boys return home, one from prison and one from the war. She thinks the solution to Henry's problems is to marry Della and throw away his zoot suit.

Enrique Reyna

Henry's father, Enrique is a first-generation Mexican American. He represents traditional values of family, honesty, hard work, infinite patience, and personal integrity. He wants his son to stay home and avoid the inevitable conflict with the police that will get Henry re-arrested, but he wisely knows that he cannot protect his son from the fate that circumstances and his son's character hold in store.

Henry Reyna

The play's protagonist, Henry is described as ''twenty-one, dark, Indian-looking.'' He becomes the primary suspect for the murder of Jose Williams because he is the leader of the 38th-street gang. The arrest spoils Henry's plan to join the Navy, and he is forced to face the problems of the barrio. His stoical resistance to interrogation only gets him beaten up, and he discovers that, guilty or not, he will pay a tremendous price for his ethnic heritage and pachuco style.

At first standoffish with Alice, he succumbs to a kind of infatuation, then reasserts his vow to Della at the play's end. The historical Henry was re-arrested and imprisoned. According to Valdez, ''Henry Renya . . . El Pachuco . . . the man . . . the myth . . . still lives.''

Lupe Reyna

Henry's younger sister, Lupe, at sixteen, wants to adopt the pachuca style, with a short skirt and fingertip coat, but her parents forbid it.

Rudy Reyna

Rudy is Henry's nineteen-year-old younger brother. He wants so much to follow in his brother's footsteps that he fashions a make-shift zoot suit out of his father's old suit. He drinks too much at the dance and gets into a fight with Rafas. After the mass arrests, he endures attacks by the Anglo sailors, who strip him of his zoot suit. He enlists in the War and returns a hero.

George Shearer

George is a middle-aged public defender assigned to the pachucos by the courts. He is athletic, strong, competent, and dedicated to his clients. He refuses to give up on Henry and the gang and finally his associates wins their release, although he himself is drafted and sent off to war at a critical moment in the trial.

Sergeant Smith

Sgt. Smith is even more brutal than his partner, Lt. Edwards. Smith tells Edwards ''you can't treat these animals like people,'' and beats Henry senseless, trying to get details about the Sleepy Lagoon murder out of the young man. Smith represents the oppressive members of the anglo majority who malign the Hispanics.

Swabbie

Swabbie is an Anglo sailor who frequents the dance hall that the pachucos frequent. It is he who strips El Pachuco of his zoot suit.

Smiley Torres

One of the members of the 38th street gang, aged twenty-three. He had started the 38th street gang with Henry, but now he has a wife and child. After getting arrested, he regrets having joined the pachucas: he feels too old for parties and jail.

Bertha Villareal

Henry's former girlfriend, who sports a tattoo and is not as pretty as Della. Rudy dates her after Henry is imprisoned.

THEMES

Culture Clash

Henry and his gang are charged with the murder of a fellow Mexican American, Jose Williams, not because there was convincing evidence of their guilt, but because of their ethnic identity and their radical style of dressing and behavior. The underlying conflict that leads to their arrest and unfair trial is a clash between Mexican Americans and the dominant Anglo culture. The zoot suiters represented a small population of Mexican Americans. They sported ducktailed haircuts and slick suits and promenaded with swaggering coolness, affectations which were seen by some Anglos as an affront to mainstream society. More common were the assimilated Mexican Americans of the 1940s, who accepted being segregated in barrios, Spanish-speaking neighborhoods, and who held low-paying, low-status jobs. They were tolerated in society as long as they limited their aspirations and kept out of the way. Enrique is a fully assimilated Mexican American, who works as a street cleaner and is proud of his son for joining the Navy to fight as an American; for Henry to do so would indicate that he would also be assimilated.

Trouble comes when groups of Mexican-American zoot-suiters, or pachucos, congregate in dance halls and begin to get rowdy. With the war hysteria of the 1940s, such rowdiness was seen as an imminent threat, and the death of Jose Williams seemed proof of the violent nature of the pachucos. The historic 38th Street Gang did not actually carry switchblades, but Valdez portrays them as quick to brandish and use such weapons; thus they seem to fulfill the violent nature suspected of them. Lt. Edwards and Sergeant Smith arrest only Mexican Americans at the dance, automatically letting the Anglos, including the violent Marine Swabbie, go free. From this point on, the harsh treatment of the prisoners is shown to emanate from ethnic hatred and distrust. They are treated like—even called-animals. The problem is perpetuated when the pachucos return the hostile treatment by distrusting Anglos.

It is not until George proves his dedication and the boys accept his help that a bond is formed across the two ethnic groups. Yet culture clash rages on while he fights for their release, and Rudy is attacked by twenty marines and stripped of his zoot suit. Even the hard-won freedom granted to the boys does not signal a resolution, since the clash continues at their celebration, when cops assume that Joey has stolen George's car. The problems of the barrio transcend the problems of one gang: El Pachuco announces that "The barrio's still out there, waiting and wanting, / The cops are still tracking us down like dogs, / The gangs are still killing each other, / Families are barely surviving."

Civil Rights

For Mexican Americans like Henry, the issues is not just ethnic conflicts, but actual civil rights abuses, and his trial is not unique in its judicial travesties. The Chicano Movement sought to correct these and other wrongs, as part of the tide of the larger Civil Rights movement taking place in the 1960s. The battle had many fronts: from the courthouse to the schoolhouse, Hispanics, African Americans, and other ethnic groups educated themselves and the public on the daily injustices committed in the United States. For Hispanics, the separate and unequal education system (there were separate, poorly equipped, schools for Mexican children), lasted far beyond the *Brown v. Board of Education* case that won legal equality in schooling for blacks. Hispanic children did not attend integrated schools until a federal ruling in 1970 forced the Texas school system to eliminate segregation.

Police brutality was another alarming civil rights issue. A group of prominent Mexican-American citizens, who created a forum in 1948 to pursue delays in veterans rights for Mexican Americans, shifted their focus to actively expose and prosecute police brutality cases. Police raids and wholesale roundups of Mexican Americans were commonplace at social gatherings, where women and children were beaten along with men; the mass arrests depicted in *Zoot Suit* were not an exaggeration. In addition, urban renewal programs targeted barrios, which were called "blighted" areas. In these "slum clearance" programs, whole neighborhoods were wiped out to make way for freeways and other works projects that, while beneficial to the dominant culture, did little to improve the lives of the Hispanic community; the uprooted Mexican-American families were often fraudulently displaced and not properly compensated for their losses.

Various groups within the Chicano movement both initiated legal reprisals and attempted to educate the American public about these civil injustices. In a 1969 conference, attendees wrote a manifesto entitled El Plan Espiritual de Aztlan, in which they sought restitution for "economic slavery, political exploitation, ethnic and cultural psychological destruction, and denial of civil and human rights." Valdez was a leading artist who contributed to this effort.

TOPICS FOR FURTHER STUDY

- What kind of influence does El Pachuco have over Henry? Is his a positive effect or a negative one?

- Revolutionary theater attempts to move the audience to reform social injustices. What techniques does Valdez's play employ in its attempt to sway the audience?

- What is the impact of the bilingual aspect of this play on Spanish-speaking and non-Spanish speaking audiences? What does this device say about American culture?

- Compare Henry Reyna's fictional life with the historical Henry Leyvas's life. Speculate on why Valdez made the choices he did in fictionalizing Henry's life for the stage.

STYLE

Valdez's Mexican Theatre Forms

Zoot Suit is a combination of *actos* (or "protest skits"), *mitos* ("myth"), and *corrido* ("ballad"); the combination draws upon traditional Mexican songs and dances, traditional stories, and the political activism of Valdez's previous work with the socially active El Teatro Campesino. The play also has a strong documentary element with its basis in historical events. The result is musical docudrama of epic proportions.

In the beginning of his career, Valdez wrote, or rather orchestrated, since he did not always commit the actos to paper, simple and brief political protest pieces aimed at audiences of migrant workers. Most lasted only fifteen minutes. These actos used masks, simple but exaggerated storylines, and minimal settings and props. Often the actors sported cards proclaiming their generic roles—"worker," or "patroncito" [manager]—rather than adopting an

actual character. Characterization is not important in social protest plays, since the purpose is to condemn acts committed against a people, not a person. Thus Henry Reyna "is" El Pachuco, representing the tragic and self-destructive genre of pachuco gangs as well as their victimization by a xenophobic society.

The mitos moves the allegorical agenda of the actos into the spiritual realm. Valdez created *mitos* to fulfill his vision of "a teatro of legends and myths." He told David Savran in an interview for *American Theatre* that to him, myth is "so real that it's just below the surface—it's the supporting structure of our everyday reality." In a Valdez *mito,* a mythical character interacts with the other, human, characters and sometimes takes controls the play like an onstage director. El Pachuco was not the first mythical character Valdez used: the Aztec god Quetzalcóatl and a precursor to El Pachuco, *La Luna* ("the moon"), appear in his allegorical play *Bernabé* (1970), and a child named Mundo ("earth") is born to skeletal figures in *El fin del mundo* (1976; the title means "The End of the Earth"). Comet sightings and symbolic sets and rituals further un-

In a flashback sequence from the film adaptation of Zoot Suit, Henry and Della recreate the events of the dance for the judge; El Pachuco stands above the proceedings on a platform in the background

derscore the presence of myth in these plays. The mythic quality of El Pachuco in *Zoot Suit* is signaled by his ability to stop and start the action with a snap of his fingers; it is confirmed when he rises, Christ-like, wearing the Christian cross but also dressed in an Aztec loincloth, in Act II, scene vii.

The *corrido* has a long history in Mexican culture; its presence adds an element of folk art to Valdez's plays, being the Hispanic version of the American musical. Valdez's fusion of these unrelated theatrical forms into a fresh, new, dramatic concept put Chicano theater onto the American theatrical map.

Brecthtian Influences and Epic Theatre

In addition to historical and traditional Hispanic elements, Valdez also looked to the Epic Theatre technique pioneered by German playwright Bertolt Brecht (*Mother Courage and Her Children*). Brecht's best-known plays were socially conscious works that sought to make audiences think about the playwright's political agenda. To achieve such results, Brecht turned to "alienation" techniques that prevented the audience from judging his plays on an

emotional level, thus freeing them to judge a play's concepts in a purely intellectual, empirical manner. These techniques included placards that informed the audience of the major plot points that would be unfolding within each act. Brecht also broke up his narratives with satirical songs that jarringly diverted the audience's attention from episodes that might allow them to form an emotional connection to characters. El Pacucho functions as an alienating device in *Zoot Suit,* often stopping the action and directly addressing the audience. Valdez's play also qualifies as Epic Theatre in its use of a wide range of characters across a considerable time period.

Mixing Spanish and English

In areas of the United States with significant Spanish-speaking populations, the practice of mixing Spanish and English in newspaper journalism, radio programming, public signs, and schools as well as in drama has become a hotly contested topic, raising issues of cultural hegemony—whether one language should dominate another. In 1978, to use whole lines of Spanish in a play was to address it primarily to a bilingual audience, although the non-

Spanish-speaking members of the audience had little trouble understanding the context of the Spanish. In *Zoot Suit,* the characters switch to Spanish in moments of intimacy, teasing, and emotional outbursts, as when the 38th Street Gang routs the Downey Gang, and Tommy elatedly proclaims the victory in mixed Spanish and English: ''Orales, you did it, ese! Se escamaron todos! [you ran them all out!].''

Julia Alvarez, author of *How the Garcia Girls Lost Their Accent,* mixes English with Spanish in her novels. She explained that Spanish is ''the language of sensations and emotions, of the day to day.'' Duke University professor and poet Gustavo Perez Fermet, author of a collection of poems called *Bilingual Blues* agreed, saying that ''English is very concise and efficient,'' while ''Spanish has sambrosura, flavor.'' In *Zoot Suit,* the scenes of the trial and the boys' discussions with George are primarily in English, while the dance and fight scenes have whole passages in Spanish, especially the insults. Official business is communicated in English, while ''street'' business is communicated in the gang's vernacular Spanish, which is not formal Spanish but ''pachuco'' Spanish, full of slang expressions.

HISTORICAL CONTEXT

The Sleeply Lagoon Murder and the Zoot Suit Riots

Valdez's play is loosely based on the events of a 1942 murder, which came to be known as the ''Sleepy Lagoon Murder.'' On August 1, 1942, a man named Jose Diaz (renamed Jose Williams in the play) was found by the side of a road, bleeding and unconscious. He later died of head trauma; he had been drunk at the time of his attack. Although his wounds could have been inflicted by an automobile, it was determined that he had been the victim of a gang fight that had occurred nearby. Public outcry, fanned by the headlines of the newspapers, resulted in a roundup of hundreds of Mexican Americans. Henry Leyvas (Henry Reyna in the play) and twenty-one of his friends, who had participated in the fight, were arrested and charged with the murder of Diaz. The young Chicanos

sported ''zoot suits,'' long, baggy trousers topped with long-tailed coats and long ''ducktail'' hairstyles, the fashion for *pachucos* or teenage Mexican gang member.

In an outright violation of the gang members' civil rights, the district attorney requested, and the judge ordered, that the defendants be required to wear their zoot suits during the trial and not be allowed to cut their hair, so that the jury would see that they were ''hoodlums.'' Further, they were required to stand up whenever their names were mentioned, even when the statements were inflammatory or indemnifying. They were also denied the right to speak with their lawyers. E. Duran Ayers, the Head of the Foreign Relations Bureau, was brought in as an ''expert'' witness to attest to the ''bloodthirsty'' nature of Mexicans, descendants of the Aztecs, renowned for their practice of human sacrifice. Ayers's formal report stated that ''the Mexican would forever retain his wild and violent tendencies no matter how much education or training he might receive.'' Nine of the men, including Henry Leyvas, were sentenced to five years' imprisonment for second-degree murder.

About six months after the end of the trial, riots broke out in Los Angeles. The riots, known alternatively as the ''Zoot Suit Riots'' and the ''Sailor Riots,'' were a xenophobic reaction to the Mexican-American youth gangs, made all the more intense by the events of World War II. In the summer of 1943, a large group of sailors traveled through the Mexican-American community in East Los Angeles in rented cabs, beating up every ''zoot suiter'' they encountered, including women and young boys who really didn't fit the pachuco image. In response, the police went after the victims: scores of Mexican Americans were rounded up in mass arrests. Although a handful of Anglos were arrested, none were charged. The local press fanned the flames of the riots by reporting a ''Mexican crime wave'' that was being valiantly controlled by the service men. It was not until military officials declared the city of Los Angeles off limits for all military personnel that they riots diminished. In October of 1944, the Court of Appeals unanimously overturned the Judge's decision on the Sleepy Lagoon case due to legal misconduct, and the 38th Street Gang members were released.

World War II

It is not a coincidence that the Zoot Suit Riots occurred during the heat of World War II. Xenopho-

COMPARE
&
CONTRAST

- **1940s:** The Hispanic community and other ethnic groups suffer obvious racism at the hands of the military, the police force, the press, and the judicial system during the xenophobic years of World War II.

   1978: Student movements of the last fifteen years seek equal opportunities in education for Chicano children and an end to civil and human rights abuses of Chicano people in the United States. By 1978, however, the Chicano movement is in decline.

   Today: Most people uphold their legal and moral obligation to treat all Americans equally. The sense that equality has been achieved has led some institutions, colleges and universities, to remove their Affirmative Action programs, even though true equality does not exist for all ethnic groups or all U. S. citizens.

- **1940s:** The United States joins World War II in 1941. At the time of the Zoot Suit Riots, enlistment in the armed services is at a fever pitch as military bases across the country prepare men and women for the war. There is almost universal support for the United States' involvement in the war.

   1978: After tremendous public pressure, the last

U.S. troops left Vietnam in 1973. Anti-war sentiment is still high in 1978, and many veterans are still seen as butchers guilty of horrible war atrocities.

   Today: In the last twenty years the United States has been involved in several military offensives but no large-scale wars. Hand-to-hand combat has given way to remote weaponry. Military personnel and veterans are viewed neither as heroes or scapegoats but as people performing assigned jobs.

- **1940s:** Fashions are fairly conservative and universal; there is not much variety in clothing styles for mainstream Americans. Zoot suits are a conspicuous marker of otherness, an attempt by Hispanic men to set themselves apart from Anglo society.

   1978: Dressing differently is a fashion rage, from paper dresses to hippies' bell-bottom jeans. Conventional fashions such as the standard business suit are considered "square" or "uncool."

   Today: Dress is much more casual than the 1940s, yet more conservative than the 1970s. Radical trends, such as body-piercing and tattoos, proclaim the wearer's statement of opposition against mainstream society.

---

bia, undue contempt or fear of foreigners, was exacerbated by a perceived threat that Americans of foreign heritage would turn against Anglo Americans. To prevent this occurrence, thousands of Japanese Americans, including two hundred Japanese-Latin Americans, were herded into internment camps throughout the West. It was not until 1988 that restitution was made to those who suffered physically, emotionally, and financially from the relocation.

In the 1940s, fear of foreigners extended to numerous cultural groups; Los Angeles had many ethnic neighborhoods, and the presence of military

bases full of personnel readying themselves for war made Los Angeles a hot spot for culture clashes and violence. Ironically, of the ethnic groups who enlisted in World War II, Mexican Americans suffered the most casualties.

CRITICAL OVERVIEW

Zoot Suit was the product of Luis Valdez's theater troupe, El Teatro Campesino, which had previously specialized in social consciousness-raising *actos,* that offered broad-brush depictions of farmworkers' plights. Valdez received a grant from the Rockefeller Foundation to research the Sleepy Lagoon murder trial so that he could create a play that would represent the experience of minorities in America. *Zoot Suit*'s April, 1978, premiere and initial ten-day run sold out in two days. The audience consisted of season-ticket holders along with members of the Mexican-American community of Los Angeles who were eager to see Valdez's latest creation. An ad for second production in August of 1978 announced the "Second Zoot Suit Riots" and tickets again sold out. The Los Angeles Drama Critics Circle honored Valdez with a best play award. The play received standing ovations every evening in Los Angeles. The following year, Valdez became the first Latino playwright to open on Broadway, and the public once again expressed its approval.

The New York critics, however, were less impressed. Richard Eder of the *New York Times* called the play "overblown and undernourished," and Douglas Watt of the *New York Daily News* condemned it as "poorly written and atrociously directed." It closed on Broadway after a disappointing four weeks. A national tour proved more successful, especially in urban areas with Mexican-American communities.

In 1980, Valdez produced a screenplay adaptation of his play under contract with Universal Pictures. The idea was to film the play live at the Aquarius Theater in Los Angeles and intersperse filmed, realistic, scenes. The film was released in 1981, having been completed on a three-million dollar budget in a mere six months. As with the stage production, Daniel Valdez played Henry, and Edward James Olmos made his film acting debut as El Pachuco, having earned his first pay as an actor in the same role in the theatre. The film's success was largely attributed to Valdez's artful weaving of filmed stage scenes and the more cinematically realized scenes. It won first place at the Cartagena Film Festival in Columbia in 1982 and the San Francisco Bay Critics award for best musical in 1983.

However, after the initial excitement, and for a decade after its release, critics accused Valdez of "selling out," of presenting stereotypical female characters with zero self initiative, and designing his productions to please Anglo audiences. In the face of such criticism, Valdez maintained his composure, as indicated by his response to David Savran who interviewed Valdez for *American Theatre* in 1988: "That [the accusation of selling out] doesn't bother me in the least. There's too much to do, to be socially conscious about. . . . In some ways it's just people sounding me out. . . . People help to keep you on course. I've strayed very little from my pronounced intentions."

CRITICISM

Carole Hamilton

Hamilton is a Humanities teacher at Cary Academy, an innovative private school in Cary, North Carolina. In this essay she discusses Valdez's treatment of the love relationship between Henry and Alice and its effects on the plot and reforming mission of the play.

Zoot Suit is a tightly written drama with each element contributing to its overt demand for social reform, specifically a correction of the social injustice suffered by Henry Reyna and his gang. Luis Valdez conducted thorough research on the Sleepy Lagoon Murder Trial of 1942 and the Zoot Suit Riots of 1943 in order to present the facts responsibly, but he also wanted to present the psychological and mythical truths of the Chicano experience. As a result, his work is a combination of documentary and myth, fact and fiction, instruction and entertainment. On the whole, both the play and the later film version succeeded beautifully in accomplishing these goals, especially in the popular arena.

Criticism was leveled at Valdez's portrayal of women (stereotypical) and complaints were leveled that the playwright turned his back on his roots with the farmworker's theater and had somehow "sold out" to the expectations of Hollywood and Broadway. To this criticism, Valdez turned a deaf ear. He did admit, however, that he had to revise the story's plot between the stage and film versions to correct a flaw that misled audience members. In a 1982 interview two weeks after the opening of the film adaptation, Valdez told Roberta Orona-Cordova in *Mexican-American Theatre* that he struggled with his portrayal of the love affair between Henry and Alice Bloomfield. The historical Henry had fallen

WHAT DO I READ NEXT?

- Julia Alvarez's novel *How the Garcia Girls Lost Their Accent* chronicles the experiences of four sisters who immigrate from the Dominican Republic to the United States, losing their Spanish language and culture before they fully acquire fluency in English. In a similar vein, Sandra Cisneros recalls her childhood in a Spanish-speaking section of Chicago in the lyrical vignettes of *House on Mango Street.*

- Ernesto Galarza's 1971 novel *Barrio Boy* and Jose Antonio Villareal's 1970 *Pocho* both explore growing up in a barrio from a young boy's perspective.

- The 1997 novel *Macho!* by Victor Villaseñor describes Cesar Chavez's strike efforts through the eyes of a seventeen-year-old boy who migrates to California from Mexico.

- The poems of Ricardo Sánchez in 1971's *Canto y grito me liberación* (title means ''The Liberation of a Chicano Mind'') explore the ambigui-ties of living in two worlds, while Rodolfo Corky Gonzales's epic poem, ''I am Joaquin'' explores the Chicano identity. Lorna Dee Cervantes's poems address the erosion of ethnic identity in transplanted families; her ''Freeway 280'' expresses frustration over urban renewal programs that razed Chicano neighborhoods.

- Several films also explore territory similar to *Zoot Suit:* Robert Redford produced and directed *The Milago Beanfield War* (1988), an endearing comedy about a group of Mexican-American citizens who resist oppressive big business owners out to abuse the farmers' civil rights; Edward James Olmos, who plays El Pachuco in *Zoot Suit,* stars in *The Ballad of Gregorio Cortez* (1982), a film about a Chicano murderer that allows the audience to believe in Cortez's guilt until the last moment; Olmos also directed and starred in a stunning film portrayal of a hardened Chicano prison inmate and his family: *American Me* (1992).

---

in love with Alice, and Valdez wanted stayed true to history in his dramatic version of the story. The inclusion of this cross-cultural affair hampered what he wanted his play to communicate, however. It alienated some members of the audience, who could not accept a white woman falling in love with a Chicano, ''They didn't like the romance or the politics of it: a white woman falling in love with a pachuco.'' The same issue came up in another interview with Gregg Barrios, who told Valdez ''The love angle between Henry and Alice Bloomfield bothered me in the play.'' Valdez responded:

> Actually, that angle in the play got me a narrower audience, especially in the confrontation scene and when Henry makes a choice between the two girls. I think what it is that led a lot of people astray was that point. That was really *not* the point I intended. Again, it was the play trying to decide what it was going to say after all . . . when I began to transfer the play to a screenplay . . . I focused more on Henry and this business with Alice was put into its proper perspective.

The affair between the historical Alice Bloomfield and Henry Leyvas (Valdez changed the name to Reyna), took place through their letters. Valdez includes fictional versions of these letters in the play, but they culminate in an intense physical encounter in the prison and the incident provides a pivotal moment in the plot. Alice's belief in Henry revitalizes his hope for release, just when he is ready to give up. Her commitment is not just to obtaining justice in his particular case but because she has ''never been able to accept one person pushing another around.'' At that moment, they understand each other, but their rapport quickly conflates with passion.

Why is this passion bothersome or ''alienating'' to some members of the audience? It would be overly simplistic to dismiss these viewers' concerns as evidence of their own prejudice. There is also the matter of Henry's obligation to Della. On the eve of the arrests, Henry promised her a big "pachuco" wedding when he returns from his tour in the Navy. She is not simply awaiting him patiently at home; she shares his misery, having been committed to a year at the Ventura State School for Girls—a prison of sorts—for her ostensible participation in the murder. Two brief scenes before his tryst with Alice, Henry complains to El Pachuco how much he misses Della. This love relationship seems permanent: for Henry to betray Della with *any* other woman seems unpardonable. That he would betray her with an Anglo woman complicates matters considerably.

In addition, a love interest between Alice and Henry muddies Alice's social reform agenda: campaigning for Henry out of love is not the same as campaigning against a social injustice. Furthermore, a love interest between these two characters, a hybrid marriage, would be a form of assimilation, which the play opposes. Enrique is the model of the assimilated Mexican American; he sweeps the dirt from the city's streets but has no power to sweep away its injustices. Assimilation is a kind of acceptance of the limitations society places on Mexican Americans. Enrique's big dream is for Henry to find a way out and up; the solution seems to be Henry's enlistment in the Navy, an event that Enrique plans to celebrate in style. However, as El Pachuco reminds Henry, joining the Navy will do nothing to solve the problems of the barrio, "Forget the war overseas, carnal. Your war is on the homefront." For Henry to marry Alice is the same as his going off to the Navy: he would be joining the culture that oppresses him, not aligning himself with his own culture and fighting for a better Hispanic lifestyle.

The staging of Henry's moment of decision between Alice and Della underscores the significance of his rejection of Alice/Anglo culture and his acceptance of the war "on the homefront." Alice stands alone, while Della is surrounded by Henry's family and the gang. This blocking of characters suggests that in choosing Della, Henry chooses his own culture, with all of its perils and promise; had he chosen Alice, he would have taken an avenue out of that culture, a move away from his social responsibilities.

One reason that Alice is able to connect with Henry is their shared experience of social oppression: she is Jewish and the year is 1943, America is fighting World War II in part to free the Jews from German leader Adolf Hitler's genocidal persecution (Hitler believed that Jews and other ethnicities were inferior and a detriment to the new society he wished to build). Alice helps him to win his battle, just as the Americans are winning the war in Europe. Henry elatedly tells El Pachuco, "We won this one because we learned to fight in a new way." Alice's experience and wisdom make her an excellent steward for Henry's transition to this new frame of mind. She helps Henry advance into social adulthood—or rather humanity, since Anglo society, as represented by Sgt. Smith and Lt. Edwards, treats him like an animal.

Henry may be an "hombre"—a man—to his doting parents, but he is a "greaseball" to the police; Sgt. Smith reminds Lt. Edwards that "You can't treat these animals like people." Alice, on the other hand, asks Henry to write for her People's World newsletter. She treats him like an educated and valuable member of society whose words are significant. She can redeem him through her conviction that he is innocent and socially worthy. She is one of the few outside of his family who accept his integrity, in a world that judges him guilty of the "crime" of looking different, of adopting a defiant style of dress, the pachuco style. She presides over his transition from an animal held in solitary confinement to a man taking part in the affairs of the world. The fact that he spent ninety days—echoing nine months—in confinement hints at a kind of rebirth, as he is released from solitary confinement (a kind of womb), into his parent's home, appearing as the guest of honor, an object of celebration, like a newborn child.

El Pachuco is with Henry at the beginning of his solitary confinement, but Henry gets fed up with his alter ego's negative attitude, his constant refrain that "No court in the land's going to set you free." Henry yells, "Fuck off," and El Pachuco departs for the streets, where he takes Rudy's place in a beating, is overwhelmed by the Anglos, and stripped of his zoot suit. El Pachuco has been Henry's confidante and alter ego up to this point but now he disappears, and Henry, who has gotten used to his ubiquitous presence, asks in vain, "Are you even there anymore?" He is not, because El Pachuco has been crucified by the Anglos. This act parallels Henry's crucifixion, in the solitary confinement cell. In the very next scene, Alice takes over the guardianship of Henry from El Pachuco, appearing at the prison and expressing devotion to his cause.

During the brawl at Sleepy Lagoon, Della (Rose Portillo) comforts a badly beaten Henry (Daniel Valdez, the playwright's brother) while El Pachuco (Edward James Olmos) watches from the car

The transfer of mentorship has completed, and Henry will be in her hands until he returns to society, rising from the dead just as El Pachuco rises after his beating.

El Pachuco rises wearing a hybrid of icons: the Christian cross and an Aztec loincloth; Henry rises from his incarceration witnessed by a Jewish mother archetype. At this point, Alice's job is finished, so El Pachuco reappears. With a snap of his fingers (signaling that he has resumed control of the play), El Pachuco speaks of the tentativeness of Henry's new social standing. He is not free, he is merely back in the barrio, with all of its prejudice and injustice. Henry's is the only voice that does not recite a version of his future—because he has so little control over it. Alice has raised this man from incarceration only to put him back into the same vicious cycle of ethnic oppression and injustice.

Alice's faith in Henry is a mark of her own integrity, making her a role model for the audience. This is revolutionary theater, not mere entertainment, and Valdez wants the audience to learn from her example. In this respect, Alice's guardianship over Henry would be complete and actually more effective without the love affair. Valdez realized this, and when he wrote the screenplay for *Zoot Suit,* he downplayed their passion. In its place he emphasized Alice's human compassion. The shift away from love to humanitarianism is at once more acceptable to the audience and more focused on the central issue of social injustice in this play.

Source: Carole Hamilton for *Drama for Students,* Gale, 1999.

Carey McWilliams

In this essay, McWilliams provides information on the historical events that shape Valdez's play. He assesses the social importance of Zoot Suit, *calling the work "more than a play: it is an event of historic importance."*

A year or so back, Luis Valdez, founder-director of El Teatro Campesino—an agitprop group formed during the Delano, Calif., farm workers' strike in 1965—came to see me in New York. It was the first time we had met. Luis had become interested in the dramatic potential of the Sleepy Lagoon murder case and wanted to talk to me about it because I had served as chairman of the defense committee. With the inevitable tape recorder at his side, he interviewed me for several hours. Since the trial had taken place in 1942, there were some big gaps in his knowledge of the facts. For example, he had not been able to find a transcript of the trial ; nor had he heard of Alice McGrath, who served as secretary of the committee. It was a good talk. I liked Luis: an authentic. rather earthy person with a robust sense of humor. He knew what he wanted to know, which is a blessed relief in an interview. After he left, I had a feeling, rather tentative I must admit, that something just might come of our talk.

On March 25, *Zoot Suit,* the play Valdez wrote based on the case, opened Winter Garden Theatre after a long and successful run in Los Angeles where it is still grossing $90,000 a week. In this odd way a legend was born—some thirty-six years after the event. Just as the case on which the play is based marked the beginning of the so-called Chicano Rebellion, so the play marks a new chapter in Mexican-American experience. As William Overend pointed out in the *Los Angeles Times* (May 9, 1978), the present has finally caught up with the past.

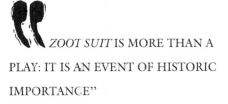

ZOOT SUIT IS MORE THAN A PLAY: IT IS AN EVENT OF HISTORIC IMPORTANCE"

Young Chicanos who were not born when the Sleepy Lagoon case was tried have flocked to see the play. Not only has *Zoot Suit* tapped a huge new audience in Los Angeles but it has been received with a general community enthusiasm that would have been unthinkable not so many years ago.

In the spring and summer of 1942 racial tensions were mounting in Los Angeles. The Japanese-Americans had been evacuated. Defense industries were booming. Rationing was an annoyance. Housing was in short supply. Manpower needs were acute. Droves of soldiers and sailors cruised through the streets in taxicabs looking for trouble. A disproportionate number of young Mexican-Americans were being drafted because they did not hold draft-deferred jobs. The likelihood of an explosion was obvious.

In this tense social setting, a free-for-all fight took place at an East Los Angeles gravel pit known as "Sleepy Lagoon," and the next day—August 2, 1942—a young Chicano was found near the scene and was rushed to the General Hospital where he died from injuries he had received. The police promptly rounded up twenty-four young Mexicans-Americans, members of one of a number of Chicano youth gangs, and a grand jury indicted them for first-degree murder. After a long trial before a gruesomely biased judge, seventeen were convicted in what was up to that time the largest mass murder trial ever held in the county. Before, after and during the trial the press, in cahoots with the police, kept up a vicious attack on Mexican-American youth gangs; better than any commentary these news stories reflected the temper of the times and the intense bias that existed against Chicanos.

After the verdict had been returned, a defense committee was formed, on which I served as chairman, to finance an appeal. New counsel was retained to prepare and argue the appeal. The costs were substantial; the trial had gone on for several months and the testimony filled 6,000 pages of transcript. But the committee was able to enlist the support of a number of Hollywood figures—Orson Welles, Joseph Cotten, Anthony Quinn—and some middle-class elements in both the Mexican-American and the larger community. On October 4, 1944, the District Court of Appeals (in *People v. Zamora*) reversed the convictions "for lack of evidence." The defendants were released after having served nearly two years in San Quentin Prison; it had been impossible to raise bail pending the appeal. The unanimous decision of the appellate court castigated the trial judge for bias, prejudicial remarks and gross misconduct. Later, all charges were dismissed.

Even before the convictions were reversed, the grand jury held open public hearings to inquire into charges of police brutality. I testified at these hearings on October 8, 1942, and warned that further trouble was to be expected if the combined press and police attacks continued. (The testimony is included in Julian Nava's *Viva la Raza,* 1973.) The following June, the "Zoot Suit Riots," which lasted a week or more, erupted in Los Angeles. This, in brief, is the factual background which Valdez has tapped for his fine play. But *Zoot Suit* is more than a play: it is an event of historic importance. The reversal of the convictions in the Sleepy Lagoon case represented the first major victory Mexican-Americans had won in the memory of the living. Slight Wonder, then, that the play has drawn such an enthusiastic response from the Hispanic community in Los Angeles.

As a footnote: during the 1943 riots a citizens' emergency meeting was called, which I chaired, to see what might be done to "cool" a dangerous situation. After the meeting I telephoned my friend, Attorney General Robert Kenny, in San Francisco and arranged for him to meet me the next morning in Los Angeles. At this early morning session I entreated him to urge Gov. Earl Warren to appoint an official committee of inquiry and suggested individuals who might be named. Warren accepted Kenny's recommendations and the commission then adopted a draft report I had prepared. Release of the report had the desired effect: if order was not fully restored, a war time truce was established.

Source: Carey McWilliams, "Second Thoughts" in the *Nation,* Vol. 228, no. 13, April 7, 1979, p. 358.

Brendan Gill

In this mixed review of Zoot Suit *, Gill compares Valdez's play to a "broadened and cheapened" version of the classic musical* West Side Story. *While the critic feels that the work is suitable entertainment and deals with important social issues, he felt that it ultimately lacks true greatness.*

In the pompous program notes accompanying "*Zoot Suit*" (at the Winter Garden), we are instructed that the show is "loosely based on the Sleepy Lagoon Murder Mystery of 1942 and the Zoot Suit Riots of 1943 in Los Angeles [which] like other historical events that pass into folklore have become a kind of myth—a mixture of fact and fancy certain to elicit strong feelings when examined from any of a variety of perspectives." A footnote in fine print further instructs us that "while some of the events portrayed did indeed occur, others did not," and continues, "The characters are merely representatives or composites. '*Zoot Suit*' is not a documentary, but a dramatization of the imagination." Now, nothing makes me more uneasy, in or out of a theatre, than phrases like "loosely based," "folklore," "myth," and "fact and fancy" (to say nothing of "dramatization of the imagination," which comes close to being gibberish). They all hint at the same ominous likelihood—that we are to be at the mercy of an author who makes words mean whatever he needs them to mean, and are therefore never to know whether our sympathies are being engaged by something that actually happened or are being manipulated by something that, for dramatic purposes, ought to have happened.

My feelings about the role of the writer as truthteller have led me to seem to take "*Zoot Suit*" and its fevered rhetoric much more seriously than it deserves. A big, noisy, brightly colored show, it is a West Coast descendant, broadened and cheapened, of "West Side Story," itself a show with a sufficiently long pedigree. In this version, Puerto Ricans have given way to Chicanos—those Mexican-Americans who make up a large portion of the population of Southern California. Within the barrios, they speak (or spoke in the forties) a lively patois of their own devising, but to judge by "*Zoot Suit*" their customs are (or were) markedly less original, resembling in thought, word, and deed those of every minority group that has ever sought to tell its story on an American stage. As a social document and a statement of protest, " *Zoot Suit* " is sorrily abreast of "Abie's Irish Rose."

In attempting to present a favorable view of the Chicano culture, Luis Valdez, the author and director of *"Zoot Suit,"* appears not to have been aware of how unpleasant his view of that culture is bound to appear to most contemporary Americans. We are shown Chicanos being brutalized by white policemen, white prosecutors, and white judges, and we cannot fail to deplore their fate; at the same time, we are being shown Valdez's Chicano ideal, which consists of a family with the father as its absolute master. His sons must kiss his hand in parting, and the only advice he can give to a son who is on his way to prison is that he must act like "a man." Women must obey men without question or protest. Men, possessing women like chattels, may sleep with anyone they please, but women must remain chaste. One must be loyal, even to the point of murder, to one's family, one's gang, one's barrio. Well! A long evening of such grisly "macho", utterances is difficult to sit through, especially when we are expected to find virtue in them.

The large cast is headed by Daniel Valdez, brother of the author. He is a handsome and dynamic young man, if no actor, and he is assisted by, among others, Charles Aidman, Abel Franco, Paul Mace, Julie Carmen, and Edward James Olmos, who, acting as a sort of spokesman for the author, vulgarly fraternizes with the audience. The choreography is by Patricia Birch, the setting is by Thomas A. Walsh, the costumes are by Peter J. Hall, and the lighting is by Dawn Chiang. The grotesquely overamplified sound was "designed" by Abe Jacob, and I understand that there have been protests as far away as Woodlawn.

Source: Brendan Gill, "Borrowings" in the *New Yorker,* Vol. LV, no. 7, April 2, 1979 , p. 94.

SOURCES

Barrios, Gregg. *"Zoot Suit:* The Man, the Myth, Still Lives: A Conversation with Luis Valdez" in *Chicano Cinema: Research, Reviews, and Resources,* edited by G. D. Keller, Bilingual Press, 1985, pp. 159-64.

Berg, Charles Ramírez. Review of *Zoot Suit* in the *Bilingual Review,* Volume 10, nos. 2-3, 1983, pp. 189-90.

Eder, Richard. Review of *Zoot Suit* in the *New York Times,* 1979.

" IN ATTEMPTING TO PRESENT A FAVORABLE VIEW OF THE CHICANO CULTURE, LUIS VALDEZ, THE AUTHOR AND DIRECTOR OF *ZOOT SUIT,* APPEARS NOT TO HAVE BEEN AWARE OF HOW UNPLEASANT HIS VIEW OF THAT CULTURE IS BOUND TO APPEAR TO MOST CONTEMPORARY AMERICANS"

Simon, John. "West Coast Story" in *New York,* April 9, 1979, p. 93.

Watt, Douglas. Review of *Zoot Suit* in the *New York Daily News,* 1979.

FURTHER READING

Acuña, Rodolfo. *Occupied America: A History of Chicanos,* 3rd edition, Harper & Row, 1988.
    Traces the development of Hispanic-American playwrights.

Alvarez, Lizette. "Spanish-English Hybrid Is Spoken with No Apologies" on *LatinoLink,* http://www.latinolink.com/ life/life97/0324lspa.htm, December 15, 1998.
    This website discusses the use of "Spanglish" as well as the employment of alternating English and Spanish in conversations and writing.

Bruce-Novoa Juan, editor. *Retrospace: Collected Essays on Chicano Literature,* Arte Público, 1990.
    Essays on Chicano, Puerto Rican, and Hispanic literatures

Electric Mercado. *El Teatro Campesino,* http://www.mercado.com/grupos/, December 13, 1998.
    A web site devoted to Latino cultural centers, with a number of pages devoted to Valdez's theater company in San Juan Bautista, California.

Elam, Harry J., Jr. *Taking It to the Streets: The Social Protest Theater of Luis Valzez and Amiri Baraka,* University of Michigan Press, 1997.
    Traces the development of social protest in drama, comparing and contrasting Valdez's work with that of African-American playwright Amiria Baraka, the author of *Dutchman.*

Huerta, Jorge A. *Chicano Theatre: Themes and Forms,* Bilingual Press, 1982.
> Explores the varied types of Chicano drama from traditional corridas and festivals to revolutionary theater.

Kanellos, Nicolàs, editor. *Mexican-American Theatre: Then and Now* Arte Público, 1983.
> Essays on the development of Mexican-American drama.

Mazón, Mauricio. *The Zoot Suit Riots,* University of Texas Press, 1984.
> Historical background and social analysis of the 1943 riots in Los Angeles.

Orona-Cordova, Roberta. "*Zoot Suit* and the Pachuco Phenomenon: An Interview with Luis Valdez" in *Mexican-American Theatre: Then and Now,* edited by Nicolás Kanellos, Arte Público, 1983.
> In this interview, Valdez discusses El Pachuco of his play and real-life gang pachucos.

Pizzato, Mark "Brechtian and Aztec Violence in Valdez's *Zoot Suit* in the *Journal of Popular Film and Television,* Volume 26, no. 2, Summer, 1998, pp. 52-61.
> Analyzes the role of violence in *Zoot Suit* as a symbol of cultural sacrifice.

Sanchez-Tranquilino, Marcos, and John Tagg. "The Pachuco's Flayed Hide: Mobility, Identity, and *Buenas Garras*" in *Cultural Studies,* edited by Lawrence Grossberger, Cary Nelson, and Paula A. Treichler, Routledge, 1992.
> The authors discuss the role of violence in the figure of the pachuco, both real and onstage.

Savran, David. "Interview with Luis Valdez" in *American Theatre,* Volume 4, no. 10, January, 1988, pp. 15-21, 56-57.
> Valdez speaks of his aspirations, influences, and work in the theater.

Suavecito *Zoot Suit Riots,* http://www.suavecito.com/history.htm3, December 13, 1998.
> A web site for Zoot Suit clothing that contains a history of the Zoot Suit Riots.

University Of Texas's *The Making of MEChA: The Climax of the Chicano Student Movement,* http://www.utexas.edu/ftp/student/mecha/research.html, December 20, 1998.
> This website presents a detailed history of and bibliography for researching the Chicano movement.

Valdez, Luis, and Stan Steiner. *Pensamiento Serpentino: A Chicano Approach to the Theatre of Reality,* Cucaracha Press, 1973.
> Contains Valdez's philosophy on the various threads of social resistance, myth, and celebration that make up Chicano theater.

Glossary of Literary Terms

A

Abstract: Used as a noun, the term refers to a short summary or outline of a longer work. As an adjective applied to writing or literary works, abstract refers to words or phrases that name things not knowable through the five senses. Examples of abstracts include the *Cliffs Notes* summaries of major literary works. Examples of abstract terms or concepts include ''idea,'' ''guilt'' ''honesty,'' and ''loyalty.''

Absurd, Theater of the: See *Theater of the Absurd*

Absurdism: See *Theater of the Absurd*

Act: A major section of a play. Acts are divided into varying numbers of shorter scenes. From ancient times to the nineteenth century plays were generally constructed of five acts, but modern works typically consist of one, two, or three acts. Examples of five-act plays include the works of Sophocles and Shakespeare, while the plays of Arthur Miller commonly have a three-act structure.

Acto: A one-act Chicano theater piece developed out of collective improvisation. *Actos* were performed by members of Luis Valdez's Teatro Campesino in California during the mid-1960s.

Aestheticism: A literary and artistic movement of the nineteenth century. Followers of the movement believed that art should not be mixed with social, political, or moral teaching. The statement ''art for art's sake'' is a good summary of aestheticism. The movement had its roots in France, but it gained widespread importance in England in the last half of the nineteenth century, where it helped change the Victorian practice of including moral lessons in literature. Oscar Wilde is one of the best-known ''aesthetes'' of the late nineteenth century.

Age of Johnson: The period in English literature between 1750 and 1798, named after the most prominent literary figure of the age, Samuel Johnson. Works written during this time are noted for their emphasis on ''sensibility,'' or emotional quality. These works formed a transition between the rational works of the Age of Reason, or Neoclassical period, and the emphasis on individual feelings and responses of the Romantic period. Significant writers during the Age of Johnson included the novelists Ann Radcliffe and Henry Mackenzie, dramatists Richard Sheridan and Oliver Goldsmith, and poets William Collins and Thomas Gray. Also known as Age of Sensibility

Age of Reason: See *Neoclassicism*

Age of Sensibility: See *Age of Johnson*

Alexandrine Meter: See *Meter*

Allegory: A narrative technique in which characters representing things or abstract ideas are used to convey a message or teach a lesson. Allegory is typically used to teach moral, ethical, or religious lessons but is sometimes used for satiric or political purposes. Examples of allegorical works include Edmund Spenser's *The Faerie Queene* and John Bunyan's *The Pilgrim's Progress.*

Allusion: A reference to a familiar literary or historical person or event, used to make an idea more easily understood. For example, describing someone as a ''Romeo'' makes an allusion to William Shakespeare's famous young lover in *Romeo and Juliet.*

Amerind Literature: The writing and oral traditions of Native Americans. Native American literature was originally passed on by word of mouth, so it consisted largely of stories and events that were easily memorized. Amerind prose is often rhythmic like poetry because it was recited to the beat of a ceremonial drum. Examples of Amerind literature include the autobiographical *Black Elk Speaks,* the works of N. Scott Momaday, James Welch, and Craig Lee Strete, and the poetry of Luci Tapahonso.

Analogy: A comparison of two things made to explain something unfamiliar through its similarities to something familiar, or to prove one point based on the acceptedness of another. Similes and metaphors are types of analogies. Analogies often take the form of an extended simile, as in William Blake's aphorism: ''As the caterpillar chooses the fairest leaves to lay her eggs on, so the priest lays his curse on the fairest joys.''

Angry Young Men: A group of British writers of the 1950s whose work expressed bitterness and disillusionment with society. Common to their work is an anti-hero who rebels against a corrupt social order and strives for personal integrity. The term has been used to describe Kingsley Amis, John Osborne, Colin Wilson, John Wain, and others.

Antagonist: The major character in a narrative or drama who works against the hero or protagonist. An example of an evil antagonist is Richard Lovelace in Samuel Richardson's *Clarissa,* while a virtuous antagonist is Macduff in William Shakespeare's *Macbeth.*

Anthropomorphism: The presentation of animals or objects in human shape or with human characteristics. The term is derived from the Greek word for ''human form.'' The fables of Aesop, the animated films of Walt Disney, and Richard Adams's *Watership Down* feature anthropomorphic characters.

Anti-hero: A central character in a work of literature who lacks traditional heroic qualities such as courage, physical prowess, and fortitude. Anti-heros

typically distrust conventional values and are unable to commit themselves to any ideals. They generally feel helpless in a world over which they have no control. Anti-heroes usually accept, and often celebrate, their positions as social outcasts. A well-known anti-hero is Yossarian in Joseph Heller's novel *Catch-22.*

Antimasque: See *Masque*

Antithesis: The antithesis of something is its direct opposite. In literature, the use of antithesis as a figure of speech results in two statements that show a contrast through the balancing of two opposite ideas. Technically, it is the second portion of the statement that is defined as the ''antithesis''; the first portion is the ''thesis.'' An example of antithesis is found in the following portion of Abraham Lincoln's ''Gettysburg Address''; notice the opposition between the verbs ''remember'' and ''forget'' and the phrases ''what we say'' and ''what they did'': ''The world will little note nor long remember what we say here, but it can never forget what they did here.''

Apocrypha: Writings tentatively attributed to an author but not proven or universally accepted to be their works. The term was originally applied to certain books of the Bible that were not considered inspired and so were not included in the ''sacred canon.'' Geoffrey Chaucer, William Shakespeare, Thomas Kyd, Thomas Middleton, and John Marston all have apocrypha. Apocryphal books of the Bible include the Old Testament's Book of Enoch and New Testament's Gospel of Peter.

Apollonian and Dionysian: The two impulses believed to guide authors of dramatic tragedy. The Apollonian impulse is named after Apollo, the Greek god of light and beauty and the symbol of intellectual order. The Dionysian impulse is named after Dionysus, the Greek god of wine and the symbol of the unrestrained forces of nature. The Apollonian impulse is to create a rational, harmonious world, while the Dionysian is to express the irrational forces of personality. Friedrich Nietzche uses these terms in *The Birth of Tragedy* to designate contrasting elements in Greek tragedy.

Apostrophe: A statement, question, or request addressed to an inanimate object or concept or to a nonexistent or absent person. Requests for inspiration from the muses in poetry are examples of apostrophe, as is Marc Antony's address to Caesar's corpse in William Shakespeare's *Julius Caesar*: ''O, pardon me, thou bleeding piece of earth, That I am meek and gentle with these butchers!. . . Woe to the hand that shed this costly blood!. . . ''

Archetype: The word archetype is commonly used to describe an original pattern or model from which all other things of the same kind are made. This term was introduced to literary criticism from the psychology of Carl Jung. It expresses Jung's theory that behind every person's ''unconscious,'' or repressed memories of the past, lies the ''collective unconscious'' of the human race: memories of the countless typical experiences of our ancestors. These memories are said to prompt illogical associations that trigger powerful emotions in the reader. Often, the emotional process is primitive, even primordial. Archetypes are the literary images that grow out of the ''collective unconscious.'' They appear in literature as incidents and plots that repeat basic patterns of life. They may also appear as stereotyped characters. Examples of literary archetypes include themes such as birth and death and characters such as the Earth Mother.

Argument: The argument of a work is the author's subject matter or principal idea. Examples of defined ''argument'' portions of works include John Milton's *Arguments* to each of the books of *Paradise Lost* and the ''Argument'' to Robert Herrick's *Hesperides.*

Aristotelian Criticism: Specifically, the method of evaluating and analyzing tragedy formulated by the Greek philosopher Aristotle in his *Poetics.* More generally, the term indicates any form of criticism that follows Aristotle's views. Aristotelian criticism focuses on the form and logical structure of a work, apart from its historical or social context, in contrast to ''Platonic Criticism,'' which stresses the usefulness of art. Adherents of New Criticism including John Crowe Ransom and Cleanth Brooks utilize and value the basic ideas of Aristotelian criticism for textual analysis.

Art for Art's Sake: See *Aestheticism*

Aside: A comment made by a stage performer that is intended to be heard by the audience but supposedly not by other characters. Eugene O'Neill's *Strange Interlude* is an extended use of the aside in modern theater.

Audience: The people for whom a piece of literature is written. Authors usually write with a certain audience in mind, for example, children, members of a religious or ethnic group, or colleagues in a professional field. The term ''audience'' also applies to the people who gather to see or hear any

performance, including plays, poetry readings, speeches, and concerts. Jane Austen's parody of the gothic novel, *Northanger Abbey,* was originally intended for (and also pokes fun at) an audience of young and avid female gothic novel readers.

Avant-garde: A French term meaning ''vanguard.'' It is used in literary criticism to describe new writing that rejects traditional approaches to literature in favor of innovations in style or content. Twentieth-century examples of the literary *avant-garde* include the Black Mountain School of poets, the Bloomsbury Group, and the Beat Movement.

B

Ballad: A short poem that tells a simple story and has a repeated refrain. Ballads were originally intended to be sung. Early ballads, known as folk ballads, were passed down through generations, so their authors are often unknown. Later ballads composed by known authors are called literary ballads. An example of an anonymous folk ballad is ''Edward,'' which dates from the Middle Ages. Samuel Taylor Coleridge's ''The Rime of the Ancient Mariner'' and John Keats's ''La Belle Dame sans Merci'' are examples of literary ballads.

Baroque: A term used in literary criticism to describe literature that is complex or ornate in style or diction. Baroque works typically express tension, anxiety, and violent emotion. The term ''Baroque Age'' designates a period in Western European literature beginning in the late sixteenth century and ending about one hundred years later. Works of this period often mirror the qualities of works more generally associated with the label ''baroque'' and sometimes feature elaborate conceits. Examples of Baroque works include John Lyly's *Euphues: The Anatomy of Wit,* Luis de Gongora's *Soledads,* and William Shakespeare's *As You Like It.*

Baroque Age: See *Baroque*

Baroque Period: See *Baroque*

Beat Generation: See *Beat Movement*

Beat Movement: A period featuring a group of American poets and novelists of the 1950s and 1960s—including Jack Kerouac, Allen Ginsberg, Gregory Corso, William S. Burroughs, and Lawrence Ferlinghetti—who rejected established social and literary values. Using such techniques as stream of consciousness writing and jazz-influenced free verse and focusing on unusual or abnormal states of mind—generated by religious ecstasy or the use of drugs—the Beat writers aimed to create works that were unconventional in both form and subject matter. Kerouac's *On the Road* is perhaps the best-known example of a Beat Generation novel, and Ginsberg's *Howl* is a famous collection of Beat poetry.

Black Aesthetic Movement: A period of artistic and literary development among African Americans in the 1960s and early 1970s. This was the first major African-American artistic movement since the Harlem Renaissance and was closely paralleled by the civil rights and black power movements. The black aesthetic writers attempted to produce works of art that would be meaningful to the black masses. Key figures in black aesthetics included one of its founders, poet and playwright Amiri Baraka, formerly known as LeRoi Jones; poet and essayist Haki R. Madhubuti, formerly Don L. Lee; poet and playwright Sonia Sanchez; and dramatist Ed Bullins. Works representative of the Black Aesthetic Movement include Amiri Baraka's play *Dutchman,* a 1964 Obie award-winner; *Black Fire: An Anthology of Afro-American Writing,* edited by Baraka and playwright Larry Neal and published in 1968; and Sonia Sanchez's poetry collection *We a BaddDDD People,* published in 1970. Also known as Black Arts Movement.

Black Arts Movement: See *Black Aesthetic Movement*

Black Comedy: See *Black Humor*

Black Humor: Writing that places grotesque elements side by side with humorous ones in an attempt to shock the reader, forcing him or her to laugh at the horrifying reality of a disordered world. Joseph Heller's novel *Catch-22* is considered a superb example of the use of black humor. Other well-known authors who use black humor include Kurt Vonnegut, Edward Albee, Eugene Ionesco, and Harold Pinter. Also known as Black Comedy.

Blank Verse: Loosely, any unrhymed poetry, but more generally, unrhymed iambic pentameter verse (composed of lines of five two-syllable feet with the first syllable accented, the second unaccented). Blank verse has been used by poets since the Renaissance for its flexibility and its graceful, dignified tone. John Milton's *Paradise Lost* is in blank verse, as are most of William Shakespeare's plays.

Bloomsbury Group: A group of English writers, artists, and intellectuals who held informal artistic and philosophical discussions in Bloomsbury, a district of London, from around 1907 to the early 1930s. The Bloomsbury Group held no uniform philosophical beliefs but did commonly express an aversion to moral prudery and a desire for greater social tolerance. At various times the circle included Virginia Woolf, E. M. Forster, Clive Bell, Lytton Strachey, and John Maynard Keynes.

Bon Mot: A French term meaning "good word." A *bon mot* is a witty remark or clever observation. Charles Lamb and Oscar Wilde are celebrated for their witty *bon mots.* Two examples by Oscar Wilde stand out: (1) "All women become their mothers. That is their tragedy. No man does. That's his." (2) "A man cannot be too careful in the choice of his enemies."

Breath Verse: See *Projective Verse*

Burlesque: Any literary work that uses exaggeration to make its subject appear ridiculous, either by treating a trivial subject with profound seriousness or by treating a dignified subject frivolously. The word "burlesque" may also be used as an adjective, as in "burlesque show," to mean "striptease act." Examples of literary burlesque include the comedies of Aristophanes, Miguel de Cervantes's *Don Quixote,,* Samuel Butler's poem "Hudibras," and John Gay's play *The Beggar's Opera.*

C

Cadence: The natural rhythm of language caused by the alternation of accented and unaccented syllables. Much modern poetry—notably free verse—deliberately manipulates cadence to create complex rhythmic effects. James Macpherson's "Ossian poems" are richly cadenced, as is the poetry of the Symbolists, Walt Whitman, and Amy Lowell.

Caesura: A pause in a line of poetry, usually occurring near the middle. It typically corresponds to a break in the natural rhythm or sense of the line but is sometimes shifted to create special meanings or rhythmic effects. The opening line of Edgar Allan Poe's "The Raven" contains a caesura following "dreary": "Once upon a midnight dreary, while I pondered weak and weary. . . ."

Canzone: A short Italian or Provencal lyric poem, commonly about love and often set to music. The *canzone* has no set form but typically contains five or six stanzas made up of seven to twenty lines of eleven syllables each. A shorter, five- to ten-line "envoy," or concluding stanza, completes the poem. Masters of the *canzone* form include

Petrarch, Dante Alighieri, Torquato Tasso, and Guido Cavalcanti.

Carpe Diem: A Latin term meaning ''seize the day.'' This is a traditional theme of poetry, especially lyrics. A *carpe diem* poem advises the reader or the person it addresses to live for today and enjoy the pleasures of the moment. Two celebrated *carpe diem* poems are Andrew Marvell's ''To His Coy Mistress'' and Robert Herrick's poem beginning ''Gather ye rosebuds while ye may. . . .''

Catharsis: The release or purging of unwanted emotions— specifically fear and pity—brought about by exposure to art. The term was first used by the Greek philosopher Aristotle in his *Poetics* to refer to the desired effect of tragedy on spectators. A famous example of catharsis is realized in Sophocles' *Oedipus Rex,* when Oedipus discovers that his wife, Jacosta, is his own mother and that the stranger he killed on the road was his own father.

Celtic Renaissance: A period of Irish literary and cultural history at the end of the nineteenth century. Followers of the movement aimed to create a romantic vision of Celtic myth and legend. The most significant works of the Celtic Renaissance typically present a dreamy, unreal world, usually in reaction against the reality of contemporary problems. William Butler Yeats's *The Wanderings of Oisin* is among the most significant works of the Celtic Renaissance. Also known as Celtic Twilight.

Celtic Twilight: See *Celtic Renaissance*

Character: Broadly speaking, a person in a literary work. The actions of characters are what constitute the plot of a story, novel, or poem. There are numerous types of characters, ranging from simple, stereotypical figures to intricate, multifaceted ones. In the techniques of anthropomorphism and personification, animals—and even places or things— can assume aspects of character. ''Characterization'' is the process by which an author creates vivid, believable characters in a work of art. This may be done in a variety of ways, including (1) direct description of the character by the narrator; (2) the direct presentation of the speech, thoughts, or actions of the character; and (3) the responses of other characters to the character. The term ''character'' also refers to a form originated by the ancient Greek writer Theophrastus that later became popular in the seventeenth and eighteenth centuries. It is a short essay or sketch of a person who prominently displays a specific attribute or quality, such as miserliness or ambition. Notable characters in lit-

erature include Oedipus Rex, Don Quixote de la Mancha, Macbeth, Candide, Hester Prynne, Ebenezer Scrooge, Huckleberry Finn, Jay Gatsby, Scarlett O'Hara, James Bond, and Kunta Kinte.

Characterization: See *Character*

Chorus: In ancient Greek drama, a group of actors who commented on and interpreted the unfolding action on the stage. Initially the chorus was a major component of the presentation, but over time it became less significant, with its numbers reduced and its role eventually limited to commentary between acts. By the sixteenth century the chorus—if employed at all—was typically a single person who provided a prologue and an epilogue and occasionally appeared between acts to introduce or underscore an important event. The chorus in William Shakespeare's *Henry V* functions in this way. Modern dramas rarely feature a chorus, but T. S. Eliot's *Murder in the Cathedral* and Arthur Miller's *A View from the Bridge* are notable exceptions. The Stage Manager in Thornton Wilder's *Our Town* performs a role similar to that of the chorus.

Chronicle: A record of events presented in chronological order. Although the scope and level of detail provided varies greatly among the chronicles surviving from ancient times, some, such as the *Anglo-Saxon Chronicle,* feature vivid descriptions and a lively recounting of events. During the Elizabethan Age, many dramas— appropriately called ''chronicle plays''—were based on material from chronicles. Many of William Shakespeare's dramas of English history as well as Christopher Marlowe's *Edward II* are based in part on Raphael Holinshead's *Chronicles of England, Scotland, and Ireland.*

Classical: In its strictest definition in literary criticism, classicism refers to works of ancient Greek or Roman literature. The term may also be used to describe a literary work of recognized importance (a ''classic'') from any time period or literature that exhibits the traits of classicism. Classical authors from ancient Greek and Roman times include Juvenal and Homer. Examples of later works and authors now described as classical include French literature of the seventeenth century, Western novels of the nineteenth century, and American fiction of the mid-nineteenth century such as that written by James Fenimore Cooper and Mark Twain.

Classicism: A term used in literary criticism to describe critical doctrines that have their roots in ancient Greek and Roman literature, philosophy, and art. Works associated with classicism typically exhibit restraint on the part of the author, unity of design and purpose, clarity, simplicity, logical organization, and respect for tradition. Examples of literary classicism include Cicero's prose, the dramas of Pierre Corneille and Jean Racine, the poetry of John Dryden and Alexander Pope, and the writings of J. W. von Goethe, G. E. Lessing, and T. S. Eliot.

Climax: The turning point in a narrative, the moment when the conflict is at its most intense. Typically, the structure of stories, novels, and plays is one of rising action, in which tension builds to the climax, followed by falling action, in which tension lessens as the story moves to its conclusion. The climax in James Fenimore Cooper's *The Last of the Mohicans* occurs when Magua and his captive Cora are pursued to the edge of a cliff by Uncas. Magua kills Uncas but is subsequently killed by Hawkeye.

Colloquialism: A word, phrase, or form of pronunciation that is acceptable in casual conversation but not in formal, written communication. It is considered more acceptable than slang. An example of colloquialism can be found in Rudyard Kipling's *Barrack-room Ballads:* When 'Omer smote 'is bloomin' lyre He'd 'eard men sing by land and sea; An' what he thought 'e might require 'E went an' took—the same as me!

Comedy: One of two major types of drama, the other being tragedy. Its aim is to amuse, and it typically ends happily. Comedy assumes many forms, such as farce and burlesque, and uses a variety of techniques, from parody to satire. In a restricted sense the term comedy refers only to dramatic presentations, but in general usage it is commonly applied to nondramatic works as well. Examples of comedies range from the plays of Aristophanes, Terrence, and Plautus, Dante Alighieri's *The Divine Comedy,* Francois Rabelais's *Pantagruel* and *Gargantua,* and some of Geoffrey Chaucer's tales and William Shakespeare's plays to Noel Coward's play *Private Lives* and James Thurber's short story ''The Secret Life of Walter Mitty.''

Comedy of Manners: A play about the manners and conventions of an aristocratic, highly sophisticated society. The characters are usually types rather than individualized personalities, and plot is less important than atmosphere. Such plays were an important aspect of late seventeenth-century English comedy. The comedy of manners was revived in the eighteenth century by Oliver Goldsmith and Richard Brinsley Sheridan, enjoyed a second revival in the late nineteenth century, and has endured

into the twentieth century. Examples of comedies of manners include William Congreve's *The Way of the World* in the late seventeenth century, Oliver Goldsmith's *She Stoops to Conquer* and Richard Brinsley Sheridan's *The School for Scandal* in the eighteenth century, Oscar Wilde's *The Importance of Being Earnest* in the nineteenth century, and W. Somerset Maugham's *The Circle* in the twentieth century.

Comic Relief: The use of humor to lighten the mood of a serious or tragic story, especially in plays. The technique is very common in Elizabethan works, and can be an integral part of the plot or simply a brief event designed to break the tension of the scene. The Gravediggers' scene in William Shakespeare's *Hamlet* is a frequently cited example of comic relief.

Commedia dell'arte: An Italian term meaning ''the comedy of guilds'' or ''the comedy of professional actors.'' This form of dramatic comedy was popular in Italy during the sixteenth century. Actors were assigned stock roles (such as Pulcinella, the stupid servant, or Pantalone, the old merchant) and given a basic plot to follow, but all dialogue was improvised. The roles were rigidly typed and the plots were formulaic, usually revolving around young lovers who thwarted their elders and attained wealth and happiness. A rigid convention of the *commedia dell'arte* is the periodic intrusion of Harlequin, who interrupts the play with low buffoonery. Peppino de Filippo's *Metamorphoses of a Wandering Minstrel* gave modern audiences an idea of what *commedia dell'arte* may have been like. Various scenarios for *commedia dell'arte* were compiled in Petraccone's *La commedia dell'arte, storia, technica, scenari,* published in 1927.

Complaint: A lyric poem, popular in the Renaissance, in which the speaker expresses sorrow about his or her condition. Typically, the speaker's sadness is caused by an unresponsive lover, but some complaints cite other sources of unhappiness, such as poverty or fate. A commonly cited example is ''A Complaint by Night of the Lover Not Beloved'' by Henry Howard, Earl of Surrey. Thomas Sackville's ''Complaint of Henry, Duke of Buckingham'' traces the duke's unhappiness to his ruthless ambition.

Conceit: A clever and fanciful metaphor, usually expressed through elaborate and extended comparison, that presents a striking parallel between two seemingly dissimilar things—for example, elaborately comparing a beautiful woman to an object like a garden or the sun. The conceit was a popular device throughout the Elizabethan Age and Baroque Age and was the principal technique of the seventeenth-century English metaphysical poets. This usage of the word conceit is unrelated to the best-known definition of conceit as an arrogant attitude or behavior. The conceit figures prominently in the works of John Donne, Emily Dickinson, and T. S. Eliot.

Concrete: Concrete is the opposite of abstract, and refers to a thing that actually exists or a description that allows the reader to experience an object or concept with the senses. Henry David Thoreau's *Walden* contains much concrete description of nature and wildlife.

Concrete Poetry: Poetry in which visual elements play a large part in the poetic effect. Punctuation marks, letters, or words are arranged on a page to form a visual design: a cross, for example, or a bumblebee. Max Bill and Eugene Gomringer were among the early practitioners of concrete poetry; Haroldo de Campos and Augusto de Campos are among contemporary authors of concrete poetry.

Confessional Poetry: A form of poetry in which the poet reveals very personal, intimate, sometimes shocking information about himself or herself. Anne Sexton, Sylvia Plath, Robert Lowell, and John Berryman wrote poetry in the confessional vein.

Conflict: The conflict in a work of fiction is the issue to be resolved in the story. It usually occurs between two characters, the protagonist and the antagonist, or between the protagonist and society or the protagonist and himself or herself. Conflict in Theodore Dreiser's novel *Sister Carrie* comes as a result of urban society, while Jack London's short story "To Build a Fire" concerns the protagonist's battle against the cold and himself.

Connotation: The impression that a word gives beyond its defined meaning. Connotations may be universally understood or may be significant only to a certain group. Both "horse" and "steed" denote the same animal, but "steed" has a different connotation, deriving from the chivalrous or romantic narratives in which the word was once often used.

Consonance: Consonance occurs in poetry when words appearing at the ends of two or more verses have similar final consonant sounds but have final vowel sounds that differ, as with "stuff" and "off." Consonance is found in "The curfew tolls the knells of parting day" from Thomas Grey's "An Elegy Written in a Country Church Yard." Also known as Half Rhyme or Slant Rhyme.

Convention: Any widely accepted literary device, style, or form. A soliloquy, in which a character reveals to the audience his or her private thoughts, is an example of a dramatic convention.

Corrido: A Mexican ballad. Examples of *corridos* include "Muerte del afamado Bilito," "La voz de mi conciencia," "Lucio Perez," "La juida," and "Los presos."

Couplet: Two lines of poetry with the same rhyme and meter, often expressing a complete and self-contained thought. The following couplet is from Alexander Pope's "Elegy to the Memory of an Unfortunate Lady": 'Tis Use alone that sanctifies Expense, And Splendour borrows all her rays from Sense.

Criticism: The systematic study and evaluation of literary works, usually based on a specific method or set of principles. An important part of literary studies since ancient times, the practice of criticism has given rise to numerous theories, methods, and "schools," sometimes producing conflicting, even contradictory, interpretations of literature in general as well as of individual works. Even such basic issues as what constitutes a poem or a novel have been the subject of much criticism over the centuries. Seminal texts of literary criticism include Plato's *Republic,* Aristotle's *Poetics,* Sir Philip Sidney's *The Defence of Poesie,* John Dryden's *Of Dramatic Poesie,* and William Wordsworth's "Preface" to the second edition of his *Lyrical Ballads.* Contemporary schools of criticism include deconstruction, feminist, psychoanalytic, poststructuralist, new historicist, postcolonialist, and reader-response.

D

Dactyl: See *Foot*

Dadaism: A protest movement in art and literature founded by Tristan Tzara in 1916. Followers of the movement expressed their outrage at the destruction brought about by World War I by revolting against numerous forms of social convention. The Dadaists presented works marked by calculated madness and flamboyant nonsense. They stressed total freedom of expression, commonly through primitive displays of emotion and illogical, often senseless, poetry. The movement ended shortly after the war, when it was replaced by surrealism. Proponents of Dadaism include Andre Breton, Louis Aragon, Philippe Soupault, and Paul Eluard.

Decadent: See *Decadents*

Decadents: The followers of a nineteenth-century literary movement that had its beginnings in French aestheticism. Decadent literature displays a fascination with perverse and morbid states; a search for novelty and sensation—the "new thrill"; a preoccupation with mysticism; and a belief in the senselessness of human existence. The movement is closely associated with the doctrine Art for Art's Sake. The term "decadence" is sometimes used to denote a decline in the quality of art or literature following a period of greatness. Major French decadents are Charles Baudelaire and Arthur Rimbaud. English decadents include Oscar Wilde, Ernest Dowson, and Frank Harris.

Deconstruction: A method of literary criticism developed by Jacques Derrida and characterized by multiple conflicting interpretations of a given work. Deconstructionists consider the impact of the language of a work and suggest that the true meaning of the work is not necessarily the meaning that the author intended. Jacques Derrida's *De la grammatologie* is the seminal text on deconstructive strategies; among American practitioners of this method of criticism are Paul de Man and J. Hillis Miller.

Deduction: The process of reaching a conclusion through reasoning from general premises to a specific premise. An example of deduction is present in the following syllogism: Premise: All mammals are animals. Premise: All whales are mammals. Conclusion: Therefore, all whales are animals.

Denotation: The definition of a word, apart from the impressions or feelings it creates in the reader. The word "apartheid" denotes a political and economic policy of segregation by race, but its connotations— oppression, slavery, inequality—are numerous.

Denouement: A French word meaning "the unknotting." In literary criticism, it denotes the resolution of conflict in fiction or drama. The *denouement* follows the climax and provides an outcome to the primary plot situation as well as an explanation of secondary plot complications. The *denouement* often involves a character's recognition of his or her state of mind or moral condition. A well-known example of *denouement* is the last scene of the play *As You Like It* by William Shakespeare, in which couples are married, an evildoer repents, the identities of two disguised characters are revealed, and a ruler is restored to power. Also known as Falling Action.

Description: Descriptive writing is intended to allow a reader to picture the scene or setting in which the action of a story takes place. The form this description takes often evokes an intended emotional response—a dark, spooky graveyard will evoke fear, and a peaceful, sunny meadow will evoke calmness. An example of a descriptive story is Edgar Allan Poe's *Landor's Cottage,* which offers a detailed depiction of a New York country estate.

Detective Story: A narrative about the solution of a mystery or the identification of a criminal. The conventions of the detective story include the detective's scrupulous use of logic in solving the mystery; incompetent or ineffectual police; a suspect who appears guilty at first but is later proved innocent; and the detective's friend or confidant—often the narrator—whose slowness in interpreting clues emphasizes by contrast the detective's brilliance. Edgar Allan Poe's "Murders in the Rue Morgue" is commonly regarded as the earliest example of this type of story. With this work, Poe established many of the conventions of the detective story genre, which are still in practice. Other practitioners of this vast and extremely popular genre include Arthur Conan Doyle, Dashiell Hammett, and Agatha Christie.

Deus ex machina: A Latin term meaning "god out of a machine." In Greek drama, a god was often lowered onto the stage by a mechanism of some kind to rescue the hero or untangle the plot. By extension, the term refers to any artificial device or coincidence used to bring about a convenient and simple solution to a plot. This is a common device in melodramas and includes such fortunate circumstances as the sudden receipt of a legacy to save the family farm or a last-minute stay of execution. The *deus ex machina* invariably rewards the virtuous and punishes evildoers. Examples of *deus ex machina* include King Louis XIV in Jean-Baptiste Moliere's *Tartuffe* and Queen Victoria in *The Pirates of Penzance* by William Gilbert and Arthur Sullivan. Bertolt Brecht parodies the abuse of such devices in the conclusion of his *Threepenny Opera.*

Dialogue: In its widest sense, dialogue is simply conversation between people in a literary work; in its most restricted sense, it refers specifically to the speech of characters in a drama. As a specific literary genre, a "dialogue" is a composition in which characters debate an issue or idea. The Greek philosopher Plato frequently expounded his theories in the form of dialogues.

Diction: The selection and arrangement of words in a literary work. Either or both may vary depending on the desired effect. There are four general types of diction: ''formal,'' used in scholarly or lofty writing; ''informal,'' used in relaxed but educated conversation; ''colloquial,'' used in everyday speech; and ''slang,'' containing newly coined words and other terms not accepted in formal usage.

Didactic: A term used to describe works of literature that aim to teach some moral, religious, political, or practical lesson. Although didactic elements are often found in artistically pleasing works, the term ''didactic'' usually refers to literature in which the message is more important than the form. The term may also be used to criticize a work that the critic finds ''overly didactic,'' that is, heavy-handed in its delivery of a lesson. Examples of didactic literature include John Bunyan's *Pilgrim's Progress,* Alexander Pope's *Essay on Criticism,* Jean-Jacques Rousseau's *Emile,* and Elizabeth Inchbald's *Simple Story.*

Dimeter: See *Meter*

Dionysian: See *Apollonian and Dionysian*

Discordia concours: A Latin phrase meaning ''discord in harmony.'' The term was coined by the eighteenth-century English writer Samuel Johnson to describe ''a combination of dissimilar images or discovery of occult resemblances in things apparently unlike.'' Johnson created the expression by reversing a phrase by the Latin poet Horace. The metaphysical poetry of John Donne, Richard Crashaw, Abraham Cowley, George Herbert, and Edward Taylor among others, contains many examples of *discordia concours.* In Donne's ''A Valediction: Forbidding Mourning,'' the poet compares the union of himself with his lover to a draftsman's compass: If they be two, they are two so, As stiff twin compasses are two: Thy soul, the fixed foot, makes no show To move, but doth, if the other do; And though it in the center sit, Yet when the other far doth roam, It leans, and hearkens after it, And grows erect, as that comes home.

Dissonance: A combination of harsh or jarring sounds, especially in poetry. Although such combinations may be accidental, poets sometimes intentionally make them to achieve particular effects. Dissonance is also sometimes used to refer to close but not identical rhymes. When this is the case, the word functions as a synonym for consonance. Robert Browning, Gerard Manley Hopkins, and many other poets have made deliberate use of dissonance.

Doppelganger: A literary technique by which a character is duplicated (usually in the form of an alter ego, though sometimes as a ghostly counterpart) or divided into two distinct, usually opposite personalities The use of this character device is widespread in nineteenth- and twentieth- century literature, and indicates a growing awareness among authors that the ''self'' is really a composite of many ''selves.'' A well-known story containing a *doppelganger* character is Robert Louis Stevenson's *Dr. Jekyll and Mr. Hyde,* which dramatizes an internal struggle between good and evil. Also known as The Double.

Double Entendre: A corruption of a French phrase meaning ''double meaning.'' The term is used to indicate a word or phrase that is deliberately ambiguous, especially when one of the meanings is risque or improper. An example of a *double entendre* is the Elizabethan usage of the verb ''die,'' which refers both to death and to orgasm.

Double, The: See *Doppelganger*

Draft: Any preliminary version of a written work. An author may write dozens of drafts which are revised to form the final work, or he or she may write only one, with few or no revisions. Dorothy Parker's observation that ''I can't write five words but that I change seven'' humorously indicates the purpose of the draft.

Drama: In its widest sense, a drama is any work designed to be presented by actors on a stage. Similarly, ''drama'' denotes a broad literary genre that includes a variety of forms, from pageant and spectacle to tragedy and comedy, as well as countless types and subtypes. More commonly in modern usage, however, a drama is a work that treats serious subjects and themes but does not aim at the grandeur of tragedy. This use of the term originated with the eighteenth-century French writer Denis Diderot, who used the word *drame* to designate his plays about middle- class life; thus ''drama'' typically features characters of a less exalted stature than those of tragedy. Examples of classical dramas include Menander's comedy *Dyscolus* and Sophocles' tragedy *Oedipus Rex.* Contemporary dramas include Eugene O'Neill's *The Iceman Cometh,* Lillian Hellman's *Little Foxes,* and August Wilson's *Ma Rainey's Black Bottom.*

Dramatic Irony: Occurs when the audience of a play or the reader of a work of literature knows something that a character in the work itself does not know. The irony is in the contrast between the intended meaning of the statements or actions of a character and the additional information understood by the audience. A celebrated example of dramatic irony is in Act V of William Shakespeare's *Romeo and Juliet,* where two young lovers meet their end as a result of a tragic misunderstanding. Here, the audience has full knowledge that Juliet's apparent ''death'' is merely temporary; she will regain her senses when the mysterious ''sleeping potion'' she has taken wears off. But Romeo, mistaking Juliet's drug-induced trance for true death, kills himself in grief. Upon awakening, Juliet discovers Romeo's corpse and, in despair, slays herself.

Dramatic Monologue: See *Monologue*

Dramatic Poetry: Any lyric work that employs elements of drama such as dialogue, conflict, or characterization, but excluding works that are intended for stage presentation. A monologue is a form of dramatic poetry.

Dramatis Personae: The characters in a work of literature, particularly a drama. The list of characters printed before the main text of a play or in the program is the *dramatis personae.*

Dream Allegory: See *Dream Vision*

Dream Vision: A literary convention, chiefly of the Middle Ages. In a dream vision a story is presented as a literal dream of the narrator. This device was commonly used to teach moral and religious lessons. Important works of this type are *The Divine Comedy* by Dante Alighieri, *Piers Plowman* by William Langland, and *The Pilgrim's Progress* by John Bunyan. Also known as Dream Allegory.

Dystopia: An imaginary place in a work of fiction where the characters lead dehumanized, fearful lives. Jack London's *The Iron Heel,* Yevgeny Zamyatin's *My,* Aldous Huxley's *Brave New World,* George Orwell's *Nineteen Eighty-four,* and Margaret Atwood's *Handmaid's Tale* portray versions of dystopia.

E

Eclogue: In classical literature, a poem featuring rural themes and structured as a dialogue among shepherds. Eclogues often took specific poetic forms, such as elegies or love poems. Some were written as the soliloquy of a shepherd. In later centuries, ''eclogue'' came to refer to any poem that was in the pastoral tradition or that had a dialogue or mono-

logue structure. A classical example of an eclogue is Virgil's *Eclogues,* also known as *Bucolics.* Giovanni Boccaccio, Edmund Spenser, Andrew Marvell, Jonathan Swift, and Louis MacNeice also wrote eclogues.

Edwardian: Describes cultural conventions identified with the period of the reign of Edward VII of England (1901-1910). Writers of the Edwardian Age typically displayed a strong reaction against the propriety and conservatism of the Victorian Age. Their work often exhibits distrust of authority in religion, politics, and art and expresses strong doubts about the soundness of conventional values. Writers of this era include George Bernard Shaw, H. G. Wells, and Joseph Conrad.

Edwardian Age: See *Edwardian*

Electra Complex: A daughter's amorous obsession with her father. The term Electra complex comes from the plays of Euripides and Sophocles entitled *Electra,* in which the character Electra drives her brother Orestes to kill their mother and her lover in revenge for the murder of their father.

Elegy: A lyric poem that laments the death of a person or the eventual death of all people. In a conventional elegy, set in a classical world, the poet and subject are spoken of as shepherds. In modern criticism, the word elegy is often used to refer to a poem that is melancholy or mournfully contemplative. John Milton's ''Lycidas'' and Percy Bysshe Shelley's ''Adonais'' are two examples of this form.

Elizabethan Age: A period of great economic growth, religious controversy, and nationalism closely associated with the reign of Elizabeth I of England (1558-1603). The Elizabethan Age is considered a part of the general renaissance—that is, the flowering of arts and literature—that took place in Europe during the fourteenth through sixteenth centuries. The era is considered the golden age of English literature. The most important dramas in English and a great deal of lyric poetry were produced during this period, and modern English criticism began around this time. The notable authors of the period—Philip Sidney, Edmund Spenser, Christopher Marlowe, William Shakespeare, Ben Jonson, Francis Bacon, and John Donne—are among the best in all of English literature.

Elizabethan Drama: English comic and tragic plays produced during the Renaissance, or more narrowly, those plays written during the last years of and few years after Queen Elizabeth's reign. William Shakespeare is considered an Elizabethan dramatist in the broader sense, although most of his work was produced during the reign of James I. Examples of Elizabethan comedies include John Lyly's *The Woman in the Moone,* Thomas Dekker's *The Roaring Girl, or, Moll Cut Purse,* and William Shakespeare's *Twelfth Night.* Examples of Elizabethan tragedies include William Shakespeare's *Antony and Cleopatra,* Thomas Kyd's *The Spanish Tragedy,* and John Webster's *The Tragedy of the Duchess of Malfi.*

Empathy: A sense of shared experience, including emotional and physical feelings, with someone or something other than oneself. Empathy is often used to describe the response of a reader to a literary character. An example of an empathic passage is William Shakespeare's description in his narrative poem *Venus and Adonis* of: the snail, whose tender horns being hit, Shrinks backward in his shelly cave with pain. Readers of Gerard Manley Hopkins's *The Windhover* may experience some of the physical sensations evoked in the description of the movement of the falcon.

English Sonnet: See *Sonnet*

Enjambment: The running over of the sense and structure of a line of verse or a couplet into the following verse or couplet. Andrew Marvell's "To His Coy Mistress" is structured as a series of enjambments, as in lines 11-12: "My vegetable love should grow/Vaster than empires and more slow."

Enlightenment, The: An eighteenth-century philosophical movement. It began in France but had a wide impact throughout Europe and America. Thinkers of the Enlightenment valued reason and believed that both the individual and society could achieve a state of perfection. Corresponding to this essentially humanist vision was a resistance to religious authority. Important figures of the Enlightenment were Denis Diderot and Voltaire in France, Edward Gibbon and David Hume in England, and Thomas Paine and Thomas Jefferson in the United States.

Epic: A long narrative poem about the adventures of a hero of great historic or legendary importance. The setting is vast and the action is often given cosmic significance through the intervention of supernatural forces such as gods, angels, or demons. Epics are typically written in a classical style of grand simplicity with elaborate metaphors and allusions that enhance the symbolic importance of a hero's adventures. Some well-known epics are Homer's *Iliad* and *Odyssey,* Virgil's *Aeneid,* and John Milton's *Paradise Lost.*

Epic Simile: See *Homeric Simile*

Epic Theater: A theory of theatrical presentation developed by twentieth-century German playwright Bertolt Brecht. Brecht created a type of drama that the audience could view with complete detachment. He used what he termed "alienation effects" to create an emotional distance between the audience and the action on stage. Among these effects are: short, self-contained scenes that keep the play from building to a cathartic climax; songs that comment on the action. and techniques of acting that prevent the actor from developing an emotional identity with his role. Besides the plays of Bertolt Brecht, other plays that utilize epic theater conventions include those of Georg Buchner, Frank Wedekind, Erwin Piscator, and Leopold Jessner.

Epigram: A saying that makes the speaker's point quickly and concisely. Samuel Taylor Coleridge wrote an epigram that neatly sums up the form: What is an Epigram? A Dwarfish whole, Its body brevity, and wit its soul.

Epilogue: A concluding statement or section of a literary work. In dramas, particularly those of the seventeenth and eighteenth centuries, the epilogue is a closing speech, often in verse, delivered by an actor at the end of a play and spoken directly to the audience. A famous epilogue is Puck's speech at the end of William Shakespeare's *A Midsummer Night's Dream.*

Epiphany: A sudden revelation of truth inspired by a seemingly trivial incident. The term was widely used by James Joyce in his critical writings, and the stories in Joyce's *Dubliners* are commonly called "epiphanies."

Episode: An incident that forms part of a story and is significantly related to it. Episodes may be either self-contained narratives or events that depend on a larger context for their sense and importance. Examples of episodes include the founding of Wilmington, Delaware in Charles Reade's *The Disinherited Heir* and the individual events comprising the picaresque novels and medieval romances.

Episodic Plot: See *Plot*

Epitaph: An inscription on a tomb or tombstone, or a verse written on the occasion of a person's death. Epitaphs may be serious or humorous. Dorothy Parker's epitaph reads, "I told you I was sick."

Epithalamion: A song or poem written to honor and commemorate a marriage ceremony. Famous examples include Edmund Spenser's

"Epithalamion" and e. e. cummings's "Epithalamion." Also spelled Epithalamium.

Epithalamium: See *Epithalamion*

Epithet: A word or phrase, often disparaging or abusive, that expresses a character trait of someone or something. "The Napoleon of crime" is an epithet applied to Professor Moriarty, arch-rival of Sherlock Holmes in Arthur Conan Doyle's series of detective stories.

Exempla: See *Exemplum*

Exemplum: A tale with a moral message. This form of literary sermonizing flourished during the Middle Ages, when *exempla* appeared in collections known as "example-books." The works of Geoffrey Chaucer are full of *exempla*.

Existentialism: A predominantly twentieth-century philosophy concerned with the nature and perception of human existence. There are two major strains of existentialist thought: atheistic and Christian. Followers of atheistic existentialism believe that the individual is alone in a godless universe and that the basic human condition is one of suffering and loneliness. Nevertheless, because there are no fixed values, individuals can create their own characters—indeed, they can shape themselves—through the exercise of free will. The atheistic strain culminates in and is popularly associated with the works of Jean-Paul Sartre. The Christian existentialists, on the other hand, believe that only in God may people find freedom from life's anguish. The two strains hold certain beliefs in common: that existence cannot be fully understood or described through empirical effort; that anguish is a universal element of life; that individuals must bear responsibility for their actions; and that there is no common standard of behavior or perception for religious and ethical matters. Existentialist thought figures prominently in the works of such authors as Eugene Ionesco, Franz Kafka, Fyodor Dostoyevsky, Simone de Beauvoir, Samuel Beckett, and Albert Camus.

Expatriates: See *Expatriatism*

Expatriatism: The practice of leaving one's country to live for an extended period in another country. Literary expatriates include English poets Percy Bysshe Shelley and John Keats in Italy, Polish novelist Joseph Conrad in England, American writers Richard Wright, James Baldwin, Gertrude Stein, and Ernest Hemingway in France, and Trinidadian author Neil Bissondath in Canada.

Exposition: Writing intended to explain the nature of an idea, thing, or theme. Expository writing is often combined with description, narration, or argument. In dramatic writing, the exposition is the introductory material which presents the characters, setting, and tone of the play. An example of dramatic exposition occurs in many nineteenth-century drawing-room comedies in which the butler and the maid open the play with relevant talk about their master and mistress; in composition, exposition relays factual information, as in encyclopedia entries.

Expressionism: An indistinct literary term, originally used to describe an early twentieth-century school of German painting. The term applies to almost any mode of unconventional, highly subjective writing that distorts reality in some way. Advocates of Expressionism include dramatists George Kaiser, Ernst Toller, Luigi Pirandello, Federico Garcia Lorca, Eugene O'Neill, and Elmer Rice; poets George Heym, Ernst Stadler, August Stramm, Gottfried Benn, and Georg Trakl; and novelists Franz Kafka and James Joyce.

Extended Monologue: See *Monologue*

F

Fable: A prose or verse narrative intended to convey a moral. Animals or inanimate objects with human characteristics often serve as characters in fables. A famous fable is Aesop's "The Tortoise and the Hare."

Fairy Tales: Short narratives featuring mythical beings such as fairies, elves, and sprites. These tales originally belonged to the folklore of a particular nation or region, such as those collected in Germany by Jacob and Wilhelm Grimm. Two other celebrated writers of fairy tales are Hans Christian Andersen and Rudyard Kipling.

Falling Action: See *Denouement*

Fantasy: A literary form related to mythology and folklore. Fantasy literature is typically set in nonexistent realms and features supernatural beings. Notable examples of fantasy literature are *The Lord of the Rings* by J. R. R. Tolkien and the Gormenghast trilogy by Mervyn Peake.

Farce: A type of comedy characterized by broad humor, outlandish incidents, and often vulgar subject matter. Much of the "comedy" in film and television could more accurately be described as farce.

Feet: See *Foot*

Feminine Rhyme: See *Rhyme*

Femme fatale: A French phrase with the literal translation ''fatal woman.'' A *femme fatale* is a sensuous, alluring woman who often leads men into danger or trouble. A classic example of the *femme fatale* is the nameless character in Billy Wilder's *The Seven Year Itch,* portrayed by Marilyn Monroe in the film adaptation.

Fiction: Any story that is the product of imagination rather than a documentation of fact. characters and events in such narratives may be based in real life but their ultimate form and configuration is a creation of the author. Geoffrey Chaucer's *The Canterbury Tales,* Laurence Sterne's *Tristram Shandy,* and Margaret Mitchell's *Gone with the Wind* are examples of fiction.

Figurative Language: A technique in writing in which the author temporarily interrupts the order, construction, or meaning of the writing for a particular effect. This interruption takes the form of one or more figures of speech such as hyperbole, irony, or simile. Figurative language is the opposite of literal language, in which every word is truthful, accurate, and free of exaggeration or embellishment. Examples of figurative language are tropes such as metaphor and rhetorical figures such as apostrophe.

Figures of Speech: Writing that differs from customary conventions for construction, meaning, order, or significance for the purpose of a special meaning or effect. There are two major types of figures of speech: rhetorical figures, which do not make changes in the meaning of the words, and tropes, which do. Types of figures of speech include simile, hyperbole, alliteration, and pun, among many others.

Fin de siecle: A French term meaning ''end of the century.'' The term is used to denote the last decade of the nineteenth century, a transition period when writers and other artists abandoned old conventions and looked for new techniques and objectives. Two writers commonly associated with the *fin de siecle* mindset are Oscar Wilde and George Bernard Shaw.

First Person: See *Point of View*

Flashback: A device used in literature to present action that occurred before the beginning of the story. Flashbacks are often introduced as the dreams or recollections of one or more characters. Flashback techniques are often used in films, where they are typically set off by a gradual changing of one picture to another.

Foil: A character in a work of literature whose physical or psychological qualities contrast strongly with, and therefore highlight, the corresponding qualities of another character. In his Sherlock Holmes stories, Arthur Conan Doyle portrayed Dr. Watson as a man of normal habits and intelligence, making him a foil for the eccentric and wonderfully perceptive Sherlock Holmes.

Folk Ballad: See *Ballad*

Folklore: Traditions and myths preserved in a culture or group of people. Typically, these are passed on by word of mouth in various forms—such as legends, songs, and proverbs— or preserved in customs and ceremonies. This term was first used by W. J. Thoms in 1846. Sir James Frazer's *The Golden Bough* is the record of English folklore; myths about the frontier and the Old South exemplify American folklore.

Folktale: A story originating in oral tradition. Folktales fall into a variety of categories, including legends, ghost stories, fairy tales, fables, and anecdotes based on historical figures and events. Examples of folktales include Giambattista Basile's *The Pentamerone,* which contains the tales of Puss in Boots, Rapunzel, Cinderella, and Beauty and the Beast, and Joel Chandler Harris's Uncle Remus stories, which represent transplanted African folktales and American tales about the characters Mike Fink, Johnny Appleseed, Paul Bunyan, and Pecos Bill.

Foot: The smallest unit of rhythm in a line of poetry. In English-language poetry, a foot is typically one accented syllable combined with one or two unaccented syllables. There are many different types of feet. When the accent is on the second syllable of a two syllable word (con- *tort*), the foot is an ''iamb''; the reverse accentual pattern (*tor* -ture) is a ''trochee.'' Other feet that commonly occur in poetry in English are ''anapest'', two unaccented syllables followed by an accented syllable as in inter-*cept,* and ''dactyl'', an accented syllable followed by two unaccented syllables as in *su*-i- cide.

Foreshadowing: A device used in literature to create expectation or to set up an explanation of later developments. In Charles Dickens's *Great Expectations,* the graveyard encounter at the beginning of the novel between Pip and the escaped convict Magwitch foreshadows the baleful atmosphere and events that comprise much of the narrative.

Form: The pattern or construction of a work which identifies its genre and distinguishes it from other genres. Examples of forms include the different genres, such as the lyric form or the short story form, and various patterns for poetry, such as the verse form or the stanza form.

Formalism: In literary criticism, the belief that literature should follow prescribed rules of construction, such as those that govern the sonnet form. Examples of formalism are found in the work of the New Critics and structuralists.

Fourteener Meter: See *Meter*

Free Verse: Poetry that lacks regular metrical and rhyme patterns but that tries to capture the cadences of everyday speech. The form allows a poet to exploit a variety of rhythmical effects within a single poem. Free-verse techniques have been widely used in the twentieth century by such writers as Ezra Pound, T. S. Eliot, Carl Sandburg, and William Carlos Williams. Also known as *Vers libre.*

Futurism: A flamboyant literary and artistic movement that developed in France, Italy, and Russia from 1908 through the 1920s. Futurist theater and poetry abandoned traditional literary forms. In their place, followers of the movement attempted to achieve total freedom of expression through bizarre imagery and deformed or newly invented words. The Futurists were self-consciously modern artists who attempted to incorporate the appearances and sounds of modern life into their work. Futurist writers include Filippo Tommaso Marinetti, Wyndham Lewis, Guillaume Apollinaire, Velimir Khlebnikov, and Vladimir Mayakovsky.

G

Genre: A category of literary work. In critical theory, genre may refer to both the content of a given work—tragedy, comedy, pastoral—and to its form, such as poetry, novel, or drama. This term also refers to types of popular literature, as in the genres of science fiction or the detective story.

Genteel Tradition: A term coined by critic George Santayana to describe the literary practice of certain late nineteenth- century American writers, especially New Englanders. Followers of the Genteel Tradition emphasized conventionality in social, religious, moral, and literary standards. Some of the best-known writers of the Genteel Tradition are R. H. Stoddard and Bayard Taylor.

Gilded Age: A period in American history during the 1870s characterized by political corruption and materialism. A number of important novels of social and political criticism were written during this time. Examples of Gilded Age literature include Henry Adams's *Democracy* and F. Marion Crawford's *An American Politician.*

Gothic: See *Gothicism*

Gothicism: In literary criticism, works characterized by a taste for the medieval or morbidly attractive. A gothic novel prominently features elements of horror, the supernatural, gloom, and violence: clanking chains, terror, charnel houses, ghosts, medieval castles, and mysteriously slamming doors. The term ''gothic novel'' is also applied to novels that lack elements of the traditional Gothic setting but that create a similar atmosphere of terror or dread. Mary Shelley's *Frankenstein* is perhaps the best-known English work of this kind.

Gothic Novel: See *Gothicism*

Great Chain of Being: The belief that all things and creatures in nature are organized in a hierarchy from inanimate objects at the bottom to God at the top. This system of belief was popular in the seventeenth and eighteenth centuries. A summary of the concept of the great chain of being can be found in the first epistle of Alexander Pope's *An Essay on Man,* and more recently in Arthur O. Lovejoy's *The Great Chain of Being: A Study of the History of an Idea.*

Grotesque: In literary criticism, the subject matter of a work or a style of expression characterized by exaggeration, deformity, freakishness, and disorder. The grotesque often includes an element of comic absurdity. Early examples of literary grotesque include Francois Rabelais's *Pantagruel* and *Gargantua* and Thomas Nashe's *The Unfortunate Traveller,* while more recent examples can be found in the works of Edgar Allan Poe, Evelyn Waugh, Eudora Welty, Flannery O'Connor, Eugene Ionesco, Gunter Grass, Thomas Mann, Mervyn Peake, and Joseph Heller, among many others.

H

Haiku: The shortest form of Japanese poetry, constructed in three lines of five, seven, and five syllables respectively. The message of a *haiku* poem usually centers on some aspect of spirituality and provokes an emotional response in the reader. Early masters of *haiku* include Basho, Buson,

Kobayashi Issa, and Masaoka Shiki. English writers of *haiku* include the Imagists, notably Ezra Pound, H. D., Amy Lowell, Carl Sandburg, and William Carlos Williams. Also known as *Hokku.*

Half Rhyme: See *Consonance*

Hamartia: In tragedy, the event or act that leads to the hero's or heroine's downfall. This term is often incorrectly used as a synonym for tragic flaw. In Richard Wright's *Native Son,* the act that seals Bigger Thomas's fate is his first impulsive murder.

Harlem Renaissance: The Harlem Renaissance of the 1920s is generally considered the first significant movement of black writers and artists in the United States. During this period, new and established black writers published more fiction and poetry than ever before, the first influential black literary journals were established, and black authors and artists received their first widespread recognition and serious critical appraisal. Among the major writers associated with this period are Claude McKay, Jean Toomer, Countee Cullen, Langston Hughes, Arna Bontemps, Nella Larsen, and Zora Neale Hurston. Works representative of the Harlem Renaissance include Arna Bontemps's poems "The Return" and "Golgotha Is a Mountain," Claude McKay's novel *Home to Harlem,* Nella Larsen's novel *Passing,* Langston Hughes's poem "The Negro Speaks of Rivers," and the journals *Crisis* and *Opportunity,* both founded during this period. Also known as Negro Renaissance and New Negro Movement.

Harlequin: A stock character of the *commedia dell'arte* who occasionally interrupted the action with silly antics. Harlequin first appeared on the English stage in John Day's *The Travailes of the Three English Brothers.* The San Francisco Mime Troupe is one of the few modern groups to adapt Harlequin to the needs of contemporary satire.

Hellenism: Imitation of ancient Greek thought or styles. Also, an approach to life that focuses on the growth and development of the intellect. "Hellenism" is sometimes used to refer to the belief that reason can be applied to examine all human experience. A cogent discussion of Hellenism can be found in Matthew Arnold's *Culture and Anarchy.*

Heptameter: See *Meter*

Hero/Heroine: The principal sympathetic character (male or female) in a literary work. Heroes and heroines typically exhibit admirable traits: idealism, courage, and integrity, for example. Famous heroes and heroines include Pip in Charles Dickens's *Great Expectations,* the anonymous narrator in Ralph Ellison's *Invisible Man,* and Sethe in Toni Morrison's *Beloved.*

Heroic Couplet: A rhyming couplet written in iambic pentameter (a verse with five iambic feet). The following lines by Alexander Pope are an example: "Truth guards the Poet, sanctifies the line,/ And makes Immortal, Verse as mean as mine."

Heroic Line: The meter and length of a line of verse in epic or heroic poetry. This varies by language and time period. For example, in English poetry, the heroic line is iambic pentameter (a verse with five iambic feet); in French, the alexandrine (a verse with six iambic feet); in classical literature, dactylic hexameter (a verse with six dactylic feet).

Heroine: See *Hero/Heroine*

Hexameter: See *Meter*

Historical Criticism: The study of a work based on its impact on the world of the time period in which it was written. Examples of postmodern historical criticism can be found in the work of Michel Foucault, Hayden White, Stephen Greenblatt, and Jonathan Goldberg.

Hokku: See *Haiku*

Holocaust: See *Holocaust Literature*

Holocaust Literature: Literature influenced by or written about the Holocaust of World War II. Such literature includes true stories of survival in concentration camps, escape, and life after the war, as well as fictional works and poetry. Representative works of Holocaust literature include Saul Bellow's *Mr. Sammler's Planet,* Anne Frank's *The Diary of a Young Girl,* Jerzy Kosinski's *The Painted Bird,* Arthur Miller's *Incident at Vichy,* Czeslaw Milosz's *Collected Poems,* William Styron's *Sophie's Choice,* and Art Spiegelman's *Maus.*

Homeric Simile: An elaborate, detailed comparison written as a simile many lines in length. An example of an epic simile from John Milton's *Paradise Lost* follows: Angel Forms, who lay entranced Thick as autumnal leaves that strow the brooks In Vallombrosa, where the Etrurian shades High over-arched embower; or scattered sedge Afloat, when with fierce winds Orion armed Hath vexed the Red-Sea coast, whose waves o'erthrew Busiris and his Memphian chivalry, While with perfidious hatred they pursued The sojourners of

Goshen, who beheld From the safe shore their floating carcasses And broken chariot-wheels. Also known as Epic Simile.

Horatian Satire: See *Satire*

Humanism: A philosophy that places faith in the dignity of humankind and rejects the medieval perception of the individual as a weak, fallen creature. "Humanists" typically believe in the perfectibility of human nature and view reason and education as the means to that end. Humanist thought is represented in the works of Marsilio Ficino, Ludovico Castelvetro, Edmund Spenser, John Milton, Dean John Colet, Desiderius Erasmus, John Dryden, Alexander Pope, Matthew Arnold, and Irving Babbitt.

Humors: Mentions of the humors refer to the ancient Greek theory that a person's health and personality were determined by the balance of four basic fluids in the body: blood, phlegm, yellow bile, and black bile. A dominance of any fluid would cause extremes in behavior. An excess of blood created a sanguine person who was joyful, aggressive, and passionate; a phlegmatic person was shy, fearful, and sluggish; too much yellow bile led to a choleric temperament characterized by impatience, anger, bitterness, and stubbornness; and excessive black bile created melancholy, a state of laziness, gluttony, and lack of motivation. Literary treatment of the humors is exemplified by several characters in Ben Jonson's plays *Every Man in His Humour* and *Every Man out of His Humour*. Also spelled Humours.

Humours: See *Humors*

Hyperbole: In literary criticism, deliberate exaggeration used to achieve an effect. In William Shakespeare's *Macbeth,* Lady Macbeth hyperbolizes when she says, "All the perfumes of Arabia could not sweeten this little hand."

I

Iamb: See *Foot*

Idiom: A word construction or verbal expression closely associated with a given language. For example, in colloquial English the construction "how come" can be used instead of "why" to introduce a question. Similarly, "a piece of cake" is sometimes used to describe a task that is easily done.

Image: A concrete representation of an object or sensory experience. Typically, such a representation helps evoke the feelings associated with the object or experience itself. Images are either "literal" or "figurative." Literal images are especially concrete and involve little or no extension of the obvious meaning of the words used to express them. Figurative images do not follow the literal meaning of the words exactly. Images in literature are usually visual, but the term "image" can also refer to the representation of any sensory experience. In his poem "The Shepherd's Hour," Paul Verlaine presents the following image: "The Moon is red through horizon's fog;/ In a dancing mist the hazy meadow sleeps." The first line is broadly literal, while the second line involves turns of meaning associated with dancing and sleeping.

Imagery: The array of images in a literary work. Also, figurative language. William Butler Yeats's "The Second Coming" offers a powerful image of encroaching anarchy: Turning and turning in the widening gyre The falcon cannot hear the falconer; Things fall apart. . . .

Imagism: An English and American poetry movement that flourished between 1908 and 1917. The Imagists used precise, clearly presented images in their works. They also used common, everyday speech and aimed for conciseness, concrete imagery, and the creation of new rhythms. Participants in the Imagist movement included Ezra Pound, H. D. (Hilda Doolittle), and Amy Lowell, among others.

In medias res: A Latin term meaning "in the middle of things." It refers to the technique of beginning a story at its midpoint and then using various flashback devices to reveal previous action. This technique originated in such epics as Virgil's *Aeneid.*

Induction: The process of reaching a conclusion by reasoning from specific premises to form a general premise. Also, an introductory portion of a work of literature, especially a play. Geoffrey Chaucer's "Prologue" to the *Canterbury Tales,* Thomas Sackville's "Induction" to *The Mirror of Magistrates,* and the opening scene in William Shakespeare's *The Taming of the Shrew* are examples of inductions to literary works.

Intentional Fallacy: The belief that judgments of a literary work based solely on an author's stated or implied intentions are false and misleading. Critics who believe in the concept of the intentional fallacy typically argue that the work itself is sufficient matter for interpretation, even though they may concede that an author's statement of purpose can be useful. Analysis of William Wordsworth's *Lyri-*

cal Ballads based on the observations about poetry he makes in his "Preface" to the second edition of that work is an example of the intentional fallacy.

Interior Monologue: A narrative technique in which characters' thoughts are revealed in a way that appears to be uncontrolled by the author. The interior monologue typically aims to reveal the inner self of a character. It portrays emotional experiences as they occur at both a conscious and unconscious level. images are often used to represent sensations or emotions. One of the best-known interior monologues in English is the Molly Bloom section at the close of James Joyce's *Ulysses.* The interior monologue is also common in the works of Virginia Woolf.

Internal Rhyme: Rhyme that occurs within a single line of verse. An example is in the opening line of Edgar Allan Poe's "The Raven": "Once upon a midnight dreary, while I pondered weak and weary." Here, "dreary" and "weary" make an internal rhyme.

Irish Literary Renaissance: A late nineteenth- and early twentieth-century movement in Irish literature. Members of the movement aimed to reduce the influence of British culture in Ireland and create an Irish national literature. William Butler Yeats, George Moore, and Sean O'Casey are three of the best-known figures of the movement.

Irony: In literary criticism, the effect of language in which the intended meaning is the opposite of what is stated. The title of Jonathan Swift's "A Modest Proposal" is ironic because what Swift proposes in this essay is cannibalism—hardly "modest."

Italian Sonnet: See *Sonnet*

J

Jacobean Age: The period of the reign of James I of England (1603-1625). The early literature of this period reflected the worldview of the Elizabethan Age, but a darker, more cynical attitude steadily grew in the art and literature of the Jacobean Age. This was an important time for English drama and poetry. Milestones include William Shakespeare's tragedies, tragi-comedies, and sonnets; Ben Jonson's various dramas; and John Donne's metaphysical poetry.

Jargon: Language that is used or understood only by a select group of people. Jargon may refer to terminology used in a certain profession, such as computer jargon, or it may refer to any nonsensical language that is not understood by most people. Literary examples of jargon are Francois Villon's *Ballades en jargon,* which is composed in the secret language of the *coquillards,* and Anthony Burgess's *A Clockwork Orange,* narrated in the fictional characters' language of "Nadsat."

Juvenalian Satire: See *Satire*

K

Knickerbocker Group: A somewhat indistinct group of New York writers of the first half of the nineteenth century. Members of the group were linked only by location and a common theme: New York life. Two famous members of the Knickerbocker Group were Washington Irving and William Cullen Bryant. The group's name derives from Irving's *Knickerbocker's History of New York.*

L

Lais: See *Lay*

Lay: A song or simple narrative poem. The form originated in medieval France. Early French *lais* were often based on the Celtic legends and other tales sung by Breton minstrels—thus the name of the "Breton lay." In fourteenth-century England, the term "lay" was used to describe short narratives written in imitation of the Breton lays. The most notable of these is Geoffrey Chaucer's "The Minstrel's Tale."

Leitmotiv: See *Motif*

Literal Language: An author uses literal language when he or she writes without exaggerating or embellishing the subject matter and without any tools of figurative language. To say "He ran very quickly down the street" is to use literal language, whereas to say "He ran like a hare down the street" would be using figurative language.

Literary Ballad: See *Ballad*

Literature: Literature is broadly defined as any written or spoken material, but the term most often refers to creative works. Literature includes poetry, drama, fiction, and many kinds of nonfiction writing, as well as oral, dramatic, and broadcast compositions not necessarily preserved in a written format, such as films and television programs.

Lost Generation: A term first used by Gertrude Stein to describe the post-World War I generation of American writers: men and women haunted by a sense of betrayal and emptiness brought about by the destructiveness of the war. The term is commonly applied to Hart Crane, Ernest Hemingway, F. Scott Fitzgerald, and others.

Lyric Poetry: A poem expressing the subjective feelings and personal emotions of the poet. Such poetry is melodic, since it was originally accompanied by a lyre in recitals. Most Western poetry in the twentieth century may be classified as lyrical. Examples of lyric poetry include A. E. Housman's elegy "To an Athlete Dying Young," the odes of Pindar and Horace, Thomas Gray and William Collins, the sonnets of Sir Thomas Wyatt and Sir Philip Sidney, Elizabeth Barrett Browning and Rainer Maria Rilke, and a host of other forms in the poetry of William Blake and Christina Rossetti, among many others.

M

Mannerism: Exaggerated, artificial adherence to a literary manner or style. Also, a popular style of the visual arts of late sixteenth-century Europe that was marked by elongation of the human form and by intentional spatial distortion. Literary works that are self-consciously high-toned and artistic are often said to be "mannered." Authors of such works include Henry James and Gertrude Stein.

Masculine Rhyme: See *Rhyme*

Masque: A lavish and elaborate form of entertainment, often performed in royal courts, that emphasizes song, dance, and costumery. The Renaissance form of the masque grew out of the spectacles of masked figures common in medieval England and Europe. The masque reached its peak of popularity and development in seventeenth-century England, during the reigns of James I and, especially, of Charles I. Ben Jonson, the most significant masque writer, also created the "antimasque," which incorporates elements of humor and the grotesque into the traditional masque and achieved greater dramatic quality. Masque-like interludes appear in Edmund Spenser's *The Faerie Queene* and in William Shakespeare's *The Tempest*. One of the best-known English masques is John Milton's *Comus*.

Measure: The foot, verse, or time sequence used in a literary work, especially a poem. Measure is often used somewhat incorrectly as a synonym for meter.

Melodrama: A play in which the typical plot is a conflict between characters who personify extreme good and evil. Melodramas usually end happily and

emphasize sensationalism. Other literary forms that use the same techniques are often labeled "melodramatic." The term was formerly used to describe a combination of drama and music; as such, it was synonymous with "opera." Augustin Daly's *Under the Gaslight* and Dion Boucicault's *The Octoroon, The Colleen Bawn,* and *The Poor of New York* are examples of melodramas. The most popular media for twentieth-century melodramas are motion pictures and television.

Metaphor: A figure of speech that expresses an idea through the image of another object. Metaphors suggest the essence of the first object by identifying it with certain qualities of the second object. An example is "But soft, what light through yonder window breaks?/ It is the east, and Juliet is the sun" in William Shakespeare's *Romeo and Juliet*. Here, Juliet, the first object, is identified with qualities of the second object, the sun.

Metaphysical Conceit: See *Conceit*

Metaphysical Poetry: The body of poetry produced by a group of seventeenth-century English writers called the "Metaphysical Poets." The group includes John Donne and Andrew Marvell. The Metaphysical Poets made use of everyday speech, intellectual analysis, and unique imagery. They aimed to portray the ordinary conflicts and contradictions of life. Their poems often took the form of an argument, and many of them emphasize physical and religious love as well as the fleeting nature of life. Elaborate conceits are typical in metaphysical poetry. Marvell's "To His Coy Mistress" is a well-known example of a metaphysical poem.

Metaphysical Poets: See *Metaphysical Poetry*

Meter: In literary criticism, the repetition of sound patterns that creates a rhythm in poetry. The patterns are based on the number of syllables and the presence and absence of accents. The unit of rhythm in a line is called a foot. Types of meter are classified according to the number of feet in a line. These are the standard English lines: Monometer, one foot; Dimeter, two feet; Trimeter, three feet; Tetrameter, four feet; Pentameter, five feet; Hexameter, six feet (also called the Alexandrine); Heptameter, seven feet (also called the "Fourteener" when the feet are iambic). The most common English meter is the iambic pentameter, in which each line contains ten syllables, or five iambic feet, which individually are composed of an unstressed syllable followed by an accented syllable. Both of the following lines from Alfred, Lord Tennyson's

"Ulysses" are written in iambic pentameter: Made weak by time and fate, but strong in will To strive, to seek, to find, and not to yield.

Mise en scene: The costumes, scenery, and other properties of a drama. Herbert Beerbohm Tree was renowned for the elaborate *mises en scene* of his lavish Shakespearean productions at His Majesty's Theatre between 1897 and 1915.

Modernism: Modern literary practices. Also, the principles of a literary school that lasted from roughly the beginning of the twentieth century until the end of World War II. Modernism is defined by its rejection of the literary conventions of the nineteenth century and by its opposition to conventional morality, taste, traditions, and economic values. Many writers are associated with the concepts of Modernism, including Albert Camus, Marcel Proust, D. H. Lawrence, W. H. Auden, Ernest Hemingway, William Faulkner, William Butler Yeats, Thomas Mann, Tennessee Williams, Eugene O'Neill, and James Joyce.

Monologue: A composition, written or oral, by a single individual. More specifically, a speech given by a single individual in a drama or other public entertainment. It has no set length, although it is usually several or more lines long. An example of an "extended monologue"—that is, a monologue of great length and seriousness—occurs in the one-act, one-character play *The Stronger* by August Strindberg.

Monometer: See *Meter*

Mood: The prevailing emotions of a work or of the author in his or her creation of the work. The mood of a work is not always what might be expected based on its subject matter. The poem "Dover Beach" by Matthew Arnold offers examples of two different moods originating from the same experience: watching the ocean at night. The mood of the first three lines— The sea is calm tonight The tide is full, the moon lies fair Upon the straights. . . . is in sharp contrast to the mood of the last three lines— And we are here as on a darkling plain Swept with confused alarms of struggle and flight, Where ignorant armies clash by night.

Motif: A theme, character type, image, metaphor, or other verbal element that recurs throughout a single work of literature or occurs in a number of different works over a period of time. For example, the various manifestations of the color white in Herman Melville's *Moby Dick* is a "specific" *motif,* while the trials of star-crossed lovers is a "conventional" *motif* from the literature of all periods. Also known as *Motiv* or *Leitmotiv.*

Motiv: See *Motif*

Muckrakers: An early twentieth-century group of American writers. Typically, their works exposed the wrongdoings of big business and government in the United States. Upton Sinclair's *The Jungle* exemplifies the muckraking novel.

Muses: Nine Greek mythological goddesses, the daughters of Zeus and Mnemosyne (Memory). Each muse patronized a specific area of the liberal arts and sciences. Calliope presided over epic poetry, Clio over history, Erato over love poetry, Euterpe over music or lyric poetry, Melpomene over tragedy, Polyhymnia over hymns to the gods, Terpsichore over dance, Thalia over comedy, and Urania over astronomy. Poets and writers traditionally made appeals to the Muses for inspiration in their work. John Milton invokes the aid of a muse at the beginning of the first book of his *Paradise Lost:* Of Man's First disobedience, and the Fruit of the Forbidden Tree, whose mortal taste Brought Death into the World, and all our woe, With loss of Eden, till one greater Man Restore us, and regain the blissful Seat Sing Heav'nly Muse, that on the secret top of Oreb, or of Sinai, didst inspire That Shepherd, who first taught the chosen Seed, In the Beginning how the Heav'ns and Earth Rose out of Chaos. . . .

Mystery: See *Suspense*

Myth: An anonymous tale emerging from the traditional beliefs of a culture or social unit. Myths use supernatural explanations for natural phenomena. They may also explain cosmic issues like creation and death. Collections of myths, known as mythologies, are common to all cultures and nations, but the best-known myths belong to the Norse, Roman, and Greek mythologies. A famous myth is the story of Arachne, an arrogant young girl who challenged a goddess, Athena, to a weaving contest; when the girl won, Athena was enraged and turned Arachne into a spider, thus explaining the existence of spiders.

N

Narration: The telling of a series of events, real or invented. A narration may be either a simple narrative, in which the events are recounted chronologically, or a narrative with a plot, in which the account is given in a style reflecting the author's artistic concept of the story. Narration is sometimes used as a synonym for "storyline." The recounting of scary stories around a campfire is a form of narration.

Narrative: A verse or prose accounting of an event or sequence of events, real or invented. The term is also used as an adjective in the sense "method of narration." For example, in literary criticism, the expression "narrative technique" usually refers to the way the author structures and presents his or her story. Narratives range from the shortest accounts of events, as in Julius Caesar's remark, "I came, I saw, I conquered," to the longest historical or biographical works, as in Edward Gibbon's *The Decline and Fall of the Roman Empire,* as well as diaries, travelogues, novels, ballads, epics, short stories, and other fictional forms.

Narrative Poetry: A nondramatic poem in which the author tells a story. Such poems may be of any length or level of complexity. Epics such as *Beowulf* and ballads are forms of narrative poetry.

Narrator: The teller of a story. The narrator may be the author or a character in the story through whom the author speaks. Huckleberry Finn is the narrator of Mark Twain's *The Adventures of Huckleberry Finn.*

Naturalism: A literary movement of the late nineteenth and early twentieth centuries. The movement's major theorist, French novelist Emile Zola, envisioned a type of fiction that would examine human life with the objectivity of scientific inquiry. The Naturalists typically viewed human beings as either the products of "biological determinism," ruled by hereditary instincts and engaged in an endless struggle for survival, or as the products of "socioeconomic determinism," ruled by social and economic forces beyond their control. In their works, the Naturalists generally ignored the highest levels of society and focused on degradation: poverty, alcoholism, prostitution, insanity, and disease. Naturalism influenced authors throughout the world, including Henrik Ibsen and Thomas Hardy. In the United States, in particular, Naturalism had a profound impact. Among the authors who embraced its principles are Theodore Dreiser, Eugene O'Neill, Stephen Crane, Jack London, and Frank Norris.

Negritude: A literary movement based on the concept of a shared cultural bond on the part of black Africans, wherever they may be in the world. It traces its origins to the former French colonies of Africa and the Caribbean. Negritude poets, novelists, and essayists generally stress four points in their writings: One, black alienation from traditional African culture can lead to feelings of inferiority. Two, European colonialism and Western education should be resisted. Three, black Africans should seek to affirm and define their own identity. Four, African culture can and should be reclaimed. Many Negritude writers also claim that blacks can make unique contributions to the world, based on a heightened appreciation of nature, rhythm, and human emotions—aspects of life they say are not so highly valued in the materialistic and rationalistic West. Examples of Negritude literature include the poetry of both Senegalese Leopold Senghor in *Hosties noires* and Martiniquais Aime-Fernand Cesaire in *Return to My Native Land.*

Negro Renaissance: See *Harlem Renaissance*

Neoclassical Period: See *Neoclassicism*

Neoclassicism: In literary criticism, this term refers to the revival of the attitudes and styles of expression of classical literature. It is generally used to describe a period in European history beginning in the late seventeenth century and lasting until about 1800. In its purest form, Neoclassicism marked a return to order, proportion, restraint, logic, accuracy, and decorum. In England, where Neoclassicism perhaps was most popular, it reflected the influence of seventeenth- century French writers, especially dramatists. Neoclassical writers typically reacted against the intensity and enthusiasm of the Renaissance period. They wrote works that appealed to the intellect, using elevated language and classical literary forms such as satire and the ode. Neoclassical works were often governed by the classical goal of instruction. English neoclassicists included Alexander Pope, Jonathan Swift, Joseph Addison, Sir Richard Steele, John Gay, and Matthew Prior; French neoclassicists included Pierre Corneille and Jean-Baptiste Moliere. Also known as Age of Reason.

Neoclassicists: See *Neoclassicism*

New Criticism: A movement in literary criticism, dating from the late 1920s, that stressed close textual analysis in the interpretation of works of literature. The New Critics saw little merit in historical and biographical analysis. Rather, they aimed to examine the text alone, free from the question of how external events—biographical or otherwise—may have helped shape it. This predominantly American school was named "New Criticism" by one of its practitioners, John Crowe Ransom. Other important New Critics included Allen Tate, R. P. Blackmur, Robert Penn Warren, and Cleanth Brooks.

New Negro Movement: See *Harlem Renaissance*

Noble Savage: The idea that primitive man is noble and good but becomes evil and corrupted as he becomes civilized. The concept of the noble savage originated in the Renaissance period but is more closely identified with such later writers as Jean-Jacques Rousseau and Aphra Behn. First described in John Dryden's play *The Conquest of Granada,* the noble savage is portrayed by the various Native Americans in James Fenimore Cooper's "Leatherstocking Tales," by Queequeg, Daggoo, and Tashtego in Herman Melville's *Moby Dick,* and by John the Savage in Aldous Huxley's *Brave New World.*

O

Objective Correlative: An outward set of objects, a situation, or a chain of events corresponding to an inward experience and evoking this experience in the reader. The term frequently appears in modern criticism in discussions of authors' intended effects on the emotional responses of readers. This term was originally used by T. S. Eliot in his 1919 essay "Hamlet."

Objectivity: A quality in writing characterized by the absence of the author's opinion or feeling about the subject matter. Objectivity is an important factor in criticism. The novels of Henry James and, to a certain extent, the poems of John Larkin demonstrate objectivity, and it is central to John Keats's concept of "negative capability." Critical and journalistic writing usually are or attempt to be objective.

Occasional Verse: poetry written on the occasion of a significant historical or personal event. *Vers de societe* is sometimes called occasional verse although it is of a less serious nature. Famous examples of occasional verse include Andrew Marvell's "Horatian Ode upon Cromwell's Return from England," Walt Whitman's "When Lilacs Last in the Dooryard Bloom'd"— written upon the death of Abraham Lincoln—and Edmund Spenser's commemoration of his wedding, "Epithalamion."

Octave: A poem or stanza composed of eight lines. The term octave most often represents the first eight lines of a Petrarchan sonnet. An example of an octave is taken from a translation of a Petrarchan sonnet by Sir Thomas Wyatt: The pillar perisht is whereto I leant, The strongest stay of mine unquiet mind; The like of it no man again can find, From East to West Still seeking though he went. To mind unhap! for hap away hath rent Of all my joy the very

bark and rind; And I, alas, by chance am thus assigned Daily to mourn till death do it relent.

Ode: Name given to an extended lyric poem characterized by exalted emotion and dignified style. An ode usually concerns a single, serious theme. Most odes, but not all, are addressed to an object or individual. Odes are distinguished from other lyric poetic forms by their complex rhythmic and stanzaic patterns. An example of this form is John Keats's "Ode to a Nightingale."

Oedipus Complex: A son's amorous obsession with his mother. The phrase is derived from the story of the ancient Theban hero Oedipus, who unknowingly killed his father and married his mother. Literary occurrences of the Oedipus complex include André Gide's *Oedipe* and Jean Cocteau's *La Machine infernale,* as well as the most famous, Sophocles' *Oedipus Rex.*

Omniscience: See *Point of View*

Onomatopoeia: The use of words whose sounds express or suggest their meaning. In its simplest sense, onomatopoeia may be represented by words that mimic the sounds they denote such as "hiss" or "meow." At a more subtle level, the pattern and rhythm of sounds and rhymes of a line or poem may be onomatopoeic. A celebrated example of onomatopoeia is the repetition of the word "bells" in Edgar Allan Poe's poem "The Bells."

Opera: A type of stage performance, usually a drama, in which the dialogue is sung. Classic examples of opera include Giuseppi Verdi's *La traviata,* Giacomo Puccini's *La Boheme,* and Richard Wagner's *Tristan und Isolde.* Major twentieth- century contributors to the form include Richard Strauss and Alban Berg.

Operetta: A usually romantic comic opera. John Gay's *The Beggar's Opera,* Richard Sheridan's *The Duenna,* and numerous works by William Gilbert and Arthur Sullivan are examples of operettas.

Oral Tradition: See *Oral Transmission*

Oral Transmission: A process by which songs, ballads, folklore, and other material are transmitted by word of mouth. The tradition of oral transmission predates the written record systems of literate society. Oral transmission preserves material sometimes over generations, although often with variations. Memory plays a large part in the recitation and preservation of orally transmitted material. Breton lays, French *fabliaux,* national epics (including the Anglo- Saxon *Beowulf,* the Spanish *El Cid,* and the Finnish *Kalevala*), Native American myths and legends, and African folktales told by plantation slaves are examples of orally transmitted literature.

Oration: Formal speaking intended to motivate the listeners to some action or feeling. Such public speaking was much more common before the development of timely printed communication such as newspapers. Famous examples of oration include Abraham Lincoln's "Gettysburg Address" and Dr. Martin Luther King Jr.'s "I Have a Dream" speech.

Ottava Rima: An eight-line stanza of poetry composed in iambic pentameter (a five-foot line in which each foot consists of an unaccented syllable followed by an accented syllable), following the abababcc rhyme scheme. This form has been prominently used by such important English writers as Lord Byron, Henry Wadsworth Longfellow, and W. B. Yeats.

Oxymoron: A phrase combining two contradictory terms. Oxymorons may be intentional or unintentional. The following speech from William Shakespeare's *Romeo and Juliet* uses several oxymorons: Why, then, O brawling love! O loving hate! O anything, of nothing first create! O heavy lightness! serious vanity! Mis-shapen chaos of well-seeming forms! Feather of lead, bright smoke, cold fire, sick health! This love feel I, that feel no love in this.

P

Pantheism: The idea that all things are both a manifestation or revelation of God and a part of God at the same time. Pantheism was a common attitude in the early societies of Egypt, India, and Greece—the term derives from the Greek *pan* meaning "all" and *theos* meaning "deity." It later became a significant part of the Christian faith. William Wordsworth and Ralph Waldo Emerson are among the many writers who have expressed the pantheistic attitude in their works.

Parable: A story intended to teach a moral lesson or answer an ethical question. In the West, the best examples of parables are those of Jesus Christ in the New Testament, notably "The Prodigal Son," but parables also are used in Sufism, rabbinic literature, Hasidism, and Zen Buddhism.

Paradox: A statement that appears illogical or contradictory at first, but may actually point to an underlying truth. "Less is more" is an example of a paradox. Literary examples include Francis Ba-

con's statement, "The most corrected copies are commonly the least correct," and "All animals are equal, but some animals are more equal than others" from George Orwell's *Animal Farm.*

Parallelism: A method of comparison of two ideas in which each is developed in the same grammatical structure. Ralph Waldo Emerson's "Civilization" contains this example of parallelism: Raphael paints wisdom; Handel sings it, Phidias carves it, Shakespeare writes it, Wren builds it, Columbus sails it, Luther preaches it, Washington arms it, Watt mechanizes it.

Parnassianism: A mid nineteenth-century movement in French literature. Followers of the movement stressed adherence to well-defined artistic forms as a reaction against the often chaotic expression of the artist's ego that dominated the work of the Romantics. The Parnassians also rejected the moral, ethical, and social themes exhibited in the works of French Romantics such as Victor Hugo. The aesthetic doctrines of the Parnassians strongly influenced the later symbolist and decadent movements. Members of the Parnassian school include Leconte de Lisle, Sully Prudhomme, Albert Glatigny, Francois Coppee, and Theodore de Banville.

Parody: In literary criticism, this term refers to an imitation of a serious literary work or the signature style of a particular author in a ridiculous manner. A typical parody adopts the style of the original and applies it to an inappropriate subject for humorous effect. Parody is a form of satire and could be considered the literary equivalent of a caricature or cartoon. Henry Fielding's *Shamela* is a parody of Samuel Richardson's *Pamela.*

Pastoral: A term derived from the Latin word "pastor," meaning shepherd. A pastoral is a literary composition on a rural theme. The conventions of the pastoral were originated by the third-century Greek poet Theocritus, who wrote about the experiences, love affairs, and pastimes of Sicilian shepherds. In a pastoral, characters and language of a courtly nature are often placed in a simple setting. The term pastoral is also used to classify dramas, elegies, and lyrics that exhibit the use of country settings and shepherd characters. Percy Bysshe Shelley's "Adonais" and John Milton's "Lycidas" are two famous examples of pastorals.

Pastorela: The Spanish name for the shepherds play, a folk drama reenacted during the Christmas season. Examples of *pastorelas* include Gomez

Manrique's *Representacion del nacimiento* and the dramas of Lucas Fernandez and Juan del Encina.

Pathetic Fallacy: A term coined by English critic John Ruskin to identify writing that falsely endows nonhuman things with human intentions and feelings, such as "angry clouds" and "sad trees." The pathetic fallacy is a required convention in the classical poetic form of the pastoral elegy, and it is used in the modern poetry of T. S. Eliot, Ezra Pound, and the Imagists. Also known as Poetic Fallacy.

Pelado: Literally the "skinned one" or shirtless one, he was the stock underdog, sharp-witted picaresque character of Mexican vaudeville and tent shows. The *pelado* is found in such works as Don Catarino's *Los effectos de la crisis* and *Regreso a mi tierra*.

Pen Name: See *Pseudonym*

Pentameter: See *Meter*

Persona: A Latin term meaning "mask." *Personae* are the characters in a fictional work of literature. The *persona* generally functions as a mask through which the author tells a story in a voice other than his or her own. A *persona* is usually either a character in a story who acts as a narrator or an "implied author," a voice created by the author to act as the narrator for himself or herself. *Personae* include the narrator of Geoffrey Chaucer's *Canterbury Tales* and Marlow in Joseph Conrad's *Heart of Darkness*.

Personae: See *Persona*

Personal Point of View: See *Point of View*

Personification: A figure of speech that gives human qualities to abstract ideas, animals, and inanimate objects. William Shakespeare used personification in *Romeo and Juliet* in the lines "Arise, fair sun, and kill the envious moon,/ Who is already sick and pale with grief." Here, the moon is portrayed as being envious, sick, and pale with grief—all markedly human qualities. Also known as *Prosopopoeia*.

Petrarchan Sonnet: See *Sonnet*

Phenomenology: A method of literary criticism based on the belief that things have no existence outside of human consciousness or awareness. Proponents of this theory believe that art is a process that takes place in the mind of the observer as he or she contemplates an object rather than a quality of the object itself. Among phenomenological critics

are Edmund Husserl, George Poulet, Marcel Raymond, and Roman Ingarden.

Picaresque Novel: Episodic fiction depicting the adventures of a roguish central character ("picaro" is Spanish for "rogue"). The picaresque hero is commonly a low-born but clever individual who wanders into and out of various affairs of love, danger, and farcical intrigue. These involvements may take place at all social levels and typically present a humorous and wide-ranging satire of a given society. Prominent examples of the picaresque novel are *Don Quixote* by Miguel de Cervantes, *Tom Jones* by Henry Fielding, and *Moll Flanders* by Daniel Defoe.

Plagiarism: Claiming another person's written material as one's own. Plagiarism can take the form of direct, word-for- word copying or the theft of the substance or idea of the work. A student who copies an encyclopedia entry and turns it in as a report for school is guilty of plagiarism.

Platonic Criticism: A form of criticism that stresses an artistic work's usefulness as an agent of social engineering rather than any quality or value of the work itself. Platonic criticism takes as its starting point the ancient Greek philosopher Plato's comments on art in his *Republic*.

Platonism: The embracing of the doctrines of the philosopher Plato, popular among the poets of the Renaissance and the Romantic period. Platonism is more flexible than Aristotelian Criticism and places more emphasis on the supernatural and unknown aspects of life. Platonism is expressed in the love poetry of the Renaissance, the fourth book of Baldassare Castiglione's *The Book of the Courtier,* and the poetry of William Blake, William Wordsworth, Percy Bysshe Shelley, Friedrich Holderlin, William Butler Yeats, and Wallace Stevens.

Play: See *Drama*

Plot: In literary criticism, this term refers to the pattern of events in a narrative or drama. In its simplest sense, the plot guides the author in composing the work and helps the reader follow the work. Typically, plots exhibit causality and unity and have a beginning, a middle, and an end. Sometimes, however, a plot may consist of a series of disconnected events, in which case it is known as an "episodic plot." In his *Aspects of the Novel*, E. M. Forster distinguishes between a story, defined as a "narrative of events arranged in their time- sequence," and plot, which organizes the events to a "sense of causality." This definition closely mirrors Aristotle's discussion of plot in his *Poetics*.

Poem: In its broadest sense, a composition utilizing rhyme, meter, concrete detail, and expressive language to create a literary experience with emotional and aesthetic appeal. Typical poems include sonnets, odes, elegies, *haiku,* ballads, and free verse.

Poet: An author who writes poetry or verse. The term is also used to refer to an artist or writer who has an exceptional gift for expression, imagination, and energy in the making of art in any form. Well-known poets include Horace, Basho, Sir Philip Sidney, Sir Edmund Spenser, John Donne, Andrew Marvell, Alexander Pope, Jonathan Swift, George Gordon, Lord Byron, John Keats, Christina Rossetti, W. H. Auden, Stevie Smith, and Sylvia Plath.

Poetic Fallacy: See *Pathetic Fallacy*

Poetic Justice: An outcome in a literary work, not necessarily a poem, in which the good are rewarded and the evil are punished, especially in ways that particularly fit their virtues or crimes. For example, a murderer may himself be murdered, or a thief will find himself penniless.

Poetic License: Distortions of fact and literary convention made by a writer—not always a poet— for the sake of the effect gained. Poetic license is closely related to the concept of "artistic freedom." An author exercises poetic license by saying that a pile of money "reaches as high as a mountain" when the pile is actually only a foot or two high.

Poetics: This term has two closely related meanings. It denotes (1) an aesthetic theory in literary criticism about the essence of poetry or (2) rules prescribing the proper methods, content, style, or diction of poetry. The term poetics may also refer to theories about literature in general, not just poetry.

Poetry: In its broadest sense, writing that aims to present ideas and evoke an emotional experience in the reader through the use of meter, imagery, connotative and concrete words, and a carefully constructed structure based on rhythmic patterns. Poetry typically relies on words and expressions that have several layers of meaning. It also makes use of the effects of regular rhythm on the ear and may make a strong appeal to the senses through the use of imagery. Edgar Allan Poe's "Annabel Lee" and Walt Whitman's *Leaves of Grass* are famous examples of poetry.

Point of View: The narrative perspective from which a literary work is presented to the reader.

There are four traditional points of view. The "third person omniscient" gives the reader a "godlike" perspective, unrestricted by time or place, from which to see actions and look into the minds of characters. This allows the author to comment openly on characters and events in the work. The "third person" point of view presents the events of the story from outside of any single character's perception, much like the omniscient point of view, but the reader must understand the action as it takes place and without any special insight into characters' minds or motivations. The "first person" or "personal" point of view relates events as they are perceived by a single character. The main character "tells" the story and may offer opinions about the action and characters which differ from those of the author. Much less common than omniscient, third person, and first person is the "second person" point of view, wherein the author tells the story as if it is happening to the reader. James Thurber employs the omniscient point of view in his short story "The Secret Life of Walter Mitty." Ernest Hemingway's "A Clean, Well-Lighted Place" is a short story told from the third person point of view. Mark Twain's novel *Huck Finn* is presented from the first person viewpoint. Jay McInerney's *Bright Lights, Big City* is an example of a novel which uses the second person point of view.

Polemic: A work in which the author takes a stand on a controversial subject, such as abortion or religion. Such works are often extremely argumentative or provocative. Classic examples of polemics include John Milton's *Aeropagitica* and Thomas Paine's *The American Crisis.*

Pornography: Writing intended to provoke feelings of lust in the reader. Such works are often condemned by critics and teachers, but those which can be shown to have literary value are viewed less harshly. Literary works that have been described as pornographic include Ovid's *The Art of Love,* Margaret of Angouleme's *Heptameron,* John Cleland's *Memoirs of a Woman of Pleasure; or, the Life of Fanny Hill,* the anonymous *My Secret Life,* D. H. Lawrence's *Lady Chatterley's Lover,* and Vladimir Nabokov's *Lolita.*

Post-Aesthetic Movement: An artistic response made by African Americans to the black aesthetic movement of the 1960s and early '70s. Writers since that time have adopted a somewhat different tone in their work, with less emphasis placed on the disparity between black and white in the United States. In the words of post-aesthetic authors such as Toni Morrison, John Edgar Wideman, and Kristin Hunter, African Americans are portrayed as looking inward for answers to their own questions, rather than always looking to the outside world. Two well-known examples of works produced as part of the post-aesthetic movement are the Pulitzer Prize-winning novels *The Color Purple* by Alice Walker and *Beloved* by Toni Morrison.

Postmodernism: Writing from the 1960s forward characterized by experimentation and continuing to apply some of the fundamentals of modernism, which included existentialism and alienation. Postmodernists have gone a step further in the rejection of tradition begun with the modernists by also rejecting traditional forms, preferring the anti-novel over the novel and the anti-hero over the hero. Postmodern writers include Alain Robbe-Grillet, Thomas Pynchon, Margaret Drabble, John Fowles, Adolfo Bioy-Casares, and Gabriel Garcia Marquez.

Pre-Raphaelites: A circle of writers and artists in mid nineteenth-century England. Valuing the pre-Renaissance artistic qualities of religious symbolism, lavish pictorialism, and natural sensuousness, the Pre-Raphaelites cultivated a sense of mystery and melancholy that influenced later writers associated with the Symbolist and Decadent movements. The major members of the group include Dante Gabriel Rossetti, Christina Rossetti, Algernon Swinburne, and Walter Pater.

Primitivism: The belief that primitive peoples were nobler and less flawed than civilized peoples because they had not been subjected to the tainting influence of society. Examples of literature espousing primitivism include Aphra Behn's *Oroonoko: Or, The History of the Royal Slave,* Jean-Jacques Rousseau's *Julie ou la Nouvelle Heloise,* Oliver Goldsmith's *The Deserted Village,* the poems of Robert Burns, Herman Melville's stories *Typee, Omoo,* and *Mardi,* many poems of William Butler Yeats and Robert Frost, and William Golding's novel *Lord of the Flies.*

Projective Verse: A form of free verse in which the poet's breathing pattern determines the lines of the poem. Poets who advocate projective verse are against all formal structures in writing, including meter and form. Besides its creators, Robert Creeley, Robert Duncan, and Charles Olson, two other well-known projective verse poets are Denise Levertov and LeRoi Jones (Amiri Baraka). Also known as Breath Verse.

Prologue: An introductory section of a literary work. It often contains information establishing the situation of the characters or presents information about the setting, time period, or action. In drama, the prologue is spoken by a chorus or by one of the principal characters. In the "General Prologue" of *The Canterbury Tales,* Geoffrey Chaucer describes the main characters and establishes the setting and purpose of the work.

Prose: A literary medium that attempts to mirror the language of everyday speech. It is distinguished from poetry by its use of unmetered, unrhymed language consisting of logically related sentences. Prose is usually grouped into paragraphs that form a cohesive whole such as an essay or a novel. Recognized masters of English prose writing include Sir Thomas Malory, William Caxton, Raphael Holinshed, Joseph Addison, Mark Twain, and Ernest Hemingway.

Prosopopoeia: See *Personification*

Protagonist: The central character of a story who serves as a focus for its themes and incidents and as the principal rationale for its development. The protagonist is sometimes referred to in discussions of modern literature as the hero or anti-hero. Well-known protagonists are Hamlet in William Shakespeare's *Hamlet* and Jay Gatsby in F. Scott Fitzgerald's *The Great Gatsby.*

Protest Fiction: Protest fiction has as its primary purpose the protesting of some social injustice, such as racism or discrimination. One example of protest fiction is a series of five novels by Chester Himes, beginning in 1945 with *If He Hollers Let Him Go* and ending in 1955 with *The Primitive.* These works depict the destructive effects of race and gender stereotyping in the context of interracial relationships. Another African American author whose works often revolve around themes of social protest is John Oliver Killens. James Baldwin's essay "Everybody's Protest Novel" generated controversy by attacking the authors of protest fiction.

Proverb: A brief, sage saying that expresses a truth about life in a striking manner. "They are not all cooks who carry long knives" is an example of a proverb.

Pseudonym: A name assumed by a writer, most often intended to prevent his or her identification as the author of a work. Two or more authors may work together under one pseudonym, or an author may use a different name for each genre he or she publishes in. Some publishing companies maintain "house pseudonyms," under which any number of authors may write installations in a series. Some authors also choose a pseudonym over their real names the way an actor may use a stage name. Examples of pseudonyms (with the author's real name in parentheses) include Voltaire (Francois-Marie Arouet), Novalis (Friedrich von Hardenberg), Currer Bell (Charlotte Bronte), Ellis Bell (Emily Bronte), George Eliot (Maryann Evans), Honorio Bustos Donmecq (Adolfo Bioy-Casares and Jorge Luis Borges), and Richard Bachman (Stephen King).

Pun: A play on words that have similar sounds but different meanings. A serious example of the pun is from John Donne's "A Hymne to God the Father": Sweare by thyself, that at my death thy sonne Shall shine as he shines now, and hereto fore; And, having done that, Thou haste done; I fear no more.

Pure Poetry: poetry written without instructional intent or moral purpose that aims only to please a reader by its imagery or musical flow. The term pure poetry is used as the antonym of the term "didacticism." The poetry of Edgar Allan Poe, Stephane Mallarme, Paul Verlaine, Paul Valery, Juan Ramoz Jimenez, and Jorge Guillen offer examples of pure poetry.

Q

Quatrain: A four-line stanza of a poem or an entire poem consisting of four lines. The following quatrain is from Robert Herrick's "To Live Merrily, and to Trust to Good Verses": Round, round, the root do's run; And being ravisht thus, Come, I will drink a Tun To my *Propertius.*

R

Raisonneur: A character in a drama who functions as a spokesperson for the dramatist's views. The *raisonneur* typically observes the play without becoming central to its action. *Raisonneurs* were very common in plays of the nineteenth century.

Realism: A nineteenth-century European literary movement that sought to portray familiar characters, situations, and settings in a realistic manner. This was done primarily by using an objective narrative point of view and through the buildup of accurate detail. The standard for success of any realistic work depends on how faithfully it transfers common experience into fictional forms. The realistic method may be altered or extended, as in stream of consciousness writing, to record highly subjec-

tive experience. Seminal authors in the tradition of Realism include Honore de Balzac, Gustave Flaubert, and Henry James.

Refrain: A phrase repeated at intervals throughout a poem. A refrain may appear at the end of each stanza or at less regular intervals. It may be altered slightly at each appearance. Some refrains are nonsense expressions—as with "Nevermore" in Edgar Allan Poe's "The Raven"—that seem to take on a different significance with each use.

Renaissance: The period in European history that marked the end of the Middle Ages. It began in Italy in the late fourteenth century. In broad terms, it is usually seen as spanning the fourteenth, fifteenth, and sixteenth centuries, although it did not reach Great Britain, for example, until the 1480s or so. The Renaissance saw an awakening in almost every sphere of human activity, especially science, philosophy, and the arts. The period is best defined by the emergence of a general philosophy that emphasized the importance of the intellect, the individual, and world affairs. It contrasts strongly with the medieval worldview, characterized by the dominant concerns of faith, the social collective, and spiritual salvation. Prominent writers during the Renaissance include Niccolo Machiavelli and Baldassare Castiglione in Italy, Miguel de Cervantes and Lope de Vega in Spain, Jean Froissart and Francois Rabelais in France, Sir Thomas More and Sir Philip Sidney in England, and Desiderius Erasmus in Holland.

Repartee: Conversation featuring snappy retorts and witticisms. Masters of *repartee* include Sydney Smith, Charles Lamb, and Oscar Wilde. An example is recorded in the meeting of "Beau" Nash and John Wesley: Nash said, "I never make way for a fool," to which Wesley responded, "Don't you? I always do," and stepped aside.

Resolution: The portion of a story following the climax, in which the conflict is resolved. The resolution of Jane Austen's *Northanger Abbey* is neatly summed up in the following sentence: "Henry and Catherine were married, the bells rang and every body smiled."

Restoration: See *Restoration Age*

Restoration Age: A period in English literature beginning with the crowning of Charles II in 1660 and running to about 1700. The era, which was characterized by a reaction against Puritanism, was the first great age of the comedy of manners. The finest literature of the era is typically witty and urbane, and often lewd. Prominent Restoration Age writers include William Congreve, Samuel Pepys, John Dryden, and John Milton.

Revenge Tragedy: A dramatic form popular during the Elizabethan Age, in which the protagonist, directed by the ghost of his murdered father or son, inflicts retaliation upon a powerful villain. Notable features of the revenge tragedy include violence, bizarre criminal acts, intrigue, insanity, a hesitant protagonist, and the use of soliloquy. Thomas Kyd's *Spanish Tragedy* is the first example of revenge tragedy in English, and William Shakespeare's *Hamlet* is perhaps the best. Extreme examples of revenge tragedy, such as John Webster's *The Duchess of Malfi,* are labeled "tragedies of blood." Also known as Tragedy of Blood.

Revista: The Spanish term for a vaudeville musical revue. Examples of *revistas* include Antonio Guzman Aguilera's *Mexico para los mexicanos,* Daniel Vanegas's *Maldito jazz,* and Don Catarino's *Whiskey, morfina y marihuana* and *El desterrado.*

Rhetoric: In literary criticism, this term denotes the art of ethical persuasion. In its strictest sense, rhetoric adheres to various principles developed since classical times for arranging facts and ideas in a clear, persuasive, appealing manner. The term is also used to refer to effective prose in general and theories of or methods for composing effective prose. Classical examples of rhetorics include *The Rhetoric of Aristotle,* Quintillian's *Institutio Oratoria,* and Cicero's *Ad Herennium.*

Rhetorical Question: A question intended to provoke thought, but not an expressed answer, in the reader. It is most commonly used in oratory and other persuasive genres. The following lines from Thomas Gray's "Elegy Written in a Country Churchyard" ask rhetorical questions: Can storied urn or animated bust Back to its mansion call the fleeting breath? Can Honour's voice provoke the silent dust, Or Flattery soothe the dull cold ear of Death?

Rhyme: When used as a noun in literary criticism, this term generally refers to a poem in which words sound identical or very similar and appear in parallel positions in two or more lines. Rhymes are classified into different types according to where they fall in a line or stanza or according to the degree of similarity they exhibit in their spellings and sounds. Some major types of rhyme are "masculine" rhyme, "feminine" rhyme, and "triple" rhyme. In a masculine rhyme, the rhyming sound falls in a single accented syllable, as with "heat"

and "eat." Feminine rhyme is a rhyme of two syllables, one stressed and one unstressed, as with "merry" and "tarry." Triple rhyme matches the sound of the accented syllable and the two unaccented syllables that follow: "narrative" and "declarative." Robert Browning alternates feminine and masculine rhymes in his "Soliloquy of the Spanish Cloister": Gr-r-r—there go, my heart's abhorrence! Water your damned flower-pots, do! If hate killed men, Brother Lawrence, God's blood, would not mine kill you! What? Your myrtle-bush wants trimming? Oh, that rose has prior claims— Needs its leaden vase filled brimming? Hell dry you up with flames! Triple rhymes can be found in Thomas Hood's "Bridge of Sighs," George Gordon Byron's satirical verse, and Ogden Nash's comic poems.

Rhyme Royal: A stanza of seven lines composed in iambic pentameter and rhymed *ababbcc.* The name is said to be a tribute to King James I of Scotland, who made much use of the form in his poetry. Examples of rhyme royal include Geoffrey Chaucer's *The Parlement of Foules,* William Shakespeare's *The Rape of Lucrece,* William Morris's *The Early Paradise,* and John Masefield's *The Widow in the Bye Street.*

Rhyme Scheme: See *Rhyme*

Rhythm: A regular pattern of sound, time intervals, or events occurring in writing, most often and most discernably in poetry. Regular, reliable rhythm is known to be soothing to humans, while interrupted, unpredictable, or rapidly changing rhythm is disturbing. These effects are known to authors, who use them to produce a desired reaction in the reader. An example of a form of irregular rhythm is sprung rhythm poetry; quantitative verse, on the other hand, is very regular in its rhythm.

Rising Action: The part of a drama where the plot becomes increasingly complicated. Rising action leads up to the climax, or turning point, of a drama. The final "chase scene" of an action film is generally the rising action which culminates in the film's climax.

Rococo: A style of European architecture that flourished in the eighteenth century, especially in France. The most notable features of *rococo* are its extensive use of ornamentation and its themes of lightness, gaiety, and intimacy. In literary criticism, the term is often used disparagingly to refer to a decadent or over-ornamental style. Alexander Pope's "The Rape of the Lock" is an example of literary *rococo.*

Roman a clef: A French phrase meaning "novel with a key." It refers to a narrative in which real persons are portrayed under fictitious names. Jack Kerouac, for example, portrayed various real-life beat generation figures under fictitious names in his *On the Road.*

Romance: A broad term, usually denoting a narrative with exotic, exaggerated, often idealized characters, scenes, and themes. Nathaniel Hawthorne called his *The House of the Seven Gables* and *The Marble Faun* romances in order to distinguish them from clearly realistic works.

Romantic Age: See *Romanticism*

Romanticism: This term has two widely accepted meanings. In historical criticism, it refers to a European intellectual and artistic movement of the late eighteenth and early nineteenth centuries that sought greater freedom of personal expression than that allowed by the strict rules of literary form and logic of the eighteenth-century neoclassicists. The Romantics preferred emotional and imaginative expression to rational analysis. They considered the individual to be at the center of all experience and so placed him or her at the center of their art. The Romantics believed that the creative imagination reveals nobler truths—unique feelings and attitudes—than those that could be discovered by logic or by scientific examination. Both the natural world and the state of childhood were important sources for revelations of "eternal truths." "Romanticism" is also used as a general term to refer to a type of sensibility found in all periods of literary history and usually considered to be in opposition to the principles of classicism. In this sense, Romanticism signifies any work or philosophy in which the exotic or dreamlike figure strongly, or that is devoted to individualistic expression, self-analysis, or a pursuit of a higher realm of knowledge than can be discovered by human reason. Prominent Romantics include Jean-Jacques Rousseau, William Wordsworth, John Keats, Lord Byron, and Johann Wolfgang von Goethe.

Romantics: See *Romanticism*

Russian Symbolism: A Russian poetic movement, derived from French symbolism, that flourished between 1894 and 1910. While some Russian Symbolists continued in the French tradition, stressing aestheticism and the importance of suggestion above didactic intent, others saw their craft as a form of mystical worship, and themselves as mediators between the supernatural and the mundane. Russian symbolists include Aleksandr Blok, Vyacheslav Ivanovich Ivanov, Fyodor Sologub, Andrey Bely, Nikolay Gumilyov, and Vladimir Sergeyevich Solovyov.

S

Satire: A work that uses ridicule, humor, and wit to criticize and provoke change in human nature and institutions. There are two major types of satire: "formal" or "direct" satire speaks directly to the reader or to a character in the work; "indirect" satire relies upon the ridiculous behavior of its characters to make its point. Formal satire is further divided into two manners: the "Horatian," which ridicules gently, and the "Juvenalian," which derides its subjects harshly and bitterly. Voltaire's novella *Candide* is an indirect satire. Jonathan Swift's essay "A Modest Proposal" is a Juvenalian satire.

Scansion: The analysis or "scanning" of a poem to determine its meter and often its rhyme scheme. The most common system of scansion uses accents (slanted lines drawn above syllables) to show stressed syllables, breves (curved lines drawn above syllables) to show unstressed syllables, and vertical lines to separate each foot. In the first line of John Keats's *Endymion,* "A thing of beauty is a joy forever:" the word "thing," the first syllable of "beauty," the word "joy," and the second syllable of "forever" are stressed, while the words "A" and "of," the second syllable of "beauty," the word "a," and the first and third syllables of "forever" are unstressed. In the second line: "Its loveliness increases; it will never" a pair of vertical lines separate the foot ending with "increases" and the one beginning with "it."

Scene: A subdivision of an act of a drama, consisting of continuous action taking place at a single time and in a single location. The beginnings and endings of scenes may be indicated by clearing the stage of actors and props or by the entrances and exits of important characters. The first act of William Shakespeare's *Winter's Tale* is comprised of two scenes.

Science Fiction: A type of narrative about or based upon real or imagined scientific theories and technology. Science fiction is often peopled with alien creatures and set on other planets or in different dimensions. Karel Capek's *R.U.R.* is a major work of science fiction.

Second Person: See *Point of View*

Semiotics: The study of how literary forms and conventions affect the meaning of language. Semioticians include Ferdinand de Saussure, Charles Sanders Pierce, Claude Levi-Strauss, Jacques Lacan, Michel Foucault, Jacques Derrida, Roland Barthes, and Julia Kristeva.

Sestet: Any six-line poem or stanza. Examples of the sestet include the last six lines of the Petrarchan sonnet form, the stanza form of Robert Burns's "A Poet's Welcome to his love-begotten Daughter," and the sestina form in W. H. Auden's "Paysage Moralise."

Setting: The time, place, and culture in which the action of a narrative takes place. The elements of setting may include geographic location, characters' physical and mental environments, prevailing cultural attitudes, or the historical time in which the action takes place. Examples of settings include the romanticized Scotland in Sir Walter Scott's "Waverley" novels, the French provincial setting in Gustave Flaubert's *Madame Bovary,* the fictional Wessex country of Thomas Hardy's novels, and the small towns of southern Ontario in Alice Munro's short stories.

Shakespearean Sonnet: See *Sonnet*

Signifying Monkey: A popular trickster figure in black folklore, with hundreds of tales about this character documented since the 19th century. Henry Louis Gates Jr. examines the history of the signifying monkey in *The Signifying Monkey: Towards a Theory of Afro-American Literary Criticism,* published in 1988.

Simile: A comparison, usually using "like" or "as", of two essentially dissimilar things, as in "coffee as cold as ice" or "He sounded like a broken record." The title of Ernest Hemingway's "Hills Like White Elephants" contains a simile.

Slang: A type of informal verbal communication that is generally unacceptable for formal writing. Slang words and phrases are often colorful exaggerations used to emphasize the speaker's point; they may also be shortened versions of an often-used word or phrase. Examples of American slang from the 1990s include "yuppie" (an acronym for Young Urban Professional), "awesome" (for "excellent"), wired (for "nervous" or "excited"), and "chill out" (for relax).

Slant Rhyme: See *Consonance*

Slave Narrative: Autobiographical accounts of American slave life as told by escaped slaves. These works first appeared during the abolition movement of the 1830s through the 1850s. Olaudah Equiano's *The Interesting Narrative of Olaudah Equiano, or Gustavus Vassa, The African* and Harriet Ann Jacobs's *Incidents in the Life of a Slave Girl* are examples of the slave narrative.

Social Realism: See *Socialist Realism*

Socialist Realism: The Socialist Realism school of literary theory was proposed by Maxim Gorky and established as a dogma by the first Soviet Congress of Writers. It demanded adherence to a communist worldview in works of literature. Its doctrines required an objective viewpoint comprehensible to the working classes and themes of social struggle featuring strong proletarian heroes. A successful work of socialist realism is Nikolay Ostrovsky's *Kak zakalyalas stal (How the Steel Was Tempered)*. Also known as Social Realism.

Soliloquy: A monologue in a drama used to give the audience information and to develop the speaker's character. It is typically a projection of the speaker's innermost thoughts. Usually delivered while the speaker is alone on stage, a soliloquy is intended to present an illusion of unspoken reflection. A celebrated soliloquy is Hamlet's "To be or not to be" speech in William Shakespeare's *Hamlet.*

Sonnet: A fourteen-line poem, usually composed in iambic pentameter, employing one of several rhyme schemes. There are three major types of sonnets, upon which all other variations of the form are based: the "Petrarchan" or "Italian" sonnet, the "Shakespearean" or "English" sonnet, and the "Spenserian" sonnet. A Petrarchan sonnet consists of an octave rhymed *abbaabba* and a "sestet" rhymed either *cdecde, cdccdc,* or *cdedce.* The octave poses a question or problem, relates a narrative, or puts forth a proposition; the sestet presents a solution to the problem, comments upon the narrative, or applies the proposition put forth in the octave. The Shakespearean sonnet is divided into three quatrains and a couplet rhymed *abab cdcd efef gg.* The couplet provides an epigrammatic comment on the narrative or problem put forth in the quatrains. The Spenserian sonnet uses three quatrains and a couplet like the Shakespearean, but links their three rhyme schemes in this way: *abab bcbc cdcd ee.* The Spenserian sonnet develops its theme in two parts like the Petrarchan, its final six lines resolving a problem, analyzing a narrative, or applying a proposition put forth in its first eight lines. Examples of sonnets can be found in Petrarch's *Canzoniere,* Edmund Spenser's *Amoretti,* Elizabeth Barrett

Browning's *Sonnets from the Portuguese,* Rainer Maria Rilke's *Sonnets to Orpheus,* and Adrienne Rich's poem "The Insusceptibles."

Spenserian Sonnet: See *Sonnet*

Spenserian Stanza: A nine-line stanza having eight verses in iambic pentameter, its ninth verse in iambic hexameter, and the rhyme scheme ababbcbcc. This stanza form was first used by Edmund Spenser in his allegorical poem *The Faerie Queene.*

Spondee: In poetry meter, a foot consisting of two long or stressed syllables occurring together. This form is quite rare in English verse, and is usually composed of two monosyllabic words. The first foot in the following line from Robert Burns's "Green Grow the Rashes" is an example of a spondee: Green grow the rashes, O

Sprung Rhythm: Versification using a specific number of accented syllables per line but disregarding the number of unaccented syllables that fall in each line, producing an irregular rhythm in the poem. Gerard Manley Hopkins, who coined the term "sprung rhythm," is the most notable practitioner of this technique.

Stanza: A subdivision of a poem consisting of lines grouped together, often in recurring patterns of rhyme, line length, and meter. Stanzas may also serve as units of thought in a poem much like paragraphs in prose. Examples of stanza forms include the quatrain, *terza rima, ottava rima,* Spenserian, and the so-called *In Memoriam* stanza from Alfred, Lord Tennyson's poem by that title. The following is an example of the latter form: Love is and was my lord and king, And in his presence I attend To hear the tidings of my friend, Which every hour his couriers bring.

Stereotype: A stereotype was originally the name for a duplication made during the printing process; this led to its modern definition as a person or thing that is (or is assumed to be) the same as all others of its type. Common stereotypical characters include the absent- minded professor, the nagging wife, the troublemaking teenager, and the kindhearted grandmother.

Stream of Consciousness: A narrative technique for rendering the inward experience of a character. This technique is designed to give the impression of an ever-changing series of thoughts, emotions, images, and memories in the spontaneous and seemingly illogical order that they occur in life. The

textbook example of stream of consciousness is the last section of James Joyce's *Ulysses.*

Structuralism: A twentieth-century movement in literary criticism that examines how literary texts arrive at their meanings, rather than the meanings themselves. There are two major types of structuralist analysis: one examines the way patterns of linguistic structures unify a specific text and emphasize certain elements of that text, and the other interprets the way literary forms and conventions affect the meaning of language itself. Prominent structuralists include Michel Foucault, Roman Jakobson, and Roland Barthes.

Structure: The form taken by a piece of literature. The structure may be made obvious for ease of understanding, as in nonfiction works, or may obscured for artistic purposes, as in some poetry or seemingly "unstructured" prose. Examples of common literary structures include the plot of a narrative, the acts and scenes of a drama, and such poetic forms as the Shakespearean sonnet and the Pindaric ode.

Sturm und Drang: A German term meaning "storm and stress." It refers to a German literary movement of the 1770s and 1780s that reacted against the order and rationalism of the enlightenment, focusing instead on the intense experience of extraordinary individuals. Highly romantic, works of this movement, such as Johann Wolfgang von Goethe's *Gotz von Berlichingen,* are typified by realism, rebelliousness, and intense emotionalism.

Style: A writer's distinctive manner of arranging words to suit his or her ideas and purpose in writing. The unique imprint of the author's personality upon his or her writing, style is the product of an author's way of arranging ideas and his or her use of diction, different sentence structures, rhythm, figures of speech, rhetorical principles, and other elements of composition. Styles may be classified according to period (Metaphysical, Augustan, Georgian), individual authors (Chaucerian, Miltonic, Jamesian), level (grand, middle, low, plain), or language (scientific, expository, poetic, journalistic).

Subject: The person, event, or theme at the center of a work of literature. A work may have one or more subjects of each type, with shorter works tending to have fewer and longer works tending to have more. The subjects of James Baldwin's novel *Go Tell It on the Mountain* include the themes of father-son relationships, religious conversion, black life, and sexuality. The subjects of Anne Frank's

Diary of a Young Girl include Anne and her family members as well as World War II, the Holocaust, and the themes of war, isolation, injustice, and racism.

Subjectivity: Writing that expresses the author's personal feelings about his subject, and which may or may not include factual information about the subject. Subjectivity is demonstrated in James Joyce's *Portrait of the Artist as a Young Man,* Samuel Butler's *The Way of All Flesh,* and Thomas Wolfe's *Look Homeward, Angel.*

Subplot: A secondary story in a narrative. A subplot may serve as a motivating or complicating force for the main plot of the work, or it may provide emphasis for, or relief from, the main plot. The conflict between the Capulets and the Montagues in William Shakespeare's *Romeo and Juliet* is an example of a subplot.

Surrealism: A term introduced to criticism by Guillaume Apollinaire and later adopted by Andre Breton. It refers to a French literary and artistic movement founded in the 1920s. The Surrealists sought to express unconscious thoughts and feelings in their works. The best-known technique used for achieving this aim was automatic writing—transcriptions of spontaneous outpourings from the unconscious. The Surrealists proposed to unify the contrary levels of conscious and unconscious, dream and reality, objectivity and subjectivity into a new level of "super-realism." Surrealism can be found in the poetry of Paul Eluard, Pierre Reverdy, and Louis Aragon, among others.

Suspense: A literary device in which the author maintains the audience's attention through the build-up of events, the outcome of which will soon be revealed. Suspense in William Shakespeare's *Hamlet* is sustained throughout by the question of whether or not the Prince will achieve what he has been instructed to do and of what he intends to do.

Syllogism: A method of presenting a logical argument. In its most basic form, the syllogism consists of a major premise, a minor premise, and a conclusion. An example of a syllogism is: Major premise: When it snows, the streets get wet. Minor premise: It is snowing. Conclusion: The streets are wet.

Symbol: Something that suggests or stands for something else without losing its original identity. In literature, symbols combine their literal meaning with the suggestion of an abstract concept. Literary symbols are of two types: those that carry complex associations of meaning no matter what their con-

texts, and those that derive their suggestive meaning from their functions in specific literary works. Examples of symbols are sunshine suggesting happiness, rain suggesting sorrow, and storm clouds suggesting despair.

Symbolism: This term has two widely accepted meanings. In historical criticism, it denotes an early modernist literary movement initiated in France during the nineteenth century that reacted against the prevailing standards of realism. Writers in this movement aimed to evoke, indirectly and symbolically, an order of being beyond the material world of the five senses. Poetic expression of personal emotion figured strongly in the movement, typically by means of a private set of symbols uniquely identifiable with the individual poet. The principal aim of the Symbolists was to express in words the highly complex feelings that grew out of everyday contact with the world. In a broader sense, the term "symbolism" refers to the use of one object to represent another. Early members of the Symbolist movement included the French authors Charles Baudelaire and Arthur Rimbaud; William Butler Yeats, James Joyce, and T. S. Eliot were influenced as the movement moved to Ireland, England, and the United States. Examples of the concept of symbolism include a flag that stands for a nation or movement, or an empty cupboard used to suggest hopelessness, poverty, and despair.

Symbolist: See *Symbolism*

Symbolist Movement: See *Symbolism*

Sympathetic Fallacy: See *Affective Fallacy*

T

Tale: A story told by a narrator with a simple plot and little character development. Tales are usually relatively short and often carry a simple message. Examples of tales can be found in the work of Rudyard Kipling, Somerset Maugham, Saki, Anton Chekhov, Guy de Maupassant, and Armistead Maupin.

Tall Tale: A humorous tale told in a straightforward, credible tone but relating absolutely impossible events or feats of the characters. Such tales were commonly told of frontier adventures during the settlement of the west in the United States. Tall tales have been spun around such legendary heroes as Mike Fink, Paul Bunyan, Davy Crockett, Johnny Appleseed, and Captain Stormalong as well as the real-life William F. Cody and Annie Oakley. Literary use of tall tales can be found in Washington Irving's *History of New York,* Mark Twain's *Life on the Mississippi,* and in the German R. F. Raspe's *Baron Munchausen's Narratives of His Marvellous Travels and Campaigns in Russia.*

Tanka: A form of Japanese poetry similar to *haiku.* A *tanka* is five lines long, with the lines containing five, seven, five, seven, and seven syllables respectively. Skilled *tanka* authors include Ishikawa Takuboku, Masaoka Shiki, Amy Lowell, and Adelaide Crapsey.

Teatro Grottesco: See *Theater of the Grotesque*

Terza Rima: A three-line stanza form in poetry in which the rhymes are made on the last word of each line in the following manner: the first and third lines of the first stanza, then the second line of the first stanza and the first and third lines of the second stanza, and so on with the middle line of any stanza rhyming with the first and third lines of the following stanza. An example of *terza rima* is Percy Bysshe Shelley's ''The Triumph of Love'': As in that trance of wondrous thought I lay This was the tenour of my waking dream. Methought I sate beside a public way Thick strewn with summer dust, and a great stream Of people there was hurrying to and fro Numerous as gnats upon the evening gleam,. . .

Tetrameter: See *Meter*

Textual Criticism: A branch of literary criticism that seeks to establish the authoritative text of a literary work. Textual critics typically compare all known manuscripts or printings of a single work in order to assess the meanings of differences and revisions. This procedure allows them to arrive at a definitive version that (supposedly) corresponds to the author's original intention. Textual criticism was applied during the Renaissance to salvage the classical texts of Greece and Rome, and modern works have been studied, for instance, to undo deliberate correction or censorship, as in the case of novels by Stephen Crane and Theodore Dreiser.

Theater of Cruelty: Term used to denote a group of theatrical techniques designed to eliminate the psychological and emotional distance between actors and audience. This concept, introduced in the 1930s in France, was intended to inspire a more intense theatrical experience than conventional theater allowed. The ''cruelty'' of this dramatic theory signified not sadism but heightened actor/audience involvement in the dramatic event. The theater of cruelty was theorized by Antonin Artaud in his *Le Theatre et son double* (*The Theatre and Its Double*), and also appears in the work of Jerzy Grotowski, Jean Genet, Jean Vilar, and Arthur Adamov, among others.

Theater of the Absurd: A post-World War II dramatic trend characterized by radical theatrical innovations. In works influenced by the Theater of the absurd, nontraditional, sometimes grotesque characterizations, plots, and stage sets reveal a meaningless universe in which human values are irrelevant. Existentialist themes of estrangement, absurdity, and futility link many of the works of this movement. The principal writers of the Theater of the Absurd are Samuel Beckett, Eugene Ionesco, Jean Genet, and Harold Pinter.

Theater of the Grotesque: An Italian theatrical movement characterized by plays written around the ironic and macabre aspects of daily life in the World War I era. Theater of the Grotesque was named after the play *The Mask and the Face* by Luigi Chiarelli, which was described as ''a grotesque in three acts.'' The movement influenced the work of Italian dramatist Luigi Pirandello, author of *Right You Are, If You Think You Are.* Also known as *Teatro Grottesco.*

Theme: The main point of a work of literature. The term is used interchangeably with thesis. The theme of William Shakespeare's *Othello*—jealousy—is a common one.

Thesis: A thesis is both an essay and the point argued in the essay. Thesis novels and thesis plays share the quality of containing a thesis which is supported through the action of the story. A master's thesis and a doctoral dissertation are two theses required of graduate students.

Thesis Play: See *Thesis*

Three Unities: See *Unities*

Tone: The author's attitude toward his or her audience may be deduced from the tone of the work. A formal tone may create distance or convey politeness, while an informal tone may encourage a friendly, intimate, or intrusive feeling in the reader. The author's attitude toward his or her subject matter may also be deduced from the tone of the words he or she uses in discussing it. The tone of John F. Kennedy's speech which included the appeal to ''ask not what your country can do for you'' was intended to instill feelings of camaraderie and national pride in listeners.

Tragedy: A drama in prose or poetry about a noble, courageous hero of excellent character who, because of some tragic character flaw or *hamartia*, brings ruin upon him- or herself. Tragedy treats its subjects in a dignified and serious manner, using poetic language to help evoke pity and fear and bring about catharsis, a purging of these emotions. The tragic form was practiced extensively by the ancient Greeks. In the Middle Ages, when classical works were virtually unknown, tragedy came to denote any works about the fall of persons from exalted to low conditions due to any reason: fate, vice, weakness, etc. According to the classical definition of tragedy, such works present the "pathetic"—that which evokes pity—rather than the tragic. The classical form of tragedy was revived in the sixteenth century; it flourished especially on the Elizabethan stage. In modern times, dramatists have attempted to adapt the form to the needs of modern society by drawing their heroes from the ranks of ordinary men and women and defining the nobility of these heroes in terms of spirit rather than exalted social standing. The greatest classical example of tragedy is Sophocles' *Oedipus Rex*. The "pathetic" derivation is exemplified in "The Monk's Tale" in Geoffrey Chaucer's *Canterbury Tales.* Notable works produced during the sixteenth century revival include William Shakespeare's *Hamlet, Othello,* and *King Lear*. Modern dramatists working in the tragic tradition include Henrik Ibsen, Arthur Miller, and Eugene O'Neill.

Tragedy of Blood: See *Revenge Tragedy*

Tragic Flaw: In a tragedy, the quality within the hero or heroine which leads to his or her downfall. Examples of the tragic flaw include Othello's jealousy and Hamlet's indecisiveness, although most great tragedies defy such simple interpretation.

Transcendentalism: An American philosophical and religious movement, based in New England from around 1835 until the Civil War. Transcendentalism was a form of American romanticism that had its roots abroad in the works of Thomas Carlyle, Samuel Coleridge, and Johann Wolfgang von Goethe. The Transcendentalists stressed the importance of intuition and subjective experience in communication with God. They rejected religious dogma and texts in favor of mysticism and scientific naturalism. They pursued truths that lie beyond the "colorless" realms perceived by reason and the senses and were active social reformers in public education,

women's rights, and the abolition of slavery. Prominent members of the group include Ralph Waldo Emerson and Henry David Thoreau.

Trickster: A character or figure common in Native American and African literature who uses his ingenuity to defeat enemies and escape difficult situations. Tricksters are most often animals, such as the spider, hare, or coyote, although they may take the form of humans as well. Examples of trickster tales include Thomas King's *A Coyote Columbus Story,* Ashley F. Bryan's *The Dancing Granny* and Ishmael Reed's *The Last Days of Louisiana Red.*

Trimeter: See *Meter*

Triple Rhyme: See *Rhyme*

Trochee: See *Foot*

U

Understatement: See *Irony*

Unities: Strict rules of dramatic structure, formulated by Italian and French critics of the Renaissance and based loosely on the principles of drama discussed by Aristotle in his *Poetics*. Foremost among these rules were the three unities of action, time, and place that compelled a dramatist to: (1) construct a single plot with a beginning, middle, and end that details the causal relationships of action and character; (2) restrict the action to the events of a single day; and (3) limit the scene to a single place or city. The unities were observed faithfully by continental European writers until the Romantic Age, but they were never regularly observed in English drama. Modern dramatists are typically more concerned with a unity of impression or emotional effect than with any of the classical unities. The unities are observed in Pierre Corneille's tragedy *Polyeuctes* and Jean-Baptiste Racine's *Phedre.* Also known as Three Unities.

Urban Realism: A branch of realist writing that attempts to accurately reflect the often harsh facts of modern urban existence. Some works by Stephen Crane, Theodore Dreiser, Charles Dickens, Fyodor Dostoyevsky, Emile Zola, Abraham Cahan, and Henry Fuller feature urban realism. Modern examples include Claude Brown's *Manchild in the Promised Land* and Ron Milner's *What the Wine Sellers Buy.*

Utopia: A fictional perfect place, such as "paradise" or "heaven." Early literary utopias were included in Plato's *Republic* and Sir Thomas More's

Utopia, while more modern utopias can be found in Samuel Butler's *Erewhon,* Theodor Herzka's *A Visit to Freeland,* and H. G. Wells' *A Modern Utopia.*

Utopian: See *Utopia*

Utopianism: See *Utopia*

V

Verisimilitude: Literally, the appearance of truth. In literary criticism, the term refers to aspects of a work of literature that seem true to the reader. Verisimilitude is achieved in the work of Honore de Balzac, Gustave Flaubert, and Henry James, among other late nineteenth-century realist writers.

Vers de societe: See *Occasional Verse*

Vers libre: See *Free Verse*

Verse: A line of metered language, a line of a poem, or any work written in verse. The following line of verse is from the epic poem *Don Juan* by Lord Byron: "My way is to begin with the beginning."

Versification: The writing of verse. Versification may also refer to the meter, rhyme, and other mechanical components of a poem. Composition of a "Roses are red, violets are blue" poem to suit an occasion is a common form of versification practiced by students.

Victorian: Refers broadly to the reign of Queen Victoria of England (1837-1901) and to anything with qualities typical of that era. For example, the qualities of smug narrowmindedness, bourgeois materialism, faith in social progress, and priggish morality are often considered Victorian. This stereotype is contradicted by such dramatic intellectual developments as the theories of Charles Darwin, Karl Marx, and Sigmund Freud (which stirred strong debates in England) and the critical attitudes of serious Victorian writers like Charles Dickens and George Eliot. In literature, the Victorian Period was the great age of the English novel, and the latter part of the era saw the rise of movements such as decadence and symbolism. Works of Victorian literature include the poetry of Robert Browning and Alfred, Lord Tennyson, the criticism of Matthew Arnold and John Ruskin, and the novels of Emily Bronte, William Makepeace Thackeray, and Thomas Hardy. Also known as Victorian Age and Victorian Period.

Victorian Age: See *Victorian*

Victorian Period: See *Victorian*

W

Weltanschauung: A German term referring to a person's worldview or philosophy. Examples of *weltanschauung* include Thomas Hardy's view of the human being as the victim of fate, destiny, or impersonal forces and circumstances, and the disillusioned and laconic cynicism expressed by such poets of the 1930s as W. H. Auden, Sir Stephen Spender, and Sir William Empson.

Weltschmerz: A German term meaning "world pain." It describes a sense of anguish about the nature of existence, usually associated with a melancholy, pessimistic attitude. *Weltschmerz* was expressed in England by George Gordon, Lord Byron in his *Manfred* and *Childe Harold's Pilgrimage,* in France by Viscount de Chateaubriand, Alfred de Vigny, and Alfred de Musset, in Russia by Aleksandr Pushkin and Mikhail Lermontov, in Poland by Juliusz Slowacki, and in America by Nathaniel Hawthorne.

Z

Zarzuela: A type of Spanish operetta. Writers of *zarzuelas* include Lope de Vega and Pedro Calderon.

Zeitgeist: A German term meaning "spirit of the time." It refers to the moral and intellectual trends of a given era. Examples of *zeitgeist* include the preoccupation with the more morbid aspects of dying and death in some Jacobean literature, especially in the works of dramatists Cyril Tourneur and John Webster, and the decadence of the French Symbolists.

Cumulative
Author/Title Index

Nationality/Ethnicity Index

African American

Baraka, Amiri
  Dutchman: V3
Childress, Alice
  The Wedding Band: V2
Hansberry, Lorraine
  A Raisin in the Sun: V2
Shange, Ntozake
  *for colored girls who have
    considered suicide/when the
    rainbow is enuf*: V2
Smith, Anna Deavere
  Twilight: Los Angeles, 1992: V2
Wilson, August
  Fences: V3

American

Albee, Edward
  *Who's Afraid of Virginia
    Woolf?*: V3
  The Zoo Story: V2
Baraka, Amiri
  Dutchman: V3
Childress, Alice
  The Wedding Band: V2
Eliot, T. S.
  Murder in the Cathedral: V4
Gibson, William
  The Miracle Worker: V2
Hammerstein, Oscar
  The King and I: V1
Hansberry, Lorraine
  A Raisin in the Sun: V2
Hart, Moss
  You Can't Take It with You: V1

Hellman, Lillian
  The Children's Hour: V3
  The Little Foxes: V1
Henley, Beth
  Crimes of the Heart: V2
Inge, William
  Come Back, Little Sheba: V3
  Picnic: V5
Kaufman, George S.
  You Can't Take It with You: V1
Kushner, Tony
  Angels in America: V5
Lawrence, Jerome
  Inherit the Wind: V2
Lee, Robert E.
  Inherit the Wind: V2
Mamet, David
  American Buffalo: V3
  Glengarry Glen Ross: V2
McCullers, Carson
  The Member of the Wedding: V5
Medoff, Mark
  Children of a Lesser God: V4
Miller, Arthur
  The Crucible: V3
  Death of a Salesman: V1
Norman, Marsha
  'night, Mother: V2
Odets, Clifford
  Waiting for Lefty: V3
O'Neill, Eugene
  The Hairy Ape: V4
  The Iceman Cometh: V5
  *Long Day's Journey into
    Night*: V2

Rabe, David
  *The Basic Training of Pavlo
    Hummel*: V3
Rodgers, Richard
  The King and I: V1
Shange, Ntozake
  *for colored girls who have
    considered suicide/when the
    rainbow is enuf*: V2
Shepard, Sam
  True West: V3
Simon, Neil
  The Odd Couple: V2
Smith, Anna Deavere
  Twilight: Los Angeles, 1992: V2
Valdez, Luis
  Zoot Suit: V5
Vidal, Gore
  Visit to a Small Planet: V2
Wasserstein, Wendy
  The Heidi Chronicles: V5
Wilder, Thornton
  Our Town: V1
  The Skin of Our Teeth: V4
Williams, Tennessee
  Cat on a Hot Tin Roof: V3
  The Glass Menagerie: V1
  A Streetcar Named Desire: V1
Wilson, August
  Fences: V3
Wilson, Lanford
  Burn This: V4

Argentinian

Dorfman, Ariel
  Death and the Maiden: V4

Subject/Theme Index